ADVANCED

VISUAL
BASIC .NET

Kip Irvine
Kaiyang Liang
Tony Gaddis

Scott/Jones, Inc.
P.O. Box 696
El Granada, CA 94018
Voice: 650-726-2436

Facsimile: 650-726-4693
E-mail: marketing@scottjonespub.com
Web page: www.scottjonespub.com
ISBN: 1-57676-098-7

Advanced Visual Basic .NET
Irvine/Liang/Gaddis

ZYX   456
ISBN: 1-57676-098-7

Printed in Canada.

The publisher wishes to acknowledge the memory and influence of James F. Leisy. Thanks, Jim. We miss you.

Text Design: GEX Publishing Services
Cover Design: Nicole Clayton
Composition: GEX Publishing Services
Book Manufacturing: WebCom Ltd.

Scott/Jones Publishing Company
Editorial Group: Richard Jones, Denise Simon, and Patricia Miyaki
Production Management: Mario Rodriguez
Marketing and Sales: Victoria Chamberlin, Richard Jones, and Leata Holloway
Business Operations: Michelle Robelet, Cathy Glenn, and Bill Overfelt

A Word About Trademarks

All product names identified in this book are trademarks or registered trademarks of their respective companies. We have used the names in an editorial fashion only, and to the benefit of the trademark owner, with no intention of infringing the trademark.

Additional Titles of Interest from Scott/Jones

Extended Prelude to Programming, Concepts and Design, Second Edition
    by Stewart Venit
Web Developer Foundations Using XHTML
    by Terry Felke Morris
Focus on Excel 2003
    by Julie Hayward Spooner
Excel 2003: Volume I, Core Concepts in Excel, Fifth Edition
Excel 2003: Volume II, Advanced Concepts in Excel, Fifth Edition
    by Karen Jolly
Starting Out with C++, Fourth Edition
Starting Out with C++ Brief, Fourth Edition
Starting Out with C++ Alternate, Fourth Edition
Starting Out with Java
Starting Out with Java Alternate
Starting Out with Visual Basic.Net, Second Edition
    by Tony Gaddis Third Edition
Starting Out with C++,Third Alternate Edition
    by Tony Gaddis
C by Discovery, Third Edition
    by L.S. and Dusty Foster
Assembly Language for the IBM PC Family, Third Edition
    by William Jones

The Visual Basic 6 Coursebook, Fourth Edition
QuickStart to JavaScript
QuickStart to DOS for Windows 9X
    by Forest Lin
Advanced Visual Basic .Net, Third Edition
    by Kip Irvine
HTML for Web Developers
Server-Side Programming for Web Developers
    by John Avila
The Complete A+ Guide to PC Repair
The Complete Computer Repair Textbook, Third Edition
    by Cheryl Schmidt
Windows 2000 Professional Step-by-Step
Windows XP Professional Step-by-Step
    by Leslie Hardin and Deborah Tice
The Windows 2000 Professional Textbook
Prelude to Programming: Concepts and Design
The Windows XP Textbook
    by Stewart Venit
The Windows 2000 Server Lab Manual
    by Gerard Morris

This book offers instruction in Visual Basic .NET programming to college students who have completed a semester course or equivalent in the same topic. After having studied the book and completed the programming exercises, students should be able to create small to medium-sized business applications involving databases that run on desktops and on the Web.

We believe effective programmers must combine theory with practice, so they can adapt to ever-changing computing environments. This book does not cover the breadth of topics found in some professional reference books, but it has a number of features that make it useful in the classroom:

- A step-by-step learning approach in which new ideas and concepts build on existing ones.
- Check-up exercises at the end of each section.
- Review questions and programming exercises at the end of each chapter.
- A student CD-ROM containing all sample programs and databases.
- A Web site actively supported by the authors.

Additional Materials for Professors

We think that one of the primary selling points of a textbook lies in the quality of support given by the authors to adopting professors. If you look at the textbook Web sites currently maintained by Tony Gaddis (http://gaddisbooks.com) and Kip Irvine (http://nuvisionmiami.com/vbnet), you will see that we have invested a great deal of time in customer support. The following materials are available at the book's Instructor Web site:

- A PowerPoint™ slide presentation for each chapter.
- A test bank for each chapter.
- Solutions to all programming exercises.
- Timely online support from the authors.

Skills We Emphasize

We believe students who plan to use Visual Basic .NET professionally should have at least the following basic areas of expertise:

- Object-oriented design and programming
- Desktop applications using relational databases
- Web applications using relational databases

We have identified a number of learning objectives addressed by our book. The objectives are divided into broad areas: Object-oriented design, object-oriented programming, user interfaces, databases, and Web programming.

Object-Oriented Design

After reading this book, students should be able to do each of the following:

◆ Recognize and understand basic UML notation.
◆ Understand design differences between inheritance, composition, and interface implementation.
◆ Understand how polymorphism contributes to effective OO design.
◆ Design applications involving classes with composition and inheritance relationships.
◆ Create use-case scenarios to describe detailed execution steps.
◆ Design applications using multi-tier design models.

Object-Oriented Programming

After reading this book, students should be able to do each of the following:

◆ Understand basic reflection and run-time type indentification.
◆ Understand early and late binding, as well as upward and downward type casting.
◆ Understand how delegates (function objects) are created.
◆ Implement exception handling with multiple catch blocks, throwing and re-throwing exceptions, and custom exception classes.
◆ Implement derived class constructors and constructors with optional parameters.
◆ Define shared methods, fields, and properties.
◆ Define structures, enums, classes, and nested classes.
◆ Overload and override class methods.
◆ Control access to members via Public, Private, Protected, and Friend modifiers.
◆ Define and implement interfaces in derived classes.
◆ Implement common .NET interfaces such as IComparable and IComparer.
◆ Use .NET collections in programs.

User Interfaces

After reading this book, students should be able to do each of the following:

◆ Be familiar with common user-interface design issues.
◆ Be able to use .NET error handling controls and event handling to trap errors at the user interface level.
◆ Customize advanced Visual Basic .NET controls such as the DataGrid, DataView, TreeView, Repeater, and DataList.
◆ Write program code that manipulates advanced Visual Basic .NET controls and responds to their events.

Databases

After reading this book, students should be able to do each of the following:

◆ Design relational databases containing multiple table relationships.

◆ Display data from related database tables.

◆ Update database tables using datasets.

◆ Implement the data tier in a multi-tier design using a database connection.

◆ Handle common database errors using exception handling.

◆ Create SQL action queries that update databases and alter the structure of databases.

◆ Create ADO.NET Command objects that execute database queries.

◆ Use DataReaders to read database data.

◆ Code applications that make extensive use of ADO.NET database objects.

◆ Create advanced SQL queries for viewing and updating databases.

◆ Create stored procedures and execute them from programs.

◆ Be familiar with database constraints and database security.

Web Programming

After reading this book, students should be able to do each of the following:

◆ Create ASP.NET applications using both flow layout and grid layout modes.

◆ Use the following basic HTML and ASP.NET controls in programs: Table, Label, TextBox, Button, LinkButton, HyperLink, and Calendar.

◆ Use all types of Web Forms validator controls.

◆ Use Web Forms list-type controls, including ListBox, DropdownList, RadioButtonList, and CheckBoxList. Create event handlers for the same controls.

◆ Upload files from Web browsers.

◆ Send mail with attachments from Web applications.

◆ Manage page-level state, session state, and application state in ASP.NET programs.

◆ Implement custom HTTP error handling at both the application level and IIS level.

◆ Create, delete, and modify browser cookies.

◆ Fill list-type controls using a DataReader.

◆ Use data binding with Web Forms controls.

◆ Use template-based controls such as DataList and Repeater.

◆ Configure advanced DataGrid options and respond to DataGrid events.

◆ Create IIS application directories and deploy Web applications.

◆ Use ADO Command objects in Web Forms to update databases.

◆ Be familiar with the protocols, languages, and processes employed by ASP.NET Web services.

◆ Create Web services that return value types and object types, including datasets.

◆ Create Visual Basic .NET applications to consume Web services.

Chapter Descriptions

Chapter 1: Classes. Object-oriented design; creating classes, properties, constructors, and destructors; multi-tier applications; composition relationships between classes, and nested classes.

Chapter 2: Exceptions and User Interfaces. User-interface design; input validation; ImageList, Toolbar, ListView and TreeView controls; structured exception handling.

Chapter 3: ADO.NET Databases. Introduction to ADO.NET; using data-bound controls; brief look at SQL; navigating, adding, and removing rows; filling list and combo boxes; selecting DataTable rows; parameterized queries.

Chapter 4: DataGrid, DataView, and ListView. DataGrid table styles and column styles; updating a DataGrid; the DataView and unbound ListView controls; Three-tier Sports Rental Income program; Sports Rental Checkout program; Command objects; inserting, updating, and deleting table rows.

Chapter 5: Databases with Related Tables. Connecting to SQL Server databases; relational database design; SQL queries that join tables; database constraints; DataGrid control with related tables; related tables with unbound controls.

Chapter 6: Using SQL Server. SQL queries; creating databases and tables; using Server Explorer; using Enterprise manager; data definition language (DDL); data manipulation language (DML); executing queries in program code; creating and executing stored procedures.

Chapter 7: Web Forms (ASP.NET). ASP.NET basics; creating ASP.NET applications; Request and Response objects; ASP.NET objects and namespaces; standard Web Forms controls; CheckBoxList and RadioButtonList controls; formatting tips.

Chapter 8: Web Forms II. Custom error handling; Calendar control; data binding with arrays; uploading files; sending mail; data validation controls; page-level state; application state; session state; browser cookies; deploying a Web application.

Chapter 9: ASP.NET Databases. Using a DataReader; CheckBoxList and RadioButtonList controls; Repeater control; DataList control; DataGrid control; adding Buttons to DataGrids.

Chapter 10: Web Services. Bookinfo Web service; creating and testing Web services; consuming Web services; connecting to a database; application state; UserList Web service.

Chapter 11: Advanced Classes. Enums, structures, objects and reflection; System.Object class; interfaces; IComparable and IComparer interfaces; inheritance; inheritance with constructors; overriding and overloading; abstract classes and methods; polymorphism; HashTable, SortedList; visual inheritance; delegates.

Chapter 12: Crystal Reports. Creating reports with Report Expert and Report Designer; selecting, sorting, and grouping records; creating totals; using parameter fields; creating charts; displaying reports from Windows and Web applications.

Sequencing the Book's Chapters

We recommend a sequential path through the book's chapters as the easiest approach for students. It is possible to delay covering Chapter 6 (*Using SQL Server*), or to omit it altogether. Chapter 6 emphasizes SQL action queries and stored procedures, which are recommended but not required when completing programming exercises in Chapter 9 (*ASP.NET Databases*). Chapter 11 (*Advanced Classes*) can immediately follow Chapter 1 (*Classes*). Chapters 7 and 8 (ASP.NET) can be covered immediately after Chapter 2 because they do not use databases. Chapters 9 and 10 require covering Chapter 5 (*Databases with Related Tables*). In summary, the following graph shows the chapter dependencies:

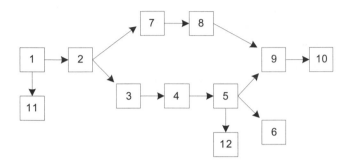

Chapters 11, 12, 6, and 10 can be skipped without affecting other chapters. Eliminating any other chapter, however, causes dependent chapters to be removed from the graph. For example, skipping Chapter 5 eliminates Chapters 6, 9, 10, and 12. Skipping Chapter 7 eliminates Chapters 8, 9, and 10.

About the Authors

Kip Irvine has a M.S. degree in Computer Science and taught computer programming at Miami-Dade College for 17 years. He now teaches in the School of Computer Science at Florida International University. He has written four college textbooks: *COBOL for the IBM-PC, C++ and Object-Oriented Programming, Assembly Language for Intel-Based Computers*, and *Advanced Visual Basic 6*. He was a founding programmer at Omega Research. His books have been translated to Russian, Korean, Chinese, Polish, and French. He also has a doctorate in Music Composition.

Kaiyang Liang has a Doctorate in Mathematics from the University of Miami. He has been a professor at Miami-Dade College for fifteen years, currently teaches in the Computer and Information Systems department. He is a Microsoft Certified Trainer (MCT), a Microsoft Certified Solution Developer (MCSD), and a Microsoft Certified Database Administrator (MCDBA). He was the co-author of the previous edition of this book, entitled *Advanced Visual Basic 6*.

Tony Gaddis teaches courses on computer programming languages, operating systems, and physics at Haywood Community College in North Carolina. He was selected as the North Carolina Community College Teacher of the Year in 1994, and received the Teaching Excellence award from the National Institute for Staff and Organizational Development in 1997. Tony has also provided training to companies and agencies, including NASA's Kennedy Space Center. He is the author of the *Starting Out with C++* series, and coauthor of *Starting Out with Visual Basic 6.0*, also published by Scott Jones.

Acknowlegements

We wish to thank the following persons for their contributions to this book:

- **Richard Jones**, editor and publisher, was the driving force behind this book. Thank you Richard, for never giving up on us.
- **Mario Rodriguez** was the editor who kept all production details on track. We had a lot of fun working together.
- **Robert Saigh** was our expert copy editor, who could always find an unnecessary word or two in every paragraph. Great job!
- **Eileen Troy and Sandra Mitchell of GEX Publishing Services** did a great job of keeping the production moving, with quality work all the way.

The following people were important reviewers and contributors:

- **Jeff Kent**, Los Angeles Valley College
- **Anita Philipp**, Oklahoma City Community College
- **Andre Poole**, Florida Community College at Jacksonville
- **Robert Phillips**, Compass Computing Group
- **Michael Olivero**, Visual Basic .NET consultant and Microsoft Student Ambassador at Florida International University, 2003.

The authors would like to thank the following professors who reviewed chapters during the book's development:

Anthony Basilico, Community College of Rhode Island
William Dorin, Indiana University Northwest
Dana Johnson, North Dakota State University
Astrid Lipp, Georgia State University
Sally Field Mullan, College of DuPage
Theresa Nagy, Northern Virgina Community College
Andre Poole, Florida Community College at Jacksonville
Ed Schott, Walsh University
Craig Van Lengen, Northern Arizona University
Sandy Wells, Gadsden State Community College

The following faculty kindly responded to a survey posed by Scott-Jones Publishing during the early development of our book:

Joan Albright, Greenville Tech
Allyson Anderson, University of Wyoming
J. Austin, St. Augustine's College
Don Bailes, East Tennessee State University
Doug Bock, Southern Illinois University
Charles Cadenhead, Brookhaven College
Betsy Campbell, Seattle Community College
Marlene Camper, Manchester Community Technical College
John Chapman, Johnson County Community College

Marg Chauvin, Palm Beach County CC, Eissey Campus
Sue Conger, University of Texas at Dallas
John J. Couture, Miramar College
Thad Crews, Western Kentucky University
John DaPonte, Southern Connecticut University
Louis DiPerna, Raritan Valley Community College
Janie Epstein, Johnson County Community College
Esther Frankel, Santa Barbara Community College
Mark Frydenberg, Bently University
David Fullerton, Yeshiva University
Joyhn Gerstenberg, Cuyamaca College
Stephen F. Hustedde, South Mountain Community College
Bill Janeway, Eastern Kentucky University
Kurt Kominek, North East State University
Paul LeCoq, Spokane Falls Community College
Jason Martinez, Clark College
Mayur Mehta, Southwest Texas University
Dave Mcdonald, Georgia State University
Gordon McNorton, Collin County Community College
Guity Ravai, Purdue University
Jeff Scott, Blackhawk Technical College
Charles Shubra, Indiana University of Pennsylvania
Ken Struckel, Hibbing Community College
Elaine Weltz, Seattle University

Recommended Reading

We highly recommend the following books for further study:

- Dino Esposito. *Programming Microsoft ASP.NET*. Microsoft Press, 2003.
- Balena, Francisco. *Programming Microsoft Visual Basic .NET (Core Reference)*. Microsoft Press, 2003.
- Walther, Stephen. *ASP.NET Unleashed, 2nd Edition*. Sams, 2003.
- David Sceppa. *Microsoft ADO.NET (Core Reference)*. Microsoft Press, 2002.

Contents at a Glance

Contents

1

Classes

▶1.1 Introduction

One of the most exciting developments in computer software over the last twenty years has been *object-oriented programming* (nicknamed *OOP*). It is a way of designing and coding applications that has led to using inter-changeable software components to build larger programs. Object-oriented programming languages first appeared in the early 1980s, with Simula, SmallTalk, and C++. The legacy from these languages is the gradual development of object-like visual tools for building programs.

A *class* is a pattern, or blueprint that defines a group of related objects that have common characteristics. House builders, for example, often use a single design to create many houses. Each house might be a different color, but the houses all derive from the same pattern. To use an analogy from nature, members of the *Canine* family have similar characteristics: four legs, paws, two ears, and an insatiable desire for food. At home, I have a couple of instances of Canines named Wolfgang and Daisy who are more alike than they are different.

In computer programs, a class identifies a specific data type. All instances of a class share common characteristics named *attributes* and *behaviors*. No doubt you have heard this before, but all entities (objects) in Visual Basic .NET are based on classes. Forms, for example, are instances of the System.Windows.Forms class. Buttons are instances of the

System.Windows.Forms.Button class. Other classes may not be visible, but they perform essential services for your programs. For example, the System.IO.StreamReader class, part of the .NET framework, provides services for reading files.

►1.2 Value Types and Reference Types

Visual Basic .NET programs contain two types of variables: value types and reference types.

◆ A *value type* is a variable that contains its own data. Examples of value types are Integer, Single, Decimal, and Boolean. Local variables that are value types are stored on the runtime stack.

◆ A *reference type* is a variable that does not contain its own data. Instead, it contains a reference to an object at some other location in memory. Strings, Collections, and Arrays are all reference types.

You might think of a reference type as a pointer, in that it points to, or indicates the address of some memory data. The memory area used by reference types is called the *managed heap*. A *null reference* is a reference that does not refer to any data. Visual Basic .NET uses the keyword **Nothing** to indicate a null reference.

> **Note:**
> *You are probably familiar with value types and reference types after having had a first course in Visual Basic .NET. We want to ensure you understand the difference in semantics (meanings, behaviors) between the two types before you start creating classes. Without this knowledge, debugging can be a perplexing experience.*

Value Type

Suppose we declare a variable named **mCount** at the module level. mCount contains its data within its own storage area:

```
Dim mCount As Integer = 25
```

We can visualize **mCount** sitting somewhere in memory, containing the binary data for the number 25:

mCount   25

If we create a second variable named **temp** and assign **mCount** to **temp**, we have two physically separate variables, each containing the value 25:

```
Dim temp As Integer = mCount
```

mCount   25

temp   25

If a new value is assigned to temp, mCount is not affected:

```
temp = 40          'mCount still equals 25
```

This relationship between mCount and temp should be no great mystery. Value types in all programming languages work the same way. Reference types, on the other hand, are different.

Reference Type

The managed heap is a large multipurpose memory area from which a program can reserve certain locations for its own data. When it reserves these locations, it obtains their addresses (we call them *references*) and stores the references in reference type variables. Let us declare a Student variable named **S1:**

```
Dim S1 As Student
```

S1 does not yet contain any references. It's empty, as the following diagram shows:

S1   ⬜   ——————(references)——————▶   (nothing)

Next, let us create a Student object and assign its refrence to S1:

```
S1 = New Student
```

Suppose we assign a value to its Name property:

```
S1.Name = "Fred Smith"
```

The following diagram helps us visualize the relationship between S1 and the data it references. The data contained in the Student object are located in the managed heap. S1 contains a reference to the data, not the data itself:

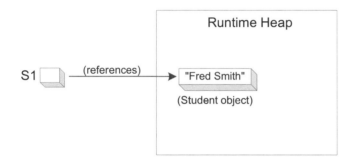

Using reference types has distinct advantages. For example, when the Student object we created is no longer needed, we can assign a value of **Nothing** to S1:

```
S1 = Nothing
```

Assuming no other references to the same Student object exist, the .NET runtime is free to destroy the object and reclaim its memory. At any later time, we can still create a new Student object and assign its reference to S1:

```
S1 = New Student
```

Reference types are convenient for accessing large-scale resources such as database connections and database tables. As long as a program has a reference to some resource, it can use the resource at will.

Assigning Reference Types

Suppose you create an array of integers, fill the array, and assign the array to another variable:

```
Dim tests() As Integer = {80, 95, 88, 76, 54}
Dim scores() As Integer = tests
```

One might imagine that the array has been copied, and we now have two separate arrays:

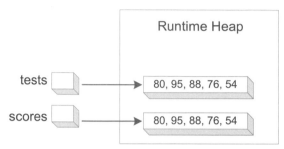

Instead, it turns out that we have only one array, referenced by both variables:

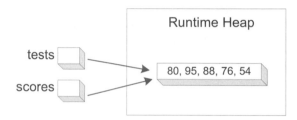

Let us prove it by modifying the first element of scores and then displaying the first element of tests:

```
Dim tests() As Integer = {80, 95, 88, 76, 54}
Dim scores() As Integer = tests
scores(0) = 99
MessageBox.Show(tests(0))
```

Of course, the displayed value is 99. When you assign a reference type to another variable, you are not copying its data. You are merely copying the reference.

If you want to copy an array, you must copy the individual elements. The following loop is an example of a *deep copy* operation:

```
Dim tests() As Integer = {80, 95, 88, 76, 54}
Dim scores(tests.Length - 1) As Integer
Dim i As Integer
For i = 0 To tests.Length - 1
   scores(i) = tests(i)
Next
```

Life and the Garbage Collector

The lifetime of a reference type is determined by whether or not references to it actively exist. We say that an object is *reachable* if at least one variable exists that holds a reference to the object. Any unreachable object can be cleaned up and removed from memory by a utility program called the *garbage collector*. The garbage collector runs continually in the background as long as a .NET application is active.

Let us illustrate the lifetime idea by creating the **tests** array inside a procedure. Array variables are reference types, though the individual array elements might be value types:

```
Sub MakeArray()
    Dim tests() As Integer = {80, 95, 88, 76, 54}
End Sub
```

When MakeArray ends, tests goes out of scope, meaning that MakeArray will be erased by the program. But what about the five integer values? They remain on the managed heap though they are no longer reachable:

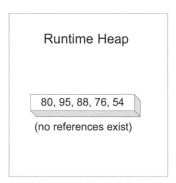

Let us imagine a different scenario, in which a function named **GetArray** creates and returns a reference to an array:

```
Function GetArray() As Integer()
    Dim tests() As Integer = {80, 95, 88, 76, 54}
    Return tests
End Function
```

Assuming GetArray is called from somewhere else in the program, the calling procedure continues to hold the reference, and the array is still reachable. We can prove it by displaying one of the array values:

```
Dim scores As Integer() = GetArray()
MessageBox.Show(scores(0))        '80
```

To remove a reference, set the reference variable to **Nothing**. From then on, an attempt to access the variable results in a runtime error:

```
scores = Nothing
MessageBox.Show(scores(0))          'runtime error!
```

Namespaces

A *namespace* is a convenient way to group one or more classes. Namespaces play a critical role in large applications. Collections of related classes are frequently grouped inside namespaces in order to provide a logical organization. The DataTable, DataRow, DataSet, and DataView classes, for example, all belong to Visual Basic .NET's System.Data namespace.

Namespaces can be used to partition groups of classes within large-scale applications created by multiple developers. Companies often organize their programmers into named groups, such as ClientUtility and StorageManagement. Suppose a developer in the **ClientUtility** group created a class named User, and suppose a developer in the **StorageManagement** group also created a class named User. In any given section of the program, instances of both classes could be used side by side. Each class name would be prefixed by its respective namespace identifier:

```
Dim StorageUser As StorageManagement.User
Dim ClientUser As ClientUtility.User
```

Every Visual Basic .NET project has a root namespace, which you can access by viewing the project's Properties window. The namespace concept is universal among modern programming languages. The Java language, for example, has *packages* which work the same way as namespaces.

Checkpoint

1.1 In one sentence, define *class* as it applies to object-oriented programming.
1.2 In which part of memory are objects stored?
1.3 What has to happen before an object can be removed from memory?
1.4 What entity in the .NET runtime is responsible for removing objects from memory?
1.5 When an object's reference is set to Nothing, when is the object removed?

▶ 1.3 Object-Oriented Design

Object-oriented design centers around the design of programs using classes and class relationships. Object-oriented design is not just a matter of randomly dropping classes into a program. The real challenge is to design classes in such a way that the resulting objects will effectively cooperate and communicate. The primary goal of design is to address the needs of the application (the problem being solved). A secondary goal is to create a design that will outlive the current application and possibly be useful in future programs.

The first step after creating program specifications is to analyze application requirements. *Object-oriented analysis*, as it is called, often starts with a detailed specification of the problem to be solved. A term often applied to this process is called *finding the classes*. In every problem and every application, there are classes waiting to be found. The designer's job is to discover those classes. A sculptor might say that inside every block of marble exists a work of art waiting to be discovered.

Finding the Classes

Classes are the fundamental building blocks of object-oriented applications. When designing object-oriented programs, first select classes that reflect physical entities in the application domain. For example, the user of a record-keeping program for a college might describe some of the application's requirements as follows:

> We need to keep a **list of students** and track the courses they have completed. Each student has a **transcript** that contains his or her information about completed courses. At the end of each semester, the system should calculate the grade point average of each **student**. At times, users will search for a particular **course** taken by a student.

Notice the highlighted nouns and noun phrases in this description: list of students, transcript, student, and course. These would ordinarily become classes in the program's design.

Looking for Control Structures

Classes can be discovered in the description of processing done by an application, or in the description of control structures. For example, what if the application involved scheduling of college classes for students? Here is another possible description that might appear in the program specifications:

> We want to schedule classes for students, using the college's master schedule to determine the times and room numbers for each student's class. When the optimal arrangement of classes for each student has been determined, each student's class schedule will be printed and distributed.

In this description, we anticipate a need for a controlling agent that could be implemented as a class. We might call it **Scheduler**, a class that matches up each student's schedule with the college master schedule.

Describing the Classes

The next step, after finding the classes in an application, is to describe the classes in terms of attributes and operations. *Attributes* are characteristics of each object that will be implemented as properties. Attributes describe the properties all objects of the same class have in common. Classes also have *operations*, which are actions the class objects may perform, or messages to which they can respond. Operations are implemented as class methods. Based on the record-keeping application we described earlier, Table 1-1 describes some of its important attributes and operations.

Table 1-1

Classes, Attributes, and Operations

Class	Attributes (properties)	Operations (methods)
Student	ID, LastName, FirstName, Transcript	Print, Input
StudentList	AllStudents, Count	Add, Remove, FindStudent
Course	Semester, Name, Grade, Credits	Print, Input
Transcript	CourseList, Count	Print, Search, CalcGradeAvg

The initial set of attributes and operations is often incomplete during the early stages of design, because anticipating all application requirements is difficult. As a design develops, the need often arises for additional properties and methods that improve communication between objects. Rather than being seen as a weakness, however, one of the strengths of the object-oriented design process is that it accommodates ongoing modifications.

Interface and Implementation

The *class interface* is the portion of the class visible to the application programmer who uses the class. The program written by such a person is also called the *client program*, in reference to the client-server relationship between a class and the programs that use it. The class interface provides a way for clients to communicate (send messages) to class objects. In Visual Basic .NET, a class interface is created by declaring public properties, methods, and events.

The class *implementation* is the portion of a class that is hidden from client programs; it is created from private instance variables, private properties, and private methods. The hiding of data and procedures inside a class is called *encapsulation*. In this, it might be helpful to visualize the class as a "capsule" around its data and procedures.

Inheritance

Inheritance lets programmers create new classes that inherit, or derive characteristics of existing classes. For example, you might want to start with a Student class containing only general attributes shared by all students. But special types of students might require the creation of classes such as GraduateStudent and StudentEmployee, shown in Figure 1-1. These new classes share all characteristics of the Student class, and add new characteristics to make them specialized.

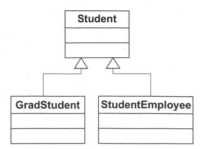

Figure 1-1 Inheritance relationships between classes

Clients and Servers

One of the most common patterns in computer software is the *client-server pattern*. This involves an entity called a *server*, which produces information consumed by one or more clients. A *client* is a program that creates a reference to a server and sends it requests in the form of method calls (Figure 1-2). The server, in return, replies to the messages by taking some action or returning some information. For example, the File class has an OpenText method that opens a file and returns a StreamReader object. A client program might contain the following line of code:

```
Dim sr As StreamReader = File.OpenText("mydata.txt")
```

The call to OpenText is the request message. The returned StreamReader object is the response message.

Figure 1-2 Client-server relationship

C h e c k p o i n t

1.6   Name an important challenge relating to object-oriented design mentioned at the beginning of this section.

1.7   (yes/no): Are class attributes specific to each instance of a class?

1.8   How is the class implementation different from the class interface?

1.9   Provide an example of the client-server pattern, using the Visual Basic .NET Form class.

▶ 1.4 Creating Classes

When you create a class, you add a new data type to your Visual Basic .NET program. A public class definition has the following general format:

```
Public Class classname
    member-declarations
End Class
```

Classname is the name of the class, which can be any valid identifier that does not conflict with the name of an existing class in the same namespace. *Member-declarations* is a list of method and variable declarations belonging to the class. **Public** is a keyword that controls the visibility of the class; for now, let us assume all classes are public.

To add a class to a Visual Basic .NET project, select *Add Class* from the Project menu. The *Add New Item* dialog window appears, as in Figure 1-3. The default name (shown as "Class1.vb" in the figure) is usually changed to reflect the name of the class you want to create. Alternatively, you can click on the *Add New Item* button on the toolbar to create a class. If you do, be sure to select the **Class** icon in the right-hand pane of the Add New Item dialog.

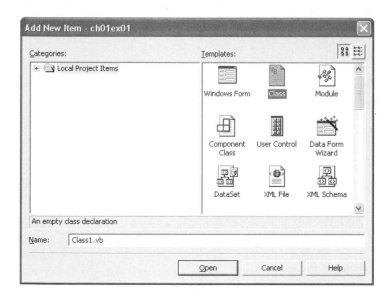

Figure 1-3 Add New Item dialog

 Note:

Option Strict: *All programs in this book will use the Option Strict-On setting, which enforces strict type checking when one variable's value is assigned to another. In particular, Option Strict does not permit the types of automatic conversions performed by Visual Basic 6. You can set Option Strict in the Project Properties dialog, under the area labeled Common Properties / Build.*

Hands-On Tutorial: Student Class

 Student1

In this hands-on tutorial, you will create a Windows desktop program containing a single class named **Student**. You will also write code that creates an instance of a Student, assigns values to its member variables, and retrieves and displays the values of the same variables.

Step 1. Create a new Windows desktop program and name it **Student1**.

Step 2. Add a ListBox to the startup form and name it **lstStudent**.

Step 3. Rename the startup form to **frmMain**. Set its Text property to a blank string. Set the project's startup form to frmMain.

Step 4. Add a class named **Student** to the project and insert the following code in the class:

```
Public Class Student
    Public mID As String       'identification number
    Public mName As String     'first and last name
    Public mAge As Integer     'age of student
End Class
```

Each member variable name is prefixed by the letter **m** (for *module-level*). The prefix is not required, but it can help identify variables that are visible throughout the current class or module.

Step 5. In the startup form, create an instance of the Student class in the **frmMain_Load** procedure:

```
Dim s1 As New Student
```

Step 6. In the same procedure, assign test values to the Student member variables:

```
s1.mID = "111111111"
s1.mName = "Bill Johnson"
s1.mAge = 20
```

Step 7. Write statements that display the Student's member variables in the list box:

```
With lstStudent.Items
    .Add(s1.mID)
    .Add(s1.mName)
    .Add(s1.mAge)
End With
```

Step 8. Save and run the program. The output should appear as in Figure 1-4.

 Note:

*If you know a bit about object-oriented programming, you know that programmers do not usually make class variables such as **mID** directly accessible. When we show how to create properties, we will hide member variables by making them private.*

(End of tutorial. You can view the completed program named Student1 in the Chapter 1 examples directory.)

Figure 1-4 Output from the Hands-On Tutorial

Code Listing 1-1 (frmMain)

```
Public Class frmMain
    Inherits System.Windows.Forms.Form
```

```
+ Windows Form Designer generated code
```

```
    Private Sub frmMain_Load(ByVal sender As System.Object, _
     ByVal e As System.EventArgs) Handles MyBase.Load

        Dim s1 As New Student
        s1.mID = "111111111"
        s1.mName = "Bill Johnson"
        s1.mAge = 20
        With lstStudent.Items()
            .Add(s1.mID)
            .Add(s1.mName)
            .Add(s1.mAge)
        End With
    End Sub
End Class
```

Methods

A *method* is a procedure declared inside a class. A method can be a *sub* procedure or a *function* procedure. It performs actions resulting from messages passed to instances of its class. For example, suppose we add a **Print** method to the Student class. It may be placed before or after the class variables. It writes the three-member variables to a message box:

```
Public Class Student
    Public mID As String
    Public mName As String
    Public mAge As Integer

    Public Sub Print()
        MessageBox.Show(mID & ", " & mName & ", " & mAge)
    End Sub
End Class
```

Methods are declared Public when they are part of the class interface (the part visible to client programs).

Function Procedures

Methods can also be function procedures. For example, let us create a method named **AsString** that returns a string representation of a Student:

```
Public Function AsString() As String
    Return mID & ", " & mName & ", " & mAge
End Function
```

A client program can call the AsString method and pass the result to the WriteLine method. The WriteLine method is used in Console-type applications, which use a plain text window for all input-output. Assuming **s1** is a Student object, we can write the following:

```
System.Console.WriteLine(s1.AsString())
```

(There is a method in the Object class named **ToString**, which returns a string representation of an object. We will show how to use that method later in this chapter.)

Private Methods

Methods should be declared Private when you only want them to be called from other methods in the same class. Suppose the Student class has a private method named ValidateStudentID that looks up the current student's ID number in a database. It can be declared as follows:

```
Private Sub ValidateStudentID()
   . . .
End Sub
```

We can call ValidateStudentID from any other method in the Student class that needs to check the current student object for correctness. By making it private, we expressly do *not* want ValidateStudentID to be called from outside the class.

Hands-On Tutorial: Adding the GetGradeAverage Method

Student1

In the following hands-on tutorial, you will add a method to the Student class that calculates a student's grade average.

Step 1. Open the **Student1** program and add the following variables to the Student class:

```
Public mCreditsEarned As Single
Public mTotalGradePoints As Single
```

Step 2. Add the following **GetGradeAverage** method to the class:

```
Public Function GetGradeAverage() As Single
   Return mTotalGradePoints / mCreditsEarned
End Function
```

Step 3. Modify the frmMain_Load procedure so it looks like the following:

```
Dim s1 As New Student
s1.mID = "111111111"
s1.mName = "Bill Johnson"
s1.mAge = 20
s1.mCreditsEarned = 20.0
s1.mTotalGradePoints = 65.5
MessageBox.Show(CStr(s1.GetGradeAverage()))
```

(Note the call to CStr, because the MessageBox function requires a String argument.)

Step 4. Run the program and look for the following output:

```
3.275
```

(End of tutorial)

Public and Private Member Access

When a class variable or method is declared Public, any client program can freely access the member belonging to a specific object. If the Private keyword is used, however, the member becomes invisible outside the class. Suppose we declared the mID field as private inside the Student class:

```
Public Class Student
    Private mID As String
```

In that case, any attempt by a client program to access the mID field would not compile:

```
Dim s1 As New Student
s1.mID = "222222222"        'error
String temp = s1.mID        'error
```

In keeping with the information hiding principle of object-oriented design, class variables are almost always private because we do not want the class user to have unrestricted access to class variables. The client program could unknowingly put the class object into an invalid state by assigning an incorrect value to a class variable. For example, suppose the ID field of a Student object must contain nine numeric digits. A client program might collect information from an input form, and because of its given user input, assign a seven-digit value to the Student object's ID. We could build error-checking statements into the input form. But what would happen if the data storage format were changed later to some other size? All input forms related to Students would have to be corrected. The result would be a maintenance nightmare.

Object-oriented programs commonly use class methods to filter access to private class variables. A Java programmer, for example, would call methods such as getID and setID to access or change a student's ID value. In Visual Basic .NET, we use property procedures to do the same thing.

Checkpoint

1.10 Show the general syntax for defining a public class.

1.11 Can a method declared Private be accessed by other methods in the same class?

1.12 Write statements that declare a class named clsEmployee, containing a String variable named mDepartmentID.

1.13 In the Hands-On Tutorial, we introduced the GetGradeAverage method. Add statements that prevent division if mCreditsEarned is equal to zero.

1.14 Why should class member variables be private?

▶1.5 Properties

Visual Basic .NET programs use *property procedures* to provide access to member variables. Property procedures are commonly referred to as *properties*. You are no doubt already familiar with properties of Forms, toolbox controls, and various other built-in objects. To the user of a class object, a property acts like a variable belonging to the object. For example, when we set a form's Text property, we are calling a property procedure:

```
frmMain.Text = "Student Record"
```

Properties nearly always have public scope so they can be accessed from outside their enclosing class module. Suppose, for example, we wanted to create a String property named **ID**. We would type the following line into the editor and press Enter:

```
Public Property ID() As String
```

The .NET editor would automatically create the following template:

```
Public Property ID() As String
   Get

   End Get
   Set(ByVal Value As String)

   End Set
End Property
```

The **Get** statement represents the block of code that executes when a client program wants to get, or retrieve the named property's value. A minimal implementation of Get would be to use the **Return** statement (as in a function procedure) to return the value of the private class variable named **mID**:

```
Get
    Return mID
End Get
```

A program wanting to display the value of the ID property in a Label control can access the property in this way:

```
lblIDNumber.Text = aStudent.ID
```

The **Set** statement indicates the client program is assigning a value to the named property. In the ID property we just proposed, the Set statement would be written as follows:

```
Set(ByVal Value As String)
    mID = Value
End Set
```

The parameter named **Value** holds the data passed by the client program to this property. The following client program code assigns a value to the property:

```
aStudent.ID = "111111111"
```

Using Properties for Data Validation

A useful purpose behind using property procedures is that they offer you a way to filter values a client program would assign to the property. Suppose we want to verify any value assigned to a Student's **Age** property is between 1 and 130. We can add an appropriate conditional statement to the Set statement:

```
Public Property Age() As Integer
    Get
        Return mAge
    End Get
    Set(ByVal Value As Integer)
        If Value >= 1 And Value <= 130 Then
            mAge = Value
        End If
    End Set
End Property
```

A question that really should be asked is, what happens to mAge if the client program tries to assign an illegal value (say, 200) to the Age property? As our code is written, mAge would keep its existing value. That may not always be desirable because the property procedure gives no indication something went wrong. There are a couple of possible alternatives: one would be to display a message on the console or in a message box. A preferred alternative would be to throw an exception that could be caught and handled by the client program. We will defer a solution to this type of problem until the next chapter, where we cover exception handling techniques.

ReadOnly Properties

Sometimes, it is useful to provide a class property that can only be read, but not modified by a client program. The **ReadOnly** qualifier must be added to the property declaration, and the **Set** statement in the property is omitted. *ReadOnly properties*, as we will call them, are useful when we either do not want a client program to modify certain variables in a class, or when the value returned by a property must be calculated from internal data. Suppose we added the following member variables to the Student class:

```
Private mCreditsEarned As Single
Private mTotalGradePoints As Single
```

We could then create a ReadOnly property named **GradePointAverage** that returns the grade point average calculated by dividing the total grade points by the credits earned. At the same time, it would give us a chance to prevent division by zero if the student has not yet earned any credits:

```
Public ReadOnly Property GradePointAverage() As Single
    Get
        If mCreditsEarned <> 0 Then
            Return mTotalGradePoints / mCreditsEarned
        Else
            Return 0.0
        End If
    End Get
End Property
```

Hands-On Tutorial: Adding Properties to the Student Class

 Student2

Let us put together some of the new information and techniques covered so far with a hands-on tutorial.

Step 1. Create a Windows application named **Student2**.

Step 2. Delete the startup form and create a new form named **frmMain**. Make this the project's startup form. Add a class to the project and name it Student.

Step 3. Declare the following variables in the Student class:

```
Private mID As String
Private mName As String
Private mAge As Integer
Private mCreditsEarned As Single
Private mTotalGradePoints As Single
```

Step 4. Insert the following line of code in the Student class that defines a property named **ID**. Press Enter at the end of the line:

```
Public Property ID() As String
```

The Visual Studio .NET editor automatically inserts the following framework for the StudentID property:

```
Public Property ID() As String
    Get
    End Get
    Set(ByVal Value As String)
    End Set
End Property
```

Step 5. Fill in the following lines, completing the property definition:

```
Public Property ID() As String
    Get
        Return mID
    End Get
    Set(ByVal Value As String)
        mID = Value
    End Set
End Property
```

Step 6. Similarly, create property procedures for Name and Age:

```
Public Property Name() As String
    Get
        Return mName
    End Get
    Set(ByVal Value As String)
        mName = Value
    End Set
End Property

Public Property Age() As Integer
    Get
```

```
            Return mAge
        End Get
        Set(ByVal Value As Integer)
            mAge = Value
        End Set
    End Property
```

Step 7. Create the CreditsEarned and TotalGradePoints properties:

```
    Public Property CreditsEarned() As Single
        Get
            Return mCreditsEarned
        End Get
        Set(ByVal Value As Single)
            mCreditsEarned = Value
        End Set
    End Property

    Public Property TotalGradePoints() As Single
        Get
            Return mTotalGradePoints
        End Get
        Set(ByVal Value As Single)
            mTotalGradePoints = Value
        End Set
    End Property
```

Step 8. Create a ReadOnly property named GradeAverage:

```
    Public ReadOnly Property GradeAverage() As Single
        Get
            If mCreditsEarned <> 0 Then
                Return mTotalGradePoints / mCreditsEarned
            Else
                Return 0.0
            End If
        End Get
    End Property
```

Step 9. Add a method named AsString that returns a string representation of the student. The GradeAverage property is used here:

```
    Public Function AsString() As String
        Return ID & ", " & Name & ", " & Age & ", " _
            & FormatNumber(GradeAverage)
    End Function
```

Step 10. In frmMain_Load, create a Student, assign properties, and display it in a message box:

```
    Dim s1 As New Student
    s1.ID = "111111111"
    s1.Name = "Bill Johnson"
    s1.Age = 20
    s1.CreditsEarned = 20.0
    s1.TotalGradePoints = 65.5
    Messagebox.show(s1.AsString())
```

Step 11. Run the program. Output should be the following:

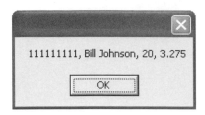

(End of tutorial)

Shared Variables and Properties

When objects are created, we expect each object to contain a copy of the variables declared inside the object's class. In Figure 1-5, for example, the three Student objects each contain a separate copy of **mName** because it is an instance variable.

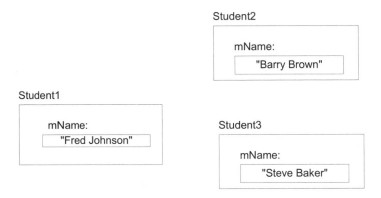

Figure 1-5 Student objects containing an instance variable

A *shared variable*, on the other hand, is shared between all class instances. If **mName** were a shared variable in the Student class, all three Student objects would have the same name (see Figure 1-6). That would be ill-advised because students do not share the same name.

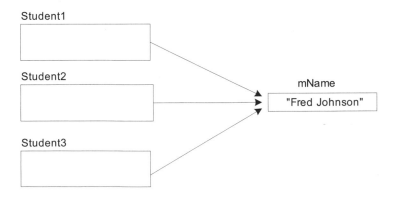

Figure 1-6 Sharing the mName variable

There are cases, however, in which shared variables can be useful. Let us add a shared variable to the Student class that keeps count of the number of Student objects created so far during the program's execution:

```
Private Shared mInstanceCount As Integer = 0
```

Note the use of the **Shared** qualifier. In the Student constructor, we increment the **mInstanceCount** variable:

```
Public Sub New()
      .
      .
   mInstanceCount += 1
End Sub
```

> **Note:**
> *The += operator is a convenient shorthand for adding to a variable. The following two statements are equivalent:*
> ```
> mInstanceCount = mInstanceCount + 1
> mInstanceCount += 1
> ```
> *The same principle holds true for the* −=, *=, /=, \=, %=, &=, *and related operators.*

Shared Property

 SharedMembers

Because shared variables tend to be private, you will usually need to create a public *shared property* if client programs are to access the shared value. The following is a shared ReadOnly property named InstanceCount in the Student class:

```
Public Shared ReadOnly Property InstanceCount() As Integer
   Get
        Return mInstanceCount
   End Get
End Property
```

A client program can obtain the shared property. A shared property is ordinarily qualified by the name of the class:

```
Student.InstanceCount
```

Although less common, you can access the property using an instance of the class:

```
Dim s As New Student
s.InstanceCount
```

Let us put some code in a client program that displays the InstanceCount property in a list box (named **myList**) after creating each Student:

```
Dim s As New Student
With myList.Items
   .Add(Student.InstanceCount & " Student exists.")
   s = New Student
   .Add(Student.InstanceCount & " Students exist.")
   s = New Student
   .Add(Student.InstanceCount & " Students exist.")
   s = New Student
   .Add(Student.InstanceCount & " Students exist.")
End With
```

Following is the **SharedMembers** program output:

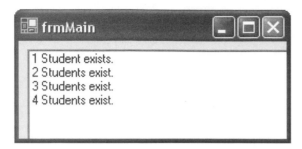

▶1.6 Constructors

A *constructor* is a class method that runs automatically when an instance of the class is created. In Visual Basic .NET, a constructor is always named **New**. Constructors typically initialize class member variables to default values, but they can also be used to perform any required class initialization. If a class is connected to a network connection, for example, the constructor could be used to open a connection to a remote computer.

A **default constructor** is a constructor with no parameters. Let us create a simple one for the Student class that assigns default values to the **mID** and **mName** members:

```
Public Sub New()
    mID = "000000000"
    mName = "(unknown)"
End Sub
```

With this constructor in the class, if a client program creates a new Student object, we know for certain what values it will have in the ID and Name properties. Notice that we did not initialize the **mAge** property; in that case, it is assigned a default value of zero.

Overloading the Constructor

Object-oriented languages, including Visual Basic .NET, have a feature called *method overloading* that permits two or more methods in the same class to have the same name as long as they have different parameter lists. We can put this feature to good use by creating another version of the constructor that contains a list of parameters. This is called a *parameterized constructor* (or *alternate constructor*). Such a constructor is a convenience because it constructs an object and initializes multiple instance fields.

Let us create a second constructor for the Student class. Notice that we are careful to use different names for constructor parameters than for private fields:

```
Public Sub New(ByVal id As String, ByVal name As String, _
   ByVal age As Integer)
   mID = id
   mName = name
   mAge = age
End Sub
```

In the client program, now construct a Student from existing data by calling the parameterized constructor:

```
Dim s2 As New Student("222222222", "Julio Gonzalez", 23)
```

If you do not create any constructors in a class, Visual Basic .NET creates an empty default constructor for you. But if you create only a parameterized constructor, a default constructor is *not* created automatically. That is so because you might have a good reason for not permitting an object to be constructed unless it is assigned meaningful values. What use would a bank account object be, for example, if it had no valid account number? You might decide to create a default constructor but restrict its visibility to functions inside the same class. You can designate the default constructor as Private, as the following code does in the Student class:

```
Private Sub New()
   mID = "000000000"
   mName = "(unknown)"
End Sub
```

It is possible to use constructor parameters having the same names as class fields. In that case, you must use the **Me** qualifier (a reference to the current object) to clarify the meaning of assignment statements:

```
Public Sub New(ByVal mID As String, ByVal mName As String, _
   ByVal mAge As Integer)
   Me.mID = mID
   Me.mName = mName
   Me.mAge = mAge
End Sub
```

Optional Constructor Parameters

Sometimes you will want to create instances of a class using varying amounts of information. You can declare optional parameters in any method (including constructors) using the **Optional** keyword, as long as you assign them default values. In the following constructor for the Student class, defaults are provided for the id number, name, and age of the student:

```
Public Sub New(Optional ByVal id As String = "000000000", _
  Optional ByVal name As String = "(unknown)", _
  Optional ByVal age As Integer = 0)

   mID = id
   mName = name
   mAge = age
End Sub
```

After this constructor is in place, client programs can create Student objects by passing zero, one, two, or three arguments:

```
Dim s3 As New Student("33333333")
Dim s4 As New Student("44444444", "Maria Rodriguez")
Dim s5 As New Student("55555555", "Henry Chen", 25)
```

There are two important rules to follow: Once a parameter is labeled Optional, all subsequent parameters in the method's parameter list must also be labeled Optional. Second, all optional parameters must be given default values.

Assigning Property Values in Constructors

A little earlier, when we showed how to create class properties, a justification was made for performing error checking and validation on property values. We could lose that advantage if invalid parameters were passed to a constructor. A sensible thing to do is to assign the constructor parameters to properties, taking advantage of the built-in validation of the property procedures. Here is an improved version of the Student constructor that assigns the ID, Name, and Age properties:

```
Public Sub New(ByVal id As String, ByVal name As String, _
   ByVal age As Integer)
   Me.ID = id
   Me.Name = name
   Me.Age = age
End Sub
```

Notice that the property values were qualified by **Me**, a keyword that references the current Student object. Because Visual Basic .NET does not distinguish between uppercase and lowercase letters, a statement such as the following would be interpreted as assigning the same variable to itself:

```
ID = id
```

Hands-On Tutorial: Adding a Parameterized Constructor to the Student Class

 Student3

In this tutorial, you will have a chance to create a constructor for the Student class having several optional parameters. You will be calling the constructor several times, experimenting with parameter lists of various sizes.

Step 1. Make a copy of the Student2 program in the Chapter 1 examples directory. Rename the copy to Student3 and open the program.

Step 2. Insert the following constructor in the Student class, which initializes all of the member variables:

```
Public Sub New(Optional ByVal pID As String = "000000000", _
  Optional ByVal pName As String = "(unknown)", _
  Optional ByVal pAge As Integer = 0, _
  Optional ByVal pCreditsEarned As Single = 0, _
  Optional ByVal pTotalGradePoints As Single = 0)

   ID = pID
   Name = pName
   Age = pAge
   CreditsEarned = pCreditsEarned
   TotalGradePoints = pTotalGradePoints
End Sub
```

Step 3. Replace the contents of the frmMain_Load procedure with the following:

```
Dim s1 As New Student("33333333")
Dim s2 As New Student("44444444", "Maria Rodriguez")
Dim s3 As New Student("55555555", "Henry Chen", 25, 95, 273)
MessageBox.Show(s1.AsString())
MessageBox.Show(s2.AsString())
MessageBox.Show(s3.AsString())
```

Step 4. Run the program. Your output should be the following lines, which appear in three separate message boxes:

```
33333333, (unknown), 0, 0.0
44444444, Maria Rodriguez, 0, 0.0
55555555, Henry Chen, 25, 2.87
```

(End of tutorial)

Checkpoint

1.19 (yes/no): Does the following statement cause the Employee constructor to execute?

```
Dim emp As Employee
```

1.20 Suppose the Account class has two member variables: **mID** and **mBalance**. Create a constructor that initializes the two variables.

1.21 Create a default constructor for the Employee class that can only be called from other methods within the same class.

1.22 Create a constructor for the Employee class that has one optional parameter that sets the value of the **mID** member variable.

▶ 1.7 Multi-Tier Applications

A number of years ago leading computer scientists recognized that large enterprise-level applications could be designed using a *multi-tier application* model. This model was included in a highly influential book named **Design Patterns** (1995), by Erich Gamma, Richard Helm, and other authors.

A multi-tier application divides program tasks into three primary tiers, or layers: **presentation** (or *interface*), **business**, and **data** (or *persistence*). Tiers are often refered to as *layers*. All program components can be included in one of these tiers, which are briefly described here:

◆ **Presentation:** Interacts with the user, provides all visual, audible, and other input-output.

◆ **Business:** Processing rules and logic, including behaviors and attributes belonging to application entities.

◆ **Data:** Information storage and retrieval system, such as Database connections, RecordSet classes, text files, and XML data.

Programs modeled after the multi-tier approach contain one or more objects representing each tier. In a strict multi-tier design, each class belongs to one tier. The classes in any tier communicate only with classes in a neighboring tier. Many software design experts believe that clear separations between tiers allows easier software maintenance and improves the reuse of software components.

Suppose your company has developed a great human resources program to handle the recruiting and hiring of employees. Let us try to imagine the changes to your company's application that have occurred over the last 15 years:

◆ **Presentation tier**: When the program was first introduced, it used a character-based interface. Later, the user interface became graphical, using a Windows desktop model. More recently, the user interface was moved to a Web interface, so users could run it with a Web browser such as Internet Explorer.

◆ **Business tier:** Because of constantly changing government regulations, it has been necessary to update the internal logic of the programs. New business classes were added to the program to handle salary and employee benefits tracking.

◆ **Data tier:** Originally, the program ran on a single-user PC. Later, a multi-user database running on a small network was used. Even later, an enterprise-level server was introduced, simultaneously serving thousands of users.

The best computer applications live for many years and undergo a great deal of maintenance. An important measure of their success is how they adapt to design modifications. Companies invest much time and money in creating large applications, and they reuse existing software whenever possible. A multi-tier design creates a clear separation between components, permitting them to be copied between programs.

Applications do not always fit neatly into a multi-tier design. For reasons of runtime efficiency, programmers sometimes bend the rules. Web forms, for example, often make direct references to ADO.NET objects. While it is possible to use generic field names in the presentation layer that can be translated by the business layer into actual database field names, the translation might prove too slow for high-traffic applications.

Hands-On Tutorial: Bank Teller Application

 BankTeller

In this tutorial, you will design and build a short interactive program that lets users deposit and withdraw money from a bank account, and check their account balance. The account information will be saved between runs of the program. The program will be a Windows desktop application, and it will use a text file to store its data. It will be structured as a two-tier application (Visual tier and combined Business/Data tier).

This program uses a text file to read and store information. If you have not used text files before, you may want to review the optional topic on text files located at the end of this chapter.

Presentation Tier

The visual tier in this program will be a single form named **frmTeller**. Table 1-2 contains a list of controls used in this program, along with their property values. Figure 1-7 shows the form in design mode.

Table 1-2

Controls Used in the Bank Teller Program

Control Type	Control Name	Properties
Form	frmTeller	Text: "Bank Teller"
		AcceptButton: btnOK
		CancelButton: btnQuit
PictureBox	pbxLogo	Image: "logo.gif"
TextBox	txtAccountNumber	Text: " "
		TabIndex: 0
TextBox	txtDeposit	Text: " "
		TabIndex: 1
TextBox	txtWithdraw	Text: " "
		TabIndex: 2

(table continues)

Table 1-2

Controls Used in the Bank Teller Program *(continued)*

Label	lblBalance	Text: "0"
		BorderStyle: FixedSingle
		TextAlign: MiddleRight
Button	btnOK	Text: O&K
		Enabled: False
		TabIndex: 3
Button	btnQuit	Text: &Quit
		TabIndex: 4
Label	lblAccountName	Text: " "
		TextAlign: MiddleCenter
Label	(default)	Text: Account Number:
Label	(default)	Text: "Deposit"
		TextAlign: MiddleRight
Label	(default)	Text: "Withdraw"
		TextAlign: MiddleRight
Label	(default)	Text: "Balance"
		TextAlign: MiddleRight

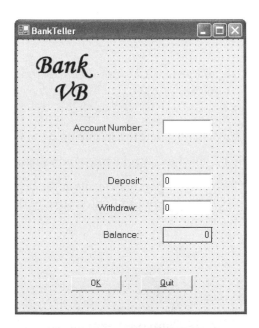

Figure 1-7 frmTeller in design mode

Business/Data Tier

The combined Business/Data tier will be implemented by the Account class, which holds information for a single bank account. Its properties are listed in Table 1-3 and its methods are listed in Table 1-4.

Table 1-3

Account Class Properties

Name	Type	Description
AccountNumber	String, ReadOnly	Unique account identifier; five numeric digits
Balance	Decimal, ReadOnly	Current account balance
Name	String, ReadOnly	Name of account holder
AccountNumberSize	Integer, Shared, ReadOnly	Number of digits in an account number

Table 1-4

Account Class Methods.

Name	Description
Deposit (amount)	Public: add amount to account balance
Open (accountNum)	Public: open account file identified by accountNum
Update	Public: save account file
Withdraw (amount)	Public: deduct amount from account balance
ReadFromFile	Private: read account information from a file

There are two important class Constraints:

◆ account balance must always be greater than zero

◆ deposits and withdrawals are positive values

Hands-On Steps

Step 1. Create a new Windows application named **BankTeller**.

Step 2. Delete the startup form and create a new form named **frmTeller**. Update the startup object to **frmMain**.

Step 3. Set up the form as shown in Figure 1-7. Refer to Table 1-2 for the control names and values.

Step 4. Add a class to the project named **Account**. Insert the following Import statements at the beginning of the module, before the class declaration. They will simplify our references to files, StreamWriters, and StreamReaders later on:

```
Imports System.IO
Imports System.IO.File
```

Step 5. Insert the following comments at the beginning of the class:

```
'Manages deposits and withdrawals for a single customer account
'at a bank, maintaining a running balance. Reads existing account
'information from a file and saves the same information on request.
```

Step 6. Add the following private variables to the class:

```
Private mAccountNumber As String
Private mAccountName As String
Private mBalance As Decimal
Private mFileName As String
Private Shared mAcctNumSize As Integer = 5
```

Step 7. Add the following properties to the class:

```
Public ReadOnly Property AccountNumber() As String
    Get
        Return mAccountNumber
    End Get
End Property

Public ReadOnly Property Balance() As Decimal
    Get
        Return mBalance
    End Get
End Property

Public ReadOnly Property Name() As String
    Get
        Return mAccountName
    End Get
End Property

Shared ReadOnly Property AccountNumberSize() As Integer
    Get
        Return mAcctNumSize
    End Get
End Property
```

Step 8. Add the **Deposit** method to the class. It receives the amount of the deposit and adds the amount to the current balance, as long as the amount is greater than zero:

```
Public Sub Deposit(ByVal amount As Decimal)
    If amount > 0 Then
        mBalance += amount
    End If
End Sub
```

Step 9. Add the **Withdraw** method to the Account class. It receives the amount of the withdrawal, and subtracts it from the current balance. It performs error checking to prevent the account from being overdrawn and returns a Boolean result indicating the success or failure of the operation:

```
Public Function Withdraw(ByVal amount As Decimal) As Boolean
    If (amount >0 And amount <= mBalance) Then
        mBalance -= amount
        Return True
    Else
        Return False
    End If
End Function
```

Step 10. Add the **Open** method to the Account class. This method receives an account number and uses it to form a filename with an extension of "txt". If the file is found in the project's **bin** directory, it is opened and the Open method returns True. If the file cannot be opened, Open returns False.

```
Public Function Open(ByVal acctNum As String) As Boolean
    mAccountNumber = acctNum
    mFileName = acctNum & ".txt"
    If Exists(mFileName) Then
        ReadFromFile()
        Return True
    Else
        Return False
    End If
End Function
```

Step 11. Add the **ReadFromFile** method to the Account class. It is marked private because it should not be called by a client program. Instead, it is called from the Open method. It uses the OpenText and ReadLine methods to open and read two records from the account file containing the customer's name and account balance:

```
Private Sub ReadFromFile()
    Dim inFile As StreamReader = OpenText(mFileName)
    With inFile
        mAccountName = .ReadLine()
        mBalance = CDec(.ReadLine())
        .Close()
    End With
End Sub
```

Notice that we were required to use the **CDec** function to convert the String returned by ReadLine into a Decimal, assigned to mBalance. This is an example of a required step when Option Strict is set to **On**.

Step 12. Add the **Update** method to the Account class. It overwrites the same account file read by the ReadFromFile method, saving the account name and balance:

```
Public Sub Update()
    Dim outFile As StreamWriter
    outFile = CreateText(mFileName)
    With outFile
        .WriteLine(mAccountName)
        .WriteLine(mBalance)
        .Close()
    End With
End Sub
```

The following steps refer to the frmTeller Form:

Step 13. Open the code window for the **frmTeller** form and add the **objAccount** variable. All Account class operations will take place via objAccount:

```
Private objAccount As Account
```

Step 14.   Select **txtDeposit** in the object pull-down list at the top of the frmTeller code window, and select the **Leave** event handler in the right-hand pulldown list. This event fires whenever the input focus leaves the txtDeposit TextBox. If the deposit amount is non-numeric, we want to inform the user immediately and return the focus to the same box:

```
Private Sub txtDeposit_Leave(ByVal sender As Object, _
 ByVal e As System.EventArgs) Handles txtDeposit.Leave

   If Not IsNumeric(txtDeposit.Text) Then
      MessageBox.Show("Deposit must be a number", "Error", _
       MessageBoxButtons.OK, _
       MessageBoxIcon.Stop)
      txtDeposit.Focus()
   End If
End Sub
```

Step 15.   Similarly, implement the Leave event for the **txtWithdraw** TextBox:

```
Private Sub txtWithdraw_Leave(ByVal sender As Object, _
 ByVal e As System.EventArgs) Handles txtWithdraw.Leave

   If Not IsNumeric(txtWithdraw.Text) Then
      MessageBox.Show("Withdrawal must be a number", "Error", _
       MessageBoxButtons.OK, _
       MessageBoxIcon.Stop)
      txtWithdraw.Focus()
   End If
End Sub
```

Step 16.   When the user selects the **OK** button, we want to add the deposit to the account balance by calling Account.Deposit. Similarly, we want to process the withdrawal amount. If Account.Withdraw returns false, a MessageBox must inform the user that insufficient funds are available. Finally, both text boxes are reset to zero to avoid accidentally processing the same transaction twice. Insert the following handler for the Click event:

```
Private Sub btnOK_Click(ByVal sender As System.Object, _
 ByVal e As System.EventArgs) Handles btnOK.Click

   objAccount.Deposit(CDec(txtDeposit.Text))
   txtDeposit.Text = "0"
   If objAccount.Withdraw(CDec(txtWithdraw.Text)) Then
      txtWithdraw.Text = "0"
   Else
      MessageBox.Show("Insufficient funds available to " _
       & "process the requested withdrawal.", "Warning", _
       MessageBoxButtons.OK, MessageBoxIcon.Warning)
   End If
   lblBalance.Text = FormatNumber(objAccount.Balance, 2)
End Sub
```

Step 17.   When the user selects the **Quit** button, we close the Form. Insert the following handler for the Click event:

```
Private Sub btnQuit_Click(ByVal sender As System.Object, _
 ByVal e As System.EventArgs) Handles btnQuit.Click

   Me.Close()
End Sub
```

Step 18. The **UpdateAccount** method creates an Account object the first time the method is called. If an Account already exists, the user is prompted to save the results of the account transactions by calling the Account.Update method. Insert the following code:

```
Private Sub UpdateAccount()
    If objAccount Is Nothing Then
        objAccount = New Account     'create for the first time
    Else
        If MessageBox.Show( _
            "Do you want to save existing account transactions?", _
            "Save Transactions", MessageBoxButtons.YesNo, _
            MessageBoxIcon.Question) = DialogResult.Yes Then
            objAccount.Update()
        End If
    End If
End Sub
```

Step 19. When the user types in an account number, the **TextChanged** event handler waits until the right number of digits have been entered (currently 5) and calls UpdateAccount. After the current account has been (possibly) saved, we want to open the new account file and fill the form labels with the new account's name and balance. We can also enable the OK button to allow transactions to begin. If the account file cannot be opened, we have to inform the user:

```
Private Sub txtAccountNumber_TextChanged(ByVal sender As Object, _
 ByVal e As System.EventArgs) Handles txtAccountNumber.TextChanged

    If txtAccountNumber.Text.Length = Account.AccountNumberSize Then
        UpdateAccount()
        'Open and view a new account
        If objAccount.Open(txtAccountNumber.Text) Then
            lblBalance.Text = FormatNumber(objAccount.Balance, 2)
            lblAccountName.Text = objAccount.Name
            btnOK.Enabled = True
        Else
            MessageBox.Show( _
             "Unable to open requested account", "Error", _
             MessageBoxButtons.OK, MessageBoxIcon.Stop)
        End If
    Else
        btnOK.Enabled = False
    End If
End Sub
```

Step 20. The **Closing** event of the form is fired either by the user selecting the Quit button, or by ending the program in any other way:

```
Private Sub frmTeller_Closing(ByVal sender As Object, _
 ByVal e As System.ComponentModel.CancelEventArgs) _
 Handles MyBase.Closing

    UpdateAccount()
End Sub
```

Step 21. Run and test the program. Here are some suggested tests:

◆ Enter a non-existent account number such as 12345. The program should notify you with a MessageBox that the account was not found.

◆ Enter account number 11111 and experiment with processing any combination of deposits and withdrawals (Figure 1-8). Be sure to attempt to overdraft the account.

◆ Enter nonnumeric characters in the deposit and withdrawal textboxes to verify their correct error handling.

◆ Enter account 22222 and expect to be prompted to save your existing account. Click Yes to save.

◆ Process new transactions for account 22222, but do not save changes to this account.

◆ Reopen account 11111 and verify that your previous balance was correctly saved.

◆ Reopen account 22222 and confirm that your previous balance was not saved.

You can easily create additional account files in the project's **bin** directory. Just use the same record format as the existing files. The Account class source code appears in Code Listing 1-2 and the frmTeller class is in Code Listing 1-3.

(End of tutorial)

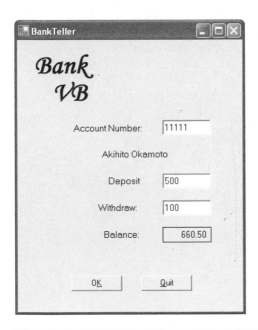

Figure 1-8 Running the Bank Teller program

Code Listing 1-2 (Account class)

```vbnet
Imports System.IO
Imports System.IO.File

'Manages deposits and withdrawals for a single customer account
'at a bank, maintaining a running balance. Reads existing account
'information from a file and saves the same information on request.
Public Class Account
    Private mAccountNumber As String
    Private mAccountName As String
    Private mBalance As Decimal
    Private mFileName As String
    Private Shared mAcctNumSize As Integer = 5

    'Deposit funds into the account if the amount is greater
    'than zero.
    Public Sub Deposit(ByVal amount As Decimal)
        If amount > 0 Then
            mBalance += amount
        End If
    End Sub

    'Attempt to locate and open the account file. Return True
    'if successful, False otherwise.
    Public Function Open(ByVal acctNum As String) As Boolean
        mAccountNumber = acctNum
        mFileName = acctNum & ".txt"
        If Exists(mFileName) Then
            ReadFromFile()
            Return True
        Else
            Return False
        End If
    End Function

    'Save account data to an account file
    Public Sub Update()
        Dim outFile As StreamWriter
        outFile = CreateText(mFileName)
        With outFile
            .WriteLine(mAccountName)
            .WriteLine(mBalance)
            .Close()
        End With
    End Sub

    'Withdraw funds from the account
    Public Function Withdraw(ByVal amount As Decimal) As Boolean
        If (amount <= mBalance) Then
            mBalance -= amount
            Return True
        Else
            Return False
        End If
    End Function

    Public ReadOnly Property AccountNumber() As String
        Get
            Return mAccountNumber
        End Get
    End Property

    Public ReadOnly Property Balance() As Decimal
        Get
            Return mBalance
        End Get
```

```
        End Property

        Public ReadOnly Property Name() As String
            Get
                Return mAccountName
            End Get
        End Property

        Shared ReadOnly Property AccountNumberSize() As Integer
            Get
                Return mAcctNumSize
            End Get
        End Property

        'Load account data from an existing account file
        Private Sub ReadFromFile()
            Dim inFile As StreamReader = OpenText(mFileName)
            With inFile
                mAccountName = .ReadLine()
                mBalance = CDec(.ReadLine())
                .Close()
            End With
        End Sub
    End Class
```

Code Listing 1-3 (frmTeller class)

```
Public Class frmTeller
    Inherits System.Windows.Forms.Form
```

```
+ Windows Form Designer generated code
```

```
    Private objAccount As Account

    Private Sub txtDeposit_Leave(ByVal sender As Object, _
     ByVal e As System.EventArgs) _
     Handles txtDeposit.Leave

        If Not IsNumeric(txtDeposit.Text) Then
            MessageBox.Show("Deposit must be a number", "Error", _
             MessageBoxButtons.OK, _
             MessageBoxIcon.Stop)
            txtDeposit.Focus()
        End If
    End Sub

    Private Sub txtWithdraw_Leave(ByVal sender As Object, _
     ByVal e As System.EventArgs) _
     Handles txtWithdraw.Leave

        If Not IsNumeric(txtWithdraw.Text) Then
            MessageBox.Show("Withdrawal must be a number", "Error", _
             MessageBoxButtons.OK, _
             MessageBoxIcon.Stop)
            txtWithdraw.Focus()
        End If
    End Sub

    Private Sub btnOK_Click(ByVal sender As System.Object, _
     ByVal e As System.EventArgs) Handles btnOK.Click

        objAccount.Deposit(CDec(txtDeposit.Text))
        txtDeposit.Text = "0"
        If objAccount.Withdraw(CDec(txtWithdraw.Text)) Then
            txtWithdraw.Text = "0"
        Else
            MessageBox.Show("Insufficient funds available to process " _
```

```
              & " the requested withdrawal.", "Warning", _
            MessageBoxButtons.OK, MessageBoxIcon.Warning)
       End If
       lblBalance.Text = FormatNumber(objAccount.Balance, 2)
   End Sub

   'If account is active, ask user to save existing transactions.
   Private Sub UpdateAccount()
       If objAccount Is Nothing Then
           objAccount = New Account        'create for the first time
       Else
           If MessageBox.Show("Do you want to save existing account " _
           & "transactions?", "Save Transactions", _
           MessageBoxButtons.YesNo, MessageBoxIcon.Question) = _
           DialogResult.Yes Then objAccount.Update()
       End If
   End Sub

   Private Sub txtAccountNumber_TextChanged(ByVal sender As Object, _
    ByVal e As System.EventArgs) Handles txtAccountNumber.TextChanged
       If txtAccountNumber.Text.Length = Account.AccountNumberSize Then
           UpdateAccount()
           'Open and view a new account
           If objAccount.Open(txtAccountNumber.Text) Then
               lblBalance.Text = FormatNumber(objAccount.Balance, 2)
               lblAccountName.Text = objAccount.Name
               btnOK.Enabled = True
           Else
               MessageBox.Show("Unable to open requested account", "Error", _
                MessageBoxButtons.OK, MessageBoxIcon.Stop)
           End If
       Else
           btnOK.Enabled = False
       End If
   End Sub

   Private Sub frmTeller_Closing(ByVal sender As Object, ByVal e _
    As System.ComponentModel.CancelEventArgs) Handles MyBase.Closing
       UpdateAccount()
   End Sub

   Private Sub btnQuit_Click(ByVal sender As System.Object, _
    ByVal e As System.EventArgs) _
    Handles btnQuit.Click
       Me.Close()
   End Sub
End Class
```

Hands-On Tutorial: Bank Teller Transaction Log

BankTeller2

In this hands-on tutorial, we make it possible for the Bank Teller program to log all transactions to a file. Transaction logging can be useful in a number of ways—when producing monthly account statements, for example, or when verifying and auditing account transactions. Our log file will contain a separate record for each deposit and withdrawal transaction on customer accounts.

Data Tier: TransactionLog Class

The **TransactionLog** class comprises the program's data tier. It is responsible for collecting transaction information and writing it to a text file. As is true with many real-world applications, data storage requirements change over time. The TransactionLog class, which currently writes to a text file, might be re-engineered to write to a database, HTML file, or XML file. Or, it could transfer transaction information through a network connection. When such changes occur, we will not want the business or presentation tiers to be affected.

Methods

Declaration	Description
Public Sub Add(ByRef trans As Transaction)	Adds a new Transaction to the log
Public Sub Save()	Appends all logged transactions to the transaction file

Internally, the TransactionLog class uses a Collection object to hold all logged transactions. The Save method iterates over the collection and writes each transaction to a file.

Business Tier: Transaction Class

The Transaction class holds information for a single bank account. Transactions are created by the Account class and passed to the TransactionLog.Add method. Here are its properties and methods:

Properties

Name	Type	Description
AccountNumber	String, ReadOnly	Unique account identifier; five numeric digits
TransDate	Date, ReadOnly	Date and time of transaction
Amount	Decimal, ReadOnly	Transaction amount (deposits are positive, withdrawals are negative)
Balance	Decimal, ReadOnly	Updated account balance

Methods

Declaration	Description
Public Sub New(ByVal acctNum As String, ByVal tdate As Date, ByVal amount As Decimal, ByVal balance As Decimal)	Constructs a transaction from account number, date, amount, and balance.
Public Overrides Function ToString() As String	Returns a comma-delimited string representation of the transaction.

Hands-On Steps:

Step 1. Copy the BankTeller program to a new directory named **BankTeller2**, and open the copied solution file (BankTeller.sln).

Step 2. Add a new class to the project named **Transaction**. Add the following variable declarations to the class:

```
'Represents a single bank account transaction. Created for
'logging purposes.

Private mAccountNum As String    'customer account number
Private mTransDate As Date       'date and time of transaction
Private mAmount As Decimal       'transaction amount
Private mBalance As Decimal      'updated account balance
```

Step 3. Add the following constructor. It creates a Transaction from an account number, transaction date (and time), transaction amount, and current balance:

```
Public Sub New(ByVal acctNum As String, ByVal tdate As Date, _
  ByVal amount As Decimal, ByVal balance As Decimal)
    mAccountNum = acctNum
    mTransDate = tdate
    mAmount = amount
    mBalance = balance
End Sub
```

Step 4. Add the following **ToString** method. The **Overrides** keyword indicates that ToString already exists in the Object (parent) class. Provide a more specific implementation of ToString for Transaction objects:

```
Public Overrides Function ToString() As String
   Return mAccountNum & ", " & mTransDate _
      & ", " & mAmount & ", " & mBalance
End Function
```

Following is an example of a string returned by Transaction.ToString:

```
"11111, 5/12/2003 11:30:39 AM, 50, 472.5".
```

Step 5. Add a new class named **TransactionLog** to the project and insert the following data definitions. The first is a collection that will hold Transaction objects. The second is a default filename to be used for the transaction log:

```
'Logs account transaction information to a text file.

Private mLog As New Collection()
Private Const FILENAME As String = "transaction.log"
```

Step 6. Add the following **Add** method to the class. The method receives a Transaction object and inserts it into the mLog collection:

```
Public Sub Add(ByRef trans As Transaction)
   mLog.Add(trans)
End Sub
```

Step 7. Add the following **Save** method to the class. The method creates the log file, iterates over the mLog collection, and writes each transaction to the file:

```
Public Sub Save()
   Dim oFile As System.IO.StreamWriter
   oFile = System.IO.File.CreateText(FILENAME)

   Dim trans As Transaction
   For Each trans In mLog
      oFile.WriteLine(trans.ToString())
   Next trans

   oFile.Close()
End Sub
```

(Optional: This would be a good time to build the program and check for any data entry errors.)

Step 8. Next, we need to make a few small changes to the **Account** class so it will be able to enable transaction logging. Open the Account class and add one new private variable to hold the transaction log:

```
Private mTransLog As New TransactionLog()
```

Step 9.   Insert an additional statement into the Deposit method that adds a record of the deposit to the transaction log. Following is the entire procedure:

```
Public Sub Deposit(ByVal amount As Decimal)
    If amount > 0 Then
        mBalance += amount
        mTransLog.Add(New Transaction(mAccountNumber, _
          Now, amount, mBalance))
    End If
End Sub
```

Step 10.   Insert three new lines into the Withdraw method that add a record of the withdrawal to the transaction log. Withdrawals will be recorded as negative values, which explains the leading negative sign:

```
Public Function Withdraw(ByVal amount As Decimal) As Boolean
    If (amount <= mBalance) Then
        mBalance -= amount
        If amount > 0 Then
            mTransLog.Add(New Transaction(mAccountNumber, _
                Now, -amount, mBalance))
        End If
        Return True
    Else
        Return False
    End If
End Function
```

Step 11.   Add a new line to the end of the Update method that saves the transaction log:

```
Public Sub Update()
    Dim outFile As System.IO.StreamWriter
    outFile = System.IO.File.CreateText(mFileName)
    outFile.WriteLine(mAccountName)
    outFile.WriteLine(mBalance)
    outFile.Close()
    mTransLog.Save()
End Sub
```

Step 12.   Compile and run the program. You can begin testing. First, enter account number **11111**, enter a combined deposit and withdrawal, and click on OK. Note the new balance.

Step 13.   Enter account number 22222, and when prompted to save the existing account, choose **Yes**.

Step 14.   Make a deposit to account 22222, click OK, and note the new balance. Save this record and end the program.

Step 15.   Go to the project's bin directory and open the transaction.log file (use the File | Open command from Visual Studio .NET to do this). You should see the transactions you just entered. Following are examples:

```
11111, 5/12/2003 11:51:38 PM, 50, 600
11111, 5/12/2003 11:51:38 PM, -100, 500
22222, 5/12/2003 11:51:46 PM, 50, 942.35
```

In the authors' test run, account 11111 began with a balance of $550. First, $50 was deposited, and then $100 was withdrawn, resulting in a balance of $500. Next, $50 was deposited in account 22222, raising its balance to $942.35. The complete source code for the Transaction class appears in Code Listing 1-4. The TransactionLog class is in Code Listing 1-5.

(End of tutorial)

Code Listing 1-4 (Transaction class)

```
Public Class Transaction
    Private mAccountNum As String      'customer account number
    Private mTransDate As Date         'date and time of transaction
    Private mAmount As Decimal         'transaction amount
    Private mBalance As Decimal        'updated account balance

    Public ReadOnly Property AccountNumber() As String
       Get
           Return mAccountNum
       End Get
    End Property

    Public ReadOnly Property TransDate() As Date
       Get
           Return mTransDate
       End Get
    End Property

    Public ReadOnly Property Amount() As Decimal
       Get
           Return mAmount
       End Get
    End Property

    Public ReadOnly Property Balance() As Decimal
       Get
           Return mBalance
       End Get
    End Property

    'Implementation Note: positive transactions are deposits.
    'Negative transactions are withdrawals.
    Public Sub New(ByVal acctNum As String, ByVal tdate As Date, _
      ByVal amount As Decimal, ByVal balance As Decimal)
        mAccountNum = acctNum
        mTransDate = tdate
        mAmount = amount
        mBalance = balance
    End Sub

    'Return a comma-delimited record suitable for writing
    'to a text file
    Public Overrides Function ToString() As String
       Return mAccountNum & ", " & mTransDate & ", " _
         & mAmount & ", " & mBalance
    End Function
End Class
```

Code Listing 1-5 (TransactionLog class)

```
Public Class TransactionLog
    'Logs Account transaction information to a text file.

    Private mLog As New Collection()
    Private Const FILENAME As String = "transaction.log"

    'Adds a new transaction to the transaction log
    Public Sub Add(ByRef trans As Transaction)
       mLog.Add(trans)
    End Sub

    'Appends all logged transactions to the transaction file
    Public Sub Save()

       Dim oFile As System.IO.StreamWriter
       oFile = System.IO.File.CreateText(FILENAME)
       Dim trans As Transaction
       For Each trans In mLog
          oFile.WriteLine(trans.ToString())
       Next trans

       oFile.Close()
    End Sub
End Class
```

Checkpoint

1.23 In the BankTeller application, what classes and methods are used in the Business logic tier?

1.24 In the BankTeller application, what classes and methods are used in the Data tier?

1.25 In the BankTeller application, what happens if the user tries to withdraw too much money from the account?

1.26 In the BankTeller application, how do the txtDeposit and txtWithdraw controls prevent the user from entering blank amounts?

1.27 In the BankTeller application, what event is fired in the frmTeller Form when the user leaves the deposit text box blank?

▶1.8 Composition Relationships Between Classes

A *composition* (or aggregation) relationship between two classes is created when one class contains object variables of the other class' type. As a design tool, composition turns out to be useful in real-world applications, because real-world objects often involve the same type of relationship. A machine, for example, is made up of parts, each of which is an object with its own attributes. A business unit consists of departments. A college transcript contains individual course records. For a slightly more specific example, an employee's personnel record contains individual components such as the following:

◆ address

◆ salary history

◆ performance evaluations

◆ employment history

◆ contact information

Object-oriented designers know that classes in real-world applications never exist in isolation. Instead, they are linked together by relationships such as composition and inheritance. We focus on composition relationships in this chapter, and defer a discussion of inheritance until Chapter 11.

Employee Information Example

We would like to create a class named **clsEmployee** that contains objects from several other classes: personal information such as ID number, name and address, current salary information, and the person's current project assignment. In all, we can create five classes, all related to each other by composition. Here's a quick overview of the classes:

- ◆ **clsEmployee** contains an employee identification number, personal information, current salary data, and current project assignment.
- ◆ **clsPersonalInfo** contains a first name, last name, and address.
- ◆ **clsAddress** contains a street address, city name, state abbreviation, zip code, and phone number.
- ◆ **clsSalaryItem** contains the date when the employee's salary level was awarded, and the employee's yearly salary amount.
- ◆ **clsProject** contains a project identification code and the date when the employee joined the project.

We could have dumped all this information into a single class named clsEmployee, but that approach would be inefficient and difficult to handle. When individual classes are kept simple, there is a greater chance they can be reused in various combinations. In a way, the principle is the same in electronics. Individual components such as transistors, resistors, logic chips, and memory chips are designed to be simple and generic. They can be combined into any number of different devices. In our example, the clsAddress class is generic enough that it could hold the address of an employee, a student, or perhaps a business.

Selecting Class Names

You may be wondering why each class name in our example was prefixed by the letters "cls". The prefix is not required, but it does help to prevent confusion regarding property names. For example, the **clsEmployee** class can have a property named **Address**, which is of type **clsAddress**. If, instead, the class name was **Address**, we would end up with statements that used the same identifier for the variable's type and the property name:

```
Dim anEmployee As New clsEmployee
Dim adr As Address = anEmployee.Address
```

The foregoing code would be legal, but awkward to read. You can lengthen class names to distinguish them from property names. For example, the **CompanyEmployee** class can have a property named **Address**, which is an **EmployeeAddress** object:

```
Dim anEmployee As New CompanyEmployee
Dim adr As EmployeeAddress = anEmployee.Address
```

Using UML to Describe Classes

Software designers commonly use a notation named *Universal Modeling Language* (UML) to describe classes and their relationships. Figure 1-9 shows a UML diagram of the classes in our Employee Information example. A class symbol is a rectangle that displays the class name in the top row, a list of the class properties in the second row, and a list of the methods in the third row. Each property is usually assigned a type, as we have in the figure. Figure 1-9 does not list any methods.

In the same figure, the lines connecting the classes indicate a composition relationship. The diamond-shaped marker in each line is closest to the class that contains an instance of the class at the other end of the connection line. For example, the line connecting clsEmployee to clsPersonalInfo shows that each clsEmployee object contains an instance of clsPersonalInfo. The digit next to the end of each connector indicates the *multiplicity* of the composition relationship. A 1..1 relationship means that one instance of clsEmployee contains one instance of clsPersonalInfo. Sometimes a class will contain multiple instances of another class. In that case, the multiplicity is "1..N".

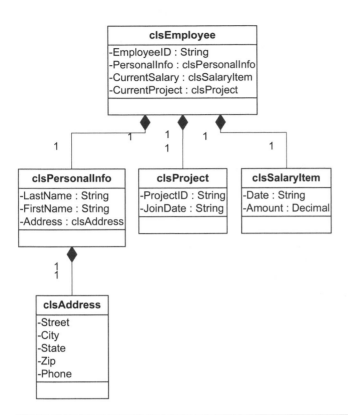

Figure 1-9 Class relationships, Employee Information example

Displaying the Objects

The classes in this program each have two methods: a constructor and a ToString method. The constructor for each class receives parameters that initialize its class properties. The ToString method converts the contents of the class properties to a string so the class can be displayed on the console. As we mentioned earlier in this chapter, ToString is a method in the Object class, and all classes we create are automatically derived from Object. The declaration of ToString in the Object class includes the **Overridable** qualifier, which permits the function to be overriden:

```
Overridable Public Function ToString() As String
```

If we override ToString and create our own version of the method, we can use it to display the contents of Employee objects:

```
123 South Street, Miami, FL, 33333, 305-333-4444
```

When we implement ToString, we must include the **Overrides** keyword:

```
Public Overrides Function ToString() As String

    Return mStreet & ", " & mCity & ", " & mState & ", " _
        & mZip & ", " & mPhone
End Function
```

Hands-On Tutorial: Employee Information

 EmployeeInfo

Using the five classes we have described, let us create the Employee Information program. We will make it a console application to keep everything to the bare essentials.

Step 1. Create a new Windows Console project named **EmployeeInfo**.

Step 2. Add a new class to the project named **clsAddress** and insert the following variables:

```
Private mStreet As String
Private mCity As String
Private mState As String
Private mZip As String
Private mPhone As String
```

Step 3. Add the following parameterized constructor to the class, which creates an address and initializes its variables:

```
Public Sub New(ByVal street As String, _
   ByVal city As String, ByVal state As String, _
   ByVal zip As String, ByVal phone As String)

   mStreet = street
   mCity = city
   mState = state
   mZip = zip
   mPhone = phone
End Sub
```

Step 4. Add the following ToString method to the class:

```
Public Overrides Function ToString() As String
   Return mStreet & ", " & mCity & ", " & mState & ", " _
      & mZip & ", " & mPhone
End Function
```

Step 5. Add the **clsPersonalInfo** class to the project and insert the following private member variables and constructor. The mAddress member is itself an instance of clsAddress:

```
Private mLastName As String
Private mFirstName As String
Private mAddress As clsAddress

Public Sub New(ByVal pLastName As String, _
   ByVal pFirstName As String, ByVal pAddress As clsAddress)

   mLastName = pLastName
   mFirstName = pFirstName
   mAddress = pAddress
End Sub
```

Step 6. Add a **ToString** method to clsPersonalInfo. It calls **mAddress.ToString** to take advantage of the work already done in the clsAddress class:

```
Public Overrides Function ToString() As String
   Return mLastName & ", " & mFirstName & ", " _
      & mAddress.ToString()
End Function
```

Step 7. Add the **clsSalaryItem** class to the project and insert the variables, constructor, and ToString method:

```
Private mDate As String      'date salary awarded
Private mAmount As Decimal    'yearly salary amount

Public Sub New(ByVal pDate As String, ByVal pAmount As Decimal)
   mDate = pDate
   mAmount = pAmount
End Sub

Public Overrides Function ToString() As String
   Return "Salary " & FormatCurrency(mAmount) _
      & " awarded " & mDate
End Function
```

Step 8. Add the **clsProject** class to the project and insert the variables, constructor, and ToString method:

```
Private mProjectID As String        'identification code
Private mJoinDate As String         'date when project joined

Public Sub New(ByVal pProjectID As String, _
   ByVal pJoinDate As String)

   mProjectID = pProjectID
   mJoinDate = pJoinDate
End Sub

Public Overrides Function ToString() As String
   Return "Project " & mProjectID & " started " & mJoinDate
End Function
```

Step 9. Finally we arrive at the clsEmployee class, which is the container for all the other classes created so far. Add **clsEmployee** to the project and insert the following code. The constructor receives parameters of type clsPersonalInfo, clsSalaryItem, and clsProject, so a client program will need to construct these objects before creating an employee:

```
Private mEmployeeID As String
Private mPersonalInfo As clsPersonalInfo
Private mCurrentSalary As clsSalaryItem
Private mCurrentProject As clsProject

Public Sub New(ByVal id As String, ByVal pInfo As clsPersonalInfo, _
ByVal pSalary As clsSalaryItem, ByVal pProject As clsProject)

   mEmployeeID = id
   mPersonalInfo = pInfo
   mCurrentSalary = pSalary
   mCurrentProject = pProject
End Sub
```

Step 10. Add the **ToString** method to clsEmployee. We have added some end-of-line characters to the string, identified by the standard constant named **ControlChars.CrLf**:

```
Public Overrides Function ToString() As String
    Return "ID: " & mEmployeeID _
    & ControlChars.CrLf _
    & mPersonalInfo.ToString() _
    & ControlChars.CrLf _
    & mCurrentSalary.ToString() _
    & ControlChars.CrLf _
    & mCurrentProject.ToString()
End Function
```

Step 11. All that remains is to create an instance of clsEmployee in the program's startup module, call its ToString method, and write the output to the console. It is easiest if we do this in steps: create an address, create some personal information, create a salary item, create a project instance, and combine all of these elements into an employee. Enter the following code in the **Main** procedure of **Module1**:

```
Sub Main()
    Dim address As New clsAddress("123 South Street", _
        "Miami", "FL", "33333", "305-333-4444")
    Dim personal As New clsPersonalInfo("Rostropovich", _
        "Ivan", address)

    Dim salary As New clsSalaryItem("02/20/1998", 35000)
    Dim project As New clsProject("AES11002", "04/20/2002")

    Dim emp As New clsEmployee("11111", personal, salary, project)
    System.Console.WriteLine(emp.ToString())
End Sub
```

Step 12. Run the program. The output should look like this:

```
ID: 11111
Rostropovich, Ivan, 123 South Street, Miami, FL, 33333, 305-333-4444
Salary $35,000.00 awarded 02/20/1998
Project AES11002 started 04/20/2002
```

(End of tutorial)

The complete source code for the clsAddress, clsPersonalInfo, and clsSalaryItem classes appears in Code Listing 1-6. The clsProject and clsEmployee classes appear in Code Listing 1-7. The class structure in this example program is a lot like a database with related tables. The main difference is that when working with classes, you do not have to have a common key field linking tables together. Instead, we embed, or contain objects of one type inside other objects.

Think about what you could do with clsEmployee and its component classes. Here are a few ideas:

◆ Provide a way for the owner of a clsEmployee object to modify the employee's address. Would you permit a change to only the street or city, or would it be easier to require the client program to create a new clsAddress object and replace the employee's existing address?

◆ Create a collection of employees. You could search for employees by ID number, add new employees, remove employees, and calculate the average salary of all employees.

◆ In clsEmployee, rather than having a single clsSalaryItem object, there could be a collection holding an employee's salary history. That would enable you to find the person's average salary, the average amount of time between promotions, the percent increase between salaries, and so on.

◆ If an employee could be working on more than one project, the clsEmployee class should contain a collection of clsProject objects. Assuming a collection of employees existed, you could generate a list of projects in which each project ID was followed by a list of employees belonging to that project.

◆ Rather than having employees containing projects, you could have projects that each contain a collection of references to employees. This would make it easier to view an employee list for each project, but harder to view a list of projects belonging to a single employee.

Code Listing 1-6 (clsAddress, clsPersonalInfo, and clsSalaryItem)

```
Public Class clsAddress
    Private mStreet As String
    Private mCity As String
    Private mState As String
    Private mZip As String
    Private mPhone As String

    Public Sub New(ByVal street As String, _
        ByVal city As String, _
        ByVal state As String, _
        ByVal zip As String, _
        ByVal phone As String)

        mStreet = street
        mCity = city
        mState = state
        mZip = zip
        mPhone = phone
    End Sub

    Public Overrides Function ToString() As String
        Return mStreet & ", " & mCity & ", " _
          & mState & ", " & mZip & ", " & mPhone
    End Function
End Class

Public Class clsPersonalInfo
    Private mLastName As String
    Private mFirstName As String
    Private mAddress As clsAddress

    Public Sub New(ByVal pLastName As String, _
        ByVal pFirstName As String, _
        ByVal pAddress As clsAddress)

        mLastName = pLastName
        mFirstName = pFirstName
        mAddress = pAddress
    End Sub

    Public Overrides Function ToString() As String
        Return mLastName & ", " & mFirstName & ", " _
          & mAddress.ToString()
    End Function
End Class

Public Class clsSalaryItem
    Private mDate As String        'date salary awarded
    Private mAmount As Decimal      'yearly salary amount

    Public Sub New(ByVal pDate As String, _
      ByVal pAmount As Decimal)
        mDate = pDate
        mAmount = pAmount
    End Sub
```

```
      Public Overrides Function ToString() As String
         Return "Salary " & FormatCurrency(mAmount) _
          & " awarded " & mDate
      End Function
   End Class
```

Code Listing 1-7 (clsProject and clsEmployee)

```
Public Class clsProject
   Private mProjectID As String     'identification code
   Private mJoinDate As String      'date project joined

   Public Sub New(ByVal pProjectID As String, _
    ByVal pJoinDate As String)
      mProjectID = pProjectID
      mJoinDate = pJoinDate
   End Sub

   Public Overrides Function ToString() As String
      Return "Project " & mProjectID _
       & " started " & mJoinDate
   End Function
End Class

Public Class clsEmployee
   Private mEmployeeID As String
   Private mPersonalInfo As clsPersonalInfo
   Private mCurrentSalary As clsSalaryItem
   Private mCurrentProject As clsProject

   Public Sub New(ByVal id As String, _
      ByVal pInfo As clsPersonalInfo, _
      ByVal pSalary As clsSalaryItem, _
      ByVal pProject As clsProject)
      mEmployeeID = id
      mPersonalInfo = pInfo
      mCurrentSalary = pSalary
      mCurrentProject = pProject
   End Sub

   Public Overrides Function ToString() As String
      Return "ID: " & mEmployeeID _
       & ControlChars.CrLf _
       & mPersonalInfo.ToString() _
       & ControlChars.CrLf _
       & mCurrentSalary.ToString() _
       & ControlChars.CrLf _
       & mCurrentProject.ToString()
   End Function
End Class
```

Checkpoint

1.28 Describe the composition relationship between an Automobile class and an Engine class.

1.29 In what ways can software classes exhibit some of the advantages of integrated circuits in electronics devices?

1.30 Draw a UML diagram that shows a composition relationship between the Employee class and the Department class. (Assume that a single department may contain multiple employees.)

1.31 In the Employee Information application presented in this section, what classes are used in composing an clsEmployee object?

►1.9 Optional Topic: Nested (Inner) Classes

When you define a class within some other class, the first class is a *nested class* or *inner class*. Nested classes tend to be used in definitions of complex objects, because they permit a data type to be hidden inside some existing type.

NestedClasses

Suppose we wished to create a class named **Address**. Many meanings of "Address" exist, depending on the context. If our program contained an Employee class, Address might imply the location of an employee's residence. But in a program containing a NetworkConnection class, Address might imply the four-part *universal resource locator* (URL) common to all networks. If Employee and NetworkConnection were within the same namespace, we might not be able to define both types of addresses.

Nested classes provide a way for both Address classes to exist within the same namespace. First, we define Address within NetworkConnection:

```
Class NetworkConnection

    Class Address
        Private mURL(3) As Integer
    End Class

End Class
```

A client program can create an instance of Address as long as it qualifies Address with its enclosing class name:

```
Public Sub main()
    Dim addr As New NetworkConnection.Address
End Sub
```

The following statement, on the other hand, is illegal:

```
Public Sub main()
    Dim addr As New Address
End Sub
```

Next, we can define an Address class inside the Employee class:

```
Class Employee

    Class Address
        Private mStreet As String
        Private mCity As String
        Private mState As String
        Private mZip As String
    End Class

End Class
```

A client program can now create an Employee.Address:

```
Public Sub main()
    Dim addr As New Employee.Address
End Sub
```

Hidden Components

Sometimes a class implementation contains component objects that would never be created on their own. We would declare their class names privately inside the surrounding class. For example, an automatic teller machine (ATM) simulation might contain individual classes such as CashDispenser, DisplayInterface, Keypad, and AccountVerifier. The ATM class would create these objects internally, but client programs would have no use for them:

```
Public Class ATM

    Private Class CashDispenser
    End Class

    Private Class DisplayInterface
    End Class

    Private Class Keypad
    End Class

    Private Class AccountVerifier
    End Class

End Class
```

The Private qualifier was used for the internal classes, making their names visible only within the ATM class. A client program can create an ATM object, but it cannot create an ATM.Keypad object:

```
Dim myATM As New ATM              'OK
Dim myKeys As New ATM.Keypad     'error: private class
```

▶1.10 Optional Topic: Using Text Files

In our first volume, *Starting Out with Visual Basic .NET*, text file processing was covered extensively in Chapter 9. In case you skipped that topic in your first VB course, we have included some supplementary material here to help you use files. First, text files have been around a long time, even before databases. Text tiles provide a valuable function in day-to-day software development:

◆ They offer a simple way to save and retrieve information without requiring the rather heavy overhead of a database management system.

◆ They are platform-independent. Even XML files, a recent development in cross-platform data transfer, are basically just made of text.

◆ You can edit text files with any text editor, such as *Windows NotePad* or *Visual Studio .NET*. You can create and modify text files without the need for a database management system such as *Microsoft Access*.

Take a moment to examine the Windows directory on your computer, and note the many files of type **Text Document.** You will see that Microsoft considers text files to be very useful. Fortunately, the creators of Visual Basic .NET provide a rich and effective set of functions for file processing.

Imports Statement

If your program is using text files, place the following Imports statements at the top of each module:

```
Imports System.IO
Imports System.IO.File
```

If you omit these statements, the function names you call will have to be qualified names, such as: System.IO.File.CreateText. Before you can read from a file or write to a file, you must open it. Reading from a text file is done using a StreamReader object. Writing data to a text file is done using a StreamWriter object. After you have finished reading and writing, you must close the appropriate StreamReader or StreamWriter.

Find Out If a Text File Exists

To find out if a file exists, call the **Exists** method, which returns True if the file is found:

```
If Exists("input.txt") Then ...
```

Open a Text File for Reading

The easiest way to open a file for reading is to call the **OpenText** method, which returns a **StreamReader** object:

```
Dim inFile As StreamReader = OpenText("input.txt")
```

If the string you pass to OpenText is just a filename, the program will look in its **bin** directory for the file. Otherwise, you can include a directory and folder name to tell the program to look in a specific place, such as *D:\MyData\VBNetFiles*.

Create a New Text File

The easiest way to create a new file and prepare it for writing is to call the **CreateText** method, which returns a **StreamWriter** object:

```
Dim outFile As StreamWriter = CreateText("output.txt")
```

The same rules regarding filenames we mentioned for OpenText apply also to CreateText.

Append to an Existing Text File

If you want to add data to an existing file without destroying existing data, call the **AppendText** method. It returns a StreamWriter:

```
Dim outFile As StreamWriter = AppendText("output.txt")
```

The same rules regarding filenames we mentioned for OpenText apply also to AppendText.

Read a Line From a Text File

To read a line of text from a file, call the StreamReader's **ReadLine** method. In the following, we assume inFile is a StreamReader:

```
Dim temp As String
temp = inFile.ReadLine()
```

Write a Line to a Text File

To write a line of text to a file, call the StreamWriter's **WriteLine** method. In the following, we assume outFile is a StreamWriter:

```
Dim temp As String = "Some data"
outFile.WriteLine(temp)
```

If you want to leave the output pointer on the same line after writing the data, call the **Write** method. The next time Write or WriteLine is called, the data will appear on the same output line:

```
outFile.Write(temp)
```

Close a StreamReader or StreamWriter

When you have finished reading from a StreamReader, call its **Close** method. Assuming inFile is an active StreamReader, we can write:

```
inFile.Close()
```

When you have finished writing to a StreamWriter, call its **Close** method:

```
outFile.Close()
```

Hands-On Example: Reading and Writing Text

FileDemo

Let us apply what was said about text files by looking at a short program that does the following:

◆ Writes a person's address to a text file.
◆ Reads the same address from the file and displays it in a list box.

Most useful text files tend to be simple. If you have a lot of data to read and write, use a database.

Step 1. Open the **FileDemo** program from the Chapter 1 examples directory.

Step 2. Inspect the startup form (frmMain) in Design view (Figure 1-10). Click on each control to note its name.

Step 3. In the Code window, note the variable holding the filename created by the program:

```
Dim mFileName As String = "address.txt"
```

Step 4. In the same window, examine the Click event handler for the **btnWrite** button. This code creates a file and writes a person's address to the file:

```
Dim outFile As StreamWriter = CreateText(mFileName)
With outFile
   .WriteLine("John Smith")
   .WriteLine("222 Mauka Street")
   .WriteLine("Kailua, HI 96734")
   .Close()
End With
MessageBox.Show("Address written to file", mFileName)
```

Step 5. Examine the Click event handler for the **btnRead** button. This code opens the address file and reads three lines. Each address line is inserted into the list box named myList:

```
Dim inFile As StreamReader = OpenText(mFileName)
With myList.Items
   .Clear()
   .Add(inFile.ReadLine())        'name
   .Add(inFile.ReadLine())        'street
```

```
        .Add(inFile.ReadLine())         'city, state, Zip
End With
inFile.Close()
```

Step 6. Run the program. Click on the **Write to File** button and note the displayed message box.

Step 7. Click on the **Read from File** button, and note the address that appears in the list box (Figure 1-11). You might want to examine the program's bin directory, looking for the address.txt file. You can open the file using Visual Studio .NET (select File | Open from the menu.).
(End of example)

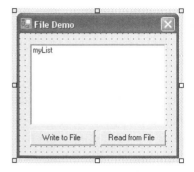

Figure 1-10 File Demo program, startup form

Figure 1-11 Output from the File Demo program

▶1.11 Summary

◆ Object-oriented programming is a way of designing and coding applications that has led to using interchangeable software components to build larger programs.

◆ A *class* is a pattern, or blueprint that defines a group of related objects having common characteristics. In computer programs, a class identifies a specific data type. All instances of a class share common characteristics named *attributes* and *behaviors*.

◆ Local variables are created on the runtime stack and they disappear when their enclosing procedure exits.

◆ When you declare an object variable (within a method), the variable itself is located in the method's runtime stack. The variable holds a reference to an actual object, which is located in the memory area called the *managed heap*.

◆ When there are no longer any active references to an object, the .NET runtime is free to remove the object from memory. Memory is freed by a .NET background program called the *garbage collector*.

◆ *Object-oriented design* centers around the design of programs using classes and class relationships. The first step after creating program specifications is to analyze the application requirements. *Object-oriented analysis*, as it is called, often starts with a detailed specification of the problem to be solved.

◆ When designing object-oriented programs, first select classes that reflect physical entities in the application domain. Classes can also be discovered in the descriptions of processing and control structures.

◆ Designers describe classes in terms of attributes and operations. *Attributes* are characteristics of each object that will be implemented as properties. *Operations* are actions the class objects may perform or messages to which they can respond.

◆ The *class interface* is visible to an Application programmer who uses the class. The class *implementation* is the portion of a class hidden from client programs.

◆ *Inheritance* lets programmers create new classes that inherit, or derive characteristics of existing classes.

◆ One of the most common patterns in computer software is the *client-server pattern*. A server produces information consumed by one or more clients. A client creates a reference to a server and sends it requests in the form of method calls.

◆ To add a new class to a Visual Basic .NET project, select *Add Class* from the Project menu.

◆ A method is a procedure or function declared inside a class. It performs actions resulting from messages passed to instances of its class.

◆ When a class variable or method is Public, any client program can freely access the member belonging to a specific object. If the Private keyword is used, however, the member becomes invisible outside the class.

◆ A *property* is a method that provides access to private class member variables. Property procedures can filter incoming values before they are assigned to private member variables.

◆ A *constructor* is a class method that runs automatically when an instance of the class is created. A *default constructor* has no parameters. A *parameterized constructor* has parameters that assign values to class variables or properties. A private constructor can only be called by other methods in the same class.

◆ *Method overloading* permits two or more methods in the same class to have the same name as long as they have different parameter lists.

◆ You can declare optional parameters in any method (including constructors) using the Optional keyword, as long as you assign them default values.

◆ Assign constructor parameters to properties, taking advantage of the built-in validation of the class property procedures.

◆ A multi-tier application divides program tasks into three primary tiers, or layers: **presentation**, **business**, and **data**. By having a clear separation between layers, individual classes can be redesigned and updated to meet changing requirements.

◆ When a class contains a variable that is shared between all instances of the class, it is called a *shared variable*. A *shared property* permits client programs to assign values to and return values of a shared variable.

- The hands-on Bank Teller application lets users deposit and withdraw money from a bank account, and check their account balance. The account information is saved between program runs.
- A *composition* relationship between classes is created when a class contains object variables of another class type. As a design tool, composition turns out to be useful in real-world applications because real-world objects often involve the same type of relationship.
- Software designers commonly use notation named *Universal Modeling Language* (UML) to describe classes and their relationships.
- You can override the ToString method from the Object class to provide a standard way of converting the properties of a class into a single String.

▶1.12 Key Terms

attribute

behavior

business tier

class

class implementation

class interface

client-server pattern

client program

composition relationship

constructor

data tier

dereference

encapsulation

finding the classes

function procedure

garbage collector

information hiding

inheritance

managed heap

method

multi-tier application model

namespace

nested class

null reference

object

object-oriented analysis

object-oriented programming

operations

optional parameters

parameterized constructor

parameters

passing by reference

passing by value

persistence

presentation tier

private (member access)

private constructor

procedure

property

public (member access)

read-only property

reference

shared property

shared variable

stack (runtime stack)

UML

value types

XML

▶1.13 Review Questions

Fill-in-the-Blank

[handwritten: Business rules]

1. The three layers of a multi-tier application are presentation, ———————, and data.

2. When describing application requirements for object-oriented programs, the nouns translate into *[handwritten: Classes (Objects)]*

3. UML stands for "Universal *[handwritten: Modeling]* Language".

4. A ——————— relationship between two classes implies that one class contains an object of the other class type. *[handwritten: containing, or aggregation]*

5. The .NET utility program named the *[handwritten: Garbage collector]* is responsible for locating all unreferenced objects and removing them from memory.

Multiple Choice

1. Local variables that are value types are stored in which area of memory?
    a. managed heap
    b. runtime stack *[circled]*
    c. static memory
    d. read-only memory

2. If a variable is a reference type, where in memory is its corresponding object stored?
    a. managed heap *[circled]*
    b. runtime stack
    c. static memory
    d. read-only memory

3. Visual Basic .NET Implements class behaviors as:
    a. properties
    b. methods *[circled]*
    c. classes
    d. private variables

4. When all references to an object are set to Nothing, what happens to the object?
    a. It is removed from memory immediately.
    b. It remains in memory until the program ends.
    c. It is removed from memory when memory runs low. *[circled]*
    d. The programmer must call a special function to remove the object from memory.

5. To create a class property that only returns a value, you must do which of the following?
    a. Include the ReadOnly qualifier in the property procedure.
    b. Not include a Set statement in the property procedure.
    c. Make the Get statement public and make the Set statement private.
    d. Two of the above are correct. *[circled]*

True or False

1. Strings are value types. *F*

2. Private methods may only be referenced by other methods in the same class. *T*

3. If a class named Account has a single constructor containing two required parameters, the following line will compile: *F*

    ```
    Dim act As New Account
    ```

4. A shared class variable must always be marked Private. *F*

5. If the Employee class had a public property named **IDSize**, one would have to write an expression such as Employee.IDSize to access the property. *F*

Short Answer

1. In which part of memory are local variables stored when the variables are value types? *runtime stack*

2. Which tier in a multi-tier application is responsible for interacting with the user? *Visual interface tier*

3. How are class behaviors implemented in Visual Basic .NET? *As methods*

4. In one or two sentences, describe the Business tier of an application that processes DVD movie rentals.

5. In a Student Registration application, which design tier would handle rules that decide if a student's grade average is high enough to enroll in 16 college credits? *Business tier*

6. In the BankTeller application, which method (in which class) saves the account file? *The account.update method*

7. In the BankTeller application, which method (in which class) adds a deposit amount to the account balance? *The account.Deposit method*

8. What type of object is returned by the OpenText method of the System.IO.File class? *Stream Reader object*

9. How is a shared class variable different from an ordinary (instance) class variable?

10. Create a shared property named Color for a class named Window. Let the property access a private shared class variable named mColor.

What Do You Think?

1. What do you think that *finding the* classes means?

2. Why is assigning constructor parameters to properties often preferred over assigning parameters to private class variables?

3. What important changes have occurred to the Data tier of most applications during the last 15 years?

4. Provide an example of a typical change to the presentation tier of an application that handles memberships for a University student club.

Algorithm Workbench

1. Draw a UML diagram for a class named Employee that has two attributes named ID and Salary.

2. Create a String property named LastName that provides access to a private class variable named mLastName.

3. Write a simple code example that demonstrates passing an object variable by reference. Show how the object variable can be reassigned to a new object.

4. Create a constructor for a class named Hero that receives two Integer parameters: pStrength and pIntelligence. Make the parameters optional. The corresponding class properties are named Strength and Intelligence.

5. Design two classes related to a Student registration application that exhibit a composition relationship.

▶1.14 Programming Challenges

1. Bank Teller with Totals

Use the Bank Teller Hands-On Tutorial program shown earlier in this chapter as a starting point for this exercise. Implement the following properties in the Account class:

◆ TotalDeposits – the total amount deposited in this account

◆ TotalWithdrawals – the total amount withdrawn from this account

Add labels to the Bank Teller form that display the new totals (Figure 1-12). The totals should be updated every time the user clicks the OK button.

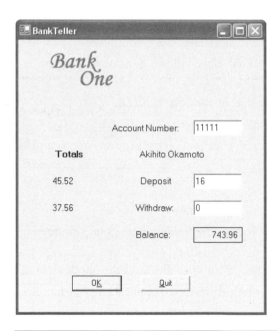

Figure 1-12 Bank Teller program with totals.

2. Employee Information – 1

Use the Employee Information Hands-On Tutorial program as a starting point for this exercise. Add a presentation tier and make it a Windows Desktop application (a Form with controls)

3. Employee Information – 2

Use the solution program form the previous Programming Challenge as a starting point for this exercise. In the clsEmployee class, rather than having only a single clsSalaryItem object, create a collection of clsSalaryItem objects that represent an employee's salary history. Add methods to the clsEmployee class that return the person's average salary, the most recent salary, and the person's starting salary.

4. Time Clock Program

Write a three-tiered application that keeps track of the amount of billable time you spend on consulting projects. The program reads a Client file and appends records to a Billing file, which it creates when the program runs for the first time.

Presentation Tier

Figure 1-13 shows a sample of the main window. When the user begins working on a project, The client name is selected from a ComboBox control, and the user clicks on the **Start** button. While the clock is running, the current elapsed time and client name appear on the form's title bar (use a Timer control to update the time every ten seconds). When the user clicks on the **Stop** button the program displays the total elapsed time in a Label and appends a corresponding row to the Billing file.

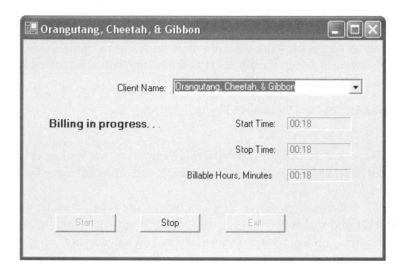

Figure 1-13 Time Clock user interface

Coordinate the command buttons carefully to make sure the user cannot click out of sequence. The following table shows the two possible program states that affect the buttons. The program is in State 1 when it starts; after clicking on Start, the program enters State 2:

State	Start	Stop	Exit
1	Enabled	Disabled	Enabled
2	Disabled	Enabled	Disabled

When the user clicks on the Start button, display a status message "Billing in Progress..." to show the clock is running. Do not permit the user to select a different client while the clock is running. When the Stop button is clicked, the stop time and the number of billable hours and minutes are displayed. The name of the selected client should appear in the window caption.

Business Tier

Create a class named **TimeClock** that encapsulates the time-related calculations performed by the program. Use a TimeSpan structure (defined in the .NET System namespace) to hold the difference between two DateTime values. The TimeSpan class includes both Hours and Minutes properties.

Properties:

Name	Type	Attributes	Description
StartTime	DateTime	read-only	
StopTime	DateTime	read-only	
Elapsed	TimeSpan	read-only	duration between the starting time and the current time
TotalElapsed	TimeSpan	read-only	duration between the starting time and ending time
ClientName	String	read-write	

Methods:

Name	Return Type	Attributes	Description
StartClock	none	public	begins the timing sequence
StopClock	none	public	ends the timing sequence

Data Tier

Create a class named **BillingData** to handle the Client and Billing text files. Use the .NET editor to create the Client file. Insert at least five records in the Client file before running the program. Each record in the Client file contains a client name. Your program will create the Billing file the first time it runs. Subsequent runs will append to the file. Each record in the Billing file contains the following fields: billing date, client name, start time, stop time, and elapsed time. The following is a sample record:

```
02-01-2003,Jones and Smith,21:51,22:10,1:19
```

5. FirstPlay Sports Rental

This project begins an ongoing series of extended projects based on requirements for a sporting goods rental store, which we have named FirstPlay Sports Rental. (We are fairly sure no actual store by this name currently exists.)

This program must display a single sports rental item in a window (Figure 1-14). Each item has an ID number, a description, daily, weekly, and monthly rental rates, and the quantity on hand. When the program starts up, it reads all item information from a text file into a collection and copies the item ID numbers into a combo box on the form. The user can select an ID number from the combo box, and display or remove existing items. The user can also add new items to the collection. When the program ends, it writes the item collection to the same text file.

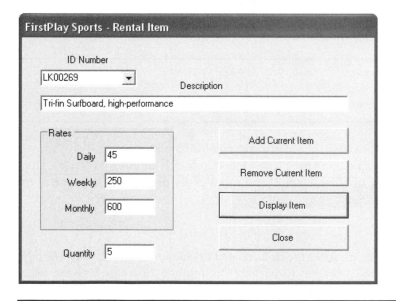

Figure 1-14 Preparing to add a new Item

Startup Module

This program uses a code startup module named **modMain** to load the inventory file before displaying the main form. Create the following Main procedure in the module:

```
Sub Main()
    Dim inventory As New clsInventory
    Dim invenFile As New clsInvenFile("inventory.txt")
    Dim itemForm As New frmItem
    invenFile.LoadData(inventory)
    itemForm.Inventory = inventory
    itemForm.ShowDialog()
    invenFile.SaveData(inventory)
End Sub
```

bring up the form

This procedure creates an instance of frmItem, loads the inventory file, assigns the Inventory collection to the form, shows the form, and saves the inventory file.

Interface Tier

The **frmItem** form displays inventory items and lets users do any of the following:

◆ Input fields for a new rental item, and add that item to the inventory.

◆ Select an item's ID Number and remove the item from the inventory.

◆ Select an item's ID Number and display the item's properties.

When the Form loads, you will need to read a list of ID numbers from a file and load them into the ComboBox control.

Looking back at Figure 1-14, recall that it showed a new item about to be added to the store inventory. When the *Add Current Item* button is clicked, the button's handler creates a new item object and passes it to the class that handles the store inventory. Figure 1-15 shows an example of searching for an item by ID Number. When the user clicks on the *Display Item* button, the remaining item fields are filled in. When the user clicks on the *Remove Current Item* button, the program first confirms the operation with the user (see Figure 1-16), then removes the item identified by the ID Number. The frmItem form has one property named **Inventory,** which exposes a clsInventory object. This is useful because the Inventory's property can be set after the program's startup module reads the inventory file. After removing an item, refill the ID Number combo box and clear all text boxes.

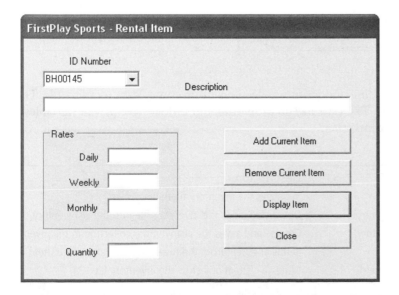

Figure 1-15 About to display an item selected by ID number

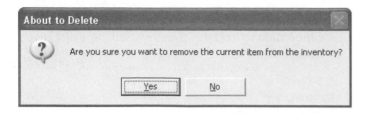

Figure 1-16   Confirm before removing item

Business Tier

The **clsItem** class describes a single type of item rented by the store. It has no methods, but it does have the following read-write properties:

Properties:

Name	Type	Description
IDNumber	String	identification number
Description	String	describes the item
DailyRate	Single	daily rental rate
WeeklyRate	Single	weekly rental rate
MonthlyRate	Single	monthly rental rate
Quantity	Integer	quantity on hand

The **clsInventory** class contains a Collection of clsItem objects. Its **Items** property exposes the Collection. The frmItem form, for instance, uses the Items collection when it fills the form's ComboBox control. Similarly, the SaveData method in the clsInvenFile class iterates over the Items collection when saving items in the data file.

Properties:

Declaration	Description
Public ReadOnly Property Items() As Collection	Returns the collection of clsItem objects.

Methods:

Declaration	Description
Public Sub AddItem(ByVal item As clsItem)	Adds a new item from the inventory.
Public Function RemoveItem(ByVal id As String)	Removes an item from the inventory.
Public Function GetItem(ByVal id As String) As clsItem	Retrieves an item from the inventory.

Data Tier

The **clsInvenFile** is responsible for reading and writing collections of inventory data to a text file. The text file is located in the project's **bin** directory. The class has no properties, but it does have private variables that hold a filename, a StreamReader, and a StreamWriter.

Methods:

Declaration	Description
Public Sub New(ByVal filename As String)	Initializes the inventory filename.
Public Sub LoadData(ByVal inven As clsInventory)	Opens and loads the inventory file into the clsInventory collection.
Public Sub SaveData(ByVal inven As clsInventory)	Creates and saves the clsInventory collection in the inventory file.
Private Function ReadOneItem() As clsItem	Reads one item from the inventory file, returns a clsItem object.
Private Sub WriteOneItem(ByVal item As clsItem)	Writes a clsItem object to the inventory file.

Exceptions and User Interfaces

▶2.1 User Interface Design

Introduction

A program's *user interface* is the part that interacts with a user. In a multi-tiered program, the Presentation tier implements the user interface. How important is it for a professional application program to have an intuitive, powerful, easy to learn, and attractive user interface? The answer is obvious for anyone who intends to buy and use the software often. In fact, a program's user interface is not just about appearances—it actually defines the program's behavior.

Suppose you have written a great program and gradually added features one by one until you are ready to offer it to the world. You have learned the program one feature at a time, run it hundreds or thousands of times, and shown it to your friends. You are the program's ultimate expert user. Following are some questions to ask:

◆ How will first-time users react to your program's user interface? Will it confuse them, or encourage them to learn more?

◆ Will users immediately recognize the "logic" behind required sequences of actions when completing tasks?

◆ Will your program's green text on a red background, with a touch of purple along the edges excite them, or will they reach for their sunglasses?

◆ After users have run your program ten or twenty times, will they be able to work faster and smarter? Or, will they fall asleep while working their way through numerous levels of menu commands?

◆ Will those humorous comments you display when users make mistakes really seem as funny to someone else?

◆ Will your program's complexity overwhelm the new user?

◆ Does your program give new users the freedom to enter a variety of data, and yet prevent them from making confusing mistakes?

◆ Does your program restrict advanced users to the point of frustration?

Some of these questions have obvious answers, but you would be surprised at what most Visual Basic teachers encounter. Programmers are by nature creative people, and they feel compelled to apply that creativity to user interface design. After all, why make a program that looks and behaves the same as everyone else's? In the following sections, we will address some of these questions.

Know Your User

Well-designed user interfaces work for users at different levels. For the moment, let's divide users into three broad categories: Novice, Intermediate, and Experienced.

◆ Novice users have no assumptions about how standard menus and keyboard shortcuts work. Selections must be obvious, and explanations should be given at every step.

◆ Intermediate users have probably used one major application, such as Microsoft Word or Internet Explorer. They can find standard menu commands, drag and drop items, and use context menus (mouse right button).

◆ Advanced users have used a number of applications over several years and expect to have certain conventions followed. Keyboard shortcuts should be consistent with other software, context menus should be abundant, and tool tips should be available for all important commands. Above all, advanced users want to work quickly and repeat certain patterns often. Such users become annoyed when tasks require too many steps to complete.

Another important consideration is a user's learning curve. Most people, as they become more skilled at using a particular program, expect the program to offer a gradual learning curve. As users progress, they may use menus less and graduate to keyboard shortcuts and drag-and-drop operations. Well-designed software must be easy for a beginner to learn and convenient for the skilled user to operate.

Task-Based Approach

A program can usually be expressed in terms of the various tasks it will perform. For example, a Sports Equipment Rental company might need software to carry out tasks such as these:

◆ Display the complete store inventory.

◆ Display detailed information on a single rental item.

◆ Print a rental invoice.

◆ Enter a hold request for an item that is unavailable.

◆ Display a list of all nonreturned items within a chosen date range.

For each task, you can create what is called a *use-case scenario* (or just *use-case*), which describes the interactions between the user and the program during the completion of the task. For example, the *Display detail information for a single item* task could be described as follows:

Step 1. User enters a full or partial description of an item.

Step 2. The program searches for and displays a list of all items that match the description.

Step 3. User selects an item from the displayed list.

Step 4. The program displays detail information on the item, including description, price, quantity available for rental, and quantity in the store's inventory.

This sequence of steps gives us some hints about the user interface. Step 1 would probably require a TextBox control. Step 2 might use either a ListBox or DataGrid control, possibly in the same window as Step 1 so the user can easily modify the description to obtain a more selective list. Step 3 would require a multicolumn (ListView has not been explained yet) DataGrid control, probably in a separate window from Step 2 because of the volume of displayed information.

There is no single best way of designing the visual interface for a particular use-case. Your user interface design must work for all the required scenarios your program implements. The final design no doubt involves considerable compromise.

Designing Forms

Assuming that you have already completed a first VB course, you have designed quite a few forms and used many standard Visual Basic .NET controls. Here are some general guidelines and suggestions relating to form design you might find useful:

- Avoid cluttering a form with more than a few command buttons. Instead, use a menu to provide logical groupings of commands, and to keep the form's interior area as simple as possible. Certain applications, notably wizards, require command buttons for navigation purposes.

- Assign buttons to a form's AcceptButton and CancelButton properties to satisfy end users who like to use the Enter and Escape (Esc) keys.

- Restrict users' variety of choices when providing input to a program. If you make it impossible to enter badly formatted data, the user will require less training. You can temporarily disable certain menu choices and command buttons until those commands are appropriate.

- Use a TabControl to partition a large number of controls into logical groups. To see an excellent example in Microsoft Word, select Print… from the File menu and click on Properties.

- Use a scrollable form when the form's contents will not fit on the screen. You need only to set the form's AutoScroll property to True. When the user resizes the form, if any controls are hidden behind the edge of the form, a scroll bar appears automatically. For example, Figure 2-1 shows a student survey form that displays a vertical scroll bar, before and after the form has been scrolled. (See the ScrollDemo program in the Chapter 2 examples directory.) Scrollable forms can be more easily reworked into Web-based applications.

- Use a TreeView control to display hierarchical information. Examples can be found everywhere in the .NET environment, such as Solution Explorer, Object Browser, Class View, and Server Explorer.

- Use a ListView control to display multicolumn information. It's quite flexible, and can be easily linked to the TreeView control. The .NET environment uses combined TreeView and ListView controls in a number of places, such as the Project Properties dialog, the Object Browser, and the Task List window.

 ScrollDemo

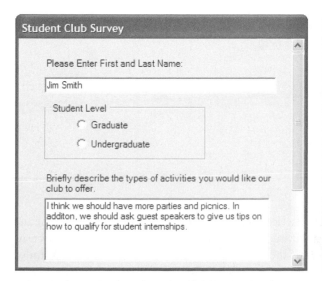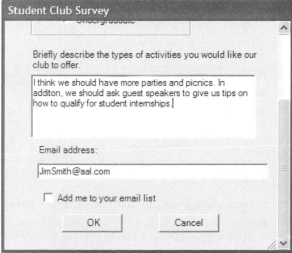

Figure 2-1 Scrollable form example.

Using Microsoft Office as a Model

Programmers should usually resist the temptation to build overly creative user interfaces. Functionality and useability nearly always win over artistic creativity. This is true particularly when creating business-oriented applications, in which users have a great deal of time already invested in learning productivity software. They have neither the time nor the inclination to master new user interfaces, but they can be persuaded to learn programs that look and act the same as software they already know. Now that we mention it, how long did you spend reading the user manual before diving into Microsoft Word or Excel? Did you expect instant results?

For better or worse, Microsoft Office has become the universally accepted standard for user interfaces in MS-Windows applications. The issue is familiarity. Users want to use software that is intuitively easy to learn and use. They will expect certain menus, keyboard shortcuts, and interface elements in all of their software to be familiar. We feel smarter when we can master new software quickly!

Menu Basics

◆ Avoid cluttering windows with too many buttons. Use drop-down menus rather than buttons whenever possible.

◆ Every button command should be duplicated by a menu command.

◆ In the top-level menu, always include File and Help. The File submenu should include an Exit option. The Help submenu should include an About option.

◆ Where appropriate, the top-level menu should include the Edit, View, and Windows submenus.

◆ If appropriate, the File menu should contain the following commands: Open, Save, Save As..., Exit, Print Preview, and Print.

◆ When a menu option launches a submenu, the option should have a "..." suffix. An example is the "Print..." option in the File menu.

◆ Use standard shortcut keys common to all MS-Windows applications, listed in Table 2-1

Table 2-1

Common shortcut keys

Menu command	Shortcut Key
File | Save	Ctrl-S
File | New	Ctrl-N
File | Open	Ctrl-O
File | Print	Ctrl-P
Edit | Copy	Ctrl-C
Edit | Cut	Ctrl-X
Edit | Paste	Ctrl-V
Edit | Select All	Ctrl-A
Edit | Undo	Ctrl-Z
Edit | Find	Ctrl-F
Edit | Replace	Ctrl-H
Edit | Go To...	Ctrl-G
Help	F1

Wizards

A *wizard* is a program that leads the user through a series of predescribed steps. Along the way, the user may be given a few choices, but the primary purpose of a wizard is to simplify decision making for the user. A common wizard application is a device driver installer such as the *Hardware Installation Wizard* in MS-Windows. When running a wizard, the average user does not want to make a lot of choices. Unfortunately, when users are presented with a choice they do not understand, they may have to make a random selection or halt the program.

A wizard must be matched to the user's knowledge and experience level. Most wizards work best when they are short and simple. Wizards with multiple execution paths can become too complex for the average person to follow.

Checkpoint

2.1 What type of user interface would probably appeal more to a novice user than an experienced one?

2.2 What software engineering tool or technique is used when you have a task-based approach to designing a user interface?

2.3 For the Sports Rental company example, create a detailed set of user interactions that would apply to the task entitled *Display a list of all nonreturned items within a chosen date range*.

2.4 What technique can you use to avoid cluttering a form with a large number of command buttons?

2.5 What user interface strategy might you use when a form has a large number of text boxes that cannot be visible all at the same time?

▶ 2.2 Input Validation

General Principles

Someday, users will input data in the same manner as expected by programmers. All misunderstandings between programmers and users will cease to exist. Until that wonderful day arrives, software companies will spend a lot of time and money on testing software.

A major component of creating user interfaces lies in the anticipation and prevention of errors resulting from user input. To be sure, error trapping is a time-consuming activity, and the required code often tends to clutter the logic of otherwise simple programs.

In every program, a question often arises as to where error-checking code should be located. In a typical three-tier application, for example, some amount of validation can occur within the Data layer. Another level of error checking can occur in the Business layer, using property procedures that validate data using logical rules. Finally, a third level of error checking can occur in the Presentation layer, using event handler procedures in visual forms.

When appropriate, you can restrict the user's ability to input bad data. For example, when asking for the user's address, the home state abbreviation is almost always selected from a preexisting list. The alternative, of having the user type the two-letter abbreviation, would introduce errors into the input data. If the address is outside the United States, on the other hand, it would be almost impossible to provide a list of states or provinces for every possible country.

When validating user input on a Windows form, you can choose from four approaches:

1. Trap individual keystrokes before they appear in the input control, and decide whether to accept or reject them. This is a powerful option, but it requires a lot of work when multiple controls are involved.

2. Trap invalid data when the user attempts to move away from a control, and force the user to correct the error before moving on. This approach gives the user immediate feedback, but it can be frustrating if the user wants to skip the input control and fill it in later.

3. Flag each control that contains invalid input, using an icon or message, as the user moves away from it. The user can either fix the error immediately or move to another control.

4. Wait for the user to input data into all appropriate controls on the form. Before the form is closed, execute code that validates all fields at once and generates a list of messages explaining what went wrong. When a large number of controls are involved, the user may have forgotten why certain input values were entered.

Web applications are not always able to perform input validation one control at a time, because of differences between Web browsers. This limitation may rule out all but option number 4 if you plan to move an application from a Windows environment to a Web environment.

Trapping Individual Keystrokes

Visual Basic .NET makes it fairly easy to intercept each keystroke as it is entered into controls such as text boxes. When a key is pressed and released, a KeyPress event is generated. Its handler receives two arguments, one of which is a KeyPressEventArgs object that contains two properties:

◆ **Handled**: Boolean property that can be set to True if you want the control to ignore the key.

◆ **KeyChar**: Holds the character pressed by the user, including special control characters, function keys, and so on. The property is read-only.

VB .NET's **Char** class has a number of useful methods you can call to examine a character for attributes, such as IsDigit, IsLetter, IsLetterOrDigit, IsLower, IsNumber, IsPunctuation, IsSeparator, IsSymbol, IsUpper, and IsWhiteSpace. The following statement, for example, tells the current control to reject the input character if it is not a letter (**e** is the input parameter):

```
If Not Char.IsLetter(e.KeyChar) Then e.Handled = True
```

It's a good idea to specifically permit control characters such as Tab, Backspace, and arrow keys. The following code exits the KeyPress event handler as soon as it finds such a character, leaving the e.Handled property equal to False:

```
If Char.IsControl(e.KeyChar) Then Exit Sub
```

Hands-On Example: Keyboard Validation

KeyboardValidation

Let's examine a short program that displays a dialog window asking the user to input a patient ID number (see Figure 2-2). The requirements are that the number must be exactly seven letters and digits, and may not contain spaces. All letters are to be stored as uppercase. The program combines a KeyPress event handler with a TextChanged event handler to get the maximum benefit for their capabilities.

The form (named **frmPatientID**) contains a text box named **txtPatientID**, a button named **cmdOK** that is disabled in design mode, and a ToolTip control named **toolTips**.

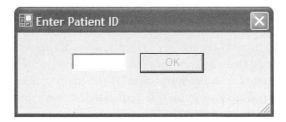

Figure 2-2 Entering a patient ID

Step 1. Open the **KeyboardValidation** program from the Chapter 2 examples directory. Run the program and experiment by entering letters and digits. Notice that letters are automatically converted to uppercase, undesired characters are rejected, and the OK button becomes enabled only when the patient ID length is 7. The status bar displays a message when exactly seven characters have been entered. Halt the program.

Step 2. In design mode, open up the form's code window and look at the Load event hander. It sets the tool tip text for the txtPatientID at runtime, to take advantage of the ID_SIZE constant:

```
Const ID_SIZE As Integer = 7


Private Sub frmPatientID_Load(ByVal sender As System.Object, _
  ByVal e As System.EventArgs) Handles MyBase.Load
```

```
        toolTips.SetToolTip(txtPatientID, "Enter " & ID_SIZE & _
          " letters or digits")
    End Sub
```

Step 3. Look at the txtPatientID_KeyPress procedure. Notice that it rejects all keyboard input when the text length equals ID_SIZE (a constant). It rejects any character that is not a letter or digit:

```
Private Sub txtPatientID_KeyPress(ByVal sender As System.Object, _
  ByVal e As System.Windows.Forms.KeyPressEventArgs) _
  Handles txtPatientID.KeyPress

    'Permit Backspace, Tab and other control keys
    If Char.IsControl(e.KeyChar) Then Exit Sub

    'Do not exceed the maximum input length
    If txtPatientID.Text.Length = ID_SIZE Then
       e.Handled = True
    End If

    'Reject any key that is not a letter or decimal digit
    If Not Char.IsLetterOrDigit(e.KeyChar) Then
       e.Handled = True
    End If
End Sub
```

Step 4. Some work is still left undone. The program must enable or disable the OK button depending on the current ID size, and it must convert input letters to uppercase. These tasks are best handled by the TextChanged event handler:

```
Private Sub txtPatientID_TextChanged(ByVal sender As Object, _
  ByVal e As System.EventArgs) Handles txtPatientID.TextChanged

    'Enable OK button only if correct ID size found
    btnOK.Enabled = txtPatientID.Text.Length = ID_SIZE

    'Convert the patient ID to uppercase, and move
    'the cursor back to the end of the string.
    txtPatientID.Text = txtPatientID.Text.ToUpper()
    txtPatientID.SelectionStart = txtPatientID.Text.Length
End Sub
```

Moving the cursor to the end of the string was an afterthought when it was discovered that assigning a new string to txtPatientID.Text reset the cursor position to the beginning of the field. The user would not understand why the input position kept jumping to the beginning of the patient ID!

Beginning programmers are often taught to use an If statement when setting a boolean property based on a conditional statement. For example:

```
If txtPatientID.Text.Length = ID_SIZE = True Then
    btnOK.Enabled = True
Else
    btnOK.Enabled = False
End If
```

Experienced programmers generally prefer the equivalent version that evaluates the Boolean expression and directly assigns the result to the Boolean property:

```
btnOK.Enabled = txtPatientID.Text.Length = ID_SIZE
```

Who would guess that so much code would be involved in validating just one input field! Yet the result is bulletproof input, so the user literally cannot make a mistake. You may want to reserve this level of error trapping for the most critical input fields. Another issue is that of ongoing maintenance. If the project designer later decides that patient ID numbers should consist of only digits or the ID length should change, our input validation would have to be updated.

(End of example. The complete source code may be seen in Code Listing 2-1.)

Code Listing 2-1 (Keyboard Validation)

```
Public Class frmPatientID
    Inherits System.Windows.Forms.Form

+ Windows Form Designer generated code

    Const ID_SIZE As Integer = 7

    Private Sub frmPatientID_Load(ByVal sender As System.Object, _
     ByVal e As System.EventArgs) Handles MyBase.Load

        toolTips.SetToolTip(txtPatientID, "Enter " & ID_SIZE & _
          " letters or digits")
    End Sub

    'Performs input validation by trapping keyboard keys.

    Private Sub txtPatientID_KeyPress(ByVal sender As System.Object, _
     ByVal e As System.Windows.Forms.KeyPressEventArgs) _
     Handles txtPatientID.KeyPress

        'Permit Backspace, Tab and other control keys
        If Char.IsControl(e.KeyChar) Then Exit Sub

        'Do not exceed the maximum input length
        If txtPatientID.Text.Length = ID_SIZE Then
            e.Handled = True
        End If
```

```
      'Reject any key that is not a letter or digit
      If Not Char.IsLetterOrDigit(e.KeyChar) Then
          e.Handled = True
      End If
  End Sub

  Private Sub txtPatientID_TextChanged(ByVal sender As Object, _
   ByVal e As System.EventArgs) Handles txtPatientID.TextChanged

      'Enable OK button only if correct ID size found
      btnOK.Enabled = txtPatientID.Text.Length = ID_SIZE

      'Convert the patient ID to uppercase, and move
      'the cursor back to the end of the string.
      txtPatientID.Text = txtPatientID.Text.ToUpper()
      txtPatientID.SelectionStart = txtPatientID.Text.Length
  End Sub

  Private Sub btnOK_Click(ByVal sender As System.Object, _
   ByVal e As System.EventArgs) Handles btnOK.Click

      Me.Close()
  End Sub
End Class
```

Handling the *Validating* Event

Programs that check for input errors can implement the **Validating** event handler for specific input controls. Text boxes, for instance, permit a wide variety of inputs and therefore require careful validation. A program might, for example, have to verify that the input string can be converted to a number, or verify that the input string is a particular length. Under specific conditions, the Validating event is fired when the user is about to shift the focus away from a control. At that moment, an error can be caught and the program can keep the focus on the control that caused the error. Events fire for a specific control in the following order: Enter, GotFocus, Leave, Validating, Validated, LostFocus.

User input to the control takes place between the GotFocus and Leave events. The Leave event fires as soon as the user moves away from the control by pressing the Tab key, clicking on another control, or typing a keyboard shortcut. GotFocus and LostFocus are low-level events that are not directly accessible in Visual Basic .NET. Table 2-2 lists the validation events for which you can write handlers.

Table 2-2

Validation events recongnized by VB .NET

Event (In Order)	Description
Leave	User has moved away from the current input field.
Validating	Handler contains code that checks the control's contents. If an error is found, focus can be kept on the control using program code.
Validated	Fires when the Validating event handler finds no error. Contains code that assumes the control's contents are valid.

The code you write in a control's Validating event handler determines whether the Validated event will fire, or the focus will be switched back to the control that was being validated. For example, the following Validating event handler is for a control named **txtLastName**. We assume that the event fired because the user attempted to move away from the control:

```
Private Sub txtLastName_Validating(ByVal sender As Object, _
  ByVal e As System.ComponentModel.CancelEventArgs) _
  Handles txtLastName.Validating

    If txtLastName.Text.Length < 1 Then
        MessageBox.Show("Last name cannot be blank")
        e.Cancel = True
    End If
End Sub
```

Our code insists that the last name field not be blank. The parameter named **e** is of type **CancelEventArgs**, which contains a property named **Cancel** (False by default). If our code sets Cancel to True, the form's input focus remains on txtLastName. Otherwise, Cancel remains False and the next event to be fired is txtLastName_Validated.

CausesValidation Property

The **CausesValidation** property is the key to understanding how and when input fields are validated. CausesValidation is True by default for all controls. It determines whether a Validating event will be fired. If you want a field to be validated, its CausesValidation must equal True. In addition, the field will not be validated until the user moves to another control whose CausesValidation property is also True. Table 2-3 shows what happens for each possible value of the CausesValidation property:

Table 2-3

CausesValidation property summary

Source Control's CausesValidation	Destination Control's CausesValidation	Validating Event Fired for Source Field?
False	(either)	Never
True	True	When focus shifts to destination control
True	False	When focus shifts to some other control whose CausesValidation property equals True

Input Validation Example

Let's use an example to make validation events seem less abstract. Assume that a form contains two text boxes named **txtLastName** and **txtAge**, and their CausesValidation properties are equal to True. Figure 2-3 graphically tracks the event sequence occurring when the user attempts to switch the focus from txtLastName to txtAge. The txtLastName_Leave procedure executes, followed by txtLastName_Validating. If the Validating procedure exits with Cancel = True, the input focus returns to txtLastName. If the Validating procedure exits with Cancel = False, the txtLastName_Validated procedure executes, and the input focus moves to txtAge.

txtLastName.CausesValidation = True and txtAge.CausesValidation = True

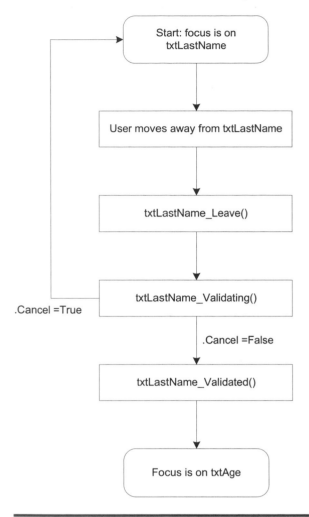

Figure 2-3   Switching focus between controls

Let's look at a program that displays events as they are fired. In addition, we will show how to use a Business-tier class to assist in the data validation process.

Hands-On Example: Name and Age Input

NameAndAgeInput

In this hands-on example, you will examine a program that contains two text boxes into which the user enters a person's last name and age. It uses a form to gather user input and perform some validation on the input data. In addition, an associated Person class performs range checking on the person's age. Figure 2-4 shows the program after the user has entered a last name and age. The list box displays the sequence of events fired when the user tabbed away from the txtAge control. In Figure 2-5, the txtLastName control was blank when the user moved away from it, so an error message displays and the LastName_Validated event does not fire.

The program's complete source code may be found in Code Listing 2-2.

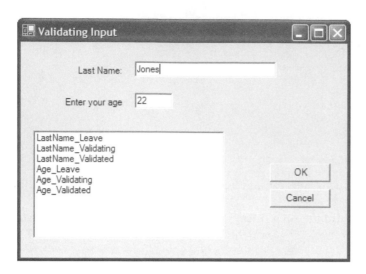

Figure 2-4 Input validation program (run mode)

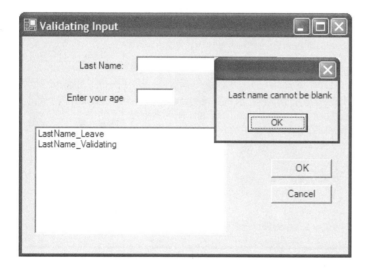

Figure 2-5 Blank last name field

Step 1. Open the **NameAndAgeInput** program from the Chapter 2 examples directory. Open the code window for the **Person** class. It contains two private variables (mLastName and mAge), properties for each, and an enumeration type named **AgeRange**:

```
Private mLastName As String
Private mAge As Integer

Public Enum AgeRange
   min = 10
   max = 120
End Enum

Public Property LastName() As String
   Get
      Return mLastName
   End Get
   Set(ByVal Value As String)
      mLastName = Value
   End Set
End Property
```

2

```
Public Property Age() As Integer
    Get
        Return mAge
    End Get
    Set(ByVal Value As Integer)
        mAge = Value
    End Set
End Property
```

References to AgeRange members by client programs must include the class name, as in **Person.AgeRange.max**.

Step 2. View the **ToString** and **IsRangeValid** methods. IsAgeValid is a shared Boolean function, which uses the AgeRange Enum to verify that the pAge parameter is within a valid range:

```
Public Overrides Function ToString() As String
    Return "[" & mLastName & ", " & mAge & "]"
End Function

Public Shared Function IsAgeValid(ByVal pAge As Integer) As Boolean
    Return pAge >= AgeRange.min And pAge <= AgeRange.max
End Function
```

Step 3. Open the code window for frmValidate. It contains a Person object that holds the data entered by the user for the last name and age. There is also a **Validating** event handler for **txtLastName**:

```
Private aPerson As New Person()

Private Sub txtLastName_Validating(ByVal sender As Object, _
  ByVal e As System.ComponentModel.CancelEventArgs) _
  Handles txtLastName.Validating

    lstEvents.Items.Add("LastName_Validating")
    If txtLastName.Text.Length < 1 Then
        MessageBox.Show("Last name cannot be blank")
        e.Cancel = True
    End If
End Sub
```

A statement in the Validating event handler writes event information to the lstEvents list box.

Step 4. Inspect the **Validating** event handler for the **txtAge** control. Two levels of validation must be performed. First, the control's event handler verifies that the txtAge control is numeric. Next, when calling the IsAgeValid method in the Person class, the code checks for a valid age range:

```
Private Sub txtAge_Validating(ByVal sender As Object, _
  ByVal e As System.ComponentModel.CancelEventArgs) _
  Handles txtAge.Validating

    lstEvents.Items.Add("Age_Validating")
    If Not IsNumeric(txtAge.Text) Then
        MessageBox.Show("Age must be a number")
        e.Cancel = True
        Exit Sub
```

```
        Else
           If Not Person.IsAgeValid(CInt(Val(txtAge.Text))) Then
              MessageBox.Show("Age must be between " & _
                 Person.AgeRange.min _
                 & " and " & Person.AgeRange.max)
              e.Cancel = True
              Exit Sub
           End If
        End If
        'if we reach this point, Age must be valid
     End Sub
```

The designer of the form does not have to know the valid range for ages. Instead, that information is encapsulated in Person.AgeRange. If at a later time the designer of the Person class changes the range of valid ages, no change will have to be made to the code in this form.

Step 5.   If the Validating events succeed for the two text boxes, the **Validated** event fires. The following event handlers assign values to the LastName and Age properties of the Person object:

```
Private Sub txtLastName_Validated(ByVal sender As Object, _
 ByVal e As System.EventArgs) Handles txtLastName.Validated

   lstEvents.Items.Add("LastName_Validated")
   aPerson.LastName = txtLastName.Text
End Sub

Private Sub txtAge_Validated(ByVal sender As Object, _
 ByVal e As System.EventArgs) Handles txtAge.Validated

   lstEvents.Items.Add("Age_Validated")
   aPerson.Age = CInt(txtAge.Text)
End Sub
```

Step 6.   The Click event handler for the OK button displays a message box showing the contents of the Person object. The Cancel handler closes the form:

```
Private Sub btnOK_Click(ByVal sender As System.Object, _
 ByVal e As System.EventArgs) Handles btnOK.Click

   MessageBox.Show("Person: " & aPerson.ToString())
   Me.Close()
End Sub

Private Sub btnCancel_Click(ByVal sender As System.Object, _
 ByVal e As System.EventArgs) Handles btnCancel.Click

   Me.Close()
End Sub
```

Step 7. Inspect the Leave event handlers for both text boxes so you can see the event sequencing when testing the program:

```
Private Sub txtAge_Leave(ByVal sender As Object, _
 ByVal e As System.EventArgs) Handles txtAge.Leave

    lstEvents.Items.Add("Age_Leave")
End Sub

Private Sub txtLastName_Leave(ByVal sender As Object, _
 ByVal e As System.EventArgs) Handles txtLastName.Leave

    lstEvents.Items.Add("LastName_Leave")
End Sub
```

Step 8. Run and test the program. Here are suggested testing actions you can use:

◆ Leave the last name text box blank and try to tab to the Age text box. An error message should alert you that the last name cannot be blank. Enter a name, and enter 22 into the Age text box. Close the form.

◆ In design mode, set the txtAge.CausesValidation property to False. Run the program again and tab from the Last name text box to the Age text box. No error message should appear. Click on either OK or cancel, and note that the error message for the Last name text box appears. Input a last name, and click on OK. Note that the input was accepted, even with a blank Age text box.

◆ Again in design mode, set the txtAge.CausesValidation property to True. Run the program again, input a last name, tab to the Age text box, and tab again. An error message should tell you that Age must be a number. Enter 2 in the Age box, and press the Tab key. The error message should tell you that Age must be between 10 and 120. Input a valid age and click on Cancel.

◆ Run the program again, leave both text boxes blank, and click on Cancel. An error message will state that the last name cannot be blank. Enter data into both fields and click Cancel to close the form.

The foregoing tests show that the form does not close when both fields are blank and the user clicks on Cancel. To change that behavior, we can set a Boolean variable named **blnClosing** to True when the user wishes to cancel the form. The variable can be checked inside both Validating event handlers. The following steps show you what to add to the program:

Step 9. Add the following variable to the form declarations area:

```
Private blnClosing As Boolean = False
```

Step 10. Insert the following statement in the first line of the txtLastName_Validating and txtAge_Validating procedures:

```
If blnClosing Then Exit Sub
```

Step 11. Insert the following statement in the first line of the btnCancel_Click procedure:

```
blnClosing = True
```

Step 12. Run and test the program again. With both text boxes blank, click on the Cancel button. The form should close without displaying any error messages.

Can we say that the input validation in this program works? Not quite. One annoying problem exists whose solution may be considered a useful programming challenge. If you run the Validation program, enter a last name, and click on OK, the txtAge_Validate procedure never executes. This is true because the focus never left (and never entered) the txtAge control. Clearly, there are difficulties in relying purely on change of focus between controls. In the next section we will show you a more elegant way to handle input validation, using the ErrorProvider control.

Code Listing 2-2 (Name and Age Input)

Person Class:

```
Public Class Person
    Private mLastName As String
    Private mAge As Integer

    Public Enum AgeRange
       min = 10
       max = 120
    End Enum

    Public Overrides Function ToString() As String
       Return "[" & mLastName & ", " & mAge & "]"
    End Function

    Public Shared Function IsAgeValid(ByVal pAge As Integer) As Boolean
       Return pAge >= AgeRange.min And pAge <= AgeRange.max
    End Function

    Public Property LastName() As String
       Get
          Return mLastName
       End Get
       Set(ByVal Value As String)
          mLastName = Value
       End Set
    End Property

    Public Property Age() As Integer
       Get
          Return mAge
       End Get
       Set(ByVal Value As Integer)
          mAge = Value
       End Set
    End Property
End Class
```

frmValidate Class:

```
Public Class frmValidate
    Inherits System.Windows.Forms.Form
```

```
+ Windows Form Designer generated code
```

2

```vb
'First program that demonstrates the Validating event
'handler. Window does not close when Cancel is clicked
'and text boxes are empty.

Private aPerson As New Person()

Private Sub txtLastName_Validating(ByVal sender As Object, _
 ByVal e As System.ComponentModel.CancelEventArgs) _
 Handles txtLastName.Validating

    lstEvents.Items.Add("LastName_Validating")
    If txtLastName.Text.Length < 1 Then
       MessageBox.Show("Last name cannot be blank")
       e.Cancel = True
    End If
End Sub

'Age must be numeric, and it must be within a valid range
Private Sub txtAge_Validating(ByVal sender As Object, _
 ByVal e As System.ComponentModel.CancelEventArgs) _
 Handles txtAge.Validating

    lstEvents.Items.Add("Age_Validating")
    If Not IsNumeric(txtAge.Text) Then
       MessageBox.Show("Age must be a number")
       e.Cancel = True
       Exit Sub
    Else
       If Not Person.IsAgeValid(CInt(Val(txtAge.Text))) Then
          MessageBox.Show("Age must be between " & Person.AgeRange.min _
           & " and " & Person.AgeRange.max)
          e.Cancel = True
          Exit Sub
       End If
    End If
    'if we reach this point, Age must be valid
End Sub

'executed when txtLastName has been validated
Private Sub txtLastName_Validated(ByVal sender As Object, _
 ByVal e As System.EventArgs) Handles txtLastName.Validated

    lstEvents.Items.Add("LastName_Validated")
    aPerson.LastName = txtLastName.Text
End Sub

'executed when txtAge has been validated
Private Sub txtAge_Validated(ByVal sender As Object, _
 ByVal e As System.EventArgs) Handles txtAge.Validated

    lstEvents.Items.Add("Age_Validated")
    aPerson.Age = CInt(txtAge.Text)
End Sub
```

```
'leaving the txtAge field
Private Sub txtAge_Leave(ByVal sender As Object, _
 ByVal e As System.EventArgs) Handles txtAge.Leave
    lstEvents.Items.Add("Age_Leave")
End Sub

'leaving the txtLastName field
Private Sub txtLastName_Leave(ByVal sender As Object, _
 ByVal e As System.EventArgs) Handles txtLastName.Leave
    lstEvents.Items.Add("LastName_Leave")
End Sub

'when OK is clicked, display the Person object
Private Sub btnOK_Click(ByVal sender As System.Object, _
 ByVal e As System.EventArgs) Handles btnOK.Click
    MessageBox.Show("Person: " & aPerson.ToString())
    Me.Close()
End Sub

'User wants to cancel
Private Sub btnCancel_Click(ByVal sender As System.Object, _
 ByVal e As System.EventArgs) Handles btnCancel.Click

    Me.Close()
End Sub
End Class
```

Hands-On Tutorial: ErrorProvider Control

ErrorProviderTest

The **ErrorProvider** control provides a powerful way to validate input fields. Rather than interrupting the user with a message box, the ErrorProvider displays a red exclamation mark icon on the right side of any field that has been found to contain invalid data. If the user hovers over the icon with the mouse, an explanatory error message appears.

A single ErrorProvider control can be used to validate all controls on the same form. When you drag it onto a form, it appears in the form's Component Tray. You may have to scroll down in the toolbox to find the ErrorProvider, which has a red circular icon containing a white exclamation mark.

If a control's event handler discovers that the contents of a control are invalid, it can call the ErrorProvider's **SetError** method, passing it a reference to **sender** (the control) and an error messsage string. The following is an example:

```
Private Sub txtLastName_TextChanged(ByVal sender As Object, _
    ByVal e As System.EventArgs) _
    Handles txtLastName.TextChanged

    If txtLastName.Text.Length = 0 Then
        errProvider.SetError(CType(sender, Control), _
            "Last name cannot be blank")
    End If
End Sub
```

(The **sender** parameter is declared type Object, so it must be cast into a Control before it can be passed to the SetError method.)

The ErrorProvider.GetError method returns the current error message associated with a control:

```
Dim st As String = errProvider.GetError( txtLastName )
```

Choosing Event Handlers

When implementing the ErrorProvider control, determine how and when you want the error checking to take effect. You have two choices:

1. **Leave** event: Check for errors when the user moves the focus away from the text box.
2. **TextChanged** event: Check for errors as the user types characters into the text box.

The Leave event fires when the program starts up and the user moves away from a text box without typing any input. The TextChanged event fires after the user has begun entering data into a text box and has either erased its contents or entered an invalid value.

You could implement the two types of checking by providing separate methods that handle both the Leave event and the TextChanged event. That would result in some amount of duplicate code, which is a bad idea. Fortunately, Visual Basic gives you the flexibility of writing a single handler procedure for multiple events. For example, the following procedure uses the same parameter list as txtLastName_TextChanged. Notice that it lists the **txtLastName.Leave** and **txtLastName_TextChanged** events in its *Handles* list:

```
Private Sub txtLastName_Validate(ByVal sender As Object, _
    ByVal e As System.EventArgs) _
        Handles txtLastName.TextChanged, txtLastName.Leave
```

You can give any name to a handler procedure. In the current example, it is named **txtLastName_Validate** because that is exactly what it does in the upcoming program example.

Begin the Hands-On Tutorial

The following tutorial takes you through the steps of creating an input validation program using the ErrorProvider control.

Step 1. Create a Windows Desktop project named **ErrorProviderTest**. Delete the startup form and create a new form named **frmValidate**.

Step 2. Add the controls listed in Table 2-4 to frmValidate. The design-mode form is shown in Figure 2-6. Be sure to place an ErrorProvider control in the form's Component Tray.

Table 2-4

frmValidate controls

Control Type	Control Name	Properties
Form	frmValidate	Text: "Validating Input"
		ControlBox: False
ErrorProvider	errProvider	
TextBox	txtLastName	Text: " "
		TabIndex: 0
TextBox	txtAge	Text: " "
		TabIndex: 1
Button	btnOK	Text: OK
		TabIndex: 2
Button	btnCancel	Text: Cancel
		TabIndex: 3
Label	(default)	Text: "Last Name:"
		TextAlign: MiddleRight
Label	(default)	Text: "Enter your age:"
		TextAlign: MiddleRight

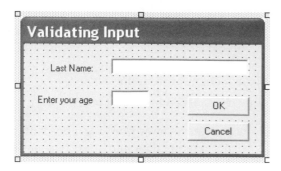

Figure 2-6 ErrorProvider test (design mode)

Step 3. In the frmValidate code, define two string constants that will be used as error messages:

```
Const nameMsg As String = "Name cannot be blank"
Const ageMsg As String = "Age must be a number"
```

Step 4. In the **Form_Load** event handler, initialize the **Tag** properties of both text boxes to false. We will use the Tag field to keep track of when the fields have passed the validation test:

```
Private Sub frmValidate_Load(ByVal sender As _
 System.Object, ByVal e As System.EventArgs) _
 Handles MyBase.Load

    txtLastName.Tag = False
    txtAge.Tag = False
End Sub
```

Step 5. Add an event handler for the **txtLastName** control that fires for the Leave and TextChanged events. If the string length is zero, pass a message string to the ErrorProvider and set the Tag field to False. Otherwise, clear the error message and set the Tag field to True:

```
Private Sub txtLastName_Validate(ByVal sender As Object, _
    ByVal e As System.EventArgs) Handles txtLastName.Leave, _
    txtLastName.TextChanged

    If txtLastName.Text.Length = 0 Then
       errProvider.SetError(CType(sender, Control), nameMsg)
       txtLastName.Tag = False
    Else
       errProvider.SetError(CType(sender, Control), "")
       txtLastName.Tag = True
    End If
End Sub
```

 Note:

When the error message string of an ErrorProvider is length zero, the ErrorProvider icon next to an input control disappears. This is a useful visual cue to the user that the input value has been corrected.

Step 6. Add an event handler for the **txtAge** control that uses the IsNumeric function to check the txtAge control. It generates an ErrorProvider message and sets the Tag property in a similar manner to the handler for the last name text box:

```
Private Sub txtAge_Validate(ByVal sender As Object, _
    ByVal e As System.EventArgs) Handles txtAge.Leave, _
    txtAge.TextChanged

    If Not IsNumeric(txtAge.Text) Then
        errProvider.SetError(CType(sender, Control), ageMsg)
        txtAge.Tag = False
    Else
        errProvider.SetError(CType(sender, Control), "")
        txtAge.Tag = True
    End If
End Sub
```

Step 7. Add Click event handlers for the **OK** and **Cancel** buttons. The btnOK handler checks the Tag fields of both text boxes before allowing the form to close:

```
Private Sub btnOK_Click(ByVal sender As System.Object, _
 ByVal e As System.EventArgs) Handles btnOK.Click

    If Not CBool(txtLastName.Tag) Then
        MessageBox.Show(nameMsg)
        Exit Sub
    End If
```

The Tag property is untyped, so it must be cast into a Boolean type before being used in an If statement:

```
    If Not CBool(txtAge.Tag) Then
        MessageBox.Show(ageMsg)
        Exit Sub
    End If

    Me.Close()
End Sub

Private Sub btnCancel_Click(ByVal sender As System.Object, _
 ByVal e As System.EventArgs) Handles btnCancel.Click

    Me.Close()
End Sub
```

Step 8. Run and test the program. Here are five suggested tests:

◆ Press the Tab key to move between the two blank text boxes. The ErrorProvider icon will appear as soon as you move away from a blank text box. Hover the mouse over the icon to read its message.

◆ While the two text boxes are still blank, click on OK. A message box should inform you that the last name cannot be blank. Fix the last name and click on OK again. This time, the message box should say that Age must be numeric.

◆ Type a name into the Last name box and note that the ErrorProvider icon disappears.

◆ Enter a non-numeric value into the Age text box. Read the error message in the ErrorProvider icon. Fix the error and watch the red icon disappear.

◆ Click on Cancel, even when the input fields contain errors. The form closes anyway.

The ErrorProvider control offers a flexible way to deal with input errors. ErrorProvider makes it easier to cancel a form having blank input controls, and it permits the user to input data into the form in any order. The program's complete source code appears in Code Listing 2-3.

(End of tutorial)

Code Listing 2-3 (ErrorProvider Test)

```
Public Class frmValidate
    Inherits System.Windows.Forms.Form
```

```
+ Windows Form Designer generated code
```

```
    Const nameMsg As String = "Name cannot be blank"
    Const ageMsg As String = "Age must be a number"

    Private Sub frmValidate_Load(ByVal sender As _
     System.Object, ByVal e As System.EventArgs) _
     Handles MyBase.Load

        txtLastName.Tag = False
        txtAge.Tag = False
    End Sub

    Private Sub txtLastName_Validate(ByVal sender As Object, _
     ByVal e As System.EventArgs) Handles txtLastName.Leave, _
     txtLastName.TextChanged

        If txtLastName.Text.Length = 0 Then
            errProvider.SetError(CType(sender, Control), nameMsg)
            txtLastName.Tag = False
        Else
            errProvider.SetError(CType(sender, Control), "")
            txtLastName.Tag = True
        End If
    End Sub

    Private Sub txtAge_Validate(ByVal sender As Object, _
     ByVal e As System.EventArgs) Handles txtAge.Leave, _
     txtAge.TextChanged

        If Not IsNumeric(txtAge.Text) Then
            errProvider.SetError(CType(sender, Control), ageMsg)
            txtAge.Tag = False
        Else
            errProvider.SetError(CType(sender, Control), "")
            txtAge.Tag = True
        End If
    End Sub

    Private Sub btnOK_Click(ByVal sender As System.Object, _
     ByVal e As System.EventArgs) Handles btnOK.Click

        If Not CBool(txtLastName.Tag) Then
            MessageBox.Show(nameMsg)
            Exit Sub
        End If
```

```
      If Not CBool(txtAge.Tag) Then
         MessageBox.Show(ageMsg)
         Exit Sub
      End If

      Me.Close()
   End Sub

   Private Sub btnCancel_Click(ByVal sender As System.Object, _
    ByVal e As System.EventArgs) Handles btnCancel.Click

      Me.Close()
   End Sub
End Class
```

Checkpoint

2.6 Complete the following sentence: " A major component of creating user interfaces lies in the anticipation and prevention of _____."

2.7 What type of error checking can be performed by a class at the Business tier level?

2.8 What advantage is there to trapping invalid data on a form as soon as the user is about to move away from a control?

2.9 What property is most important when causing a control's Validating event to be fired?

2.10 What advantage does the ErrorProvider control offer over the Validating event in terms of checking input data?

▶2.3 ImageList and ToolBar Controls

The ImageList and ToolBar controls go together so well that we decided to present them as a combined section. Both can be configured in design mode. The ImageList control provides a simple way to invisibly store a set of icons or bitmaps in a form, and then associate those images with other controls. The Button, ToolBar, TabControl, ListView, and TreeView controls all have an ImageList property which can assigned the name of an ImageList control contained in the same form.

The ToolBar control, used in nearly every MS-Windows application program, acts as a container for command buttons. The ToolBar is nearly always joined to an ImageList control, so the latter can provide images for the ToolBar buttons. If you are looking for useful bitmaps, cursors, and icons for your programs, a number of graphical resources are supplied in the following directories:

◆ \Program Files\Microsoft Visual Studio .NET\Common7\Graphics\bitmaps

◆ \Program Files\Microsoft Visual Studio .NET\Common7\Graphics\cursors

◆ \Program Files\Microsoft Visual Studio .NET\Common7\Graphics\icons

A form can contain multiple ImageList controls, so it's possible to have a separate set of images for each control. In design mode, the ImageList control has a convenient dialog window that lets you select image files and insert them into the ImageList. The first image you place in an ImageList dictates the size of all subsequently inserted images.

Responding to Click Events

When a ButtonClick event is generated for a Toolbar, you have to find some way of determining which button was selected. The parameter **e** (a ToolBarButtonClickEventArgs object) has a property named Button that matches the button clicked by the user. Some references suggest using a Select Case statement to compare the button's Text property against known values:

```
Private Sub tlbMain_ButtonClick(ByVal sender As System.Object, _
 ByVal e As System.Windows.Forms.ToolBarButtonClickEventArgs) _
 Handles tlbMain.ButtonClick

    Select Case e.Button.Text
       Case "New"
          MessageBox.Show("New button clicked")
       Case "Open"
       etc.
```

Unfortunately, if your ToolBar does not display text below each button, this technique is useless. Ideally, we would like to access the name of each button in the ToolBar.Buttons collection, but the Name property is not accessible. A possible alternative is to use the Equals method to compare the clicked button to the button at each index position in the ToolBar's Buttons collection. The following statement, for example, compares to the button at index position 0:

```
If e.Button.Equals(tlbMain.Buttons(0)) Then
   MessageBox.Show("New button clicked")
End If
```

The use of a numeric index is not too self-documenting, and might prove to be a problem if the order of the buttons was changed at a later time. There is an alternative solution: you can store a string that uniquely identifies each button in its **Tag** property. For the ToolBar button that represents the *New document* command, for example, we can set its Tag property to "**new**" and check for the same value in the ButtonClick event handler:

```
Private Sub tlbMain_ButtonClick(ByVal sender As System.Object, _
 ByVal e As System.Windows.Forms.ToolBarButtonClickEventArgs) _
 Handles tlbMain.ButtonClick

    Select Case e.Button.Tag
       Case "new"
          MessageBox.Show("New button clicked")
       Case "open"
       etc.
```

This is the technique used in the following tutorial.

Hands-On Tutorial: Simple ToolBar

SimpleToolBar

In this tutorial, you will create a Windows Desktop program that contains ImageList and ToolBar controls. The ImageList will contain bitmaps from the Visual Studio .NET directory, and the ToolBar buttons will display the bitmaps.

Step 1.   Create a Windows Desktop project named **SimpleToolBar**. Rename the form to frmMain and change the project's startup object to frmMain.

Step 2.   Add an ImageList control to the main form and name it **imlToolBar**.

Step 3.   Click on the **Images** property of the ImageList control. When the Image Collection Editor window appears, click on the Add button to add the first bitmap (see Figure 2-7). Navigate to the **\Common7\Graphics\bitmaps\OffCtlBr\Small\Color** directory in your Visual Studio .NET installation and add the following bitmaps, in order: New, Open, Save, Preview, Print, and Help.

Step 4.   Add a ToolBar control to the form and name it **tlbMain**. Set its ImageList property to **imlToolBar**. Click on the Buttons property and display the dialog shown in Figure 2-8. Add the first button, set its ImageIndex property to **0**, its Tag property to "**new**", and its ToolTip property to "**Create a new document**".

The **ImageIndex** property identifies the index position of an image in the ImageList that will be used for the current button. The **ToolTipText** property holds the text that displays at runtime when the user hovers the mouse over the button. The **Tag** property will be used to indentify each button when we respond to Click events.

Step 5.   Add similar buttons to the toolbar for Open, Save, Preview, Print, and Help. Each ImageIndex property value increases by 1. The Tag properties for the buttons should be set to "open", "save", "preview", "print", and "help", respectively.

Step 6.   Run the program and verify that all buttons have bitmaps, as in Figure 2-9. Hover the mouse over each button and observe the button's tool tip text.

Step 7.   Stop the program. In Design mode, double-click on the ToolBar and insert the following ButtonClick handler procedure:

```
Private Sub tlbMain_ButtonClick(ByVal sender As System.Object, _
  ByVal e As System.Windows.Forms.ToolBarButtonClickEventArgs) _
  Handles tlbMain.ButtonClick
    Select Case (e.Button.Tag)
      Case "new"
        MessageBox.Show("New button clicked")
      Case "open"
        MessageBox.Show("Open button clicked")
      Case "save"
        MessageBox.Show("Save button clicked")
      Case "preview"
        MessageBox.Show("Preview button clicked")
      Case "print"
        MessageBox.Show("Print button clicked")
      Case "help"
        MessageBox.Show("Help button clicked")
    End Select
End Sub
```

Step 8. Run the program again, click on each ToolBar button, and verify that the appropriate message box appears.

(End of tutorial.)

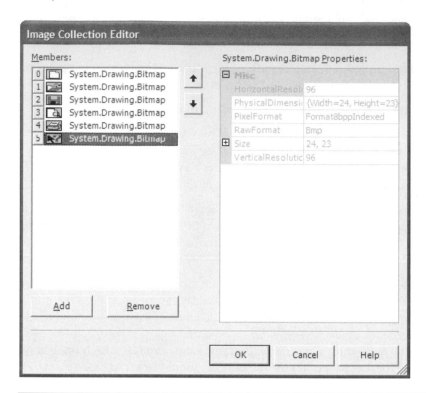

Figure 2-7 Adding bitmaps to an ImageList control

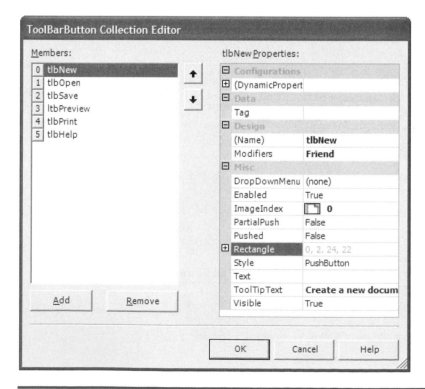

Figure 2-8 Adding buttons to a tool bar

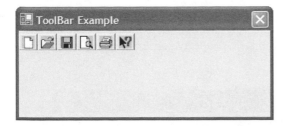

Figure 2-9 Running the ToolBar program

Checkpoint

2.11 What ToolBar property identifies the particular ImageList that contains images for the toolbar's buttons?

2.12 Once a button has been added to a ToolBar, what property identifies the image to be displayed on the button?

2.13 (yes/no) If the first image in an ImageList is a 32 x 32 icon, can the next image be a 16 x 16 icon?

2.14 (yes/no) Can a form contain more than one ImageList control?

2.15 How do you add buttons to a ToolBar control in design mode?

▶ 2.4 ListView Control

One of the most commonly used controls in all MS-Windows software, the ListView control stands out for its flexibility and power. The effort you take to master the ListView is well rewarded, as it can give your programs a distinctly professional appearance. It offers a number of features:

◆ The user can switch between display formats: large icons, small icons, list, or details.

◆ Data can easily be aligned in columns, without the need for tabs.

◆ Columns can be resized by the user, by dragging the column headings with the mouse.

◆ Column widths can be set at runtime by program statements.

◆ Column headers can respond to click events.

◆ Text appearing in columns can be centered, left justified, or right justified.

◆ List items are stored in a collection, making it easy to find individual items.

◆ List items can be edited by the user at runtime.

A well-known example of the ListView control is the Microsoft Windows Explorer. The left-hand panel displays a TreeView containing directory folders, and the right side displays the contents of the currently selected folder. You may also have noticed that in the .NET environment, property pages often contain ListView controls (Figure 2-10).

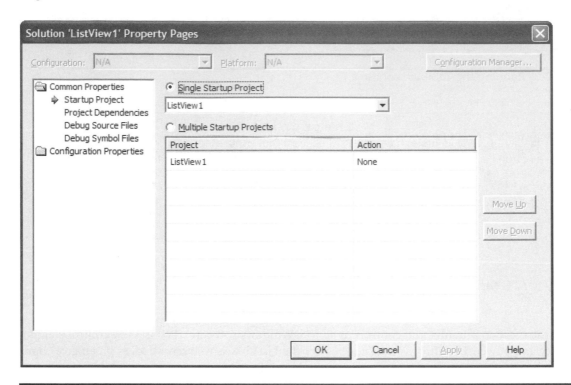

Figure 2-10 Solution property pages (using ListView)

The ListView control stores each row of its display in a **ListViewItem** object. The ListViewItem objects belong to a collection named **Items**. Each column heading belongs to a collection named **Columns**.

Creating Column Headings

If you want a ListView to display data in a table-like format (called the *Detail* view), you must add column headings. You can create column headings in design mode by clicking on the **Columns** entry in the ListView control's properties window. The property page is reasonably self-explanatory.

For greater flexibility, programmers often create column headings at runtime. To do this, call the Columns.Add method, passing the column title, its width (in pixels), and the type of aligment. The possible alignment values are HorizontalAlignment.Left, HorizontalAlignment.Center, and HorizontalAlignment.Right. The following, for example, creates a column heading named **Name**, which is 150 pixels wide and left-aligned:

```
lvwContacts.Columns.Add("Name", 150, HorizontalAlignment.Left)
```

In fact, our statement added a ColumnHeader object to the ListView. A longer way to add the column would have been the following:

```
Dim column As New ColumnHeader()
With column
    .Text = "Name"
    .Width = 150
    .TextAlign = HorizontalAlignment.Left
End With
lvwContacts.Columns.Add(column)
```

A nice trick is to calculate column header widths as percentages of the ListView's Width property. Each calculated expression returns a Double, so it must be cast into an Integer argument when passed to the Add method:

```
With lvwContacts
    .Columns.Add("Name", CInt(.Width * 0.3), HorizontalAlignment.Left)
    .Columns.Add("Phone", CInt(.Width * 0.3), HorizontalAlignment.Left)
    .Columns.Add("Email", CInt(.Width * 0.4), HorizontalAlignment.Left)
End With
```

 Note:

Class names everywhere! The preceding discussion purposely glossed over some details about column headings. If we were to be completely correct, we'd have to mention that the Columns property is really an instance of the ColumnHeaderCollection class. In other words, the ListView designers created a unique collection type to handle column headers in a ListView control. Why didn't they just create a standard collection object and avoid the extra work? First, the Add method in a standard .NET collection would permit one to add any type of object. Obviously, it wouldn't be smart to allow random objects to be inserted in a header collection. Second, they were able to overload the Add method so you can add a new column heading simply by passing a string, an integer, and the HorizontalAlignment constant:

```
lvwContacts.Columns.Add("Name", 150, HorizontalAlignment.Left)
```

Similarly, the Items collection in a ListView control is an instance of the ListViewItemCollection class. Its Add method is overloaded, so you can add a ListViewItem object, a String, or a String plus an integer to the collection.

ListViewItem Class

The **ListViewItem** class defines the appearance, behavior and data associated with each row in a ListView control. Depending on which View is selected, the items may appear in a table-like format, or as large icons, small icons, or a list of items. If you plan to display icons, they must be stored in an ImageList control associated with the ListView. Each ListViewItem contains an ImageIndex property that identifies the index of the item's icon in an ImageList.

You can construct a ListViewItem in a number of different ways, a few of which are listed here:

```
New ListViewItem( )
New ListViewItem( itemText As String )
New ListViewItem( itemArray As String() )
New ListViewItem( itemText As String, imageIndex As Integer )
```

Following are examples of each:

```
Dim item As ListViewItem
item = New ListViewItem()                         '1
item = New ListViewItem("John Smith")             '2
Dim strArray As String() = {"Tennis Racket", _
    "10.25", "40.50", "200.00", "15"}
item = New ListViewItem(strArray)                 '3
item = New ListViewItem("John Smith",0)           '4
```

Creating and Inserting a ListViewItem

To insert a new row in a ListView, you can create a ListViewItem using the text you want to display in the first column. To add more columns to the item, pass the columns to the item's SubItems.Add method. Finally, call the Items.Add method to add the complete ListViewItem to the ListView control. The following statements, for example, create a ListViewItem containing a person's name, phone number, and email address:

```
With lvwContacts
    Dim item As ListViewItem
    item = New ListViewItem("John Smith")
    item.SubItems.Add("305-222-3333")
    item.SubItems.Add("smithj@nuvisionmiami.com")
    item.ForeColor = Color.White
    item.BackColor = Color.DarkBlue
    .Items.Add(item)
End With
```

(Notice that you can set individual item colors.)

When you are ready to display a ListView containing multiple columns, set the View property to show all column details:

```
lvwContacts.View = View.Details
```

Other possible values for the View property are related to the same view options available in Windows Explorer:

◆ View.LargeIcon

◆ View.List

◆ View.SmallIcon

Changing Font Styles

You can set font styles such as Bold and Italic for ListViewItem objects. The way to do it is to create a Font object, passing it the existing Font as well as the desired font style. For example, the following lines create a ListViewItem and set its font style to Bold:

```
Dim item As New ListViewItem("John Smith")
item.Font = New Font(item.Font, FontStyle.Bold)
```

FontStyle is a standard Enum type that includes Bold, Italic, Regular, Strikeout, and Underline.

ListViewItem Properties

Table 2-5 contains descriptions of ListViewItem properties you are most likely to use.

TIP   If you forget to define column headings for a ListView and set the View property to Details, the ListView will appear empty when the program runs.

Table 2-5

ListViewItem Properties

Property	Description
BackColor	Background text color
Checked	Boolean: indicates whether or not the item is currently checked
Font	Font object: defines a format for text, including font face, size, and style attributes
Selected	Boolean: indicates whether or not the item is currently selected
ForeColor	Foreground text color
ImageIndex	Index of the image associated with the item (the image is stored in an ImageList control.)

Hands-On Tutorial: Contacts ListView

ListView 1

This tutorial will take you through the steps to fill a ListView control containing employee contact information. There will be three columns and two employees, as shown in Figure 2-11. The item data will be inserted by code in the form's Load event handler.

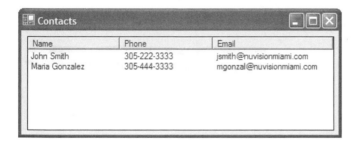

Figure 2-11 ListView holding contact information

Step 1. Create a Windows Desktop project named **ListView1**. Rename the form to **frmContacts** and set the project's startup object to **frmContacts**.

Step 2. Add a ListView control to the form and name it **lvwContacts**. Size the ListView so it fills the entire form, and set its Anchor property to (**top, bottom, left, right**). Optionally, you can change the BorderStyle property to **FixedSingle**.

Step 3. Insert the following code into the form's Load event handler:

```
With lvwContacts()
    .Columns.Add("Name", CInt(.Width * 0.3), HorizontalAlignment.Left)
    .Columns.Add("Phone", CInt(.Width * 0.3), HorizontalAlignment.Left)
    .Columns.Add("Email", CInt(.Width * 0.4), HorizontalAlignment.Left)
    .Width += 2
    .View = View.Details          'show all column details

    Dim item As ListViewItem
    item = New ListViewItem("John Smith")
    item.SubItems.Add("305-222-3333")
    item.SubItems.Add("jsmith@nuvisionmiami.com")
    .Items.Add(item)

    item = New ListViewItem("Maria Gonzalez")
    item.SubItems.Add("305-444-3333")
    item.SubItems.Add("mgonzal@nuvisionmiami.com")
    .Items.Add(item)
End With
```

Step 4. Run the program and confirm the output shown earlier in Figure 2-11.

Step 5. In design mode, set the ListView's **FullRowSelect** property to true. This will permit the user to select a row by clicking on any column within the row. Also, set the **CheckBoxes** property to True. This will display a checkbox at the beginning of each row.

Step 6. Run the program again and verify that the row selection and checkboxes work correctly.

(End of tutorial)

Useful ListView Techniques

Responding to ItemCheck

The **ItemCheck** event fires when the user clicks on a ListViewItem's checkbox. The Index property of the parameter **e** indicates the row index checked by the user. The following code displays the contact name of the person whose checkbox was clicked (Figure 2-12):

```
Private Sub lvwContacts_ItemCheck(ByVal sender As Object, _
  ByVal e As System.Windows.Forms.ItemCheckEventArgs) _
  Handles lvwContacts.ItemCheck

    MessageBox.Show(lvwContacts.Items(e.Index).Text _
      & " was checked/unchecked")
End Sub
```

The Text property of an item contains the contents of the first column. Row indexes begin at zero.

Figure 2-12 Selecting a check box

Selecting Items

When the user clicks on a single ListItem, the item reference is stored at index 0 in the SelectedItems collection. The following code displays that item:

```
Private Sub lvwContacts_Click(ByVal sender As Object, _
  ByVal e As System.EventArgs) Handles lvwContacts.Click

    MessageBox.Show(lvwContacts.SelectedItems.Item(0).Text _
        & " has been selected")
End Sub
```

If multiple items have been selected (by clicking and holding down the Ctrl or Shift key), you can iterate through the SelectedItems collection. The following code concatenates a list of all items that have been selected into a string and displays it:

```
Private Sub lvwContacts_Click(ByVal sender As Object, _
  ByVal e As System.EventArgs) Handles lvwContacts.Click

    Dim temp As String
    Dim item As ListViewItem
    For Each item In lvwContacts.SelectedItems
      temp = temp + item.Text & ", "
```

```
    Next item
    MessageBox.Show(temp, "Selected Contacts")
End Sub
```

Removing Items

You can remove an item from a ListView control by calling the Items.Remove method. Pass an object to the method that matches the one to be removed from the collection. The following code removes a single selected item:

```
Dim item As ListViewItem = lvwContacts.SelectedItems(0)
    .
    .
    .
lvwContacts.Items.Remove(item)
```

The CheckedItems collection contains references to all items in the ListView that are currently checked. You can use it in the same way as the SelectedItems collection.

Other ListView Features

The ListView control is rich with special properties, methods and events. We do not have enough space to describe them all, but here are a few that you are most likely to use. In Table 2-6, you can see a list of ListView properties you would commonly set in either design mode or at runtime. Table 2-7 contains a list of properties that can only be accessed at run time. Table 2-8 contains a list of commonly used ListView runtime events.

Table 2-6

Common ListView properties

Property	Description
AllowColumnReorder	When set to True, the user can rearrange columns by dragging their headers with the mouse. (The altered column order is not saved.)
CheckBoxes	When True, every item will have a checkbox.
CheckedItems	Collection of currently checked items.
Columns	Collection of ColumnHeader objects that each describe a column heading when the Details view is active.
GridLines	When True, horizontal and vertical gridlines appear between rows and columns.
Items	Collection of ListViewItem objects in the ListView.
LabelEdit	When True, the first column of each item can be modified by the user (or by program code).
LargeImageList	Reference to the ImageList control that holds large icons associated with the Items collection.
MultiSelect	If set to True, permits the user to select more than one item at a time.
SmallImageList	Reference to the ImageList control that holds small icons associated with the Items collection.
Sorting	Permits sorting of the first column in ascending or descending order.
View	Selects the active view (values are: LargeIcon, SmallIcon, List, Details).

Table 2-7

ListView run-time properties

Property	Description
CheckedIndices	Returns a collection containing the indexes of the currently checked items (ListViewItem objects).
CheckedItems	Returns a collection of the currently checked items .
SelectedIndices	Returns a collection containing the indexes of the currently selected items.
SelectedItems	Returns a collection of the currently selected items.
TopItem	Returns the first visible item in the control (useful when the user scrolls the items).

Table 2-8

ListView events

Property	Description
AfterLabelEdit	Occurs when the user has finished editing the label of an item.
BeforeLabelEdit	Occurs when the user starts editing the label of an item.
ColumnClick	Occurs when the user clicks on a column header.
ItemActivate	Occurs when an item is activated.
ItemCheck	Occurs when the check state of an item changes.
SelectedIndexChanged	Occurs when the index of the selected item in the list view control changes.

Hands-On Example: Removing ListView Items

ListView2

In this example, we will show off some of the more interesting features of the ListView control. Each item will have a leading check box, which the user will use to select and remove items from the ListView. The user will be able to reorder columns and edit a list item's text. The list will be sorted alphabetically, and the ListView will display grid lines.

Step 1. Open the **ListView2** project from the Chapter 2 example programs. The following ListView properties have been modified in design mode:

Property	Value
AllowColumnReorder	True
CheckBoxes	True
FullRowSelect	True
GridLines	True
Sorting	Ascending
View	Details

Step 2. Open the code window for the main form and inspect the **btnRemove_Click** procedure. The following statements remove all ListView items that have been checked by the user:

```
Private Sub btnRemove_Click(ByVal sender As System.Object, _
 ByVal e As System.EventArgs) Handles btnRemove.Click
    Dim item As ListViewItem
    For Each item In lvwContacts.CheckedItems
       lvwContacts.Items.Remove(item)
    Next item
End Sub
```

Step 3. Run the program and observe that a third contact has been added to the ListView, and each contact has a check box (Figure 2-13). The items are sorted in order by name, and vertical grid lines appear. Use the mouse to rearrange the columns by dragging their headers.

Step 4. Click on an item's Name, wait for a second, and click again. You should be able to edit the contact's name.

Step 5. Run the program, check one or more contact persons, and click on the Remove button. Verify that the contacts were removed from the list.

You may want to experiment with the BackColor property of the ListView, to see what looks best when combined with the grid lines. The program source code appears in Code Listing 2-4.

(End of example)

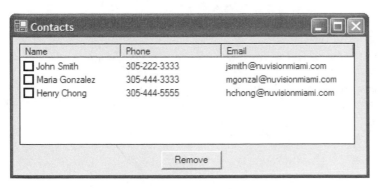

Figure 2-13 ListView contacts with check boxes

Code Listing 2-4 (Removing ListView Items)

```vb
Public Class frmMain
    Inherits System.Windows.Forms.Form
```

```
+ Windows Form Designer generated code
```

```vb
    Private Sub frmMain_Load(ByVal sender As System.Object, _
     ByVal e As System.EventArgs) Handles MyBase.Load

        With lvwContacts()
            .Columns.Add("Name", CInt(.Width * 0.3), HorizontalAlignment.Left)
            .Columns.Add("Phone", CInt(.Width * 0.3), HorizontalAlignment.Left)
            .Columns.Add("Email", CInt(.Width * 0.4), HorizontalAlignment.Left)
            .Width += 2

            Dim item As ListViewItem
            item = New ListViewItem("John Smith")
            item.SubItems.Add("305-222-3333")
            item.SubItems.Add("jsmith@nuvisionmiami.com")
            .Items.Add(item)

            item = New ListViewItem("Maria Gonzalez")
            item.SubItems.Add("305-444-3333")
            item.SubItems.Add("mgonzal@nuvisionmiami.com")
            .Items.Add(item)

            item = New ListViewItem("Henry Chong")
            item.SubItems.Add("305-444-5555")
            item.SubItems.Add("hchong@nuvisionmiami.com")
            .Items.Add(item)
        End With
    End Sub

    'Remove all checked items
    Private Sub btnRemove_Click(ByVal sender As System.Object, _
     ByVal e As System.EventArgs) Handles btnRemove.Click

        Dim item As ListViewItem
        For Each item In lvwContacts.CheckedItems
            lvwContacts.Items.Remove(item)
        Next item
    End Sub
End Class
```

▶ 2.5 TreeView Control

The TreeView control organizes information in a hierarchical structure known as a *tree*. Each element in the tree is a *node*. If a node has other nodes grouped under it, those nodes are called *child nodes*, and the node itself is a *parent* node. In Figure 2-14, the node named *Air* is a parent node and its child nodes are *Blimp*, *Balloon*, and *Glider*. When a plus sign (+) appears next to Air, the user clicks to display the child nodes. When a minus sign (−) appears, the user clicks to collapse the node's child nodes.

Because of its power and flexibility, the TreeView control seems to appear everywhere in MS-Windows applications. In Visual Studio .NET, for example, tree structures appear in the Solution Explorer window, the Class View window, the Object Browser, the Data Connections window, and elsewhere.

Figure 2-14 Travel tree example

Basic Techniques

A TreeView control contains a collection named **Nodes**, each element of which is a **TreeNode** object. A TreeNode can be constructed from a string, and can include additional information. The following statements, for example, add nodes to a TreeView control named **tvwTravel**:

```
With tvwTravel
   .Nodes.Add("Air")
   .Nodes.Add("Land")
   .Nodes.Add("Water")
End With
```

The Nodes collection only represents the top-level nodes in a tree. In order to create a hierarchical structure, you must attach child nodes to top-level nodes. Use the return value from the Add method to obtain a reference to the node you just added. Then you can access the Nodes collection of that node. The following statements, for example, add child nodes to the "Air" node in the tvwTravel control.

```
Dim aNode As TreeNode
With tvwTravel
   aNode = .Nodes.Add("Air")
   aNode.Nodes.Add("Blimp")
```

```
    aNode.Nodes.Add("Balloon")
    aNode.Nodes.Add("Glider")

    .Nodes.Add("Land")
    .Nodes.Add("Water")
End With
```

Figure 2-14 (page 96) contains the TreeView display after our code has executed.

Expanding the Tree

When new child nodes are added to a TreeView, the nodes are grouped under an icon that looks like a plus sign (+). You can call the ExpandAll method to expand all subtrees, thus displaying all nodes. Or, you can select a single node and call Expand to expand only the subtree belonging to the node:

```
tvwTravel.ExpandAll()        'expand all subtrees
aNode.Expand()               'expand one node's subtree
```

Inserting Multiple Nodes

When a large number of nodes are inserted in a TreeView all at once, a noticeable delay can result. This happens because the control redisplays itself after every insertion. You can get better performance by calling the **AddRange** method to insert an entire array of nodes all at once:

```
Dim nodeArray(2) As TreeNode
nodeArray(0) = New TreeNode("Air")
nodeArray(1) = New TreeNode("Land")
nodeArray(2) = New TreeNode("Water")
tvwTravel.Nodes.AddRange(nodeArray)
```

An alternative approach is to call the **BeginUpdate** method, which turns off the automatic redraw mode. After all nodes are inserted, call **EndUpdate** to restore the default redraw mode:

```
With tvwTravel
    .BeginUpdate()
    .Nodes.Add("Air")
    .Nodes.Add("Land")
    .Nodes.Add("Water")
    .EndUpdate()
End With
```

Getting Selected Nodes

The user can select individual tree nodes by clicking once with the mouse, or by using the cursor arrow keys. The control keeps track of the most recently selected node in the tree's **SelectedNode** property. Here's an example:

```
Dim aNode As TreeNode = tvwTravel.SelectedNode
```

The selected node has an **Index** property that returns the index position of the node in the collection. Be aware, however, that the index of a node changes when nodes before it are added or removed.

Sorting a Tree

A TreeView's **Sorted** property, when set to True, causes all subsequent node insertions to be in alphabetical order. The top-level nodes are ordered, and each subtree is ordered within itself. When Sorted is False, the Nodes. Add method appends nodes to the end of the tree.

Removing a Node

You can remove a node from the tree by calling the **Nodes.Remove** method, passing a TreeNode object. In the following code, we remove the currently selected node:

```
tvwTravel.Nodes.Remove(tvwTravel.SelectedNode)
```

Removing a Subtree

You can remove a node's subtree (its child nodes) by calling the Nodes.Clear method. The following statement removes all child nodes of the currently selected node:

```
tvwTravel.SelectedNode.Nodes.Clear()
```

Inserting a Node

If you want to insert a node in a specific position in a TreeView, you must obtain the index of an existing node. When the new node is inserted, the existing node is shifted downward. The following code inserts a node just before the selected node:

```
With tvwTravel
    Dim index As Integer = .SelectedNode.Index
    .Nodes.Insert(index, New TreeNode("Space"))
End With
```

Attaching a Child Node

If you want to insert a node and attach it as a child to an existing node, call the Nodes.Add method. The following code adds a child node to the selected node:

```
tvwTravel.SelectedNode.Nodes.Add("Dirigible")
```

Hands-On Tutorial: Contact Categories

TreeViewContacts
In this tutorial, you will fill a TreeView control with a list of category names that could be used to manage phone and email contacts. The user will be able to initialize several default categories, insert, and delete entries. The TreeView will maintain itself in alphabetical order. An About window will be displayed on demand, and the program will be menu-driven.

Operation

When the program starts up, the list of contacts is empty. When the user selects **Initialize** from the Edit menu, a default list of contacts appears in the tree (see Figure 2-15). All controls used in the main Form (frmMain) are listed in Table 2-9. In addition there is an About window named **frmAbout**, shown in Figure 2-16.

Table 2-9

Control properties, frmMain

Control Type	Control Name	Properties
Form	frmMain	Menu: MainMenu1
		MinimizeBox: False
		MaximizeBox: False
		Text: Contacts
TreeView	tvwContacts	Anchor: Top, Left, Bottom, Right
MainMenu	MainMenu1	
MenuItem	mnuFile	Text: &File
MenuItem	mnuEdit	Text: &Edit
MenuItem	mnuHelp	Text: &Help
MenuItem	mnuFileExit	Text: E&xit
		ShortCut: CtrlQ
MenuItem	mnuEditInit	Text: &Initialize
MenuItem	mnuEditInsert	Text: I&nsert…
		ShortCut: Ins
MenuItem	mnuEditRemove	Text: &Remove…
		ShortCut: Del
MenuItem	mnuHelpAbout	Text: &About Contacts…

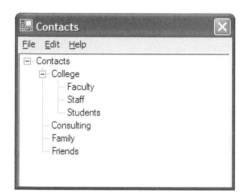

Figure 2-15 Default contact list

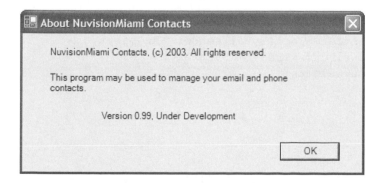

Figure 2-16 About window

Let's create the program:

Step 1. Open the **TreeViewContacts** program located in the Chapter 2 examples directory. The startup form (frmMain) and its menu have been created for you, as well as the frmAbout form.

Step 2. Define the following variable at the beginning of the frmMain class:

```
Dim mCurrNode As TreeNode
```

Step 3. When the user selects **Initialize** from the **Edit** menu, the TreeView is to be populated with a default set of nodes. First, a root node named "Contacts" is inserted. The Sorted property is set to True, and the top-level categories are inserted as subnodes of the root. One of the subnodes, "College", has its own set of subnodes. Create the following Click event handler for mnuEditInit:

```
Private Sub mnuEditInit_Click(ByVal sender As System.Object, _
    ByVal e As System.EventArgs) Handles mnuEditInit.Click

    Dim root As TreeNode, aNode As TreeNode
    With tvwContacts
        .BeginUpdate()
        .Sorted = True
        root = .Nodes.Add("Contacts")
        root.Nodes.Add("Family")
        root.Nodes.Add("Friends")
        aNode = root.Nodes.Add("College")
        aNode.Nodes.Add("Faculty")
        aNode.Nodes.Add("Students")
        aNode.Nodes.Add("Staff")
        root.Nodes.Add("Consulting")
        root.Expand()
        .EndUpdate()
    End With
    mnuEditInsert.Enabled = True
End Sub
```

Unless the **Expand** method is called, the entire tree remains hidden inside the "Contacts" node, with a plus symbol next to it. We call the method so the user can see the top-level category names. The Edit | Insert menu choice is enabled after the tree is initialized.

Step 4. The **AfterSelect** event fires each time the user selects a tree node. In its handler procedure, the parameter **e** contains a reference (through its Node property) to the selected node. We save that reference in **mCurrNode**:

```
Private Sub tvwContacts_AfterSelect(ByVal sender As Object, _
 ByVal e As System.Windows.Forms.TreeViewEventArgs) _
 Handles tvwContacts.AfterSelect

    mCurrNode = e.Node
End Sub
```

Step 5. When the user selects **Insert** from the **Edit** menu, we want to display a message box that prompts for the name of a node to insert. The new node is inserted as a child of the currently selected node. Create the following Click event handler for **mnuEditInsert**:

```
Private Sub mnuEditInsert_Click(ByVal sender As System.Object, _
 ByVal e As System.EventArgs) Handles mnuEditInsert.Click

    Dim nodeStr As String = InputBox("Enter a value to insert " _
    & "as a sub-category: ", "Insert Sub-Category")

    If nodeStr.Length > 0 Then
       mCurrNode = mCurrNode.Nodes.Add(nodeStr)
       mCurrNode.Expand()
       tvwContacts.SelectedNode = mCurrNode
    End If
End Sub
```

The code expands the current node so the user can see the added child node, and it selects (highlights) the new node.

Step 6. When the user selects **Remove** from the Edit menu, we want to make sure they understand that all child nodes (sub-categories) of the current node will also be erased. Create the following Click event handler for mnuEditRemove:

```
Private Sub mnuEditRemove_Click(ByVal sender As System.Object, _
 ByVal e As System.EventArgs) Handles mnuEditRemove.Click

    'Cannot remove the root node
    If mCurrNode.Equals(tvwContacts.TopNode) Then Exit Sub

    Dim ans As Integer
    ans = MessageBox.Show("Removing the selected node " _
    & "will also remove its child nodes. Do you want " _
    & "to continue?", "Removing Node", _
    MessageBoxButtons.YesNo, MessageBoxIcon.Question, _
    MessageBoxDefaultButton.Button2)

    If ans = DialogResult.Yes Then
       tvwContacts.Nodes.Remove(mCurrNode)
    End If
End Sub
```

We want to prevent the user from deleting the root node because it is the reference point for all other nodes. You cannot compare two nodes using an = sign, but you can call the Equals method to find out if mCurrNode and tvwContacts.TopNode both reference the same object:

```
If mCurrNode.Equals(tvwContacts.TopNode) Then Exit Sub
```

The last parameter passed to the MessageBox function selects Cancel as the default button. Therefore, if the user presses the Enter key, the message box will return the constant named DialogResult.Cancel.

Step 7. Run and test the program by initializing the tree, inserting new entries, and removing entries. You can also use the Ins and Del keys as shortcuts.

(End of tutorial. The program's complete source appears in Code Listing 2-5.)

We have only covered a small subset of what is possible with the TreeView control. It's probably the most advanced visual control in the .NET toolbox, and possibly the most commonly used in professional applications. If you are inspired, read the complete .NET documentation for the TreeView control and look at Microsoft's sample programs.

Code Listing 2-5 (TreeView Contacts)

```
Public Class frmTreeView
    Inherits System.Windows.Forms.Form
```

```
+ Windows Form Designer generated code
```

```
    Dim mCurrNode As TreeNode

    Private Sub tvwContacts_AfterSelect(ByVal sender As Object, _
     ByVal e As System.Windows.Forms.TreeViewEventArgs) _
     Handles tvwContacts.AfterSelect

        mCurrNode = e.Node
    End Sub

    'Initialize the tree with default nodes
    Private Sub mnuEditInit_Click(ByVal sender As System.Object, _
     ByVal e As System.EventArgs) Handles mnuEditInit.Click

        Dim root As TreeNode, aNode As TreeNode
        With tvwContacts
          .BeginUpdate()
          .Sorted = True
          root = .Nodes.Add("Contacts")
          root.Nodes.Add("Family")
          root.Nodes.Add("Friends")
          aNode = root.Nodes.Add("College")
          aNode.Nodes.Add("Faculty")
          aNode.Nodes.Add("Students")
          aNode.Nodes.Add("Staff")
          root.Nodes.Add("Consulting")
          root.Expand()
          .EndUpdate()
        End With
    End Sub
```

2

```
'Insert a new child node
Private Sub mnuEditInsert_Click(ByVal sender As System.Object, _
 ByVal e As System.EventArgs) Handles mnuEditInsert.Click

    Dim nodeStr As String = InputBox("Enter a value to insert " _
     & "as a sub-category: ", "Insert Sub-Category")

    If nodeStr.Length > 0 Then
       'mCurrNode = mCurrNode.Nodes.Add(nodeStr)
       mCurrNode.Nodes.Add(nodeStr)
       'mCurrNode now points to the inserted node
       mCurrNode.Expand()
       tvwContacts.SelectedNode = mCurrNode
    End If
End Sub


'Remove the current node
Private Sub mnuEditRemove_Click(ByVal sender As System.Object, _
 ByVal e As System.EventArgs) Handles mnuEditRemove.Click

    'Cannot remove the root node
    If mCurrNode.Equals(tvwContacts.TopNode) Then Exit Sub

    Dim ans As Integer
    ans = MessageBox.Show("Removing the selected node " _
     & "will also remove its child nodes. Do you want " _
     & "to continue?", "Removing Node", _
     MessageBoxButtons.YesNo, MessageBoxIcon.Question, _
     MessageBoxDefaultButton.Button2)

    If ans = DialogResult.Yes Then
       tvwContacts.Nodes.Remove(mCurrNode)
    End If
End Sub

Private Sub mnuFileExit_Click(ByVal sender As _
 System.Object, ByVal e As System.EventArgs) _
 Handles mnuFileExit.Click

    Me.Close()
End Sub

Private Sub mnuHelpAbout_Click(ByVal sender As _
 System.Object, ByVal e As System.EventArgs) _
 Handles mnuHelpAbout.Click

    Dim aboutForm As New frmAbout
    aboutForm.ShowDialog()
End Sub
End Class
```

Hands-On Example: Disk Directory TreeView

DirectoryTree

For our final TreeView example, we will show how to display a disk directory tree. We will call upon the **System.IO.DirectoryInfo** class, which has a method named **GetDirectories** that returns a collection of DirectoryInfo objects. In other words, the directories form a recursive relationship, in which a directory contains a list of subdirectories, and each of the subdirectories contains its own list of subdirectories, and so on. The TreeView control has the same type of recursive relationship, in which each node in the Nodes collection has its own collection of nodes. Sounds like a perfect match!

Step 1. Open the **DirectoryTree** program from the Chapter 2 samples directory. It has a TreeView control named **tvwDirectory** that is anchored on all four sides to a resizable window.

Step 2. Note that the program imports the System.IO namespace:

```
Imports System.IO
```

Step 3. The Form_Load event handler uses a variable named **path** to hold the starting path for our directory display (C:\Windows), which is also displayed in the form's title bar:

```
Private Sub frmDirectory_Load(ByVal sender As System.Object, _
   ByVal e As System.EventArgs) Handles MyBase.Load

   Dim path As String = "C:\Windows"
   Me.Text = path
   tvwDirectory.BeginUpdate()
   getDirectory(tvwDirectory.Nodes, path)
   tvwDirectory.EndUpdate()
End Sub
```

The call to **ShowDirectory** passes the TreeView's Nodes collection, along with the starting directory path we want to display.

Step 4. The GetDirectory method is the focal point of the program. It sets up a DirectoryInfo object named currentDir, which holds a list of all subdirectories attached to the current directory:

```
Sub GetDirectory(ByVal nodes As TreeNodeCollection, _
   ByVal path As String)

   Dim currentDir As New DirectoryInfo(path)
   Dim dirInfo As DirectoryInfo
   Dim aNode As TreeNode

   For Each dirInfo In currentDir.GetDirectories()
      aNode = nodes.Add(dirInfo.Name)
      GetDirectory(aNode.Nodes, dirInfo.FullName)
   Next dirInfo
End Sub
```

The For-Each loop iterates through the directories, adding each one's name to the **nodes** collection. (Remember, nodes was passed into this method as tvwDirectory.Nodes.) What is really interesting about this loop is that GetDirectory calls itself (a technique known as *recursion*), passing the Nodes collection of the current TreeView node, as well as the name of the current subdirectory. GetDirectory will find all the subdirectories of the current subdirectory, and add them all to the tree as child nodes. The recursive approach used by GetDirectory makes it possible to locate all subdirectories attached to the starting directory (C:\Windows), no matter how deeply nested.

Step 5. Run the program. You may notice a momentary delay due to the large number of directory names inserted in the tree. After you expand some of the subtrees by clicking the "+" symbols with the mouse, you should see your computer's directory structure. A sample is shown in Figure 2-17.

(End of example)

Figure 2-17 Sample TreeView directory display

Recursion

Recursion is the general term for what happens when a procedure calls itself. We call such a procedure a *recursive* procedure, and a *recursive call* is the actual moment when the procedure call happens. If this program is your first encounter with recursion, you may think it's a bit odd. In fact, beginning programmers sometimes create recursion by mistake, causing their programs to stop responding and eventually run out of memory. When used properly, however recursion is a great tool for using only a few lines of code to accomplish a great deal of work. Our ShowDirectory procedure is a good example, because it handles any level of directory nesting. Imagine how such a search would be accomplished without using recursion!

A sequence of recursive procedure calls must have a way to stop. In our ShowDirectory procedure, for example, the recursive calls stop when no more subdirectories are attached to the current directory. That's when the deeply nested procedure calls begin to back up to the point where ShowDirectory was first called (from the form's Load event handler). We do not have the space to fully explain recursion here, but you can find a full tutorial in almost any intermediate-level C++, Java, or C# programming textbook.

►2.6 Structured Exception Handling

Introduction

In general terms, when any program encounters an error while running, we say that a *runtime error* occurred. In .NET and other environments like it, we can go further and say that a runtime error is the result of an *exception* being *thrown*.

An exception is thrown when a program encounters an error severe enough to cause the program's behavior to become unreliable. The error must be dealt with before the program can continue. There are two general types of exceptions:

Exceptions caused by faulty programming logic, such as dividing by zero or accessing an object using a null reference. Such exceptions can always be prevented by checking values prior to performing an operation that would throw an exception.

Exceptions caused by events outside the control of the programmer. For example, a data file might be missing, a program might run out of memory, or the user might enter an invalid data item.

T
I
P

Exception handling has a lot in common with automobile insurance. We do our best to prevent accidents, but insurance helps when the unforseen happens. It would be madness to drive recklessly with the intention of filing lots of insurance claims.

Visual Basic .NET, using the legacy of languages such as C++ and Java, has the ability to perform what is known as *structured exception handling*. Programs can detect and respond to specific exceptions when they happen. When an exception occurs, a program can (in many cases) recover from the exception and continue running. For example, if a data file cannot be found, a program can display an Open File dialog that lets the user browse to the file's actual location.

Before exception handling was invented, programmers had to create complicated schemes for signalling and dealing with errors. In earlier versions of Visual Basic, a statement named **On Error Goto** would be used to jump to a block of code when a runtime error occurred, and the block of code would ask the user to enter a new filename, input a different number, or somehow try to fix the problem that caused the error. But On Error Goto was difficult to use, and tended to make program code difficult to follow.

A vexing problem has long plagued programmers: one part of a program might be able to detect errors, but doesn't know what to do about them. Another part of the program cannot detect errors, but it knows what to do about them. It sometimes helps to relate this problem to a real-world example involving machines:

> Imagine a bottling plant running various machines that fill bottles, move them between locations, attach caps, and pack them in boxes. Suppose the bottle-mover machine overheats. The person monitoring the machine has no idea what to do about this error, other than perhaps shutting the machine down. (It might not be such a good idea to shut down only the machine that moves bottles!) Instead, this person calls the plant manager, who evaluates the overall operation of the assembly line and decides to bring a different bottle-mover online.

No doubt, computer software shows many of the same characteristics as manufacturing and processing plants, with many interdependent parts and processes that communicate both objects and information.

When a procedure throws an exception, it creates an instance of either the Exception class or some class derived from Exception. Exceptions are of three general types:

- ◆ **SystemException**: Exceptions of this type can occur at any time when a program is running, so they are also called *runtime exceptions*. Most of the exceptions thrown by .NET are of this type. Table 2-10 contains a list of exceptions found in .NET's System namespace that are derived from the SystemException class.

- ◆ **ApplicationException**: Exceptions of this type are usually thrown by application programs (ones that you write).

- ◆ **IOException**: Exceptions of this type result from file and stream input-output errors.

Table 2-10

Common SystemException classes

Class Name	Description
ArgumentException	Invalid argument was passed to a procedure. Application programs can throw this exception. Includes ArgumentNullException, ArgumentOutOfRangeException.
ArrayTypeMismatchException	Attempt is made to store an element of the wrong type within an array.
ArithmeticException	Arithmetic operation produced an invalid result. Includes DivideByZeroException, NotFiniteNumberException, OverflowException
UnauthorizedAccessException	File or directory might be write-protected, or the current user may not have access privileges.
StackOverflowException	Often caused by runaway recursion or excessive number of local variables in a procedure. Program must terminate.
FormatException	Format of an argument in a method invocation does not match the format of the corresponding formal parameter type.
IndexOutOfRangeException	Array subscript is out of bounds.
OutOfMemoryException	Program is out of memory, requiring it to terminate.
InvalidCastException	Cast operator function (such as CType, CInt or CSng) applied to an incompatible value.
InvalidOperationException	A method call is invalid for the object's current state.
NullReferenceException	Attempt to reference an object variable which has been set to Nothing.

The Common Language Runtime (CLR) built into the .NET Framework is the agent responsible for throwing exceptions. The CLR looks for a block of code named an *exception handler*, written by the application programmer. We alternatively say that the exception handler *catches* the exception, or that it *handles* the exception. If an exception handler cannot be found for a thrown exception, the exception becomes an *unhandled exception* (or *uncaught exception*).

You can see a complete list of .NET exception classes by selecting Exceptions... from the Debug menu.

Integer Conversion Example

Exceptions 1

Let's create a simple program with an text box that asks the user to input an integer (see Figure 2-18). When the OK button is clicked, we will attempt to convert the contents of the text box into an integer. If we were to call the CInt function, any string containing either an integer or real value would be successfully converted to an Integer.

Instead, let's call the **ToInt32** method from the .NET Framework class named **Convert**. It specifically requires the input string to be in integer format. Otherwise, it throws an exception. For example:

```
Dim n As Integer
n = Convert.ToInt32("123")      'ok
n = Convert.ToInt32("12.3")     'throws an exception
```

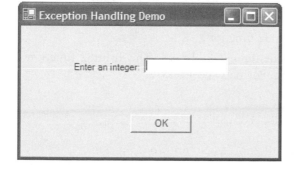

Figure 2-18 Integer conversion example

The following code executes in the program's startup form:

```
Dim n As Integer
If IsNumeric(txtInput.Text) Then
    n = Convert.ToInt32(txtInput.Text)
    stsMessage.Text = "OK"
Else
    stsMessage.Text = "That's not a number!"
End If
```

When we run this program, enter "xxx" into the text box, and click on OK, the status bar displays "That's not a number!". Most competent programmers would include at least this level of error checking. But if we run the program again and enter "22.5" into the text box, the program displays an *unhandled exception* message, shown in Figure 2-19. If the the user clicks on Continue, the program continues to run, presumably with invalid data. This type of message might be ok for the programmer, but it would not be very useful for end users. In most cases, they would quit the program and be somewhat displeased with the software.

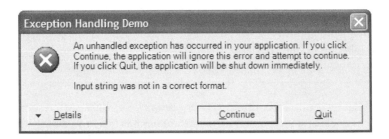

Figure 2-19 Unhandled exception dialog

If you click on the Details button, the runtime system displays a description of the exception, followed by a *stack trace*. The latter is a history of procedure calls listed in reverse order, leading back to the code in our program that caused the error. Following is an abbreviated version of the Details display of our sample program, assuming the program was compiled to a Debug target:

```
************** Exception Text **************
System.FormatException: Input string was not in a correct format.
   at System.Number.ParseInt32(String s, NumberStyles style,
   NumberFormatInfo info)
   at System.Convert.ToInt32(String value)
   at Exceptions1.frmMain.Example1() in
   C:\Data\_vbook3\chapters\ch02\examples\Exceptions1\Form1.vb:line 93
   at Exceptions1.frmMain.btnOK_Click(Object sender, EventArgs e) in
   C:\Data\_vbook3\chapters\ch02\examples\Exceptions1\Form1.vb:line 129
```

The error message is repeated, followed by a stack trace. The latter is the sequence of function calls that led to the throwing of the exception. To follow the sequence of events, we can start at the end and work backward:

◆ On line 129 in the **btnOK_Click** procedure, we called the **Example1** procedure.

◆ On line 93 (inside Example1), we called the **ToInt32** function.

◆ (At this point, the function call sequence is inside the .NET library.) The ToInt32 function called the ParseInt32 function, and the latter threw a System.FormatException.

If the program is compiled to a Release target, we will get similar information, most notably without source code line numbers:

```
************** Exception Text **************
System.FormatException: Input string was not in a correct format.
   at System.Number.ParseInt32(String s, NumberStyles style,
   NumberFormatInfo info)
   at Exceptions1.frmMain.Example1()
   at Exceptions1.frmMain.btnOK_Click(Object sender, EventArgs e)
```

In this example, we could not prevent the user from entering a non-integer value. Our only recourse might have been to trap every keystroke and lock out non-digit characters. Instead, we will use exception handling to provide a simpler, more general way to catch user input errors.

Exception Classes

An exception's type is often a good indication of what went wrong. For example, if a program tries to open a file from a directory that does not exist, a **DirectoryNotFoundException** is thrown. Or, if the directory exists but the file does not, a **FileNotFoundException** is thrown. If the file exists but cannot be loaded, a **FileLoadException** is thrown. A well-written exception handler compares a thrown exception with specific exception types, permitting the exception to be handled in a way most appropriate to its type.

Though numerous exception classes exist, all have a common ancestor named **Exception**. Using terminology from human genealogy, some exception classes are *children* of the Exception class, others *grandchildren*, inheriting from a child class of the Exception class, and still others are great *grandchildren*, inheriting from a grandchild class of the Exception class. Figure 2-20 shows that DirectoryNotFoundException, FileLoadException, and FileNotFoundException extend IOException, which extends SystemException, which extends Exception.

The Exception class is part of the System namespace, so it is named System.Exception. You can view a list of all exception types in the Common Language Runtime by selecting **Exceptions** from the **Debug** menu.

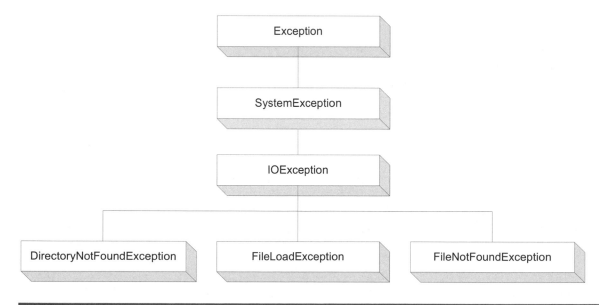

Figure 2-20 IOException class hierarchy (excerpt)

Setting Exception Breakpoints in the Debugger

You can set up the .NET debugger to break on specific exceptions. To do that, select **Exceptions...** from the Debug menu, open up the list of exceptions under **System**, and select an exception name. In our example, we will select the **FormatException**. In the "When the exception is thrown" option group, select "Break into the debugger". From that point on, any exception having this option will display with a red icon containing a white "X".

If we run the Integer Conversion example program in Debug mode (selecting **Start** from the Debug menu), the thrown exception causes the following breakpoint window to display:

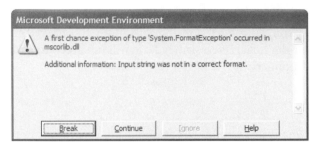

When you click on the **Break** button, the source code line that threw the exception is shown with green highlighting.

```
        Inherits System.Windows.Forms.Form

    Windows Form Designer generated code

    'Allow an uncaught exception to be thrown
    Sub Example1()
        Dim n As Integer
        If IsNumeric(txtInput.Text) Then
            n = Convert.ToInt32(txtInput.Text)
            stsMessage.Text = "OK"
        Else
            stsMessage.Text = "That's not a number!"
        End If
    End Sub

    'Use structured exception handling, with a
    'nonspecific Catch block
```

This type of display is only useful to the programmer, when the program is being tested. We also need to think about the end users of a program. In the next section, we show you how to catch and handle exceptions in your own code.

Try...Catch...Finally Statement

Handling an exception is accomplished using a Try...Catch statement. An optional statement, **Finally,** is often used as well (see Figure 2-21). We will discuss the *exception-type* parameter in the next section. A structured exception handler begins with **Try** and ends with **End Try**. There are three blocks:

1. The **Try** block starts with **Try** and ends at **Catch**. The Try block contains code that might cause an exception to be thrown.

2. The **Catch** block starts with **Catch** and ends at **Finally**, or at the beginning of a new Catch block. The code in the Catch block executes when an exception is thrown. The Catch block is known as the exception handler.

3. The **Finally** block begins with **Finally** and ends at **End Try**. If no exceptions are thrown, the Finally block executes immediately after the last statement in the Try block. If an exception is thrown, the Finally block executes immediately after the last statement in the appropriate Catch block.

Figure 2-22 shows the alternate paths that may be taken through Try...Catch...Finally blocks, depending on whether an exception was thrown. Use the optional Finally block to release resources created inside the Try block, or to perform any other type of cleanup.

```
Try
    try-block
Catch [optional filters]
    catch-block
[additional Catch blocks]
    catch-block
Finally
    [finally-block]
End Try
```

Figure 2-21 Syntax of the Try...Catch...Finally statement

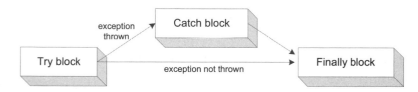

Figure 2-22 Alternate execution paths

Integer Conversion Example

Exceptions 1

Let's return the to the Integer Conversion program that recently threw an unhandled exception. The following code attempts to convert the contents in the text box to an integer and displays an appropriate message depending on the outcome:

```
Try
    Dim n As Integer
    n = Convert.ToInt32(txtInput.Text)
    stsMessage.Text = "OK"
Catch
    stsMessage.Text = "That's not an Integer!"
End Try
```

Figure 2-23 shows the result when the user enters "xxx" into the text box and clicks on OK. At least this program is more stable than the previous version. What would happen, however, if the user entered an integer outside the range −2,147,483,648 to 2,147,483,647? The same message "That's not an Integer" would display, which is not quite appropriate. Our program should catch two types of exceptions:

◆ FormatException: Input string not in correct format
◆ OverflowException: Conversion yields an integer that is either too large or too small

Fortunately, it is possible to create Catch blocks that look for specific exception types.

Figure 2-23 Handling the Exception

Catch Block- Optional Filters

When statements in the Try block could generate more than one type of exception, the Catch block should contain a filter specifying an exact exception type:

Catch [*filter*]

filter can be one of the following:

◆ The name of the exception type, such as:

```
FormatException
```

◆ An exception object declaration, such as:

```
except As InvalidCastException
```

◆ An exception object declaration, followed by a When clause:

```
except As Exception _
  When except.GetType.ToString() = "System.OverflowException"
```

By specifying an object name, you have access to Exception properties and methods, several of which are listed in Table 2-11. They make it easier to customize information displayed to the user.

Table 2-11

System.Exception properties and methods

Property/Method	Description
GetType()	Gets the exact type of the exception object. You can display the exception's type name by calling GetType.ToString()
Message	Gets a message string describing the current exception.
Source	Gets or sets the name of the application or object in which the error occurred.
StackTrace	Gets a string representation of the call stack when the exception was thrown, enabling you to trace the error through several procedure calls.
TargetSite	Gets the method that throws the current exception. Returns a MethodBase object.
ToString()	Returns a string representation of the exception, including the Message and StackTrace property values.

All classes that inherit from System.Exception contain at least the same properties as Exception. They may contain additional properties relating to the particular type of exception they represent. For example, the FileLoadException class has a **FileName** property that gets the name of the file being read when the exception was thrown.

Examples

The following Catch block catches any exception type:

```
Catch
   MessageBox.Show("An exception was thrown")
```

The following Catch block names the exception type:

```
Catch InvalidCastException
   MessageBox.Show("InvalidCastException was thrown")
```

The following Catch block declares the exception object that was caught so we can display the object's Message property:

```
Catch except As InvalidCastException
   MessageBox.Show(except.Message)
```

The following catches any type of exception and displays the exception's type in the messsage box caption:

```
Catch except As Exception
    MessageBox.Show(except.Message, except.GetType.ToString())
```

Integer Conversion Example

Let's return to the Integer Conversion program and create Catch blocks for two specific exception types: InvalidCastException and OverflowException. We will also display the Exception object's Message property on the form's status bar:

```
Try
    Dim n As Integer
    n = Convert.ToInt32(txtInput.Text)
    stsMessage.Text = "OK"
Catch except As FormatException
    stsMessage.Text = except.Message
Catch except As OverflowException
    stsMessage.Text = except.Message
End Try
```

Figure 2-24 shows how the program responds when the user enters either "xxx" or a very large integer into the text box. The messages produced on the status bar might be a little impersonal, but you can replace them with your own. You might want to display the exception's StackTrace property, as we have in Figure 2-25. You can also display the name of the method that was executing when the exception was thrown. The TargetSite property returns a MethodBase object, which in turn has a Name property:

```
MessageBox.Show("Method name: " & except.TargetSite.Name())
```

In our conversion program, the method name displayed is **FromString**, which is a method inside the IntegerType class. This property is more useful when our own classes throw exceptions.

The ToString method of the Exception class produces the same information we saw when an unhandled exception was thrown (see earlier in this chapter). Figure 2-26 shows our program's output when calling ToString:

```
MessageBox.Show(except.ToString())
```

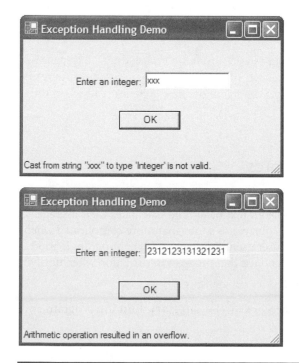

Figure 2-24 Handling specific exceptions

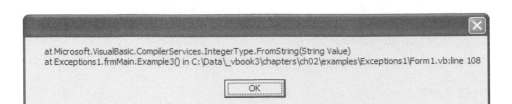

Figure 2-25 Displaying a stack trace

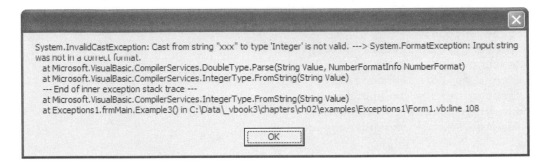

Figure 2-26 Calling Exception.ToString

System.IO Exceptions

Programs that handle file I/O often have to deal with error conditions outside their control. As we mentioned earlier in this chapter, a program might try to open a file that doesn't exist. Or, a program might attempt to write data to a read-only file. In general, the programmer has little control over the situation, other than to catch exceptions, notify the user, and ask how to proceed. System.IO Exceptions belong to the System.IO namespace. For example, a Catch block for FileNotFoundException is written as follows:

```
Catch except As IO.FileNotFoundException
```

The following exception classes belong to the System.IO namespace:

- DirectoryNotFoundException
- EndOfStreamException
- FileLoadException
- FileNotFoundException
- InternalBufferOverflowException
- IOException
- PathTooLongException

Hands-On Example: Averaging Test Scores

TestScores

We will look at a program that inputs a set of test scores from text boxes and calculates their average. This would seem a simple task, suitable for a beginning programming course. It is somewhat more complicated when exception handling is introduced, particularly if we want to give the user useful information. The program is good example of how a program can track its progress through a Try block, and use that progress information when notifying the user about a thrown exception.

Step 1. Open the **TestScores** program from the Chapter 2 examples directory. Run the program and view the startup form, shown in Figure 2-27.

Step 2. Stop the program and open the code window for the startup form. Inspect the code in the first Try block in the **cmdOK_Click** procedure. Notice how the variable named **count** is incremented each time we convert the contents of a text box into a value of type Single. Each value is inserted into the **scores** collection:

```
Dim scores As New Collection()
Dim count As Integer = 0

'Convert all text boxes to numbers and store the
'values in a collection of scores.
Try
    scores.Add(Convert.ToSingle(txtScore_1.Text))
    count += 1
    scores.Add(Convert.ToSingle(txtScore_2.Text))
    count += 1
    scores.Add(Convert.ToSingle(txtScore_3.Text))
    count += 1
    scores.Add(Convert.ToSingle(txtScore_4.Text))
    count += 1
    scores.Add(Convert.ToSingle(txtScore_5.Text))
    count += 1
    scores.Add(Convert.ToSingle(txtScore_6.Text))
    count += 1
    scores.Add(Convert.ToSingle(txtScore_7.Text))
    count += 1
    scores.Add(Convert.ToSingle(txtScore_8.Text))
    count += 1
Catch except As FormatException
    MessageBox.Show("Bad number in test score #" _
      & (count + 1))
Catch except As Exception
    MessageBox.Show(except.Message)
End Try
```

If any text box is blank or it contains a non-numeric value, the ToSingle method throws a FormatException. Because this method is called eight times, we would like to be able to know exactly which text box caused the error. (The user can easily tell by looking, but not all steps in a Try block will be this obvious.)

The message box in the FormatException Catch block displays the test score number of the score that caused an exception to be thrown. This is possible because we incremented **count** during each conversion inside the Try block.

Step 3. Still inside the Click procedure, look at the second Try block, which calculates and displays the average of the test scores. We iterate through the collection of scores, add each to a sum, and count the number of nonzero scores:

```
'Start a new Try block to calculate and display
'the sum of the test scores.
Try
    Dim sumScores As Single = 0.0, iscore As Single
    count = 0

    'calculate the sum of all nonzero scores
    For Each iscore In scores
        sumScores += iscore
        If iscore > 0 Then count += 1
    Next iscore
```

When the average is calculated, there may not be any scores at all. As a precaution, we catch any exception that might occur:

```
        Dim testAverage As Single
        If count <> 0 Then
            testAverage = sumScores / count
        Else
            testAverage = 0
        End If
        lblAverage.Text = FormatNumber(testAverage)
    Catch except As Exception
        MessageBox.Show("Exception thrown while calculating " _
          & "the sum & average.", except.Message)
    End Try
```

Step 4. Run and test the program by entering a few valid test scores. The average calculates correctly. Next, leave one of the scores blank and click on OK. The error message should tell you which text box had an invalid value (Figure 2-28). If multiple boxes are invalid, only the first will be flagged, and you will have to fix them one by one.

(End of tutorial. The program's source code can be found in Code Listing 2-6.)

It would have been possible to use a single Try block for the entire Click handler procedure, but using two shorter blocks is a better idea. In general, using a shorter Try block makes it easier for you to tailor your Catch blocks for the type of exceptions most likely to be thrown. In the current sample program, two logically separate tasks existed: The first Try block validated the input data, and the second block performed the calculations.

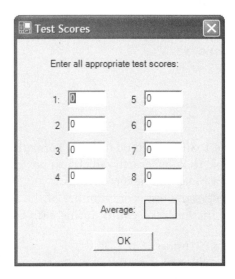

Figure 2-27 Test score program

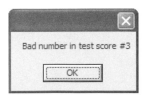

Figure 2-28 Error message resulting from a blank text box

Code Listing 2-6 (Averaging Test Scores)

```
Public Class Form1
    Inherits System.Windows.Forms.Form

┌─────────────────────────────────────┐
│ + Windows Form Designer generated code │
└─────────────────────────────────────┘

    Private Sub cmdOK_Click(ByVal sender As System.Object, _
     ByVal e As System.EventArgs) Handles cmdOK.Click

        Dim scores As New Collection()
        Dim count As Integer = 0

        'Convert all text boxes to numbers and store the
        'values in a collection of scores.
        Try
            scores.Add(Convert.ToSingle(txtScore_1.Text))
            count += 1
            scores.Add(Convert.ToSingle(txtScore_2.Text))
            count += 1
            scores.Add(Convert.ToSingle(txtScore_3.Text))
            count += 1
            scores.Add(Convert.ToSingle(txtScore_4.Text))
            count += 1
            scores.Add(Convert.ToSingle(txtScore_5.Text))
            count += 1
            scores.Add(Convert.ToSingle(txtScore_6.Text))
            count += 1
            scores.Add(Convert.ToSingle(txtScore_7.Text))
            count += 1
            scores.Add(Convert.ToSingle(txtScore_8.Text))
            count += 1
        Catch except As FormatException
            MessageBox.Show("Bad number in test score #" _
             & (count + 1))
        Catch except As Exception
            MessageBox.Show(except.Message)
        End Try

        'Start a new Try block to calculate and display
        'the sum of the test scores.
        Try
            Dim sumScores As Single = 0.0, iscore As Single
            count = 0

            'calculate the sum of all nonzero scores
            For Each iscore In scores
                sumScores += iscore
                If iscore > 0 Then count += 1
            Next iscore

            'Calculate and display the average score. Note that
            'count might be zero.
            Dim testAverage As Single
            If count <> 0 Then
                testAverage = sumScores / count
            Else
                testAverage = 0
```

```
            End If
            lblAverage.Text = FormatNumber(testAverage)
        Catch except As Exception
            MessageBox.Show("Exception thrown while calculating " _
            & "the sum & average.", except.Message)
        End Try
    End Sub
End Class
```

Hands-On Example: Handling File Exceptions

FileExceptions

Let's look at a short program that handles file-related exceptions. The program displays a form (see Figure 2-29) containing a text box into which the user types a filename with an optional path. When the **Read File** button is clicked, the program attempts to open and read the file. Two text files have been placed in the project's \bin directory: **myfile.txt**, and a read-only file named **locked.txt**. You can set the read-only property of a file in Windows Explorer by right-clicking the filename, selecting *Properties*, and checking the *Read-only* box.

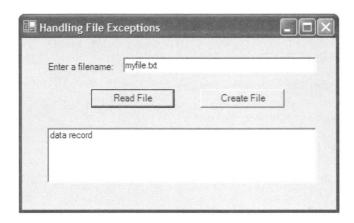

Figure 2-29 Reading an input file

Two Imports statements are required:

```
Imports System.IO
Imports System.IO.File
```

The System.IO namespace holds the various exception types caught by the program, as well as the StreamReader and StreamWriter classes. The System.IO.File namespace contains all file-related functions, such as OpenText and CreateText.

Step 1. Open the project named **FileExceptions** from the Chapter 2 examples directory. Open the code window for the startup form and inspect the **btnReadFile_Click** handler:

```
Private Sub btnReadFile_Click(ByVal sender As System.Object, _
 ByVal e As System.EventArgs) Handles btnReadFile.Click

    Dim reader As StreamReader
    Dim record As String
    Try
        Me.Cursor = Cursors.WaitCursor
        reader = OpenText(txtFileName.Text)
        lstText.Items.Add(reader.ReadLine())
        reader.Close()
    Catch except As DirectoryNotFoundException
```

```
      MessageBox.Show(except.Message, "DirectoryNotFoundException")
   Catch except As FileNotFoundException
      MessageBox.Show(except.Message, "FileNotFoundException")
   Catch except As IOException
      MessageBox.Show(except.Message, "Unknown IOException")
   Finally
      Me.Cursor = Cursors.Default
   End Try
End Sub
```

In this procedure, the Try block changes the mouse cursor to an hourglass, opens the file (named in the text box), reads a line from the file, and closes the file. The Catch block looks for exceptions thrown under the following error conditions:

◆ directory name not found (DirectoryNotFoundException)

◆ input file not found (FileNotFoundException)

◆ other IO-related error (IOException)

The Finally block returns the mouse cursor to its default shape.

Step 2. Run the program and click the Read File button. A single line of data from the *myfile.txt* file should appear in the list box.

Step 3. Enter a new filename, such as "otherfile.txt" and click the Read File button. Figure 2-30 shows the dialog box displayed by the exception handler. Note that the exception class name appears in the message box title bar. This can be useful for testing purposes.

Step 4. Change the filename in the text box to "c:\myprogs\myfile.txt" and click the Read File button. Figure 2-31 shows the dialog box displayed by the exception handler.

Step 5. Change the filename path in the text box so it points to your CD drive or diskette drive, and remove any disk from the drive. Click the Read File button, and note the message displayed by the exception handler (see Figure 2-32).

Step 6. Open the btnCreateFile_Click handler procedure and inspect the following code. It creates a file named by the text box control, writes a string to the file, and closes the file:

```
Private Sub btnCreateFile_Click(ByVal sender As _
 System.Object, ByVal e As System.EventArgs) _
 Handles btnCreateFile.Click

   Dim writer As StreamWriter
   Try
      writer = CreateText(txtFileName.Text)
      writer.WriteLine("data record")
      writer.Close()
   Catch except As UnauthorizedAccessException
      MessageBox.Show(except.Message & ControlChars.CrLf _
         & "The file may be locked by another process, or it may be " _
         & "a read-only file.", "UnauthorizedAccessException")
   Catch except As IOException
      MessageBox.Show(except.Message, "Unknown IOException")
   End Try
End Sub
```

We handle an UnauthorizedAccessException error, which is generally thrown when a program tries to create or write to a file that is either locked or has a read-only attribute. Alternatively, the current user might not have sufficient permissions to write to the directory.

Step 7. Run the program, entering "locked.txt" into the text box, and click the Create File button. The exception handler should display the message shown in Figure 2-33, with a different file path, of course.

(End of example)

Figure 2-30 FileNotFoundException

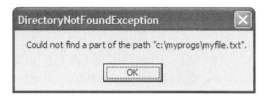

Figure 2-31 DirectoryNotFoundException

Figure 2-32 Device not ready (IOException)

Figure 2-33 UnauthorizedAccessException

Propagating Exceptions

Programs often call procedures several levels deep, knowing that eventually each procedure will end and return to its calling procedure. For a simple example, let's name the procedures A, B, C, D, and E. If A calls B, which calls C, and so on, the normal sequence of calls and returns can be expressed by the following figure:

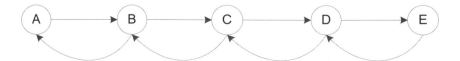

Suppose an exception is thrown during the execution of procedure D, and it turns out that no Catch clause exists in procedures B and C. Then the exception is *propagated backward* to procedure A. Designers often choose not to catch exceptions near where they are thrown, because not enough is known about the context at that point to make a good decision.

Adding a twist to the bottling plant scenario, suppose assembly-line worker **E** discovers that a bottling machine cannot handle a new type of bottle. Worker E informs shift manager **D**, who does not have the authority to solve the problem, so she relays the problem back to general manager **C**. General manager **C** realizes that a purchase of a new bottling machine may be required, so he informs Vice-President **B** that a major problem has been discovered. Vice-president **B** brings up the problem at the next Directors meeting, and President **A** decides to invest several hundred thousand dollars in a new machine.

If President A does not do anything, the assembly line breaks down when the new type of bottle arrives and cannot be processed. Similarly, Visual Basic programs halt with an *unhandled exception* error when exceptions are propagated back to their startup procedures, and the exceptions are not handled.

Exception Handling at the Business Tier Level

In Chapter 1 we introduced the multi-tier application structure that has become widespread today. The Business tier, you may recall, consists of classes that hold data and rules to process the data. The same classes should not interact directly with the user, because doing so would make the class less portable to different platforms (Windows Forms versus Web Forms, for example).

There is often a reason why you do not want to handle an exception inside the method from which it was thrown. For example, the method might not know which part of the overall program called it. Therefore, it would have no idea what to do about the error. Instead, the method must find a way to inform the client program that something has gone wrong. Throwing an exception is a good way to do so.

Consider the following business-tier **Person** class, which contains one private member (mAge) and one property procedure named Age. We mentioned back in Chapter 1 that property procedures have a difficult time letting their client programs know when a bad input value has been received. Displaying a message box is a poor way to handle the problem since the Person class is supposed to be detached from the user interface layer:

```
Class Person
   Private mAge As Integer
   Private Const AGE_MIN As Integer = 1
   Private Const AGE_MAX As Integer = 120

   Public Property Age() As Integer
     Get
        Return mAge
     End Get
     Set(ByVal Value As Integer)
        If Value < AGE_MIN Or Value > AGE_MAX Then
           MessageBox.show("Age is out of range", "Error")
        Else
           mAge = Value
        End If
     End Set
   End Property
End Class
```

A much better way of handling such an error condition is to throw an exception, passing an informative message to the caller. At the same time, the integrity of the class data is preserved:

```
Class Person
   Private mAge As Integer
   Private Const AGE_MIN As Integer = 1
   Private Const AGE_MAX As Integer = 120
```

```
Public Property Age() As Integer
   Get
      Return mAge
   End Get
   Set(ByVal Value As Integer)
      If Value < AGE_MIN Or Value > AGE_MAX Then
         Throw New ArgumentException("Age must be between " _
           & AGE_MIN & " and " & AGE_MAX)
      Else
         mAge = Value
      End If
   End Set
End Property
End Class
```

Usually we try to choose an existing exception type that suggests the type of error condition. As we will see later in this chapter, you can define your own exception types.

A calling program (from the user interface layer, for example) can catch the exception. It has the option of alerting the user in any number of ways. In the following code, we assign the contents of a text box to the Age property:

```
Dim aPerson As New Person()

Try
   aPerson.Age = CInt(txtAge.Text)
Catch except As Exception
   MessageBox.Show(except.Message, "Error")
End Try
```

Rather than using a MessageBox, the interface-tier class might choose to use an ErrorProvider control or write the error message to a text file.

Designing Your Own Exception Types

Exceptions2

Visual Basic .NET lets you design your own exception classes. This can be useful when you might want to store custom information in a thrown exception. You can also name the exception class in a descriptive way, such as SalaryRangeException, or MemberNotFoundException. When a client program catches exceptions with specific names, it can provide customized responses.

Your exception class should inherit from ApplicationException, to ensure that it retains the behavior of standard exceptions. Recall from Chapter 1 that *inheritance* means creating a more specific class from a more general one. Because class inheritance is not covered until a later chapter, we will guide you through the relevant elements in the current example.

We will create a class named **PropertyException** that can be thrown when an invalid value is assigned to a class property. The following Student.ID property procedure, for example, throws a PropertyException if the ID number is the wrong length:

```
Public Property ID() As String
   Get
      Return mID
   End Get
   Set(ByVal Value As String)
      If Value.Length = IDSIZE Then
         mID = Value
```

```
      Else
         Throw New PropertyException("Student ID must be " _
           & IDSIZE & " digits. ", Value)
      End If
   End Set
End Property
```

PropertyException has a private variable named **mBadValue** that holds a String representation of the data that caused the exception:

```
Public Class PropertyException
   Inherits System.ApplicationException

   Private mBadValue As String
```

The PropertyException constructor has two parameters: The first is the same message string passed to all Exception objects, and the second is the property value that we want to store:

```
Sub New(ByVal message As String, ByVal badVal As String)
   MyBase.New(message)       'call base constructor
   mBadValue = badVal
End Sub
```

The first line of the constructor makes a reference to the **ApplicationException** class, identified using the keyword **MyBase**. The statement calls the base class constructor, passing it the message parameter. This step is important because the ApplicationException class constructor contains code that must be executed by all exception-type objects.

The PropertyException class has a **BadValue** property that returns the contents of **mBadValue**:

```
      Public ReadOnly Property BadValue() As String
         Get
            Return mBadValue
            End Get
         End Property
      End Class
```

Hands-On Example: Testing PropertyException

Exceptions3

In this tutorial, we will examine and test a short program that lets the user enter Student property values into text boxes. When a Test button is clicked, the text box values are assigned to the properties of a Student object. The program catches several types of exceptions.

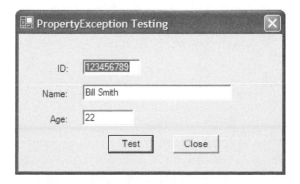

Figure 2-34 PropertyException program

Step 1. Open the **Exceptions3** project from the Chapter 2 examples directory. The startup form is shown in Figure 2-34.

Step 2. Open and inspect the PropertyException class. The constructor takes two parameters:

```
Public Class PropertyException
    Inherits System.ApplicationException

    Private mBadValue As String

    Sub New(ByVal message As String, ByVal badVal As String)
        MyBase.New(message)        'call base constructor
        mBadValue = badVal
    End Sub

    Public ReadOnly Property BadValue() As String
        Get
            Return mBadValue
        End Get
    End Property
End Class
```

Step 3. Open the Student class and note the recent changes to the property procedures. All three throw PropertyException objects:

```
Public Class Student
    Private mID As String
    Private mName As String
    Private mAge As Integer
    Const IDSIZE As Integer = 9
    Const AGE_MIN As Integer = 10
    Const AGE_MAX As Integer = 120

    Public Property ID() As String
        Get
            Return mID
        End Get
        Set(ByVal Value As String)
            If Value.Length = IDSIZE Then
                mID = Value
            Else
                Throw New PropertyException("Student ID must be " _
                  & IDSIZE & " digits. ", Value)
            End If
        End Set
    End Property

    Public Property Name() As String
        Get
            Return mName
        End Get
        Set(ByVal Value As String)
            If Value.IndexOf(" ") >= 0 Then
                mName = Value
            Else
                Throw New PropertyException("Both first and last names" _
                    & " are required. ", Value)
```

```
            End If
         End Set
      End Property

      Public Property Age() As Integer
         Get
            Return mAge
         End Get
         Set(ByVal Value As Integer)
            If Value >= AGE_MIN And Value <= AGE_MAX Then
               mAge = Value
            Else
            Throw New PropertyException("Age must be between " _
               & AGE_MIN & " and " & AGE_MAX & ". ", CStr(Value))
            End If
         End Set
      End Property

   End Class
```

Step 4. Open the code window of the main form (frmMain). The Click handler for the Test button assigns Student properties, using the three text boxes. Catch blocks exist for PropertyException, InvalidCastException, and Exception:

```
Dim aStudent As New Student()

Private Sub btnTest_Click(ByVal sender As System.Object, _
 ByVal e As System.EventArgs) Handles btnTest.Click

   Try
      aStudent.ID = txtID.Text
      aStudent.Name = txtName.Text
      aStudent.Age = CInt(txtAge.Text)
      MessageBox.Show("All fields tested successfully")
   Catch except As PropertyException
      MessageBox.Show(except.Message & "Given value: " _
        & except.BadValue, "PropertyException")
   Catch except As InvalidCastException
      MessageBox.Show(except.Message, "InvalidCastException")
   Catch except As Exception
      MessageBox.Show(except.Message, "Unknown exception.type")
   End Try
End Sub
```

Step 5. Run and test the program. Table 2-12 lists some suggested tests you can run, along with the displayed exception messages.

- ◆ Input a five-digit ID number and click the Test button.
- ◆ Change the ID number to nine digits, remove the space between the first and last names, and click the Test button.
- ◆ Insert a space between the first and last names, and erase the Age text box. Click the Test button.
- ◆ Enter an Age value of 2 and click the Test button.

In general, this program reports exceptions in a more meaningful way than the earlier version that displayed ApplicationException objects. This should help show some benefits of using custom exception classes.
(End of example)

Table 2-12

Testing the PropertyException class

Action	Display

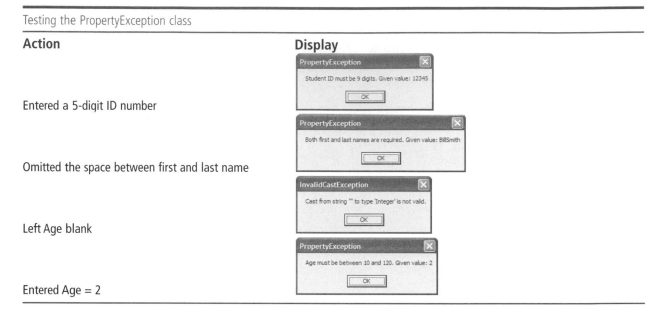

Entered a 5-digit ID number

Omitted the space between first and last name

Left Age blank

Entered Age = 2

Ignoring Exceptions

You can Catch an exception and then pretend it did not happen. Suppose our Student class checks the Age property to make sure the age is between 10 and 120, but we have imported the class into a program that tracks elementary students. The relevant code in the program's main form is shown here:

```
Try
    aStudent.ID = txtID.Text
    aStudent.Name = txtName.Text
    aStudent.Age = CInt(txtAge.Text)
    MessageBox.Show("All fields tested successfully")
Catch except As PropertyException _
    When except.BadValue = txtAge.Text
    'no action taken
Catch except As PropertyException
    MessageBox.Show(except.Message & "Given value: " _
     & except.BadValue, "PropertyException")
```

The When class in a Catch block lets us add an extra condition. In addition to being a PropertyException, the Catch block will only be executed if the BadValue property of the exception contains the same value as the Age text box. Otherwise, the second Catch block will handle all other PropertyExceptions. If you make this change to the Exceptions3 program, no error messsage will display when you enter Age values less than 10.

Exception Handling Tips

Tip #1: Whenever possible, try to prevent exceptions before they are thrown, rather than cleaning up after them after they happen. Isn't that a bit like real life?

Tip #2: When a Try block contains multiple statements (and it usually does), not all statements in the block may be executed. If an exception is thrown part-way through the execution of the block, control immediately transfers to the appropriate Catch block. The remaining statements in the Try block are skipped.

Tip #3: Catch blocks should always begin with the most specific exception types and end with the most general. Once a Catch block is entered, no Catch block can be executed. In the following example, the Catch block for Exception class is first. It catches all exceptions before more specific Catch blocks can execute:

```
Catch except As Exception            'catches all exceptions
    . . .
Catch except As FormatException      'never reached
    . . .
Catch except As OverflowException    'never reached
    . . .
```

Place Catch...Exception at the end of the list, to guarantee that all exceptions will be caught.

Tip #4: Throw predefined .NET exception types whenever possible. You can customize the Message property by passing a string to the Exception object's constructor.

Tip #5: If you must define your own exception class, always inherit from ApplicationException.

Checkpoint

2.21 What type of exception causes a program to halt?
2.22 Does the Common Language Runtime look for Catch handlers only in the procedure in which an exception is thrown?
2.23 Must a Catch block include an exception object variable?
2.24 Will the code in the Finally section execute regardless of whether any exception was thrown?

▶2.7 Chapter Summary

- A program's user interface defines the program's behavior. With that idea in mind, design the interface so beginning users can learn it quickly, and advanced users can complete tasks with a minimum of effort.

- A *task-based approach* to program design lets you focus on the various tasks a program must perform. Given a particular program task, you can use a *use-case scenario* to clarify the interactions between the user and a program.

- Avoid cluttering a form with many command buttons. Instead, use a menu to logically group commands. Also, restrict the user's variety of choices when providing input to a program.

- Use a TreeView control to display hierarchical information, and use a ListView control to display multicolumn information.

- Take advantage of the users' familiarity with Microsoft Office, since it is the accepted standard for user interfaces in MS-Windows applications.

◆ Wizard-type programs should be tailored to the expected knowlede and experience level of the user.

◆ A major component of creating user interfaces lies in the anticipation and prevention of errors resulting from user input.

◆ When validating user input on a Windows form, you have four alternatives: (1) trap individual keystrokes before they appear in the input control; (2) trap invalid data as the user moves away from each control; (3) flag controls that contain invalid input, using an icon or message; and (4) validate all fields at once after the user has finished entering data.

◆ Programs that check for input errors can implement the Validating event handler for specific input controls. Text boxes, for example, permit a wide variety of inputs, and therefore require careful validation.

◆ The CausesValidation property is instrumental in causing the Validating event to fire for a particular control.

◆ The code you write in a control's Validating event handler determines whether the Validated event will fire, or the focus will be switched back to the control that was being validated.

◆ The ErrorProvider control provides a simple way to validate input fields by displaying an icon and error message for any field containing invalid data.

◆ One of the most commonly used controls in all MS-Windows software, the ListView control stands out for its flexibility and power. Mastering the ListView is well worth the effort, as it can give your programs a distinctly professional appearance.

◆ If you want a ListView to display data in a table-like format, you must add column headings, which can be created in either design mode or run mode.

◆ The ListViewItem class defines the appearance, behavior and data associated with each row in a ListView control.

◆ The TreeView control, found in so many professional MS-Windows applications, organizes information in a hierarchical structure known as a *tree*. Each element in the tree is a *node*. If a node has other nodes grouped under it, those nodes are called *child nodes*, and the node itself is a *parent* node.

◆ A TreeView contains a collection named Nodes, each element of which is a TreeNode object. The Nodes collection, however, represents only the top level of nodes in the tree. In order to create a hierarchical structure, you have to attach child nodes to top-level nodes.

◆ When a program encounters an error while running, we say that a *runtime error* occurred. In .NET and other environments like it, we go a step further and say that a runtime error is the result of an *exception* being *thrown*.

◆ *Structured exception handling* makes it possible for programs to detect and respond to specific exceptions when they happen.

◆ There are two general types of exceptions: those caused by faulty programming logic, and those caused by events outside the control of the programmer. The second type of exception must be handled, using a Try—End Try statement that contains at least one Catch block.

◆ When a procedure throws an exception, it creates an instance of either the Exception class or some class derived from Exception. The most general types of exceptions are SystemException, ApplicationException, and IOException.

◆ The Common Language Runtime (CLR) built into the .NET Framework is the agent responsible for throwing exceptions.

◆ A Catch block can handle either a specific exception type or an entire class of exception types. If a Catch block names ApplicationException as its type, the block will also handle all exceptions derived from ApplicationException.

◆ When an exception is thrown, the Common Language Runtime backs up through the series of procedure calls that led to the moment when the exception was thrown. Any procedure in the call chain can handle the error with a Catch block.

◆ If a method in one of your classes must throw an exception, Microsoft recommends creating and throwing an ApplicationException object. Throw predefined .NET exception types whenever possible.

◆ When necessary, you can design a custom exception class that contains additional information about the cause of an error. Your exception class should inherit from ApplicationException.

◆ When a Try block contains multiple statements, all statements in the block may not be executed. If an exception is thrown part-way through execution of the block, control immediately transfers to the appropriate Catch block.

◆ Catch blocks should always be ordered starting with specific exception types, and proceeding to more general exception types. Once a Catch block is entered, no other subsequent Catch block can execute.

▶2.8 Key Terms

Catch block	Read-only file
catching an exception	runtime error
CausesValidation property	scrollable form
Common Language Runtime (CLR)	stack trace
configuration utility	structured exception handling
data browser	task-based approach
DirectoryInfo	TextChanged event
document editor	throwing an exception
ErrorProvider control	ToolBar control
exception	TreeNode
Finally block	TreeView control
ImageList control	Try block
KeyPress event	unhandled exception
Leave event	use-case scenario
ListView control	user interface
ListViewItem	Validated event
monitor	Validating event
propagated backward	wizard
propagating an exception	workspace

▶2.9 Review Questions

Fill-in-the-Blank

1. A program's _____ is the part of a program that interacts with a user.

2. A _____ scenario describes the interactions between a user and a program for a particular task.

3. Microsoft _____ has become the universally accepted standard for user interfaces in Windows applications.

4. The Validated event fires for a control when the _____ is set to True.

5. Each row in a ListView control is an instance of the _____ class.

Multiple Choice

1. Which of the following was not recommended as a way to simplify a form containing a great deal of information?

   a. Use a Tab control
   b. Use a scrollable form
   c. Use a multicolumn ListBox control
   d. Use a TreeView control
   e. none of the above

2. Which of the following controls display hierarchical information?

   a. Tab control
   b. ListView control
   c. TreeView control
   d. Menu control
   e. Two of the above are correct

3. Which of the following approaches to validating user input was not suggested in this chapter?

   a. Flag controls containing invalid input with an icon or message.
   b. Intercept each input character.
   c. Trap invalid data when the user attempts to move away from a control.
   d. When the user clicks on OK, validate all the fields at once.
   e. None of the above.

4. Which of the following names the correct sequence of events that occur when the user switches the focus from one control to another?

   a. Validating, Leave, LostFocus, Validated
   b. Validating, Validated, Leave, LostFocus
   c. Leave, LostFocus, Validating, Validated
   d. Leave, Validating, Validated, LostFocus
   e. LostFocus, Validating, Validated, Leave

5. What are the four possible View property values in the ListView control?

   a. LargeIcon, SmallIcon, List, Details
   b. LargeIcon, SmallIcon, Details, Table
   c. Tabular, LargeIcons, SmallIcons, List
   d. ColumnList, SmallIcon, LargeIcon, Details
   e. LargeIcon, SmallIcon, List, Columns

6. Which statement adds a top-level node containing "Sample" to a TreeView control named tvwTest?

   a. tvwTest.AddNode("Sample")
   b. tvwTest.Insert("Sample")
   c. tvwTest.Add("Sample")
   d. tvwTest.Nodes.Add("Sample")
   e. none of the above

True or False

1. When the user presses the Esc button, the Click event handler for the button named in the form's CancelButton property is executed.

2. In order to create a scrollable form, you must add a ScrollBar control to the form.

3. The Ctrl-X keyboard shortcut is ordinarily assigned to the File | Exit menu command.

4. If the Validating event handler sets the e.Cancel parameter to True, the Validated event handler does not execute.

5. A separate ErrorProvider control is required for each TextBox on a form.

6. ToolBar buttons have an ImageIndex property that identifies which image will appear on each button.

7. When a ListView control is set to the Details view, you can display at least one column without having to define any column headings.

8. A ListViewItem has a property named Selected.

9. If an exception is thrown mid-way through a Try block, the appropriate Catch block executes immediately.

10. After a Catch block executes, any remaining statements in the Try block are executed.

11. The Finally block always executes, whether or not an exception was thrown.

12. An exception must be caught inside the same procedure as the procedure throwing the exception.

13. Catch blocks should be sequenced so the most specific types of exceptions occur first, followed by more general exception types last.

14. A Catch block does not have to declare an exception variable.

15. Only the first Catch block (in a series of Catch blocks) is permitted to have a When clause.

Short Answer

1. What characteristics define a wizard-type program?

2. If errors are trapped when the user switches the focus from one control to another, what aspect of this may frustrate the user?

3. Which ErrorProvider method must be called in order to create a pop-up error message for a particular control?

4. Which ToolBar property must be selected when you want to add buttons to the tool bar?

5. Which ListView property must be True before the columns can be dragged to new locations by the user?

6. Which event fires when the user clicks on a check box next to a row in a ListView control?

7. Which TreeView method causes all child nodes to be displayed?

8. What do we call an exception that is never caught?

9. What type of exception should be thrown by methods in your own classes?

10. What type of exception is thrown when the format of an argument passed to a method does not match the format of the formal parameter?

11. Which Exception property returns a string containing the sequence of procedure calls that led up to the exception being thrown?

What Do You Think?

1. Why might the user prefer to have all fields on a form validated at the same time?

2. Name five foreground/background color combinations you find most restful to your eyes.

3. Do you prefer that programs prevent you from making input mistakes, or would you rather make the mistakes and be notified later?

4. Which interface features are most useful for advanced users of Microsoft Word?

5. How might a TreeView control be useful when designing a Student Registration program for a college?

6. If you were planning to transfer a Destop application to the Web, how would you handle user input validation?

7. Explain how the CausesValidation property influences the Validating event for a control.

8. What advantages, if any, would there be to designing a custom exception class for a program that processes Employee payroll records?

9. Do you think an OutOfMemoryException should be caught by application programs?

10. How might the Finally block be useful in a program that reads from a file?

Algorithm Workbench

1. In the Sports Rental application (earlier in this chapter) there was a task named "Display the complete store inventory." Create an imaginary use-case scenario for this task.

2. Suppose you wanted to create a wizard program to help the user set up a sprinkler system with a timer that would turn off and on at the same time daily. Make a list of the questions the wizard would ask the user.

3. Write one or more statements that set e.Cancel to True if the txtZIP TextBox does not contain five decimal digits.

4. Write a statement that passes an error message to an ErrorProvider control named errProvider under the following condition: txtName.Text does not contain two words.

5. Write a statement that adds a column named **Address** to a ListView control named lvwCustomer. Make the column one-fourth the width of the ListView, and left-align the column.

6. Add a row to a ListView control that contains two columns. In the row being added, the first column contains "Surfboards Hawaii" and the second column contains "100 North King Street".

7. Add a top-level node containing "Hawaii" to a TreeView control named **tvwSurfspots**. Add two child nodes: "Maui", and "Oahu".

8. Attach two child nodes to "Oahu" in the TreeView control from the previous question. The child nodes should contain "VelzyLand" and "Pupukea".

▶2.10 Programming Challenges

1. Sports Rental Exceptions

Make a copy of your completed FirstPlay Sports Rental program from the Chapter 1 exercises. Add expection handling to the program for the following conditions: 1) Attempt to add duplicate ID number; 2) blank description; 3) nonnumeric values for daily rate, weekly rate, monthly rate, or quantity. 4) attempt to remove nonexistent item.

2. Bank Teller Program

Make a copy of the solution program you wrote for the **Bank Teller with Totals** program at the end of Chapter 1. In the current program, you will add the following exception handling:

- The Account.Deposit method must throw an ApplicationException if the amount parameter is less than zero. Catch the exception in frmTeller and display the following message: "Deposit must be a positive value."

- The Account.Withdraw method must throw an ApplicationException if the amount parameter is less than zero. Catch the exception in frmTeller and display the following message: "Withdrawal must be a positive value."

- The Account.Withdraw method must throw an ApplicationException if the amount parameter is greater than the current account balance. Display the following message: "Insufficient funds available for the attempted withdrawal."

- When the program tries to update the account file and fails, your program should catch the exception and display the following message: "Cannot update the account file.", Also, display the Message property of the exception that was thrown by the .NET Common Language Runtime. (You can test this runtime error by using Windows Explorer to set the read-only property of one of the account files. We explained how to do this earlier in this chapter, in the section entitled *Handling File Exceptions*.)

All exceptions are to be caught by frmTeller, so you must not display any message boxes from classes in the Business layer (Transaction, TransactionLog, and Account).

3. Bank Teller with ErrorProvider

The second Bank Teller example program in Chapter 1 performed input validation inside the Leave event handler procedures of the input controls. Make a copy of that program (*BankTeller2*) to use as a starting point for this exercise.

Use an ErrorProvider control to validate the txtDeposit and txtWithdraw controls. When the user clicks on the OK button, do not process the deposit and withdrawal unless both input controls contain valid numeric values.

4. ListView Disk Directory

Write a program that uses a ListView control to display a list of all files in the current directory. For each file, display the filename, file length, date created, and date last modified. The sample in Figure 2-35 shows that your program will list all files in your project's \bin directory.

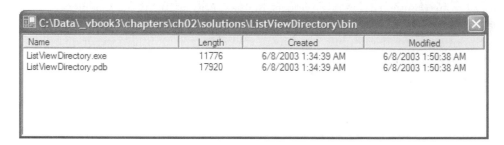

Name	Length	Created	Modified
ListViewDirectory.exe	11776	6/8/2003 1:34:39 AM	6/8/2003 1:50:38 AM
ListViewDirectory.pdb	17920	6/8/2003 1:34:39 AM	6/8/2003 1:50:38 AM

Figure 2-35 Files in the current directory

Notes

◆ The Directory.GetCurrentDirectory method returns the current directory at runtime.

◆ The DirectoryInfo.GetFiles method returns a collection of FileInfo objects.

◆ A FileInfo object contains properties such as Name, Length, CreationTime, and LastWriteTime.

◆ You will have to insert an **Imports System.IO** statement at the beginning of the form's source code (before the class declaration).

5. Disk Directory TreeView

Make a copy of the Disk Directory TreeView example program shown earlier in this chapter. You must make the following enhancement to the program: When the user double-clicks on a directory name, reload the tree, using the selected name as the root of the directory tree.

Hint: Each node in the TreeView stores only a directory name, not the full path, in the node's Text property. You must find a way to save (or rebuild) the node's full path before passing it to the ShowDirectory method. Otherwise, the directory will not be found.

6. FirstPlay Sports Rental

Make a copy of your completed **FirstPlay Sports Rental** program from the Chapter 1 exercises before beginning this project. Rename the program to **SportsListView**. You will not need the Rental Item form for this project. Intead, you must create a new form, which we will call the **Product Listing** form (see Figure 2-36). The ListView must fill as soon as the form displays, without any actions on the part of the user. The Product Listing form should include an Inventory property (with associated private class variable), that holds a clsInventory object passed from the Main procedure in Module1.vb.

The Product Listing form must contain a ListView control. Also, it must contain a menu having the following selections:

Menu Item	Description
File	Exit	Exit program
View	Large Icons	Set View property to large icons
View	Small Icons	Set View property to small icons
View	List	Set View property to list
View	Details	Set View property to details

Set the form's BorderStyle to FixedSingle. Anchor the ListView to the form on all sides. Minimize and maximize boxes are optional. Find at least one icon, add it to an ImageList control, and identify the icon's index when you insert items into the ListView.

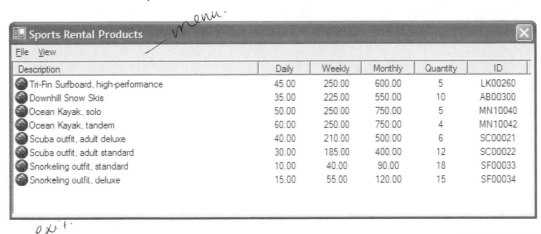

menu.

List view.
need for labs

exit

Figure 2-36 Sports rental program

This project focuses on the presentation tier, so you will not be making any changes to the clsInvenFile or clsInventory classes. You will need to add a **ToString** method to the clsItem class that displays the names of the properties along with the property values. A sample is shown in Figure 2-37, where the string returned by ToString has been placed in a message box.

Your program will be reading a data file named *inventory.txt*, found in the Chapter 2 sample programs directory. Copy the file into your project's *bin* directory.

Modify the Main startup procedure in Module1.vb so it catches any exceptions thrown while loading the inventory file. Display the error messages shown in Figure 2-38 under the following conditions:

◆ The inventory file could be opened.

◆ Nonnumeric data was found in a file field that should have been numeric.

When the user double-clicks on an item in the ListView, your program should display the item details. You will need to create a handler procedure for the ListView's DoubleClick event. You should include exception handling so that if the index is out of range, your program displays the error message shown in Figure 2-39. Admittedly, this error is not like to happen by itself, but you are creating this program partly to learn how to handle errors when they do occur.

Testing Your Program

Perform the following runtime tests on your program:

1. Run the program and double-click on any item. Verify that it displays a message box containing all the item's fields (with labels).

2. Rename the data file and run the program. Your program should display the error shown in Figure 2-38. Fix the filename, and edit the file, changing one of the numeric fields to a non-numeric string. When you run the program, the error message should correctly identify the problem. Now you can restore the file to its previous contents.

3. Modify the DoubleClick event in the form so the index value is out of range. Run the program and check that your program shows the message from Figure 2-39.

Figure 2-37   Displaying item details

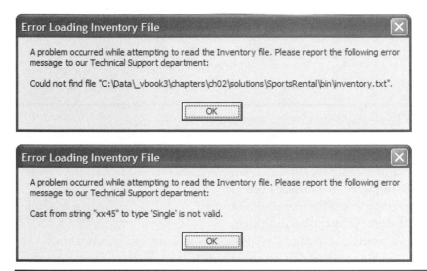

Figure 2-38   Errors loading inventory file

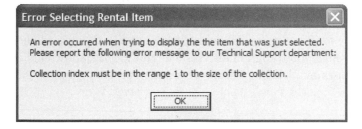

Figure 2-39   Error selecting item from ListView

ADO.NET Databases

Major Topics

▶3.1 Introduction to ADO.NET

 Note:

*All of the example programs in this chapter use Microsoft Access databases installed by the setup program on the book's CDROM. If you have installed the sample databases at a different location than the default, you will have to open each program's app.config file and modify the **Data Source** entry in the **ConnectionString** property.*

Overview

ADO.NET provides consistent access to data sources such as Microsoft SQL Server, as well as data sources exposed via OLE DB and XML. Data-sharing consumer applications can use ADO.NET to connect to these data sources and retrieve, manipulate, and update data.

Step back a moment and remember how it used to be. Years ago, microcomputer programmers used to create their own formats for storing data in files, sometimes in text, and sometimes in binary. Programmers came up with clever ways of efficiently retrieving and updating files containing multiple data fields. The problem was that every implementation was different. If a programmer left their code behind for someone else to maintain, it was often difficult to learn.

Later, as database software emerged for microcomputers, programmers had to write code geared toward several well-known database formats. One of the great conveniences that appeared around the time Visual Basic became popular was the ODBC (*Open Database Connectivity*) library. This library exported a list of functions that could be used to open, read, and update databases, without gearing one's code to a specific database format.

Early versions of Visual Basic introduced DAO (*Data Access Objects*), which enabled object-oriented database programming. Visual Basic 6.0 later developed a more sophisticated model named ADO (*ActiveX Data Objects*). ADO still had some drawbacks when scaling applications from the desktop to large numbers of users. It could only able to run on a Windows platform and did not initially provide a way to stream a database over an Internet connection. ADO followed a tightly coupled *client-server* model, where a client program remains continually connected to a database, and interactions are synchronized between the two.

ADO.NET represents Microsoft's most recent data access software, with a number of design features. To a great extent, it was influenced by the needs of Internet applications, in which Web pages do not keep a continuous connection to a server. Instead, much of the processing can be done on the user's machine, and contact between the user and the database server can be as brief as possible. In short, ADO.NET does the following:

- Moves away from the client-server model to a loosely connected relationship between application programs and their data sources.

- Provides excellent support for multi-tier application development.

- Keeps a database connection open only long enough to retrieve data required by the program. This approach makes programs more *scalable*, referring to their ability to continue to run efficiently when the number of users greatly increases.

- Fully supports XML (*Extensible Markup Language*), a universal format for data exchanged between different computer platforms and across the Internet. XML is a fundamental part of ADO.NET's design.

- Represents database tables and relationships between tables as strongly typed objects in a way that is natural for object-oriented programs.

ADO.NET functions in two modes: connected and disconnected:

- In *connected mode*, database connection is kept open. Database rows can only be accessed in a forward direction, and they cannot be modified.

- In *disconnected mode*, a database table is copied into memory and then the connection is closed. From that point on, the application program works exclusively with an in-memory copy of the data (called a *dataset*).

If a program simply has to list a large amount of data, connected mode runs more quickly. It requires that a connection to the database server machine be kept active. If one were to use disconnected mode with a large database table, it might be difficult to keep all the required data in memory at the same time.

On the other hand, disconnected mode permits network servers to handle greater numbers of users because valuable resources are not consumed by maintaining continuous database connections.

We will concentrate on disconnected mode in this chapter for two reasons: First, disconnected datasets are well-suited to creating multi-tier applications, and second, datasets represent an easy-to-use object-oriented programming model.

Connecting to a Database

In this chapter we will be using various databases in each program. Each program will be linked to a database table, using a connection and a data adapter. The table data will be copied into a dataset.

You can set up a database for use in a program by following three basic steps:

1. Create a *connection* to a database.
2. Create a *data adapter* to enable transfer of data from the database to a dataset.
3. Create a *dataset* to hold the data in memory while it is manipulated by your program.

After changes have been made to a dataset, you have the option of writing the changes back to the underlying database.

Database Basics

Let's review a few basic concepts and terms relating to databases. A *database* is a collection of one or more tables, each containing data related to a particular topic. A *table* is often called a logical grouping of related information. Suppose a database contains employee information for a company, including a table named **Departments** that contains the ID number, name, and size of each department in the company:

dept_id	dept_name	dept_size
1	Human Resources	10
2	Accounting	5
3	Computer Support	30
4	Research & Devel	15

Each row of the table can also be called a *record*. In the Departments table, the first row contains "**1, Human Resources, 10**". When discussing tables, we refer to their columns by name. In the Departments table, the columns are named **dept_id**, **dept_name**, and **dept_size**. Table columns are also called *fields*.

The **dept_id** column is also called a *primary key* because it uniquely identifies each department. To say this another way, no two departments can ever have the same department ID. Primary keys can be either numbers or strings, but numeric values are processed by the database software more efficiently. Primary keys are not always comprised of just one column; sometimes they include multiple columns joined together (called a clustered *key*).

The following table represents product sales. No single column produces a unique value, so we can combine the values in the date, product_id, and customer_id columns. The primary key consists of the three combined fields:

date	product_id	customer_id	amount
5/20/2004	25	36	$500.00
5/20/2004	25	32	$400.00
5/22/2004	25	32	$620.00

Designing Database Tables

A *database schema* is the design of tables, columns, and relationships between tables for the database. Let's look at some of the elements that belong to a schema, beginning with tables. Most well-designed databases contain multiple tables in order to avoid duplicating data. It might be tempting when designing a table of employees, for example, to include the complete name of the department in which an employee works. Here are a few sample rows:

emp_id	first_name	last_name	dept_name
001234	Ignacio	Fleta	Accounting
002000	Christian	Martin	Computer Support
002122	Orville	Gibson	Human Resources
003000	Jose	Ramirez	Research & Devel
003400	Ben	Smith	Accounting
003780	Allison	Chong	Computer Support

There are problems with this approach. We can imagine that the same department name appears many times within the Employee table, leading to wasted storage space. Also, a data entry clerk might easily misspell a department name. Finally, if the company decided to rename a department, it would become necessary to find and correct every occurrence of the department name in the employee table (and possibly other tables).

Rather than inserting a department name in each employee record, we prefer to store the department's ID number in the employee table:

emp_id	first_name	last_name	dept_id
001234	Ignacio	Fleta	2
002000	Christian	Martin	3
002122	Orville	Gibson	1
003000	Jose	Ramirez	4
003400	Ben	Smith	2
003780	Allison	Chong	3

If we rename a department, the name must only be changed once, in the Departments table. A data entry clerk requires less time to input a numeric department ID, and the department ID numbers use less storage space than complete department names.

When looking up the name of an employee's department, we can use the department ID number in the Employees table to find the same ID in the Departments table. The department name will be in the same table row. Relational databases make the linking of two tables extremely easy.

One-To-Many Relationship

Relational databases are designed around what is known as a *relational model*. This model promotes the use of multiple tables linked by common values. A *relation* is a link or relationship that relies on a common field to join together rows from two different tables. In the following relationship diagram, **dept_id** is the common field that links the Departments and Employees tables:

In the Departments table, we already know that **dept_id** is the primary key. In the Employees table, dept_id is called a *foreign key*. There can be multiple occurrences of a foreign key in a table. Along the line connecting the two tables, the "1" and "∞" symbols indicate a one-to-many relationship. A particular dept_id (such as 4) occurs only one time in the Departments table, but it can appear many times (or not at all) in the Employees table.

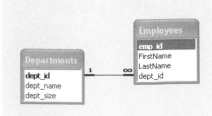

In this chapter, we will usually work with one table at a time. But there will be times when we use information from one table to find data in another related table. In Chapter 5 we will examine other types of table relationships, and build datasets from multiple tables.

Microsoft Access Data Types

When you design a database table, it is important to select column types appropriate to the data being used. Fortunately, there is a close correlation between Access data types and Visual Basic data types. Table 3-1 cross-references the types, along with descriptions. In general, if you already know which Visual Basic data type is appropriate for the contents of a database column, you can select the Access type that is the closest match.

When storing ID numbers, you can use either Text type or one of the integer types. But if the ID numbers contain leading zeros, use Text. An integer-type column would truncate leading zeros, thereby altering the values.

Table 3-1

Comparing Microsoft Access types to Visual Basic types

Access Type	Visual Basic	Description
AutoNumber	Long	Auto-generated integer, created either randomly or sequentially. Sequential values begin at 1. *— 64 byte.*
Currency	Decimal	Use for monetary values. Does not perform rounding during calculations. Fixed number of digits to the right of the decimal.
Date/Time	Date, DateTime	Dates and times. Internally, the date is stored as the integer part of a floating-point value, and the time is stored as the fractional part.
HyperLink	String	Text or combinations of text and numbers stored as text and used as a hyperlink address.
Memo	String	Lengthly text, may contain up to 65,535 characters (1.2 billion in recent versions of Access).
Number, byte	Byte	1-byte integer
Number, integer	Integer	Integer between −32,768 and +32,767
Number, long integer	Long Integer	Integer between −1.2 million and +1.2 million
Number, single	Single	Single precision floating-point number
Number, double	Double	Double precision floating-point number
OLE Object	String	An object (such as a Microsoft Excel spreadsheet, a Microsoft Word document, graphics, sounds, or other binary data) linked to or embedded in a Microsoft Access table.
Text	String	Up to 255 characters. Use for names, address, etc.
Yes/No	Boolean	Holds values of yes/no, true/false, on/off.

Default Values

You can designate a default value to be inserted into selected fields when new rows are added to a table. Suppose, for example that a table named **invoice** has a default value of 0 for the **discount** column. Then, when new rows are inserted, the discount is automatically set to 0 unless specifically assigned a different value.

You can use built-in functions to assign default values. Suppose a table named **enroll** holds college course ID numbers, student ID numbers, and the date and time when the row was added to the table. Figure 3-1 shows how to insert a call to the Now() function in the Default value property for the field. When rows are added to the table, only the course ID and student ID need to be assigned, and the registDate field will be initialized automatically.

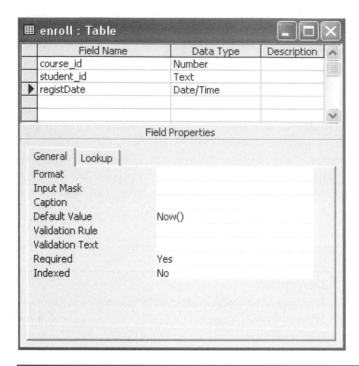

Figure 3-1 Enroll table.

Data Sources and Connections

Before programming in ADO.NET, it is important to have a clear idea of the connections, objects, and data flow in a typical database application. All data-related classes belong to the System.Data namespace. Figure 3-2 displays the general data flow used in an ADO.NET application. The arrows point in both directions because the data in a dataset must often be written back to the database. The data adapter provides the copying mechanism.

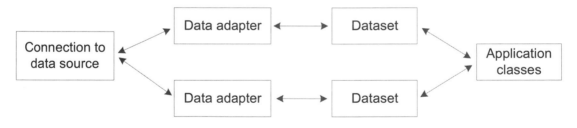

Figure 3-2 ADO.NET Data Flow.

Data access begins with a data source, which is typically a database. A program must provide a *Connection* object that opens the database, provides the proper security permissions, and specifies its registered name or location. A *data adapter* reads data from the appropriate database table, provided by the open connection. The data adapter copies the table rows into a *dataset*, which is held in memory. A program interacts with the dataset by displaying or modifying its data. ADO.NET uses classes to represent connections, data adapters, and datasets.

Data Source

A *data source* is usually a relational database such as Microsoft Access or SQL Server, but it can also be a spreadsheet or stream of data in XML (extensible markup language) format. A data source can be on the same machine as the program using it, or it can be located on a network connected to the machine running the program.

The standard .NET installation includes at least two data providers:

◆ OLE DB .NET Data Provider
◆ SQL Server .NET Data Provider

The OLE DB provider will be used in this chapter and the next to connect to Microsoft Access desktop databases. We will introduce the SQL Server provider in Chapter 5 for networked databases, and continue using it throughout the rest of the book.

Connection

A *Connection* object provides the ability to interact with a data source. It is an instance of a specific class such as **OleDbConnection** or **SqlConnection**, depending on what type of data source is used. Typically, it contains a reference to the database location, security information, and provider-specific information. As new connection classes are created for the .NET environment, programs can connect to an increasingly wide variety of data sources. Table 3-2 lists the most important properties and methods.

Table 3-2

Connection properties and methods

Name	Description
ConnectionString	Gets or sets the command string used to open a database.
Database	Gets the name of the database (read-only).
DataSource	Gets the location (path) and name of the database (read-only).
Open()	Opens the connection to the database, using the information encoded in the ConnectionString property.
Close()	Closes the connection.

Following is a minimal OLE DB ConnectionString containing two subproperties (Provider and Data Source) separated by semicolons:

```
Provider=Microsoft.Jet.OLEDB.4.0;Data Source=C:\vbData\SalesStaff.mdb
```

Example

Visual Studio .NET makes it easy to set up a database connection. Figure 3-3 shows how to select a data provider. In the examples shown in this chapter, we use the Microsoft Jet 4.0 provider for Microsoft Access databases. The list of providers changes over time, so your list may vary slightly from the one shown in the figure.

Figure 3-4 shows the next step in setting up a data connection. You locate the database file (in this case, *SalesStaff.mdb*) by clicking on the browse (...) button. The file path in the figure is not real, but you would select the actual file path on your system. Finally, you can click the *Test Connection* button to make sure the connection works.

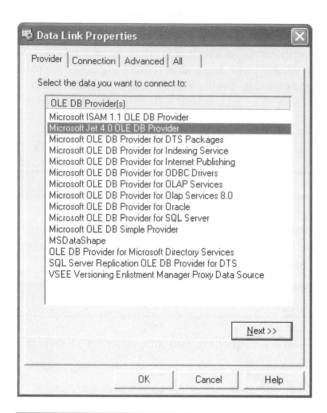

Figure 3-3 Selecting the data provider.

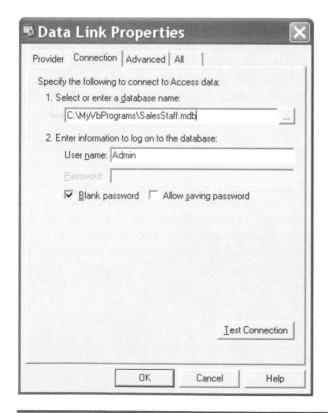

Figure 3-4 Setting connection properties.

Data Adapter

A *data adapter* acts as a bridge between a data source and a dataset. Specific types of data adapters include **OleDbDataAdapter** and **SqlDataAdapter**, depending on which type of database connection is being used. A data adapter has two primary duties:

◆ Reads data from a data source into a dataset.

◆ Writes data from a dataset back to a data source.

In this chapter, we will only read one table at a time, and in later chapters we show how to link multiple tables. Data adapters use statements written in SQL, an industry-standard database processing language named *Structured Query Language*. The statements are stored in Command objects. Command objects can also execute *stored procedures*, which are procedures containing SQL queries stored within the database itself.

A data adapter can be created by dragging a table name from the Server Explorer window into a form or database component. In the following figure, we have exposed the SalesStaff table in the Server Explorer window, in preparation for dragging it onto a form:

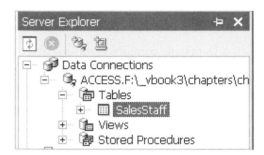

Data Reader

A d*ata reader* directly connects to a data source to provide high-speed access to read-only data. It can only read data in a forward direction, and it cannot be used to update data in a data source. We will show how to use data readers in Chapter 9 when connecting databases to ASP.NET programs.

Datasets

A *dataset* is an in-memory cache of records that holds table data retrieved from one or more data sources. A dataset is completely disconnected from the data source that provides its data, a feature that reduces back-and-forth network traffic between applications and data sources (such as database servers). A program that uses a dataset will write all table updates to its local dataset. When the program decides to make existing dataset changes permanent, it performs a single operation to write the updated dataset back to the underlying data source.

The **DataSet** class in the .NET framework contains properties, methods, and events relating to datasets. You never actually use instances of DataSet, but your programs contain instances of classes derived from DataSet. The Visual Studio .NET compiler builds specific dataset classes according to the tables specified in each program's data adapters.

When you connect a database to an application and select a table to be used by a data adapter, Visual Studio provides a command named **Generate Dataset** that uses the data adapter to create a DataSet-derived class whose properties match the columns in the database table. For example, a program using the Departments table (seen earlier) might have a data adapter named **daDepartments**. The Generate Dataset command would create a DateSet-derived class named **dsDepartments**. If we then looked at the Class View window, the following hierarchy would appear under the application name:

```
(ApplicationName)
  dsDepartments
     Bases and Interfaces
        DataSet
     DepartmentsDataTable
     DepartmentsRow
        dept_id() As Integer
        dept_name() As String
        dept_size() As Integer
```

The dsDepartments class contains nested classes named **DepartmentsDataTable** and **DepartmentsRow**. The DepartmentsRow class contains properties named dept_id, dept_name, and dept_size, which match the database column names.

A DataSet object contains two important properties: Tables, and Relations. The **Tables** property is a collection of DataTable objects that describe the database tables used to create the dataset. The **Relations** property is a collection of objects that describe relationships between the tables in a dataset.

DataTable Class

The **DataTable** class describes a single table of in-memory data. A DataTable contains **DataRow** objects, each of which contains a collection of columns. Table 3-3 lists some essential DataTable properties.

Table 3-3

Essential DataTable properties.

Property	Description
Columns	A collection of DataColumn objects
Rows	A collection of DataRow objects
Constraints	A collection of Constraint objects
TableName	A String containing the name of the table
DefaultView	The DataView associated with the DataTable
PrimaryKey	An array of DataColumn objects that make up the table's primary key (value that makes each row unique)

The **Tables** property of a dataset contains a zero-based collection of DataTable objects. You can easily iterate over the collection to find all the table names. The following code, for example, lists the names of all tables belonging to a dataset named DsDepartments1:

```
Dim tbl As DataTable
For Each tbl In DsDepartments1.Tables
   List1.Items.Add(tbl.TableName)
Next
```

(See the ExploreCompany program in the Chapter 3 examples directory to test the examples shown in this section.)

You can get a reference to an individual table by indexing into the collection with an integer or table name. Both ways are shown here:

```
tbl = DsDepartments1.Tables(0)
tbl = DsDepartments1.Tables("Departments")
```

Assuming that the DsDepartments1 dataset was generated from a data adapter, it would also have a specific property name for each of its DataTable objects. The following statement, for example, gets a reference to the Departments table:

```
tbl = DsDepartments1.Departments
```

The **PrimaryKey** property contains a collection of all columns that make up the key. (In most of our programs, key fields will require only one column.) The following code displays the name of the column containing the primary key:

```
MessageBox.Show(tbl.PrimaryKey(0).ColumnName)
```

DataRow Class

The **DataRow** class describes a single row in a DataTable. The row contains all the column data passed into the dataset by the data adapter. The following statement declares a DataRow object:

```
Dim row As DataRow
```

The following expression returns the first row of the DataTable named DsDepartments1.Departments:

```
DsDepartments1.Departments.Rows(0)
```

DataColumn Class

The **DataColumn** class describes a single column in a DataTable. The column has a name and type, among other properties. You can get the column names for a specific table by iterating through the table's Columns collection. The following retrieves column names for a table named **mCurrentTable** and adds them to a list box:

```
Dim col As DataColumn
For Each col In mCurrentTable.Columns
   List1.Items.Add(col.ColumnName)
Next
```

The following statement returns the column named **dept_id**:

```
col = mCurrentTable.Columns("dept_id")
```

DataViews and DataRowViews

A **DataView** object represents a customized view of a DataTable that permits you to sort, filter, search, edit, and navigate through the table rows. For example, a DataView's **Sort** property lets you control the sort order of its rows. Similarly, the **RowFilter** property lets you select which rows (called *filtering*) are viewed in the DataView.

A **DataRowView** object represents a single row in a DataView. It has an **Item** property that lets you set or get a value in a specified column.

Checkpoint

3.1 Does ADO.NET emphasize a tight connection, or loose connection between a client program and its data source?

3.2 How does XML fit into ADO.NET?

3.3 (Fill-in-the-blank) A database may contain multiple _____., which in turn contain multiple rows.

3.4 What are the three primary steps required when accessing a database in ADO.NET?

3.5 (Fill-in-the-blank) In a database, another term for *column* is _____.

▶ 3.2 Using Data-Bound Controls

If you want to display database data inside controls appearing on a form, use a VB.NET feature called *data binding*. It permits individual controls to be bound (connected) to dataset columns. Such data-aware controls can display the contents of database columns at runtime. As the user moves from one row to another, the contents of the data-aware control are automatically refreshed. If the user changes the contents of the control, the corresponding column in the current row is updated when the user moves to a different row. A data-aware control has a **DataBindings** property that links (binds) the control to a table. The most common DataBindings subproperty is **Text**, which holds the name of the bound column.

Hands-On Tutorial: SalesStaff 1

SalesStaff1

Our first hands-on tutorial takes you through the steps to set up a connection to a Microsoft Access database and display a single row on a form with data-bound controls. Although the steps seem detailed, they require little time to complete.

 Note:
Before you begin, find out where the file SalesStaff.mdb is located on your computer. The adminstrator of your college's computer lab may have designated a special directory to hold databases for Visual Basic classes.

This program will read a table named **SalesStaff**, which represents information collected about sales employees. Its design is shown in Figure 3-5, and some sample rows are shown in Figure 3-6.

Column Name	Type
StaffId	Text (primary key)
LastName	Text
FirstName	Text
IsFullTime	Yes/No
HireDate	Date/Time
Salary	Currency

Figure 3-5 SalesStaff table design.

StaffId	LastName	FirstName	IsFullTime	HireDate	Salary
104	Adams	Adrian	Yes	05/20/1996	$35,007.00
114	Franklin	Fay	Yes	08/22/1995	$56,001.00
115	Franklin	Adiel	No	04/20/1986	$41,000.00
120	Baker	Barbara	Yes	04/22/1993	$32,000.00
135	Ferriere	Henri	Yes	01/01/1990	$57,000.00
292	Hasegawa	Danny	No	05/20/1997	$45,000.00
302	Easterbrook	Erin	No	07/09/1994	$22,000.00
305	Kawananakoa	Sam	Yes	10/20/1987	$42,000.00
396	Zabaleta	Maria	Yes	11/01/1985	$29,000.00
404	Del Terzo	Daniel	Yes	07/09/1994	$37,500.00
407	Greenwood	Charles	No	04/20/1996	$23,432.00

Figure 3-6 SalesStaff table, sample data.

Step 1. Open the **SalesStaff1** program from the Chapter 3 examples directory. The main form's design is shown in Figure 3-7.

Step 2. Open the **Server Explorer** window (the icon just above the Visual Studio ToolBox, on the left side of the .NET window). Right-click on **Data Connections** and select **Add Connection....** The **Data Link Properties** window will appear.

Step 3. Select the **Provider** tab, and select **Microsoft Jet 4.0 OLE DB Provider** from the list. Click on **Next**.

Figure 3-7 Startup form (design mode).

Step 4. With the **Connection** tab selected, click on the ellipsis (. . .) button next to "1. Select or enter a database name:". Browse to the location of **SalesStaff.mdb**. Click on the **Test Connection** button to verify that the connection is valid.

Step 5. Expand the **Data Connections** tree in the Server Explorer window until you see the **SalesStaff** table.

Step 6. Drag the SalesStaff table name onto the program's form, and notice that two items appear in the component tray: **OleDbConnection1** represents the Connection object, and **OleDbDataAdapter1** is the data adapter. When you drag the table onto the form, a dialog window (Figure 3-8) appears, asking you if you want to include the password in the connection string. Accept the default choice (*Don't include password*) by pressing Enter. Click the mouse in an empty area of the component tray to deselect the connection and data adapter.

Figure 3-8 Password-related dialog.

Step 7. Select OleDbConnection1 with the mouse and rename it (using its Name property) to **conSalesStaff**. Select OleDbDataAdapter1 and rename it to **daSalesStaff**.

Step 8. Right-click on daSalesStaff and select **Generate Dataset** from the context menu. In the Generate Dataset window (Figure 3-9), select **New**, enter the name **dsSalesStaff**, and click on OK to close the window.

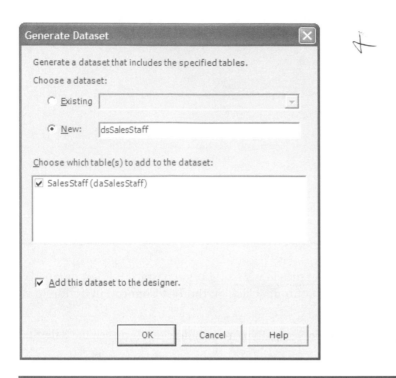

Figure 3-9 Generate Dataset window.

The name **dsSalesStaff** is a new class generated by Visual Studio .NET. The tool also created an instance of dsSalesStaff named **DsSalesStaff1**, which appears in the form's component tray.

Step 9. Take a moment to inspect dsSalesStaff's design by double-clicking its XSD filename in the Solution Explorer window.

Step 10. Select the **txtStaffId** text box and click on the + next to its **DataBindings** property. Select the **Text** subproperty and notice that the dataset name **DsSalesStaff1** appears. Expand its tree until you can select the **StaffId** field. You have now bound the StaffId field from the SalesStaff table to the txtStaffId text box on your form.

Step 11. As in the previous step, set up the DataBindings property for the remaining text boxes on the form. The **chkFullTime** check box's DataBindings property includes a subproperty named **Checked**. Bind it to the **IsFullTime** database column.

Step 12. Next, you have to add a single line of code to the **Form_Load** event handler that loads the dataset at run time:

```
daSalesStaff.Fill(DsSalesStaff1)
```

(An easy way to generate a Form_Load event handler is to double-click on an open area of the form.)

Step 13. Run the program. Your program should display the first row of the SalesStaff table, shown in Figure 3-10.

A complete listing of the program can be seen in Code Listing 3-1.
(End of tutorial)

Figure 3-10 SalesStaff: displaying the first row

Code Listing 3-1 (SalesStaff 1)

```
Public Class frmMain
    Inherits System.Windows.Forms.Form

+ Windows Form Designer generated code

    Private Sub Form1_Load(ByVal sender As System.Object, _
    ByVal e As System.EventArgs) Handles MyBase.Load

        'Fill the DataSet object (named dsSalesStaff1)
        daSalesStaff.Fill(dsSalesStaff1)
    End Sub

    Private Sub btnOK_Click(ByVal sender As System.Object, _
    ByVal e As System.EventArgs) Handles btnOK.Click

        Me.Close()
    End Sub
End Class
```

Moving Programs and Databases

Moving a Program on the Same Computer

If you **copy** a database program from one directory to another on the same computer, the program will still compile and run.

You can also rename both the Solution and the Project in the Project Solution window. There are, however, a few complications that you might want to avoid:

◆ If you modify any data adapter properties after **moving** a program, you will have to add a new database connection to the Server Explorer. (It just takes a few seconds to do this.)

◆ If you change the project's Root Namespace property, the program will not compile unless you re-create the database connection from scratch.

Moving a Database

In general, it is best to avoid moving a Microsoft Access database that has connections to existing programs. The programs will cease to run unless you fix each program's database path inside the ConnectionString property of the Connection object. The best way to modify a connection string is to select an option that causes the connection string to display in the project's **app.config** file. Here's how to do it:

◆ Select the Connection object and open its Properties window.

◆ In the Properties window, open the **DynamicProperties** group and select **ConnectionString**. Click on the ellipsis (...) button, and when the dialog window appears, check the option: **Map property to a key in configuration file**. Click on OK to close the dialog.

◆ Open the app.config file and inspect the *<databasename>*.ConnectionString property. The directory path appearing after the **DataSource** keyword is the absolute location of the database.

You may prefer to take this opportunity to simplify the connection string. Microsoft Access databases require only the Provider and Data Source properties:

```
Provider=Microsoft.Jet.OLEDB.4.0;Data Source=C:\vbData\SalesStaff.mdb
```

If your database path includes spaces, you must embed quotation mark characters in the Data Source:

```
Data Source=&quot;C:\visual basic data\SalesStaff.mdb;&quot;
```

If you later move the database to a new location, change the DataSource entry to the database's new directory path.

A Brief Look at SQL

SQL was developed as a universal language for creating, updating, and retrieving data from databases. The American National Standards Institute (ANSI) has ratified different levels of standard SQL, which are followed to a greater or lesser degree by database vendors. ANSI standards are identified by their year of ratification and a level number. The *Microsoft Jet Database Engine*, for example, uses Jet 4.x SQL, which is generally ANSI-89 Level 1 compliant. Jet 4.x is used by Visual Basic .NET, along with the MSDE (Microsoft Database Engine).

SELECT Statement

The data adapter retrieves rows from an underlying data source using a command written in **SQL**. The command is stored as a string in the **CommandText** subproperty of the data adapter's **SelectCommand** property. For example, the command used by the SalesStaff program's data adapter to load the SalesStaff table was the following:

```
SELECT
    FirstName, HireDate, IsFullTime, LastName, Salary, StaffId
FROM
    SalesStaff
```

This is called a SELECT statement—it tells the database to read all the named columns from the SalesStaff table. It can be written on a single line, or it can be spread across several lines, as we have done here. Later, you will experiment with using the SelectCommand property to modify a data adapter's SELECT statement.

As a shortcut, you can automatically select all columns from a table using the * (wildcard) character:

```
SELECT
    *
FROM
    SalesStaff
```

If a column name contains embedded spaces, you must surround it with brackets:

```
SELECT
    [Hire Date]
FROM
    SalesStaff
```

There is no required formatting for SQL queries. The following statement, for example, is valid:

```
SELECT * FROM SalesStaff
```

Aliases for Column Names

It is simple to rename existing table columns when selecting the columns to be generated by a SELECT statement. The following statement renames the existing HireDate column to DateHired:

```
SELECT
    FirstName, LastName, Salary, HireDate AS DateHired
FROM
    SalesStaff
```

If the alias column name contains embedded spaces, you must surround it with square brackets:

```
SELECT
    FirstName, LastName, Salary, HireDate AS [Date Hired]
FROM
    SalesStaff
```

Renaming columns is useful for two reasons: First, you might want to hide the real column names from users for security purposes. Second, column headings in reports can be made more user-friendly if you substitute your own names for the column names used inside the database.

Calculated Columns

You can create new columns that are calculated from existing columns in a SELECT statement. Suppose a table named Payroll contains columns named employeeId, hoursWorked and hourlyRate. The following statement creates a new column named **amtPay** using hoursWorked and hourlyRate:

```
SELECT employeeId,
    hoursWorked * hourlyRate AS amtPay
FROM PayRoll
```

Setting the Row Order (ORDER BY)

The SELECT statement has an ORDER BY clause that lets you control the display order of the table rows. In other words, you can sort the data on one or more columns. The general form for sorting on a single column is the following:

```
ORDER BY columnName [ASC | DESC]
```

ASC indicates ascending order (the default), and DESC indicates descending order. Both are optional, and you can use only one at a time. For example, we can sort the SalesStaff table in ascending order by last name,

```
ORDER BY LastName ASC
```

We can do this more simply:

```
ORDER BY LastName
```

The following sorts the data in descending order by Salary:

```
ORDER BY Salary DESC
```

You can sort on multiple columns. The following statement sorts in ascending order first by last name, then within each last name, it sorts in ascending order by first name:

```
ORDER BY LastName, FirstName
```

For a more complete example, the following SELECT statement returns all columns from SalesStaff, sorting by last name and first name:

```
SELECT
    FirstName, HireDate, IsFullTime, LastName, Salary, StaffId
FROM
    SalesStaff
ORDER BY LastName, FirstName
```

XML Designer

Visual Studio .NET has a great editing tool for viewing and editing datasets named the *XML Designer*. It has three views: Schema, Data, and XML:

◆ The *Schema view* can be used to visually create and modify XML Schemas and datasets.

◆ The *Data view* lets you visually modify XML data files in a structured data grid.

◆ The *XML view* lets you directly view and edit XML code.

In the SalesStaff 1 tutorial, you created a dataset named dsSalesStaff. You can find the dataset's XML schema definition in the Solution Explorer window. It is named **dsSalesStaff.xsd**. If you double-click the filename, the XML Designer window displays the dataset as in Figure 3-11. If you select XML from the View menu, you will see the XML source code shown in Figure 3-12. The definition includes a constraint asserting that the StaffId column holds the table's *primary key*.

E SalesStaff	(SalesStaff)
E FirstName	string
E HireDate	dateTime
E IsFullTime	boolean
E LastName	string
E Salary	decimal
⚷E StaffId	string

Figure 3-11 dsSalesStaff Definition.

```
<?xml version="1.0" standalone="yes" ?>
<xs:schema id="dsSalesStaff" targetNamespace="http://www.tempuri.org/dsSalesStaff.xsd"
xmlns:mstns="http://www.tempuri.org/dsSalesStaff.xsd"
xmlns="http://www.tempuri.org/dsSalesStaff.xsd" xmlns:xs="http://www.w3.org/2001/XMLSchema"
xmlns:msdata="urn:schemas-microsoft-com:xml-msdata" attributeFormDefault="qualified"
elementFormDefault="qualified">
  <xs:element name="dsSalesStaff" msdata:IsDataSet="true">
    <xs:complexType>
      <xs:choice maxOccurs="unbounded">
        <xs:element name="SalesStaff">
          <xs:complexType>
            <xs:sequence>
              <xs:element name="FirstName" type="xs:string" minOccurs="0" />
              <xs:element name="HireDate" type="xs:dateTime" minOccurs="0" />
              <xs:element name="IsFullTime" type="xs:boolean" minOccurs="0" />
              <xs:element name="LastName" type="xs:string" minOccurs="0" />
              <xs:element name="Salary" type="xs:decimal" minOccurs="0" />
              <xs:element name="StaffId" type="xs:string" />
            </xs:sequence>
          </xs:complexType>
        </xs:element>
      </xs:choice>
    </xs:complexType>
    <xs:unique name="Constraint1" msdata:PrimaryKey="true">
      <xs:selector xpath=".//mstns:SalesStaff" />
      <xs:field xpath="mstns:StaffId" />
    </xs:unique>
  </xs:element>
</xs:schema>
```

Figure 3-12 dsSalesStaff Definition (XML).

Checkpoint

3.6 Describe *binding* as it relates to controls on a form.

3.7 Which object in a form provides a way to navigate between table rows?

3.8 Which data adapter property contains SQL query commands?

3.9 What action must you take to add a data adapter to your program?

3.10 Where can you find the XML schema definition of a dataset?

▶3.3 Navigating, Adding, and Removing Rows

A few basic operations are easy to perform on table rows: moving between rows, adding new rows, and removing rows. Any form containing DataAdapter and DataSet components has a CurrencyManager object, which you can use to move between dataset rows, remove rows, or reload a dataset.

BindingContext and CurrencyManager

To navigate between rows of a dataset that is bound to controls on a form, use the form's CurrencyManager object. Here are its important properties and methods:

◆ **Count**: Number of rows in the dataset.

◆ **Current**: Returns the current table row, which is a **DataRowView** object.

◆ **Position**: Sets or gets the index position in the dataset of the current row. Its range is 0 to Count −1.

◆ **Refresh**: (method) Reloads all bound controls on a form.

Every Windows form has a property named **BindingContext** that manages data bindings for the form's controls. The following code shows how to get the CurrencyManager object, assuming that Option Strict is Off:

```
Private currManager As CurrencyManager
currManager = Me.BindingContext(dsSalesStaff1, "SalesStaff")
```

BindingContext returns a BindingManagerBase object, which is the superclass (base class) of CurrencyManager. If you have Option Strict set On (our default setting), use the CType function to cast the return value into a CurrencyManager object:

```
currManager = CType( _
    Me.BindingContext(DsSalesStaff1, "SalesStaff"), _
    CurrencyManager)
```

Using WithEvents

Nearly all Visual Basic programs contain methods that respond to events. When a button is clicked by the user, for example, a Click event is fired. What about object variables? It turns out that a good many object types have the ability to fire events. You can find out which events are available by looking at a list of class members in MSDN help.

For example, take a moment to find the **CurrencyManager** class in the MSDN help index, and double-click on its subentry entitled **all members**. Scroll through the list of properties and methods until you get to Public Events. Note three events:

Event Name	Description
CurrentChanged	Occurs when the bound value changes.
ItemChanged	Occurs when the current item has been altered.
PositionChanged	Occurs when the Position has changed.

To handle these events, use the WithEvents qualifier when defining a CurrencyManager variable. For example, see the following:

```
Private WithEvents currManager As CurrencyManager
```

After you do this, you can use the code editor to paste in a handler for any of the three events. In the members pull-down list (top left of the code window), select currManager. In the right-hand pull down list, select one of the event names. For example, this is the skeleton handler created for PositionChanged:

```
Private Sub currManager_PositionChanged(ByVal sender As Object, _
    ByVal e As System.EventArgs) Handles currManager.PositionChanged
End Sub
```

Then you can write code that executes whenever the CurrencyManager's position moves from one dataset row to another.

Altering the Position Property

Our first example program displayed only the first row in the SalesStaff table. A CurrencyManager's **Count** property indicates the number of rows in the table, and the **Position** property identifies the zero-based index of the current row. To move to the next row, add 1 to Position. If you reach the last row, adding 1 to Position will have no effect:

```
currManager.Position += 1
```

To move to the previous row, subtract 1. You will not be able to set Position any lower than zero:

```
currManager.Position -= 1
```

To move to the first row, set Position to 0. To move to the last row, set Position to Count minus 1:

```
currManager.Position = currManager.Count - 1
```

Adding a New Row

Adding a new row to a table can be done as follows:

1. Create a new empty row that has the same columns as the current table.

2. Fill in the row's columns (fields).

3. Add the row to the table.

When you add a row to a table, the row must be a System.Data.DataRow object. Following is the general format for the Add method:

```
DataSet.Table.Rows.Add( datarow )
```

You can access dataset tables via property names. Strongly typed dataset classes mimic the structure of the underlying database. For example, the **DsSalesStaff1** table created in the previous hands-on tutorial contains a property named **SalesStaff**. Using that property, we can access the rows and columns of the table.

Let's define a variable named **newRow** and assign it the value returned by the **SalesStaff** table's NewRow method. We are using a specific type of DataRow object named SalesStaffRow:

```
Dim newRow As DsSalesStaff1.SalesStaffRow
newRow = DsSalesStaff1.SalesStaff.NewRow
```

After creating a new row, we usually assign values to its columns. The DataRow.Item property is a collection of column values, indexed by either integers or column names. The following statements insert values in the first three columns of **newRow**:

```
newRow.StaffId = "104"
newRow.FirstName = "Andrew"
newRow.LastName = "Chang"
```

After filling in a row, call the Rows.Add method:

```
DsSalesStaff1.SalesStaff.Rows.Add(newRow)
```

The Add method only affects a dataset object, not its underlying database.

Catching Exceptions

Throwing an exception is common when adding a new row to a dataset. For example, a ConstraintException is thrown if you try to add a row containing a duplicate key value. It is always a good idea to surround your code with a Try-Catch block:

```
Try
   newRow.StaffId = "104"
   newRow.FirstName = "Andrew"
   newRow.LastName = "Chang"
   '(assign other column values . . .)
   dsSalesStaff1.SalesStaff.Rows.Add(newRow)
Catch except As Exception
   MessageBox.Show(except.Message)
   newRow.CancelEdit()
End Try
```

If an exception is thrown, call **CancelEdit** to roll back (undo) all changes to the current row. If your form has bound controls, they will be refreshed with the row that was current before the Add operation began.

Removing a Table Row

There are two ways to remove a row from a DataTable; the first is to call the CurrencyManager's RemoveAt method; the second is to call the table's Rows.Remove method.

When calling the CurrencyManager's **RemoveAt** method, pass the index position of the row you want to remove. Here is the general format for the RemoveAt method:

```
CurrencyManager.RemoveAt( index )
```

An IndexOutOfRange exception may be thrown. The following statement removes the current row (referenced by Position) from a dataset:

```
currManager.RemoveAt(currManager.Position)
```

Calling Rows.Remove

If you want to remove a row by calling Remove on the Rows collection of a DataTable, you need to pass it a DataRow having the same column properties as the table. Here is the general format:

```
DataTable.Rows.Remove( DataRow )
```

Suppose we want to remove the first row of the SalesStaff table. We can get a reference to that row and pass it to the Remove method:

```
Dim aRow As System.Data.DataRow
With DsSalesStaff1.SalesStaff
   aRow = .Rows(0)
   .Rows.Remove(aRow)
End With
```

To be slightly more clever, the following code does the same job:

```
With DsSalesStaff1.SalesStaff
   .Rows.Remove(.Rows(0))
End With
```

Updating the Database

Changes made to a dataset are not permanent until they are copied back to the dataset's underlying database. To do this, call the Update method on the associated DataAdapter object. Here is the general format:

```
DataAdapter.Update( dataset )
```

The data adapter examines each row (in index order) for changes, and executes any required insert, update, or delete statements on the row. It might be well to explain why the exceptions may be thrown, and more importantly how to aviod them and how to correct them. The following statement updates the database attached to daSalesStaff, using the table in DsSalesStaff1:

```
daSalesStaff.Update(DsSalesStaff1)
```

Reloading the Dataset

To reload a dataset from its underlying data source, call the **Fill** method of the data adapter, passing it the DataSet object. Here is the general form:

```
DataAdapter.Fill( dataset )
```

The following reloads DsSalesStaff1, using the daSalesStaff data adapter:

```
daSalesStaff.Fill(DsSalesStaff1)
```

If your form has bound controls, you will want to call the CurrencyManager's Refresh method to update the values in the controls:

```
currManager.Refresh()
```

Example: Updating the SalesStaff Table

SalesStaff2

This program example shows you how to add, remove, and update rows of a dataset, and then copy all changes back to the underlying database. It is a continuation of the SalesStaff program from the first tutorial in this chapter. The startup form (frmMain) is shown in Figure 3-13. The user can move between rows using commands from the Move menu. The Edit menu contains two selections: Add and Remove. If the user selects Add, the **Add New Person** window (Figure 3-14) is displayed.

> ☞ *Reminder:*
> *If you installed the sample databases at a different location than the default used by the setup program on the book's CDROM, you will have to open the project's app.config file and modify the **Data Source** entry in the **ConnectionString** property. Set Data Source to the actual location of the SalesStaff.mdb database on your computer.*

Figure 3-13 SalesStaff program, Version 2.

Figure 3-14 Add New Person window.

Implementaiton

The frmMain class defines the program's startup form:

```
Public Class frmMain
    Inherits System.Windows.Forms.Form
```

```
+ Windows Form Designer generated code
```

```
    Dim currManager As CurrencyManager

    Private Sub frmMain_Load(ByVal sender As System.Object, _
     ByVal e As System.EventArgs) Handles MyBase.Load

        daSalesStaff.Fill(DsSalesStaff1)
        currManager = Me.BindingContext(DsSalesStaff1, "SalesStaff")
    End Sub
```

The CurrencyManager object allows the program to move between rows in the dataset by modifying the Position property. Following are four Click event handlers for the menu commands: mnuMoveFirst, mnuMoveLast, mnuMovePrev, and mnuMoveNext:

```
    Private Sub mnuMoveFirst_Click(ByVal sender As System.Object, _
     ByVal e As System.EventArgs) Handles mnuMoveFirst.Click
        currManager.Position = 0
    End Sub

    Private Sub mnuMoveLast_Click(ByVal sender As System.Object, _
     ByVal e As System.EventArgs) Handles mnuMoveLast.Click
        currManager.Position = currManager.Count - 1
    End Sub

    Private Sub mnuMovePrev_Click(ByVal sender As System.Object, _
     ByVal e As System.EventArgs) Handles mnuMovePrev.Click
        currManager.Position = currManager.Position - 1
    End Sub

    Private Sub mnuMoveNext_Click(ByVal sender As System.Object, _
     ByVal e As System.EventArgs) Handles mnuMoveNext.Click
        currManager.Position = currManager.Position + 1
    End Sub
```

The Click event handler for the **mnuEditAdd** command creates and displays an instance of the frmAdd window. The same method also inserts a new row in the SalesStaff table by calling the **NewRow** method:

```
    Private Sub mnuEditAdd_Click(ByVal sender As System.Object, _
     ByVal e As System.EventArgs) Handles mnuEditAdd.Click

        Dim addForm As New frmAdd
        Dim newRow As System.Data.DataRow
        Try
            newRow = DsSalesStaff1.SalesStaff.NewRow()
            addForm.newRow = newRow
            If addForm.ShowDialog() = DialogResult.OK Then
                DsSalesStaff1.SalesStaff.Rows.Add(newRow)
            End If
        Catch except As Exception
            MessageBox.Show(except.Message)
            newRow.CancelEdit()
        End Try
    End Sub
```

If the user wants to remove the current row from the table, the Click event handler calls the CurrencyManager object's RemoveAt method:

```
Private Sub mnuEditRemove_Click(ByVal sender As System.Object, _
 ByVal e As System.EventArgs) Handles mnuEditRemove.Click

    Try
        currManager.RemoveAt(currManager.Position)
    Catch except As Exception
        MessageBox.Show(except.Message)
    End Try
End Sub
```

When the user selects **Update** from the File menu, the program displays a confirmation message box and calls the Update method on the data adapter (daSalesStaff):

```
Private Sub mnuFileUpdate_Click(ByVal sender As System.Object, _
 ByVal e As System.EventArgs) Handles mnuFileUpdate.Click

    If MessageBox.Show("Save all changes to database?", _
     "Update Database", MessageBoxButtons.YesNo, _
     MessageBoxIcon.Question) = DialogResult.Yes Then
        'The next three lines use a little trick to force the
        'DataSet to save changes to the current record:
        Dim savePos As Integer = currManager.Position
        currManager.Position += 1
        currManager.Position = savePos
        daSalesStaff.Update(DsSalesStaff1)
    End If
End Sub
```

The three lines in mnuFileUpdate_Click move the current position ahead by one and then return to the previous position. These actions force the dataset to save changes to the current record.

If the user wants to reload the dataset, the **mnuFileReload_Click** event handler calls the Fill method on the data adapter, and refreshes the CurrencyManager:

```
Private Sub mnuFileReload_Click(ByVal sender As System.Object, _
 ByVal e As System.EventArgs) Handles mnuFileReload.Click

    'Fill the data set and refresh the CurrencyManager
    If MessageBox.Show("Warning: This command will cancel all " _
        & "changes you have made to the database since the File | " _
        & "Update command was last executed. Do you wish to continue?", _
        "Reload Database", MessageBoxButtons.YesNo, _
        MessageBoxIcon.Warning) = DialogResult.Yes Then
        daSalesStaff.Fill(DsSalesStaff1)
        currManager.Refresh()
    End If
End Sub

Private Sub mnuFileExit_Click(ByVal sender As System.Object, _
 ByVal e As System.EventArgs) Handles mnuFileExit.Click
    Me.Close()
End Sub
End Class
```

frmAdd Source Code

The source code for the Add New Person form appears next:

```
Public Class frmAdd
    Inherits System.Windows.Forms.Form
```

+ Windows Form Designer generated code

The newRow variable, declared publicly, is initialized by the main form before displaying frmAdd:

```
Public newRow As System.Data.DataRow
```

The btnOK_Click handler activates after the user has entered data into the input fields. It assigns values to the dataset fields and catches exceptions:

```
Private Sub btnOK_Click(ByVal sender As System.Object, _
  ByVal e As System.EventArgs) Handles btnOK.Click
    Try
        newRow("StaffId") = txtStaffId.Text
        newRow("FirstName") = txtFirstName.Text
        newRow("LastName") = txtLastName.Text
        newRow("Salary") = txtSalary.Text
        newRow("IsFullTime") = chkFullTime.Checked
        newRow("HireDate") = txtHireDate.Text
        Me.DialogResult = DialogResult.OK
        Me.Close()
    Catch ex As Exception
        MessageBox.Show(ex.Message)
        newRow.CancelEdit()
    End Try
End Sub

Private Sub btnCancel_Click(ByVal sender As System.Object, _
  ByVal e As System.EventArgs) Handles btnCancel.Click
    Me.DialogResult = DialogResult.Cancel
    Me.Close()
End Sub
End Class
```

Writing Code for DataTables

A useful way to move between rows in a dataset is to combine a subscript with one of the dataset's DataTable objects. The following expression, for example, refers to the first row (row 0) of the SalesStaff table that belongs to the DsSalesStaff1 dataset:

```
DsSalesStaff1.SalesStaff(0)
```

In fact, we are really accessing the table's **Item** property, as if the following notation had been used:

```
DsSalesStaff1.SalesStaff.Item(0)
```

Once you can access a table row, you can get or set individual field values from a specific row by using the field name as a property:

```
DsSalesStaff1.SalesStaff(0).Salary
```

We are seeing some of the .NET magic here, because the compiler generated all the source code for the **dsSalesStaff** class. The class includes a DataTable property named **SalesStaff**, which in turn includes property names for all of the table fields. (Remind me to send Microsoft a thank-you letter.) If you would like to see the dsSalesStaff source code, open up the SalesStaff2 program from the last tutorial, and open the ClassView window (Figure 3-15). Double-click on any one of the properties or methods inside the dsSalesStaff or SalesStaffDataTable classes.

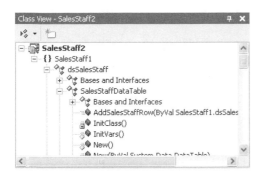

Figure 3-15 dsSalesStaff Class (Class View)

Continuing with our discussion of the DataTable associated with a dataset, you can use an integer counting loop to traverse the table. Use the table's **Count** property in the loop condition. The following lines, for example, add each row's Salary field to a total:

```
Dim i As Integer
For i = 0 To DsSalesStaff1.SalesStaff.Count - 1
    totalSalary += DsSalesStaff1.SalesStaff(i).Salary
Next i
```

Using Visual Studio .NET Query Builder

Query Builder is a tool provided by Visual Studio .NET for creating and modifying SQL queries. When a data adapter is created from a DataConnection, a default SQL query is created that retrieves all fields from the table. (A *query* is a command written in SQL.) You can see the query by locating the **SelectCommand** property of the data adapter, and examining its **CommandText** subproperty. Subproperties are often notated in the format *property.subproperty*, so we would call this the **SelectCommand.CommandText** property. When you click on the button containing an ellipsis (…) in the property's entry, the **Query Builder** window appears (see Figure 3-16).

You can modify the SQL query, thereby changing the set of fields and rows returned from the data source. It consists of four panes (panels):

◆ The **diagram** pane displays all the tables used in the query, with a check mark next to each field that will be used in the dataset.

◆ The **grid** pane displays the query in a spreadsheet-like format, which is particularly well-suited to choosing a sort order and entering selection criteria.

◆ The **SQL** pane displays the actual SQL query that corresponds to the tables and fields selected in the diagram and grid panes. Advanced SQL users usually write queries directly into this pane.

◆ The **results** pane displays the rows returned by executing the current SQL query. To fill the results pane, right-click in the Query Builder window and select **Run** from the context menu.

To remove and restore panes, do the following:

◆ To remove a pane, right-click it and select **Remove Pane** from the popup menu.

◆ To restore a pane that was removed, right-click in the window, select **Show Panes** from the popup menu, and select a pane from the list that appears.

To add a new table to the Query Builder window, right-click inside the *diagram* pane and select **Add Table** from the popup menu. In our next hands-on tutorial, we will use the Query Builder to change the sort order of the SalesStaff table.

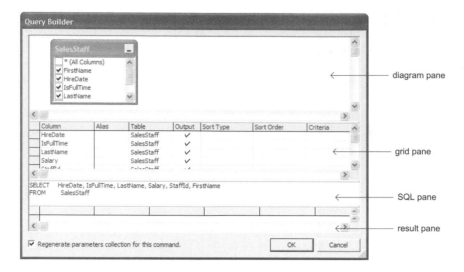

Figure 3-16 Query Builder Window.

Hands-On Example: SalesStaff 3

SalesStaff3

In this example, we will show how to iterate through a dataset table and display the resulting information in a list box. We will also examine the SQL query that the data adapter uses to fill the dataset.

Step 1. Open the **SalesStaff3** program from the Chapter 3 examples directory. The program has two forms: frmMain, and frmNames.

Step 2. Open frmMain and view the properties of **daSalesStaff** (the data adapter). Examine its **SelectCommand.CommandText** property and open the Query Builder window. In the **Grid** pane (Figure 3-17), the integers in the Sort Order column specify a sort by both last name and first name. The equivalent SQL query contains the ORDER BY clause:

```
SELECT FirstName, HireDate, IsFullTime, LastName, Salary, StaffId
FROM SalesStaff
ORDER BY LastName, FirstName
```

Step 3. Run the program and select **Average Salary** from the Tools menu. The program should display a message box containing the average salary of all SalesStaff personnel.

Step 4. Select **Name List** from the Tools menu. The program should display all first and last names in a multicolumn list box (Figure 3-18). Note that the names are sorted in alphabetical order.

A complete listing of this program may be seen in Code Listing 3-2.
(End of Example)

Column	Alias	Table	Output	Sort Type	Sort Order	Criteria
FirstName		SalesStaff	✓	Ascending	2	
HireDate		SalesStaff	✓			
IsFullTime		SalesStaff	✓			
LastName		SalesStaff	✓	Ascending	1	
Salary		SalesStaff	✓			
StaffId		SalesStaff	✓			

Figure 3-17 Controlling the Sort Order.

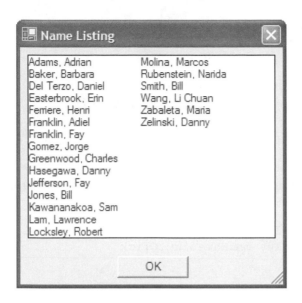

Figure 3-18 List of SalesStaff Names.

Code Listing 3-2 (SalesStaff 3)

```
Public Class frmMain
    Inherits System.Windows.Forms.Form
```

```
+ Windows Form Designer generated code
```

```
    Dim currManager As CurrencyManager

    Private Sub frmMain_Load(ByVal sender As System.Object, _
     ByVal e As System.EventArgs) Handles MyBase.Load

        daSalesStaff.Fill(DsSalesStaff1)
        currManager = Me.BindingContext(DsSalesStaff1, "SalesStaff")
End Sub
End Class
```

The **mnuAvgSalary_Click** method uses a loop to iterate through the SalesStaff table, accumulating all the values in the Salary column:

```
    Private Sub mnuAvgSalary_Click(ByVal sender As System.Object, _
     ByVal e As System.EventArgs) Handles mnuAvgSalary.Click

        Dim totalSalary As Single = 0, avgSalary As Single
        Try
            With DsSalesStaff1
                Dim count As Integer = .SalesStaff.Count
                Dim i As Integer
                For i = 0 To count - 1
                    totalSalary += .SalesStaff(i).Salary
                    'totalSalary += .SalesStaff.Item(i).Salary
                Next
                If count > 0 Then
                    avgSalary = totalSalary / count
                    MessageBox.Show("The average person's salary is " & _
                      FormatCurrency(avgSalary), count & " Records Found")
                Else
```

```
            MessageBox.Show("No table rows were found. Cannot " _
              & "calculate the average salary.")
          End If
        End With
    Catch except As Exception
        MessageBox.Show(except.Message, except.GetType.ToString())
    End Try
End Sub
```

The **mnuNameList_Click** method loops through the SalesStaff table and concatenates each person's last name and first name. The names are added to the lstNames list box on **namesForm** (an instance of frmNames) and the form is displayed:

```
Private Sub mnuNameList_Click(ByVal sender As System.Object, _
  ByVal e As System.EventArgs) Handles mnuNameList.Click

    Dim namesForm As New frmNames
    Try
       With DsSalesStaff1
          Dim count As Integer = .SalesStaff.Count
          Dim i As Integer
          For i = 0 To count - 1
             namesForm.lstNames.Items.Add( _
              .SalesStaff(i).LastName & ", " & _
              .SalesStaff(i).FirstName)
          Next
       End With
    Catch except As Exception
        MessageBox.Show(except.Message, except.GetType.ToString())
    End Try
    namesForm.ShowDialog()
End Sub

Private Sub mnuMoveFirst_Click(ByVal sender As System.Object, _
  ByVal e As System.EventArgs) Handles mnuMoveFirst.Click

    currManager.Position = 0
End Sub

Private Sub mnuMoveLast_Click(ByVal sender As System.Object, _
  ByVal e As System.EventArgs) Handles mnuMoveLast.Click

    currManager.Position = currManager.Count - 1
End Sub

Private Sub mnuMovePrev_Click(ByVal sender As System.Object, _
  ByVal e As System.EventArgs) Handles mnuMovePrev.Click

    currManager.Position = currManager.Position - 1
End Sub

Private Sub mnuMoveNext_Click(ByVal sender As System.Object, _
  ByVal e As System.EventArgs) Handles mnuMoveNext.Click

    currManager.Position = currManager.Position + 1
End Sub
```

```
Private Sub mnuFileExit_Click(ByVal sender As System.Object, _
  ByVal e As System.EventArgs) Handles mnuFileExit.Click

    Me.Close()
  End Sub
End Class
```

Filling List and Combo Boxes

In the foregoing example, we showed how to fill a list box by iterating over a dataset and inserting each row into the control's Items collection. Fortunately, there is an easier way to do the same thing: Assign the name of your dataset to the list box's **DataSource** property, and assign the appropriate column name to the list box's **DisplayMember** property.

Using the SalesStaff table as an example, if we want a list box to display the **LastName** column, the properties should be assigned as follows:

Property	Value
DataSource	DsSalesStaff1.SalesStaff
DisplayMember	SalesStaff.LastName

The same properties are used in the ComboBox control. Always set the DataSource property first. Then, when you set the DisplayMember property, a drop-down list will appear containing a list of columns belonging to the DataSource.

As in the case of any bound controls, the dataset must be filled by the data adapter when the form loads:

```
daSalesStaff.Fill(DsSalesStaff1)
```

If you are using a combo box, you may want to set its SelectedIndex to –1 so the initial selection will be blank:

```
cboLastName.SelectedIndex = -1
```

SelectedIndexChanged Event

The DataSet.Fill method has an interesting side effect—it fires SelectedIndexChanged events for any ListBox and ComboBox controls bound to the dataset. Often, the handler procedure for SelectedIndexChange contains code designed to react to selection events by the user. If this code executes prematurely, unintended errors result. If you want to see this behavior for yourself, start with a program that fills a dataset in its Load event procedure, and insert the following statement inside the SelectedIndexChanged event for a combo box or list box:

```
MessageBox.Show("SelectedIndexChanged event fired")
```

Run the program, and watch the MessageBox pop up twice before the form is displayed.

A common solution to this problem of prematurely fired events involves the use of an on/off switch. We will demonstrate it with a combo box, but the same techniques would apply to a list box. Declare a variable such as **mbComboLoaded** at the class level and set it to False:

```
Private mbComboLoaded As Boolean = False
```

Inside the form's Load event handler, after filling the dataset, set the combo box's SelectedIndex to –1 and set mbComboLoaded to True:

```
Private Sub frmMain_Load(ByVal sender As System.Object, _
  ByVal e As System.EventArgs) Handles MyBase.Load

    daLastName.Fill(DsLastName1)
```

```
      cboLastName.SelectedIndex = -1
      mbComboLoaded = True
   End Sub
```

Any subsequent SelectedIndexChanged events will be caused by either the user or code in your program that explicitly sets the SelectedIndex property. In the SelectedIndexChanged event handler, exit the procedure if mbComboLoaded equals False:

```
Private Sub cboLastName_SelectedIndexChanged(ByVal sender As _
   System.Object, ByVal e As System.EventArgs) _
   Handles cboLastName.SelectedIndexChanged

   If mbComboLoaded = False Then Exit Sub
```

If your program contains other statements that set SelectedIndex to –1 (indicating no selection), you may also find it useful to insert the following statement near the beginning of the SelectedIndexChanged event handler:

```
   If cboLastName.SelectedIndex = -1 Then Exit Sub
```

Otherwise, the event handler may try to do some odd things with the combo box and database that make no sense and cause annoying runtime errors.

Using the ValueMember Property

ListBox and ComboBox controls both have a useful property named **ValueMember**, which contains a reference to a table column. The column is not displayed, but it contains a lookup value belonging to the same row as the current list/combo selection.

Suppose we want a combo box to display a list of LastName values from the SalesStaff table. We can set the following properties:

Property	Value
DataSource	DsSalesStaff1
DisplayMember	SalesStaff.LastName
ValueMember	SalesStaff.StaffId

At runtime, when a user clicks on a person's last name in the combo box, the combo's **SelectedValue** property is automatically filled with the same person's StaffId. We can write code such as the following to display the ID number in the combo's SelectedIndexChanged event handler:

```
   MessageBox.Show("StaffId = " & cboNames.SelectedValue)
```

We can also use StaffId to look up a table row. That technique will be shown in an upcoming tutorial named *Selecting Karate School Members*.

C h e c k p o i n t

3.11 Which CurrencyManager property lets you change the index of the current row?

3.12 Which three steps are required when adding a new row to a table?

3.13 If an exception is thrown while you are trying to add a new row to a dataset, how to you cancel all changes?

3.14 How do you remove a row from a dataset's table?

3.15 What method copies changes from a dataset back to its underlying table?

▶3.4 Selecting DataTable Rows

Introducing the SQL WHERE Clause

The SQL SELECT statement has an optional WHERE clause that you can use to *filter*, or select zero or more rows retrieved from a database table. The simplest form of the WHERE clause is:

```
WHERE columnName = value
```

In this case, *columnName* must be one of the table columns, and *value* must be in a format that is consistent with the column type. The following SELECT statement, for example, specifies that LastName must be equal to Gomez:

```
SELECT FirstName, LastName, Salary
FROM SalesStaff
WHERE LastName = 'Gomez'
```

Because LastName is a Text column, it must be assigned a string literal enclosed in single quotes. If the person's name contains an apostrophe (such as O'Leary), the apostrophe must be repeated:

```
SELECT FirstName, LastName, Salary
FROM SalesStaff
WHERE LastName = 'O''Leary'
```

Relational Operators

You can use the following relational operators in a WHERE clause:

Operator	Meaning
=	equal to
<>	not equal to
<	less than
<=	less than or equal to
>	greater than
>=	greater than or equal to
BETWEEN	between two values (inclusive)
LIKE	similar to (wildcard match)

The following expression matches last names starting with letters B..Z:

```
WHERE LastName >= 'B'
```

The following expression matches non-zero salary values:

```
WHERE Salary <> 0
```

Numeric and Date Values

Numeric columns, on the other hand, do not require quotes. The following expression matches all rows in which Salary is greater than $30,000:

```
WHERE (Salary > 30000)
```

Date/Time values must be delimited by # characters:

```
WHERE (HireDate > #12/31/1999#)
```

The following expression matches rows containing hire dates falling between (and including) January 1, 1992, and December 31, 1999:

```
WHERE (HireDate BETWEEN #1/1/1992# AND #12/31/1999#)
```

 Note:

SQL Server uses the apostrophe as its date delimiter. For example, the WHERE clause we just looked at would be written as follows:
```
WHERE (HireDate BETWEEN '1/1/1992' AND '12/31/1999')
```

LIKE Operator

The LIKE operator can be used to create partial matches with Text column values. When combined with LIKE, the underscore character matches a single unknown character. For example, the following expression matches all StaffId values that begin with a '1' and end with a '4':

```
WHERE StaffId LIKE '1_4'
```

The % character matches multiple unknown characters. We also call % a *wildcard* symbol. For example, the following matches all last names that start with the letter A:

```
WHERE LastName LIKE 'A%'
```

You can combine wildcard characters. For example, the following matches all FirstName values in the table that have 'dr' in the second and third positions:

```
WHERE FirstName LIKE '_dr%'
```

Compound Expressions (AND, OR, NOT)

SQL uses the NOT, AND, and OR operators to create compound expressions. In most cases, you should use parentheses to clarify the order of operations.

The following expression matches rows in which the person was hired after 1/1/1990 and their salary is greater than $40,000:

```
WHERE (HireDate > #1/1/1990#) AND (Salary > 40000)
```

The following expression matches rows in which the person was hired either before 1992 or after 1999:

```
WHERE (HireDate < #1/1/1992#) OR (HireDate > #12/31/1999#)
```

The following expression matches two types of employees: (1) ones that were hired after 1/1/1990 and whose salary is greater than $40,000; and (2) part-time employees:

```
WHERE (HireDate > #1/1/1990#) AND (Salary > 40000)
   OR (IsFullTime = 0)
```

The following expression matches rows in which the hire date was either earlier than 1/1/1999, or later than 12/31/1999:

```
WHERE (HireDate NOT BETWEEN #1/1/1999# AND #12/31/1999#)
```

The following expression matches rows in which the last name does not begin with the letter A:

```
WHERE (LastName NOT LIKE 'A%')
```

Using Embedded Variables

The primary drawback to the examples shown so far is that they use constant values which cannot change at runtime. More often, filtering values are stored in variables and properties, and their identifiers can be embedded into SQL SELECT statements.

Using the familiar SalesStaff table as an example, suppose we want to retrieve the table row matching a name currently stored in txtLastName.Text. We can assign a complete SQL query to the data adapter's SelectCommand.CommandText property:

```
daSalesStaff.SelectCommand.CommandText = _
    "SELECT FirstName, LastName FROM SalesStaff " & _
    "WHERE LastName = '" & txtLastName.Text & "'"
```

Notice that single quote delimiters must be inserted into the string.

After assigning a query to the CommandText property, you normally clear existing records from the dataset and call the data adapter's Fill method to refill the dataset:

```
DsSalesStaff1.Clear()
daSalesStaff.Fill(DsSalesStaff1)
```

A WHERE clause involving numeric fields is fairly simple. The following filter selects records in which the Salary field has a value greater than the contents of txtSalary:

```
"WHERE Salary > " & CSng(txtSalary.Text)
```

Date fields must be surrounded by # delimiters:

```
"WHERE HireDate > #" &  txtHireDate.Text & "#"
```

Adding Expressions to Datasets

ProposedSalaryExpression

The *Dataset Schema Designer*, launched when you double-click on an XSD file in the Solution Explorer Window, permits you to add new columns to a dataset. Specifically, you can add a column containing an expression. The expression is usually based on the values of fields within each dataset row. You can, for example, concatenate the FirstName and LastName fields to form a complete name. You can also perform a calculation using numeric field values, or modify the way a field is presented in the dataset table.

In the SalesStaff application, we can display the **dsSalesStaff** schema, shown in Figure 3-19. The following steps are required to add an expression that calculates a proposed salary increase. You can compare the steps to Figure 3-20:

1. In the line below StaffId, select **E** for Element in the pull-down list.
2. Enter **ProposedSalary** into the field name column.
3. Select **decimal** from a pull-down list in the field type column.
4. In the Properties window, enter **Salary * 1.10** into the Expression property.
5. Select **Rebuild Solution** from the Build menu.

To display the proposed salary, all you have to do is add a new text box to the program and set its DataBindings.Text property to the following: **DsSalesStaff1 - SalesStaff.ProposedSalary**. The result is shown in Figure 3-21, where the proposed salary appears to the right of the current salary.

Figure 3-19 Schema for dsSalesStaff dataset.

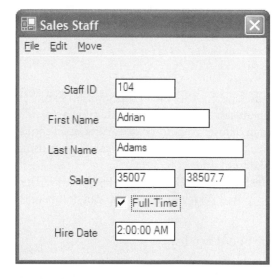

Figure 3-20 Adding an expression to dsSalesStaff.

Figure 3-21 Displaying the proposed salary.

Hands-On Tutorial: Selecting Karate School Members

Karate1

In this tutorial, you will work with a new database named **karate.mdb** that contains a table named **Members** (Figure 3-22). The rows represent members of a Karate school. A ComboBox control will be filled with names from the Members table. When the user selects a name, the program will display all remaining columns in the same table row.

MemberId	LastName	FirstName	Phone	Street	City	Zip	BirthDate
00001	Kahumanu	Keoki	111-2222	42 Pipeline Ave.	Sunset Beach	93444	2/20/1972
00002	Chong	Anne	232-2323	44 Makapuu Place	Waimanalo	91123	2/20/1991
00003	Hasegawa	Elaine	313-3455	1101 Haliewa St.	Kahala	93233	2/20/1975
00004	Kahane	Brian	646-9387	967 Pupukea Road	Hauula	93311	5/20/1974
00005	Gonzalez	Aldo	123-2345	999 Kamehameha Hwy	Haliewa	94555	6/6/1976
00006	Kousevitzky	Jascha	414-2345	88 Chuns Reef	Haliewa	93171	2/20/1982
00007	Taliafea	Moses	545-2323	6606 Laniakea Lane	Lihue	93176	5/20/1981
00008	Concepcion	Rafael	602-3312	64-021 Waimea St.	Laie	93188	5/20/1983
00009	Taylor	Winifred	333-2222	544 Honolua Bay Rd.	Wailuku	93411	2/20/1983
00010	Kyoshi	Sensei	232-2342	88 Velzyland Ct.	Kahuku	93133	3/29/1942

Figure 3-22 Members table, karate.mdb database.

We will show two ways to handle SQL in this program. In the first version, we will use a SELECT statement with an embedded variable. In the second version, we will use a parameterized query.

Step 1. Open the **Karate1** program from the Chapter 3 examples directory. Open the frmMain form's Designer window.

Step 2. In the Server Explorer, create a new connection. For the *Provider* entry, select **Microsoft Jet 4.0 OLE DB Provider**, and for the *Connection* entry, select **karate.mdb**.

Step 3. First, you will bind the ComboBox control to the LastName field in the Members table. Drag the Members table in the Server Explorer to frmMain. Rename the Connection to **conMembers** and rename the data adapter to **daLastName**.

Step 4. Right-click on **daLastName** in the component tray and select **Generate Dataset**. Name the dataset **dsLastName**.

Step 5. Set the ComboBox's DataSource property to **DsLastName1**. Set the DisplayMember property to **Members.LastName**. Set the ValueMember property to **Members.MemberId**.

Step 6. In the frmMain code window, declare the following variable at the class level:
```
Private mbComboLoaded As Boolean = False
```

Step 7. Insert the following code in the **frmMain_Load** procedure:
```
daLastName.Fill(DsLastName1)
cboLastName.SelectedIndex = -1
mbComboLoaded = True
```

Step 8. Run the program and verify that the combo box contains a list of last names. Return to design mode.

The names in the combo box do not appear in alphabetical order. Instead, they appear in the same sequence as their physical order in the database (see Figure 3-22, shown earlier). Our next task is to modify the data adapter's SQL query so it orders the records by last name.

Step 9. Edit the **SelectCommand.CommandText** property of the **daLastName** data adapter. In the Query Builder window, change the SQL command to:

```
SELECT LastName, MemberId
FROM Members
ORDER BY LastName
```

(Spacing and line breaks are unimportant, as long as keywords and identifiers are surrounded by at least one space.)

Step 10. Run the program again and verify that the names appear in alphabetical order. Return to design mode. Next, we will bind the other controls on this form to a new data adapter, based on the complete Members table.

Step 11. With frmMain's Designer window open, drag the **Members** table from the Server Explorer onto the form. Notice that a new data adapter was created, but we will still be using the same Connection object. Rename the data adapter to **daMembers**.

Step 12. Right-click on daMembers and select Generate Dataset. Name the new dataset **dsMembers**. When you click on OK, an object named **DsMembers1** appears in the component tray.

Step 13. Bind all the TextBox controls on the form to matching fields in the DsMembers1 dataset. For example, bind the txtFirstName control to **DsMembers1, Members.FirstName**. (The Name property of each text box will indicate which field is to be bound.)

Step 14. Locate the **cboLastName_SelectedIndexChanged** procedure in frmMain's Code window. When the user selects a last name in the combo box, this procedure creates an SQL command that displays all rows in which the LastName field matches the name stored in the combo box's Text property. Insert the following statements:

```
If mbComboLoaded = False Then Exit Sub

daMembers.SelectCommand.CommandText = _
   "SELECT * from Members WHERE MemberId = '" _
   & cboLastName.SelectedValue & "'"

DsMembers1.Clear()
daMembers.Fill(DsMembers1)
```

(**SELECT *** is an abbreviated way to select all columns from the table.) The DsMembers1 dataset must be cleared before being filled with the new row selection. Otherwise, we would append to existing rows in the dataset.

Step 15. Run the program and select various names from the combo box. As you select each name, its matching columns should appear in the bound controls. Figure 3-23 shows the row displayed when the name **Gonzalez** was selected.

The program has a weakness: If a particular last name were to appear more than once in the Members table, the user would see duplicate names in the combo box. In the chapter exercises, you will be asked to insert combined first and last names into the combo box. The complete program source code is shown in Code Listing 3-3.

(End of tutorial. You can find a finished version of this program in the Karate1_done directory.)

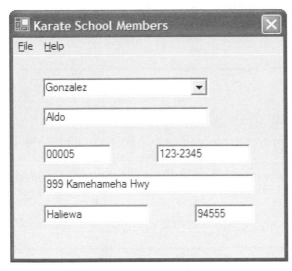

Figure 3-23 Last name selected.

Code Listing 3-3 (Karate 1)

```
Public Class frmMain
    Inherits System.Windows.Forms.Form

+ Windows Form Designer generated code

    Private mbComboLoaded As Boolean = False

    Private Sub frmMain_Load(ByVal sender As System.Object, _
     ByVal e As System.EventArgs) Handles MyBase.Load

        'Fill the DataSet (used by the combo box)
        daLastName.Fill(DsLastName1)
        cboLastName.SelectedIndex = -1
        mbComboLoaded = True
    End Sub

    Private Sub cboLastName_SelectedIndexChanged(ByVal sender As _
     System.Object, ByVal e As System.EventArgs) _
     Handles cboLastName.SelectedIndexChanged

        If mbComboLoaded = False Then Exit Sub

        daMembers.SelectCommand.CommandText = _
         "SELECT * from Members WHERE MemberId = '" _
          & cboLastName.SelectedValue & "'"
        DsMembers1.Clear()
        daMembers.Fill(DsMembers1)
    End Sub

    Private Sub mnuFileExit_Click(ByVal sender As System.Object, _
     ByVal e As System.EventArgs) Handles mnuFileExit.Click
        Me.Close()
    End Sub

    Private Sub mnuHelpAbout_Click(ByVal sender As System.Object, _
     ByVal e As System.EventArgs) Handles mnuHelpAbout.Click
```

```
        Dim aForm As New frmAbout()
        aForm.ShowDialog()
    End Sub
End Class
```

Parameterized Queries

A *parameterized query* is a query in which certain elements of the query (called *query parameters*) are assigned values at runtime. In the same way that you pass parameters to procedures to make them more flexible, you can do the same with SQL queries.

A query parameter can be identified by the use of a question mark (?) in place of what is usually a literal value. For example, insead of writing **WHERE (LastName = 'Gonzalez')**, we would write **WHERE (LastName=?)**.

The following SELECT statement selects rows from the Members table using a query parameter for the LastName field:

```
SELECT BirthDate, City, FirstName, LastName, MemberId, Phone,
       Street, Zip
FROM   Members
WHERE (LastName = ?)
```

Review the **SelectCommand** property of a data adapter for a moment. It has two important subproperties:

♦ **CommandText**: Contains a SQL SELECT statement that fills the dataset.

♦ **Parameters**: Contains a collection of query parameters that correspond to parameters marked by the ? character in CommandText.

When your program is ready to fill a dataset, you must pass values to the appropriate query parameters. For example, the following statement assigns the contents of txtLastName.Text to the **LastName** query parameter:

```
daMembers.SelectCommand.Parameters("LastName").Value = txtLastName.Text
```

The Parameters property is a zero-based collection, so the LastName parameter is located at index 0. The following code is equivalent to the previous example:

```
daMembers.SelectCommand.Parameters(0).Value = txtLastName.Text
```

If additional query parameters existed, their indices would be 1, 2, ... etc.

After assigning a new value to a query parameter, you must clear the old dataset contents and refill the dataset from the data adapter:

```
DsMembers1.Clear()
daMembers.Fill(DsMembers1)
```

In general, parameterized queries are preferred over queries containing embedded variables. The latter type of query involves substantial processing time when queries contain multiple uses of the concatenation (&) operator. Parameterized queries, on the other hand, can be compiled before a program runs, so they execute quickly.

☞ *Note:*

In this section, we are using the OLE DB syntax for parameterized queries. SQL Server, however, requires query parameters to be named. Each parameter name must begin with the @ sign. For example:

```
SELECT BirthDate, City, FirstName, LastName, MemberId,
       Phone, Street, Zip
FROM   Members
WHERE LastName = @lastName
```

Hands-on Tutorial: Selecting Members Using Query Parameters

Karate2

Now you will modify the Selecting Karate Members Tutorial so that it uses a parameterized query.

Step 1. Copy the **Karate1** program that you developed in the previous Tutorial to a new directory named **Karate2**. Open the program from the Karate2 directory.

Step 2. At this time, you may want to rename both the solution name and project name to Karate2. Be careful, however, *not* to change the project's Root namespace property.

Step 3. Find the SelectCommand.CommandText property of the daMembers data adapter. Click on its button to open the Query Builder window. In the SQL pane, change the SELECT statement to the following:

```
SELECT BirthDate, City, FirstName, LastName, MemberId, Phone,
        Street, Zip
FROM Members
WHERE (MemberId = ?)
```

Click on OK to close the Query Builder. If a dialog window asks: "Some column information may be lost...", click on **Yes**.

Step 4. Open the Code window for frmMain, and modify the combo box's SelectedIndexChanged procedure so it contains the following statements:

```
If mbComboLoaded = False Then Exit Sub

daMembers.SelectCommand.Parameters("MemberId").Value _
    = cboLastName.SelectedValue
DsMembers1.Clear()
daMembers.Fill(DsMembers1)
```

Step 5. Run the program and select various names from the combo box. The output should be the same as it was in the Karate1 program.

The program's complete source code appears in Code Listing 3-4.
   (End of tutorial)

Code Listing 3-4 (Karate 2)

```
Public Class frmMain
    Inherits System.Windows.Forms.Form

+ Windows Form Designer generated code

    Private mbComboLoaded As Boolean = False

    Private Sub frmMain_Load(ByVal sender As System.Object, _
     ByVal e As System.EventArgs) Handles MyBase.Load

        'Fill the DataSet (used by the combo box)
        daLastName.Fill(DsLastName1)
        cboLastName.SelectedIndex = -1
        mbComboLoaded = True
    End Sub
```

```
Private Sub cboLastName_SelectedIndexChanged(ByVal sender As _
  System.Object, ByVal e As System.EventArgs) _
  Handles cboLastName.SelectedIndexChanged

    If mbComboLoaded = False Then Exit Sub

    daMembers.SelectCommand.Parameters("MemberId").Value _
      = cboLastName.SelectedValue
        DsMembers1.Clear()
        daMembers.Fill(DsMembers1)
End Sub

Private Sub mnuFileExit_Click(ByVal sender As System.Object, _
  ByVal e As System.EventArgs) Handles mnuFileExit.Click

    Me.Close()
End Sub

Private Sub mnuHelpAbout_Click(ByVal sender As System.Object, _
  ByVal e As System.EventArgs) Handles mnuHelpAbout.Click

    Dim aForm As New frmAbout()
    aForm.ShowDialog()
End Sub
End Class
```

Changing the Root Namespace. It is possible to change the Root Namespace of a project, but once you do so, you must search through your program's code for the old namespace name and replace it with the new one. In the Windows Generated code for frmMain in the Karate program, for example, the **Karate1** namespace appears in the following dataset definitions:

```
Friend WithEvents DsLastName1 As Karate1.dsLastName
Friend WithEvents DsMembers1 As Karate1.dsMembers
Me.DsLastName1 = New Karate1.dsLastName()
Me.DsMembers1 = New Karate1.dsMembers()
```

You can use a search and replace operation from the Edit menu to change every **Karate1** to **Karate2**.

Checkpoint

3.16 Which SQL clause lets you control which rows from a database will be retrieved from a database table?

3.17 Write a query statement in SQL that retrieves only rows from a table named **Employees** in which the **Years** column is > 9.

3.18 Which data adapter method must be called after assigning a new value to the data adapter's SelectCommand.CommandText property?

3.19 What basic steps are required to add an expression column to a dataset?

3.20 In the Karate1 program, which ComboBox event handler was used to alter the SQL query that retrieves records?

▶3.5 Chapter Summary

◆ ADO.NET provides consistent access to databases such as Microsoft Access and Microsoft SQL Server. It also connects to XML data sources.

◆ ADO.NET moves away from an earlier client-server model to a loosely connected relationship between application programs and their data sources.

◆ ADO.NET represents database tables and relationships between tables as strongly typed objects in a natural way for object-oriented programs.

◆ ADO.NET functions in two modes: connected and disconnected.

◆ A database is a collection of one or more tables, each of which contains data related to a particular topic.

◆ A *database schema* is the design of tables, columns, and relationships between tables for the database.

◆ Databases are usually designed around a relational model, meaning that relations exist between tables. A relation uses a common field value to link records from two different tables.

◆ A database query is a command written in SQL, which extracts information from one or more linked tables.

◆ A Connection object opens a database.

◆ A data adapter reads data from a database table. It acts as a bridge between a data source and a dataset, by retrieving rows from the underlying data source.

◆ A data reader directly connects to a data source to provide high-speed access to read-only data.

◆ A dataset is an in-memory cache of records that holds table data retrieved from one or more data sources. The DataSet class contains standardized methods and properties for datasets.

◆ A DataTable object represents a single table of in-memory data.

◆ A data-aware control is a control that can bind itself to a database field and display the contents of the field at runtime. It has a DataBindings property that links the control to a DataTable field.

◆ Every Windows form has a built-in object named BindingContext that manages the data bindings for the form's controls. A form's CurrencyManager object is required when a form is connected to a data source. It provides a way to navigate between the rows in a table.

◆ You can display a table's structure by double-clicking on its XML schema definition file in the Solution Explorer window.

◆ When you add a row to a table, the row must be a System.Data.DataRow object. Exceptions can be thrown when adding new rows to datasets. If an exception is thrown while adding or modifying a row, call CancelEdit to undo changes to the row.

◆ Changes made to a disconnected dataset are not permanent until they are copied back to the data set's underlying data source.

◆ You can move between dataset rows using a subscript combined with one of the dataset's DataTable objects.

◆ Query Builder is a tool provided by .NET for creating and modifying SQL queries. Use it to modify the CommandText subproperty of a data adapter's SelectCommand.

◆ You can fill a list box or combo box by assigning the name of a dataset to the list/combo box's DataSource property, and assigning the appropriate column name to the list/combo box's DisplayMember property.

◆ SQL has a WHERE clause that you can use to filter, or select which row (or rows) you want to retrieve from a database table. A program variable's value can be embedded into a filter, making it more flexible at runtime.

◆ A parameterized query contains query parameters that are assigned values at runtime.

▶3.6 Key Terms

ADO (ActiveX Data Objects)

ADO.NET

binding

client-server model

column

connected mode

DAO (Data Access Objects)

data adapter

data-aware control

data reader

database schema

datasource

database connection

database query

dataset

DataTable

disconnected dataset

disconnected mode

Extensible Markup Language (XML)

field

filter

parameterized query

query

record

relation

relational model

row

Structured Query Language (SQL)

table

table relation

update operation

XML schema definition

▶3.7 Review Questions

Fill-in-the-Blank

1. ADO.NET features a ————————— coupled relationship between application programs and their data sources.

2. XML stands for ————————— Markup Language.

3. A data ————————— transfers data from a data source to a dataset.

4. A ————————— is a connection that relies on a common field value to link rows from two different database tables.

5. A disconnected ————————— holds database tables in memory so they can be viewed and updated by a program.

6. The ————————— property of a DataTable contains multiple DataRow objects.

7. The ————————— property of a CurrencyManager can be used to set the current row index of a DataSet.

8. The ————————— subproperty of a data adapter's SelectCommand contains an SQL query.

Multiple Choice

1. Which of the following characteristics is **not** associated with ADO.NET?

    a. It is capable of using disconnected datasets.
    b. It supports Extensible Markup Language.
    c. It is based on the client-server application model.
    d. It supports multi-tier application development.
    e. Tables and relationships are represented by strongly typed objects.

2. Which of the following choices lists the design steps to set up a database in the correct order?

    a. create dataset, create data adapter, create connection
    b. create data adapter, create connection, create dataset
    c. create connection, create data adapter, create dataview
    d. create connection, create data adapter, create dataset
    e. create connection, create dataview, create data adapter

3. In a database table containing addresses of employees, which of the following terms describes all the information relating to one employee?

    a. column
    b. row
    c. record
    d. answers a and b
    e. answers b and c

4. Which of the following was **not** listed as a DataTable property in this chapter?

    a. Columns
    b. Rows
    c. Connection
    d. TableName
    e. PrimaryKey

5. Which of the following controls is not data-aware?

    a. TextBox
    b. Label
    c. ComboBox
    d. ListView
    e. CheckBox

6. Which of the following SQL commands was **not** discussed in this chapter?

    a. SELECT
    b. FROM
    c. EXCEPT
    d. WHERE
    e. none of the above

True or False

1. When a dataset row is modified, the change is immediately copied to the underlying dataset.
2. A data reader uses a disconnected dataset to hold the application data.
3. A CurrencyManager has a property named Current that holds a DataRowView object.
4. A data adapter has an Update method that copies dataset changes to the underlying database.
5. You can use a subscript to move through the rows of a dataset's DataTable object.
6. You can add an expression to a DataSet using the DataAdapter's Expression property.
7. The Parameters property of a DataSet object contains values that will be passed to a parameterized query at runtime.

Short Answer

1. What specific class creates a connection to an Microsoft Access database?
2. Which type of object manages the data bindings for a form's controls?
3. Suppose you have just created a data adapter from the Members table of the Karate database. What must you do next before you can bind the Members table to any controls?
4. Which exception is thrown if you try to add a dataset row containing a duplicate key value?

5. Which CurrencyManager method removes a row from a dataset?

6. Which Visual Studio .NET tool is used for creating and modifying queries?

What Do You Think?

1. If you had to display a database table containing 100,000 rows, would you prefer to use ADO.NET's connected mode, or disconnected mode?

2. If you had to build a dataset from two different tables, how many data adapters would you need?

Algorithm Workbench

1. Write a statement that fills a dataset named DsEmployees1 from a data adapter named daEmployees.

2. Write a statement that initializes a CurrencyManager object named currManager from a dataset named DsEmployees1, containing a table named Employees.

3. Write an SQL SELECT statement that retrieves all rows from the Departments table, including the DeptID and ManagerName columns.

4. Given a CurrencyManager named myCurr, write a statement that sets its position to the last row of the data table.

5. Write a statement that creates a new DataRow named myRow, having the same column format as the DsEmployees1.Employees dataset.

6. Write a statement that removes row 0 from the DsEmployees1 dataset, using a CurrencyManager named myCurr.

7. Write an SQL SELECT statement that retrieves the DeptID and Salary columns from the Departments table, including only rows where Salary is less than or equal to 50000.

8. Assume that the daEmployees data adapter contains a SELECT statement with a query parameter named Salary. Write a statement that assigns 30000 to the Salary parameter.

▶3.8 Programming Challenges

1. Selecting Sales Staff

Create a program that lets the user select rows from the SalesStaff table. Fill a ComboBox control with the names (last, first). Use a parameterized query to retrieve the matching table row and display it in databound controls. A sample is shown in Figure 3-24.

Figure 3-24 Selecting Sales Staff

2. Selecting Karate Members

Create a program that displays rows from the Members table in the Karate.mdb database. Display the full name of each member in a ComboBox control, in the format *LastName, FirstName*. Sort the names in ascending order on both the last name and first name. When the user selects a name, fill in the remaining text boxes, using the arrangement shown in Figure 3-25.

You will need two data adapters—one for the complete Members table, and a second one that extracts the MemberId, FirstName, and LastName from the Members table. Each data adapter will have a related dataset. You will probably find it helpful to add an expression to one of your dataset definitions that concatenates the first and last names. The expression will be: **LastName + ', ' + FirstName**.

You may want to use the Karate1 program from earlier in this chapter as a guide when completing this program.

Figure 3-25 Selecting Karate Members.

3. Adding Karate Members

Create a program that uses the Members table of the Karate.mdb database. Let the user add new members. Optionally, the program can save the dataset changes to the underlying database. A sample is shown in Figure 3-26.

Figure 3-26 Adding a Karate School member

4. Finding Member Birth Dates

Create a program that uses the Members table of the Karate.mdb database. Let the user select a birth date from a DateTimePicker control. The program must display the first and last names of all members whose birth dates are earlier than the selected date (see Figure 3-27). Use a parameterized query.

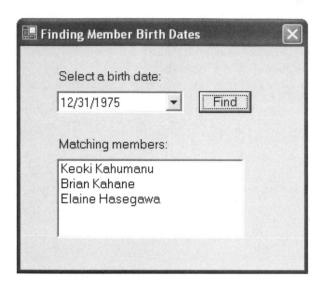

Figure 3-27   Finding members by birth date

5. Finding a Date Range

Using the program from the previous exercise as a starting point, let the user input two dates, using a DateTimePicker control. Display the first and last names of all members whose birth dates fall within the selected range (Figure 3-28).

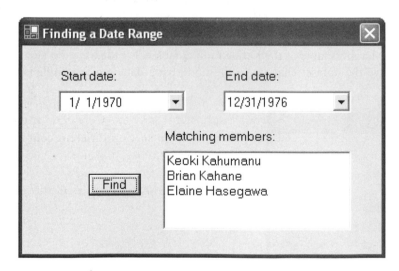

Figure 3-28   Finding a date range

DataGrid, DataView, and ListView

►4.1 DataGrid Control

Introduction

A DataGrid conveniently displays a spreadsheet-like view of a dataset. In nearly every database application, we have to show existing data or data we have collected. We usually want to sort on different columns, and we want to select only certain columns to display. The DataGrid control is easy to use, fills quickly, and can be customized in many different ways.

So much capability is included with the DataGrid that you only need to set a few important properties to get instant output. For example, you may want to use the CaptionText property to set the title above the column headings line. Or, you may want to use the TableStyles property to identify and label the columns to be displayed in the grid. Naturally, the colors of the fonts, lines, and background can all be configured for a professional design.

A DataGrid is directly linked to a dataset, so any change made to the grid's data also changes the attached dataset. The underlying database, on the other hand, is not updated until the data adapter's Update method is called.

Figure 4-1 shows a DataGrid holding the contents of the Items table in the Sports Rental database. The column headings contain the dataset field names.

By default, the user can modify data in the grid by selecting items and overtyping their contents. The user can select a row by clicking on the button to the left of the row, and can delete the row by pressing the Del key. The user can also insert a new row by typing on the bottom line of the grid and filling in the field values. Changes made to an individual cell are not saved until the user moves away from the cell.

DataGrid columns are generated in a specific order based on the SQL command in the data adapter. Table 4-1 contains descriptions of DataGrid properties you are most likely to use.

item_id	description	daily_rate	weekly_rate	monthly_rate	quantity
1	Surfboard, short fiberglass	40	200	450	5
2	Ocean kayak, solo	50	250	650	3
3	Ocean kayak, tandem	60	250	650	4
4	Snorkeling outfit	15	40	100	10
5	Outrigger canoe, solo	62	250	550	2
6	Surfboard, long fiberglass	40	200	450	8
7	Boogie board, standard	15	55	180	15
8	Wind surfer, beginner	50	250	550	8
9	Wind surfer, intermediate	55	260	580	4
10	Wind surfer, advanced	60	270	600	2
11	Surfboard, long epoxy	30	120	400	5
12	Surfboard, short epoxy	25	100	300	8

Figure 4-1 DataGrid Showing Sports Items.

Table 4-1

Important DataGrid Properties.

Property	Type	Description
AllowSorting	Boolean	Enables or disables column sorting when the user clicks on the column headings.
CaptionText	String	Gets or sets the caption displayed on the line above the column headings.
CaptionVisible	Boolean	Determines whether or not the caption will be visible.
CurrentRowIndex	Integer	Gets or sets the index of the currently selected row.
DataSource	Object	Gets or sets the DataSource object associated with the DataGrid.
Enabled	Boolean	Determines whether or not the user can interact with the DataGrid.
ReadOnly	Boolean	Determines whether or not the user can add or modify the grid's data. Set it to False if you want the user to be able to add, delete, and modify rows.

In Chapter 5, we will show how to use the DataGrid control to display datasets having multiple related tables. It can let the user automatically navigate from a parent table to a child table when a one-to-many relationship exists between the tables.

Hands-On Tutorial: Rental Inventory DataGrid

 RentalInventory

In this tutorial, you will attach a DataGrid control to the SportsRental database, so the grid can display the Items table. The program's complete source code may be seen in Code Listing 4-1.

Step 1. Create a new Windows Application named **RentalInventory**. Change the startup form's Text property to **Sports Rentals**.

Step 2. Add a DataGrid control to the form and name it **dgdItems**. Size the control so it fills the entire open area of the form. Set its Anchor property to **Top, Bottom, Left, Right**. Set its CaptionVisible property to **False**.

Step 3. Add a MainMenu control to the form. Insert a submenu named **File,** and insert two items in the submenu: **Save** and **Exit**. Name them **mnuFileSave** and **mnuFileExit,** respectively.

Step 4. In Server Explorer, create a connection to the **SportsRental.mdb** database and drag the Items table onto your form. Rename the connection to **conSportsRental**, and rename the data adapter to **daItems.**

Step 5. Select the daItems data adapter and open its **SelectCommand.CommandText** property. Use Query Builder to replace the existing SQL statement with with the following:

```
SELECT item_id, description, daily_rate, weekly_rate, monthly_rate,
quantity FROM Items
```

Select the table fields in the same order (from left to right) as shown earlier in Figure 4-1.

Step 6. Right-click on **daItems** and generate a dataset class named **dsItems**.

Step 7. Set the grid's DataSource property to **DsItems1.Items.**

Step 8. Add the following statement to the form's **Load** event handler:

```
daItems.Fill(DsItems1)
```

Step 9. When the user clicks on File | Save, the program updates the underlying database. Insert the following statements in the **mnuFileSave_Click** procedure:

```
MessageBox.Show("Saving changes in database")
daItems.Update(DsItems1)
```

Step 10. Insert the following line in the mnuFileExit_Click event handler:

```
Me.Close()
```

Step 11. Run the program. After some adjusting of the column widths, the output should appear as in Figure 4-1 (shown previously). Click on each column heading to sort the column. Clicking on the same heading a second time reverses the column sort order.

Step 12. Still running the program, add new rows to the grid, delete existing rows, and edit individual cells. The grid control is designed so editing changes are not saved until you move away from the current cell. A small problem with that approach appears when you want to update the underlying database (by clicking on File | Save in the menu). The user might not realize that one has to move away from the current cell before updating the database. We dealt with a similar problem when working with data-bound text boxes. We can use a similar solution in this program, except that now we're working with cell positions rather than row indexes.

Step 13. Return to design mode and replace the contents of the **mnuFileSave_Click** procedure with the following lines:

```
Dim saveCell As DataGridCell = dgdItems.CurrentCell
If dgdItems.CurrentRowIndex > 0 Then
    dgdItems.CurrentCell = New DataGridCell(0, 0)
Else
    dgdItems.CurrentCell = New DataGridCell(1, 0)
End If
MessageBox.Show("Saving changes in database")
Try
    daItems.Update(DsItems1)
    dgdInventory.CurrentCell = saveCell
Catch ex As Exception
    MessageBox.Show(ex.Message)
End Try
```

The **CurrentCell** property holds a **DataGridCell** object that indicates the row and column position of the currently selected cell. We have to move away from that cell, update the Items table, and then move back to the original cell. In all cases but one, we can move to cell 0,0 with assurance that the current cell position will have moved. If the user is editing cell 0,0, we move to the next row, update the table, and move back again.

Step 14. Run the program again, modify a cell, and click on File | Save before you move away from the cell. Add a new row to the table and click on File | Save before moving away from the row. When you run the program a second time, check that your previous editing changes were saved.

(End of tutorial)

Code Listing 4-1 (Rental Inventory DataGrid)

```
Public Class frmInventory
    Inherits System.Windows.Forms.Form
```

    + Windows Form Designer generated code

```
    Private Sub frmInventory_Load(ByVal sender As Object, _
        ByVal e As System.EventArgs) Handles MyBase.Load

        daItems.Fill(DsItems1)
    End Sub

    Private Sub mnuFileExit_Click(ByVal sender As System.Object, _
     ByVal e As System.EventArgs) Handles mnuFileExit.Click

        Me.Close()
    End Sub

    Private Sub mnuFileSave_Click(ByVal sender As System.Object, _
     ByVal e As System.EventArgs) Handles mnuFileSave.Click

        'Move away from the current cell, update the database,
        'and move back to the same cell. Must be done in order
        'to save changes to current row.
        Dim saveCell As DataGridCell = dgdInventory.CurrentCell
        If dgdInventory.CurrentRowIndex > 0 Then
            dgdInventory.CurrentCell = New DataGridCell(0, 0)
        Else
            dgdInventory.CurrentCell = New DataGridCell(1, 0)
        End If
        Try
            daItems.Update(DsItems1)
            dgdInventory.CurrentCell = saveCell
        Catch ex As Exception
            MessageBox.Show(ex.Message)
        End Try
    End Sub

    'Demonstrates one of the DataGrid tips by preventing changes to
    'column 0. Also prevents user from inserting new rows.
    Private Sub dgdInventory_CurrentCellChanged(ByVal sender As Object, _
     ByVal e As System.EventArgs) Handles dgdInventory.CurrentCellChanged

        'dgdInventory.ReadOnly = (dgdInventory.CurrentCell.ColumnNumber = 0)
    End Sub
```

```
    Private Sub dgdInventory_Click(ByVal sender As Object, _
     ByVal e As System.EventArgs) Handles dgdInventory.Click

        Dim drItem As DataRow = DsItems1.Items(dgdInventory.CurrentRowIndex)

    End Sub
End Class
```

Table Styles and Column Styles

In the previous tutorial, you may have noticed that the default DataGrid column headings show all columns from the Items table, using column headings taken directly from the dataset table. You may want to customize the column headings for several reasons:

◆ The default column names might be cryptic and not easily recognized by users.

◆ The default column widths may not be wide enough to view the column data.

◆ You may want to change either the order or selection of display columns.

◆ You may want to change the default column alignment (left, right, or center).

You can improve the appearance of columns and headings by editing the DataGrid's **TableStyles** property. TableStyles is a collection of **DataGridTableStyle** objects. It's possible to create such objects in code, but you may prefer to do it interactively. The best way to learn how to create table and column styles is to try it yourself, so we will continue the Rental Inventory program begun in the previous section.

Rental Inventory DataGrid, Continued

RentalInventoryColumns

Step 1. Copy the RentalInventory program to a new directory and rename the directory to **RentalInventoryColumns**.

Step 2. Open the program and display the program's startup form.

Step 3. With the DataGrid selected in the design window, click next to its **TableStyles** property, causing the DataGridTableStyle Collection Editor window to display (Figure 4-2).

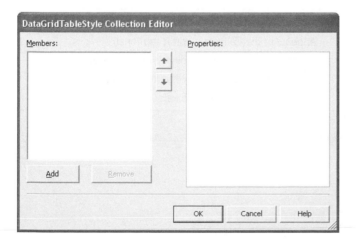

Figure 4-2 DataGridTableStyle Collection Editor.

Step 4. Click the **Add** button to create a new table style. Set its **MappingName** property to the name of the dataset table you plan to display (in this case, **Items**). Optionally, you can set its Name property to **Items** in case you later want to identify the TableStyle definition by name (Figure 4-3).

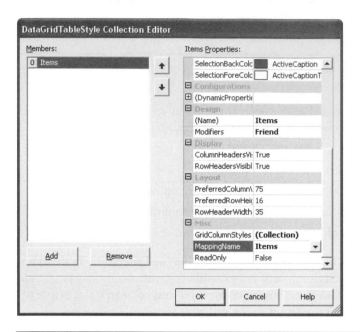

Figure 4-3 Setting Name and MappingName properties.

The same editor window lets you hide column headers using the ColumnHeadersVisible property, and lets you hide row headers using the RowHeadersVisible property. Next, you will create columns for the Description and Daily Rate columns from the Items table.

Step 5. While still in the DataGridTableStyle editor, click on the **GridColumnStyle** property, which causes the **DataGridColumnStyle Collection Editor** to appear (Figure 4-4).

Step 6. Click the **Add** button, and set the following property values:

Property	Value	Description
Name	colDescription	Appears in the Collection editor (optional)
HeaderText	Description	Appears in the column heading when grid is displayed
MappingName	description	Names the database table column suppling the data
Width	200	Specifies column width, in pixels

Figure 4-5 shows the editor window with the defined column.

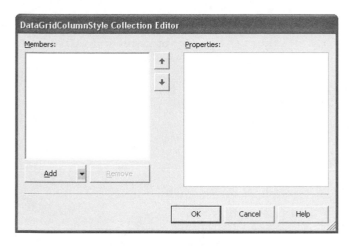

Figure 4-4 DataGridColumnStyle Collection Editor.

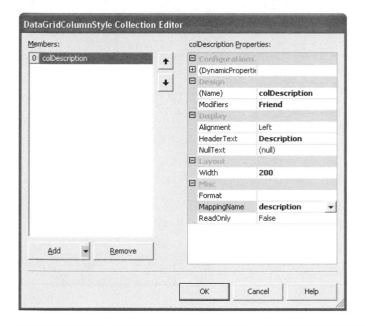

Figure 4-5 Defining the Description Column.

Step 7. Create a second column to display the daily rental rate and set the following properties:

Property	Value	Description
Name	colDailyRate	Appears in the Collection editor (optional)
Alignment	Center	Aligns column to the left, right, or center
HeaderText	Daily Rate	Appears in the column heading when the grid is displayed
MappingName	daily_rate	Names the database table column supplying the data

Figure 4-6 shows the Rental Inventory program, using custom column definitions.

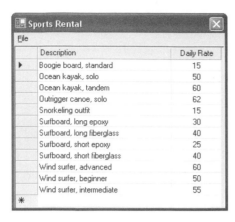

Figure 4-6 Sports Rental Inventory Grid.

Step 8. We will make the grid read-only and remove the row headers. Set the grid's ReadOnly property to **True**. Open the DataGridTableStyle Collection Editor, select the **Items** table, and set RowHeadersVisible to **False**.

Step 9. Save and run the program. Figure 4-7 shows the program's output after making these changes.

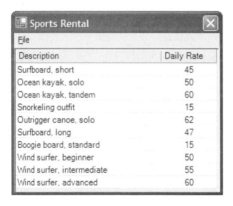

Figure 4-7 Removing the row headers.

(End of tutorial)

DataGrid Events

Navigate Event

Navigate is the default event for the DataGrid control. Navigate is fired when the grid contains related tables, and the user is currently moving from one table to the next. We will explore this capability in Chapter 5.

Click Event

The **Click** event fires when the user selects a DataGrid row, using one of the buttons located along the left side of the grid rows. Setting RowHeadersVisible to False hides the buttons, preventing the user from selecting rows.

To select any event for a control, open the form's Code window, select the control name from the Class Name pulldown list at the top left, and select an event name from the Method Name pulldown list at the top right.

The **CurrentRowIndex** property returns the row index (starting at zero) of the selected row. In the following code, for example, we display the index in a message box:

```
Private Sub dgdInventory_Click(ByVal sender As Object, _
 ByVal e As System.EventArgs) Handles dgdInventory.Click

   MessageBox.Show("CurrentRowIndex is " &
     dgdInventory.CurrentRowIndex)
End Sub
```

If the grid is connected to a dataset, you can obtain the current dataset row (a DataRow object) with the following statement:

```
Dim drItem As DataRow = DsItems1.Items(dgdInventory.CurrentRowIndex)
```

Once you have the row (named drItem in this example), you can obtain individual field values using the row's Item property.

Updating a DataGrid

Chapter 3 showed how to remove and update dataset rows. You can use that knowledge to modify datasets attached to DataGrids. For our examples, we will use the Karate database, which contains a table named Payments:

Column Name	Description
PaymentId	Integer (autonumber)
MemberId	Text
PaymentDate	Date/Time
Amount	Currency

Deleting a Row

Using the CurrentRowIndex property of a datagrid, you can locate its matching row in the dataset referenced by the grid's DataSource property. Then you can call the row's Delete method to remove it from the dataset. Exception handling should be used for this type of operation. For example, suppose a DataGrid named **dgrPayments** displays the Payments table, and the dataset is named **DsPayments1**. The following statement gets the DataRow referenced by the grid:

```
Dim row As DataRow = DsPayments1.Payments(dgrPayments.CurrentRowIndex)
```

The following statement deletes the row from the dataset:

```
row.Delete()
```

Updating a Row

Given a DataRow object from a dataset, you can modify the contents of individual colums. Suppose, for example, we want to modify the Amount column of the DsPayments1 dataset. The DataGrid displaying the payments is named dgrPayments. The following code obtains the row and copies a value from a text box into the Amount column:

```
Dim row As DataRow = DsPayments1.Payments(dgrPayments.CurrentRowIndex)
row("Amount") = txtAmount.Text
```

Karate Updates Example

KarateUpdates

The Karate Updates program, shown in Figure 4-8, displays the Payments table from the Karate database. The user selects a payment from the grid by clicking on the buttons to the left side of the grid. He/she enters a new payment amount in the text box at the bottom of the form and clicks on **Update**. The payment amount is updated and the rows in the grid are refreshed. If the user selects a grid row and clicks on the **Delete** button, the payment row disappears. Modifications are made only to the dataset, and are not permanent unless the user selects the **Update database** checkbox prior to performing Update and Delete operations.

The program has a Connection named conKarate, a data adapter named daPayments, a dataset class named dsPayments, and a dataset object named DsPayments1. The grid is named dgrPayments, and the CheckBox is named chkUpdate. The program source code may be seen in Code Listing 4-2.

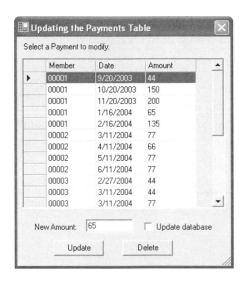

Figure 4-8 Updating the payments table.

Code Listing 4-2 (Karate Updates)

```
Public Class frmUpdate
    Inherits System.Windows.Forms.Form

    + Windows Form Designer generated code

    Private Sub frmUpdate_Load(ByVal sender As System.Object, _
     ByVal e As System.EventArgs) Handles MyBase.Load
        daPayments.Fill(DsPayments1)
    End Sub

    'The event handler for the Update button gets the current row number
    'of the grid and uses it to locate the corresponding row in the
    'DsPayments1 dataset. The row's Amount column is assigned the value
    'in the txtAmount text box.

    Private Sub btnUpdate_Click(ByVal sender As System.Object, _
     ByVal e As System.EventArgs) Handles btnUpdate.Click
        Try
            DsPayments1.Payments(dgrPayments.CurrentRowIndex).Item("Amount") _
            = txtAmount.Text
            If chkUpdate.Checked Then daPayments.Update(DsPayments1)
        Catch ex As Exception
            MessageBox.Show(ex.Message, "Error")
```

```
            End Try
      End Sub


      'The event handler for the delete button gets the current row number
      'of the grid and uses it to locate the corresponding row in the
      'DsPayments1 dataset. The row's Delete method removes it from the
      'dataset.

      Private Sub btnDelete_Click(ByVal sender As System.Object, _
       ByVal e As System.EventArgs) Handles btnDelete.Click
          Try
              DsPayments1.Payments(dgrPayments.CurrentRowIndex).Delete()
              If chkUpdate.Checked Then daPayments.Update(DsPayments1)
          Catch ex As Exception
              MessageBox.Show(ex.Message, "Error")
          End Try
      End Sub
End Class
```

DataGrid Tips

Tip #1: One way to change the ordering of the DataGrid columns is to alter the field order in the SELECT statement in the data adapter's CommandText property. After doing that, right-click on the data adapter and choose **Generate Dataset**.

Tip #2: Another way to change the ordering of DataGrid columns is to define DataGrid table styles and DataGrid column styles. In addition, you can change many characteristics of the displayed columns.

Tip #3: To prevent the user from modifying a particular column in a DataGrid, you can write code in the CurrentCellChanged event handler that checks the current cell location. If, for example, we want to prevent the user from modifying ID numbers in the Rental Inventory grid, the following statement sets the grid's ReadOnly property to True only when the current cell is in column 0 (the ID column):

```
dgdItems.ReadOnly = (dgdItems.CurrentCell.ColumnNumber = 0)
```

A side effect of this code is that the user will not be able to add new rows to the DataGrid.

Checkpoint

4.1 (yes/no): When a DataGrid cell is modified, is the change written to the attached dataset?

4.2 How can the user add a new row to the data in a DataGrid?

4.3 Which DataGrid property must be True before the user can modify data in its cells?

4.4 Which DataGrid property permits a program to move to a particular cell?

4.5 Which DataGrid event fires when the user moves to a different cell?

▶4.2 DataViews and ListViews

Using a DataView Control

We have shown how to filter and sort records in a dataset. Sometimes, however, you're better off leaving the dataset unchanged and, instead, using a DataView to sort or filter the data. You can create multiple simultaneous DataViews, each sorting or filtering the table data in different ways. A DataView control has two properties that sort and filter its attached dataset:

- **Sort**: Contains the field name to be sorted.
- **RowFilter**: Contains an expression that selects which rows will be viewed.

To add a DataView to your program, drag the DataView component from the Data tab of the ToolBox to an open form or component. Only two additional steps are required:

◆ Set the **Name** property to a name that reflects the table being viewed, such as dvMembers.

◆ Set the **Table** property to the name of a dataset table, such as dsMembers1.Members.

You can bind DataView columns to individual controls as you would bind them to a dataset table.

Sorting

To sort the **Members** table in ascending order by last name, set the DataView's Sort property to **LastName**. To sort a field in descending order, append DESC to the sort field name. For example, to sort the Members table in descending order by birth date, set Sort equal to **BirthDate DESC**.

Filtering (selecting) Rows

To filter the rows in a DataView, enter a relational expression into the DataView's **RowFilter** property. For example, to select only rows from the SalesStaff table having a Salary greater than 30,000, assign the following string to the RowFilter property:

Salary > 30000

In a tutorial later in this section, we will show how to sort and filter a DataView using data from the Karate School application.

Accessing Rows in Code

You can access any row of a DataView using an integer subscript. For example, the following loop iterates through the **dvMembers** DataView, adding each last name to a list box named lstNames:

```
Dim i As Integer
For i = 0 To dvMembers.Count - 1
   lstNames.Items.Add(dvMembers(i).Item("LastName"))
Next i
```

The DataView's **Count** property is useful when programming a loop. The **Item** property is a column collection, indexed by a zero-based integer or by a field name. Each row of a DataView is a DataRowView object. The following statement copies row i of the dvMembers DataView into **oneRow**:

```
Dim oneRow As DataRowView = dvMembers(i)
```

Finally, when referencing a particular column within a row, it helps to know that Item is a DataRowView's default property. The following two expressions are equivalent:

```
oneRow.Item("LastName")
oneRow("LastName")
```

Null Data

A datatable row may contain uninitialized columns. Such columns are automatically assigned a special value by the database named NULL. You can check for null values in your code by comparing the value of a column to the predefined identifier **DbNull.Value**. The following statements, for example, display a message that shows the contents of the LastName field:

```
Dim obj As Object = oneRow.Item("LastName")
If obj Is DbNull.Value Then
   MessageBox.Show("LastName is NULL")
Else
   MessageBox.Show("LastName is equal to " & CStr(obj))
EndIf
```

If you attempt to assign a null field to a specific variable type such as String or Integer, your program will throw an exception.

Filling a ListView Control

The ListView control, with its multiple columns, provides an ideal way to display a database table. Microsoft Access, for example, uses a ListView to do just that. The ListView control contains no data binding fields, so some coding is required if you want to fill it from a data source. You can fill a ListView from either a dataset or DataView, but the latter has a slight advantage because of its RowFilter and Sort properties.

Suppose a DataView named **dvPayments** holds a view of a table named **Payments** from the Karate School database. The table (shown in Figure 4-9) holds membership dues paid by schoool members. It has four columns:

◆ **PaymentId**: Autonumber field that guarantees a unique integer value for each row

◆ **MemberId**: ID number of the member who made a payment

◆ **PaymentDate**: Date when the member paid

◆ **Amount**: Amount paid by the member

PaymentId	MemberId	PaymentDate	Amount
1	00001	10/20/2003	$150.00
2	00001	11/20/2003	$200.00
3	00006	11/16/2003	$25.00
4	00006	12/16/2003	$50.00
5	00001	1/16/2004	$65.00
6	00001	2/16/2004	$135.00
7	00002	3/11/2004	$77.00
8	00003	2/27/2004	$44.00
9	00003	3/11/2004	$77.00
10	00002	4/11/2004	$66.00
11	00002	5/11/2004	$77.00
13	00002	6/11/2004	$77.00
14	00006	10/16/2003	$77.00
15	00003	3/11/2004	$44.00
16	00003	3/28/2004	$43.00
17	00004	3/27/2004	$44.00
19	00001	9/20/2003	$44.00
22	00004	3/21/2004	$55.00
23	00004	3/21/2004	$60.00
25	00004	3/23/2004	$50.00
30	00007	6/7/2004	$75.00
31	00008	6/7/2004	$55.00
32	00008	6/7/2004	$77.00
33	00009	6/8/2004	$50.25

Figure 4-9 Payments Table.

Let's review the structure of a ListView control for a moment. The Items collection holds all the rows. Each row is a ListViewItem object. The first column in the row is stored in the item's Text property, and the remaining columns are stored in the item's SubItems collection. Each element of SubItems is itself a ListViewItem object.

The following code fills a ListView control named **lvwPayments** with the contents of a DataView named **dvPayments**:

```
lvwPayments.Items.Clear()
Dim count As Integer = dvPayments.Count
Dim i As Integer
Dim item As ListViewItem
```

```
For i = 0 To count - 1
   With dvPayments(i)
      item = New ListViewItem(Format(.Item("PaymentDate"), _
         " MM/dd/yyyy"))
      lvwPayments.Items.Add(item)
      item.SubItems.Add(.Item("MemberId"))
      item.SubItems.Add(FormatNumber(.Item("Amount")))
   End With
Next i
```

If you wanted to sort on different ListView columns, you could just modify the DataView's Sort property and reload the ListView. That's exactly what we will do in the next tutorial.

Hands-On Tutorial: Karate School Payments

KaratePayments

In this tutorial, you will create a program that fills a ListView control from a DataView. Your program will have a fairly advanced feature: It will sort on any column, switching between ascending and descending order when the user clicks twice on the same column. The user interface is shown in Figure 4-10.

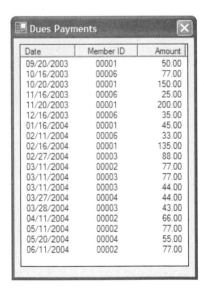

Figure 4-10 Ascending Sort by Date.

Step 1. Open the **KaratePayments** program from the Chapter 4 examples directory.

Step 2. Create a connection to the Karate.mdb database.

Step 3. Drag the Payments table from the Server Explorer to the frmPayments form.

Step 4. Rename the connection to **conKarate**, and rename the data adapter to **daPayments**.

Step 5. Generate a dataset from the daPayments adapter named **dsPayments**.

Step 6. Drag a DataView control from the Data tab of the Toolbox onto your form. Rename the DataView to **dvPayments**. Set its Table property to **DsPayments1.Payments**.

Step 7. Open the Code window of the frmPayments form and insert the **FillListView** procedure, which fills the ListView control from the dvPayments DataView:

```
Sub FillListView()
    lvwPayments.Items.Clear()
    Dim count As Integer = dvPayments.Count
    Dim i As Integer
    Dim item As ListViewItem

    For i = 0 To count - 1
      With dvPayments(i)
          item = New ListViewItem(Format(.Item("PaymentDate"), _
            " MM/dd/yyyy"))
          lvwPayments.Items.Add(item)
          item.SubItems.Add(.Item("MemberId"))
          item.SubItems.Add(FormatNumber(.Item("Amount")))
      End With
    Next i
End Sub
```

We did a bit of fancy formatting of the PaymentDate field to make it line up properly in the ListView columns.

Step 8. Insert the following code into the Form_Load procedure, which fills the dataset, sets the DataView's Sort property, and fills the ListView:

```
daPayments.Fill(DsPayments1)
dvPayments.Sort = "PaymentDate"
FillListView()
SortAscending = True
LastColumn = 0
```

Step 9. Run the program and confirm that the rows are sorted in ascending order by payment date. Wasn't that easy? Return to design mode.

Step 10. You must add code to sort the data on any column the user chooses. Insert the following two lines in the form's declarations area. The first is a toggle that helps us decide whether to sort in ascending or descending order. The second variable keeps track of the last column selected by the user:

```
Private SortAscending As Boolean
Private LastColumn As Integer
```

Step 11. When the user clicks on a column heading, the ListView's **ColumnClick** event handler is called. Find the procedure and insert the following code:

```
Dim FieldArray As String() = {"PaymentDate","MemberId","Amount"}
If e.Column = LastColumn Then SortAscending = Not SortAscending
```

The first line declares an array of strings containing the names of the table fields, in the same order as the ListView column headings. The second line reverses the sort order if the user clicks twice in a row on the same column heading.

Step 12. The next few lines (same procedure) modify the Sort property of the DataView. For an ascending sort, we use the field name optionally followed by " ASC". For a descending sort, follow the field name with " DESC":

```
If SortAscending Then
    dvPayments.Sort = FieldArray(e.Column) & " ASC"
Else
    dvPayments.Sort = FieldArray(e.Column) & " DESC"
End If
```

In case you're wondering where the ASC and DESC came from, it's part of standard SQL syntax, in the ORDER BY clause. SQL is everywhere in ADO.NET.

Step 13. The last two lines in the same procedure fill the ListView control and copy the current ListView column number into our variable named LastColumn:

```
FillListView()
LastColumn = e.Column
```

In the ColumnClick event handler, the parameter named **e** is a ColumnClickEventArgs object. It has a property named **Column** that indicates which column number was clicked. Columns are numbered starting at zero.

Step 14. Save and run the program. Click on various columns, and note that if you click on the same column twice, it reverses the sort direction. A complete listing of the program appears in Code Listing 4-3.

(End of tutorial)

Code Listing 4-3 (Karate Payments)

```
Public Class frmPayments
    Inherits System.Windows.Forms.Form

+ Windows Form Designer generated code

    Private SortAscending As Boolean
    Private LastColumn As Integer

    Sub FillListView()
        lvwPayments.Items.Clear()
        Dim count As Integer = dvPayments.Count
        Dim i As Integer
        Dim item As ListViewItem

        For i = 0 To count - 1
            With dvPayments(i)
                item = New ListViewItem(Format(.Item("PaymentDate"), _
                 " MM/dd/yyyy"))
                lvwPayments.Items.Add(item)
                item.SubItems.Add(.Item("MemberId"))
                item.SubItems.Add(FormatNumber(.Item("Amount")))
            End With
        Next i
    End Sub
```

```
    Private Sub Form1_Load(ByVal sender As System.Object, _
     ByVal e As System.EventArgs) Handles MyBase.Load

       daPayments.Fill(DsPayments1)
       dvPayments.Sort = "PaymentDate"
       FillListView()
       SortAscending = True
       LastColumn = 0
    End Sub

    Private Sub lvwPayments_ColumnClick(ByVal sender As Object, _
     ByVal e As System.Windows.Forms.ColumnClickEventArgs) _
     Handles lvwPayments.ColumnClick

       'Array containing the table field names (from the data adapter)
       Dim FieldArray As String() = {"PaymentDate", "MemberId", "Amount"}

       'If the same column was clicked twice in a row, reverse
       'the sort order
       If e.Column = LastColumn Then SortAscending = Not SortAscending

       'Each column header's Text property corresponds to a table column name:
       If SortAscending Then
          dvPayments.Sort = FieldArray(e.Column) & " ASC"
       Else
          dvPayments.Sort = FieldArray(e.Column) & " DESC"
       End If

       FillListView()
       LastColumn = e.Column
    End Sub
End Class
```

Checkpoint

4.6 For a DataView named dvMembers, show how to modify its properties to sort on the LastName field.

4.7 How does a program using a DataView know which table and dataset it will be reading?

4.8 Show an example of sorting a DataView named dvEmployees in descending order by Salary.

4.9 Show how to get the LastName column value from row 5 of the dvEmployees table.

4.10 What advantage does a DataView have over a dataset when filling a ListView control?

▶4.3 Three-Tier Sports Rental Income

 RentalIncome

Chapter 1 introduced the *three-tier application* concept in which programs are divided into three *tiers*, or *layers*: Presentation, Business, and Data. Many software design experts believe that clear separations between tiers permit software to be more easily maintained, and improve the reuse of software components. Using what you have learned about databases in this chapter, you should be able to create a Data tier that encapsulates a database connection. Use a Component class when creating the data tier. It is the same as an ordinary class, except that it holds data-related controls such as DataConnections, DataAdapters, DataSets, and DataViews.

Classes in the Business tier often use properties and methods to provide class users with an abstracted view of the program's data. Rules can be implemented to provide an extra layer of validation of data properties, and properties can be added that result from calculations rather than database fields. Classes in this tier provide services to the Presentation tier, but they do not generate any visual output.

Classes in the Presentation tier communicate only with Business-tier classes. For this reason, the Presentation classes often do not need to know specific database field names. Code written in this tier is almost completely focused on the visual user interface.

Sports Rental Income Program

In the next few tutorials, we will interactively build an application that reads the Sports Rental database and displays information calculated from the Items table (Figure 4-11). We would like to compare the income received when the store rents items by the day, versus renting by the week. For each item category, we should know how the rental income varies depending on the number of days per week the item is rented. In addition, we want to display totals for all items, rented both daily and weekly.

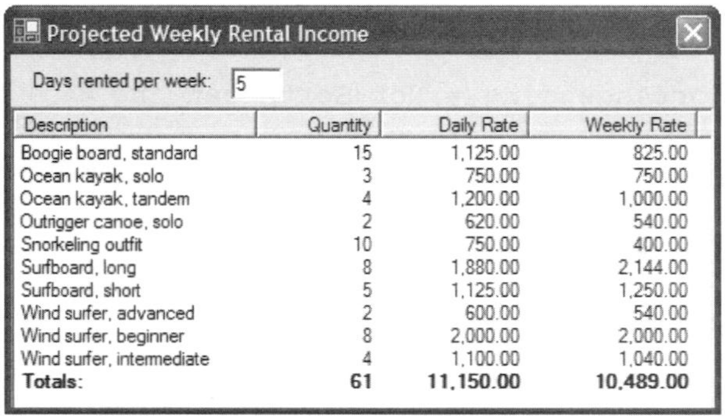

Description	Quantity	Daily Rate	Weekly Rate
Boogie board, standard	15	1,125.00	825.00
Ocean kayak, solo	3	750.00	750.00
Ocean kayak, tandem	4	1,200.00	1,000.00
Outrigger canoe, solo	2	620.00	540.00
Snorkeling outfit	10	750.00	400.00
Surfboard, long	8	1,880.00	2,144.00
Surfboard, short	5	1,125.00	1,250.00
Wind surfer, advanced	2	600.00	540.00
Wind surfer, beginner	8	2,000.00	2,000.00
Wind surfer, intermediate	4	1,100.00	1,040.00
Totals:	**61**	**11,150.00**	**10,489.00**

Days rented per week: 5

Figure 4-11 Weekly Sports Rental Income.

Theoretically, it would be possible to build this program using only Data and Presentation tiers, but that approach would force us to decide where to perform application-related calculations. If placed in the Data tier, the calculations would render the Data tier unsuited to other programs that need to use the Items table. If the calculations were located in the Presentation tier, they would be almost unusable in any other program because they would be closely associated with user interface controls. Our program will benefit from using a Business tier to perform calculations.

Creating the Data and Business Tiers

Data Tier (SportsRental Class)

The goal of this tutorial is to create a generic, portable data component for the SportsRental database. The component could be inserted into any other program that needs the same data. The component will hold DataConnection, DataView, and DataSet objects relating to the Items table in the SportsRental database. Its only public property will be a reference to a DataSet object.

You will create a separate folder within the project to hold the SportsRental class. (Later, we may decide to include this folder in another program that uses the same data.)

Step 1. Create a new Windows Application program named **RentalIncome**. Set Option Strict = On in the Project Properties window.

Step 2. From the Server Explorer, create a connection to the **SportsRental.mdb** database.

Step 3. In the Solution Explorer, right-click on the Project name, select **Add**, and select **New Folder**. Name the folder **SportsRental**.

Step 4. Right-click on the new folder and select **Add Component** from the context menu. Name the new component **SportsRental**.

Step 5. Drag the Items table from the Server Explorer into the SportsRental component's designer window. Rename the connection to **conSportsRental**. Rename the data adapter to **daItems**.

Step 6. Right-click on **daItems** and generate a dataset class named **dsItems**. Before clicking on OK, place a check next to *Add this dataset to the designer*.

Step 7. In the Code view for SportsRental.vb, expand the section labeled "Component designer generated code." Find the class constructor (New) and look for the following comment line:

```
'Add any initialization after the InitializeComponent() call
```

Insert the following statement after the comment line, and collapse the Component designer generated code area when you're done.

```
daItems.Fill(DsItems1)
```

Step 8. Add a read-only property named ItemsDs that returns a reference to the DsItems1 dataset:

```
Public ReadOnly Property ItemsDs() As dsItems
    Get
        Return DsItems1
    End Get
End Property
```

Step 9. Build the program to check for any syntax errors, and save it one more time.

Business Tier (Items Class)

The Business tier consists of a class named **Items** that performs application-specific calculations and provides access to columns from the Items table. The Items class will be added to the SportsRental project folder, along with the SportsRental class we just created.

Step 1. In the Solution Explorer, right-click the SportsRental folder, select **Add Class**, and add a new class to the folder named **Items**.

Step 2. Add the following declaration to the class, which creates an instance of SportsRental and copies its ItemsDs property (a strongly typed dataset) into the mItemsDs variable:

```
Private mItemsDs As dsItems = New SportsRental().ItemsDs
```

We did not declare mItemsDs as a DataSet because the more specific type (dsItems) contains an Items property (a DataTable). The Items property gives us direct access to properties that match database field names such as description, quantity, and daily_rate.

Step 3. Declare and initialize a DataView component named dvItems:

```
Private WithEvents dvItems As DataView = New DataView()
```

Step 4. Create **mPosition**, which tracks the current row position within the DataView, much like CurrencyManager.Position did when we worked with bound controls in Chapter 3. Create **mCurrentRow**, which contains the contents of the row of the DataView indexed by mPosition:

```
Private mPosition As Integer = 0
Private mCurrentRow As DataRowView
```

Step 5. Create three variables, which will be calculated and returned as property values by this class:

```
Private mTotalQuantity As Integer
Private mTotalDailyRevenue As Single
Private mTotalWeeklyRevenue As Single
```

Step 6. The class constructor sets the Table and Sort properties of the DataView and fills the current row with data at the starting row position (mPosition). Totals are calculated:

```
Public Sub New()
    dvItems.Table = mItemsDs.Items
    dvItems.Sort = "description"
    mCurrentRow = dvItems(mPosition)
    CalculateTotals()
End Sub
```

Step 7. The Count and Position properties permit the client program to find out how many rows are in the DataView, and either get or set the current row number:

```
Public ReadOnly Property Count() As Integer
    Get
        Return dvItems.Count
    End Get
End Property

Public Property Position() As Integer
    Get
        Return mPosition
    End Get
    Set(ByVal Value As Integer)
        If Value >= 0 And Value < dvItems.Count Then
            mPosition = Value
            mCurrentRow = dvItems(mPosition)
        End If
    End Set
End Property
```

Step 8. A number of properties set and get specific column values from the current row. One example is the ItemID property, which returns the value of the item_id column. The property name and the column name do not have to be the same:

```
Public ReadOnly Property ItemID() As Integer
    Get
        Return CInt(mCurrentRow.Item("item_id"))
    End Get
End Property
```

The cast function (CInt) is required here and for all other column values because the Item method in the DataRowView class returns an Object. When Option Strict is On, you cannot directly assign an Object to another type.

Many property procedures in this class make references to mCurrentRow.Item( ). Because Item is the default property of a DataRowView, you can simplify the expression as: mCurrentRow( ). For example, mCurrentRow("item_id") returns the item_id column value.

Step 9. Another field-related property is Description:

```
Public Property Description() As String
   Get
      Return CStr(mCurrentRow("description"))
   End Get
   Set(ByVal Value As String)
      mCurrentRow("description") = Value
   End Set
End Property
```

One small disadvantage to providing column names as strings is that the program would throw an exception if the actual column name (in the database) were to change. Some developers prefer a more object-oriented way to specify column names:

```
Public Property Description() As String
  Get
    Return CStr(mCurrentRow.Item(mItemsDs.Items.descriptionColumn.ToString()))
  End Get
  Set(ByVal Value As String)
     mCurrentRow.Item(mItemsDs.Items.descriptionColumn.ToString()) = Value
  End Set
End Property
```

(You can decide how you want to code the remaining column properties. Our examples will use the string approach.)

Step 10. Following are property procedures for the remaining columns:

```
Public Property DailyRate() As Single
   Get
      Return CSng(mCurrentRow("daily_rate"))
   End Get
   Set(ByVal Value As Single)
      mCurrentRow("daily_rate") = Value
   End Set
End Property

Public Property WeeklyRate() As Single
   Get
      Return CSng(mCurrentRow("weekly_rate"))
   End Get
   Set(ByVal Value As Single)
      mCurrentRow("weekly_rate") = Value
   End Set
End Property

Public Property MonthlyRate() As Single
   Get
      Return CSng(mCurrentRow("monthly_rate"))
   End Get
   Set(ByVal Value As Single)
      mCurrentRow("monthly_rate") = Value
   End Set
End Property
```

```
Public Property Quantity() As Integer
    Get
        Return CInt(mCurrentRow("quantity"))
    End Get
    Set(ByVal Value As Integer)
        mCurrentRow("quantity") = Value
    End Set
End Property
```

Step 11. Add various calculated properties useful to client programs: DailyRevenue, WeeklyRevenue, TotalQuantity, TotalDailyRevenue, and TotalWeeklyRevenue:

```
'Revenue earned by all items of the same type in a day.
Public ReadOnly Property DailyRevenue() As Single
    Get
        Return DailyRate * Quantity
    End Get
End Property


'Revenue earned by all items of the same type in a week.
Public ReadOnly Property WeeklyRevenue() As Single
    Get
        Return WeeklyRate * Quantity
    End Get
End Property


'Total quantity of all rental items.
Public ReadOnly Property TotalQuantity() As Integer
    Get
        Return mTotalQuantity
    End Get
End Property


'Total revenue earned in a single day when all items
'are rented.
Public ReadOnly Property TotalDailyRevenue() As Single
    Get
        Return mTotalDailyRevenue
    End Get
End Property


'Total revenue earned in a single week when all items
'are rented.
Public ReadOnly Property TotalWeeklyRevenue() As Single
    Get
        Return mTotalWeeklyRevenue
    End Get
End Property
```

Step 12. Add a private method that accumulates totals:

```
Private Sub CalculateTotals()
   Dim i As Integer
   mPosition = 0
   mTotalQuantity = 0
   mTotalDailyRevenue = 0
   mTotalWeeklyRevenue = 0
   For i = 0 To Count - 1
      mTotalQuantity += Quantity
      mTotalDailyRevenue += DailyRevenue
      mTotalWeeklyRevenue += WeeklyRevenue
      mPosition += 1
   Next i
End Sub
```

Step 13. Build the program to check for syntax errors, and save it one more time.

You are finished creating the Business tier of the Sports Rental Income application. All this hard work will have benefits, because you can easily lift out the data and business classes from this program and use them in other programs. You might later customize the Items class by providing ways to sort on different columns, but the existing properties and methods should always be useful. Next, we begin the Presentation tier, which is very simple.

Adding the Presentation Tier

The presentation tier consists of controls and code written in the program's startup form. Table 4-2 lists the controls used on this form.

Step 1. Open the RentalIncome program and rename the startup form to **frmRentalIncome.vb**. Change the Project's startup object setting to the same name.

Step 2. Place a label and text box named **txtDaysRented** at the top of the form, as in Figure 4-12. Set the form's caption property as shown in the figure.

Step 3. Place a ListView control on the form and name it **lvwItems**. Set its column values as shown in Table 4-2. All columns are right-aligned except for Description.

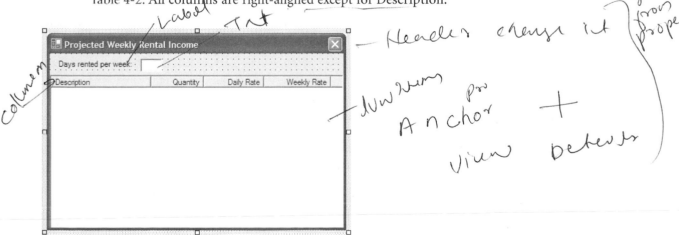

Figure 4-12 The frmRentalIncome form, design view.

Table 4-2

Control Properties, frmMain.

Control Type	Name	Properties
Label	(default)	Text: "Days rented per week"
		TextAlign: MiddleRight
TextBox	txtDaysRented	Text: (blank)
ListView	lvwItems	Anchor: Top, Bottom, Left, Right
		Columns: Description, Quantity, Daily Rate, Weekly Rate
		View: Details

Step 4. In the Code window, declare an Items object that provides all the properties and methods of the business tier. Add a variable to hold the number of days rented:

```
Private objItems As New Items
Private mDaysRented As Integer = 5
```

Step 5. Insert the following line in the frmMain_Load procedure:

```
txtDaysRented.Text = mDaysRented
```

Cleass

Step 6. Whenever the user modifies the number in the txtDaysRented text box, the program must redisplay the contents of the ListView control. Therefore, create a **txtDaysRented_TextChanged** event handler containing the following line:

```
FillListView()
```

Step 7. Begin writing the main driver procedure, named **FillListView**. We will build it in stages and explain each part. First, if the text box contains a valid number, store its integer value in **mDaysRented**. Then the contents of the ListView are cleared:

```
Private Sub FillListView()
   If IsNumeric(txtDaysRented.Text) Then
      mDaysRented = CInt(txtDaysRented.Text)
   End If
   lvwItems.Items.Clear()
```

Step 8. The procedure loops through the Items table, adding a row to the ListView on each pass. The ListView row contains an item description, quantity on hand, daily revenue times the days rented, and weekly revenue:

```
Dim item As ListViewItem
With objItems
   Dim i As Integer
   For i = 0 To .Count - 1
      .Position = i
      item = New ListViewItem(.Description)
      lvwItems.Items.Add(item)
      item.SubItems.Add(CStr(.Quantity))
      item.SubItems.Add(FormatNumber(.DailyRevenue * mDaysRented))
      item.SubItems.Add(FormatNumber(.WeeklyRevenue))
   Next i
End With
```

It might be helpful here to remember the purpose of the columns. We want to know how much revenue is generated by renting items daily, depending on the number of days per week we keep them rented. If we rent items five days a week, for example, we will earn five times the daily revenue. That amount is compared to revenue calculated using the weekly rental rate for the same item type.

Step 9. Concluding the FillListView procedure, you need to add a row to the end of the ListView that displays the total quantity on hand, the total daily revenue times days rented, and the total weekly revenue:

```
item = New ListViewItem("Totals:")
item.Font = New Font(item.Font, FontStyle.Bold)
lvwItems.Items.Add(item)
item.SubItems.Add(CStr(objItems.TotalQuantity))
item.SubItems.Add(FormatNumber(objItems.TotalDailyRevenue *
    mDaysRented))
item.SubItems.Add(FormatNumber(objItems.TotalWeeklyRevenue))
End Sub
```

(We showed how to set font properties for a ListViewItem in Chapter 2.)

Step 10. Run the program and compare your output to that shown earlier in Figure Figure 4-11. Experiment by changing the number of days rented to a value between zero and seven. Note the differences in daily rental income. How many days per week, minimum, do you need to rent in order to equal the weekly revenue?

(End of tutorial)

Checkpoint

4.11 Name the tiers in a typical three-tier application.

4.12 DataAdapter objects belong in which application tier?

4.13 (yes/no) When you write code in the Presentation tier, should it reflect a knowledge of specific database field names?

4.14 (yes/no) Is it possible to use a DataView control in a non-component class?

4.15 In the Sports Rental Income application, name the tier to which each of the classes belongs.

▶ 4.4 Sports Rental Checkout Example

 RentalCheckout

In this section, we will design an important part of a sporting goods rental application. The task we will implement is the rental checkout procedure, which takes place when a customer rents some equipment. The clerk, who is operating the computer, conducts all user input. The project will be named **RentalCheckout**.

Let's construct a *scenario*, or series of steps that describe the likely input by the sales clerk and the responses given by the program. The description is kept as general as possible, to avoid referring to specific user interface controls such as buttons and combo boxes. The equipment rental checkout procedure is divided into two subtasks: first to input the username and password, and second to create a rental invoice.

Main task: Equipment rental checkout procedure

Subtask: The clerk enters a username and password

1. The program displays a dialog window containing a list of employee names.

2. The clerk selects a name from the list and inputs a corresponding user password.

3. The program checks the password against the database and does one of the following:

   ◆ If the password is correct, the program closes the login window and proceeds to the next subtask.

   ◆ If the password is incorrect, the program displays an error message and asks the clerk to reenter the password. The clerk is given three tries before the program ends.

Subtask: The clerk creates a Rental Invoice

1. The clerk selects the customer's name from a list.

2. The program displays the current customer information.

3. The clerk selects a rental item from a list of item descriptions.

4. The program displays the selected item's price and quantity information.

5. The clerk enters the anticipated rental duration, in days.

6. The program calculates the suggested prepayment amount (only daily rental rates are used.

7. The clerk optionally modifies the prepayment amount or any other input fields.

8. The clerk confirms the rental.

9. The program verifies that all required entries have been completed and displays a message indicating which, if any entry fields are missing.

10. If the verification in the previous step is successful, the program displays and prints a rental checkout invoice listing the date, time, customer name, employee name, item description, daily rental rate, prepayment amount, and rental duration, in days. The clerk can do one of the following:

◆ Clear all entries and prepare for a new rental

◆ Log out

◆ Terminate the program.

A scenario like this cannot anticipate every possible action on the part of the user, nor can it anticipate error conditions. It can, however, provide an excellent guide for designing the user interface. Before we take the latter step, let's examine the database used by both this program and related programs we will write later.

Sports Rental Database Design

The Sports Rental database consists of five tables, listed below:

Table Name	Description
Customers	Customer information such as name and phone.
Employees	Employee identification and logon information.
Items	Items currently available for rental.
RentalsOut	Items that are currently checked out.
RentalsIn	Items that were rented and later returned.

Figures 4-13, 4-14, 4-15, 4-16, and 4-17 contain individual database table descriptions.

Field Name	Type	Description
customer_id	Long Integer	Unique record key
first_name	Text	Customer's first name
last_name	Text	Customer's last name
phone	Text	Customer phone (999-999-9999)
total_rentals	Currency	Total dollar amount of past rentals

Figure 4-13 Customers table.

Field Name	Type	Description
emp_id	Long Integer	Unique record key
last_name	Text	Employee's last name
password	Text	Logon password

Figure 4-14 Employees table.

Field Name	Type	Description
item_id	Long Integer	Unique record key
description	Text	Description of item
daily_rate	Currency	Daily rental rate
weekly_rate	Currency	Weekly rental rate
monthly_rate	Currency	Monthly rental rate
quantity	Integer	Number of available items of this type

Figure 4-15 Items table.

Field Name	Type	Description
rental_id	Long Integer	Unique record key
item_id	Long Integer	Foreign key, links to Items table
customer_id	Long Integer	Foreign key, links to Customers table
emp_id	Long Integer	Foreign key, links to Employees table
date_out	Date/Time	Date and time when item was checked out
duration	Integer	Expected rental duration, in days
prepayment	Currency	Amount prepaid by customer

Figure 4-16 RentalsOut table.

Field Name	Type	Description
rental_id	Long Integer	Unique record key
item_id	Long Integer	Foreign key, links to Items table
customer_id	Long Integer	Foreign key, links to Customers table
emp_id	Long Integer	Foreign key, links to Employees table
date_out	Date/Time	Date and time when item was checked out
date_ret	Date/Time	Date and time when item was checked in
amt_paid	Currency	Amount paid by customer for the rental

Figure 4-17   RentalsIn table.

Relationships in the Sports Rental Database

Figure 4-18 shows a total of six one-to-many relationships between tables in the Sports Rental database. The following table lists the linking key field in each relationship:

Parent (record key)	Child (foreign key)
Customers (customer_id)	RentalsOut (customer_id)
Customers (customer_id)	RentalsIn (customer_id)
Employees (emp_id)	RentalsOut (emp_id)
Employees (emp_id)	RentalsIn (emp_id)
Items (item_id)	RentalsOut (item_id)
Items (item_id)	RentalsIn (item_id)

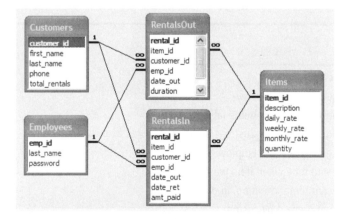

Figure 4-18   SportsRental table relationships.

User Interface Design

The user interface for this program could be designed in many ways, so let us start with a few criteria that we can apply to the design:

- ◆ The program should prevent data entry by unathorized persons.
- ◆ The clerk should be able to fill out a rental form in less than 30 seconds.
- ◆ The number of screen controls and display items should be kept to a minimum.
- ◆ Because of high turnover among sales clerks, the program should be easy to learn.
- ◆ Cash and credit card transactions will be handled outside the program.

When the program starts, the user has only two options: Log in, or exit (Figure 4-19). Unauthorized users will not be able to view sensitive information or input data.

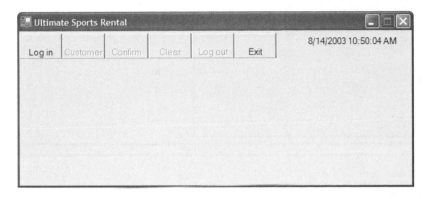

Figure 4-19 Program startup window.

The sales clerk login will be handled by a separate dialog window (Figure 4-20). The clerk selects their last name from a combo box and a password is entered into a text box. Code inside the Login window validates the password and permits the user a limited number of invalid password attempts. If the clerk cancels the login dialog, control returns to the program startup window, with no changes to the toolbar buttons. The following names and passwords are in the Employees table.

emp_id	last_name	password
1	Brewer	c
2	Jacobs	d
3	Alter	b
4	Aipa	a
5	Lopez	e
6	Yates	f

Figure 4-20 Logging in the sales clerk.

After the clerk has logged in, the remaining toolbar buttons are activated (Figure 4-21) and the clerk's name appears in the form's caption bar. The clerk proceeds to the next step, which is to select a customer name from a combo box located in a separate dialog window (Figure 4-22).

Figure 4-21 Sales clerk is logged in.

Figure 4-22 Customer selection dialog.

After the clerk selects a customer name, information from the customer's database record is displayed in a single-line DataGrid control (Figure 4-23). At the same time, a new combo box containing a list of rental items appears.

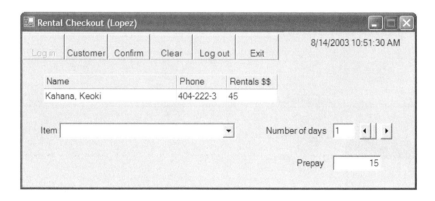

Figure 4-23 A customer has been selected.

When the clerk selects a rental item description from the combo box, the program displays the item's price and available quantity in another DataGrid (Figure 4-24). The program uses the item's daily price and number of days to calculate the suggested prepayment amount.

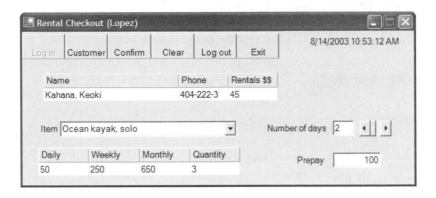

Figure 4-24 Rental item selected.

The clerk can enter the number of rental days in a text box, or use the horizontal scroll bar to increase and reduce the number of days. The clerk can also change the amount in the Prepay box, in case the customer decides to pay a different amount. (The balance due will be collected when the item is returned.)

When the clerk has entered all relevant data, he/she clicks on the Confirm button. The program displays a separate window containing a rental invoice (Figure 4-25). The clerk can manually edit this window and insert comments.

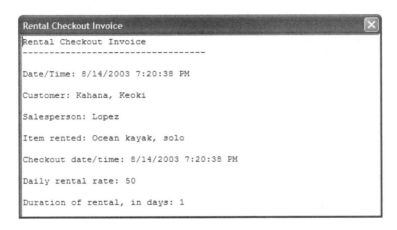

Figure 4-25 Rental invoice.

The Invoice window has a File menu containing Print and Close commands. When the clerk selects Print, a copy of the invoice is sent to the default printer.

Data-Related and Visual Components

The program's startup form is frmRental, shown in Figure 4-26 in design mode.

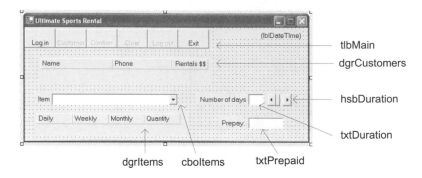

Figure 4-26 The frmRental form (design mode)

The form's components are listed in Table 4-3. The form is easy to set up, given the experience gained from the programs in Chapter 3. Table 4-4 lists the controls and properties found in the frmRental form.

Table 4-3

Components in the frmRental form.

Name	Type	Description
conSportsRental	Connection	Connects to the SportsRental.mdb database (Microsoft Access)
daCustomers	DataAdapter	Selects all columns from the Customers table
daEmployees	DataAdapter	Selects all columns from the Employees table, sorted on last_name
daItems	DataAdapter	Selects all columns from the Items table, sorted by description
DsCustomers1	dsCustomers	Dataset generated from daCustomers
DsEmployees1	dsEmployees	Dataset generated from daEmployees
DsItems1	dsItems	Dataset generated from daItems
dvCustomers	DataView	Connected to DsCustomers1.Customers
dvItems	DataView	Connected to DsItems1.Items
Timer1	Timer	Refreshes date/time display every 1000 milliseconds

The dsCustomers dataset includes an expression field (full_name) that concatenates the fname and lname columns from the customers table. (You can view its structure by opening *dsCustomers.xsd* from the Solution Explorer Window.)

Table 4-4

Controls in the frmRental form.

Name	Type	Properties
frmRental	Form	FormBorderStyle: FixedSingle
		MaximizeBox: False
		Text: Ultimate Sports Rental
tlbMain	ToolBar	Dock = none
tlbLogin	ToolBarButton	Tag: login
		Text: Log in

(table continues)

Table 4-4

Controls in the frmRental form. *(continued)*

tlbCustomer	ToolBarButton	Tag: customer
		Text: Customer
tlbConfirm	ToolBarButton	Tag: confirm
		Text: Confirm
tlbClear	ToolBarButton	Tag: clear
		Text: Clear
tlbLogout	ToolBarButton	Tag: logout
		Text: Log out
tlbExit	ToolBarButton	Tag: exit
		Text: Exit
lblDateTime	Label	
dgrCustomers	DataGrid	BackgroundColor: Control
		BorderStyle: None
		CaptionVisible: False
		DataSource: dvCustomers
		ReadOnly: True
		TableStyle/MappingName: Customers
		GridColumnStyle/MappingNames:
		full_name, phone, total_rentals
		Visible: False
dgrItems	DataGrid	BackgroundColor: Control
		BorderStyle: None
		CaptionVisible: False
		DataSource: dvItems
		ReadOnly: True
		TableStyle/MappingName: Items
		GridColumnStyle/MappingNames:
		daily_rate, weekly_rate, monthly_rate, quantity
		Visible: False
cboItems	ComboBox	DataSource: DsItems1.Items
		DisplayMember: description
		DropDownStyle: DropDownList
		ValueMember: Items.item_id
lblDuration	Label	Text: Number of days
lblPrepay	Label	Text: Prepaid
txtDuration	TextBox	
txtPrepaid	TextBox	
hsbDuration	HScrollBar	LargeChange: 5
		Minimum: 1
		Value: 1

The Visible properties of the two DataGrid controls must be set to False in design mode to prevent vertical scroll bars from appearing next to them when the controls are made visible at runtime.

Table 4-5 lists the controls found in the **frmLogin** form, used for entering the clerk's name and password.

Table 4-5

Controls in the frmLogin form.

Name	Type	Properties
cboName	ComboBox	DropDownStyle: DropDownList
txtPassword	TextBox	PasswordChar: *
btnOK	Button	Text: OK
btnCancel	Button	Text: Cancel
frmLogin	Form	AcceptButton: btnOK
		CancelButton: btnCancel
		ControlBox: False
		FormBorderStyle: FixedDialog
		Text: Sales Clerk Login

The frmInvoice form (Table 4-6) has a text box named txtPassword that fills the entire form. The form also has a MainMenu component and a PrintDocument component. (For more information on using PrintDocument objects, see *Starting Out with Visual Basic .NET*, page 573.)

Table 4-6

Controls in the frmInvoice form.

Name	Type	Properties
txtReport	TextBox	Anchor: top, bottom, left, right
		MultiLine: True
		ScrollBars: Vertical
frmInvoice	Form	ControlBox: False
		Font: Courier New, 10 pt
		Menu: MainMenu1
		Text: Rental Checkout Invoice
MainMenu1	MainMenu	
mnuFilePrint	Menu Item	ShortCut: CtrlP
		Text: &Print
mnuFileClose	MenuItem	ShortCut: CtrlX
		Text: &Close
pdPrint	PrintDocument	DocumentName: Rental Checkout Invoice

The frmCustomer form (Table 4-7) lets the user select a customer by name from a combo box. It also has a Cancel button that lets the user close the dialog without making a choice.

Table 4-7

Controls in the frmCustomer form.

Name	Type	Properties
frmCustomer	Form	CancelButton: btnCancel
		ControlBox: False
		FormBorderStyle: FixedDialog
		Text: Select Customer
btnCancel	Button	DialogResult: Cancel
		Text: Cancel
cboNames	ComboBox	DropDownStyle: DropDownList
dvCustomers	DataView	

frmRental Class

Let's examine the code in the frmRental class, taking time to understand the details. It contains a number of class-level variables, primarily used to hold the database values collected from the user:

```
Const DEFAULT_DURATION As Integer = 1
Private bmSelectingItems As Boolean
Private mPrepayAmount As Decimal
Private mDailyRate As Decimal
Private mDuration As Integer
Private mItemDescription As String
Private mRentalDate As Date
Private mCustomerName As String
Private mEmployeeID As Integer
Private mEmployeeName As String
```

We have added an enumeration named **tb** to help identify the toolbar buttons. Each enumeration constant corresponds with the index position of a button in the toolbar:

```
Private Enum tb    'Toolbar button indices
   login = 0
   customer = 1
   confirm = 2
   clear = 3
   logout = 4
   [exit] = 5
End Enum
```

The Tick event handler for the Timer control updates the current date/time display in the upper-right corner of the form once each second:

```
lblDateTime.Text = CStr(Now)
```

Load Event Handler

The form's Load event handler fills the three datasets (DsEmployees1, DsCustomers1, and DsItems1), and calls a procedure named ClearFields that resets a number of important controls and class-level variables to default values:

```
daEmployees.Fill(DsEmployees1)
daCustomers.Fill(DsCustomers1)
daItems.Fill(DsItems1)
ClearFields()
```

SelectedIndexChanged

When a SelectedIndexChanged event is fired for the cboItems combo box, we want to know if the user made a selection or if the event fired because of other related form events (such as making the combo box visible). The bmSelectingItems variable is only set to True when the list of rental items has been made visible:

```
If Not bmSelectingItems Then Exit Sub
```

Assuming the user made a selection, we want to filter the DataView control attached to the dgrItems grid so it only displays the selected rental item. We show the grid by setting its Visible property to True:

```
Dim itemID As Integer = CInt(cboItems.SelectedValue)
vItems.RowFilter = "item_id = " & itemID
dgrItems.Visible = True
```

The item description and daily rate values are stored in a single row of the table attached to the dvItems DataView. We can save the values in class-level variables:

```
mItemDescription = CStr(dvItems(0).Item("description"))
mDailyRate = CDec(dvItems(0).Item("daily_rate"))
```

An expressions such as Item("description") returns an Object. It must therefore be cast into a specific type such as String or Decimal before it can be asssigned to a variable. We always set Option Strict to On, which requires type-safe conversions to be used.

The prepayment amount is calculated in a separate procedure, and various controls are made visible so the rental duration and prepayment can be displayed:

```
CalculatePrepayment()
lblDuration.Visible = True
txtDuration.Visible = True
hsbDuration.Visible = True
lblPrepaid.Visible = True
txtPrepaid.Visible = True
```

CalculatePrepayment

The CalculatePrepayment procedure multiplies the daily rental rate by the rental duration, and copies the resulting value to a class-level variable and a text box:

```
Private Sub CalculatePrepayment()
    If dvItems.Count > 0 Then
        mPrepayAmount = mDuration * CDec(dvItems(0).Item("daily_rate"))
        txtPrepaid.Text = FormatCurrency(mPrepayAmount)
    End If
End Sub
```

Rental Duration

The user can change the rental duration by typing a number into a text box or by manipulating a horizontal scroll bar. We have included code that synchronizes the two controls. When the user types in a number, the TextChanged event handler for the text box (txtDuration) verifies that the user entered a numeric value and updates the horizontal scroll bar control. The prepayment amount is also recalculated:

```
If IsNumeric(txtDuration.Text) Then
    mDuration = CInt(txtDuration.Text)
    hsbDuration.Value = mDuration
    CalculatePrepayment()
End If
```

The hsbDuration scroll bar updates the txtDuration text box when the user scrolls the number of days:

```
txtDuration.Text = CStr(hsbDuration.Value)
```

Validating the Order

When all input fields have been entered, the user clicks a button to confirm the rental transaction. This action causes the **Validate_Order** function to be called, which does the following:

◆ Verifies that a customer was selected (mCustomerName is not blank)

◆ Verifies than a rental item was selected (mItemDescription is not blank)

◆ Verifies that the prepayment amount is numeric

◆ Verifies that the rental duration is numeric

The function returns False if (and only if) any of the four tests fail:

```
Private Function Validate_Order() As Boolean
    If mCustomerName = "" Then
        MessageBox.Show("A customer must be selected", "Error")
        Return False
    End If

    If mItemDescription = "" Then
        MessageBox.Show("A rental item must be selected", "Error")
        cboItems.Focus()
        Return False
    End If

    If Not IsNumeric(txtPrepaid.Text) Then
        MessageBox.Show( "The Prepayment amount must be numeric",
            "Error")
        txtPrepaid.Focus()
        txtPrepaid.SelectionStart = 0
        txtPrepaid.SelectionLength = txtPrepaid.Text.Length
        Return False
    End If

    If Not IsNumeric(txtDuration.Text) Then
        MessageBox.Show( "Number of days must be numeric", "Error")
        txtDuration.Focus()
        txtDuration.SelectionStart = 0
        txtDuration.SelectionLength = txtDuration.Text.Length
```

```
            Return False
        End If
        Return True        'success!
    End Function
```

When a text box validation fails, we set the focus back to the text box and highlight the box's contents using the SelectionStart and SelectionLength properties. For more information on selecting text, see *Starting Out with Visual Basic .NET*, page 311.

Class Code Listing

A complete listing of the frmRental class appears in Code Listing 4-4.

Code Listing 4-4 (frmRental class)

```vb
Imports Microsoft.VisualBasic.ControlChars

Public Class frmRental
    Inherits System.Windows.Forms.Form

+ Windows Form Designer generated code

    Const DEFAULT_DURATION As Integer = 1
    Private bmSelectingItems As Boolean
    Private mPrepayAmount As Decimal
    Private mDailyRate As Decimal
    Private mDuration As Integer
    Private mItemDescription As String
    Private mRentalDate As Date
    Private mCustomerName As String
    Private mEmployeeID As Integer
    Private mEmployeeName As String

    Private Enum tb    'Toolbar button indices
        login = 0
        customer = 1
        confirm = 2
        clear = 3
        logout = 4
        [exit] = 5
    End Enum

    Private Sub Timer1_Tick(ByVal sender As System.Object, _
        ByVal e As System.EventArgs) Handles Timer1.Tick
        lblDateTime.Text = CStr(Now)
    End Sub

    Private Sub frmRental_Load(ByVal sender As System.Object, _
        ByVal e As System.EventArgs) Handles MyBase.Load

        daEmployees.Fill(DsEmployees1)
        daCustomers.Fill(DsCustomers1)
        daItems.Fill(DsItems1)
        ClearFields()
    End Sub

    Private Sub cboItems_SelectedIndexChanged(ByVal _
        sender As System.Object, ByVal e As System.EventArgs) _
        Handles cboItems.SelectedIndexChanged
```

```
        If Not bmSelectingItems Then Exit Sub

        'Filter the DataView attached to the dgrItems grid so it
        'displays only the selected rental item.
        Dim itemID As Integer = CInt(cboItems.SelectedValue)
        dvItems.RowFilter = "item_id = " & itemID
        dgrItems.Visible = True
        mItemDescription = CStr(dvItems(0).Item("description"))
        mDailyRate = CDec(dvItems(0).Item("daily_rate"))
        CalculatePrepayment()
        lblDuration.Visible = True
        txtDuration.Visible = True
        hsbDuration.Visible = True
        lblPrepaid.Visible = True
        txtPrepaid.Visible = True
    End Sub

    Private Sub CalculatePrepayment()
        If dvItems.Count > 0 Then
            mPrepayAmount = mDuration * CDec(dvItems(0).Item("daily_rate"))
            txtPrepaid.Text = FormatCurrency(mPrepayAmount)
        End If
    End Sub

    Private Sub txtDuration_TextChanged(ByVal sender As System.Object, _
        ByVal e As System.EventArgs) Handles txtDuration.TextChanged

        If IsNumeric(txtDuration.Text) Then
            mDuration = CInt(txtDuration.Text)
            hsbDuration.Value = mDuration
            CalculatePrepayment()
        End If
    End Sub

    Private Sub hscDuration_Scroll(ByVal sender As System.Object, _
        ByVal e As System.Windows.Forms.ScrollEventArgs) _
        Handles hsbDuration.Scroll
        txtDuration.Text = CStr(hsbDuration.Value)
    End Sub

    Private Function Validate_Order() As Boolean
        If mCustomerName = "" Then
            MessageBox.Show("A customer must be selected", "Error")
            Return False
        End If

        If mItemDescription = "" Then
            MessageBox.Show("A rental item must be selected", "Error")
            cboItems.Focus()
            Return False
        End If

        If Not IsNumeric(txtPrepaid.Text) Then
            MessageBox.Show("The Prepayment amount must be numeric", "Error")
            txtPrepaid.Focus()
            txtPrepaid.SelectionStart = 0
            txtPrepaid.SelectionLength = txtPrepaid.Text.Length
```

```
            Return False
        End If

    If Not IsNumeric(txtDuration.Text) Then
        MessageBox.Show( _
         "Number of days must be numeric", "Error")
        txtDuration.Focus()
        txtDuration.SelectionStart = 0
        txtDuration.SelectionLength = txtDuration.Text.Length
        Return False
    End If
    Return True          'success!
End Function

Private Sub tlbMain_ButtonClick(ByVal sender As System.Object, _
 ByVal e As System.Windows.Forms.ToolBarButtonClickEventArgs) _
 Handles tlbMain.ButtonClick

    Select Case CStr(e.Button.Tag)
        Case "login"
            'Create and show a login dialog. If the password is not
            'entered correctly, exit.
            Dim myLogin As New frmLogin
            myLogin.DsEmployees1 = DsEmployees1
            If myLogin.ShowDialog() = DialogResult.Cancel Then Exit Sub

            'Retrieve the employee's name and ID from the login dialog
            mEmployeeName = myLogin.cboName.Text
            mEmployeeID = myLogin.EmployeeID
            Me.Text = "Rental Checkout (" & mEmployeeName & ")"

            'adjust the toolbar button states
            tlbMain.Buttons(tb.login).Enabled = False
            tlbMain.Buttons(tb.customer).Enabled = True
            tlbMain.Buttons(tb.confirm).Enabled = True
            tlbMain.Buttons(tb.clear).Enabled = True
            tlbMain.Buttons(tb.logout).Enabled = True

        Case "customer"
            'Display a list of all customers & let the user select one
            ClearFields()
            Dim custForm As New frmCustomer
            custForm.dvCustomers.Table = DsCustomers1.Customers
            If custForm.ShowDialog() = DialogResult.OK Then
                Dim custID As Integer = CInt(custForm.cboNames.SelectedValue)
                dvCustomers.RowFilter = "customer_id = " & custID
                mCustomerName = CStr(dvCustomers(0).Item("full_name"))
                dgrCustomers.Visible = True
                cboItems.Visible = True
                lblItem.Visible = True
                cboItems.SelectedIndex = -1
                bmSelectingItems = True
            End If

        Case "confirm"
            If Validate_Order() Then
                mRentalDate = Now
                Dim myInvoice As New frmInvoice
                myInvoice.txtReport.Text = _
```

```
                    "Rental Checkout Invoice" & CrLf _
                  & "────────────────" & CrLf _
                  & CrLf _
                  & "Date/Time: " & Now & CrLf _
                  & CrLf _
                  & "Customer: " & mCustomerName & CrLf _
                  & CrLf _
                  & "Salesperson: " & mEmployeeName & CrLf _
                  & CrLf _
                  & "Item rented: " & mItemDescription & CrLf _
                  & CrLf _
                  & "Checkout date/time: " & mRentalDate & CrLf _
                  & CrLf _
                  & "Daily rental rate: " & FormatCurrency(mDailyRate) & CrLf _
                  & CrLf _
                  & "Duration of rental, in days: " & mDuration & CrLf _
                  & CrLf _
                  & "Prepayment amount: " & FormatCurrency(mPrepayAmount) _
                  & CrLf
                myInvoice.txtReport.SelectionLength = 0
                myInvoice.ShowDialog()
            End If

        Case "clear"
            ClearFields()

        Case "logout"
            tlbMain.Buttons(tb.login).Enabled = True
            tlbMain.Buttons(tb.customer).Enabled = False
            tlbMain.Buttons(tb.confirm).Enabled = False
            tlbMain.Buttons(tb.clear).Enabled = False
            tlbMain.Buttons(tb.logout).Enabled = False
            ClearFields()

        Case "exit"
            Me.Close()
    End Select
End Sub

Private Sub ClearFields()
    bmSelectingItems = False
    txtDuration.Text = CStr(DEFAULT_DURATION)
    cboItems.SelectedIndex = -1
    mCustomerName = ""
    mItemDescription = ""
    dgrCustomers.Visible = False
    cboItems.Visible = False
    dgrItems.Visible = False
    lblItem.Visible = False
    lblDuration.Visible = False
    txtDuration.Visible = False
    hsbDuration.Visible = False
    lblPrepaid.Visible = False
    txtPrepaid.Visible = False
End Sub
End Class
```

ToolBar Click Event

When the user clicks on a ToolBar button, a Select Case statement checks the button's Tag property to determine which action to take. For example, if the Login button is clicked, the program creates and shows the Login dialog window. If the user cancels, no further actions are taken:

```
Select Case CStr(e.Button.Tag)
   Case "login"
       Dim myLogin As New frmLogin()
       myLogin.DsEmployees1 = DsEmployees1
       If myLogin.ShowDialog() = DialogResult.Cancel Then Exit Sub
```

If a valid username and password are entered, we retrieve the employee's name and ID number from the dialog and activate the appropriate toolbar buttons (Customer, Confirm, Clear, and Logout):

```
mEmployeeName = myLogin.cboName.Text
mEmployeeID = myLogin.EmployeeID
Me.Text = "Rental Checkout (" & mEmployeeName & ")"
tlbMain.Buttons(tb.login).Enabled = False
tlbMain.Buttons(tb.customer).Enabled = True
tlbMain.Buttons(tb.confirm).Enabled = True
tlbMain.Buttons(tb.clear).Enabled = True
tlbMain.Buttons(tb.logout).Enabled = True
```

Recall from Chapter 2 that Toolbar buttons can be accessed using their index position in the Buttons array. The indexes used here are from the **tb** Enumeration defined at the top of this class.

After the user logs in and clicks on the Customer toolbar button, the program displays the frmCustomer form. The following code passes the form a reference to the DsCustomers1 dataset so the form can display a list of customer names:

```
Case "customer"
   ClearFields()
   Dim custForm As New frmCustomer()
   custForm.dvCustomers.Table = DsCustomers1.Customers
```

ClearFields was called here, which is the procedure that erases all other selections on the form and hides controls the user should not see.

Once a customer has been selected, the customer ID is available from the combo box in the frmCustomer form. We use the ID to create a row filter for the dvCustomers DataView. The DataView then yields the customer's name:

```
If custForm.ShowDialog() = DialogResult.OK Then
   Dim custID As Integer = CInt(custForm.cboNames.SelectedValue)
   dvCustomers.RowFilter = "customer_id = " & custID
   mCustomerName = CStr(dvCustomers(0).Item("full_name"))
```

This is a good moment to make the dgrCustomers grid and the cboItems combo box visible, and to set the bmSelectingItems switch so we can begin processing SelectedIndexChanged events in the combo box:

```
   dgrCustomers.Visible = True
   cboItems.Visible = True
   lblItem.Visible = True
   cboItems.SelectedIndex = -1
   bmSelectingItems = True
End If
```

The user clicks the Confirm toolbar button when they want to print an invoice. First, we validate the input vields by calling Validate_Order. An instance of the frmInvoice form is created, and it is assigned all the necessary field values to display a report:

```
Case "confirm"
   If Validate_Order() Then
      mRentalDate = Now
      Dim myInvoice As New frmInvoice()
      myInvoice.txtReport.Text = _
       "Rental Checkout Invoice" & CrLf _
       & "——————————" & CrLf _
       & CrLf _
       & "Date/Time: " & Now & CrLf _
       & CrLf _
       & "Customer: " & mCustomerName & CrLf _
       & CrLf _
       & "Salesperson: " & mEmployeeName & CrLf _
       & CrLf _
       & "Item rented: " & mItemDescription & CrLf _
       & CrLf _
       & "Checkout date/time: " & mRentalDate & CrLf _
       & CrLf _
       & "Daily rental rate: " & mDailyRate & CrLf _
       & CrLf _
       & "Duration of rental, in days: " & mDuration & CrLf _
       & CrLf _
       & "Prepayment amount: " & FormatCurrency(mPrepayAmount) _
       & CrLf
      myInvoice.txtReport.SelectionLength = 0
      myInvoice.ShowDialog()
   End If
```

When first testing the program, we noticed that assigning a string to the Text property of the myInvoice.txtReport control (a text box) causes the entire block to be selected. To avoid this effect, SelectionLength is set to zero.

When the user clicks on the Clear toolbar button, we call ClearFields to clear the form:

```
Case "clear"
   ClearFields()
```

When the user clicks on the Logout toolbar button, most of the toolbar buttons are disabled (except for login). We also call ClearFields:

```
Case "logout"
   tlbMain.Buttons(tb.login).Enabled = True
   tlbMain.Buttons(tb.customer).Enabled = False
   tlbMain.Buttons(tb.confirm).Enabled = False
   tlbMain.Buttons(tb.clear).Enabled = False
   tlbMain.Buttons(tb.logout).Enabled = False
   ClearFields()

   Case "exit"
      Me.Close()
End Select
```

ClearFields is called from several different places in this class. As unsightly as it looks, it performs the important task of resetting variables and controls to their starting values. Many of the controls are made invisible, to limit the user's choices when beginning to build a new rental invoice:

```
Private Sub ClearFields()
    bmSelectingItems = False
    txtDuration.Text = CStr(DEFAULT_DURATION)
    cboItems.SelectedIndex = -1
    mCustomerName = ""
    mItemDescription = ""
    dgrCustomers.Visible = False
    cboItems.Visible = False
    dgrItems.Visible = False
    lblItem.Visible = False
    lblDuration.Visible = False
    txtDuration.Visible = False
    hsbDuration.Visible = False
    lblPrepaid.Visible = False
    txtPrepaid.Visible = False
End Sub
End Class
```

frmLogin Class

FindBy<key> Method

Before we look at the implementation of the frmLogin class, we need to digress for a moment and introduce a useful method named **FindBy<key>**. It's syntax is the following:

```
FindBy<key>( <keyvalue> ) As DataRow
```

Its name looks odd because the *<key>* portion is the same as the dataset's primary key. It returns a DataRow object, specific to the dataset's type. The *<keyvalue>* parameter is a primary key value we want to find in the dataset. For example, in the Employees table, the primary key is **emp_id**, so the method in question is named **FindByemp_id**. The following statement searches for an emp_id value of 5 in the DsEmployees1.Employees table and assigns the resulting row to drEmployees:

```
Dim drEmployees As DataRow
drEmployees = DsEmployees1.Employees.FindByemp_id(5)
```

If the given emp_id is not found, drEmployees equals Nothing.

frmLogin Class Implementation

Let's now return to the frmLogin class (Code Listing 4-5) in the Sports Rental Income application. A class-level variable named **mAttempts** counts the number of times the user attempts to enter a password. A class-level variable named **DsEmployees1** holds a reference to the dataset by the same name in the program's startup form. The form's Load event handler sets up the combo box properties needed to display a list of employee last names. The EmployeeID property returns the sales clerk's employee ID value (after logging in) from the emp_id field of the Employees database table.

When the user clicks on OK, the program gets the emp_id value from the combo box and passes it to the FindByemp_id method. The latter returns a matching DataRow from the Employee table, which we use to get the person's password:

```
Dim drEmployees As DataRow
drEmployees = DsEmployees1.Employees.FindByemp_id( _
   CInt(cboName.SelectedValue))
Dim password As String = CStr(drEmployees("password"))
```

If the password input by the user matches the password from the database, the window closes and returns a predefined constant, DialogResult.OK. Otherwise, we increment the number of attempts and wait for the user to try again:

```
If password = txtPassword.Text Then
   Me.DialogResult = DialogResult.OK
   Me.Close()
Else
   MessageBox.Show("Password rejected")
   mAttempts += 1
   If mAttempts = MAX_ATTEMPTS Then Me.Close()
End If
```

If the user clicks on Cancel, the predefined constant DialogResult.Cancel is returned to the caller of ShowDialog.

Code Listing 4-5 (frmLogin Class)

```
Public Class frmLogin
   Inherits System.Windows.Forms.Form

+ Windows Form Designer generated code

   Const MAX_ATTEMPTS As Integer = 3
   Private mAttempts As Integer = 0
   Friend DsEmployees1 As dsEmployees

   Private Sub frmLogin_Load(ByVal sender As System.Object, _
      ByVal e As System.EventArgs) Handles MyBase.Load

      cboName.DataSource = DsEmployees1.Employees
      cboName.DisplayMember = "last_name"
      cboName.ValueMember = "emp_id"
   End Sub

   Public ReadOnly Property EmployeeID() As Integer
      Get
           Return CInt(cboName.SelectedValue)
      End Get
   End Property

   Private Sub btnOK_Click(ByVal sender As System.Object, _
      ByVal e As System.EventArgs) Handles btnOK.Click

      Dim drEmployees As DataRow
      drEmployees = DsEmployees1.Employees.FindByemp_id( _
       CInt(cboName.SelectedValue))
      Dim password As String = CStr(drEmployees("password"))

      If password = txtPassword.Text Then
          Me.DialogResult = DialogResult.OK
```

```
            Me.Close()
        Else
            MessageBox.Show("Password rejected")
            mAttempts += 1
            If mAttempts = MAX_ATTEMPTS Then Me.Close()
        End If
    End Sub

    Private Sub btnCancel_Click(ByVal sender As System.Object, _
      ByVal e As System.EventArgs) Handles btnCancel.Click

        Me.DialogResult = DialogResult.Cancel
        Me.Close()
    End Sub
End Class
```

frmCustomer Class

The frmCustomer class (Code Listing 4-6) defines a form containing a DataView control named dvCustomers, which is initialized from the DsCustomers1 dataset we saw earlier. You may recall the following two lines from the frmRental class that were executed when the user clicked on the **Customer** toolbar button:

```
Dim custForm As New frmCustomer()
custForm.dvCustomers.Table = DsCustomers1.Customers
```

The **mbComboFilled** variable lets us know when the the DataView has filled the combo box and the combo box is ready to respond to user selections. The form's Load event handler sorts the dvCustomers DataView on the full_name column, and initializes the cboNames combo box to the DataView. We set the ValueMember property to make it easy to retrieve the customer ID number when the user makes a selection.

The **SelectedIndexChanged** event fires when the user selects a customer name. We assume the user wants to close the dialog, so we do it for them. The part of the program that displayed this dialog can check the DialogResult property and decide what action to take.

Code Listing 4-6 (frmCustomer class)

```
Public Class frmCustomer
    Inherits System.Windows.Forms.Form

  +─────────────────────────────────────┐
  │ + Windows Form Designer generated code │
  └─────────────────────────────────────┘

    'This form has its own DataView (dvCustomers) that lists the
    'customers in alphabetical order. We could not borrow the DataView
    'from frmRental, because it may have been filtered to show only one
    'customer. Similarly, we could not pass DsCustomers1, because the
    'rows are not sorted.

    Private mbComboFilled As Boolean = False

    Private Sub frmFindCustomer_Load(ByVal sender As System.Object, _
      ByVal e As System.EventArgs) Handles MyBase.Load

        dvCustomers.Sort = "full_name"
        With cboNames
          .DataSource = dvCustomers
          .DisplayMember = "full_name"
          .ValueMember = "customer_id"
          .SelectedIndex = -1
```

```
            End With
            mbComboFilled = True
         End Sub

         Private Sub cboNames_SelectedIndexChanged(ByVal sender As _
            System.Object, ByVal e As System.EventArgs) Handles _
            cboNames.SelectedIndexChanged

            If Not mbComboFilled Or cboNames.SelectedIndex = -1 _
               Then Exit Sub
            Me.DialogResult = DialogResult.OK
            Me.Close()
         End Sub

         Private Sub btnOK_Click(ByVal sender As System.Object, _
            ByVal e As System.EventArgs)
            Me.DialogResult = DialogResult.OK
            Me.Close()
         End Sub

         Private Sub btnCancel_Click(ByVal sender As System.Object, _
            ByVal e As System.EventArgs) Handles btnCancel.Click
            Me.Close()
         End Sub
      End Class
```

frmInvoice Class

Look at the frmInvoice class in Code Listing 4-7. When the user clicks on the File >> Print command, the program executes the **Print** method of the PrintDocument control named pdPrint. The File >> Close event handler closes the form. The PrintPage event handler executes the DrawString method attached to the Graphics property of the object passed as as the parameter named **e**. The printed output for this example is plain, but you could easily format the invoice with different font styles. For more information on printing, see *Starting Out with Visual Basic .NET*, page 573.

Code Listing 4-7 (frmInvoice class)

```
Public Class frmInvoice
   Inherits System.Windows.Forms.Form

 + Windows Form Designer generated code

      Private Sub mnuFilePrint_Click(ByVal sender As System.Object, _
       ByVal e As System.EventArgs) Handles mnuFilePrint.Click

         pdPrint.Print()
      End Sub

      Private Sub mnuFileClose_Click(ByVal sender As System.Object, _
       ByVal e As System.EventArgs) Handles mnuFileClose.Click

         Me.Close()
      End Sub

      Private Sub pdPrint_PrintPage(ByVal sender As Object, _
       ByVal e As System.Drawing.Printing.PrintPageEventArgs) _
        Handles pdPrint.PrintPage
```

```
        e.Graphics.DrawString(txtReport.Text, New Font("Times New Roman", _
          12, FontStyle.Regular), Brushes.Black, 50, 50)
    End Sub
End Class
```

Summary

Details, details. Even a program with a narrowly defined scope such as the Rental Checkout program is not so simple if you make it reasonably robust. You must anticipate the user's actions and provide for every possible sequence of inputs. This program does provide quite a few opportunities for improvement, some of which you might want to pursue:

1. Use various fonts and line spacing in the frmInvoice window to improve the appearance of the displayed and printed reports.

2. Implement exception handling to trap database-related errors.

3. Permit the user to add a new customer to the database if the customer's name does not appear in the existing list of names.

4. Use the type of rental rate (daily, weekly, or monthly) that gives the customer the optimal lowest rental fee.

5. Append the rental invoice information to the RentalsOut database table, shown earlier in Figure 4-16.

Checkpoint

4.16 What was the first step in the scenario created for the Equipment Rental Checkout procedure?

4.17 After selecting the customer's name from a list, what action does the program take?

4.18 When the customer enters the anticipated rental duration, how does the program respond?

4.19 Which table holds information about the sales clerk and his/her password?

4.20 What was the reason for using an Enumeration definition in the program?

4.21 At what point in the program's execution was bmSelectingItems set to True?

▶4.5 Command Objects

Introduction

When you create a data adapter, Visual Studio automatically creates four queries: Select, Update, Insert, and Delete. The latter three require your database table to have a primary key, because they must uniquely identify the table row to be updated, inserted, or deleted.

If you select OleDbDataAdapter from the Data tab of the ToolBox, the Data Adapter Configuration Wizard generates SQL **select**, **insert**, **update**, and **delete** statements and inserts them in your program (see Figure 4-27). In previous examples, we avoided using this wizard by dragging tables directly from Server Explorer onto a form. But it is helpful to note that the SQL statements are inserted directly into a program's code, in the Windows Form Designer Generated Code area. Later, we will show how to use them in programs.

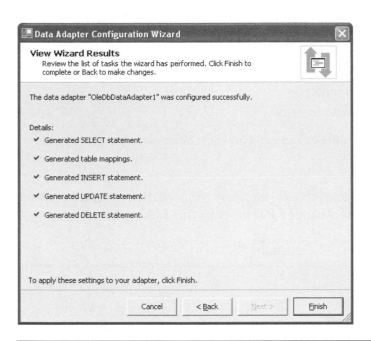

Figure 4-27 Queries generated by the Data Adapter Configuration Wizard.

Direct Updates

Chapter 3 showed how to add and remove rows from datasets. In those examples, the underlying database was not modified immediately; instead, changes were deferred until the corresponding data adapter's Update method was called

It is also possible to update a database table by directly executing queries in Command objects, without involving datasets. The *direct update* approach, as we will call it, has advantages over the deferred update approach used by datasets. Consider the following scenario:

> A certain hotel reservation system has a number of users who are reservations agents. Each has built a dataset filled with a list of available rooms. One agent assigns the last available room to a customer and adds their reservation to the dataset. A few minutes later, when the program updates the underlying database using the data adapter, it turns out that another user has already taken the room. The agent's customer is upset, because they assumed the room was available.

When the dataset update approach is used, it is possible the dataset may contain obsolete data. It must be said that direct updates can create increased network traffic and server requests. In Chapter 9 we will show that direct updates are often preferred in Web-based applications.

Properties

A Command object is used when executing SQL update commands on a database. Table 4-8 lists important Command object properties and methods.

Table 4-8

Command objects.

Name	Description
CommandText property	Gets or sets the SQL statement that will be executed by the command. May also be the name of a stored procedure.
Connection property	Gets or sets the database connection that will be used by this command.
Parameters property	Collection of query parameters.
ExecuteNonQuery method	Executes a query (insert, update, delete) that does not return any rows.
ExecuteReader method	Sends the CommandText to the connection and returns a DataReader object.

There is no actual Command class; instead, there are four different Command-type classes:

◆ OleDbCommand: Used with Microsoft Access connections
◆ SqlCommand: Used with SQL Server connections
◆ OdbcCommand: Used with ODBC connections
◆ OracleCommand: Used with Oracle connections

In this book, we will only use the first two: OleDbCommand and SqlCommand.

Data Adapter Commands

Visual Studio .NET creates four command objects for every data adapter. The data adapter classes (OleDbDataAdapter and SqlDataAdapter) contain the following properties which return command objects that select, insert, delete, and update rows:

Property	Description
SelectCommand	Selects table rows
InsertCommand	Inserts rows into the table
DeleteCommand	Deletes rows from the table
UpdateCommand	Updates table rows

Suppose there is a data adapter named daPayments. The following expression references the command that inserts rows:

```
daPayments.InsertCommand
```

Each command has Parameters property that contains a collection of parameters belonging to the query. When Visual Studio creates a data adapter, it selects parameter names based on the names of the columns used in the query. For example, the Payments table in the Karate database contains columns named Amount, MemberId, and PaymentDate. An update query would choose those names for the query parameters.

You can assign values to query parameters, or retrieve their names and values. The following example copies the names of INSERT query parameters into a listbox named lstParameters:

```
lstParameters.Items.Clear()
Dim param As OleDbParameter
For Each param In daPayments.InsertCommand.Parameters
    lstParameters.Items.Add(param.ParameterName)
Next
```

Example: Karate Commands

KarateCommands

The Karate Commands program displays information about the Command objects inside a data adapter named daPayments. The data adapter is associated with the Payments table in the Karate database. Figure 4-28 lists sample rows from the Payments table. The PaymentId field is an autonumber field, so it is not included in the INSERT INTO statement. Its values are automatically inserted by the database.

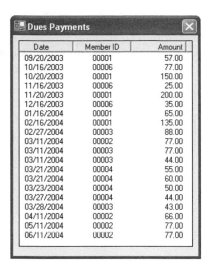

Figure 4-28 Payments table.

In Figure 4-29, the user has selected the InsertCommand property of the data adapter. The program displays the names of the parameters and in the bottom of the window, the text of the query. Figure 4-30 shows the parameters and contents of the DeleteCommand property of the data adapter. The query is somewhat long, because it must check for possible null field values.

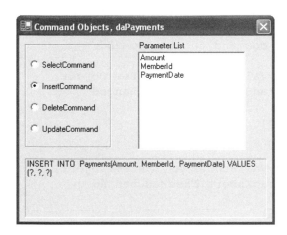

Figure 4-29 Displaying the InsertCommand property

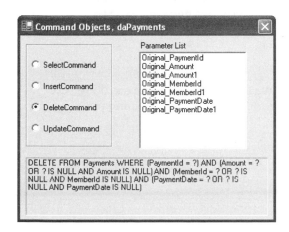

Figure 4-30 Displaying the DeleteCommand property

The RadioButton controls are named radSelect, radInsert, radDelete, and radUpdate. The ListBox control is named lstParameters. The Label control at the bottom is named lblCommandText.

Code Listing 4-8 contains a complete listing of the program, with embedded comments. The System.Data.OleDb namespace is imported because the program makes references to the OleDbParameter class.

Code Listing 4-8 (Karate Commands)

```vb
Imports System.Data.OleDb

Public Class frmMain
    Inherits System.Windows.Forms.Form
```

```
+ Windows Form Designer generated code
```

```vb
    'Display the parameter list and CommandText of a Command object.

    Private Sub showCommand(ByVal cmd As OleDbCommand)
        lstParameters.Items.Clear()
        Dim param As OleDbParameter
        For Each param In cmd.Parameters
            lstParameters.Items.Add(param.ParameterName)
        Next
        lblCommandText.Text = cmd.CommandText
    End Sub


    'For each radio button, access the appropriate Command property of
    'the daPayments data adapter. Pass the command to showCommand.

    Private Sub radSelect_CheckedChanged(ByVal sender As System.Object, _
      ByVal e As System.EventArgs) Handles radSelect.CheckedChanged

        showCommand(daPayments.SelectCommand)
    End Sub

    Private Sub radInsert_CheckedChanged(ByVal sender As System.Object, _
      ByVal e As System.EventArgs) Handles radInsert.CheckedChanged

        showCommand(daPayments.InsertCommand)
    End Sub

    Private Sub radDelete_CheckedChanged(ByVal sender As System.Object, _
      ByVal e As System.EventArgs) Handles radDelete.CheckedChanged

        showCommand(daPayments.DeleteCommand)
    End Sub

    Private Sub radUpdate_CheckedChanged(ByVal sender As System.Object, _
      ByVal e As System.EventArgs) Handles radUpdate.CheckedChanged

        showCommand(daPayments.UpdateCommand)
    End Sub
End Class
```

Inserting Table Rows

The SQL statement INSERT INTO inserts a new row into a table, using the following syntax:

```
INSERT INTO target
[(field1[,field2[,...]])]
VALUES(value1,[,value2[,...])
```

Target is the table name. Field (column) names must be specified unless you are willing to assign values in exactly the same order as they occur in the database's table structure.

The following query, for example inserts a row into the Payroll table of the Karate database. All column names are specified:

```
INSERT INTO Payroll (SSN, PaymentDate, HoursWorked, HourlyRate)
    VALUES('400-33-2555', #1/15/1998#, 47.5, 17.50)
```

Text (string) values must be enclosed in single quotes, and date/time literals must be enclosed in #...#. The following statement inserts a row into the Payments table of the Karate database:

```
INSERT INTO Payments( Amount, MemberId, PaymentDate )
    VALUES( '00004', #3/15/2004#, 82.00 )
```

Query Parameters

Generally, INSERT INTO statements do not contain literal column values. More often, values from controls and variables are inserted in queries. Therefore, parameterized queries are the best tools for updating a database. The following statement inserts a row in the Payments table using query parameters:

```
INSERT INTO Payments( Amount, MemberId, PaymentDate )
    VALUES (?, ?, ?)
```

This is exactly the INSERT query generated by Visual Studio .NET when you create a data adapter for the Payments table.

Executing Commands

You can create your own command objects from scratch, but it's a lot easier to use commands created by Visual Studio .NET for data adapters. You must carry out the following steps in your code when executing a command object:

1. Open the database connection.
2. Assign a value to each parameter.
3. Execute the command by calling ExecuteNonQuery.
4. Close the connection.

As we saw earlier, data adapters already contain appropriate command objects, accessible via property names such as InsertCommand and DeleteCommand. The following example executes the InsertCommand for the daPayments data adapter. Always include exception handling to handle database errors and display appropriate messages:

```
Try
    conKarate.Open()
    With daPayments.InsertCommand
        .Parameters("Amount").Value = CDec(txtAmount.Text)
        .Parameters("MemberId").Value = txtMemberId.Text
        .Parameters("PaymentDate").Value = Now
        .ExecuteNonQuery()
```

```
      End With
      lblMessage.Text = "New row was added successfully"
   Catch ex As Exception
      lblMessage.Text = ex.Message
   Finally
      If conKarate.State = ConnectionState.Open Then conKarate.Close()
   End Try
```

The Finally clause of the Try-Catch statement is the best place to close the connection. An exception might have been thrown while trying to open the connection, so you should check the connection's state before calling the Close method.

Updating Table Rows

The SQL UPDATE statement modifies the contents of one or more rows in a database table. It has the following basic syntax:

```
UPDATE table
  SET fieldname = newvalue
  [ SET fieldname = newvalue ] ...
  WHERE criteria
```

The UPDATE statement has the potential to modify every row in a table. For example, the following query increases the hourly pay rate in all rows of the Payroll table by 5%:

```
UPDATE Payroll
SET HourlyRate = HourlyRate * 1.05
```

If you want to update only some of the rows in a table, use a WHERE clause with selection criteria. The following query, for example, increases the hourly pay rate for employees who were paid after a given payment date:

```
UPDATE Payroll
SET HourlyRate = HourlyRate * 1.05
WHERE PaymentDate > #05/01/1999#
```

If you want to update a single row, the WHERE clause must uniquely identify the selected row. Ordinarily, you would use an expression containing the table's primary key. For example, the following increases the hourly pay rate for a single employee:

```
UPDATE Payroll
SET HourlyRate = HourlyRate * 1.05
WHERE SSN = '111223333'
```

Karate Database Example

The following query sets Amount to $60 in the Payments table of the Karate database for the payment identified by PaymentId value 23:

```
UPDATE Payments
SET Amount = 60
WHERE PaymentId = 23
```

The following example uses a Command object to execute an UPDATE query on the Payments table:

```
Dim paymentId As Integer
Dim cmd As OleDb.OleDbCommand = New OleDb.OleDbCommand
```

```
conKarate.Open()
With cmd
   .Connection = conKarate
   .CommandType = CommandType.Text
   .CommandText = "UPDATE Payments SET amount = " & txtAmount.Text _
      & " WHERE PaymentId = " & paymentId
   .ExecuteNonQuery()
End With
conKarate.Close()
```

As in the INSERT example shown earlier, we would normally add a Try-End Try block to the code and catch exceptions.

Deleting Table Rows

The DELETE statement removes rows from a table. The WHERE clause can be used to select the rows. The following format is used when deleting from a single table:

```
DELETE
   FROM table
   WHERE criteria
```

Once a row has been deleted, it cannot be recovered. It is also possible to delete from multiple tables. When you're deleting a single row from a table, the WHERE clause must uniquely identify the row you want to delete. The easiest thing to do is to specify a value for the primary key field.

Examples

The following statement deletes all rows from the Payroll table in which the payment date is before January 1, 1998:

```
DELETE FROM Payroll
WHERE PaymentDate < #1/1/1998#
```

The following command deletes all rows from the Payroll table and retains the empty table in the database:

```
DELETE FROM Payroll
```

The following statement deletes a single row from the Payments table, identified by Payment ID 19:

```
DELETE FROM Payments
WHERE PaymentId = 19
```

The following code could be used in a program that deletes a single row from the Payments table:

```
Dim paymentId As Integer
Dim cmd As OleDb.OleDbCommand = New OleDb.OleDbCommand
conKarate.Open()
With cmd
   .Connection = conKarate
   .CommandType = CommandType.Text
   .CommandText = "DELETE FROM Payments " _
      & " WHERE PaymentId = " & paymentId
   .ExecuteNonQuery()
End With
conKarate.Close()
```

As usual, surround this code with a Try-End Try block.

Example: Inserting Karate Payments

KarateInsertPayments

To conclude, we present a short program that uses a command object to execute an INSERT query. In Figure 4-31, a DataGrid shows the current contents of the Payments table. The user enters a member ID, date, and payment amount, and clicks on the Insert button. If the payment is added to the dataset, a message appears confirming the new payment and the grid display is refreshed. If an exception is thrown, an error message appears (Figure 4-32). The complete program appears in Code Listing 4-9.

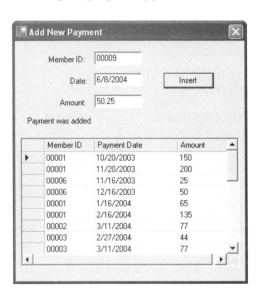

Figure 4-31   Adding a new payment.

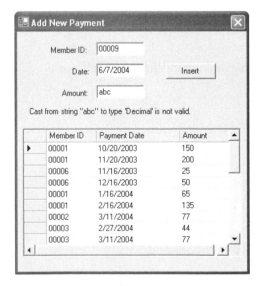

Figure 4-32   Error handling

Code Listing 4-9 (Inserting Karate Payments)

```
Public Class frmInsert
    Inherits System.Windows.Forms.Form

┌──────────────────────────────────────┐
│ + Windows Form Designer generated code │
└──────────────────────────────────────┘

    Private Sub frmInsert_Load(ByVal sender As System.Object, _
     ByVal e As System.EventArgs) Handles MyBase.Load

        txtDate.Text = FormatDateTime(Today, DateFormat.ShortDate)
    End Sub

    Private Sub btnInsert_Click(ByVal sender As System.Object, _
     ByVal e As System.EventArgs) Handles btnInsert.Click
      Try
          conKarate.Open()
          With daPayments.InsertCommand
             .Parameters("MemberId").Value = txtMemberId.Text
             .Parameters("PaymentDate").Value = CDate(txtDate.Text)
             .Parameters("Amount").Value = CDec(txtAmount.Text)
             .ExecuteNonQuery()
             lblMessage.Text = "Payment was added"
          End With
      Catch ex As Exception
          lblMessage.Text = ex.Message
      Finally
          If conKarate.State = ConnectionState.Open Then conKarate.Close()
      End Try
    End Sub
End Class
```

Checkpoint

4.22 When you create a data adapter, which four SQL queries are created automatically?

4.23 What are the two specific types of command objects?

4.24 Which SQL statement adds a new row to a table?

4.25 Which Command object property holds values that are passed from a program to a query before the query executes?

▶4.6 Chapter Summary

◆ A DataView permits you to sort, filter, search, edit, and navigate through the rows of a table.

◆ A DataRowView object represents a single row in a DataView. It has an Item property that lets you set or get a value in a specified column.

◆ The DataGrid control is an ideal tool for simultaneously displaying the rows and columns of a dataset. The DataGrid is directly linked to a dataset, so any change made to the grid's data changes the attached dataset.

◆ A DataView sorts and/or filters dataset rows. It does not modify the dataset's contents; instead, it displays a particular view, or version of the data.

◆ The ListView control provides a flexible way to display table data. You can fill a ListView from a dataset or a DataView, but the latter has a slight advantage because of its RowFilter and Sort properties.

◆ A three-tier application is divided into three tiers, or layers, named Presentation, Business, and Data. Classes in the Data tier typically include Connection, DataAdapter, DataSet, and DataView objects. Classes in the Business tier often provide properties and methods that provide class users with an abstracted view of the program's data. Classes in the Presentation tier communicate only with Business tier classes.

◆ Data adapters contain Select, Update, Insert, and Delete queries. The Data Adapter Configuration wizard creates these queries.

◆ A direct update approach modifies database tables directly, without the use of datasets. One advantage to this approach is that other users of the database can immediately access the updated table rows.

◆ Data adapters have four properties that expose command objects for SQL queries: SelectCommand, InsertCommand, DeleteCommand, and UpdateCommand.

◆ The SQL statement INSERT INTO inserts a new row into a table.

◆ Parameterized queries are usually used when executing INSERT INTO statements.

▶4.7 Key Terms

column styles	parameterized queries
Command object	Query parameters
DataGrid	scenario
DataView	subtask
DELETE query	task
INSERT query	three-tier application
ListView	UPDATE query

►4.8 Review Questions

True or False

1. A DataView object has a Sort property that can alter the sequence of rows
2. You can add an expression to a DataSet using the DataAdapter's Expression property

Short Answer

1. Which control displays table rows and columns in a spreadsheet-like format?
2. If you had to display table rows and columns, and planned to add a totals line in the last row, which control would be better—DataGrid or ListView?
3. Which DataView property can limit the choice of rows returned from a dataset?
4. If you wanted to prevent the user from making any changes to the contents of a DataGrid, which property would you set to True?

What Do You Think?

1. What advantages, if any, does a DataView have over a DataTable?
2. Would there be any disadvantages to making the ListView control data-aware?
3. The DataGrid control does not save any changes to a cell until the user moves away from the cell. Explain why you think that was (or was not) a good design decision.
4. The Sales Rental Inventory program uses a three-tier design, which admittedly requires quite a bit of source code. Do you think the program could have been written more easily by eliminating one of the tiers? Explain your answer.

►4.9 Programming Challenges

1. Three-Tier Sports Rental Income

In the Three-Tier Sports Rental Income program (Section 4.3), the Items class contains a DataView control that sorts items by their descriptions. As a consequence, each dataset row is of type DataRowView, and it contains no predefined properties that match column names. Ideally, we would prefer to replace awkward-looking statements such as the following...

```
Return CSng(mCurrentRow("weekly_rate"))
```

With code that uses the properties of a strongly typed data set:

```
Return mCurrentRow.weekly_rate
```

Your task is to redesign the Items class so it uses the latter type of notation, and still sorts items by their descriptions. (You may find more than one way to solve this problem.)

2. Sporting Goods Equipment Rental

Write a program that displays an equipment rental form. This form, shown in Figure 4-33, is filled out by the clerk when a customer rents an item from a store. The SportsRental database contains a table named **ch04Rentals** having the following design:

Field	Type	Description
InvoiceNumber	Integer	Autonumber (guarantees a unique key)
Date	Date/Time	Date and time of the rental
Customer	String	Customer name
Phone	String	Customer phone number
ItemID	String	ID number of Item (matches Items table)
ReturnDate	Date/Time	Anticipated return date
AmtPaid	Single	Amount paid by customer

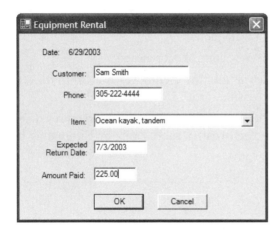

Figure 4-33 Filling Out a Rental Form.

You will need two data adapters in this program: one for the ch04Rentals table and another for the Items table. The latter will be used to fill a combo box with item descriptions. Set the ValueMember of this combo box to item_id.

When the program starts, the user fills in each of the text boxes and selects an item description from the combo box. When the user clicks on OK, all information on the form is inserted into a new table row, which is added to the ch04Rentals table. The value in the Item.item_id field is the same value you will insert into the ch04Rentals.ItemID column of your new data row. A message box confirms the new invoice number:

3. Sporting Goods Equipment Rental EC

Using your solution program from the previous exercise as a starting point, add error checking. If your program detects any of the following errors, notify the user and let them correct the error:

◆ Exception thrown while assigning field values.

◆ Exception thrown while adding the new row to the ch04Rentals table.

◆ Neither the customer name nor the phone number may be blank.

◆ A rental item must be selected.

◆ The return date must be 1 to 60 days from the current date.

◆ The amount paid must be greater than or equal to zero.

The DateDiff function finds the time interval between two dates. There is no need to use data binding for the text boxes on your form.

4. **Sports Inventory, Query Parameter**

Write a program that uses a DataGrid to display the SportsRental Items table. Do not permit the user to modify any data. The main menu should have the following entries:

Menu Entry	Description
File | Exit	End the program
Query | Select Daily Rate	Select daily rates for row filtering

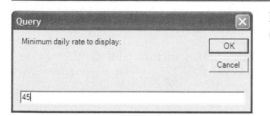

Permit the user to filter the displayed rows by selecting a lowest (minimum) daily rental rate value. Use an InputBox:

Allow user edit = false properties

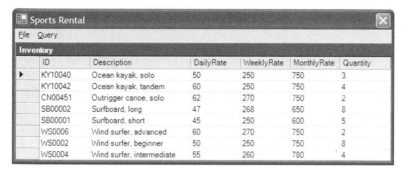

Refresh the DataGrid display with rows that match the given criteria. For example, the following rows all have a daily rental rate greater than or equal to 45. The rows are sorted by Description:

Use a parameterized query in the SelectCommand.CommandText property of the data adapter for the Items table. In your SQL query, **ORDER BY description** should be placed on the line following the WHERE clause.

5. **Sports Inventory, Multiple Query Parameters**

Using the solution program from the previous exercise as a starting point, make the following changes:

- The menu entries should be changed to the following:

Menu Entry	Description
File | Exit	End the program
Query | Minimum Daily Rate...	Input the minimum daily rate, for row filtering

- Use a dialog box entitled **Set Ranges** to input two range values from the user: minimum daily rate, and maximum daily rate.

- Using the minimum and maximum daily rental rate values, display matching rows in the DataGrid.

- The **Set Ranges** dialog should retain and display any range values previously entered during the same program run. (A user might want to change one value without having to retype both values.)

Implementation Notes

You will need to specify two query parameters in the data adapter's SELECT statement. The WHERE clause will be as follows:

```
WHERE (daily_rate >= ?) AND (daily_rate <= ?)
```

In your program code, the two query parameters are located at indices 0 and 1 in the Parameters array of the SelectCommand property of the data adapter. The following is the general format for assigning a value to the first query parameter:

```
DataAdapter.SelectCommand.Parameters(0).Value = paramValue
```

6. Karate Instructors Update

Write a short program that allows the user to update the Instructors table in the Karate database. Specifically, the functions are:

◆ Add a new instructor

◆ Modify an instructor entry

◆ Remove an instructor

7. Concert Hall Ticketing

Write a program that could be used in the box office of a concert hall. The easiest way to describe the program's operations is to construct a scenario, or sequence of events:

1. A customer calls in and requests a particular concert. The office receptionist (the user of our program) verifies the concert's date, time, and ticket availability, and quotes the ticket prices to the customer.
2. The customer decides to buy some tickets in a particular section of the hall. The attendant notifies the customer of the total price.
3. The customer confirms the purchase.
4. The program updates the database containing the number counts of available tickets in each concert hall section. When tickets are sold, the appropriate count is reduced.

Tickets purchased for a particular seating section can be used anywhere within that section. There are three seating sections: AA, AB, and AC. Your program must do the following:

1. List all concert titles in a combo box control.
2. When a concert title and seating section are selected, display the price per ticket and the number of available seats in the section.
3. When the user enters the number of tickets to purchase, the program must calculate the total cost of the tickets and display a confirmation dialog.
4. After displaying the confirmation dialog, the program must subtract the number of tickets sold from the database field holding the number of available tickets for the selected seating section.

Figure 4-34(a) shows the program's startup window, with all controls empty. Figure 4-34 (b) shows the same window after the user has selected a concert title and a seating section. Note how the concert date, ticket price and available seats have appeared. Figure 4-35 shows the calculated subtotal after the customer wants to purchase two tickets. Figure 4-36 shows the confirmation dialog window displayed after the user clicks on the Confirm button. After this dialog window closes, all controls are reset to their default values. If the user selects the same concert title and seating section again, the number of available seats must reflect the number of tickets already sold (Figure 4-37).

The program should be fairly flexible with regard to user input. If the user selects a concert, section, and number of tickets to purchase, they might decide to change the seating section. In that case, the program must recalculate all relevant values.

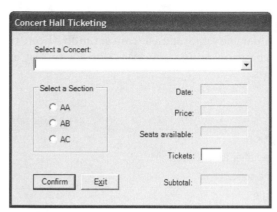

(a) Startup Window

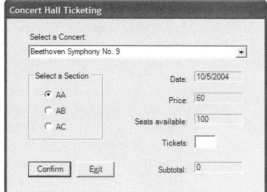

(b) Concert Selected

Figure 4-34 Concert Hall Ticketing Program

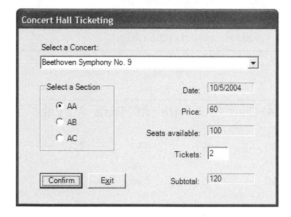

Figure 4-35 Number of Tickets Entered.

Figure 4-36 Confirmation Dialog.

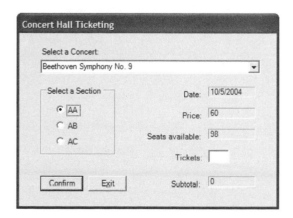

Figure 4-37 Updated Seat Count.

Database

Your program will read a table named **Concerts** in a database file named **concert.mdb** (from the book's CD-ROM). The **Concerts** table contains information about upcoming concerts, along with seat availability information. You can see the table design and sample rows:

Concerts Table Design

Name	Type	Description
ConcertId	Autonumber (integer)	Unique identifier for each concert
Date	Date/Time	Date of the concert
Title	String	Concert title
AA_Price	Single	Price per seat in section AA
AA_Seats	Integer	Number of available seats in section AA
AB_Price	Single	Price per seat in section AB
AB_Seats	Integer	Number of available seats in section AB
AC_Price	Single	Price per seat in section AC
AC_Seats	Integer	Number of available seats in section AC

Sample Rows

Concert Id	Date	Title	AA_Price	AA_Seats	AB_Price	AB_Seats	AC_Price	AC_Seats
1	8/1/2004	Paganini Concerto No. 2	60	100	45	150	35	200
2	9/2/2004	Music of Haydn	60	100	45	150	35	200
3	10/5/2004	Beethoven Symphony No. 9	60	100	45	150	35	200
4	10/17/2004	Mozart Piano Concerto	70	100	55	150	40	200
5	11/2/2004	Brahms Symphony No. 4	70	100	55	150	40	200
6	11/15/2004	Stravinsky Rite of Spring	60	100	45	150	35	200

Databases with Related Tables

▶5.1 Connecting to SQL Server Databases

In this chapter, we switch from using MS-Access databases to SQL Server databases. There are many advantages to using SQL Server in the professional world, primarily when multiple users share the same database. SQL Server 2000 includes two powerful tools which you are likely to use in the future:

◆ Enterprise Manager: Lets you perform a number of essential tasks, including creating new databases, attaching existing databases, adding and removing tables, modifying the contents of tables, and creating views and stored procedures.

◆ Query Analyzer: Lets you interactively create, modify, run, and debug queries.

Visual Studio.NET includes the **SQL Server Desktop Engine** (MSDE), a reduced version of SQL Server that lets your programs connect to SQL Server databases. MSDE is missing Enterprise Manager and Query Analyzer, but can be used for most standard tasks related to Visual Basic.NET programming.

When you install MSDE and the example databases that come with it, you will notice an icon on your computer's taskbar that looks like a gray rectangle with a green triangular arrow: 🔧 When the server is stopped, the green arrow turns into a red square.

In this book we will use the pubs database supplied with both MSDE and SQL Server. In addition, we have supplied several databases on the enclosed CD-ROM that can easily be attached to your lab's database server. Your server administrator will assign appropriate usernames and passwords, which can be included in the ConnectionString property of your Connection objects.

If you are running .NET on your home computer, we recommend that you install a full version of SQL Server. If your college is a member of the MSDN Academic Alliance (MSDNAA), you can probably download Visual Studio .NET and SQL Server for free. Otherwise, you may be able to get a 120-day evaluation of copy of the server by buying a book on SQL Server.

If it's not possible for you to get SQL Server, you can install MSDE after installing .NET, using the following directions.

Installing SQL Server Desktop Engine (MSDE)

To install MSDE, use Windows Explorer to navigate to the **\Setup\MSDE** folder in your installed Visual Studio .NET folder. For example, the default directory for .NET 2003 is the following:

```
c:\Program Files\Microsoft Visual Studio .NET 2003\Setup\MSDE\
```

If you find a file named setup.exe in the directory, double-click to open it. Otherwise, if you find a file named **msde_readme.htm** in the directory, double-click to open it. It will probably contain a message such as the following:

```
Visual Studio .NET 2003 does not include Microsoft SQL Server Desktop
Engine (MSDE). To download MSDE, go to http://go.microsoft.com/fwlink/?linkid=
13962.
```

 Click on the link and follow the download instructions. The installation instructions are somewhat minimal, so we recommend that you follow the setup instructions at http://www.kipirvine.com/vbnet/setup/#MSDE. After you install MSDE and reboot the computer, the MSDE service will start automatically. Your server will be named *machine*\NETSDK, where *machine* is your computer name.

If you do not install either SQL Server or MSDE, you can create all programs in this chapter using MS-Access databases. You will have to modify the connection strings and refer to the upcoming section (Programming Differences) for details. All of the sample databases on the CD-ROM have MS-Access versions.

Attaching SQL Databases to a Server

When you install an instance of SQL Server, certain databases are included automatically. Ordinarily, you see at least the following:

◆ Pubs: A simple database related to book publshing
◆ NorthWind: An advanced database for managing retail stores, suppliers, and shipping.

From time to time, you will want to add more databases to your SQL server instance. You can create new databases from scratch, and you can attach existing databases from files supplied on disk. This book's CD-ROM supplies several databases that must be attached to your SQL Server before you can run the example programs and complete some programming projects:

Database	Description
pubs	Authors, publishers, and book titles.
Campus	Students and college courses
Company	Departments, employees, payroll, and sales
Karate	A martial arts school
KayakStore	A kayak store
SportsRental	A sporting goods rental store

SQL server database files can be located in any directory of your hard drive. They consist of two files, with extensions .mdf and .ldf. For example, the Campus database consists of Campus.mdf and campus.Idf.

Using Enterprise Manager

If you have the standard version of SQL Server 2000, you can attach an existing database using the **Enterprise Manager** utility. Here, for example, are the steps to attach the Campus database:

Step 1. Right-click on the **Databases** entry, select **All Tasks**, and select **Attach Database**.

Step 2. Locate the Campus.mdf file with the browse button (...) and click on OK. An example is shown in Figure 5-1.

If you should ever want to move a database to a new location, you can detach it, copy the files, and reattach it to the server. To detach a database, right-click on the database name, select **All Tasks**, and select **Detach Database**.

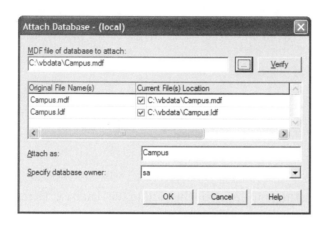

Figure 5-1 Attaching a database using Enterprise Manager

Using MDSE

The instructions shown here for attaching databases to the MSDE Server may not work correctly, because of changing installation instructions provided by Microsoft. Please check our book's Web site for the latest instructions (at http://www.kipirvine.com/vbnet/setup.).

If you are using the NETSDK server with Microsoft Server Desktop Engine, you can attach external databases using the OSQL utility supplied with Visual Studio .NET. Let's assume that you have run the setup program on the book's CD-ROM and all of your database files are located on drive C, in the c:\vbdata directory. The following steps would attach the Campus database to your server:

Step 1. Select **Run** from the **Start** menu.

Step 2. Enter **cmd** in the input box and click on OK.

Step 3. Type the following command:

```
OSQL  -E  -S  (local)\NETSDK
```

Step 4. When prompted by line numbers (1>, 2>, etc.), type the following (Figure 5-2):

```
1> EXEC sp_attach_db @dbname = 'Campus',
2> @filename1 = 'C:\vbdata\Campus.mdf',
3> @filename2 = 'C:\vbdata\Campus.ldf'
4> go
```

Step 5. Refresh the Server name in Visual Studio .NET Server Explorer window, and verify that the database exists.

The setup instructions on our Web site shows how to attach all of the book's databases.

Figure 5-2 Attaching the Campus database.

Programming Differences

In this chapter we head into new territory by writing programs that connect to SQL Server databases. There are a few important programming differences between MS-Access and SQL Server. Briefly, they can be summarized as:

◆ connection strings

◆ naming of query parameters

◆ wildcard characters in queries

◆ object names

Connection Strings

If you are using MS-Access, a minimal connection string must include the path to the database. Here, we show it for the pubs.mdb database:

```
Provider=Microsoft.Jet.OLEDB.4.0;Data Source=C:\vbdata\pubs.mdb
```

Similarly, a minimal connection string for an SQL Server database would be as follows:

```
user id=sa;data source=(local);initial catalog=pubs
```

Query Parameters

An important difference between SQL Server and MS-Access is in the naming of query parameters. In MS-Access, query parameters are identified by the ? mark:

```
INSERT INTO Payments( Amount, MemberId, PaymentDate )
    VALUES (?, ?, ?)
```

When parameters are assigned, they are automatically assigned their respective field names:

```
Dm cmd as OleDb.OleDbCommand
cmd.Parameters("Amount").Value = 50
cmd.Parameters("MemberId").Value = "12345"
cmd.Parameters("PaymentDate").Value = Now
```

If you are using SQL Server, parameters are given specific names, always starting with the @ character:

```
INSERT INTO Payments( Amount, MemberId, PaymentDate )
    VALUES (@amount, @memberId, @paymentDate )
```

The parameter values would be assigned as follows:

```
Dim cmd as SqlCommand
cmd.Parameters("@amount").Value = 50
cmd.Parameters("@MemberId").Value = "12345"
cmd.Parameters("@PaymentDate").Value = Now
```

Object Names

In this chapter we create and use objects associated with SQL Server. If you decide to use MS-Access instead, you will need to use certain equivalent object types. To assist you, Table 5-1 compares SQL Server object types to matching types used with MS-Access:

Table 5-1

SQL Server Object Types vs MS-Access Types.

SQL Server	MS-Access
SqlConnection	OleDbConnection
SqlDataAdapter	OleDbDataAdapter
SqlCommand	OleDbCommand

Date Literals

In SQL Server, date literals must be surrounded by single quotation marks. The following is an example:

```
SELECT id, enrollDate from students
WHERE enrollDate > '01/20/2004'
```

Also, in Chapter 3, we showed how to assign a default value to a datetime field using the Now function in MS-Access. The equivalent function is named **getdate** in SQL Server.

▶5.2 Relational Database Design

In this section, we will briefly look at how tables in a database can be linked using common key columns. The links are called *relations*, and they offer many useful advantages:

◆ Multiple related tables can be inserted into a single dataset.

◆ Detailed information for a column can be retrieved from a separate table.

◆ Relations can reduce the amount of data duplication.

We will also show how constraints (rules) can be used to control the content of individual columns, and how constraints affect Visual Basic .NET database programming.

Pubs Database Tables

The **pubs** database is an SQL server database centered around the business operations of a book distributor. The database is one of the samples supplied with both SQL Server and the Microsoft SQL Server Desktop Engine. For the moment, we will focus on two tables, named **jobs** and **employee**.

Jobs Table

The **jobs** table contains information about job categories relating to employees. It holds a job identification number, a job description, and numeric classification levels:

Column Name	Type	Description
job_id	smallint	Unique job ID number (primary key)
job_desc	varchar(50)	Job description
min_lvl	tinyint	Minimum classification level
max_lvl	tinyint	Maximum classification level

The **job_id** column, the primary key, uniquely identifies each table row in the table. Following are sample table rows:

job_id	job_desc	min_lvl	max_lvl
1	New Hire - Job not specified	10	10
2	Chief Executive Officer	200	250
3	Business Operations Manager	175	225
4	Chief Financial Officier	175	250
5	Publisher	150	250

Employee Table

The **employee** table contains information about individual employees. The following table describes its organization:

Column Name	Type	Description
emp_id	char(9)	Unique ID number
fname	varchar(20)	First name
minit	char(1)	Middle initial
lname	varchar(30)	Last name
job_id	smallint	Job ID number
job_lvl	tinyint	Job level number
pub_id	char(4)	Publisher ID
hire_date	datetime	Date employee was hired

Following are sample rows from the employee table:

emp_id	fname	minit	lname	job_id	job_lvl	pub_id	hire_date
PMA42628M	Paolo	M	Accorti	13	35	0877	8/27/1992
PSA89086M	Pedro	S	Afonso	14	89	1389	12/24/1990
VPA30890F	Victoria	P	Ashworth	6	140	0877	9/13/1990
H-B39728F	Helen		Bennett	12	35	0877	9/21/1989
L-B31947F	Lesley		Brown	7	120	0877	2/13/1991
F-C16315M	Francisco		Chang	4	227	9952	11/3/1990
PTC11962M	Philip	T	Cramer	2	215	9952	11/11/1989

Table Relationships

In Chapter 3 we introduced the idea that database tables can be related via two types of columns: primary key and foreign key. At the time, we used a one-to-many relationship to show how to look up information that cannot be held in a single table. In the current chapter, we can expand on the same idea, showing three types of table relationships that provide flexibility for database programming: one-to-one, one-to-many, and many-to-many.

One-to-One Relationship

When a single table would contain too much detailed information, it can be split into two tables. The same primary key occurs in both tables, and it links the two in a one-to-one relationship. Such a relationship exists between the orders and order_details tables in the pubs database. In Figure 5-3, the relationship diagram created in MS-Access uses a line to connect the primary key columns of the two tables. The digit 1 at each end identifies a primary key column. Therefore, by knowing just the publisher ID (pub_id) of a publisher, you can gain access to its logo, name, city, state, and country.

Three reasons for using a one-to-one relationships are (1) supplementary text or graphics information may be too large to be practical to store in a single dataset; (2) a large table might have so many columns that it exceeds the number permitted by the database software; (3) some columns might contain sensitive information that should not be stored in a single table. Columns that require a special security level can be in a separate table, accessible only to selected users and programs.

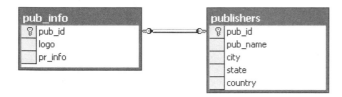

Figure 5-3 One-to-one relationship.

One-to-Many Relationship

A one-to-many relationship exists between two tables when the primary key of one table links to a column called a *foreign key* in another table. For example, the employee and jobs tables have such a relationship, shown in Figure 5-4. The infinity sign (°) next to the job_id column of the employee table implies that the same job_id value can occur multiple (many) times in the employee table. Table 5-2, for example, shows rows in the employee table having the same job_id value.

The relationship between the employee and jobs tables is useful because we might want to display the job description for an employee. That information is not in the employee table, but the foreign key (job_id) allows us to find the person's job description (job_desc) in the jobs table.

When a one-to-many relation exists between two tables, the table on the **one** side is called the *parent* table. The table on the **many** side is the *child* table. In our current example, **jobs** is the parent table and **employee** is the child table.

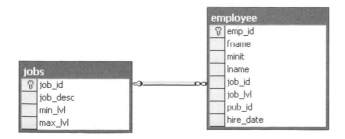

Figure 5-4 One-to-many relationship.

Table 5-2

Selected employee rows

emp_id	fname	minit	lname	job_id	job_lvl	pub_id	hire_date
PXH22250M	Paul	X	Henriot	5	159	0877	8/19/1993
CFH28514M	Carlos	F	Hernandez	5	211	9999	4/21/1989
JYL26161F	Janine	Y	Labrune	5	172	9901	5/26/1991
LAL21447M	Laurence	A	Lebihan	5	175	0736	6/3/1990
RBM23061F	Rita	B	Muller	5	198	1622	10/9/1993
SKO22412M	Sven	K	Ottlieb	5	150	1389	4/5/1991
MJP25939M	Maria	J	Pontes	5	246	1756	3/1/1989

Many-To-Many

A many-to-many relationship exists between two tables when the connecting column is a foreign key in both tables. We could say that many rows in one table can link to many rows in the second table. Most database systems do not directly support many-to-many relationships, so the usual solution is to create a third table that acts as an intermediary between the tables. In effect, the relationship is divided into two one-to-many relationships.

In the pubs database, the **titles** table contains a list of book titles, and the **authors** table contains a list of authors. It is easy to imagine that a single book could have multiple authors, leading us to imagine that a one-to-many relationship exists between the titles and authors tables (Figure 5-5).

Notice that the "one" side is titles, the "many" side is authors, and **title_id** is a foreign key in the authors table. But what if a single author has written more than one book? Then the relationship is reversed, and the titles table has a foreign key named **au_id** (Figure 5-6).

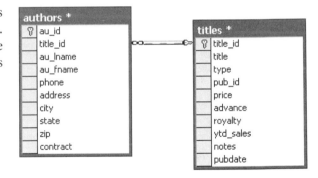

Figure 5-5 Titles as the parent table

The contradiction created by the two possible one-to-one relationships is resolved in the pubs database by a table named **titleauthor** (Figure 5-7), which has a one-to-many relatioship with both the authors and titles tables. The au_id and title_id fields are both (individually) foreign keys, so we know the table can contain multiple instances of each key value.

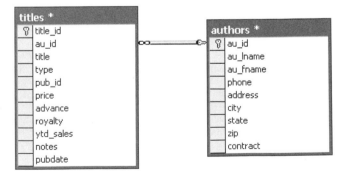

Figure 5-6 Authors as the parent table

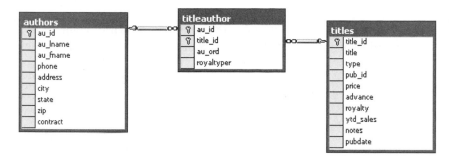

Figure 5-7 The titleauthor table.

As we look at selected rows in the titleauthor table (Table 5-3) sorted by title_id, we see that two different authors wrote the book with title_id equal to BU1032.

Table 5-3

The titleauthor table, sorted by title_id

au_id	title_id	au_ord	royaltyper
213-46-8915	**BU1032**	**2**	**40**
409-56-7008	**BU1032**	**1**	**60**
267-41-2394	BU1111	2	40
724-80-9391	BU1111	1	60
213-46-8915	BU2075	1	100
274-80-9391	BU7832	1	100

If we sort the titleauthor table by au_id (Table 5-4), we see that author 213-46-8915 has written two books.

Table 5-4

The titleauthor table, sorted by au_id

au_id	title_id	au_ord	royaltyper
172-32-1176	PS3333	1	100
213-46-8915	**BU1032**	**2**	**40**
213-46-8915	**BU2075**	**1**	**100**
238-95-7766	PC1035	1	100
267-41-2394	BU1111	2	40
267-41-2394	TC7777	2	30
274-80-9391	BU7832	1	100

Other Relationships in the Pubs Database

The eleven tables in the pubs database have many one-to-many relationships, shown in Figure 5-8. Using this diagram, you can piece together related information that you might want to place in the same dataset.

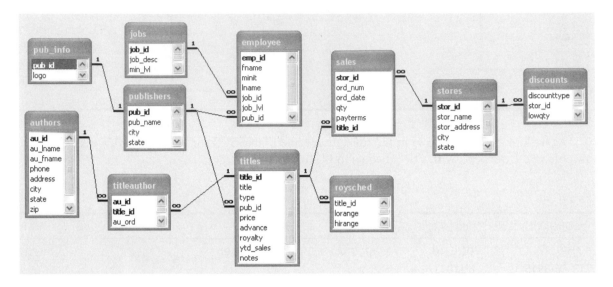

Figure 5-8 Relationships in the pubs database.

Cascading Deletes and Updates

When you create relationships between tables, you have the option of selecting cascading deletes and/or cascading updates. Suppose a primary key value in a parent table is changed. If *cascading updates* are enabled, all rows in the child table that match this key are updated. This is generally very desirable, so that referential integrity is maintained in the database. Recall, for example, that a parent-child relationship exists between the jobs and employee tables in the pubs database. Suppose job_id 5 were changed to 6 in the jobs table (Table 5-5). Then every row in the employee table having job_id 5 would automatically be updated, with its job_id changed to 6. The affected rows are shown in Table 5-6

Table 5-5

Jobs table.

job_id	job_desc	min_lvl	max_lvl
1	New Hire - Job not specified	10	10
2	Chief Executive Officer	200	250
3	Business Operations Manager	175	225
4	Chief Financial Officier	175	250
5	Publisher	150	250

Table 5-6

Selected employee rows.

emp_id	fname	minit	lname	job_id	job_lvl	pub_id	hire_date
PXH22250M	Paul	X	Henriot	5	159	0877	8/19/1993
CFH28514M	Carlos	F	Hernandez	5	211	9999	4/21/1989
JYL26161F	Janine	Y	Labrune	5	172	9901	5/26/1991
LAL21447M	Laurence	A	Lebihan	5	175	0736	6/3/1990
RBM23061F	Rita	B	Muller	5	198	1622	10/9/1993
SKO22412M	Sven	K	Ottlieb	5	150	1389	4/5/1991
MJP25939M	Maria	J	Pontes	5	246	1756	3/1/1989

Cascading Deletes

If cascading deletes are enabled, deleting a parent row causes all matching child rows to be deleted. Needless to say, this is a dangerous option! In the pubs database, for example, suppose we deleted job_id 3 from the jobs table. Then all the employees with the same job id would disappear from the employee table. If our intention had been to reassign the affected employees to another job, it would have to be done before deleting job_id 3 from the jobs table. Generally, cascading updates are a good idea, but cascading deletes should be used only when you are willing to lose rows from child tables.

Creating SQL Queries that Join Tables

Queries

Query Builder is a powerful tool that makes table joining easy. You can access Query Builder by selecting SqlDataAdapter from the Data tab of the Visual Studio .NET ToolBox. Query Builder can build queries for inserting, deleting, and updating table rows, but it needs to know which column uniquely identifies each row (the primary key). If you omit the primary key when adding tables to Query Builder, it will still be able to generate a SELECT query. Now we will build four hands-on examples that experiment with various combinations of tables from the **pubs** database.

Example 1: Book Titles and Store IDs

We will create a dataset containing sales of books, using the title of the book and the store ID of the store that sold the book. Using Query Builder, do the following steps, in order:

Step 1. Create a new program named **Queries**.

Step 2. From the Data tab of the ToolBox window, drag an SqlDataAdapter control onto the program's startup form. This action will launch the Data Adapter Configuration Wizard, as in Figure 5-9. Click on the Next button.

Figure 5-9   Configuring a data adapter

Step 3. Assuming that the pubs database is not currently in your list of connections, select **New Connection**.

Step 4. When the Data Link Properties window displays (Figure 5-10), you will need to supply connection information appropriate to your college laboratory setup. The values shown in the figure are appropriate if you are running the SQL Server Desktop Engine on your local computer. If you are running SQL Server 2000, Figure 5-11 shows a typical connection configuration.

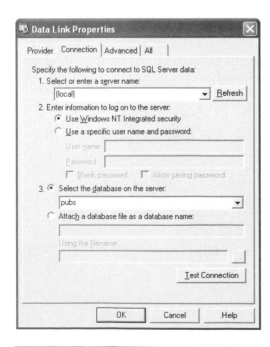

Figure 5-10   Data Link Properties window (MSDE).

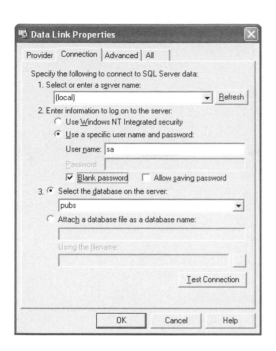

Figure 5-11 Data Link Properties window (SQL Server 2000).

Step 5. When you are prompted to choose the query type (Figure 5-12), use the default selection (Use SQL Statements). Visual Studio will generate SQL queries and insert them in your program's source code.

Step 6. Begin creating an SQL query (Figure 5-13) by selecting **Query Builder**. A dialog window appears containing names of tables in the pubs database (Figure 5-14).

Figure 5-12 Choose the query type.

Figure 5-13 Generate the SQL statements.

Figure 5-14 Adding tables.

Step 7. Add the **sales** and **titles** tables to the upper pane of Query Builder (Figure 5-15). Because the necessary table relations already exist in the database, lines automatically connect the related primary keys and foreign keys. The linking column name is title_id.

Step 8. Place a check next to **title** in the titles table, and place a check next to **stor_id** in the sales table. Query Builder automatically generates the following SQL SELECT statement that joins the sales and titles tables on the title_id column:

```
SELECT titles.title, sales.stor_id
FROM    sales INNER JOIN
        titles ON sales.title_id = titles.title_id
```

Step 9. To see the table rows generated by the query, right-click and select Run. Table 5-7 displays sample rows, which may not be in the same order as your query's display.

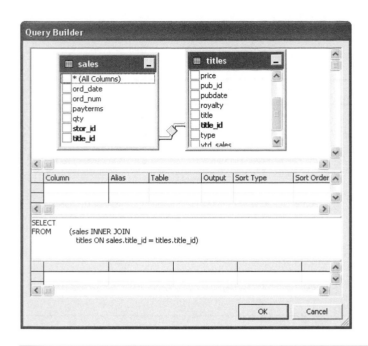

Figure 5-15 Sales and titles tables.

Table 5-7

Sample rows generated by SELECT query.

title	stor_id
The Busy Executive's Database Guide	6380
The Busy Executive's Database Guide	8042
Cooking with Computers: Surreptitious Balance Sheets	8042
You Can Combat Computer Stress!	7896
Straight Talk About Computers	7896
Silicon Valley Gastronomic Treats	7896
The Gourmet Microwave	7131
The Gourmet Microwave	8042
But Is It User Friendly?	8042

Step 10. Close Query Builder and click on Finish to end the wizard. A warning message will tell you that update queries cannot be generated because you did not select a primary key column. Ignore the message, because we will only be using the SELECT query.

Example 2: Title IDs and Store Names

Let's create a dataset containing the identification numbers of books that were sold, along with the names of the stores selling the books.

Step 1. Drag another SqlDataAdapter control onto your program's startup form. Run the configuration wizard as in the previous example.

Step 2. Add the **sales** and **stores** tables to the upper pane of the Query Builder.

Step 3. Select the title_id and stor_name columns. The following query is generated:

```
SELECT sales.title_id, stores.stor_name
FROM      sales INNER JOIN
          stores ON sales.stor_id = stores.stor_id
```

Step 4. Run the query, and compare the resulting rows to those in Table 5-8.

Table 5-8

Sales/Stores query.

title_id	stor_name
PC8888	Barnum's
PS2091	Barnum's
BU1032	Eric the Read Books
PS2091	Eric the Read Books
PS2091	News & Brews
TC3218	News & Brews
TC4203	News & Brews
TC7777	News & Brews
PS2091	Doc-U-Mat: Quality Laundry and Books
(continued)	

Example 3: Job Descriptions and Employee Names

The following query creates a dataset containing an employee's job description, along with the person's first and last names. The required information is located in the jobs and employee tables:

```
SELECT jobs.job_desc, employee.fname, employee.lname
FROM    jobs INNER JOIN
           employee ON jobs.job_id = employee.job_id
```

Table 5-9 contains sample rows from the resulting dataset.

Table 5-9

Jobs/Employees query.

job_desc	fname	lname
Sales Representative	Paolo	Accorti
Designer	Pedro	Afonso
Managing Editor	Victoria	Ashworth
Editor	Helen	Bennett
Marketing Manager	Lesley	Brown
Chief Financial Officier	Francisco	Chang
Chief Executive Officer	Philip	Cramer
Productions Manager	Aria	Cruz
Business Operations Manager	Ann	Devon
Public Relations Manager	Anabela	Domingues
(continued)		

Example 4: Author IDs, Titles, and Publishers

Next, you will create a dataset containing author IDs, book titles, and publisher names, and sort the rows in ascending order by the author ID. Because some authors have written more than one book, we can expect duplicate author IDs to appear. Try the followng steps in Query Builder:

Step 1. Add the publishers, titles, and titleauthor tables.

Step 2. Select the au_id, title, and pub_name columns.

Step 3. Sort on the au_id column.

Step 4. Following is the SQL query created by Query Builder:

```
SELECT
    titleauthor.au_id,
    titles.title,
    publishers.pub_name
FROM publishers
INNER JOIN titles ON publishers.pub_id = titles.pub_id
INNER JOIN titleauthor ON titles.title_id = titleauthor.title_id
ORDER BY titleauthor.au_id
```

The query involves more than two tables, so Query Builder may use parentheses to specify the order in which tables are joined. First, the titleauthor and titles tables are joined. The resulting table is then joined to the publishers table. Table 5-10 contains sample rows from the resulting dataset.

Table 5-10

Titleauthor/titles/publishers query.

au_id	title	pub_name
172-32-1176	Prolonged Data Deprivation: Four Case Studies	New Moon Books
213-46-8915	The Busy Executive's Database Guide	Algodata Infosystems
213-46-8915	You Can Combat Computer Stress!	New Moon Books
238-95-7766	But Is It User Friendly?	Algodata Infosystems
267-41-2394	Sushi, Anyone?	Binnet & Hardley
267-41-2394	Cooking with Computers: Surreptitious Balance Sheets	Algodata Infosystems
274-80-9391	Straight Talk About Computers	Algodata Infosystems
409-56-7008	The Busy Executive's Database Guide	Algodata Infosystems
427-17-2319	Secrets of Silicon Valley	Algodata Infosystems
472-27-2349	Sushi, Anyone?	Binnet & Hardley
(continued)		

When adding multiple tables to the Query Builder, the order is important. Any adjacent tables must have a common joining column. In the previous example, if we had added the titleauthor table followed by the publishers table, Query Builder would not have created a join relationship between the tables.

You must be running Visual Studio 2003 or later to join more than two tables using the Visual Studio .NET Query Builder.

Checkpoint

5.1 What special property does a primary key column (field) have?

5.2 Name several reasons why two tables might have a one-to-one relationship.

5.3 If a database does not support many-to-many relationships, what is a common way to make the tables usable?

5.4 Which tables in the pubs database have a one-to-many relationship with the sales table?

▶5.3 Database Constraints

Primary Key Constraints

Database constraints are rules inserted into a database by the designer or administrator. They help to preserve the integrity of the data, preventing errors caused by the insertion of invalid data. By doing so, they take some of the burden off of individual application programs that use the database. Rather than inserting validation statements into every program that uses a shared database, it's more efficient to embed constraints in the database. Sometimes the constraints check ranges of numbers, such as a person's age. In other cases, constraints look for prescribed sets of characters.

A *primary key constraint* is violated if an attempt is made to add a table row containing a primary key value that already exists in the table. The database signals that a primary key constraint has been violated, and refuses to add the row. In the employee table, for example, if we add a new row containing a duplicate emp_id, Figure 5-16 shows the resulting error message displayed by Visual Studio .NET's Server Explorer.

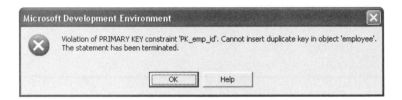

Figure 5-16 Primary key constraint violation.

Referential Integrity Constraints

One of the most important types of database constraints is a *referential integrity constraint*, also called a *foreign key constraint*. It applies to the relationship between two tables. For example, in a one-to-many relationship, the parent table is required to contain a primary key value for every foreign key value found in the child table. We examined one such relationship (Figure 5-17) between the jobs and employee tables.

Suppose that your program were to add a new row to the employee table, setting its job_id column equal to 50. Assuming that the jobs table contains no job_id equal to 50, a referential integrity constraint would be violated, and a runtime error would result (Figure 5-18). The program would have to add a new row to the jobs table containing job_id = 50; only then could the program create an employee whose job_id was equal to 50.

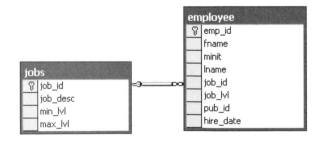

Figure 5-17 One-to-many relationship.

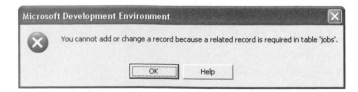

Figure 5-18 Referential integrity constraint error message.

Column Check Constraints

A *column check constraint* is a rule that governs the contents of any arbitrary column in a database table. Databases include column check constraints to validate data inserted into various columns, relieving application programs of having to do the same task. The database integrity is more easily preserved when constraints are used. In the pubs database, for example, the **emp_id** column of the employee table has a constraint that requires the key to begin with one of two patterns, where X is an alphabetic character:

◆ XXX

◆ X-X

The next position must be a digit between 1 and 9. The next four digits must be between 0 and 9. The final character must be either letter M or F. As it turns out, the first three characters represent the person's initials, and the dash (-) is a placeholder for employees having no middle initial. For example, the name "Paolo M. Accorti" is assigned PMA as the first three characters in the employee ID: "PMA42628M". The trailing M indicates the person's gender. The employee "Victoria P. Ashworth" has employee ID "VPA30890F".

Example: Column Check Constraint in SQL Server

You can view the constraint for a particular column from the Server Explorer window. Right-click on the table name, and choose **Design Table**. Right click on the column name, and select **Check Constraints**. Let's look at the constraint expression for the **emp_id** column. There are two expressions in this constraint, connected by an OR operator:

```
([emp_id] like '[A-Z][A-Z][A-Z][1-9][0-9][0-9][0-9][0-9][FM]' or
[emp_id] like '[A-Z]-[A-Z][1-9][0-9][0-9][0-9][0-9][FM]')
```

The first expression begins with the following:

```
[emp_id] like '[A-Z][A-Z][A-Z]...
```

The expression [A-Z] specifies character in the range A to Z. Because there are three [A-Z] in a row, the emp_id column starts with three letters. Next, the expression [1-9] requires the next character to be a digit between 1 and 9:

```
...[1-9]...
```

The next 4 characters must be digits between 0 and 9:

```
...[0-9][0-9][0-9][0-9]...
```

The last character must be either letter F or M:

```
...[FM]...
```

The OR operator at the end of the first line asserts that if the emp_id column does not conform to the expression in the first line, it must match the expression in the second line:

```
[emp_id] like '[A-Z]-[A-Z][1-9][0-9][0-9][0-9][0-9][FM]
```

The expression specifies that an employee ID can begin with a letter, followed by a dash, followed by a letter, followed by a digit between 1 and 9, followed by four digits between 0 and 9, followed by either letter F or M. The following are examples of valid emp_id values, showing which constraint expression applies:

Example	Which Expression?
ABC10000M	Line 1
GBS20202F	Line 1
X-B50010M	Line 2
M-A20101F	Line 2
ZYP30002M	Line 1

Enforcing Constraints

How, then, are constraints enforced? One important factor is how the constraint is specified. In Figure 5-19, the option entitled *Enforce constraint for INSERTs and UPDATEs* is checked. In other words, if we try to add a new row or modify an existing row, we can expect the constraint to be enforced by the database itself. If, for example, you were to modify the emp_id column in such a way that a constraint was volated, the message shown in Figure 5-20 would be displayed.

You can use Enterprise Manager to view table constraints. Right-click on a table name and select **Design Table**. Inside the designer window, right-click and select **Check Constraints**.

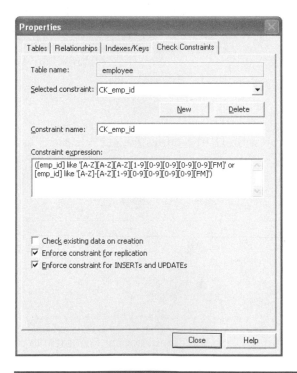

Figure 5-19   Constraints for emp_id column.

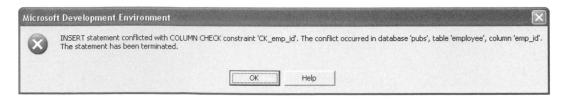

Figure 5-20   Constraint violation, emp_id column.

Checkpoint

5.5 Describe a primary key constraint.

5.6 What type of relationship is there between the pub_info and publishers tables in the pubs database?

5.7 What type of relationship is there between the authors and titles tables in the pubs database?

5.8 In a One-to-many relationship, how can you tell which table contains the foreign key?

5.9 Between the employee and publishers tables, which column would be involved in a referential integrity constraint?

▶ 5.4 DataGrid Control with Related Tables

In this section we will explore various ways to use the DataGrid control in connection with multiple related tables. First, we will examine two tables from the pubs database more closely: **jobs** and **employee**. Then we will show how to use a ComboBox control to *filter*, or control the selection of table rows displayed in a data grid. After that, we will show how to display parent and child tables within the same data grid.

A combo box provides a simple way to select a single item from one column of a database table. It's usually easiest to attach the combo box to a data view, to allow easy sorting on the displayed list of values. The combo box's SelectedValue property can be used to filter the records in a second data view attached to a data grid.

Figure 5-21 shows how the combo box and data grid coordinate with two DataView controls named dvJobs and dvEmployee. The combo box's DataSource property equals **dvJobs**, and the grid's DataSource property equals **dvEmployee**. The combo box's ValueMember property equals **job_id**, so when the user selects a job description, SelectedValue contains a specific job_id value. Using program code, assign job_id to the RowFilter property of the dvEmployee data view, causing the grid to display only rows from the employee table having the same job_id value.

One-to-many relationship:

Control Properties:

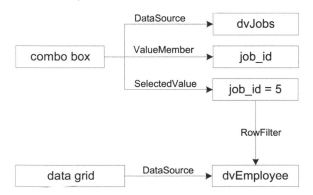

Figure 5-21 Combo box, grid, and data views.

Hands-On Tutorial: Using a ComboBox to Filter DataGrid Rows

SelectingJobs

Let's create a program that first displays a list of job descriptions from the jobs table in a ComboBox control. When the user selects a job description, a DataGrid displays the names and hire dates of all employees who work at the selected job. At startup, only the ComboBox control appears, as in Figure 5-22. When the user selects a job category such as *Designer*, the DataGrid appears and is populated with the names of all employees who have that type of job (Figure 5-23). The employee names are built from an expression column in the dsEmployee dataset. Note from the figure that by altering the grid's BorderStyle, BackgroundColor, and CaptionVisible properties, you can make it blend with its enclosing window.

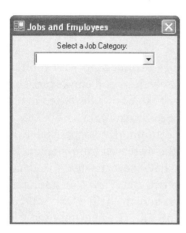

Figure 5-22 Program startup.

Figure 5-23 Job category selected, data grid filled.

Step 1. Create a new Windows Desktop program named **SelectingJobs**.

Step 2. Delete the startup form and create a new form named **frmMain**.

Step 3. Create a connection to the **pubs** database.

Step 4. Drag the **jobs** table onto the program's form. Rename the connection to **conPubs**, and rename the data adapter to **daJobs**.

Step 5. Generate a dataset class named **dsJobs** from the daJobs data adapter. The dataset variable will be named DsJobs1.

Step 6. Drag the **employee** table onto the program's form. Rename the data adapter to **daEmployee**.

Step 7. Generate a dataset class named **dsEmployee** from the daEmployee data adapter. The dataset variable will be named **DsEmployee1**.

Step 8. Add an expression column named **fullName** (type Text) to the dsEmployee schema definition, and set its Expression property to: **lname + ', ' + fname + ' ' + minit + '.'**

Step 9. Place a DataView control on frmMain and name it **dvJobs**. Set its Table property to **DsJobs1.Jobs** and set its Sort property to **job_desc**.

Step 10. Place another DataView on the form and name it **dvEmployec**. Set its Table property to **DsEmployee1.Employee** and set its Sort property to **fullName**.

Step 11. Add a ComboBox control to the form named **cboJobs**. Set its DataSource property to **dvJobs** (the DataView name) and set its DisplayMember property to **job_desc**. Set its ValueMember property to **job_id**.

Step 12. Add a Label just above the combo box and set its Text property to "**Select a Job Category**".

Step 13. Place a DataGrid control on the form below the combo box and name it **dgrEmployee**. Set the following property values:

Property	Value
BackGroundColor	Control
BorderStyle	None
CaptionVisible	False
ReadOnly	True
Visible	False

Step 14. Select the DataGrid's **TableStyles** property and add a single table style with the following properties:

Property	Value
Name	Employee
MappingName	employee
RowHeadersVisible	False

(Chapter 3 has a short tutorial on using the DataGridTableStyle Collections editor.) The MappingName property refers to a table in the database. The name is case-sensitive.

Step 15. Select the TableStyle's **GridColumnStyles** property. In the DataGridColumnStyle Collection editor, add two GridColumnStyles with the following properties:

Column Name	Properties
DataGridTextBoxColumn1	MappingName: fullName
	HeaderText: Name
DataGridTextBoxColumn2	MappingName: hire_date
	HeaderText: Date Hired

Step 16. Open up the form's code window and add the following code to the **frmMain_Load** event handler.

```
daJobs.Fill(DsJobs1)
daEmployee.Fill(DsEmployee1)
cboJobs.SelectedIndex = -1
```

Step 17. Create the **cboJobs_SelectedIndexChanged** event handler:

```
Private Sub cboJobs_SelectedIndexChanged(ByVal sender As _
    System.Object, ByVal e As System.EventArgs) _
    Handles cboJobs.SelectedIndexChanged

    If cboJobs.SelectedIndex = -1 Then Exit Sub

    dvEmployee.RowFilter = "job_id = " & CStr(cboJobs.SelectedValue)
    dgrEmployee.DataSource = dvEmployee
    dgrEmployee.Visible = True
End Sub
```

Note that if SelectedIndex is –1, the user has not yet selected a job category from the combo box.

Step 18. Run the program, select various job categories, and watch the DataGrid fill with lists of employees having identical jobs.

(End of tutorial. The program source code is in Code Listing 5-1.)

Code Listing 5-1 (Selecting Jobs)

```
Public Class frmMain
    Inherits System.Windows.Forms.Form

    +  Windows Form Designer generated code

    Private Sub Form1_Load(ByVal sender As System.Object, _
     ByVal e As System.EventArgs) Handles MyBase.Load

        daJobs.Fill(DsJobs1)
        daEmployee.Fill(DsEmployee1)
        cboJobs.SelectedIndex = -1
    End Sub

    Private Sub cboJobs_SelectedIndexChanged(ByVal sender As System.Object, _
     ByVal e As System.EventArgs) Handles cboJobs.SelectedIndexChanged

        If cboJobs.SelectedIndex = -1 Then Exit Sub

        dvEmployee.RowFilter = "job_id = " & CStr(cboJobs.SelectedValue)
        dgrEmployee.DataSource = dvEmployee
        dgrEmployee.Visible = True
    End Sub
End Class
```

Displaying Parent and Child Tables in the Same Data Grid

In the previous tutorial we used a data grid to display a single database table. Now that we've learned how database tables can be related using key columns, it makes sense to display information from more than one table. Fortunately, the data grid has a built-in mechanism that lets the user navigate between parent and child tables. Following are the general steps to set up a data grid to display parent and child tables:

1. Create data adapters for both the parent and child tables, related to each other by a common key value.
2. Generate a single dataset from the two data adapters.

3. Add a relation to the dataset's schema definition that identifies the parent and child tables.

4. Set the grid's DataSource property to the dataset object, and set its DataMember property to the name of the parent table.

5. Write code in the Form_Load event that loads the dataset from the two data adapters.

6. *Optional:* Create grid table style definitions for both tables that specify, among other things, the names and widths of the displayed columns.

Let's look at a simple example that links two tables and displays them in a DataGrid. Assume that two data adapters exist named **daJobs** and **daEmployee**. We can generate a single dataset that contains rows from both data adapters. In the **Generate Dataset** dialog (Figure 5-24), both data adapters are selected, and the dataset is named **dsJobsEmployee**. Any name for the dataset is possible, of course, but it's good style to include both the parent and child table names.

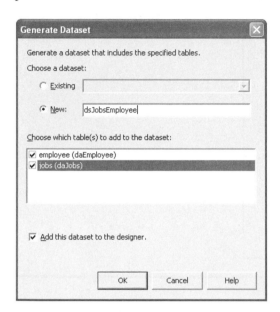

Figure 5-24 Generating a dataset.

The next step is to add a relation to the dataset's schema definition. A *schema* is a description of the columns and relationships contained in a dataset (or database). Visual Studio .NET displays dataset schema in either graphical or XML format.

To add a relation to the dataset schema, double-click the dataset's XSD file in the Solution Explorer window. Position the mouse pointer over a table, right-click, select **Add,** and then select **New Relation** (Figure 5-25). In the *Parent element* drop-down list, **jobs** is selected, and in the *Child element* drop-down list, **employee** is selected. You can name the relation; we called it JobsEmployee in the current example. *Note: The OK button is not enabled until you explicitly select both the parent and child elements.*

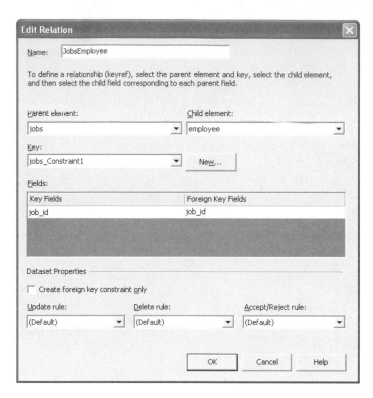

Figure 5-25   Adding a relation to the dataset.

We then set the DataGrid's DataSource property to **DsJobsEmployee1,** and its DataMember property to **jobs.** Last of all, code that loads the dataset from the two data adapters is placed in the Form_Load event handler:

```
daJobs.Fill(DsJobsEmployee1)
daEmployee.Fill(DsJobsEmployee1)
```

When you call the Fill method for two data adapters having a parent-child relationship, the parent table must be filled first. This requirement has to do with the referential integrity rule that requires the foreign key in the child table to have a matching value in the parent table. The following is an example of the dialog that appears when the Fill methods are called in the wrong order.

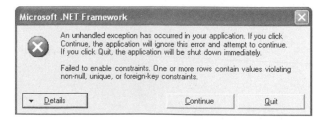

When running the program (Figure 5-26), the jobs table is displayed with a + sign next to each row. The user might want to know the names of all employees that fit under each of these job categories. If you select "Publisher" for example, the grid displays the names and related information of all employees who are publishers. The user can click on any + sign to expand a row, revealing a link to the row's child table.

job_id	job_desc	min_lvl	max_lvl
1	New Hire - Job not specified	10	10
2	Chief Executive Officer	200	250
3	Business Operations Manager	175	225
4	Chief Financial Officier	175	250
5	Publisher	150	250
6	Managing Editor	140	225
7	Marketing Manager	120	200
8	Public Relations Manager	100	175
9	Acquisitions Manager	75	175
10	Productions Manager	75	165
11	Operations Manager	75	150
12	Editor	25	100
13	Sales Representative	25	100
14	Designer	25	100

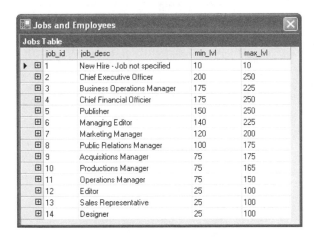

Figure 5-26 Jobs table in the DataGrid

In Figure 5-27, the row having **job_id = 5** is selected, revealing a hyperlink named **JobsEmployee** (the name of the relation we created in Figure 5-25). When the user clicks on the hyperlink, the grid contents are replaced with all rows in the Employee table having job_id = 5 (see Figure 5-28).

job_id	job_desc	min_lvl	max_lvl
1	New Hire - Job not specified	10	10
2	Chief Executive Officer	200	250
3	Business Operations Manager	175	225
4	Chief Financial Officier	175	250
5	Publisher	150	250
6	Managing Editor	140	225
7	Marketing Manager	120	200
8	Public Relations Manager	100	175
9	Acquisitions Manager	75	175
10	Productions Manager	75	165
11	Operations Manager	75	150
12	Editor	25	100
13	Sales Representative	25	100

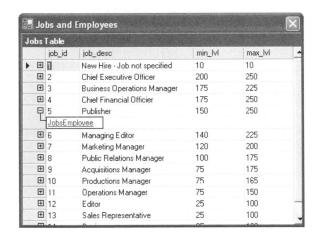

Figure 5-27 Revealing the publisher link.

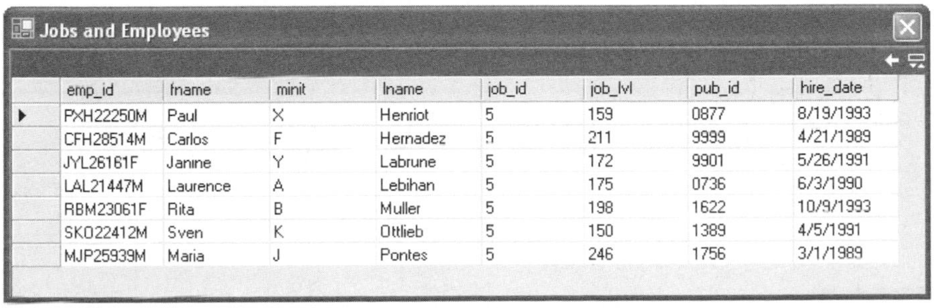

emp_id	fname	minit	lname	job_id	job_lvl	pub_id	hire_date
PXH22250M	Paul	X	Henriot	5	159	0877	8/19/1993
CFH28514M	Carlos	F	Hernadez	5	211	9999	4/21/1989
JYL26161F	Janine	Y	Labrune	5	172	9901	5/26/1991
LAL21447M	Laurence	A	Lebihan	5	175	0736	6/3/1990
RBM23061F	Rita	B	Muller	5	198	1622	10/9/1993
SKO22412M	Sven	K	Ottlieb	5	150	1389	4/5/1991
MJP25939M	Maria	J	Pontes	5	246	1756	3/1/1989

Figure 5-28 Employees with job_id = 5.

Notice in Figure 5-28 that the corresponding row from the jobs table can be displayed at the top of the grid; it can be hidden at design time by setting the ParentRowsVisible property to False. Or, at runtime, the user can click the icon on the farthest right side of the grid's title bar to toggle the display of the parent row. The left-pointing arrow next to the icon returns the user to the parent table (jobs).

When the user moves between the parent and child tables, the grid fires a **Navigate** event. You can examine the event handler's input parameter to find out if the user is moving *forward* from the parent table to the child table, or *backward* from the child to the parent. For example, the following code uses the Navigate event handler to set the data grid's caption to the name of the table currently displayed, depending on which direction the user just moved:

```
Private Sub dgrJobsEmployee_Navigate(ByVal sender As System.Object, _
    ByVal ne As System.Windows.Forms.NavigateEventArgs) _
    Handles dgrJobsEmployee.Navigate

    If ne.Forward Then
        dgrJobsEmployee.CaptionText = "Employee Table"
    Else
        dgrJobsEmployee.CaptionText = "Jobs Table"
    End If
End Sub
```

Hands-On Tutorial: Jobs-Employees DataGrid

JobsEmployeeGrid

We've already explained the concepts and most of the mechanics behind parent-child DataGrid applications, so this tutorial will begin with a partially completed program. The JobsEmployeesGrid program already contains data adapters for the Jobs and Employees tables, as well as a dataset class named dsJobsEmployee.

Step 1.   Open the **JobsEmployeeGrid** program.

Step 2.   Open the dsJobsEmployee XSD definition file and examine the data relation between the Jobs table and the Employee table, shown in Figure 5-29. (You may have to scroll the employee table to view the job_id column definition.) For practice, delete the relation by clicking on the diamond-shaped icon and pressing the Del key. Then, recreate the relation using the techniques explained in the previous section (see Figure 5-25).

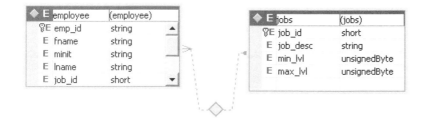

Figure 5-29   XML schema with relation.

Step 3. Place a DataGrid on the form and set the following properties:

Property Name	Value
Name	dgrJobsEmployee
Anchor	Top, Bottom, Left, Right
CaptionText	Jobs Table
DataSource	DsJobsEmployee1
DataMember	jobs
ParentRowsVisible	True
ReadOnly	True

Step 4. Click on the DataGrid's **TableStyles** property and open the TableStyles Collection editor. Define a table style name **jobs**, with MappingName = jobs. Define a single column for the table, containing the job_desc column (see Figure 5-30). Note that the column heading is **Description**.

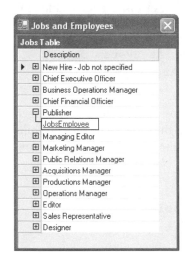

Figure 5-30 Jobs table.

Step 5. Define a second table style named **employee** with MappingName = employee. Define three column styles, based on the following columns in the employee table: fname, lname, and hire_date (see Figure 5-31). Note that the heading in the third column is **Date Hired**.

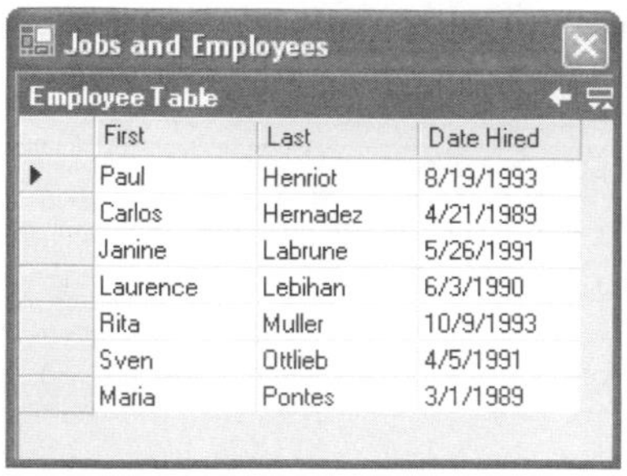

Figure 5-31 Employee table.

Step 6. Open the form's code window and insert the following lines into the Form_Load handler. Notice that each data adapter fills part of the DsJobsEmployee dataset:

```
daJobs.Fill(DsJobsEmployee1)
daEmployee.Fill(DsJobsEmployee1)
```

Step 7. Finally, you will add a nice finishing touch. When the user navigates from the Jobs table to the Employee table, display the table name in the DataGrid's heading by trapping the Navigate event:

```
Private Sub dgrJobsEmployee_Navigate(ByVal sender As System.Object, _
  ByVal ne As System.Windows.Forms.NavigateEventArgs) _
  Handles dgrJobsEmployee.Navigate
```

Notice the parameter named **ne**, which is of type NavigateEventArgs. It has a single ReadOnly property named **Forward**, which is set to True when the user has just begun to move from the parent table to the child table. All we have to do is set the CaptionText property of the grid to one table name when the user is moving forward, and another when the user is moving backward:

```
    If ne.Forward Then
        dgrJobsEmployee.CaptionText = "Employee Table"
    Else
        dgrJobsEmployee.CaptionText = "Jobs Table"
    End If
End Sub
```

Step 8. Save and run the program. If all goes well, a list of job descriptions should appear first. When you expand a job description and click on its child hyperlink, the related employee rows should display, as in Figure 5-31.

(End of tutorial. The program source code is in Code Listing 5-2.)

Code Listing 5-2 (JobsEmployeeGrid)

```
Public Class frmMain
    Inherits System.Windows.Forms.Form
```

```
+ Windows Form Designer generated code
```

```
    Private Sub frmMain_Load(ByVal sender As System.Object, _
     ByVal e As System.EventArgs) Handles MyBase.Load

      daJobs.Fill(DsJobsEmployee1)
      daEmployee.Fill(DsJobsEmployee1)
```

```
      End Sub

      Private Sub dgrJobsEmployee_Navigate(ByVal sender As System.Object, _
       ByVal ne As System.Windows.Forms.NavigateEventArgs) _
       Handles dgrJobsEmployee.Navigate

          If ne.Forward Then
              dgrJobsEmployee.CaptionText = "Employee Table"
          Else
              dgrJobsEmployee.CaptionText = "Jobs Table"
          End If
      End Sub
  End Class
```

Checkpoint

5.10 Which column name joins the jobs and employee tables?

5.11 When using a ComboBox to display rows from a parent table, which property is useful when selecting rows in a DataView attached to a child table?

5.12 In the SelectingJobs program (first hands-on tutorial in this section), which table is displayed in the data grid?

5.13 When a single DataGrid control is used to display both parent and child tables, what identifier is used in the hyperlink that navigates from the parent to the child table?

5.14 When filling a dataset from data adapters for both parent and child tables, which table must be filled first?

▶ 5.5 Related Tables with Unbound Controls

Stores and Sales Tables

We have shown how to use a DataGrid control to display related tables having a parent-child relationship (also called one-to-many). Now we would like to show how to perform the same type of task using code with unbound controls. We will focus on two tables from the pubs database, stores and sales. The **stores** table (Table 5-11) contains a list of stores, in which **stor_id** is the primary key:

Table 5-11

The stores table in the pubs database.

stor_id	stor_name	stor_address	city	state	zip
6380	Eric the Read Books	788 Catamaugus Ave.	Seattle	WA	98056
7066	Barnum's	567 Pasadena Ave.	Tustin	CA	92789
7067	News & Brews	577 First St.	Los Gatos	CA	96745
7131	Doc-U-Mat: Quality Laundry and Books	24-A Avogadro Way	Remulade	WA	98014
7896	Fricative Bookshop	89 Madison St.	Fremont	CA	90019
8042	Bookbeat	679 Carson St.	Portland	OR	89076

The **sales** table contains sales transactions for individual book titles. Table 5-12 contains several sample rows. We might assume that various quantities of books are sold by a distributor to individual bookstores. The sales table has a two foreign keys: **stor_id** and **title_id**, and a composite primary key built from the **stor_id**, **ord_num**, and **title_id** colums. The table's XML schema definition in Figure 5-32 shows key-shaped icons next to the primary key columns.

There is a one-to-many relationship between the store table and the sales table, using the store_id field as the link between the two. **Store** is parent table, and **sales** is the child table.

Table 5-12

The sales table from the pubs database.

stor_id	ord_num	ord_date	qty	payterms	title_id
6380	6871	9/14/1994	5	Net 60	BU1032
6380	722a	9/13/1994	3	Net 60	PS2091
7066	A2976	5/24/1993	50	Net 30	PC8888
7066	QA7442.3	9/13/1994	75	ON invoice	PS2091

Figure 5-32 XML schema definition, sales table.

DataRelation Objects

In Section 5.4 we showed how to create a relation between two tables (employee and jobs). We opened the Schema Definition window and used the Edit Relation dialog (Figure 5-25) to create the relation. We didn't mention it at the time, but Visual Studio .NET creates a corresponding DataRelation object that can be manipulated using program code. Since we're about to create a new program that manipulates the stores and sales tables, let's assume that a DataRelation named **relStoresSales** has been created, as in Figure 5-33. We will use this relation when searching for child rows (rows in the sales table) linked to the stores table using the store_id key.

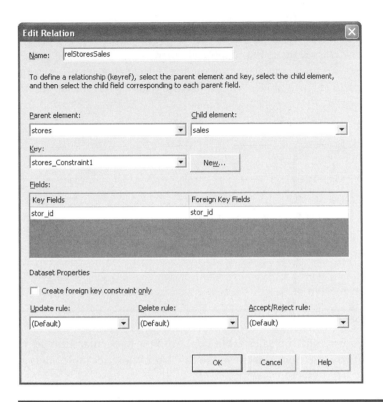

Figure 5-33 DataRelation for stores and sales.

GetChildRows Method

The **GetChildRows** method of the DataRow class uses the current row of a parent table to find all rows in a child table related to the parent row. Its input parameter is a DataRelation object. It returns an array of DataRow objects (specific to the dataset, of course). Here's an example. Assuming that **drStores** is a DataRow from the **stores** table, let's declare **salesRows** as an array of DataRow objects. We pass the name of the **relStoreSales** DataRelation to the GetChildRows method:

```
Dim salesRows As DataRow()
salesRows = drStores.GetChildRows("relStoresSales")
```

GetChildRows returns an array of DataRows from the sales table whose primary key values match the sales_id value in the drStores DataRow. For example, if the following were the current row in drStores:

6380	Eric the Read Books	788 Catamaugus Ave.	Seattle	WA	98056

The following child rows from the sales table would be copied to the salesRows array:

stor_id	ord_num	ord_date	qty	payterms	title_id
6380	6871	9/14/1994	5	Net 60	BU1032
6380	722a	9/13/1994	3	Net 60	PS2091

GetParentRow Method

The GetParentRow method of the DataRow class returns the parent table row that links to the current row in the child table. For example, suppose that a one-to-many relation named **relTitlesSales** exists between the titles and sales tables, linked by the **title_id** column (Figure 5-34). We can use the relation to look up the title of any book listed in the sales table.

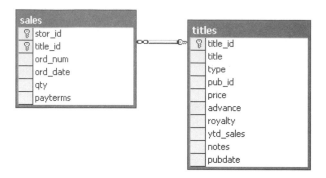

Figure 5-34   Relation between titles and sales.

Let's assume that drSales contains a row from the sales table containing a particular title_id value. The following code calls the **drSales.GetParentRow** method to retrieve the row from the titles table having the same title_id value:

```
Dim drTitles As DataRow
drTitles = drSales.GetParentRow("relTitlesSales")
```

Note that we pass the name of the relation binding the two tables as an input argument. Using drTitles, we can retrieve any field, such as the book title:

```
Dim bookTitle As String = CStr(drTitles("title"))
```

It's safe to assume that GetParentRow is successful as long as referential integrity has been preserved in the database. Otherwise, the title_id value from the sales table would have no counterpart in the titles table.

Hands-On Tutorial: Sales by Store

SalesByStore

In this tutorial, you will create a program that demonstrates three new methods we've introduced in this chapter: FindBystor_id, GetChildRows, and GetParentRow. It uses three tables from the pubs database: stores, sales, and titles. The program is very similar in function to the SelectingJobs program presented in Section 5.4. In contrast to the bound DataGrid control used in the earlier program, we now use an unbound ListView control.

The program starts with a combo box containing a list of store names (Figure 5-35). When the user selects a store, the program displays the titles of all books sold by the store (Figure 5-36). The list of titles changes each time the user selects a store.

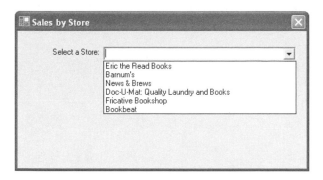

Figure 5-35 Sales by Store program startup.

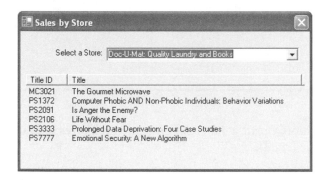

Figure 5-36 Sales for one store.

Step 1. Create a new Windows application named **SalesByStore**.

Step 2. Delete the startup form and create a new startup form named **frmSales**. Set the form's Text property to **Sales by Store**. Set the form's MinimizeBox and MaximizeBox properties to False.

Step 3. Add the **stores** table from the pubs database to frmSales. Rename the connection to **conPubs** and rename the data adapter to **daStores**.

Step 4. Create data adapters for the sales and titles tables, naming them **daSales** and **daTitles**.

Step 5. Let's create a single dataset that includes the stores, sales, and titles tables. Right-click on daStores, select **Generate Dataset**, and name the dataset **dsStoresSales** (Figure 5-37). Place checks next to all three tables before closing the window.

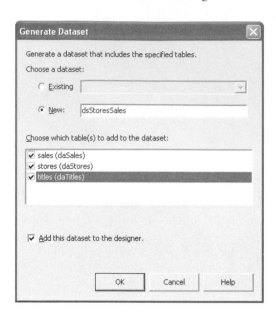

Figure 5-37 Creating the dsStoresSales dataset.

Step 6. Open the dsStoresSales.xsd schema definition. Create a data relation named **relStoresSales** between the stores table (parent) and the sales table (child).

Step 7. Similarly, create a data relation named **relTitlesSales** between the titles and sales tables. Titles is the parent element and sales is the child element. Close the xsd file viewer.

Step 8. Add a combo box to the form named **cboStores**. Set its DataSource property to **DsStoresSales1.stores**, its DisplayMember property to **stor_name**, and its ValueMember property to **stor_id**.

Step 9. Place a label to the left of the combo box and set its Text property set to "Select a Store".

Step 10. Add a ListView control to the form and name it **lvwSales**. Set its BackColor property to **Control**, and set its BorderStyle property to **None**. Set its View property to **Details**, and its Visible property to **False**. Create two columns, with captions "Title ID" and "Title". Adjust the column widths to look approximately like those shown earlier in Figure 5-36.

Step 11. In the form's code window, create the following variable that lets us know at runtime if the combo box is in the process of being initialized:

```
Dim mbStoresLoaded As Boolean = False
```

Step 12. Create a Load event handler for the form that fills the dataset from the stores, titles, and sales tables. Insert the following code:

```
daStores.Fill(DsStoresSales1)
daTitles.Fill(DsStoresSales1)
daSales.Fill(DsStoresSales1)
cboStores.SelectedIndex = -1
mbStoresLoaded = True
```

The mbStoresLoaded variable is set to True at the end of the form load event, letting the combo box know that it may begin responding to selection events.

Step 13. Create a **cboStores_SelectedIndexChanged** event handler and begin by inserting code that searches the dataset for the stor_id returned by the SelectedValue property of the combo box:

```
If Not mbStoresLoaded Then Exit Sub

Dim drStores As DataRow
drStores = DsStoresSales1.stores.FindBystor_id( _
    cboStores.SelectedValue.ToString())
```

The drStores DataRow returned by FindBystor_id will be used in the next step.

 Note:

The FindBystor_id method was automatically generated by Visual Studio when the deStoresSales dataset was created. For more details about FindBy, see page 228 in Chapter 4.

Step 14. Still inside the SelectedIndexChanged procedure, write code that uses drStores to call its GetChildRows method and get the array of rows from the sales table that matches the current store:

```
Dim matchingSalesRows As DataRow() = _
    drStores.GetChildRows("relStoresSales")
```

Step 15. The next step is to iterate through matchingSalesRows. For each row in the array, find its title by calling GetParentRow, using the relation between the sales and titles tables:

```
Dim drSales, drTitles As DataRow
lvwSales.Items.Clear()
For Each drSales In matchingSalesRows
    drTitles = drSales.GetParentRow("relTitlesSales")
    . . .
```

Step 16. Once each book's title is found, create a ListViewItem and add the title ID and book title to the list view:

```
    Dim lvItem As New ListViewItem(CStr(drSales("title_id")))
    lvItem.SubItems.Add(CStr(drTitles("title")))
    lvwSales.Items.Add(lvItem)
Next
```

The expression drSales("title_id") returns an Object. Since we always have Option Strict set on, an Object must be explicitly converted into a String before being assigned to list boxes, list views, and other similar controls.

Step 17. If at least one row was found in the sales table, make the list view visible:

```
If matchingSalesRows.Length > 0 Then lvwSales.Visible = True
```

Step 18. You're done. Save the program and begin testing it.

(End of tutorial. The program source code appears in Code Listing 5-3.)

Code Listing 5-3 (SalesByStore)

```
Public Class frmSales
    Inherits System.Windows.Forms.Form
```

```
+ Windows Form Designer generated code
```

```
Dim mbStoresLoaded As Boolean = False

Private Sub frmSales_Load(ByVal sender As System.Object, _
 ByVal e As System.EventArgs) Handles MyBase.Load

    'Must fill stores and titles tables first, to avoid foreign-key
    'Constraint violation when filling sales table.

    daStores.Fill(DsStoresSales1)
    daTitles.Fill(DsStoresSales1)
    daSales.Fill(DsStoresSales1)
    cboStores.SelectedIndex = -1
    mbStoresLoaded = True
End Sub

Private Sub cboStores_SelectedIndexChanged(ByVal sender As _
 System.Object, ByVal e As System.EventArgs) _
 Handles cboStores.SelectedIndexChanged

    If Not mbStoresLoaded Then Exit Sub

    Dim drStores As DataRow
    drStores = DsStoresSales1.stores.FindBystor_id( _
     cboStores.SelectedValue.ToString())

    Dim matchingSalesRows As DataRow() = _
     drStores.GetChildRows("relStoresSales")
    Dim drSales, drTitles As DataRow
    lvwSales.Items.Clear()

    For Each drSales In matchingSalesRows
        drTitles = drSales.GetParentRow("relTitlesSales")
        Dim lvItem As New ListViewItem(CStr(drSales("title_id")))
        lvItem.SubItems.Add(CStr(drTitles("title")))
        lvwSales.Items.Add(lvItem)
    Next
    If matchingSalesRows.Length > 0 Then lvwSales.Visible = True
   End Sub
End Class
```

Using Query Builder to Join Tables

Up to this point, we've used a separate data adapter for each table and pulled together multiple data adapters into datasets. Using a separate data adapter for each table does provide some flexibility in how the tables are used. For example, individual tables can be manipulated separately.

By taking advantage of the power of SQL, you can also use a single data adapter to combine columns from multiple tables. Use the Query Builder tool that appears when activating the SelectCommand.CommandText property of a data adapter.

Suppose, for example, you would like to display the name and job titles of employees in the pubs database. You can activate the Query Builder, and insert the employee and jobs tables in the upper pane. To add a table to the upper pane, right-click and select Add Table from the pull-down menu. A list of tables appears, allowing you to select one (see Figure 5-38).

Figure 5-38 Adding a table to the Query Builder.

Selected tables appear in the upper pane of the Query Builder, where you can place check marks next to fields you want to select. Query Builder automatically displays database relations between tables.

Let's select fname, lname, and hire_date from the employee table, along with job_desc (job description) from the jobs table:

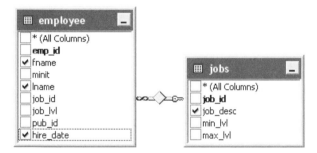

Query Builder uses the INNER JOIN clause to link together the employee and jobs table, using the job_id key as the common element. Following is the SQL code generated by Query Builder, reformatted slightly for the printed page:

```
SELECT employee.fname, employee.lname,
    employee.hire_date, jobs.job_desc
FROM employee
INNER JOIN jobs ON employee.job_id = jobs.job_id
```

In other words, the rows returned by this query will be such that each job_id value in employee will be paired up with a row in the jobs table that has the same job_id.

To run and test the query, right-click anywhere in the window and select Run. The output from the sample query is shown in Figure 5-39.

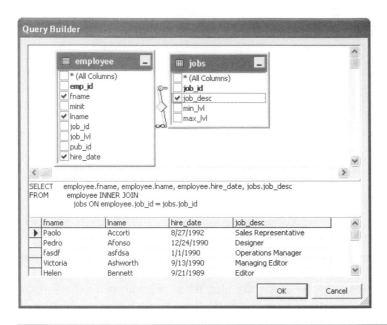

Figure 5-39 Joining the employee and jobs tables.

Nested Join

We might want to add a third table to the employee/jobs example, by adding the publishers table. We could then display the name of the publisher each employee works for. Let's add the publishers table to the Query Designer window, remove the hire_date field, and add the pub_name field:

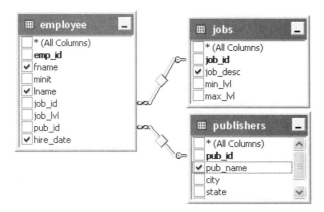

The resulting query uses two INNER JOIN clauses to build the resultset:

```
SELECT employee.fname, employee.lname,
       jobs.job_desc, publishers.pub_name
FROM employee
INNER JOIN jobs ON employee.job_id = jobs.job_id
INNER JOIN publishers ON employee.pub_id = publishers.pub_id
```

Following are some sample output rows:

fname	lname	job_desc	pub_name
Paolo	Accorti	Sales Representative	Binnet & Hardley
Pedro	Afonso	Designer	Algodata Infosystems
Victoria	Ashworth	Managing Editor	Binnet & Hardley
Helen	Bennett	Editor	Binnet & Hardley
Lesley	Brown	Marketing Manager	Binnet & Hardley
Francisco	Chang	Chief Financial Officier	Scootney Books
Philip	Cramer	Chief Executive Officer	Scootney Books

When possible, try to create queries at design time that will reduce the amount of program code you must write and debug. Queries can also reduce the number of data adapters in your programs. It is still useful to remember that tables from multiple data adapters can be combined into a single dataset. One of the data adapters can contain a parent table, and the other data adapter can contain a table built by joining other tables. In the next hands-on tutorial, we join the store table (parent) to a combined sales/titles table created by a JOIN query.

Hands-On Tutorial: Joining Tables in Sales by Store

SalesByStoreJoin

The SalesByStore hands-on tutorial from the previous section used separate data adapters for the sales and titles tables. Let's use a new approach, which will use the Query Builder to create a table using SQL statements. A single data adapter will retrieve only the fields from the sales and titles tables that we plan to display, or that participate in the data relation between the stores and sales tables.

Step 1. Make a copy of the SalesByStore program and call it **SalesByStoreJoin**. Optionally, you can rename the Solution, Project, and Assembly to SalesByStoreJoin.

Step 2. Change the caption of the startup form to "Sales by Store – Join".

Step 3. Remove the daTitles data adapter.

Step 4. Select the **SelectCommand.CommandText** property of daSales and open the Query Builder window.

Step 5. Right-click in the top panel of the Query Builder and select **Add Table**. Select the **titles** table from the list and close the Add Table dialog. Notice that a line automatically appears between the two tables, showing their relationship.

Step 6. Remove all checks next to the columns in the sales table except **stor_id** and **title_id**.

Step 7. Place a check mark next to the **title** column of the titles table. Notice the SELECT command created by your actions (rearranged here slightly):

```
SELECT sales.stor_id, titles.title, sales.title_id
FROM sales
INNER JOIN titles ON sales.title_id = titles.title_id
```

The INNER JOIN clause builds a temporary table from existing tables by joining their rows based on a table relationship.

Step 8. Right-click in the window and select **Run**. You should see a long list of title IDs, store IDs, and book titles in the output pane. Close the Query Builder window.

Step 9. Right-click on the daSales adapter and select **Generate Dataset**. In the dialog window (Figure 5-40), select the existing dataset (dsStoresSales) and place checks next to both data adapters.

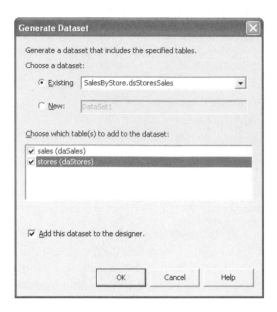

Figure 5-40   Regenerating the dsStoreSales dataset.

Step 10. Edit the contents of the Form_Load event handler so it looks like the following. Notice that we removed the line that references daTitles:

```
daStores.Fill(DsStoresSales1)
daSales.Fill(DsStoresSales1)
cboStores.SelectedIndex = -1
mbStoresLoaded = True
```

Step 11. In the SelectedIndexChanged event handler, find the line that declared both drSales and drTitles, and change it to the following:

```
Dim drSales As DataRow
```

Step 12. The loop that fills the ListView no longer needs to call GetParentRow to locate each book title:

```
For Each drSales In matchingSalesRows
    Dim lvItem As New ListViewItem(CStr(drSales("title_id")))
    lvItem.SubItems.Add(CStr(drSales("title")))
    lvwSales.Items.Add(lvItem)
Next
```

Step 13. Save and run the program. The output should appear as in Figure 5-41.

(End of tutorial. The program's source code appears in Code Listing 5-4.)

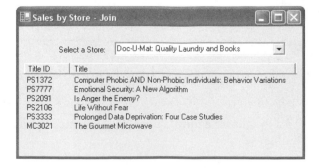

Figure 5-41   SalesByStoreJoin program output.

Code Listing 5-4 (SalesByStoreJoin)

```
Public Class frmSales
    Inherits System.Windows.Forms.Form

┌─────────────────────────────────────┐
│ + Windows Form Designer generated code │
└─────────────────────────────────────┘

    Dim mbStoresLoaded As Boolean = False

    Private Sub frmSales_Load(ByVal sender As System.Object, _
     ByVal e As System.EventArgs) Handles MyBase.Load

        'Must fill stores table first, to avoid
        'foreign key Constraint violation when filling sales table.
        daStores.Fill(DsStoresSales1)
        daSales.Fill(DsStoresSales1)
        cboStores.SelectedIndex = -1
        mbStoresLoaded = True
    End Sub

    Private Sub cboStores_SelectedIndexChanged(ByVal sender As _
        System.Object, ByVal e As System.EventArgs) _
        Handles cboStores.SelectedIndexChanged

        If Not mbStoresLoaded Then Exit Sub

        Dim drStores As DataRow
        drStores = DsStoresSales1.stores.FindBystor_id( _
         cboStores.SelectedValue.ToString())

        Dim matchingSalesRows As DataRow() = _
           drStores.GetChildRows("relStoresSales")
        Dim drSales As DataRow
        lvwSales.Items.Clear()

        For Each drSales In matchingSalesRows
            Dim lvItem As New ListViewItem(CStr(drSales("title_id")))
            lvItem.SubItems.Add(CStr(drSales("title")))
            lvwSales.Items.Add(lvItem)
        Next
        If matchingSalesRows.Length > 0 Then lvwSales.Visible = True
    End Sub
End Class
```

Checkpoint

5.15 Where in Visual Studio .NET can you see a graphical representation of a DataRelation object?

5.16 What input parameter is required by the GetChildRows method?

5.17 Assume that a DataRelation exists between the stores and sales tables in a dataset. From which table would rows be returned by a call to GetChildRows?

5.18 Write a SELECT statement in SQL that joins the employee and jobs tables, returning rows containing the employee's last name and job description.

▶5.6 Chapter Summary

◆ Database relations permit multiple database tables to be included in the same dataset.

◆ The pubs database provides information centered on the business operations of a book distributor. It contains tables that store information about employees, jobs, publishers, stores, and book sales.

◆ A one-to-one relationship between database tables is often used to break up a table with too many columns, or to isolate certain columns that contain sensitive information.

◆ A one-to-many relationship between database tables is used when the tables share a common key field, and in one of the tables, the key field values are unique.

◆ In the pubs database, examples of one-to-many relationships can be found between jobs and employees, publishers and employees, publishers and titles, and between stores and sales.

◆ A many-to-many relationship exists when the connecting key column does not contain unique values in either table. An example is the relationship between the authors and titles tables in the pubs database.

◆ A common solution to the problem of expressing a many-to-many relationship is to use an intermediate table that contains one-to-many relationships with the outside tables. An example is the titleauthor table in the pubs database.

◆ A referential integrity constraint verifies that when a row is inserted or updated, its foreign key value has a matching primary key value in its parent table.

◆ A column check constraint verifies that the contents of a single column in a row conforms to certain rules.

◆ The DataGrid control can easily display tables having a parent-child relationship (one-to-many) as long as both tables belong to the same dataset.

◆ When filling a dataset from two data adapters, be sure to load the parent table before a related child table. Otherwise, a runtime error results (due to a referential integrity error).

◆ The GetChildRows method retrieves all rows from a child table in a DataRelation.

◆ The GetParentRow method retrieves the parent row from a parent table in a DataRelation.

◆ The SalesByStore program shows how to manage two related tables and display their contents in a ListView control.

◆ SQL Server uses the INNER JOIN statement to join two related tables.

▶5.7 Key Terms

child table	Navigate event
column check constraint	nested join
constraint	one-to-many relationship
DataRelation object	one-to-one relationship
foreign key	parent table
GetChildRows method	primary key
GetParentRow method	primary key constraint
inner join	relation
many-to-many relationship	table relationship

►5.8 Review Questions

Fill-in-the-blank

1. Links between —————————— in a database are called relations.

2. When the same primary key field exists in two related tables, the tables have a —————————— relationship.

3. A one-to-many relationship connects a primary key in one table to a —————————— key in a second table.

4. In the pubs database, the authors table has a many-to-many relationship with the —————————— table.

5. In SQL, the —————————— —————————— statement connects two tables using a common column.

6. A —————————— —————————— constraint is violated if an attempt is made to add a table row containing a primary key value that already exists in the table.

7. A DataGrid's —————————— event fires when the user moves between the parent and child tables.

Multiple Choice

1. Which of the following would **not** be a reason to create a one-to-one relationship between two database tables?

   a. Supplementary text or graphics information may be too large to store in a single dataset
   b. Certain columns may contain sensitive information that should be placed in a separate table.
   c. A table with an excessive number of columns might have to be divided into two tables.
   d. Database access is faster for separate tables than for a single table.
   e. Two of the above answers are correct.

2. The method in the DataRow class that uses the current row of a parent table to find all rows in a child table is called

   a. GetRelatedRows
   b. ReadChildRows
   c. GetChildRows
   d. GetParentRows
   e. none of the above

3. The type of SQL SELECT statement created by Query Builder when three or more tables are related is called

   a. query join
   b. nested join
   c. outer join
   d. multiple join
   e. none of the above

4. Which of the following tables in the pubs database have a one-to-one relationship?

   a. authors and titleauthor
   b. jobs and employee
   c. stores and discounts
   d. publishers and pub_info
   e. two of the above

True or False

1. In the pubs database, the jobs and employee tables have a one-to-many relationship.
2. In a one-to-many relationship, the child table uses its primary key field to form a relationship with the parent.
3. An example of a column check constraint would be to say that an employee salary cannot be greater than $100,000.
4. A DataGrid control can only show data from a single table.
5. To display both parent and child tables in a DataGrid, you must create a single dataset that defines a DataRelation between the tables.
6. A DataRelation object is created using the Query Builder.

Short Answer

1. Which table in the pubs database has a one-to-one relationship with the publishers table?
2. When a child table contains a foreign key with no matching value in the related parent table, what type of constraint is violated?
3. What do you call the automatic action performed by a database when a primary key value is changed in a table that belongs to a parent-child relationship?
4. Which DataGrid property lets you assign a table name to the MappingName property in the grid?
5. Which DataGrid property lets you define the appearance of individual column headings?
6. What is the name of the DataRow method that returns the row in the parent table which is linked to the current child row?

What Do You Think?

1. In a database that records information about sporting goods rentals, one table might contain the ID numbers of items rented during the past month. Another table might contain the ID numbers of the store's inventory items. What type of relationship would the two tables likely have?
2. Suppose you were to create separate datasets for parent and child tables in a one-to-many relationship (jobs and employees, for example). Would it still be possible to display both datasets in a single DataGrid control?
3. In the **SelectingJobs** program (Section 5.4), if no DataView control were used, how might we still be able to display a list of employees having a particular job category?
4. When two tables have a parent-child relationship, what happens if a dataset is filled by the child table's data adapter before being filled by the parent table's data adapter?
5. Suppose you want to display a DataGrid containing a list of all book titles and the names of their authors, sorted in ascending by book title. Assume that you don't want the user to have to navigate between parent and child tables. Should you use a single SQL query and place the data in a single data adapter, or should you use two separate data adapters and join them into a single dataset?

Algorithm Workbench

1. Write an SQL query that joins the sales and stores tables, using **stor_id** as the linking column. The returned rows should contain the title_id and stor_name columns.

2. Write a Visual Basic statement that filters a DataView named dvEmployee in such a way that job_id (an integer) is equal to the contents of the SelectedValue property of a combo box named cboJobs.

3. Write a Visual Basic statement that filters a DataView named dvSales in such a way that stor_id (an integer) is equal to the contents of the SelectedValue property of a combo box named cboStores.

4. Assume that a one-to-many DataRelation named relJobsEmployee connects the jobs and employee tables in the pubs database. Write a Visual Basic statement that gets the child rows of drJobs, a DataRow object. Assign the rows to a variable named employeeRows.

5. Write an SQL query that returns rows from the pubs database containing jobs.job_desc, employee.lname, and employee.hire_date.

▶ 5.9 Programming Challenges

1. Finding Authors by State

Write a program that lets the user select rows from the authors table in the pubs database, using the author's state of residence as the selection criteria. When the program starts up (see Figure 5-42), a list of state abbreviations appears in a list box (with no duplicates, of course). The datagrid on the form is blank.

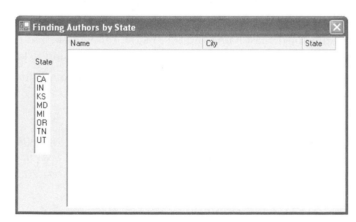

Figure 5-42 Startup window.

When the user selects a state abbreviation from the list box, the grid fills with all authors who live in the selected state (Figure 5-43). Each author's first and last name appear in the first column, and the rows are sorted in ascending order by last name.

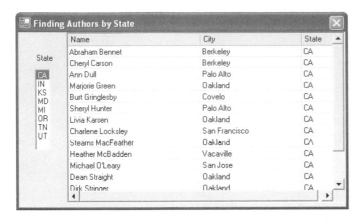

Figure 5-43 California selected.

Row headers are not visible. The grid should be read-only, and only the Name, City, and State columns should display in the grid. Here are a few hints to get you started:

◆ Use separate data adapters for the list box and the data grid.

◆ Use a DataView control to filter the rows in the data grid.

◆ To ensure a unique list of state abbreviations in the list box, use a SELECT DISTINCT statement in the data adapters SelectCommand.CommandText property.

◆ The authors table has separate columns for the last name and first name. You will need to find a way to add a new column to the dataset that joints the names together using an Expression field.

◆ When a state abbreviation is selected, the list box's SelectedItem property will hold a DataRowView object; its row.Item(0) property will contain the state abbreviation.

2. SalesByStore

Using the SalesByStore program from Section 5.5 as a starting point, make the following improvement: For each book found in the sales table, display the book's title and author in the same ListView control. To simplify your program, you can use a single data adapter for the sales, titles, stores, authors, and titleauthor tables.

3. Books by Authors

Write a program that displays a list of authors' first and last names in a data grid, using the **pubs** database. When the user expands an author entry and clicks on a hyperlink, the grid displays the titles and publisher IDs of all books by the selected author. In the startup window shown in Figure 5-44, the user has selected the author Marjorie Green. In Figure 5-45, the grid displays all books by the selected author. The File menu contains the Exit command, which halts the program.

Implementation: You will need to link the titles and authors tables to the titleauthor table. You can use two separate data adapters, and create a relation named "Books_by_Author".

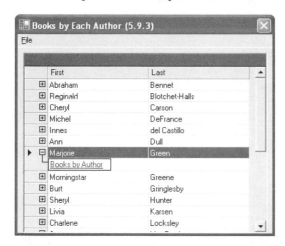

Figure 5-44 Startup window, Books by Authors program.

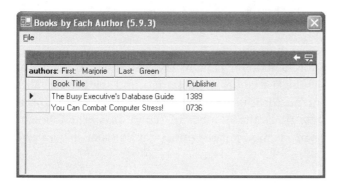

Figure 5-45 List of books by one author.

4. Publisher Employees

Create a dataset containing an employee's first and last names, publisher name, and job description. Display the information in a single DataGrid panel. Hide the DataGrid's caption and row headers. The first and last names must appear in a single column, in alphabetical order by last name. Suggested steps:

◆ Use an SQL query to join the three tables in a single data adapter.

◆ Generate a dataset, and add the expression field for the full name (first + ' ' + last).

◆ Use a data adapter to sort the dataset.

◆ Connect the data adapter to the DataGrid, and define the latter's table and column styles.

Following is a sample:

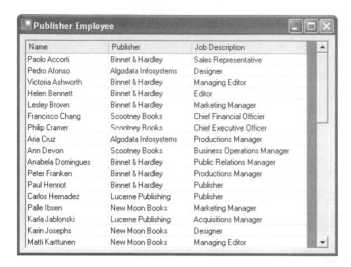

5. Saving a Rental Reservation

Write a program that adds a new row to the RentalsOut table of the SportsRentals database using an INSERT query. Use combo boxes to display the last names of customers and sales clerks, and descriptions of rental items. Input the number of rental days using a text box. The prepayment amount is calculated by multiplying the item's daily rate times the number of rental days. The following sample shows how the program calculates the prepayment amount based on a 3-day rental of an item priced at $62 per day:

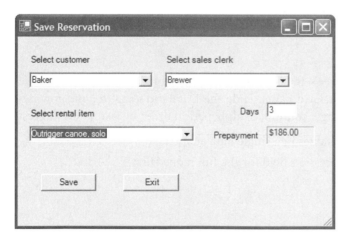

When the user clicks on the Save button, your program must open the Connection object, assign values to the query parameters of a Command object, and call ExecuteNonQuery. Then display a message on the status bar saying the reservation was saved.

Here's a partial listing of code that inserts a new row in the table:

```
conSportsRentals.Open()
With daRentalsOut.InsertCommand
    .Parameters("item_id").Value = cboItems.SelectedValue
    .Parameters("customer_id").Value = cboCustomers.SelectedValue
    (and so on, with the other parameters)
    .ExecuteNonQuery()
End With
conSportsRentals.Close()
```

However, you must also use a Try-Catch block to handle exeptions. The rental_id field is automatically generated, so you do not have to assign it a value.

6. Book Royalties

Using the titles table in the pubs database, fill a combo box with an alphabetical list of book types. The list should not contain duplicates, so use the SELECT DISTINCT clause in the data adapter.

When the user selects a book type, fill a DataGrid with books having the selected type, as in Figure 5-46. The grid must contain the following fields, with customized column headings:

◆ title

◆ ytd_sales

◆ price

◆ publisher name

(The publisher name is from in the publishers table.) Sort the rows by title. When the user clicks on a selection button to the left of a grid row, display the total royalty amount in a label below the grid.

When the user clicks on the button at the left side of a grid row, your program must calculate the amount of royalties due for the book (see Figure 5-47). (You may recall that Chapter 4 showed how to respond to the Click event of a DataGrid.)

To calculate the royalty, multiply the book price by the sales count, and then by the royalty rate. The royalty rate is stored as a whole number in the titles table, so it must be divided by 100 to produce a percent value.

If the user clicks on a row that contains null values for sales, price, or royalty rate, use a Try-Catch block to prevent a runtime error, and display an appropriate message (Figure 5-48).

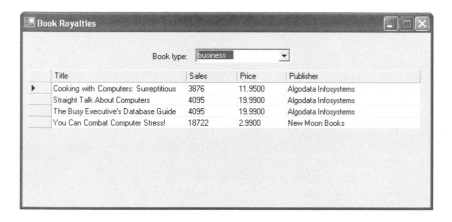

Figure 5-46 Selecting a book in the combo box fills a grid with matching books.

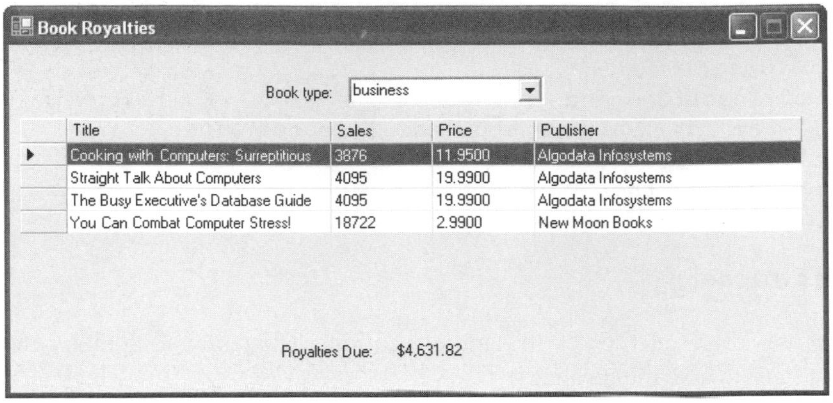

Book Royalties

Book type: business

Title	Sales	Price	Publisher
Cooking with Computers: Surreptitious	3876	11.9500	Algodata Infosystems
Straight Talk About Computers	4095	19.9900	Algodata Infosystems
The Busy Executive's Database Guide	4095	19.9900	Algodata Infosystems
You Can Combat Computer Stress!	18722	2.9900	New Moon Books

Royalties Due: $4,631.82

Figure 5-47   Selecting a book in the grid produces the book's royalties.

Cannot Calculate Royalty Amount

The current book's price, sales, and/or royalty rate contain null values

[OK]

Figure 5-48   Response to null field values.

Using SQL Server

▶6.1 INTRODUCTION

Structured Query Language (SQL)

In past chapters, we mainly used SQL to retrieve data from tables using SELECT statements. In this chapter, our goal is to help you to become more independent of data adapters and datasets, and to write SQL statements on your own. We will use SQL to create new tables, insert rows in tables, remove tables, and modify table data. The flexibility and skills learned here will be invaluable as you move into ASP.NET database programming in Chapter 9.

The ADO.NET database driver passes SQL statements to the database engine. Some database operations are more efficient when written in SQL. For example, if you need to delete all the records in a dataset, a single statement in SQL can do the job. Without SQL, you would have to loop through all the rows of a dataset and remove them one by one.

ADO.NET uses a standard version of SQL named **ANSI SQL**, designed by the American National Standards Institute (ANSI). Previously, Visual Basic used a version of SQL named **Jet SQL**, the same one still used by MS-Access. The two versions of SQL are nearly compatible, with some minor exceptions that we will point out later.

Row-Returning Queries

SQL queries that use the SELECT statement are called *row-returning queries*. Such queries return a result set made up of rows from one or more tables.

Action Queries

Queries that do not return result sets are called *action queries*. Such queries modify the database by changing the contents of tables or by changing the structure of the database. Action queries are also called *non row-returning queries*. Two subsets of SQL are used in action queries:

◆ Data Manipulation Language (DML): Queries that modify the contents of tables by adding, deleting, or updating rows.

◆ Data Definition Language (DDL): Queries that modify the database structure by adding or removing tables, or by modifying table structures.

All the above actions can be carried out in design mode, using tools such as SQL Server Enterprise Manager, or Visual Studio .NET Server Explorer. In this chapter, you will learn how to perform action queries from within program code.

Column Types

If you plan to create or modify SQL Server database tables, you must be familiar with the basic column types, listed in Table 6-1. Here are a few guidelines to follow when selecting column types:

◆ Use the varchar type for text columns in which the contents vary in length.

◆ Use the char type for text columns that have a fixed size. If necessary, column contents are automatically padded at the end with spaces to match the column size. For example, if you insert the string "ABC" into a char(6) column, the column contents become "ABC   ", including three trailing spaces.

Table 6-1

SQL Server Column Types.

SQL Data Type	Corresponding VB Data Type	Description
binary[(n)]		Fixed-length binary data with a maximum length of 8,000 bytes.
varbinary[(n)]	Array of Byte	Variable-length binary data with a maximum length of 8,000 bytes.
char[(n)]	Array of Char	Fixed-length non-Unicode character data with a maximum length of 8,000 characters.
varchar[(n)]	String	Variable-length non-Unicode data with a maximum of 8,000 characters.
datetime	DateTime	Date and time data from January 1, 1753, through December 31, 9999, with an accuracy of three-hundredths of a second, or 3.33 milliseconds. Date literals inserted into datetime columns must be surrounded by single quotes, as in '05/15/2004'.
smalldatetime	DateTime	Date and time data from January 1, 1900, through June 6, 2079, with an accuracy of one minute.
decimal	Decimal	Fixed precision and scale numeric data from $-10^{38} +1$ through $10^{38} -1$.
numeric	Decimal	Functionally equivalent to **decimal.**
float	Double	Floating precision number data from $-1.79E + 308$ through $1.79E + 308$.
real	Single	Floating precision number data from $-3.40E + 38$ through $3.40E + 38$.
int	Integer	Integer (whole number) data from -2^{31} ($-2,147,483,648$) through $2^{31} - 1$ ($2,147,483,647$).
smallint	Short	Integer data from 2^{15} ($-32,768$) through $2^{15} - 1$ ($32,767$).

(table continues)

Table 6-1

SQL Server Column Types. *(continued)*

SQL Data Type	Corresponding VB Data Type	Description
tinyint	Byte	Integer data from 0 through 255.
money	Decimal	Monetary data values from -2^{63} ($-922,337,203,685,477.5808$) through $2^{63} - 1$ ($+922,337,203,685,477.5807$), with accuracy to a ten-thousandth of a monetary unit.
Smallmoney	Decimal	Monetary data values from $-214,748.3648$ through $+214,748.3647$, with accuracy to a ten-thousandth of a monetary unit.
Bit	Boolean	Integer data with either a 1 or 0 value.
timestamp		A database-wide unique number that is updated when a row is updated.
user-defined		Data that matches the definition of a user-defined data type.
text	String	Variable-length non-Unicode data with a maximum length of $2^{31} - 1$ ($2,147,483,647$) characters.
image		Variable-length binary data with a maximum length of $2^{31} - 1$ ($2,147,483,647$) bytes.

Primary Key

When you create a table, always designate one or more columns as the primary key. The key is essential when performing update, delete, and insert operations on individual table rows. In general, the primary key is the best way to uniquely identify a table row.

Every table can have at most one clustered key as its primary key. A clustered key is formed by combining columns in such a way that they uniquely identify each table row. You may recall the **titleauthor** table from the pubs database, for example (0). Any author ID can appear multiple times, and any title ID can appear multiple times. The primary key, therefore is clustered, combining the au_id and title_id columns (Table 6-2).

Table 6-2

The titleauthor table, sorted by title_id.

au_id	title_id	au_ord	royaltyper
213-46-8915	BU1032	2	40
409-56-7008	BU1032	1	60
267-41-2394	BU1111	2	40
724-80-9391	BU1111	1	60
213-46-8915	BU2075	1	100
274-80-9391	BU7832	1	100

Indexes

An *index* is a logical structure encoded within a database that provides a way for the database to efficiently search for information. Generally, indexes are created on two types of columns: primary keys and foreign keys. By definition, a primary key is a unique index. In the case of foreign keys, the entries are not unique, but the index can optimize searches for entries.

Views

A view is a tool you can use to select certain columns or rows from a table, or from multiple related tables. In other words, a view is basically a named query that can be used in other table relationships. Some common reasons for creating Views are the following:

◆ To restrict certain users from accessing columns containing senstive information.
◆ To join together existing tables or views.
◆ To rename table columns, making them more user-friendly.
◆ To filter table rows.

Views use the principle of abstraction to remove the user one or more steps from the original data. We could use table X to supply data when creating a view named Y. At the same time, we could rename the columns. Any program using view Y from that point on would have no knowledge of the column names in table X that supply the data.

Authentication Methods

SQL Server offers two types of authentication choices for databases:

◆ **Windows NT Integrated Security:** The current user's username and ID are automatically used when opening and modifying the database. When you run Visual Studio .NET applications, the current user automatically becomes **ASP.NET Machine A....** Whatever rights are assigned to that user will be the rights given to the application.
◆ **SQL Server Authentication:** You can encode a separate user id and password into the database connection string. These values are used when authenticating the user, before the database can be opened.

Checkpoint

6.1 Which version of SQL is supported by Microsoft ADO?
6.2 Which version of SQL is used when you use an OleDb Connection to connect to a Microsoft Access database?
6.3 Which language within SQL is used for modifying the contents of tables?
6.4 Which Visual Basic type corresponds most closely to the SQL Server varchar column type?
6.5 Which SQL server type corresponds to the Visual Basic Byte data type?
6.6 Why are indexes useful?
6.7 Identify at least two common reasons for creating Views.
6.8 What is a clustered key?

▶6.2 Creating Databases and Tables

Using Server Explorer

Microsoft Visual Studio .NET Server Explorer is a convenient tool that makes it easy to interactively design and modify databases on your local machine. It is not as complete as the tools supplied with a full version of SQL Server, but it is good enough for most tasks. If you use a shared database in a computer lab, check with your lab adminstrator on the best way to create and modify databases.

If you have already installed SQL Server 2000, you will probably want to skip this section and go directly to the one entitled **Using SQL Server Enterprise Manager**.

Creating a Database

To create a database in Server Explorer, locate the NETSDK server name in the list of available servers. Server Explorer only lets you create databases on the NETSDK server.

Right-click on the NETSDK server name and select **New Database**. When the Create Database dialog appears, select Use Windows NT Integrated Security (Figure 6-1).

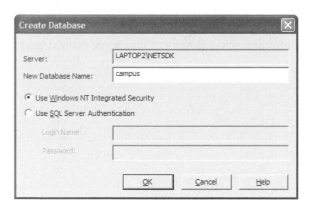

Figure 6-1 Creating a database in Server Explorer.

Creating, Deleting, and Modifying Tables

To create a table in an existing database, right-click on the **Tables** entry under the database name, and select **Add Table**. To delete a table, right-click on the table name and select **Delete**. To add new rows or modify the contents of a table, right-click on the table name and select **Retrieve Data from Table**.

Always create a primary key for a new table. A primary key is required by Visual Studio .NET when it generates UPDATE, DELETE, and INSERT queries for a data adapter. The only type of query that will work without a primary key is a SELECT query.

Hands-On Tutorial: Campus Database (Server Explorer)

This tutorial takes you through the steps required to create a database. You will use Server Explorer to add tables and create stored procedures. The name of the database is **campus**. If your server already has a database named Campus, delete the database from the server. Database names are not case-sensitive.

Step 1. Locate the NETSDK server under *SQL Servers* in the Server Explorer window. Right-click on the server name and select **New Database**. In the Create Database window, name the database **campus** and leave the default option set to *Use Windows NT Integrated Security.*

Step 2. Find the new entry named **campus** in the list of SQL Server databases, and right-click on its **Tables** entry. Create a new table and define the column names and types shown in Figure 6-2.

Column Name	Data Type	Length	Allow Nulls
id	char	9	
firstname	varchar	30	
lastname	varchar	30	
gpa	float	8	
birthdate	varchar	10	✓
status	int	4	

Figure 6-2 Designing the students table.

 Note:
If you want to reorder the table columns in the design window, use the mouse to drag the button on the left side of any column to a new location in the column list.

Step 3. Next, you will designate a primary key. Right-click on the **id** column in the designer window and select **Set Primary Key**. When you save the table, name it **students** and close the designer window.

Step 4. Create an index on the **status** column, which is the foreign key that will connect the students table to another table. Right-click on the students table design and select **Indexes/Keys**. In the Property Pages window (Figure 6-3), click on **New** and create an index named **IX_status**. Set the column name and index name properties as shown in the figure.

Step 5. Right-click the students table in Server Explorer and select **Retrieve Data from Table**. Input several records into the table, as shown in Figure 6-4.

Figure 6-3 Creating an Index on status.

id	firstname	lastname	gpa	birthdate	status
111223333	Julio	Gonzalez	3.56	10/5/82	4
222334444	Maria	Sanchez	3.22	5/15/83	3
333445555	Anson	Chong	2.89	4/1/84	2
555662222	Michael	Johnson	3.4	6/18/85	1

Figure 6-4 Input data into the students table.

Step 6. Create a second table named **status** and insert two columns: **status_id** (type int), and **description** (20 characters). Set status_id as the primary key.

Step 7. Input the following data into the status table:

```
1, freshman
2, sophomore
3, junior
4, senior
5, graduate
```

Step 8. In Server Explorer, find the college database and right-click on **Database Diagrams**. Select **New Diagram**.

Step 9. When prompted by a dialog window, add the status and students tables to the diagram.

Step 10. Drag the mouse from the students.status column to the status.status_id column. When the Create Relationship window appears, check the Cascade Update option. Verify that the entries in the window appear as in Figure 6-5.

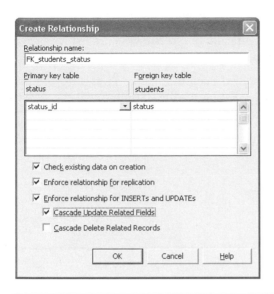

Figure 6-5 Create Relationship window.

Note:
We discussed cascading deletes and updates in Section 5.2.

Step 11. Click Ok to close the Create Relationship window and when prompted, name the relationship **Student-Status**.

Step 12. Right click on the **Views** entry for the college database, and select **New View**. Notice that the window that appears is identical to the Query Designer we have always used with data adapters. Select both the students and status tables in the Add Table window.

Step 13. Select the columns in the upper pane as shown in Figure 6-6. In the grid pane, insert names in the alias column to make the display more user-friendly: Student ID, First, Last, GPA Birth Date, and Status. Run the query, showing the alias names as column headings (Figure 6-7). Save the view and name it **studentView**.

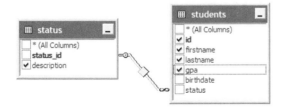

Figure 6-6 Creating the studentView.

Student ID	First	Last	GPA	Birth Date	Status
111223333	Julio	Gonzalez	3.56	10/5/82	senior
222334444	Maria	Sanchez	3.22	5/15/83	junior
333445555	Anson	Chong	2.89	4/1/84	sophomore
555662222	Michael	Johnson	3.4	6/18/85	freshman

Figure 6-7 StudentView with alias column names.

Step 14. Next, create a second view containing a more public list of students that does not include sensitive information. When the Query Designer window opens, click on the **Views** tab of the Add Table window and select **studentView**. Select the First, Last, and Status columns.

Step 15. Sort the rows first by the column named **Last**, then by the column named **First**. Run and test the query. If it looks like the output in Figure 6-8, save the view as **publicStudent**.

Notice from this example that you can build new views from both database tables and other existing views. This powerful capability lets you create customized views of database tables for various groups of users.
(End of tutorial)

First	Last	Status
Anson	Chong	sophomore
Julio	Gonzalez	senior
Michael	Johnson	freshman
Maria	Sanchez	junior

Figure 6-8 PublicStudent view.

Using SQL Server Enterprise Manager

Microsoft SQL Server 2000 Enterprise Manager is an easy-to-use, powerful tool you can use to design and modify databases on your local machine. Understandably, it has many more capabilities than Visual Studio Server Explorer. If you plan to become a practicing Visual Basic professional, you will have to become an expert at using SQL Server, Oracle, or a similar enterprise-level database. If your computer lab has SQL Server 2000 installed, be sure to ask your lab administrator for access to Enterprise Manager.

Creating a Database

To create a new database in Enterprise Manager, double-click on the SQL Server instance you have been instructed to use. The default instance on the local machine is named LOCAL by default (Figure 6-9). The list of databases under your server name may be different from those shown in the figure.

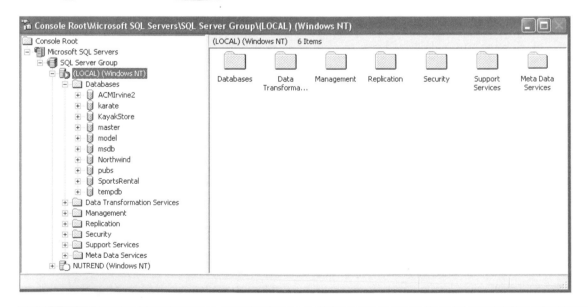

Figure 6-9 Creating a new database in Enterprise Manager.

To create a new database, right-click on the Databases folder and select **New Database**. When the Database Properties dialog appears, enter the database name (Figure 6-10). You do not have to set any other properties, unless specifically instructed by your system administrator.

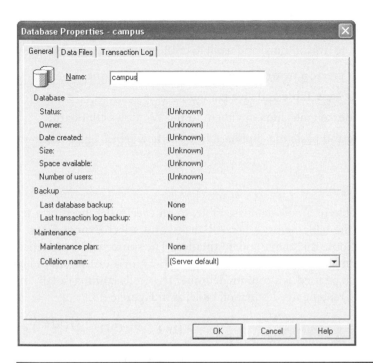

Figure 6-10 Database Properties dialog.

When you select the database name in the left panel, various types of containers associated with the database appear in the right-hand panel (Figure 6-11). In this chapter, we will show you how to use Diagrams, Tables, Views, and Stored Procedures.

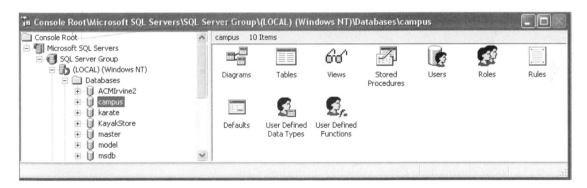

Figure 6-11 Database objects (campus database).

Creating, Deleting, and Modifying Tables

If you open up the list under campus in the left-hand pane and select **Tables**, notice that databases automatically have quite a few system tables. Following is a short summary of commands you are likely to use:

- ◆ To add a table to a database, right-click on the Tables entry and select **New Table**.
- ◆ To delete a table, right-click on the table name and select **Delete**.
- ◆ To view or modify the contents of a table, right-click on the table name and select **Retrieve Data from Table**.

Copying a Table's Structure

If you want to make a copy of a table's structure (its columns) and use it to create a new table, do the following steps:

1. Open the **Diagrams** window. Either create a new diagram or open an existing one.
2. Right click in the window and select **New Table** and give it a name.
3. Select all column names from the source table and copy them to the Windows clipboard.
4. Select the new table with the mouse and paste the clipboard into the new table. The column definitions should appear.

Exporting Table Data

You can easily copy (export) an existing table to a new database table, to an excel worksheet, or a text file. To export one or more tables, right-click on the table name, select **All Tasks**, and select **Export Data**. When the Export Wizard starts, you will be asked to choose the source and destination. The source will automatically be the currently selected database. The destination might be a database, as in Figure 6-12, or a text file, as in Figure 6-13. For the latter, you can choose the character to be used as a column delimiter (typically comma or tab). If you copy the table to a new table in the same database, rename the destination table, as in Figure 6-14.

Figure 6-12 Choose destination database when exporting data.

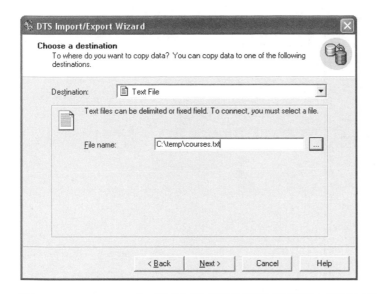

Figure 6-13 Exporting to a text file.

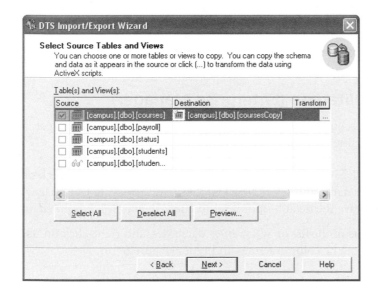

Figure 6-14 Selecting the table to be copied.

Creating an Index

To create an index, you must open a table in design mode. Then, right-click in the table design window and select **Indexes/Keys**. In the Properties window, click on the **New** button and assign a name to your index. For example, in Figure 6-15 an index named IX_status was created based on a column named **status** from a table named **students**.

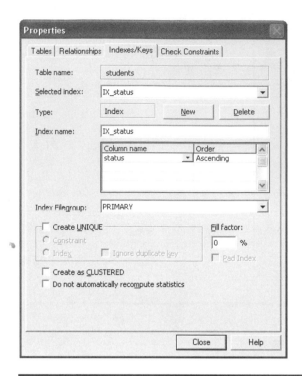

Figure 6-15 Creating an index.

Hands-On Tutorial: Campus Database (Enterprise Manager)

This tutorial takes you through the steps required to create a database using Enterprise Manager, add some tables, and create stored procedures. The name of the database is **campus**.

Step 1. Locate your SQL server under *SQL Servers* in the Enterprise Manager window. Right-click on the **Databases** folder under the server name and select **New Database**. In the Create Database window, name the database **campus** and leave the default option set to *Use Windows NT Integrated Security*.

Step 2. Find the new entry named **campus** in the list of SQL Server databases, and right-click on its **Tables** entry. Create a new table and define the column names and types (Figure 6-16).

Column Name	Data Type	Length	Allow Nulls
id	char	9	
firstname	varchar	30	
lastname	varchar	30	
gpa	float	8	
birthdate	varchar	10	✓
status	int	4	

Figure 6-16 Designing the students table.

 Note:
If you want to reorder the table columns in the design window, use the mouse to drag the button on the left side of any column to a new location in the column list.

Step 3. Next, you will designate the id column as the primary key. Right-click on the column in the designer window and select *Set Primary Key*. When you save the table, name it **students** and close the designer window.

Step 4. Create an index on the **status** column, which is the foreign key that connects the students table to another table. Right-click on the students table design and select Indexes/Keys. In the Properties window, (previously shown in Figure 6-15), click on the New button and create an index named IX_status. Set the column name and index name properties as shown.

Step 5. Right-click the students table in Enterprise Manager, select **Open Table**, and select **Return all rows**. Input several records into the table (Figure 6-17).

id	firstname	lastname	gpa	birthdate	status
111223333	Julio	Gonzalez	3.56	10/5/82	4
222334444	Maria	Sanchez	3.22	5/15/83	3
333445555	Anson	Chong	2.89	4/1/84	2
555662222	Michael	Johnson	3.4	6/18/85	1

Figure 6-17 Input data into the students table.

Step 6. Create a second table named **status** and insert two columns: **status_id** (type int), and **description** (type varchar(20)). Make status_id the primary key, and do not allow either column to be null.

Step 7. Input the following data into the status table:

```
1, freshman
2, sophomore
3, junior
4, senior
5, graduate
```

Step 8. In the left-hand pane, right-click on **Diagrams**. Select **New Database Diagram.**

Step 9. When prompted by the wizard, add the status and students tables to the diagram.

Step 10. Drag the mouse from the students.status column to the status.status_id column. When the Create Relationship window appears, check the **Cascade Update** option. Verify that the entries in the window appear as in Figure 6-18.

Figure 6-18 Create Relationship window.

Step 11. Click Ok to close the Create Relationship window and when prompted, name it **Student-Status**.

(If in the future you want to inspect a table relationship, select Diagrams in the left-hand pane and double-click on the relationship name.)

Step 12. Next, you will create a view that joins the student and status tables. Right-click on the **Views** entry for the college database, and select **New View**. The displayed window is identical to the Query Designer we use to design data adapters. Select the students and status tables in the **Add Table** window.

Step 13. Select the columns in the upper pane (Figure 6-19). Insert names in the alias column to make the display more user-friendly: Student ID, First, Last, GPA Birth Date, and Status. Run the query again, showing the new column headings (Figure 6-20). Save the view as **studentView**.

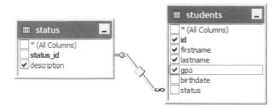

Figure 6-19 Creating studentView.

Student ID	First	Last	GPA	Birth Date	Status
► 111223333	Julio	Gonzalez	3.56	10/5/82	senior
222334444	Maria	Sanchez	3.22	5/15/83	junior
333445555	Anson	Chong	2.89	4/1/84	sophomore
555662222	Michael	Johnson	3.4	6/18/85	freshman

Figure 6-20 StudentView with alias column names.

Step 14. Create a second view containing a more restricted view of students that omits sensitive information. When the Query Designer window opens, click on the **Views** tab of the Add Table window and select **studentView**. Select the First, Last, and Status columns. Sort on last name, then on first name. Run and test the query. If it looks like Figure 6-21, save the view as **publicStudent**.

(End of tutorial)

First	Last	Status
Anson	Chong	sophomore
Julio	Gonzalez	senior
Michael	Johnson	freshman
Maria	Sanchez	junior

Figure 6-21 PublicStudent view.

Checkpoint

6.9 When creating a database using Server Explorer, what type of security must be used?

6.10 In the Query Designer window, how do you assign alias names to existing columns?

6.11 How is the Diagrams window used in Enterprise Manager?

▶6.3 Data Definition Language (DDL)

Earlier, we mentioned that action queries modify either the database structure or the contents of the database's data. Let's now focus on the SQL subset that lets you perform one type of action query: Data Definition Language (DDL). You can use it to create or modify databases, tables, indexes, and views. We will limit our examples to the following DDL statements:

◆ CREATE TABLE

◆ DROP TABLE

◆ ALTER TABLE

CREATE TABLE

The CREATE TABLE statement creates a new database table. You must supply all column names and types:

```
CREATE TABLE tablename
(  col1 type [(size)] [NULL | NOT NULL]
   [, col2 type [(size)] [NULL | NOT NULL]
   [, ...]]
)
```

Tablename is the name of a table that does not exist, *type* is the column type, and *size* is only relevant for binary, varbinary, char, and varchar columns. Optionally, you can include a column constraint that prevents a column from being empty (equal to null).

Examples

The following example creates a table named **students** containing columns named id, firstname, lastname, and gpa:

```
CREATE TABLE students
   (id int PRIMARY KEY,        'defaults to NOT NULL
   firstname varchar(30),
   lastname varchar(30),
   gpa float NOT NULL)
```

We permit only the firstname and lastname columns to contain null values, and **id** is the primary key. The following example creates a table named **payroll** in which none of the columns may contain null values:

```
CREATE TABLE payroll
   (employeeId int PRIMARY KEY,
   paymentDate datetime NOT NULL,
   hoursWorked real NOT NULL,
   hourlyRate real NOT NULL
   )
```

DROP TABLE

The **DROP TABLE** statement removes an existing table from a database. This is the basic syntax:

```
DROP TABLE tablename
```

For example, the following statement removes the Students table:

```
DROP TABLE Students
```

In a parent-child relationship, the child table must be dropped before the parent. Any views or stored procedures associated with the table must be dropped before the table can be dropped.

ALTER TABLE

The ALTER TABLE command can do any of the following:

◆ Add a column to a table
◆ Modify the attributes of an existing column
◆ Drop a column from a table

There are three basic formats:

```
ALTER TABLE tablename
   ALTER COLUMN column_name
   new_data_type[(size)]
   [NULL | NOT NULL]

ALTER TABLE tablename
   ADD column_name
   data_type[(size)]
   [NULL | NOT NULL]

ALTER TABLE tablename
   DROP COLUMN column_name
```

Examples

The following examples create and modify columns in a table named payroll:

◆ Add a column named hourlyRate of type int to the table:

```
ALTER TABLE payroll
   ADD hourlyRate int
```

◆ Change the hourlyRate column to type real and do not permit the column to be null:

```
ALTER TABLE payroll
   ALTER COLUMN hourlyRate real NOT NULL
```

◆ Add a hireDate column of type datetime and permit the column to be null:

```
ALTER TABLE payroll
   ADD hireDate datetime NULL
```

◆ Drop the hireDate column:

```
ALTER TABLE payroll
   DROP COLUMN hireDate
```

Adding a Primary Key

If a table does not have a primary key, you can use the ALTER TABLE statement to add one. The following example sets the employeeId column as the primary key:

```
ALTER TABLE payroll
   ADD PRIMARY KEY employeeId
```

You can add a clustered primary key to a table. The following clusters the employeeId and paymentDate columns:

```
ALTER TABLE payroll
   ADD PRIMARY KEY CLUSTERED
   (employeeId, paymentDate
   )
```

Checkpoint

6.12 Which SQL statement adds a new table to a database?

6.13 When creating a table, show an example of declaring a column named **address**, which contains a variable amount of text up to 50 characters.

6.14 What information, aside from the table name, must be supplied to the DROP TABLE statement?

6.15 Write a statement that modifies the structure of a table named **employees**: Add a new integer column named **serviceYears**.

6.4 Data Manipulation Language (DML)

Data Manipulation Language is used to create action queries that modify the contents of database tables. The commands we will discuss here are UPDATE, DELETE, and INSERT INTO.

UPDATE

The UPDATE statement modifies one or more table rows. Here's the basic syntax:

```
UPDATE table
  SET colname = newvalue
  WHERE criteria
```

You can update single or multiple rows, modifying one or more column values.

Examples

The following query increases the hourly pay rate in all rows of the payroll table by 5 percent:

```
UPDATE payroll
  SET hourlyRate = hourlyRate * 1.05
```

The following query increases the hourly pay rate for employees who were paid after a given payment date:

```
UPDATE payroll
  SET hourlyRate = hourlyRate * 1.05
  WHERE paymentDate > '05/01/1999'
```

Sales Table Example

Let's use a new table named **Sales**, shown in Figure 6-22. The Jan and Feb columns list the amount of goods sold by each employee, in thousands of dollars. The PctIncrease column represents the percent increase in sales between January and February. Initially, the column is blank, so we can write an update query that calculates the percent increase:

```
UPDATE Sales
  SET PctIncrease = (Feb - Jan) / Jan * 100
```

empId	Jan	Feb	PctIncrease
1001	1000	2000	100
1002	1500	1800	20
1003	760	850	12
1004	1900	2400	26

Figure 6-22 Sales table.

Updating with Parameters

Update queries usually require a complete set of parameters because multiple column values must be replaced. The following example updates a single row in the payroll table, using a simplified version of the one auto-generated for data adapters. We assume the @id parameter is used to locate the record, and only the remaining three columns are updated:

```
UPDATE payroll
   SET paymentDate = @paymentDate, hoursWorked = @hoursWorked,
      hourlyRate = @hourlyRate
   WHERE id = @id
```

If the ID column will be modified during the update, we must include an additional parameter that locates the record to be updated before we modify the ID column:

```
UPDATE payroll
   SET id = @id, paymentDate = @paymentDate,
      hoursWorked = @hoursWorked,
      hourlyRate = @hourlyRate
   WHERE id = @original_id
```

DELETE

The DELETE statement removes one or more rows from a table. The WHERE clause can be used to select the rows. This is the syntax:

```
DELETE
  FROM tablename
  [WHERE criteria]
```

Once a row has been deleted, it cannot be recovered. If you delete rows from a parent table in a parent-child relationship there is a potential for making orphans in the child table. That is, rows may exist in the child table that have no counterpart in the parent table. The following command deletes all rows from the payroll table in which the payment date is before January 1, 1998:

```
DELETE FROM payroll
  WHERE paymentDate < '1/1/1998'
```

The following command deletes all rows from the payroll table and retains the empty table in the database:

```
DELETE FROM payroll
```

INSERT INTO

The INSERT INTO statement, known as an *append* query, inserts new rows in a table. You can add a single row by supplying all of its column data, or multiple rows can be appended from another table.

Single-Row Append

A single-row append query has the following syntax:

```
INSERT INTO target
  [(column1[,column2[,...]])]
  VALUES(value1,[,value2[,...])
```

Column names must be specified unless you assign column values in exactly the same order as they occur in the table. The following query appends a new row to the payroll table. All column names are specified:

```
INSERT INTO payroll(id, paymentDate, hoursWorked, hourlyRate)
   VALUES( 1001, '1/15/1998', 47.5, 17.50 )
```

Assuming that the columns are in order, the following query produces the same result as the previous one:

```
INSERT INTO payroll
   VALUES( 1001, '1/15/1998', 47.5, 17.50 )
```

Notice that dates and text (string) values must be enclosed in single quotes.

 Microsoft Access requires date literals to be surrounded by # delimiters, as in #1/15/1998#. Do not use this delimiter with SQL Server.

Multi-Row Append

You can use the INSERT INTO statement to copy one or more rows from one table to another. Here is the general syntax:

```
INSERT INTO target
   SELECT col1,col2[,...]
   FROM source
```

The data in the specified columns are copied from the table named *source* to the table named *target*. For example, the following query copies the id and hourlyRate columns from all rows of the payroll table to the payTemp table:

```
INSERT INTO payTemp
   SELECT id, hourlyRate
   FROM payroll
```

The following query copies all columns of all rows from the payroll table to the payTemp table:

```
INSERT INTO payTemp
   SELECT *
   FROM payroll
```

You can apply a Boolean condition to an append query. The following statement copies only rows in which hoursWorked is greater than 40 from the payroll table to the payTemp table:

```
INSERT INTO payTemp
   SELECT *
   FROM payroll
   WHERE hoursWorked >= 40
```

Checkpoint

6.16 Write a statement that sets the **bonus** column to 0 in all rows of the **employees** table.

6.17 Write a statement that multiplies the **salary** column by 1.10 in all rows of the **employees** table.

6.18 Write a statement that sets **bonus** to 1000 in the **employees** table, only in rows where the person's **hireDate** is less than 01/01/1998.

6.19 Write a statement that deletes all rows from the **payroll** table in which **hoursWorked** is less than 40.

▶6.5 Executing Queries in Program Code

You can create and execute SQL queries in program code, without using Visual Studio components. There are some basic steps to follow, assuming you are using a SQL Server database:

1. Import the System.Data.SqlClient namespace.
2. Create a database connection, using Visual Basic code or by selecting **SqlConnection** from the Data tab of the Visual Studio ToolBox.
3. Create a command object (SqlCommand), passing a query to its constructor. The query can be any of the DDL query types we have discussed in this chapter.
4. Set the command object's CommandType property to CommandType.Text, a constant defined in the SqlClient namespace.
5. Set the command object's Connection property to your database connection.
6. Open the connection and call ExecuteNonQuery on the command object.

You will want to enclose these steps in a Try-Catch block. One additional required step, closing the connection, should be located in the Finally block of the exception handler. Doing this ensures that the connection will be closed even when an exception is thrown. But what if the exception was thrown before the connection could be successfully opened? You can check the connection's Status property before trying to close it. Here's a sample:

```
Finally
   If myConn.State = ConnectionState.Open Then
      myConn.Close()
   End If
End Try
```

Campus Database Example

If you do not choose to create a Connection component using the Visual Studio Connection Wizard, you can create a connection string for the campus database using program code. If you are using the NETSDK server, the string would be the following:

```
Dim conStr As String = "integrated security=SSPI;data source=" _
   & "(local)\NETSDK;initial catalog=campus"
```

Or, if you are using a local SQL server under SQL Server 2000, the string would be the following (assuming that your database username is **sa**):

```
Dim conStr As String = "user id=sa;data source=(local);" _
   & "initial catalog=campus"
```

You would then create the connection object using the following statement:

```
Dim conCampus As SqlConnection = New SqlConnection(conStr)
```

Next, you would create a command object named **cmd**, set its CommandType and Connection properties, open the connection, execute the query, display either a success message or an error message and close the connection. Here's a complete example in which the query string is contained in a TextBox control named txtQuery:

```
Try
   Dim cmd As New SqlCommand(txtQuery.Text)
   cmd.CommandType = CommandType.Text
   cmd.Connection = conCampus
   conCampus.Open()
   cmd.ExecuteNonQuery()
```

```
      lblResult.Text = "Query executed successfully"
   Catch ex As SqlClient.SqlException
      lblResult.Text = ex.Message
   Finally
      If conCampus.State = ConnectionState.Open Then
         conCampus.Close()
      End If
   End Try
```

Hands-On Tutorial: Action Query Program

ActionQueryDemo

Let's create a program that executes action queries interactively selected by the user. We will make it easy for the user to modify and test a variety of queries, and to see the queries' effect on the database. Figure 6-23 shows the program while running. The user has selected a query that creates the payroll table. The query appears in a textbox, giving the user a chance to modify the query before it executes. The status line at the bottom indicates the success or failure of the query after the Execute button is clicked.

One reason this program is so useful is that the user can experiment by running the various queries in different sequences. By being able to modify the queries, the user can introduce new column names and values. The Display Payroll button displays the contents of the payroll table in a DataGrid (Figure 6-24) so the user can see the results of running the queries.

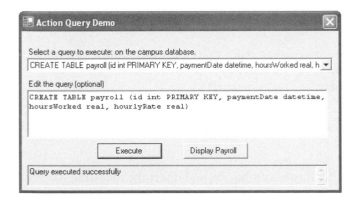

Figure 6-23 Running the Action Query Demo program.

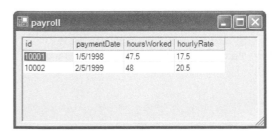

Figure 6-24 Displaying the payroll table.

To create the program, do the following:

Step 1. Create a new program named **ActionQueryDemo**. Add System.Data.SqlClient to the program's Imports list in the Project Properties window.

Step 2. Design the startup form using the sample already shown in Figure 6-23. Table 6-3 lists the nontrivial controls used on the startup form. Add an SqlConnection component named conCampus to the form, and attach it to the campus database.

Table 6-3

Startup form properties (ActionQueryDemo).

Control Type	Control Name	Property Values
SqlConnection	conCampus	(connect to campus database)
TextBox	txtQuery	
ComboBox	cboQueries	DropDownStyle: DropDownList
Button	btnExecute	Text: Execute
Button	btnDisplay	Text: Display Payroll
TextBox	txtResult	Multiline: True
		ReadOnly: True
		ScrollBars: Vertical
Form	frmMain	Title: Action Query Demo

Step 3. Insert the following queries into the Items collection of the ComboBox, leaving out the line numbers:

```
1:  CREATE TABLE payroll (id int PRIMARY KEY, paymentDate
    datetime, hoursWorked real, hourlyRate real)
2:  CREATE TABLE payTemp (id int PRIMARY KEY, paymentDate
    datetime, hoursWorked real, hourlyRate real)
3:  DELETE FROM payroll
4:  DELETE FROM payTemp
5:  DROP TABLE payroll
6:  DROP TABLE payTemp
7:  INSERT INTO payroll (id, PaymentDate, HoursWorked, HourlyRate)
    VALUES (10001, '1/5/1998', 47.5, 17.50)
8:  INSERT INTO payTemp SELECT * FROM payroll
9:  UPDATE payTemp SET hourlyRate = hourlyRate * 1.20
```

Each query should be a separate item. The lines wrap around on the printed page, but should not wrap around in the Items collection.

Step 4. Create a SelectedIndexChanged handler for the combo box and insert the following statement that copies the query from the combo box to the text box:

```
txtQuery.Text = CStr(cboQueries.SelectedItem)
```

Step 5. Insert the following code into the Click event handler for the btnExecute button:

```
Try
    Dim cmd As New SqlCommand(txtQuery.Text)
    cmd.CommandType = CommandType.Text
    cmd.Connection = conCampus
    conCampus.Open()
    cmd.ExecuteNonQuery()
    txtResult.Text = "Query executed successfully"
Catch ex As SqlClient.SqlException
    txtResult.Text = ex.Message
Finally
    If conCampus.State = ConnectionState.Open Then
        conCampus.Close()
    End If
End Try
```

Step 6. Create a Click event handler for the Display Payroll button and insert the following code:

```
Dim frm As New frmPayroll
frm.ShowDialog()
```

Step 7. Add a second form to the program and name it **frmPayroll**. Insert a DataGrid control and use Server Explorer to create a connection component, data adapter, and dataset for the payroll table. Refer back to Figure 6-24 for the form's design. Set the grid's DataSource property to **DsPayroll1**, and its DataMember property to **payroll**.

Step 8. In the form's Load event handler, use a Try-Catch block to let the program recover if the user tries to display the payroll table after it has been deleted:

```
Try
    daPayroll.Fill(DsPayroll1)
Catch ex As SqlClient.SqlException
    MessageBox.Show("Unable to open the payroll table. " _
        & "Did you drop it from the database?", "Error")
    Me.Close()
End Try
```

Step 9. Run and test the program. Experiment with different queries. For example, what happens if you try to create the same table twice in a row? What happens if you drop a table twice? Try modifying some of the queries, perhaps by creating new table names.

(End of tutorial)

9

Program Listing

Following is a complete listing of the startup form code (frmMain.vb):

```
Public Class frmMain
    Inherits System.Windows.Forms.Form

┌────────────────────────────────────────┐
│ + Windows Form Designer generated code │
└────────────────────────────────────────┘

    Private Sub cboQueries_SelectedIndexChanged(ByVal sender _
     As System.Object, ByVal e As System.EventArgs) _
     Handles cboQueries.SelectedIndexChanged

       txtQuery.Text = CStr(cboQueries.SelectedItem)
    End Sub

    Private Sub btnExecute_Click(ByVal sender As _
     System.Object, ByVal e As System.EventArgs) _
     Handles btnExecute.Click

       Try
          Dim cmd As New SqlCommand(txtQuery.Text)
          cmd.CommandType = CommandType.Text
          cmd.Connection = conCampus
          conCampus.Open()
          cmd.ExecuteNonQuery()
          txtResult.Text = "Query executed successfully"
       Catch ex As SqlClient.SqlException
          txtResult.Text = ex.Message
       Finally
          If conCampus.State = ConnectionState.Open Then
             conCampus.Close()
          End If
```

```
            End Try
        End Sub

        Private Sub btnDisplay_Click(ByVal sender As System.Object, _
          ByVal e As System.EventArgs) Handles btnDisplay.Click

            Dim frm As New frmPayroll
            frm.ShowDialog()
        End Sub
    End Class
```

Following is the source code for the frmPayroll form:

```
    Public Class frmPayroll
        Inherits System.Windows.Forms.Form
```

```
+ Windows Form Designer generated code
```

```
        Private Sub payroll_Load(ByVal sender As System.Object, _
          ByVal e As System.EventArgs) Handles MyBase.Load

            Try
                daPayroll.Fill(DsPayroll1)
            Catch ex As SqlClient.SqlException
                MessageBox.Show("Unable to open the payroll table. " _
                & "Did you DROP it from the database?", "Error")
                Me.Close()
            End Try
        End Sub
    End Class
```

Checkpoint

6.20 When we executed the SqlCommand object at the beginning of Section 6.5, what was passed to the object's constructor?

6.21 What other properties must be set in the SqlCommand before calling ExecuteNonQuery?

6.22 Where is the call to the SqlConnection.Close method located when you execute an SqlCommand?

6.23 How is a NETSDK database connection string different from a local database running under SQL Server 2000?

▶ 6.6 Stored Procedures

A *stored procedure* is a named block of code stored within a database that contains one or more database query transactions. Stored procedures can have parameters, making them particularly useful when executing parameterized queries.

Until this point in the book, we have always assumed that SQL queries were embedded directly in our program's source code. Such queries are alternately called *inline queries* or *text queries*. As you have seen, inline queries can be quite messy.

Stored procedures are automatically compiled the first time they are run, resulting in much faster execution than possible with inline queries. SQL server uses a low-level protocol named Tabular Data Stream (TDS) that is many times faster than the OleDb methods used for MS-Access databases.

Companies often create a library of procedures for a database that can be efficiently shared between numerous applications. By sharing the procedures, they reduce the amount of required maintenance by individual programmers, and reduce the potential for errors in the queries. If a single person is responsible for creating and maintaining the database, they can verify that all stored procedures are consistent with table and column attributes.

Security is tighter when stored procedures are used. If a program uses text queries, hackers can insert their own queries and retrieve sensitive data from the database. Stored procedures can also be encrypted, preventing them from being viewed by unauthorized persons.

Queries, if written improperly, can have a huge impact on database performance. An excellent way to prevent the use of inefficient queries is to have a database adminstrator inspect and approve all queries. Consequently, many companies insist that only stored procedures be used for database transactions.

At the end of this section, a tutorial will show how to create and execute stored procedures using the Server Explorer tool in Visual Studio .NET. First, let's look at SQL statements that create, modify, and delete stored procedures.

CREATE / ALTER PROCEDURE

The CREATE PROCEDURE statement creates a stored procedure and inserts it in the current database. The ALTER PROCEDURE statement modifies an existing procedure. Both have the same syntax, shown here for CREATE:

```
CREATE PROCEDURE procedureName
   [{@parameter data_type}
      [VARYING] [=default] [OUTPUT]
   ][,...]
AS
   sql_statements
```

Stored procedures can have parameters, allowing them to include runtime information supplied by calling programs. Keywords are not case-sensitive. Comments in stored procedures occur between the /* and */ delimiters. Comments can be on a single line or they can span multiple lines. The following is an example:

```
/* This procedure creates a new table
   named courses. */
```

Examples

The following statement creates a stored procedure that returns all rows in the **Students** table:

```
CREATE PROCEDURE spListStudents
AS
   SELECT * FROM Students
```

Stored procedures usually have input parameters to make them more flexible. The caller can pass an argument that is incorporated into the query. For example, the following procedure has a parameter named **StudentId**. The procedure returns all rows in the table matching the StudentId value:

```
CREATE PROCEDURE spFindStudent
   @StudentId int
AS
   SELECT *
   FROM Students
   WHERE StudentId = @StudentId
```

When multiple parameters are declared, programmers commonly surround them with optional parentheses. Such is the case with the following query, which updates a single row of a table named payroll:

```
CREATE PROCEDURE spUpdatePayroll
(
   @id int,
   @paymentDate datetime,
   @hoursWorked real,
   @hourlyRate real
)
AS
   UPDATE payroll
   SET paymentDate = @paymentDate, hoursWorked = @hoursWorked,
      hourlyRate = @hourlyRate
   WHERE id = @id
```

Stored procedures can assign default parameter values. In the following spEmployeeInsert procedure, if the caller does not pass a value to the @phone parameter, the column value will equal "(unknown)".

```
CREATE PROCEDURE spEmployeeInsert
(
    @ssn char(11),
    @last varchar(30),
    @first varchar(30),
    @phone varchar(10) = '(unknown)'
)
AS
   INSERT INTO Employee
   VALUES
   ( @ssn, @last, @first, @phone )
```

The following example modifies a stored procedure so it returns all rows from the Students table, sorted by StudentId:

```
ALTER PROCEDURE spListStudents
AS
   SELECT *
   FROM Students
   ORDER BY StudentId
```

The following modifies a stored procedure that displays three columns from the Students table, selecting only rows that match a specific last name:

```
ALTER PROCEDURE spFindStudent
   @last varchar(30)
AS
   SELECT FirstName, MiddleName, LastName
   FROM Students
   WHERE lastname = @last
```

DROP PROCEDURE

The DROP PROCEDURE statement removes a stored procedure from a database:

```
DROP PROCEDURE
   procedureName [,procedureName-2,...procedureName-n]
```

The following statement removes the spFindStudent procedure:

```
DROP PROCEDURE spFindStudent
```

Creating Stored Procedures (VS Server Explorer)

Visual Studio .NET's Server Explorer provides all the tools you need to create stored procedures for MSDE (NETSDK) databases. When you use it to create a new procedure, it creates one with a default name and displays an editor window containing the CREATE PROCEDURE statement. Comments are included that show how to create parameters, and the procedure always ends with a RETURN statement:

```
CREATE PROCEDURE dbo.StoredProcedure1
/*
   (
       @parameter1 datatype = default value,
       @parameter2 datatype OUTPUT
   )
*/
AS
   /* SET NOCOUNT ON */
   RETURN
```

The RETURN statement is optional, as are the parentheses before and after the parameter list. When you modify the procedure name, it is automatically saved under the new name. All you have to do is insert the appropriate SQL query into the procedure to make it useful.

Server Explorer can only create and edit stored procedures for MSDE databases. You cannot use it to view stored procedures created by SQL Server Enterprise Manager or by Visual Studio's Data Adapter Wizard.

If you want to rename a stored procedure, open it and edit the name shown in the CREATE PROCEDURE statement.

Hands-On Tutorial: Server Explorer

In this short hands-on exercise you will use Server Explorer to create two stored procedures: The first, named **spCreateCourseTable**, adds a new table named **courses** to the campus database. The second procedure, named **spDeleteCourseTable**, removes the courses table from the database.

Step 1. Open Server Explorer and locate the **campus** database that we created earlier in this chapter. If you have not done so already, create the database using Server Explorer.

Step 2. Right-click on the **Stored Procedures** category and select **New Stored Procedure**. Edit the procedure so it becomes the following:

```
CREATE PROCEDURE spCreateCourseTable
/* Adds the courses table */
AS
CREATE TABLE courses
    (courseid int PRIMARY KEY,
    yearsem char(7) NOT NULL,
    coursenum varchar(10) NOT NULL,
    credits int NOT NULL)
```

Close the editor window and note that the procedure name now appears in Server Explorer under Stored Procedures.

Step 3. Right-click on the procedure name and select **Run Stored Procedure**. Right-click on the database's **Tables** entry and select **Refresh**. The courses table name should appear. Take a moment to examine the table's design.

Step 4. Add the following stored procedure named **spDeleteCourseTable**. Save it when you are done:

```
CREATE PROCEDURE spDeleteCourseTable
/* Removes the courses table */
AS
    DROP TABLE courses
```

Next, let's create stored procedures that add and remove rows from the courses table.

Step 5. Add a new stored procedure named **spAddCourseRows** that inserts rows into the courses table:

```
CREATE PROCEDURE spAddCourseRows
/* Adds three rows to the courses table */
AS
INSERT INTO courses VALUES(11111,'2002-02','COP 2100',3)
INSERT INTO courses( courseid, yearsem, coursenum, credits)
    VALUES(22222,'2002-02','COP 3337',3)
INSERT INTO courses( courseid, yearsem, coursenum, credits)
    VALUES(33333,'2002-02','COP 4338',3)
```

The first INSERT INTO demonstrates the short form, in which the order of the data is identical to the order of the table columns.

Step 6. Add another procedure named **spRemoveCourseRows** that removes all rows from the courses table:

```
CREATE PROCEDURE spRemoveCourseRows
/* Removes all rows from the courses table */
AS
    DELETE from courses
```

Step 7. Create the **spUpdateCourse** procedure, a parameterized query that updates the course number and credits columns:

```
CREATE PROCEDURE spUpdateCourse
    @courseid int,
    @coursenum varchar(10),
    @credits int
AS
    UPDATE courses
    SET coursenum = @coursenum, credits = @credits
    WHERE courseid = @courseid
```

Step 8. It's time to do some testing. If you didn't do it before, run the spCreateCourseTable procedure.

Step 9. Run the spAddCourseRows procedure. Use Server Explorer to view the rows you just added.

Step 10. Open the spUpdateCourse procedure. Enter the following parameter values into the dialog: courseid = 22222, coursenum = COP 4000, credits = 4. Run the procedure and use Server Explorer to verify that course 22222 has been modified.

Step 11. Run the spRemoveCourseRows procedure. Use Server Explorer to verify that the table is empty.

Step 12. Run the spDeleteCourseTable procedure. Refresh the Tables listing and verify that the courses table no longer exists.

(End of tutorial)

Creating Stored Procedures (SQL Server 2000)

SQL Server 2000 provides two great tools for creating and testing stored procedures:

◆ **Enterprise Manager** creates and edits stored procedures.

◆ **SQL Query Analyzer** executes stored procedures. Run this tool from the Tools menu of Enterprise Manager.

Enterprise Manager

The Enterprise Manager utility makes it easy to create and edit stored procedures. When you create a new procedure, the window in Figure 6-25 appears. You can enter the source code and check the syntax of your procedure. You cannot run it here. For that, you need to use the Query Analyzer tool.

Figure 6-25 New Stored Procedure window.

SQL Query Analyzer

When you open a query using the SQL Query Analyzer tool, you can execute the query, and optionally pass it the values of input parameters (Figure 6-26). When you click on Execute, a result dialog appears (Figure 6-27) that shows whether or not the execution was successful. A return code equal to 0 indicates success.

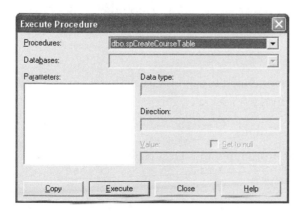

Figure 6-26 Executing a stored procedure.

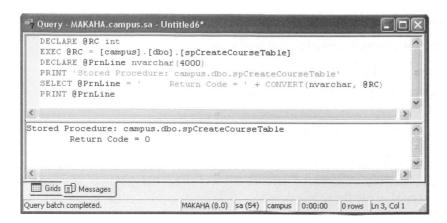

Figure 6-27   Results after executing a stored procedure.

You can modify a query and test the results of the modification. For example, in Figure 6-28, a comma was removed after the PRIMARY KEY clause, and the Query analyzer displayed an appropriate message.

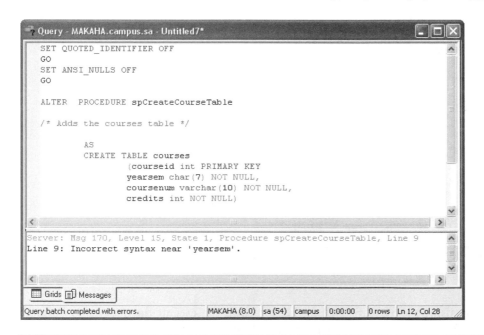

Figure 6-28   Flagging a syntax error.

Query Analyzer has many more capabilities than we have room to show here, and we think you'll find many advantages to using the full version of SQL Server.

Hands-On Tutorial

Before you try the following steps, look over the corresponding tutorial for Visual Studio Server Explorer.

Step 1. Run Enterprise Manager and locate your SQL Server. Right-click on Databases under the server name and select **New Database**. Name the database **campus**.

Step 2. In the campus database, right-click on **Stored Procedures** and select **New Stored Procedure**. Insert the following code for the spCreateCourseTable procedure into the edit window and save the procedure:

```
CREATE PROCEDURE spCreateCourseTable
/* Adds the courses table */
AS
    CREATE TABLE courses
        (courseid int PRIMARY KEY,
        yearsem char(7) NOT NULL,
        coursenum varchar(10) NOT NULL,
        credits int NOT NULL)
```

Step 3. Create and save the spDeleteCourseTable procedure:

```
CREATE PROCEDURE spDeleteCourseTable
/* Removes the courses table */
AS
    DROP TABLE courses
```

Step 4. Create the spAddCourseRows procedure:

```
CREATE PROCEDURE spAddCourseRows
/* Adds three rows to the courses table */
AS
    INSERT INTO courses VALUES(11111,'2002-02','COP 2100',3)
    INSERT INTO courses( courseid, yearsem, coursenum, credits)
        VALUES(22222,'2002-02','COP 3337',3)
    INSERT INTO courses( courseid, yearsem, coursenum, credits)
        VALUES(33333,'2002-02','COP 4338',3)
```

Step 5. Create the spRemoveCourseRows procedure:

```
CREATE PROCEDURE spRemoveCourseRows
    /* Removes all rows from the courses table */
AS
    DELETE from courses
```

Step 6. Create the spUpdateCourse procedure, a parameterized query that updates the course number and credits columns:

```
CREATE PROCEDURE spUpdateCourse
    @courseid int,
    @coursenum varchar(10),
    @credits int
AS
    UPDATE courses
    SET coursenum = @coursenum, credits = @credits
    WHERE courseid = @courseid
```

Step 7. Let's do some testing. From the Tools menu, select **SQL Query Analyzer**. Find the list of stored procedures under the campus database heading.

Step 8. Right-click on the spCreateCourseTable procedure name and select **Open**. When the dialog opens, execute the query (shown earlier in Figure 6-26).

Step 9. Run spCreateCourseTable a second time. You should see the following message in Query Analyzer, showing that it is properly doing its job:

```
Server: Msg 2714, Level 16, State 6,
    Procedure spCreateCourseTable, Line 7
    There is already an object named 'courses' in the database.
```

Step 10. Open and execute the spAddCourseRows procedure. Use Enterprise Manager to view the rows you just added.

Step 11. Open the spUpdateCourse procedure. Enter the following parameter values into the dialog: courseid = 22222, coursenum = COP 4000, credits = 4. Execute the procedure, and then use Enterprise Manager to view the row you just modified.

Step 12. Open and execute the spRemoveCourseRows procedure. From Enterprise Manager, verify that the table is now empty.

Step 13. Open and execute the spDeleteCourseTable procedure. The table name should disappear from the database after you refresh the Tables listing in Enterprise manager.

(End of tutorial)

Checkpoint

6.24 Why do stored procedures execute more quickly than text (inline) queries?

6.25 How can database adminstrators prevent programmers from embedding inefficient queries in their programs?

6.26 How are comments marked in stored procedures?

6.27 Can Visual Studio Server Explorer view queries created by Enterprise Manager?

▶6.7 Executing Stored Procedures

Earlier in this chapter, we showed how to create command objects and use them to execute inline SQL queries. Now we can show how to create command objects that execute stored procedures. Assuming that a database connection already exists, executing a stored procedure is done using a few simple steps:

1. Construct a command object, passing it the name of the stored procedure and a reference to a database connection.

2. Set the CommandType property of the command object to CommandType.StoredProcedure.

3. If the stored procedure has parameters, add the same parameters to the command object.

4. Open the connection.

5. Call ExecuteNonQuery method on the command object.

6. Close the connection.

Always use Try-Catch-Finally to perform exception handling.

Example without Parameters

Suppose **spMyProc** is the name of the stored procedure, **conCampus** is a database connection, and the stored procedure has no parameters. The following code executes the procedure:

```
Try
    'Create the command.
    Dim cmd As New SqlCommand("spMyProc", conCampus)

    'Set the command type.
    cmd.CommandType = CommandType.StoredProcedure

    'Open the connection.
    conCampus.Open()
```

```
    'Execute the procedure.
    cmd.ExecuteNonQuery()

Catch ex As SqlException
   stsMsg.Text = ex.Message

Finally
   'Close the connection.
   If conCampus.State = ConnectionState.Open Then
      conCampus.Close()
   End If
End Try
```

Stored Procedures with Parameters

If a stored procedure has parameters, you must add each parameter name and value to the Command object's Parameters collection before executing the procedure. Parameter types are defined in the .NET enumeration named SqlDbType. Examples are SqlDbType.Int, SqlDbType.VarChar, and SqlDbType.DateTime.

Suppose, for example, that a procedure has a integer parameter named @courseid. The following statement adds an SqlParameter object to the Parameters collection:

```
cmd.Parameters.Add("@courseid", SqlDbType.Int)
```

The following line sets the @courseid parameter value to 22222:

```
cmd.Parameters("@courseid").Value = 22222
```

Because the Add method returns the parameter object, you can use a single statement that adds the parameter and sets its value:

```
cmd.Parameters.Add("@courseid", SqlDbType.Int).Value = 22222
```

An alternative way to add a parameter is to omit the parameter type, and assign the value directly:

```
cmd.Parameters.Add("@courseid", 22222)
```

However, there may be times when you have to pass the column's SqlDbType to the Add method, to avoid throwing an exception.

When a parameter's type is varchar, you may optionally supply a length value when adding the parameter. The following parameter, for example, is type varchar(10):

```
cmd.Parameters.Add("@coursenum", SqlDbType.VarChar, 10).Value = "COP
1120"
```

Parameters can be added to a Command object in any order.

Hands-On Example: College Courses Program

College_Courses

Let's take a look at a short program that uses SQL to modify the campus database created earlier in this chapter. It creates and removes tables and inserts and deletes table rows. It executes the same stored procedures we created in Section 6.6. In fact, it will not run until you add the following stored procedures to the campus database:

- spCreateCourseTable
- spDeleteCourseTable
- spAddCourseRows
- spRemoveCourseRows
- spUpdateCourse

Interface

Open the **College_Courses** program from the Chapter 6 examples. The program starts up with the window shown in Figure 6-29. The user selects each possible action from a list box. If the courses table contains rows, they are displayed in the DataGrid. A TextBox with a vertical scroll bar below the grid displays error messages.

The user can experiment with executing the commands in different sequences. Some sequences will generate error messages, depending on whether the requested operation is possible. The following errors can occur, for example:

- **Create courses table** fails if the courses table already exists.
- **Delete table** fails if the courses table does not exist.
- **Add rows, Remove rows,** and **Update rows** fail if the courses table does not exist.

Error trapping is an important aspect of this program. We use Try-Catch blocks whenever an operation could throw an exception. Error messages appear in a TextBox control at the bottom of the form. Figure 6-30, for example, shows the error message generated when the user tries to add rows to a nonexistent table. The somewhat terse error messages displayed by the program are generated by the SqlException class (part of the System.Data.SqlClient namespace).

If the user creates the courses table and selects Add rows, the datagrid will be filled with the contents of the courses table (Figure 6-31). If they try to add the same rows again, the following error message is issued by the database because adding the same primary key value again would create a duplicate key:

```
Violation of PRIMARY KEY constraint 'PK__courses__5EBF139D'.
Cannot insert duplicate key in object 'courses'.
```

When the user selects Update rows, the coursenum column of course 22222 is modified (Figure 6-32). When the user selects Remove rows, all rows are removed from the table and the list box is cleared. When the user deletes the course table, the list box is also cleared.

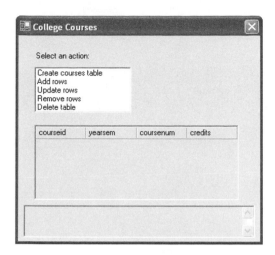

Figure 6-29 College Courses program.

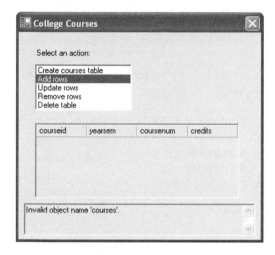

Figure 6-30 Error: Adding rows to a nonexistent table.

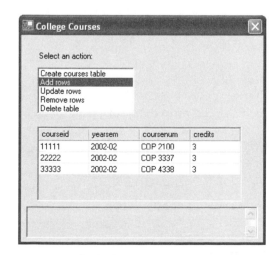

Figure 6-31 Adding rows to the courses table.

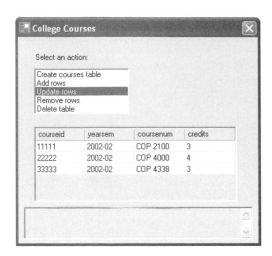

Figure 6-32 Updating course 22222.

Implementation

The program's component tray contains a Connection component (conCampus), a data adapter, and a dataset used for filling the DataGrid.

The ExecuteStoredProc method executes any stored procedure having no parameters. It receives the name of a stored procedure and returns False if an exception is thrown:

```
Public Function ExecuteStoredProc(ByVal procname As String) As Boolean
   Try
      Dim cmd As New SqlCommand(procname, conCampus)
      cmd.CommandType = CommandType.StoredProcedure
      conCampus.Open()
      cmd.ExecuteNonQuery()
      Return True
   Catch ex As SqlException
      stsMsg.Text = ex.Message
      Return False
   Finally
      If conCampus.State = ConnectionState.Open Then
         conCampus.Close()
      End If
   End Try
End Function
```

A second function (ExecuteUpdateProc) executes a specific stored procedure, spUpdateCourse, which has three parameters:

```
Public Function ExecuteUpdateProc(ByVal courseId As Integer, _
 ByVal courseNum As String, ByVal credits As Integer) As Boolean
   Try
      Dim cmd As New SqlCommand("spUpdateCourse", conCampus)
      With cmd
         .CommandType = CommandType.StoredProcedure
         .Parameters.Add("@courseid", courseId)
         .Parameters.Add("@coursenum", courseNum)
         .Parameters.Add("@credits", credits)
         conCampus.Open()
         .ExecuteNonQuery()
      End With
```

```
            Return True
        Catch ex As SqlException
            stsMsg.Text = ex.Message
            Return False
        Finally
            If conCampus.State = ConnectionState.Open Then
                conCampus.Close()
            End If
        End Try
    End Function
```

Finally, the **SelectedIndexChanged** event handler for the list box has the job of deciding which stored procedure should execute, based on the list box entry selected by the user:

```
    Private Sub lstActions_SelectedIndexChanged(ByVal sender As _
      System.Object, ByVal e As System.EventArgs) _
        Handles lstActions.SelectedIndexChanged

        stsMsg.Text = ""
        Select Case lstActions.SelectedIndex
            Case 0
                If ExecuteStoredProc("spCreateCourseTable") Then
                    stsMsg.Text = "courses table created"
                End If
            Case 1
                If ExecuteStoredProc("spAddCourseRows") Then
                    DsCourses1.Clear()
                    daCourses.Fill(DsCourses1)
                End If
            Case 2
                If ExecuteUpdateProc(22222, "COP 4000", 4) Then
                    DsCourses1.Clear()
                    daCourses.Fill(DsCourses1)
                End If
            Case 3
                If ExecuteStoredProc("spRemoveCourseRows") Then
                    DsCourses1.Clear()
                    daCourses.Fill(DsCourses1)
                End If
            Case 4
                If ExecuteStoredProc("spDeleteCourseTable") Then
                    DsCourses1.Clear()
                    stsMsg.Text = "courses table deleted"
                End If
        End Select
    End Sub
```

Using a Data Adapter to Create Stored Procedures

Visual Studio .NET has a useful wizard that activates when you select the SqlDataAdapter from the Data tab of the ToolBox. Suppose you want to use the courses database and create a data adapter for the students table. When asked for the Query Type, select **Create new stored procedures**, as in Figure 6-33. Notice in the same window that you can choose to use existing stored procedures and attach them to the data adapter. When the Query Builder window appears, you can select the students table (Figure 6-34).

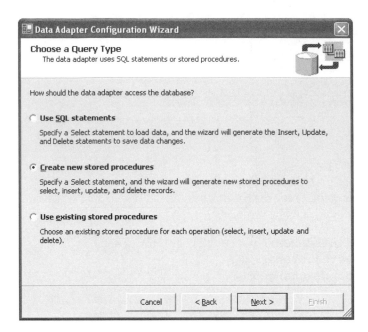

Figure 6-33 Data Adapter wizard.

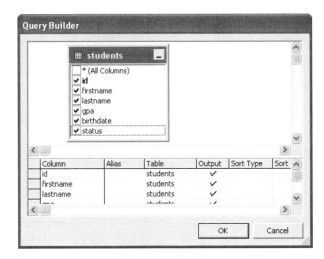

Figure 6-34 Selecting the students table.

Next, you are given a chance to assign meaningful names to the stored procedures, shown in Figure 6-35. You have the option of viewing the SQL script that will be used to create the procedures. When you click on Finish, the procedures are created. You can then view and edit the procedures using SQL Server Enterprise Manager. (Be sure to right-click on Stored Procedures and select Refresh so you can see the new procedure names.)

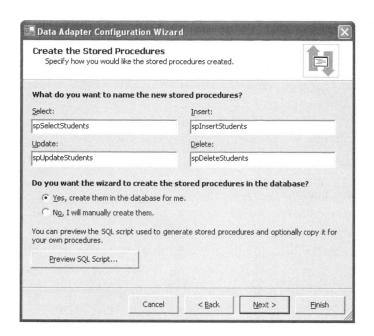

Figure 6-35 Naming the stored procedures.

Following is a listing of the spInsertStudents procedure created by the Wizard:

```
CREATE PROCEDURE dbo.spInsertStudents
(
    @id char(9),
    @firstname varchar(30),
    @lastname varchar(30),
    @gpa float,
    @birthdate varchar(10),
    @status int
)
AS
    SET NOCOUNT OFF;
    INSERT INTO students(id, firstname, lastname, gpa, birthdate, status)
        VALUES (@id, @firstname, @lastname, @gpa, @birthdate, @status);
        SELECT id, firstname, lastname, gpa, birthdate, status FROM students
        WHERE (id = @id)
GO
```

The SET NOCOUNT option gives you the option of suppressing the count that queries return indicating the number of rows affected by a query. If NOCOUNT is ON, the count will not be returned. You may have noticed that in our queries shown earlier in the chapter, we did not use this option.

Checkpoint

6.28 Write a statement that constructs an SqlCommand object named **cmd** that could used to execute a stored procedure named **spMyproc**. Assume that the connection is named myConn.

6.29 What value should be assigned to the CommandType property of an SqlCommand object when executing a stored procedure?

6.30 What types of action queries are carried out by the College Courses program?

6.31 Write a statement that adds an Integer parameter named **@age** to an SqlCommand object named **cmd**.

6.32 Which class generates exception error messages when errors occur during the execution of SQL database queries?

►6.8 Chapter Summary

◆ Microsft ADO.NET uses a standardized version of SQL named **ANSI SQL**, designed by the American National Standards Institute (ANSI).

◆ A *view* is table-like object that makes references to other tables and views. It does not contain data, but it permits you to include or exclude individual table columns, and to combine existing tables and views.

◆ Queries that do not return result sets are called *action queries*. They modify the database, either by changing the contents of tables or by changing the database structure.

◆ Queries using Data Manipulation Language modify the contents of tables by adding, deleting, or updating the rows. Queries using Data Definition Language modify the database structure by adding or removing tables, or by modifying table structures.

◆ When selecting database column types, use **varchar** for columns in which the contents vary in length, and use **char** for columns having a fixed size.

◆ A primary key column is essential when performing update, delete, and insert operations on individual table rows. Every table can have at most one clustered key as its primary key.

◆ An index is a tool that lets the database rapidly search for information. Generally, indexes are created on two types of columns: primary keys and foreign keys.

◆ Microsoft Visual Studio .NET Server Explorer is a convenient tool you can use to interactively design and modify databases.

◆ Microsoft SQL Server 2000 Enterprise Manager is an easy-to-use powerful tool you can use to design and modify databases.

◆ The CREATE TABLE statement creates a new database table and DROP TABLE removes a table.

◆ The ALTER TABLE command adds a column to a table, modifies the attributes of an existing column, or drops a column from a table

◆ The UPDATE statement modifies one or more table rows. You can choose to modify one or more column values.

◆ The DELETE statement removes one or more rows from a table.

◆ The INSERT INTO statement, known as an *append query*, inserts new rows in a table.

◆ The Action Query program example lets users interactively select, modify, and execute queries on the campus database.

◆ A *stored procedure* is a named block of code stored within a database that can contain one or more SQL statements.

◆ Stored procedures are automatically compiled the the first time they are run, resulting in much faster execution than possible with inline queries.

◆ An important benefit to storing queries in a database is that any number of programs can execute the queries without having to encode their own inline queries. Security is improved when stored procedures are used rather than inline queries.

◆ Stored procedures usually have input parameters that make them more flexible. The caller can pass an argument that is incorporated into the query.

◆ The CREATE PROCEDURE statement creates a stored procedure and inserts it in the database.

◆ The ALTER PROCEDURE statement modifies an existing procedue.

◆ The DROP PROCEDURE statement removes a stored procedure from a database.

◆ To execute a stored procedure from a program, create a command object, pass it the name of the stored procedure and a database connection, open the connection, and call ExecuteNonQuery.

◆ If a stored procedure has parameters, you must add each parameter name and type to the Command object's Parameters collection before calling ExecuteNonQuery.

◆ The College Courses example program executes stored procedures located in the **campus** database.

▶6.9 Key Terms

action query
ALTER TABLE
ALTER PROCEDURE
ANSI SQL
CREATE DATABASE
CREATE TABLE
CREATE PROCEDURE
CREATE VIEW
Data Definition Language (DDL)
Data Manipulation Language (DML)
DataColumn
DataRows
DataTable
DELETE
DROP TABLE
DROP PROCEDURE
index
INSERT INTO
Jet SQL
non row-returning query
primary key
row-returning query
SqlCommand
SqlConnection
stored procedure
UPDATE
view

▶6.10 Review Questions

Fill-in-the-blank

1. Microsoft ADO.NET uses a version of SQL called _____ SQL.

2. Queries that do not return result sets are called _____ queries.

3. Data _____ Language is used when creating queries that modify a database's structure.

4.   A column that is guaranteed to have unique values in all rows of a table is called a _____ key.

5.   The _____ statement in SQL adds a new row to a table.

Multiple Choice

1.   Which of the following steps is not required when preparing to execute a query in program code?

   a.   Create a database connection.
   b.   Create an SqlCommand object.
   c.   Create a data adapter from the SqlCommand object.
   d.   Set the SqlCommand object's Connection property.
   e.   Open the connection.

2.   Which statement is not true about the Action Query Demo program?

   a.   Lets the user select queries from a ComboBox.
   b.   Calls a stored procedure named spUpdateTable.
   c.   Lets the user modify existing queries before executing them.
   d.   Displays the contents of the payroll table in a DataGrid.
   e.   Displays error messages generated by thrown exceptions.

3.   Which of the following is not an advantage to using stored procedures versus inline queries?

   a.   stored procedures execute more quickly.
   b.   stored procedures have greater security against unauthorized access to databases.
   c.   inline procedures are more flexible than stored procedures because the query parameters can change at runtime.
   d.   stored procedures can be shared by multiple applications.
   e.   none of the above.

4.   Which of the following would be the correct way to add an integer parameter named @count to an SqlCommand object?

   a.   cmd.Parameters.Add("@count", Integer)
   b.   cmd.Parameters.Add("@count", SqlDbType.Int)
   c.   cmd.Parameters.Add(Integer, "@count")
   d.   cmd.Parameters.Add(SqlDbType.Int).Value = "@count"
   e.   none of the above are correct

5.   Which of the following SQL Server column types does **not** match the Decimal type in Visual Basic?

   a.   float
   b.   numeric
   c.   money
   d.   small money
   e.   decimal

True or False

1.   The SELECT statement in SQL is called a row-returning query.

2.   Data Definition Queries modify the contents of tables.

3.   If you insert "abc" in a column defined as char(10) in SQL Server, the column will contain seven spaces.

4.   Date literals must be surrounded by the "#" delimiter in SQL Server queries.

5.   Visual Studio Server Explorer cannot open stored procedures created by Enterprise Manager.

6.   A view can only show columns from a single table.

7.   The Query Analyzer tool is available in Visual Studio as part of the NETSDK package.

8.   Query Analyzer can be used to create a new query.

9.   A clustered index may only be created on the primary key column.

10. A view does not contain any data.

11. A common reason for creating views is to restrict groups of users from access to certain table columns.

12. The REMOVE TABLE statement removes a table from a database.

13. If a parent-child relationship exists in a database, the child table must be removed before the parent table.

14. If the WHERE clause is omitted from the UPDATE statement, all rows in the table will be affected by the query.

15. If you want to remove a single row using DELETE, you must use the DISTINCT clause to uniquely identify a row.

16. The INSERT INTO statement requires all column names to be identified.

17. When executing a query in program code, you must open the connection before setting the CommandType property.

18. An error is generated when you try to delete the same table twice.

Short Answer

1. What is the most common server name used for SQL Server names in connection strings?

2. Which SQL Server window displays table relationships?

3. What type of security is required for NETSDK databases?

4. Write a query that removes a table named temp.

5. Write a query that deletes all rows from a table named temp.

What Do You Think?

1. What advantages do you think SQL Server Authentication might have over Windows NT Integrated Security in regard to using a database in application programs?

2. What advantages would stored procedures offer in an online bookstore application that has thousands of simultaneous users?

3. The College Courses example program in section 6.7 executes a number of stored procedures that affect the courses table in the campus database. Suppose you wanted this program to run on another database such as **pubs**. What changes would be required?

4. Do you think it is possible for a data adapter component to call existing stored procedures?

5. Find one of the programming exercises from Chapter 5 and briefly explain how it could be revised to use stored procedures.

Algorithm Workbench

1. Write an SQL query that copies all rows from a table named **source** to a table named **target**.

2. Write an SQL query that creates a table named **employee** with columns **id** (int), **name** (varchar 30), and **salary** (real). None of the columns may contain null values, and the id column is the primary key.

3. Write an SQL query that adds a column to the employee table named **hireDate**, type datetime.

4. Write an SQL query that modifies the salary column by changing its type to decimal.

5. Write an SQL query that inserts a row into the employee table used in the previous question.

6. Write an SQL query that removes all rows from the employee table in which hireDate is prior to January 1, 1995.

7. Write an SQL query that removes the salary column from the employee table used in the previous question.

▶6.11 Programming Challenges

1. **Create the Company Database**

   Create a database named Company. Use a stored procedure to create the following table named **Employee:**

Column Name	Type	Attributes
ssn	char(11)	primary key
lastName	varchar(30)	not null
firstName	varchar(30)	not null
phone	varchar(12)	

   Use a stored procedure to create the **Payroll** table, which uses a clustered primary key:

Column Name	Type	Attributes
ssn	char(11)	primary key
paymentDate	datetime	primary key
hoursWorked	real	not null
hourlyRate	money	not null
dept_id	smallint	

   Use a stored procedure to create the **Department** table:

Column Name	Type	Attributes
dept_id	smallint	primary key
dept_name	varchar(30)	not null

   Use a stored procedure to create the **Sales** table:

Column Name	Type	Attributes
ssn	char(11)	primary key
Jan	int	
Feb	int	
PctIncrease	real	

   Run and test your stored procedures. Verify that all tables were added to the Company database.

2. **Company Database Diagram**

   Create the database diagram for the database that was created in the previous programming challenge problem.

3. **Company Database INSERT Procedures**

Create the following stored procedures that insert rows in the Company database:

◆ spEmployeeInsert inserts a row in the Employee table, using query parameters for all columns.

◆ spPayrollInsert inserts a row in the Payroll table, using query parameters for all columns.

◆ spDepartmentInsert inserts a row in the Department table, using query parameters for all columns.

Run and test your procedures.

4. **Company Database SELECT Procedures**

Create the following stored procedures in the Company database that select rows:

◆ spEmployeeSelect returns a specific row in the Employee table based on the value of **ssn**. Use a query parameter named @ssn.

◆ spEmployeePay selects an Employee by ssn and paymentDate and returns the first and last name, as well as the person's pay for a specific payment date.

◆ spSalesAll returns all rows and columns in the Sales table that match a particular ssn value.

5. **Company Database UPDATE Procedures**

Create the following stored procedures that update rows in the Company database:

◆ spPayrollUpdate updates a single row in the Payroll table.

◆ spDepartmentUpdate updates a single row in the Department table.

6. **Inserting Employee Rows**

Using the INSERT stored procedure spEmployeeInsert, create an application that activates the stored procedure from a Visual Basic program. The user interface should be similar to the user interface in Figure 6-36. When the Insert button is clicked, the data in the text boxes are inserted into the Employee table. When the Clear button is clicked, the text boxes are cleared. When the Exit button is clicked, the application ends. Use exception handling to catch and report all database errors. Do not worry about input validation.

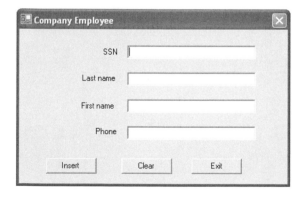

Figure 6-36 Inserting Employee rows.

7. **Updating Employee Rows**

Modify your solution to the previous programming exercise as follows: Let the user update existing Employee rows. When the user enters the SSN, use the spEmployeeSelect stored procedure to retrieve the matching row from the Employee table and populate the text boxes on the form with the returned data. After the record has been retrieved from the database, lock the SSN text box. When the user clicks the Clear button, clear the text boxes and unlock the SSN text box. Create a menu that includes options to add employees and update employees.

8. **Company Employee Pay**

Using the spEmployeePay stored procedure you created in Programming challenge #4, display an employee's pay based on a specific payment date. When the user selects the SSN and payment date from combo boxes, retrieve the employee's payment record. Fill the Label controls with the returned dataset row. Figure 6-37 and Figure 6-38 show the program's user interface.

Figure 6-37   Company Employee Pay program.

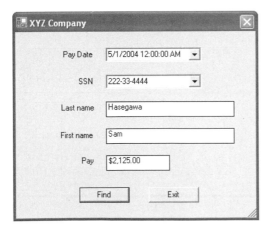

Figure 6-38   Finding the employee's pay.

Web Forms (ASP.NET)

▶7.1 ASP.NET Basics

Introduction

Until a few years ago, Web development with databases was out of reach of average programmers unless they invested a lot of time in learning specialized technologies. The languages and tools for Web programming required programmers to insert JavaScript and VBScript functions directly into Web pages along with the rest of the page content. These script functions did not perform compile-time type checking, so many data conversion errors were not discovered until the programs were running. There was no way to perform the kind of exception handling that Visual Basic uses to avoid runtime errors.

Web programming environments have changed. With ASP.NET, for example, you can create Web applications using object-oriented programming languages such as Visual Basic and C#. Database connections can be fully expressed as objects.

As you can imagine, a good deal of competition exists between language developers to offer top-rate Web programming tools. Users can choose from tools such as Java Server Pages (JSP), IBM WebSphere, and of course, ASP.NET. In this chapter and the ones that follow, we will use ASP.NET as the tool of choice, but many concepts and techniques explained here are common to other Web development products.

Types of Internet Applications

There are a number of ways that applications can access the Internet, depending on what one is trying to accomplish. Although we focus on Web applications in the next few chapters, it's important to take a broader look at what can be done:

◆ A *Web application* is an interactive program that communicates with Web browsers over a network. A *Web server* is a utility program that hosts Web applications.

◆ A *Web service* provides data on demand to other programs running on the Internet. This type of application has no visual interface.

◆ An *Internet-enabled application* is an application program that uses the Internet to send and receive data. It is a stand-alone application, meaning that it does not require a Web browser to run.

◆ A *Peer-to-peer application* is a program that runs on one or more computers connected via a network. The program does not require any external services to run, and it could run on a local network not connected to the Internet.

How Web Applications Work

Web applications are designed around a *client-server model*, which means an entity called a *server* produces data consumed by another entity called a *client*. Put another way, clients make requests satisfied by responses from servers.

When you use a Web browser such as Internet Explorer to access a Web site, your browser is the client, and the Web site provides the server. A program called a *Web server* runs on the computer hosting the Web site. Microsoft Internet Information Services (IIS) is the Web server used most often for ASP.NET applications, but other servers such as *Apache Tomcat* are also available.

Browsers display data encoded in HTML (HyperText Markup Language). Microsoft Internet Explorer is the browser used when running most ASP.NET applications.

You will find it helpful to learn some basic HTML as you begin to write ASP.NET applications. You can find tutorials all over the Web, but you may want to start with the World Wide Web Consortium's Web site (nicknamed W3C):

```
http://www.w3.org
```

Look for a link to HTML, then look for a link to Tutorials.

Displaying a Web Page

Let's go through the steps that take place whenever you display a Web page using a browser. This scenario applies to the basic mechanism of displaying HTML pages as well as Web programming.

Preparation: The Web server is started on the server computer and begins waiting for connection requests.

Step 1. An end user running a Web browser connects to the server by opening a network connection and passing a URL (Uniform Resource Locator) to the connection. An example of a URL is http://scottjonespub.com.

Step 2. Using the URL it receives from the client, the Web server translates the URL into a physical location within the server computer's file system. The server reads the requested file, now called a *Web page*. The server sends the Web page over the network connection to the client computer. The Client browser renders (interprets) the HTML on the client computer. Output consists of text, graphics, and sound.

As soon as the server sends the Web page to the client, it immediately breaks the connection. The server becomes free to handle Web page requests from other clients.

Postback

After a Web page is displayed, the user will often click on a button control or press the Enter key, causing the page contents to be sent back to the web server. This action is called a *postback*. The server processes the page contents and resends the modified page to the browser. The processing might involve updating controls and executing functions in the application's compiled code.

The postback process takes a little time for Windows desktop programmers to get used to. In Web applications, you have to take special steps to preserve the values of variables and the states of controls when a postback occurs. We will focus on those steps, called *preserving program state*, in Chapter 8.

Uniform Resource Locator (URL)

A Uniform Resource Locator (URL) is the name given to a string such as *http://microsoft.com*, which can be entered into the address field of a Web browser. A URL contains several parts, some of which are required, others optional:

- ◆ **Protocol (required):** The protocol specifies how the Web server should interpret the URL's connection request. The two primary Web protocols are HTTP (*hypertext transfer protocol*) and HTTPS (*secure hypertext transfer protocol*). Another protocol you may have seen is FTP (*file transfer protocol*), which uses its own server to transfer files from one computer to another.

- ◆ **Host address (required):** The host address may consist of either an IP (*Internet protocol*) address or domain name: An *IP address* is the host computer's unique network address, displayed as four integers in the range 0 to 255, separated by periods. An example is 123.45.66.21. A *domain name* is an identifying name followed by a standard domain extension such as .com, .org, or .edu. The Web browser sends the domain name to a remote computer called a *Domain Name Server* (DNS), which looks up the domain name in a database and returns a matching IP address.

- ◆ **File path:** The optional file path shows how to reach a file from the server's root directory.

- ◆ **Anchor:** An anchor is an optional named location within a Web page, prefixed by the # character. Examples of anchors are #top and #summary.

- ◆ **Port number:** The port number may optionally follow the host address. The number defaults to port 80 for Web servers. Occasionally, you might see another port number used for specialized servers. The following URL, for example, uses port 8080 to connect to a Web server:

```
http://localhost:8080/myProg.aspx
```

URL Examples

Only the protocol and host address are required in a URL. Here are a few example URLs:

```
http://microsoft.com
http://127.0.0.1
http://localhost
https://CreditCardCompany.com
http://scottjonespub.com/catalog.html#vbasic
```

The second URL (127.0.0.1), is the default location of a Web server running on the user's own computer. Its corresponding domain name is **localhost**. When developing ASP.NET applications on your own computer, it's easiest to test them using the localhost domain.

When a URL does not contain an actual filename, the Web server looks for one of several default filenames in the requested directory. Examples of default filenames are: index.html, index.htm, and Default.aspx. These names may vary from one Web site to another. If only a domain name is supplied, the Web server assumes the URL refers to the server's root Web directory.

Not all computers run Web servers, of course, but Windows 2000, Windows XP Professional, and Windows 2003 all have the option to install the Internet Information Services (IIS) server.

History of Web Programming

For a number of years, HTML has provided a way for users to input information into a Web page using what is called an *HTML form*. By providing a supplementary type of program named *Common Gateway Interface* (CGI), Web sites could receive and process information entered into HTML forms. CGI programs are still used, but must be carefully designed to prevent intrusions by hackers.

Web pages can also contain short programs named *scripts*. Scripts are usually written in languages such as VBScript, JavaScript, Perl, PHP, or Python. A *server-side script* is executed by the Web server, and therefore has access to all the resources on the server computer. A *client-side script* is executed by the client Browser, so it does not require any processing by the Web server. Client-side scripts are often used to perform validation of user input, fancy animations on Web pages, and in general to simulate the kind of user interfaces found in Windows Desktop applications. Scripting languages are tricky to use because they do not perform compile-time type checking. As a result, runtime errors occur at unpredictable moments, confusing end users.

The technology for processing Web pages and creating Web applications has evolved quite a bit during the past several years. ASP.NET and competing products make it easy to create Web applications as powerful as desktop applications. Best of all, the power of object-oriented programming, with features such as runtime exception handling, inheritance, and database classes have become available to Web programmers.

What is ASP.NET?

ASP.NET is called a *platform* because it provides development tools, code libraries, and visual controls for Web programming. It contains Web-friendly counterparts of the Windows Forms classes that we have already been using in this book. You can use ASP.NET from Visual Basic or C# because both languages share the same tools, libraries, and controls. The essential elements of the ASP.NET platform are listed here:

◆ System.Web namespaces, containing classes specifically designed for Web programming.

◆ Web forms controls (also known as *server controls*)

◆ Visual Basic and C# programming languages

◆ The .NET framework (integrated collection of classes and methods)

◆ ADO.NET database classes

ASP.NET gives end users the illusion that Web applications behave almost like desktop applications. The programmer, on the other hand, is given tools that assist in creating visual interfaces and in writing object-oriented code. ASP.NET lets programmers use object-oriented classes and interactive controls similar to those used in desktop applications. Finally, Visual Studio .NET is an excellent integrated development environment for building and testing .NET applications.

Creating ASP.NET Web Applications

Web applications written for ASP.NET consist of several parts:

◆ Content: Web forms, HTML code, Web forms controls, images, and other multimedia

◆ Program logic: both scripted and compiled executable code

◆ Configuration information

The computer running a Web application must be running a Web server such as Internet Information Services (IIS). Windows XP Professional and Windows 2000 include IIS as an optional service.

When you create a Web application in ASP.NET, you usually start with a Web page having a special filename extension: aspx. This page is commonly known as a *Web form* because it contains an HTML form and HTML-based controls such as buttons and text boxes. HTML controls and Web forms controls are added to the page, using an ordinary text editor or an integrated tool such as Visual Studio .NET. This part of the application is called *content*.

Web forms controls are interactive controls such as buttons, list boxes, and text boxes that execute on the server. Though they look like HTML controls, they are more powerful because they can use event handler procedures to carry out actions based on user input. In effect, they behave a lot like Windows desktop controls.

The source code related to a Web form is stored in a related file called a *codebehind* file, with the filename extension **aspx.vb**. This part of the application is called the *program logic*.

Configuration information is stored in two files: One of them, **Web.config**, describes the runtime environment. For example, you might use it to specify a connection to a database. Another file, **Styles.css**, is a *Cascading Style Sheet* (CSS) file that contains HTML styles for customizing the appearance of Web forms. (Most Web designers use cascading style sheets for ordinary Web pages.)

A Web application can contain any number of Web forms, each of which is assigned a codebehind file. When the program is compiled, the codebehind file is translated into a *Dynamic Link Library* (DLL) file containing compiled *Intermediate Language* (IL) code. When the program runs, the IL code is converted to native machine code by the Microsoft *Just-In-Time* (JIT) compiler.

A Web application executes when the URL of its startup Web form is requested by a Web browser. The Web server interprets the contents of the startup form. An application can run on localhost, or it can be run over a network (including the Internet) by users connected to the Web server.

HTML Designer

The HTML Designer is a tool supplied inside Visual Studio .NET that simplifies the design of ASP.NET pages. It generates HTML source code and embeds the ASP.NET tags required for Web forms controls. You don't have to use the HTML designer. Some prominent Web developers prefer to use a plain text editor. In this book, we will use the HTML Designer because it's the easiest way to go. The Visual Studio .NET ToolBox has two tabs that identify groups of controls:

HTML: The HTML group contains standard *HTML controls* that might be found on any Web page. They are 100-percent compatible with standard HTML, and as such have a limited number of properties, no event handling, and no associated classes. Any HTML control can be turned into server-side control by setting its **RunAtServer** property to True. This action causes the control to be interpreted and translated into HTML by the Web server. In any event, such a control would still not have the rich set of properties found in a corresponding Web forms control.

Web Forms: The Web Forms group contains *Web forms controls* that run on a Web server. These easy-to-use controls have a rich set of properties and supporting classes. Browsers do not understand the various properties found in Web forms controls, so the Web server must interpret each control and translate it into standard HTML. Because of their power and flexibility, you will use Web forms controls most of the time when writing ASP.NET applications.

Comparing TextField to TextBox

To help illustrate differences between HTML and Web forms controls, we can compare a Text Field (HTML control) to a TextBox (Web forms control). Both controls look identical on a Web page, and both permit the user to enter text. Table 7-1 lists the TextField properties and Table 7-2 lists the TextBox properties. A Web designer who uses only HTML would have to go to great lengths to simulate the richness of the TextBox control using client-side scripts. But such efforts are no longer necessary in ASP.NET. The differences we have seen between the TextField and TextBox controls are typical of the differences between other HTML and Web forms controls.

Table 7-1

TextField HTML control properties.

Property Name	Description
HTML Tag	<INPUT>
id	Unique identifier
maxlength	Maximum characters that can be entered by the user
name	Name of the control
size	Length of the enclosing box
type	Text (read-only)
value	Initial contents assigned to the control

Table 7-2

TextBox Web forms control properties.

Property Name	Description
ID	Unique identifier
AutoPostBack	Indicates whether the Web page should immediately post back to the server when the text changes
BackColor, ForeColor, BorderColor, BorderStyle, BorderWidth	Color of background, color of foreground, color of border, line style of border, width of border (in pixels)
Columns	Width of the text box, in characters
CSSclass	Name of associated cascading style-sheet class
DataBindings	Binds the text box to a column within a database table
Enabled	Indicates whether the control is enabled
EnableViewState	Indicates whether the contents will be saved in a ViewState bag, so its contents will not be lost when the page is refreshed
Font	Various font properties (name, size, bold, etc.)
MaxLength	Maximum number of characters that can be entered
ReadOnly	Indicates whether or not the field contents can be modified by the user
Rows	Number of rows (for a multiline text box)
TabIndex	Index within the form's tab order
Text	Contents of text box
TextMode	Single-line, multi-line, or password
ToolTip	Text displayed when mouse is hovered over the control
Visible	Indicates whether the control is visible
Height, Width	Height and width, in pixels
Wrap	Indicates whether word wrap is enabled

Form Layout Options

Visual Studio.NET offers two layout options for Web forms:

◆ **Grid layout** is the default. Controls can be positioned on a grid by dragging them with the mouse or by pressing keyboard arrow keys.

◆ **Flow layout** is what HTML developers use for Web pages. Controls appear on the form in sequential order, much like the words in a text document. You can use HTML tables to position controls anywhere on the Web page.

To select the layout method, click the mouse in an open area of a new Web form, and select the **pageLayout** property.

Browser Support

Web pages would be easier to create if all end users ran the same Web browser. Unfortunately, browsers have different capabilities and characteristics. To make it easier to adapt to different browsers, the Web server automatically detects the browser type and makes the information available to ASP.NET programs. The programs automatically generate HTML appropriate for the user's browser.

Microsoft classifies Web browsers as either uplevel or downlevel: An *uplevel* Web browser refers to a browser based on Internet Explorer versions 5.5 or later. A *downlevel* Web browser applies to all other Web browsers. Browser differences can create subtle differences in program behavior. When an uplevel browser is used, for example, a Web control that performs error checking on user input can alert users as they change the focus from one control to another. When a downlevel browser is used, errors are only reported when users post the page back to the server.

Before publishing your Web applications for end users, test them with more than one Web browser. Netscape and Mozilla are good choices.

Files in Web Projects

The following files are found in a typical web project: Web forms with their codebehind files, an Application file, an AssemblyInfo file, an XML discovery file, a CSS file, a Web configuration file, and a DLL file. Let's examine each in turn.

Web Form

A project may contain one or more Web forms. A *Web form* consists of two files having filename extensions **aspx** and **aspx.vb**. The aspx file contains the visible HTML code, and the aspx.vb file is the codebehind file that supports the Web page with program code. When the latter file is compiled, its code is stored in a DLL.

ASP.NET Application File

An ASP.NET project's *application file,* named **Global.asax**, contains program code that manipulates Application and Session objects.

◆ An *Application* object contains properties and methods relating to the ASP.NET application as a whole. Application data are shared between all client connections active at a given moment.

◆ A *Session* object contains properties and methods relating to an individual client connection (called a *session*). The client can, for example, create session variables that pertain only to a single end user.

AssemblyInfo.vb

The file named **AssemblyInfo.vb** contains project information in a text file that can be configured by the developer. It contains information such as the company name, copyright, and program version number.

ProjectName.vsdisco

Every project contains a single **XML discovery file** that holds links to required Web services. Its filename consists of the project name followed by the filename extension **vsdisco**.

Styles.css

A project always has a *cascading style sheet* file named **Styles.css** containing definitions of paragraph and font styles. You can use style sheets to redefine existing HTML tags such as H1 (heading level 1) or P (paragraph). You can also define new style tags that customize your program's appearance. You might, for example, like to have certain text change color when the user hovers above it with the mouse. Or, you might like to use right-justified text to display currency values in text boxes.

Web.config

The *Web configuration file,* named **Web.config**, contains information about each URL resource used in the project. For example, you can use it to customize error messages displayed to the user, set the authentication policy of the program, or store a database connection string.

DLL files

A *compiled code* file is created the first time an ASP.NET application runs. The file has the same name as the project, along with a filename extension of DLL. This file is loaded by the server when a Web application is started, and stays in memory as long as the application is running.

Checkpoint

4.1 Name at least one disadvantage to using scripting languages commonly available before ASP.NET.
4.2 Describe a Web application in your own words.
4.3 Describe the client-server relationship in a Web application.
4.4 What is a postback?
4.5 Why is ASP.NET called a platform?
4.6 What is meant by *content* in an ASP.NET application?
4.7 Give an example of how an uplevel browser might behave differently than a downlevel browser.

▶ 7.2 Creating ASP.NET Programs

A Simple ASP.NET Program

Let's create a simple program that shows how easy it is to program in ASP.NET. When a client connects to the program, a button is displayed (Figure 7-1). When the user clicks on the button, the program displays a message (Figure 7-2). Notice that the address bar of the browser displays the program's URL. The server is at **localhost**, the project is stored in a Web directory named **Cool**, and the startup Web form is named *Default.aspx*.

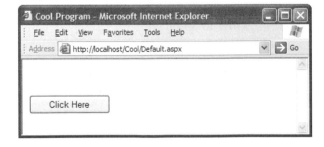

Figure 7-1 Cool program – startup page.

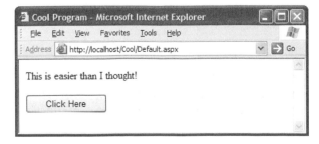

Figure 7-2 After clicking the button.

Let's look at the HTML code inside the Web form named **cool.aspx**. The line numbers shown here are for reference and are not stored in the file:

```
1: <%@ Page Language="vb" AutoEventWireup="false"
2:          Codebehind="Default.aspx.vb" Inherits="Cool.WebForm1"%>
3: <!DOCTYPE HTML PUBLIC "-//W3C//DTD HTML 4.0 Transitional//EN">
4: <HTML>
5: <HEAD>
6:     <title>Cool Program</title>
7: </HEAD>
8: <body>
9: <form id="Form1" method="post" runat="server">
10:         <asp:Label id="lblMessage" runat="server" Width="246px">
11:         </asp:Label>
12:         <P>
13:         <asp:Button id="btnCool" runat="server" Width="121px"
14:            Text="Click Here" Height="28px">
15:         </asp:Button>
16:         </P>
17:     </form>
18:     </body>
19:</HTML>
```

Lines 1-2 declare this to be an ASP.NET file. They identify the filename (cool.aspx.vb) and the name of the class (cool.WebForm1) containing Visual Basic.NET code that supports this page. Our project namespace is **Cool**. Line 9 identifies the beginning of a form, of which at least one is on an ASP.NET page. All controls must be placed within a form:

```
<form id="Form1" method="post" runat="server">
```

Web forms controls are easy to spot because they begin with the "<asp:" tag. Lines 13-15 define a Button control named btnCool. The runat="server" attribute on line 13 says that the Web server will process this control before generating standard HTML for the user's browser.

It may require some time, but your success as a Web programmer will depend in part on your understanding of HTML code. We recommend that you read a beginning HTML reference and become familiar with standard tags.

Codebehind File

If our example program only consisted of the HTML code shown so far, it would not do anything when the user clicked on the button. To implement actions, we must open the codebehind file (cool.asxp.vb):

```
Public Class WebForm1 Inherits System.Web.UI.Page

    Private Sub btnCool_Click(ByVal sender As System.Object, _
        ByVal e As System.EventArgs) Handles btnCool.Click

        lblMessage.Text = "This is easier than I thought!"
    End Sub
End Class
```

At first glance, the code in this file is similar to that of desktop applications. Microsoft designers did their best to make ASP.NET code look as much as possible like desktop application code. One important difference is that a Web form inherits from the System.Web.UI.Page class, whereas a Windows form inherits from the System.Windows.Forms.Form class.

Web controls such as buttons respond to events, and you have already written event handlers for Windows forms. You will soon find out, however, that event handling on Web forms does have some important differences from events on Windows forms.

Rendering HTML Output

If we were to view the source code in the HTML page displayed by the Browser in Figure 7-1, we would find little resemblance to the code in we saw earlier in cool.aspx:

```
<!DOCTYPE HTML PUBLIC "-//W3C//DTD HTML 4.0 Transitional//EN">
<HTML>
<HEAD>
<title>Cool Program</title>
</HEAD>
<body>
<form name="Form1" method="post" action="Default.aspx" id="Form1">
<input type="hidden" name="__VIEWSTATE"
   value="dDwtOTk1MjE0NDA4O3Q8O2w8aTwxPjs+O2w8dDw7bDxpPDE+Oz47bDx0PHA8cDxsPFRleHQ7Pjts
   PFRoaXMgaXMgZWFzaWVyIHRoYW4gSSB0aG91Z2h0ITs+Pjs+Ozs+Oz4+Oz73UEQSi65+ZUHoPsPbJhB
   b5R73Ag==" />
<span id="lblMessage" style="width:246px;">This is easier than I
   thought!</span>
<P>
<input type="submit" name="btnCool" value="Click Here" id="btnCool"
   style="height:28px;width:121px;" />
</P>
</form>
</body>
</HTML>
```

The content of this page is generic HTML, understood by all Web browsers. All references to Web forms controls are gone, and the message we generated in the Click event handler has now become literal text embedded in the HTML page. Notice the reference to a special hidden field containing encrypted data named **__ViewState**. It stores the runtime properties of Web controls directly inside the page's HTML, so the values will not be lost when the server disconnects from the client browser.

We know that Web browsers do not understand ASP.NET code, but they do understand HTML. Our ASP.NET code was executed by the Web server, which in turn generated HTML, which was sent to the browser. One advantage to the ASP.NET approach is that end users cannot see the ASP.NET page's source code. By comparison, pages containing VBscript and JavaScript source code reveal their source code to end users.

HTML controls do not, by default, save their contents in ViewState. If a user enters data into an HTML TextField control, for example, the field is erased when a postback occurs.

Hands-on Tutorial: Student Picnic Program

Picnic

You will create a simple ASP.NET signup form for a computer department picnic. It will have a title, labels, text boxes for users to enter their names, and a button that displays a confirmation message. Figure 7-3 shows the program's output after the Save button has been clicked. It looks similar to a Windows desktop application, except the text box and button styles are more typical of Web applications. We will use the grid layout method when positioning controls on the form.

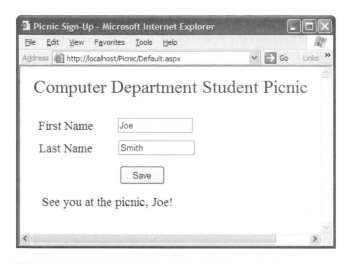

Figure 7-3 The Student Picnic program.

Preparation Step

Before you create a project, become familiar with Visual Studio .NET's default project path. Select Tools > Options from the menu; under the *Environment* heading, select *Projects and Solutions*. Note the contents of *Visual Studio projects location*. Certain project files will be stored at this location when you create ASP.NET projects. You may wish to change this value to a more convenient location in your working directory.

Let's create the new project.

Step 1. From the menu, select File > New > Project. Select **ASP.NET Web Application** from the list of templates, as in Figure 7-4. The location of your project is shown relative the Web server running on the local machine (http://localhost). Ordinarily, you will create the project in either localhost or in one of its subfolders.

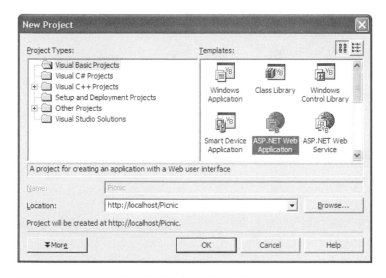

Figure 7-4 Creating a new ASP.NET project.

Step 2. Enter **http://localhost/Picnic** as the project location.

Step 3. In the Solution Explorer window, rename Webform1.aspx to **Default.aspx**. (This name is used as a default name for ASP.NET startup pages, much in the same way that index.html is the default for ordinary Web pages.)

Step 4. Click inside the form once and change the Title property of the page to "Picnic Sign-Up". This text will appear in the browser's title bar when the application runs.

Step 5. From the Web Forms tab in the ToolBox, insert four Label controls, two TextBox controls and a Button control. Refer to Figure 7-5 for their placement, and set the properties according to Table 7-3. (Web controls have an ID property rather than a Name property.)

Step 6. Double-click on the Button control to add a handler procedure to the form. Insert the following code:

```
Private Sub btnSave_Click(ByVal sender As System.Object, _
 ByVal e As System.EventArgs) Handles btnSave.Click

    'Make sure that neither input field is blank.
    If txtFirstName.Text = "" Or txtLastName.Text = "" Then
        lblMessage.Text = "Please enter both your first and last names"
        Exit Sub
    End If

    'Display a confirmation message.
    lblMessage.Text = "See you at the picnic, " & _
        txtFirstName.Text & "!"
End Sub
```

Step 7. Change the class name from Webform1 to **Picnic**.

Step 8. Save and run the program. Enter a person's name, and click on the button. The output should be similar to that shown earlier in Figure 7-3.

(End of tutorial)

Table 7-3

Controls on the Picnic Web form.

Control Type	ID	Property Values
Label	(default)	Text: Computer Department Student Picnic
		Font.Size: Larger
Label	(default)	Text: First Name
Label	(default)	Text: Last Name
Label	lblMessage	Text: (*empty*)
TextBox	txtFirstName	
TextBox	txtLastName	
Button	btnSave	Text: Save

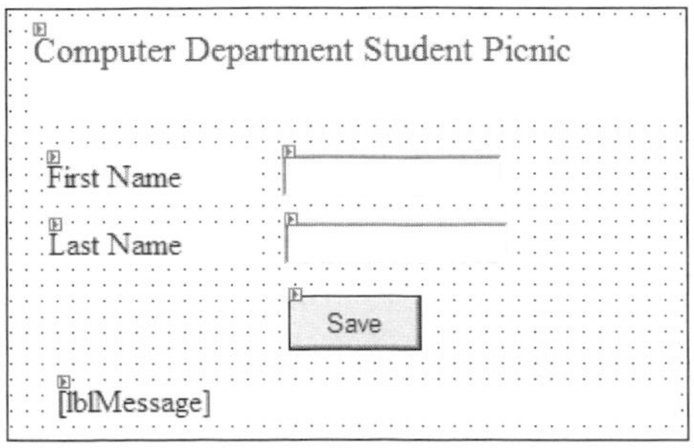

Figure 7-5 Student Picnic program in design mode.

Physical File Locations

If you selected **http://localhost/Picnic** as your project location, its actual physical location on your hard drive is in the default Web server directory. On most computers, the default Web server is located at **c:\Inetpub\wwwroot**. Assuming that is the case, the program we just created is located at **c:\Inetpub\wwwroot\Picnic**.

Aside from your program's project files, Visual Studio .NET places your project's .sln and .suo files in the default Visual Studio .NET projects folder. From the menu, select Tools > Options > Projects and Solutions > Visual Studio projects location, and look for a folder named Picnic. In that folder, look for **Picnic.sln** and **Picnic.suo**. These two files are saved separately from the rest of your project.

If you plan to copy your project to another computer at a later time, you'll have to copy the Picnic.sln and Picnic.suo files to the same folder as the rest of your project (\Inetpub\wwwroot\Picnic). Later, you can copy the entire project folder to the same location on the target machine.

Links and Navigation

In any multipage Web application, the user will need to navigate from one Web page to another, and some of the pages may even be located on other Web servers. In fact, two basic types of hypertext links are used in Web forms:

◆ An *absolute link* contains the complete URL of the destination. An example is http://localhost/myProg/Default.aspx.

◆ A *relative link* stores only the path from the current page to some other page. Suppose your program was located at *localhost/myProg/Default.aspx*, and you wanted the user to navigate to a page named Confirm.aspx in the *localhost/myProg/special* folder. The following relative link would accomplish the navigation:

```
special/Confirm.aspx"
```

An easy way to navigate from one page to another is to use a HyperLink control, located in the HTML section of the Visual Studio .NET Toolbox. Simply assign the destination URL to the control's NavigateUrl property. On the other hand, if you want to write an event handler that navigates between pages, there are two common ways to write it: call the Server.Transfer method or the Response.Redirect method.

Server.Transfer

When you call Server.Transfer to move to a different page, pass it the relative path of the destination page. This method requires the destination page to be located on the same Web server as the current page. Suppose the file confirm.aspx was in the same directory as the current page; then you could write:

```
Server.Transfer("confirm.aspx")
```

One consideration should be noted: The user's Web browser is not informed that the current page's URL has changed, so users may get unpredictable results if they click on their browser's Refresh button.

Response.Redirect

You can navigate to another Web page by calling Response.Redirect, passing it either a relative path or a complete URL. The destination can be either on the same server or on a different server. If we wanted to load the Florida International University home page, the required statement would be:

```
Response.Redirect("http://www.fiu.edu")
```

Response.Redirect is slightly less efficient than Server.Transfer, because it forces a roundtrip to the server (a postback). If the user clicks the Refresh button after a Response.Redirect has taken place, the browser is aware that the current page's URL has changed.

Losing Runtime Control Properties

As soon as you write a program that inputs data and lets the user navigate to a new page, you are in for a surprise: Input controls lose their contents. Consider the simple program in Figure 7-6 that inputs a person's name and uses a HyperLink control to navigate to a second page. On the second page, the user clicks on a link that returns them to the first page (Figure 7-7). Upon returning to the first page, the person's name disappears from the text box. Similarly, if a user enters a name on the first page and clicks on their browser's **Refresh** button, the name is erased from the text box.

If the user clicks on their browser's **Back** button, they can return to the first page without losing the contents of controls. The data remains on the page because the browser has kept a copy of the page in memory on the client computer. It's not wise, however, to assume that users will always use the Back button when returning to previously visited Web pages. The challenge of preserving runtime control properties will be addressed in Chapter 8, using a collection named *Session state*.

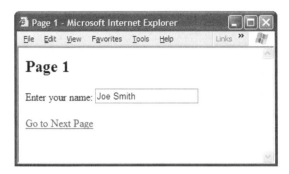

Figure 7-6 Navigation example, first page.

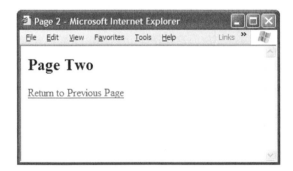

Figure 7-7 Navigation example, second page.

Request and Response Objects

ASP.NET Web pages have two important properties named **Request** and **Response** that permit you to transfer information between pages and write text directly to an HTML page.

Request Object

The Request object, an instance of the HttpRequest class, holds HTTP values sent by the client to the server during a Web request. The easiest way to send Request parameters to a Web page is to append the parameters to the page's URL.

Response Object

The Response object can be used to create data passed from the server to the client browser. You can use a Response to do the following:

◆ Write HTML directly to the client browser from an ASP.NET page

◆ Redirect (transfer control) to another Web page.

◆ Save small files named cookies on the client computer.

For example, the following writes a line of text on the page sent to the client browser:

```
Response.Write("Thank you for registering!<p>")
```

You can embed HTML tags (such as <p>) in the text. The <p> tag inserts a paragraph break.

Modifying the URL

You can append information to a URL when loading a Web form. This information, expressed as name/value pairs, becomes available to the Request object in the Web form. The pairs are in the following general format:

```
?name=value[&name=value]...
```

The *name* is any identifier, and *value* is a string. Use the & character to separate multiple name/value pairs.

Suppose we want our browser to open the **Confirm.aspx** Web form from the **myProg** folder, and pass a student ID on the browser's address line. We can use the following URL:

```
http://localhost/myProg/Confirm.aspx?studentId=12345
```

Or, if we're using Response.Redirect to load the page from an existing Web form in the same directory, we can use the following statement:

```
Response.Redirect ("Confirm.aspx?studentId=12345");
```

The following statement passes a name/value pair, using the Text property of a text box as the value:

```
Response.Redirect("Confirm.aspx?studentId=" & txtStudentId.Text)
```

The following example passes two name/value pairs, using the & character to separate them:

```
Response.Redirect("Confirm.aspx?studentId=12345&lastName=Jones")
```

In some cases, the value added to the URL may contain spaces or special characters. ASP.NET automatically inserts placeholders in the passed information to make it a valid URL. If we write the following,

```
Response.Redirect("Confirm.aspx?lastName=del Rey")
```

The space in "del Rey" will be replaced by %20, the hexadecimal ASCII code for a space:

```
Confirm.aspx?lastName=del%20Rey
```

HttpRequest Object

The **Request** property of a page is used by a Web form to retrieve name/value pairs passed from another page. It's actually an *HttpRequest* object that contains a **Params** collection, which in turn contains all name/value pairs passed to the Web form. Each parameter value is returned as a string. The following example statement retrieves the studentId parameter from the page's Request object:

```
Dim idVal As String = Request.Params.Item("studentId")
```

Because Params is the default property of Request, and Item is the default property of Params, we can shorten the foregoing statement:

```
Dim idVal As String = Request("studentId")
```

Hands-On Tutorial: Student Picnic Confirmation

PicnicConfirm

Let's enhance the Student Picnic program by adding a confirmation page. We will show how to transfer information from the signup page to the confirmation page. Figure 7-8 shows a sample of the program's output after having entered Joe Smith as the student name when registering for the picnic. The new page name is Confirm.aspx. Attached to the URL is a name-value pair assigned when the program transferred from the Default.aspx form to this one.

HyperLink Control

We will introduce a new Web control on the confirmation page named **HyperLink**. This control looks exactly like an HTML hyperlink, and provides a simple way for the client's browser to move to a new Web page. You can display a label in its Text property or you can insert a reference to a graphic image file in its **ImageUrl** property. If used, the graphic image overrides the text. The **NavigateUrl** property holds the URL of the page you'll be branching to. The HyperLink control does not generate any programmable events.

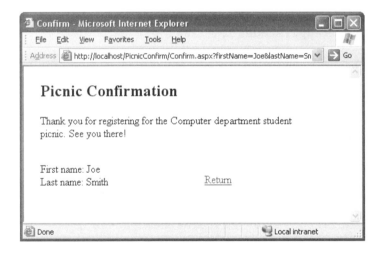

Figure 7-8 Confirmation page.

Here are the steps:

Step 1. Open the Picnic application you created in the previous hands-on tutorial.

Step 2. Add a new Web form to the project and name it **Confirm.aspx**. (Use the Project menu to add the form.)

Step 3. Place a Label control on the form, set its Text property to **Picnic Confirmation**, set its Font.Size property to Large, and set its Font.Bold property to True.

Step 4. Select the HTML ToolBox tab and place another Label control on the form. Stretch its dimensions a bit, and type directly into the label. Enter "Thank you for registering for ...", as shown earlier in Figure 7-8. HTML labels are easier to use than Web form labels when you have a lot of text to enter.

Step 5. Select the Web Forms ToolBox tab and place a third Label control on the form. Set its Id property to **lblName**.

Step 6. Add a HyperLink control to the form, set its Text property to **Return**, and set its NavigateURL property to **Default.aspx**.

Step 7. Open the form's code window and enter the following code into the Page_Load event handler. Notice how we inserted the
 HTML tag after the first name to make the last name appear on a separate line:

```
lblName.Text = "First name: " & Request.Params("firstName") & "<br>" _
   & "Last name: " & Request.Params("lastName")
```

Step 8. Open the code window for Default.aspx (the startup form) and change the code in the btnSave_Click handler to the following:

```
'Make sure that neither input field is blank.
If txtFirstName.Text = "" Or txtLastName.Text = "" Then
   lblMessage.Text = "Please enter both your first and last names"
   Exit Sub
End If

'Display a confirmation message.
Response.Redirect ("Confirm.aspx?firstName=" & txtFirstName.Text _
   & "&lastName=" & txtLastName.Text)
```

Step 9. Save and run the program. Enter a name in the startup form, click on Save, and verify the confirmation message.

(End of tutorial. The complete source code is shown in Code Listing 7-1.)

Code Listing 7-1 (Student Picnic Confirmation)

```
Public Class StudentPicnic
   Inherits System.Web.UI.Page
```

+ Web Form Designer generated code

```
   Private Sub btnSave_Click(ByVal sender As System.Object, _
   ByVal e As System.EventArgs) Handles btnSave.Click

      'Make sure that neither input field is blank.
      If txtFirstName.Text = "" Or txtLastName.Text = "" Then
         lblMessage.Text = "Please enter both your first and last names"
         Exit Sub
      End If

      'Display a confirmation message.
      Response.Redirect("Confirm.aspx?firstName=" & txtFirstName.Text _
         & "&lastName=" & txtLastName.Text)
   End Sub
End Class

Public Class Confirm
   Inherits System.Web.UI.Page
```

+ Web Form Designer generated code

```
   Private Sub Page_Load(ByVal sender As System.Object, _
   ByVal e As System.EventArgs) Handles MyBase.Load

      lblName.Text = "First name: " & Request.Params("firstName") & "<br>" _
         & "Last name: " & Request.Params("lastName")

      'Alternative display method:
      'lblFirst.Text = "First name: <b>" & Request.Params("firstName") & "</b>"
```

```
      'lblLast.Text = "Last name: <b>" & Request.Params("lastName") & "</b>"
    End Sub
End Class
```

Text Output

Another way we might have generated the user's first and last names on the confirmation form would have been to insert the values in separate Label controls:

```
lblFirst.Text = "First name: " & Request.Params("firstName")
lblLast.Text = "Last name: " & Request.Params("lastName")
```

Another possibility would be to embed <b> (bold) and </b> (end bold) tags in the text to highlight the first and last names:

```
lblFirst.Text = "First name: <b>" & Request.Params("firstName") & "</b>"
lblLast.Text = "Last name: <b>" & Request.Params("lastName") & "</b>"
```

Using Server.Transfer to Move Between Pages

In the Default.aspx page, we used the Response.Redirect method to transfer control to the confirmation page. You may have noticed that the request parameters appeared in the URL in the browser's address line:

```
http://localhost/PicnicConfirm/Confirm.aspx?firstName=Joe&lastName=Smith
```

A URL containing request parameters can easily be bookmarked or added to the Favorites menu of the browser, allowing a user to return to this page later. The Server.Transfer method, on the other hand, hides the target Web page name and the request parameters from users. If we used the following statement in the Save button in the Picnic program, the browser's command line would continue to display the following URL after moving to the confirmation form:

```
http://localhost/PicnicConfirm/Default.aspx
```

Checkpoint

7.8 Name at least two attributes that appear in the Page directive at the beginning of a Web form file.

7.9 Which class is the superclass of all Web forms?

7.10 What is the purpose of the codebehind file?

7.11 How can all browsers display the contents of a Web form after it has been processed by the Web server?

7.12 What is ViewState?

▶ 7.3 ASP.NET Objects and Namespaces

Important Namespaces

Before we write any more programs in ASP.NET, let's examine the two primary namespaces: System.Web and System.Web.UI.

System.Web Namespace

The System.Web namespace includes classes that provide Web capability to programs. They permit you to tap into the considerable power of both the Web server and client browser. Many of these classes are instantiated as Page class properties.

◆ The **HttpApplication** class defines the methods, properties, and events common to all application objects in ASP.NET programs. It is the base class for applications defined by the user in the global.asax file.

◆ The **HttpBrowserCapabilities** class lets an ASP.NET application collect information about the client's browser.

◆ The **HttpCookie** class lets you create and read the values of HTTP cookies. Cookies are name-value pairs stored on the client's computer that can remain after the user has disconnected.

◆ The **HttpCookieCollection** class defines a collection of HttpCookie objects. It provides methods that let you add, remove, and set the values of cookies. Every Page object has such a property named **Cookies.**

◆ The **HttpException** class provides a way to generate HTTP exceptions.

◆ The **HttpRequest** class lets a program read the HTTP values sent by a client during a Web request. Every Page object has such a property named **Request**.

◆ The **HttpResponse** class lets a program generate HTTP values sent by the server to a client browser. Every Page object has such a property named **Response**. You can use the standard HttpResponse object to write text directly to the user's displayed Web page.

◆ The **HttpServerUtility** class represents the Web server processing Web forms. Every Page object, for example, has a property named **Server** that returns the Web server associated with the page.

◆ The **HttpSessionState** class provides access to Session-state data, that is, data which you want to preserve when the user navigates from one Web page to another. Every Web page has a property named **Session**, which is an HttpSessionState object.

System.Web.UI Namespace

◆ The **System.Web.UI.WebControls** namespace contains classes that provide properties, methods, and events for Web forms controls.

◆ The **System.Web.UI.HTMLControls** namespace contains classes that hold HTML control properties.

◆ The **System.Web.UI namespace** includes the Page and HtmlTextWriter classes, as well as others. The Page class represents an .aspx file (Web form) requested from a server that hosts an ASP.NET Web application. The HtmlTextWriter class makes it possible to write specific HTML characters and text to a Web form. It provides formatting for HTML content when Web pages are sent to the client browser.

Other Namespaces

◆ The **System.Web.Caching** namespace provides facilities for caching (saving) frequently-used objects on the server to improve application performance. The Cache class belongs to this namespace.

◆ The **System.Web.Mail** namespace creates and sends messages to a mail server, using Simple Mail Transfer Protocol (SMTP).

◆ The **System.Web.Security** namespace contains classes that implement security in Web applications.

Checkpoint

7.13 Which class contains methods, properties, and events common to application objects in ASP.NET programs?

7.14 Which two classes make it possible to read, write, add, and remove HTTP cookies?

7.15 Which class lets programs write text directly to the user's browser window?

7.16 Which class lets programs preserve data when the user navigates from one Web page to another?

7.17 Which class sends messages to a mail server?

▶7.4 Standard Web Forms Controls

Let's turn to the practical aspects of programming, as we study the various types of Web forms controls. The following are ones you are likely to use often:

- ◆ ImageButton
- ◆ LinkButton
- ◆ RadioButton
- ◆ CheckBox
- ◆ CheckBoxList
- ◆ RadioButtonList
- ◆ ListBox
- ◆ DropDownList
- ◆ Panel

Most Web controls have similar properties as their Windows forms counterparts. Examples of those properties are Text, Enabled, Visible, Font, BorderStyle, ReadOnly, and TabIndex. There are, however, a few important differences between Web forms and Windows forms controls:

- ◆ The ID property replaces the Name property used in Windows forms controls.
- ◆ The AutoPostBack property is not found in Windows forms controls.
- ◆ Web forms controls lose their runtime property values when the user moves away from the current page.

The AutoPostBack Property

When a control's AutoPostBack property is True, clicking on the control causes the form to be posted back to the server. You might, for example, want to trigger a database row lookup when the user makes a selection in a list box. The server will redisplay the form quickly or slowly, depending on how busy it is handling other requests. AutoPostBack defaults to False for the following controls: CheckBox, CheckBoxList, DropDownList, ListBox, ListControl, RadioButton, RadioButtonList, and TextBox. Setting AutoPostBack to True in a TextBox has no effect, so you have no way to generate a postback event every time a character is typed. You probably would not want to do it anyway, because the program would eat up a lot of server time. Not all controls need an AutoPostBack property. In particular, the Button, LinkButton, and ImageButton controls automatically post the current page back to the server.

Event Handling in Web Forms

Events are fired in a different sequence in Web forms than they are in Windows forms. In a Web form, the Page_Load event occurs when the page is first loaded into the user's browser, and again every time the page is posted back to the server. The program shown in Figure 7-9 inserts a message in the list box every time the Page_Load event fires. From the program display, we can see that Page_Load fired when the page was first displayed.

Figure 7-9 Loading a Web form.

When the user types in a name and clicks the OK button (Figure 7-10), the Page_Load event fires again because of a postback. Next, the TextChanged event handler executes. This unusual event sequence can be unsettling if you expect the TextChanged event to fire immediately, as it does in Windows forms applications. ASP.NET programmers are careful not to execute any code in the Page_Load event handler that would change the state of controls whose event handlers have not yet had a chance to execute.

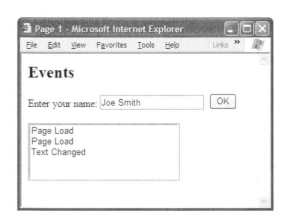

Figure 7-10 After entering a name and clicking on OK.

Renaming Web Forms Controls

In Windows forms and Web forms, the Handles clause in an event handler procedure forms a vital link between the handler and the event fired by the .NET runtime. Using the following Click event handler as an example, the Handles clause names the actual event:

```
Private Sub Button1_Click(ByVal sender As System.Object, _
    ByVal e As System.EventArgs) Handles btnMode.Click
```

If you rename a Web forms control after having created one or more event handlers, Visual Studio .NET automatically drops the Handles clause from each of the handlers. The same is true if you cut or copy a control to the Windows clipboard and then paste it back onto the form. If we rename Button1 to btnOk, the Handles clause disappears:

```
Private Sub btnOk_Click(ByVal sender As System.Object, _
    ByVal e As System.EventArgs)
```

The event procedure no longer executes when the button is clicked, so we must manually add back a Handles clause to make the button work.

Rather than using the Windows clipboard to move controls between table cells, drag them with the mouse. Then you can avoid losing the Handles clause from the control's event handlers.

Page (Document) Properties

When you select the design area of a new Web page, the Properties window displays the object known as **Document**. Table 7-4 lists some properties you are likely to use.

Table 7-4

Page (Document) Properties.

Property	Description
aLink	Color of hypertext links.
background	Secify a graphic file that will be used as a background picture.
bgColor	Background color for the page.
errorPage	The URL of a page that can be used to display unhandled errors.
pageLayout	Select FlowLayout or GridLayout mode for editing.
text	Foreground color of text placed directly on the page.
title	String that appears in the browser's title bar.
vLink	Color of links that have already been visited.

ImageButton and LinkButton

 SampleControls

Examples of different types of button controls are shown in Figure 7-11. We discussed the HyperLink and Button controls earlier in this chapter. The Button, ImageButton, and LinkButton controls provide identical functions; they differ only in their appearance. The HyperLink control is a lightweight HTML-like control that does not generate events. The RadioButton and CheckBox controls are quite similar to their WinForms counterparts.

Figure 7-11 Examples of various ASP button controls.

ImageButton Control

The ImageButton control lets you make a graphic image work like a button. You insert the image by placing a filename in the button's ImageUrl property. The button generates a Click event when the image is clicked by the user.

LinkButton Control

The LinkButton control looks and behaves much like an ordinary HTML hyperlink: it displays underlined text, and when the user clicks on the text, a Click event is generated.

RadioButton and CheckBox

SampleControls

RadioButton Control

The RadioButton control has a Checked property that is True or False depending on whether the button has been selected. Use the **GroupName** property to form a group of radio buttons, so only one button in the group can be selected at a time. In Figure 7-12, for example, the GroupName of the first three buttons equals **shift**. The GroupNames of the last two buttons equals **department**. The two button groups operate independently. You can use the CheckedChanged event handler to respond when individual buttons are clicked:

```
Private selectedShift As String

Private Sub radDaytime_CheckedChanged(ByVal sender As System.Object, _
    ByVal e As System.EventArgs) Handles radDaytime.CheckedChanged

    selectedShift = "daytime"
End Sub
```

The event handler does not execute until the page is posted back to the server. Alternatively, you can use the same handler to respond to clicks by all buttons within a group by adding their names to the procedure's Handles list:

```
Handles radDaytime.CheckedChanged, radEvening.CheckChanged,
    radNight.CheckChanged
```

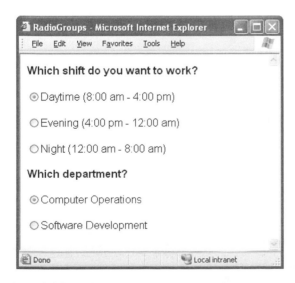

Figure 7-12 Using RadioButton groups.

CheckBox Control

The CheckBox control has a Checked property that equals True when the user has checked the box. Each check box works independently of all other check boxes on the page. When the user clicks on a check box, its CheckChanged event fires.

CheckBoxList and RadioButtonList

SampleControls

The CheckBoxList and RadioButtonList controls each provide a convenient way to group a set of controls under a single name and single event handler. Each has an Items collection, which you can use to create multiple instances of the button or check box. The items can appear in the form either vertically or horizontally, using the RepeatDirection property. Figure 7-13 shows examples of both types of lists. Use the RepeatColumns property to determine the number of columns to display when the buttons wrap around. Figure 7-14 shows a RadioButtonList with RepeatColumns equal to 3.

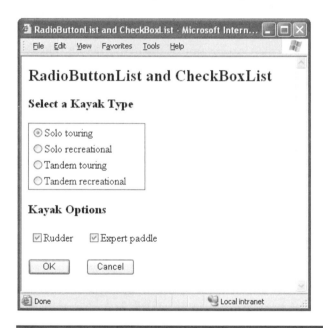

Figure 7-13 RadioButtonList and CheckBoxList examples.

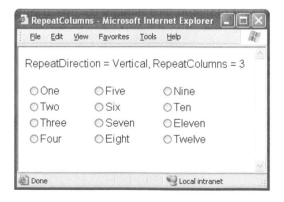

Figure 7-14 Using the RepeatColumns property.

Building the Items Collection in Design Mode

In design mode, you can click on the Items property of a RadioButtonList (or CheckBoxList) and use the collection editor to insert values into the Items collection. Figure 7-15 shows how the editor is used. Each item has three properties that you can set: Selected, Text, and Value.

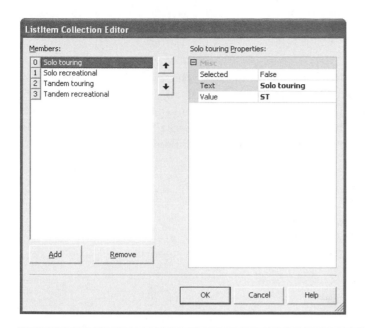

Figure 7-15 Building the Items collection.

Determining the Selected Item

As is true for Windows forms, the SelectedIndexChanged event fires when the user makes a selection in a list-type control on a Web form. You can find out which item has been selected by examining any of three properties:

◆ **SelectedIndex**: Returns the zero-based index of the selected item. You can use this property to assign a default selection for the list.

◆ **SelectedItem**: Returns the currently selected item, a ListItem object.

◆ **SelectedValue**: Returns the contents of the field that was specified by the DataValueField property.

The DataValueField property is the analog to the ValueMember property found in ListBox and ComboBox controls on Windows forms. Following are examples of querying RadioButtonList selections. For the SelectedItem example, we display the item's Text property:

```
lblResult.Text = "Selected index = " & radKayakType.SelectedIndex
lblResult.Text = "Kayak name = " & radKayakType.SelectedItem.Text
lblResult.Text = "Kayak value = " & radKayakType.SelectedValue
```

The kayak at index position 0, for example, has Text = "Solo touring", and Value = "ST".

Page_Load Considerations

The Page_Load event handler always executes before the SelectedIndexChanged handler. Therefore, be careful not to reinitialize your RadioButtonList, CheckBoxList, ListBox, or DropDownList controls each time a page is posted back. If you do, the user's selections will be erased. The usual way to avoid postback problems is to surround initialization statements with an IF statement as we have done here for the radKayakType list:

```
Private Sub Page_Load(ByVal sender As System.Object, _
    ByVal e As System.EventArgs) Handles MyBase.Load

    If Not IsPostBack Then
        radKayakType.SelectedIndex = -1
    End If
End Sub
```

Therefore, SelectedIndex is initialized only the first time the page is loaded.

Determining CheckBoxList Selections

Unlike the RadioButtonList, multiple items in a CheckBoxList can be selected at the same time. In such cases, the SelectedIndex, SelectedItem, and SelectedValue properties only apply to the first selected item. If you want to locate all selected items, you must iterate through the Items collection (a ListItemCollection object). As you inspect each item, use its Selected property to find out if it has been checked. Each item in the collection is a ListItem object. The following code shows how to iterate through a CheckBoxList named chkOptions and build a string containing descriptions of the selected items:

```
lblResult.Text = "Selected options: "
Dim item As ListItem
For Each item In chkOptions.Items
    If item.Selected Then
        lblResult.Text &= item.Text & ", "
    End If
Next
```

Figure 7-16 shows the output from this code when two kayak options are selected.

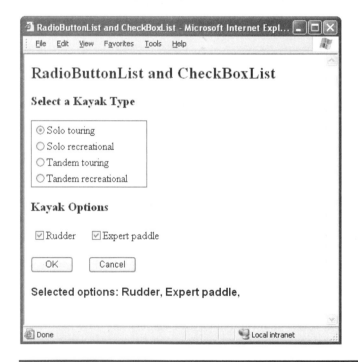

Figure 7-16 Selected CheckBoxList items.

ListBox

SampleControls

In many ways, the Web forms ListBox control is similar to the Windows forms ListBox control. It has an Items collection and a SelectedIndexChanged event. You can retrieve the following properties at runtime:

◆ **SelectedIndex**: returns the index of the selected item.

◆ **SelectedItem**: returns the currently selected item, a ListItem object.

◆ **SelectedValue**: returns the contents of the selected item's Value property.

The following examples retrieve the three properties from a ListBox named lstStaff:

```
lblResult.Text = "Selected Index: " & lstStaff.SelectedIndex
lblResult.Text = "Selected Item: " & lstStaff.SelectedItem.Text
lblResult.Text = "Selected Value: " & lstStaff.SelectedValue
```

In Figure 7-17 the index of the selected item from a list of sales staff members is displayed in a label below the OK button.

Figure 7-17 Displaying the SelectedIndex of a Listbox.

SelectionMode

You can use the SelectionMode property to determine whether users can select only a single item, or multiple items from a ListBox. The two possible choices are **Single** and **Multiple**. In Multiple mode, the user can hold down the Ctrl key to select multiple individual items or hold down the Shift key to select a range of items.

SelectedIndexChanged Event

You can use a **SelectedIndexChanged** event handler to respond to selections by the user in any list-type control. There is one important consideration, however: the **AutoPostBack** property must be set to True if you want the user's selection to be detected immediately. Otherwise, the SelectedIndexChanged event will not fire until the form is posted back to the server by some other control (such as a button).

When you set AutoPostBack to True for a list-type control, the user experiences a short delay every time they click on the list. Depending on the Web server's response time, the delay could cause performance problems. Most Web applications do not post back to the server every time users select from list-type controls. Instead, the sites use button controls to post all selections on the page back to the server at the same time.

DropDownList

 ### SampleControls

The DropDownList control displays a list of items from which you can choose only one. In this sense, it is similar to the RadioButtonList control. The DropDownList does not permit multiple items to be selected. There are two noticeable differences between the DropDownList and its Windows forms counterpart, the ComboBox: In a DropDownList, the initial value of SelectedIndex is always 0, causing the first item to display. Second, users cannot enter an arbitrary string into the DropDownList, as they can in a ComboBox. Figure 7-18 shows a simple example of a list when first displayed on a Web form. We have inserted an initial entry named "(none)" in the first row.

Figure 7-18 DropDownList demo.

When the user selects a kayak tour, its date appears in a Label, as in Figure 7-19. Ordinarily we would have to wait for the user to click on a button before a postback would occur. Instead, by setting AutoPostBack to True, the page posts back as soon as the user makes a selection. The following code handles the SelectedIndexChanged event handler for the ddlTours list:

```
Private Sub ddlTours_SelectedIndexChanged(ByVal sender As _
    System.Object, ByVal e As System.EventArgs) _
    Handles ddlTours.SelectedIndexChanged

    lblDate.Text = ddlTours.SelectedValue
End Sub
```

Figure 7-19 Selecting a kayak tour

Panel

SampleControls

The Panel control is a container that can hold other controls. The Panel allows controls to be moved, displayed, or hidden as a unified group. You may find it useful when providing a set of alternative displays on the same Web form. When you set the Visible property of a panel to False, all controls within the panel are hidden. Similarly, when the panel is made visible, all enclosed controls become visible.

Figure 7-20 shows the design of a Web form for a kayak store in which the user can sign up for either kayak tours or kayak classes. Assume that the form would be too cluttered if both tours and classes were displayed simultaneously. We will use the two buttons at the top to determine which panel is visible. Initially, the Visible property of both panels is set to False. The form is designed in flow layout mode so invisible panels do not take up space on the Web page. In effect, both panels will appear to occupy the same position on the page.

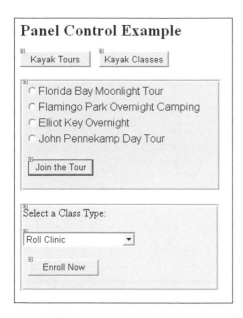

Figure 7-20 Two panels on the same page (design mode)

Showing and Hiding the Panels

To show and hide the two panels, we insert code in the Click event handlers for the two buttons at the top of the page. For example in the btnTours_Click handler, we write:

```
pnlTours.Visible = True
pnlClasses.Visible = False
```

In the btnClasses_Click handler, the following lines are used:

```
pnlClasses.Visible = True
pnlTours.Visible = False
```

At runtime, users are presented with only the page title and two buttons. Depending on which button users select, they see either the Kayak Tours panel or the Kayak Classes panel. In Figure 7-21, the user has selected Kayak Classes; in Figure 7-22, the user has selected Kayak Tours.

Figure 7-21 Showing the Kayak Classes panel.

Figure 7-22 Showing the Kayak Tours panel.

Binding List Controls to Arrays

A little-publicized feature of list-type controls is that you can bind them not only to databases, but also to arrays. If you don't want to enter a lot of data into a control in design mode, array binding is a good alternative. Suppose that our program used a ListBox control named **lstKayakTypes**. We could declare the following public array at the class level:

```
Public kayakTypes As String() = {"Owner supplied", _
    "Solo touring", "Tandem touring", _
    "Solo recreational", "Tandem recreational"}
```

We would insert the array name into the ListBox's DataSource property. The program would fill the ListBox by calling its DataBind method from the Page_Load event handler:

```
If Not IsPostBack Then
    lstKayakType.DataBind()
End If
```

Only fill the ListBox once and not after each postback. Otherwise, any selection made by the user is erased.

Checkpoint

7.18 How does setting AutoPostBack to True affect a ListBox control?

7.19 What is the first event to fire when the user clicks on a Button control?

7.20 How is the LinkButton control different from the HyperLink control?

7.21 How can several individual RadioButton controls be grouped in such a way that only one button can be selected at a time?

7.22 Which event is fired when the user clicks on a CheckBox control?

7.23 Which property in a CheckBoxList holds the text displayed next to the individual check boxes?

7.24 How do you find out which items have been selected in a CheckBoxList control?

7.25 Which list-type control automatically initializes its SelectedIndex property to zero?

7.26 How do you initialize the Items property of a ListBox with the contents of an array?

▶7.5 Formatting Tips

In this section we would like to share with you a few useful tips to use when designing forms:

◆ Setting the tab order for input controls

◆ Using text boxes with multiple lines

◆ Using flow layout mode rather than grid layout when designing forms.

◆ Using the HTML Table Control to position text and controls on a form.

Setting the Tab Order

To set the tab order on a Web form, manually set the TabIndex property of each control. The index values start at 1 rather than 0. In Internet Explorer, the first time the user presses Tab, the browser's Address bar gets the focus; when Tab is pressed again, the focus moves to the first field in your tab sequence. Not all browsers support the TabIndex property, but you can definitely use it with Internet Explorer 4.0 and later.

Text Boxes with Multiple Lines

For proper compatibility with non-Microsoft browsers, a text box containing multiple lines should not be dragged with the mouse to increase its size. Instead, specify values for the Rows and Columns properties. The Rows property specifies the height in terms of text lines. The Columns property specifies the character width of the text box.

Grid Layout Versus Flow Layout

Grid_vs_Flow_Layout

Every Page object has a property named **pageLayout**, which has one of two possible values: GridLayout or FlowLayout. The default is *GridLayout*, perhaps to accommodate programmers who are accustomed to creating Windows forms. Grid layout, however, is not typically used by HTML designers. There are a few disadvantages to using grid layout:

◆ You cannot type text directly onto the form. All text must be placed in Label controls.

◆ Grid layouts do not work if you are using HTML tables elsewhere on the form.

◆ When the user changes the default text size setting in their browser, the contents of Label controls may wrap around and look ugly.

Less importantly, the form's HTML code is complicated by having to introduce LEFT and TOP property values into each control's definition. For example, in flow layout mode, we could insert a level-2 heading on a page with just one line of HTML:

```
<H2>Label Controls</H2>
```

But in grid layout mode, the following HTML is required. Curiously enough, it includes a property that indicates the temporary use of flow layout:

```
<DIV style="DISPLAY: inline; Z-INDEX: 103; LEFT: 24px;
   WIDTH: 312px; POSITION: absolute; TOP: 16px; HEIGHT: 32px";
   ms_positioning="FlowLayout">
   <H2>Label Controls</H2>
</DIV>
```

Wraparound Text

Wraparound text can be a problem in grid layout mode when users switch to larger fonts in their Web browser. In Figure 7-23, the Web page looks fairly good, running under the programmer's browser. Label controls are placed just to the left of text boxes, and a Label control is used to display the page title. Suppose the end user prefers larger fonts and has changed their browser settings as in Figure 7-24. The text in the labels wraps around, creating a mess. The developer is forced to anticipate possible ranges of text sizes and must lengthen the Label controls accordingly.

Figure 7-23 Simple input form, designed in GridLayout mode.

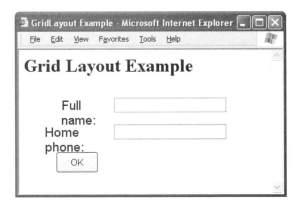

Figure 7-24 GridLayout form, after user increases the text size.

Let's now create the same Web form, using flow layout. Figure 7-25 shows the Web page running in a browser after the text size has been increased. There is a slight misalignment of the two text boxes, but the page still looks usable.

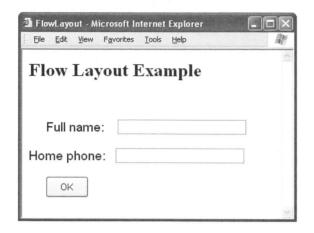

Figure 7-25 Converting to flow layout.

The slight alignment problem we just mentioned can be eliminated by placing text and controls in cells of an HTML table control. The next section describes how to do this.

HTML Table Control

The HTML Table control is particularly useful when working in flow layout mode. You can use it to align text and Web controls. Normally, we avoid HTML controls because they do not generate programmable events. The Table control is an exception because it is only used for formatting.

You can use Visual Studio's Table menu command to insert, delete, and select rows and columns. The following keyboard shortcuts speed up the building of tables:

◆ Insert a new row above the current row: Ctrl + Alt + Up Arrow

◆ Insert a new row below the current row: Ctrl + Alt + Down Arrow

◆ Insert a new column to the left of the current row: Ctrl + Alt + Left Arrow

◆ Insert a new column to the right of the current row: Ctrl + Alt + Right Arrow

In Figure 7-26, a Table control is used to position text and controls on our Web form. Although table lines show in design mode, we can make them disappear at runtime by setting the Table's **border** property equal to zero. When the program runs (Figure 7-27), the alignment is exact, regardless of the text size selected by the user.

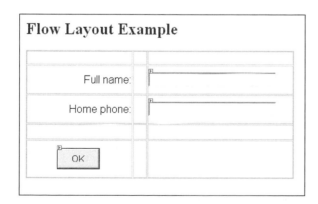

Figure 7-26 Flow layout example, using a table for alignment.

Figure 7-27 Results of using a table to align controls.

Using Tables to Design Forms

You may find a few tricks and guidelines useful when creating forms with many controls. First, decide on an overall organizational format for the page. You might, for example, divide up the page into three large columns with only one cell in each column. In Figure 7-28 we set the **valign** (vertical alignment) property of each column to **top**, and insert a single character in each column to act as a place-holder. We will call this a *column-major* layout scheme.

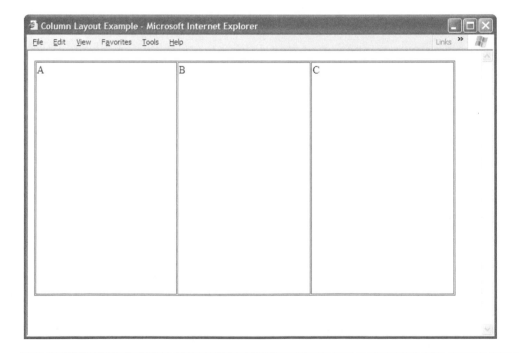

Figure 7-28 Organizing a page into columns.

Next, insert a new HTML table into each cell of the first table (Figure 7-29). This action allows each column to be independent of the other two. Leave at least two columns in each of these tables, to make it easier to provide empty space between columns A, B, and C. Also, it is easier to view the individual cells if you insert a space in each cell. As you build each column, always leave one table row between controls. You will need to use the empty rows to fine-tune the vertical spacing.

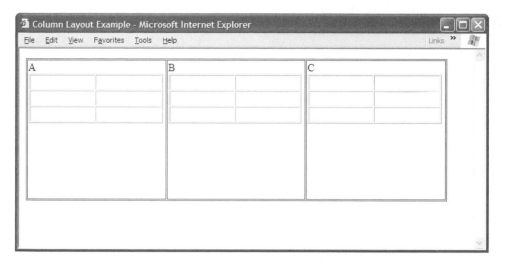

Figure 7-29 Inserting tables in each column.

After you have inserted an ample number of rows in each table, begin inserting text and controls in the table columns. For example, let's insert a DropDownList and CheckBoxList along with some text in the first column (Figure 7-30). We have set the border thicknesses of the alignment tables to zero so they will be invisible at runtime. The second column just to the right of each control acts as a convenient spacer, to prevent the controls from running into column B. Also, there is a blank row between the DropDownList and the "Choose a Topping" text.

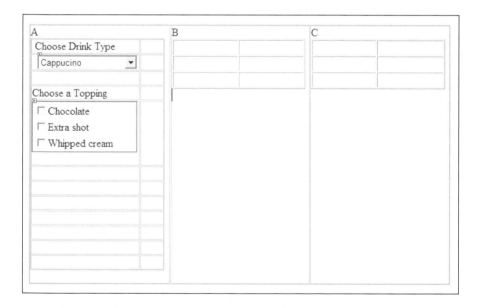

Figure 7-30 Inserting controls (design mode).

When we run the program (Figure 7-31), the first column has a clean appearance. (We deleted the letter A.) The vertical spacing can be adjusted by dragging the borders of the blank table rows.

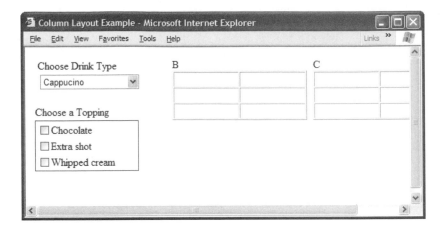

Figure 7-31 Showing the drink selections at runtime.

Row-Major Layout

Instead of dividing a page into columns, you can divide it into rows (called a *row-major* layout scheme). Insert a separate table into each row, as is done in Figure 7-32. This approach works well for input fields that vary in length. Labels are easily right-justified by setting the align property of their enclosing table cells to **right**. The RadioButtonList in this figure uses RepeatDirection = Horizontal, and RepeatColumns = 3. Figure 7-33 shows the same form at runtime.

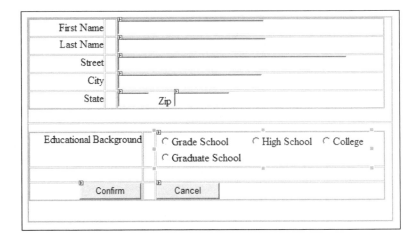

Figure 7-32 Row-major layout, design mode.

Merging Cells

Merging cells together to create larger cells can be a little tricky, but is very useful when you have too much data for one cell.

◆ Merge all the cells in a row together by first selecting the Table | Select | Row menu command, followed by the Table | Merge Cells command.

◆ Merge all the cells in a column together by first selecting the Table | Select | Column menu command, followed by the Table | Merge Cells command.

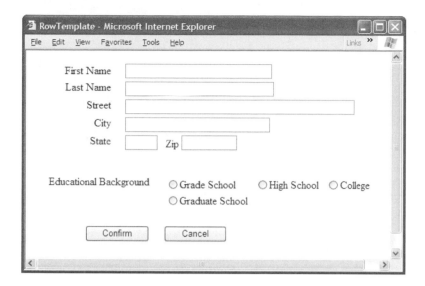

Figure 7-33 Row-major layout, at runtime.

Be cautious when using merging rows and columns. Doing so can have drastic effects on other rows and columns in your table. Fortunately, using a separate table for each column helps to minimize the need for row and column spans.

Final Suggestions

If the height of a row seems to change when you switch from design mode to run mode, drag the bottom of the row with the mouse. This causes a specific row height to be encoded in the Style property of each cell in the row.

Start with more columns and rows than you think you need. It's much easier to delete an existing column than to insert a new one without messing up the original table alignment.

In design mode, avoid pressing the Enter key as the last action while editing a cell. Doing so inserts a paragraph tag which is difficult to remove. You can do it by editing the HTML directly, and removing the <P> and </P> tags from the cells. In HTML, a table cell is defined by the <TD> and </TD> tags.

If you're an expert, go ahead and edit the HTML in your forms. However, be careful, because you can mess things up. If Visual Studio .NET is unable to understand your HTML, it will refuse to load some or all of the controls on your Web form. We have sometimes had to remove everything from a Web page and rebuild the page from scratch!

After reading our suggestions about flow layout, you may be thinking that grid layout looks better all the time. Consider the following, however:

◆ Flow layout is more compatible with existing HTML design programs, making it easier for you to customize your program's appearance with third-party Web editing tools.

◆ Flow layout automatically adjusts to changes in the size of the text content in Web forms. Grid layout requires significant manual adjustments to accommodate such changes.

Example: Kayak Tour Signup

KayakTour

Let's look at a short program (named KayakTour) that demonstrates many of the standard Web forms controls used in this chapter. The Kayak Tour Signup program lets users register for an exciting South Florida kayak tour. They can select several features, including the type of kayak, extra equipment, and the method of payment. In Figure 7-34, a user has signed up for a tour and made a number of other selections. When they click on the Confirm button, a summary of their choices appears on the right side of the form. The techniques used in this program to harvest list selections will be useful in Chapter 9 when we start saving Web forms data in databases.

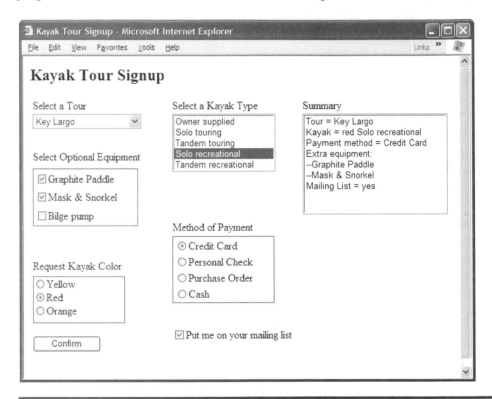

Figure 7-34 Signing up for a kayak tour.

Table 7-5 lists the more important controls on the Web form, along with their essential property values. The remaining property values can be seen from the screen snapshot.

Table 7-5

Kayak Tour Signup, essential control properties.

Control Type	Control Name	Properties
DropDownList	ddlTour	Items: (collection)
CheckBoxList	chkEquipment	Items: (collection)
RadioButton	radYellow	GroupName: ColorChoice
RadioButton	radRed	GroupName: ColorChoice
RadioButton	radOrange	GroupName: ColorChoice
ListBox	lstSummary	
CheckBox	chkMailingList	Text:: Put me on your mailing list
ListBox	lstKayakType	DataSource: KayakTypes
RadioButtonList	radPaymentType	Items: (collection)
Button	btnConfirm	Text: Confirm
Label	lblMessage	Color: Red

Program Implementation

The complete program source code appears in Code Listing 7-2. The **Page_Load** event handler fills the lstKayakType list box from the array of kayak types declared at the class level. The **ValidInputs** function checks to make sure the user has selected a kayak tour (ddlTour), a kayak type (lstKayakType), and a payment type (radPaymentType). If all three are selected, the function returns True. When the user clicks on the Confirm button, the program adds all selections made by the user to the lstSummary list box.

Code Listing 7-2 (Kayak Tour Signup)

```
Public Class KayakTour
   Inherits System.Web.UI.Page


+ Web Form Designer Generated Code


   'Array definition, bound to the list box
   Public kayakTypes As String() = {"Owner supplied", _
    "Solo touring", "Tandem touring", _
    "Solo recreational", "Tandem recreational"}


   Private Sub Page_Load(ByVal sender As System.Object, _
    ByVal e As System.EventArgs) Handles MyBase.Load

      If Not IsPostBack Then
         lstKayakType.DataBind()
      End If
   End Sub


   Private Function ValidInputs() As Boolean
      If ddlTour.SelectedIndex = 0 Then
         lblMessage.Text = "Error: A tour must be selected"
         Return False
      End If
      If lstKayakType.SelectedIndex = -1 Then
         lblMessage.Text = "Error: Kayak type must be selected"
         Return False
      End If
      If radPaymentType.SelectedIndex = -1 Then
         lblMessage.Text = "Error: Payment method must be selected"
         Return False
      End If
      lblMessage.Text = ""
      Return True                      'everthing's ok
   End Function


   Private Sub btnConfirm_Click(ByVal sender As System.Object, _
    ByVal e As System.EventArgs) Handles btnConfirm.Click

      'Check for required selections.
      If Not ValidInputs() Then Exit Sub
      With lstSummary.Items
         .Clear()
         'Get the name of the tour from the drop-down list
         .Add("Tour = " & ddlTour.SelectedItem.Text)

         'Get the color selection from the radio buttons
         Dim color As String = "yellow"                'default
```

```
        If radRed.Checked Then
            color = "red"
        ElseIf radOrange.Checked Then
            color = "orange"
        End If

        'Get the kayak type from the listbox
        .Add("Kayak = " & color & " " & lstKayakType.SelectedItem.Text)

         'Get the payment method from the radio button list
        Dim ix As Integer = radPaymentType.SelectedIndex
        .Add("Payment method = " & radPaymentType.Items(ix).Text)

        'Get the equipment list
        .Add("Extra equipment:")
        Dim item As ListItem
        For Each item In chkEquipment.Items
            If item.Selected Then .Add("—" & item.Text)
        Next

        'Get the mailing list choice
        If chkMailingList.Checked Then .Add("Mailing List = yes")
        End With
    End Sub
End Class
```

Checkpoint

7.27 Which property is used to control the tab order on a Web page?

7.28 Which Page property selects flow layout for the page design?

7.29 Which HTML control is useful for positioning other controls in flow layout mode?

7.30 What is meant by row-major layout when designing a Web form?

7.31 Which list-type controls are demonstrated in the Kayak Tour Signup program?

▶7.6 Copying and Deleting ASP.NET Projects

With a little bit of effort, you can copy a Web project using Windows Explorer. You will often do this when working on incremental versions of the same program. There are four steps involved in this process:

1. Open the project and select **Copy Project** from the Project menu. Figure 7-35, for example, shows the Picnic program from Section 7.2 being copied to a new program named **Copy_of_Picnic**. (You can select a better name.) The **File share** option is selected, which permits us to specify the exact file path of the copied project. Be sure to select the **All project files** option.

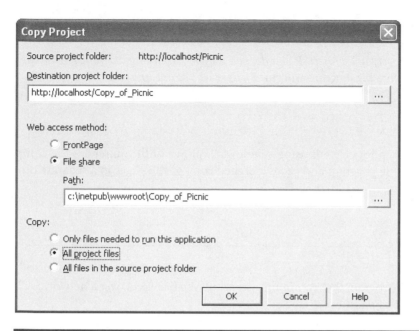

Figure 7-35 Copying a project.

2. Copy the .suo and .sln files from your source folder to the copied folder. In our example, the files are named Picnic.suo and Picnic.sln. As mentioned earlier in this chapter, we suggest that you keep these two files in their main project folder rather than leaving them in the Visual Studio .NET default projects folder.

3. Next, go to the new project folder you created and right-click the sln file of the copied project and select **Edit**. Our example folder is named Copy_of_Picnic. Use any text editor to do the editing, such as Windows NotePad. Look at the third line, which contains the project path. Suppose that we had just copied the Picnic application; this is what the relevant line in Picnic.sln would look like:

```
"http://localhost/Picnic/Picnic.vbproj",
    "{D71DA5F1-54AB-48DB-9F74-56F1EF064C23}"
```

Modify the path so it points to the copied project. For example:

```
"http://localhost/Copy_of_Picnic/Picnic.vbproj",
    "{D71DA5F1-54AB-48DB-9F74-56F1EF064C23}"
```

4. After saving and closing the sln file, double-click on it to open the project in Visual Studio .NET. In the Solution Explorer window, right-click on the Web form that should start the program and select **Set as Start Page.**

Using Windows Explorer

You can, by the way, directly copy projects using Windows Explorer using the following steps:

1. Copy the entire project folder, giving the copied folder a new name.

2. Set the Web sharing properties of the folder by doing the following: Right-click on the folder, select the **Web Sharing** tab, and select **Share this folder**. Click OK twice to close the Properties dialog window.

3. Next, edit the project's SLN file as explained before, editing the project path to the new directory name.

4. Finally, open the project and set the program's startup form.

Caution:
Do not alter the Root Namespace property of a project. If you do, you will be forced to make multiple modifications to your project's configuration files before the program will run. Believe us, it's not much fun.

Deleting a Project

Once you run a Web project, you cannot delete it using Windows Explorer until you reboot the computer. The Web server locks the files used by the program and keeps a cached copy of the pages in a separate directory.

▶ 7.7 Chapter Summary

- ◆ A *Web application* is an interactive program that communicates with Web browsers over a network. A *Web server* is a utility program that hosts Web applications.

- ◆ Web applications use a client-server architecture model, which applies to any information-processing situation where an entity called a *server* produces data consumed by another entity called a *client*.

- ◆ Traditionally, Web applications were a combination of HTML, CGI programs, and scripts. Two kinds of scripts exist: client-side and server-side.

- ◆ ASP.NET lets you create Web applications using object-oriented programming languages such as Visual Basic and C#.

- ◆ A postback occurs when a Web page is sent back to the Web server. This would happen when a Button, LinkButton, or ImageButton is clicked. Other controls such as ListBoxes must have their AutoPostBack property set to True before they can cause a postback.

- ◆ A Uniform Resource Locator (URL) consists of a protocol, a host, and optional port number, file path and anchor. A host can be an IP address or a domain name.

- ◆ ASP.NET is called a platform because it provides development tools, code libraries, and visual controls for Web programming. The essential elements of the ASP.NET platform are namespaces, Web Forms controls, the programming languages, the .NET framerwork library, and ADO.NET database classes.

- ◆ An ASP.NET application consists of three basic parts: content (Web Forms, HTML), program logic (code behind file), and configuration information.

- ◆ The ToolBox in Visual Studio .NET has two types of ASP.NET controls: HTML controls and Web forms controls. HTML controls do not generate events, and are designed to be 100-percent compatible with standard HTML. Web Forms controls are represented by underlying classes, and offer a rich set of properties beyond standard HTML.

- ◆ There are two methods for arranging text and controls on a Web form: Grid layout and Flow layout.

- ◆ Each project has an ASP.NET application file named Global.asax that contains application and session event handlers. A Web configuration file named Web.config holds project information such as user authentication, database connection strings, and error handling options.

- ◆ When you create an ASP.NET project, it is stored in a virtual directory configured by a currently running Web server. Ordinarily, you create and test your programs from the localhost/name directory, where name is the name of your project.

- ◆ The Server.Transfer method transfers control to another page on the same server. The Response.Redirect method transfers control to a page on any server.

- ◆ Property values entered by the user at runtime are lost when the user navigates to a new Web page. Special methods must be used to preserve such information.

◆ The Request object holds HTTP values sent by the client to the server during a Web request. Name/value pairs can be appended to a URL when passing Request information to a Web form.

◆ The Response object can be used to create data that are passed from the server to the client browser.

◆ The System.Web namespace includes classes that provide Web capability to programs. The System.Web.UI.WebControls namespace contains classes for Web forms controls.

◆ The Page_Load event handler always executes before event handlers such as SelectedIndexChanged or TextChanged.

◆ RadioButton controls must have a common GroupName property value to make them behave as a unified group.

◆ The CheckBoxList and RadioButtonList controls fire a SelectedIndexChanged event. Both have SelectedIndex, SelectedItem, and SelectedValue properties.

◆ The DropDownList control is the ASP.NET counterpart to the ComboBox control in Windows desktop applications.

◆ The Panel control is a useful container into which you can drop other controls. The panel allows grouped controls to be moved, displayed, or hidden.

◆ Controls such as ListBox and RadioButtonList can be bound to arrays and collections.

◆ The HTML Table control is an effective tool for arranging multiple controls on a form in Flow layout mode.

◆ If you rename a control, the Handles clause is automatically dropped from any of the control's handler methods. The same is true if you cut or copy a control to the Windows clipboard and then paste it back onto the form.

▶7.8 Key Terms

absolute link

Application object

ASP.NET application file

ASP.NET

AutoPostBack

Cascading Style Sheet (CSS)

client-server model

client-side script

codebehind file

column-major layout

Common Gateway Interface (CGI)

domain name

Domain Name Server (DNS)

downlevel Web browser

flow layout

grid layout

HTML controls

HTML form

HyperText Markup Language (HTML)

HyperText Transfer Protocol (HTTP)

Internet Information Services (IIS)

localhost

Internet-enabled application

Internet Protocol (IP)

Java Server Pages (JSP)

peer-to-peer application

postback	Uniform Resource Locator (URL)
relative link	uplevel Web browser
Request object	ViewState
Response object	Web application
row-major layout	Web configuration file
Secure Hypertext Transfer Protocol (HTTPS)	Web form
server controls	Web forms controls
server-side script	Web page
Session object	Web server
TextBox	Web service
TextField	XML discovery file

▶7.9 Review Questions

Fill-in-the-blank

1. A _____ is a utility program that hosts Web applications.

2. The acronym for *HyperText Markup Language* is _____.

3. When a Web page is sent back to the server, a _____ occurs.

4. A _____ provides development tools, code libraries, and visual controls for programming.

5. The two types of controls used in Web forms are HTML controls and _____ controls.

6. Configuration information for an ASP.NET application is stored in a file named _____.

Multiple Choice

1. A Web service is a program that...

   a. lets two interconnected computers interactively exchange data.
   b. uses a Web browser to display pages for users.
   c. uses the Internet to distribute data on demand.
   d. is a stand-alone program that uses the Internet to send and receive data.
   e. specializes in removing spider webs from homes.

2. Which one of the following would not be part of a Uniform Resource Locator (URL)?

   a. protocol
   b. host address
   c. network machine name
   d. anchor
   e. port number

3. Which one of the following would not appear in an ASP.NET Web form file (aspx file)?

   a. class definition
   b. Web forms controls
   c. HTML controls
   d. images
   e. plain text

4. Which of the following statements is *not* true about Server.Transfer?

   a. It is a method that loads a new page into the user's browser.
   b. It preserves the contents of input controls when moving away from the page.
   c. It can only transfer to Web pages located on the same server as the current page.
   d. It permits name/value pairs to be appended to the target URL.
   e. Two of the above statements are not true.

5. Which of the following method calls can be used to write text to the user's browser?

   a. Request.Write
   b. HTML.Write
   c. Response.Redirect
   d. Response.Write
   e. Page.Write

6. Which ListBox property or event causes the current page to be posted back immediately when the user makes a selection?

   a. PostBack
   b. AutoRefresh
   c. AutoPostBack
   d. SelectedIndexChanged
   e. SelectedValue

7. How can you find out which button was selected by the user in a RadioButtonList control?

   a. Examine the SelectedIndex property.
   b. Examine the Index property.
   c. Examine the input parameter to the SelectedIndexChanged event handler.
   d. Loop through the buttons and examine the Selected property of each.
   e. Loop through the buttons and examine the Checked property of each.

True or False

1. Internet Explorer is a typical example of a Web server.

2. When a postback occurs, the Web server resends the page to the browser.

3. A URL must include both the protocol and host address.

4. A Web application can run directly from Windows, without requiring a Web server.

5. The domain name *localhost* is equivalent to the URL 127.0.0.1.

6. Web forms controls are completely compatible with standard HTML.

7. HTML controls cannot fire events.

8. A TextBox control automatically saves its contents when a postback occurs.

9. The two layout options for a Web form are *grid layout* and *form layout*.

10. Netscape is considered an uplevel browser.

11. A page's Request object is used when retrieving name/value pairs appended to a URL.

12. The following URL uses correct syntax to pass request parameters to the Confirm.aspx Web page:

```
http://localhost/Confirm.aspx?id=12345&name=Jones
```

Short Answer

1. Suppose you create an ASP.NET project named Coffee. How can you determine where the files Coffee.suo and Coffee.sln are saved?

2. Which method call requires less processing on the part of the Web server: Response.Redirect, or Server.Transfer?

3. What must you do before deleting a Web project, once the project has been executed?

4. Which control looks like a HTML hyperlink, but provides a Click event handler?

5. What is the name of the class that describes the Request object in a Web form?

6. Which control displays an image that when clicked by the user, generates a Click event?

7. Which RadioButton event fires when the user selects a button?

8. Which property of a RadioButtonList control lets you arrange the buttons either vertically or horizontally?

9. Which ListBox property controls whether or not the user can make select multiple items?

10. When AutoPostBack is true for a DropDownList control, which event fires first when the user selects an item?

11. Which control is a container for other controls, making it easy to alternately hide and display groups of controls?

12. What is the initial value of SelectedIndex when a DropDownList control is displayed?

What do You Think?

1. Why would using absolute links in a Web application be a problem?

2. Why do Web servers hide the physical locations of Web applications from users?

3. Suppose you were asked to write an Internet application that supplied stock-market data to Web applications. Would you make your program a Web service or Web application? Explain your answer.

4. Why do you suppose that the ListBox control does not automatically cause a postback when the user selects an item?

5. What advantages does compiled Visual Basic code have over interpreted script code that appears in a Web page's HTML?

6. HTTP is commonly called a *stateless protocol* because it immediately terminates a connection after sending out a Web page. Suppose instead that it were possible for a Web server to retain a connection to each user. What would be some disadvantages to such an approach?

Algorithm Workbench

1. Write code that does the following the first time a Web page is loaded: Declare an array of four college department names and bind the array to a ListBox control named lstDepts.

2. Write code that adds a new item to the lstDepts ListBox, using the contents of a TextBox named txtDepartment. In addition, select the new item in the ListBox.

3. Write a statement that navigates to Page2.aspx, passing the value of the item selected from a ListBox control named lstDepts.

4. Write statements that receive a Request parameter named **dept** and write the value of that parameter to the user's browser window along with a descriptive label. An example of the output might be: "Department = Chemistry".

5. Suppose a CheckBoxList named chkDepts contained the names of four college departments. Write code that builds a string containing the names of the departments selected by the user. Insert a single space between each name in the string.

6. Refer to the CheckBoxList introduced in the previous question. Suppose an integer value was associated with each item in the list. Build a string that contains the values of the selected items. Insert a single space between each value.

▶ 7.10 Programming Challenges

1. Best Brew Coffee Shop, Version 1

Write a program that displays several types of coffee and tea drinks in a list box (Figure 7-36). When the user selects an item and clicks on the OK button, the price is displayed in a label. You can put the prices into the value property associated with item when you build the Items collection from the Properties window. Display the price using a currency format.

Figure 7-36 Best Brew Coffee Shop, Version 1.

2. Best Brew Coffee Shop, Version 2

Start with the Best Brew Coffee Shop Program from the previous exercise. Add a CheckBoxList so the user can select extra items such as chocolate and whipped cream (Figure 7-37). Each item should have a add-on price, such as 25 cents for whipped cream. When the user clicks the OK button, display the basic price of the drink plus the price of the combined extras.

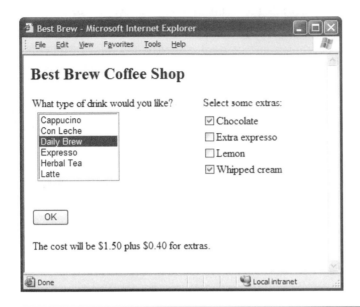

Figure 7-37 Best Brew Coffee Shop, Version 2.

3. Best Brew Coffee Shop, Version 3

Start with the Best Brew Coffee Shop program from the previous exercise. When the user makes selections to order a drink, do not display the price on the same Web page. Instead, when the user clicks on the OK button, display a separate Web page showing a Receipt. Figure 7-38 shows the user ordering a drink, and Figure 7-39 shows the corresponding receipt. We have elongated the window so you can see that the order information was passed as a set of Request parameters appended to the URL. Assume that the sales tax rate is 7 percent.

Figure 7-38 Best Brew Coffee Shop, Version 3.

Figure 7-39 Displaying the receipt.

8

Web Forms II

 Note:
    All example programs shown in this chapter can be found in the book's *examples\ASP_NET* directory.

▶8.1 Custom Error Handling

Custom error handling refers to the ability ASP.NET programs have to configure the display of runtime error messages for both end users and program developers. You've probably encountered unhandled exceptions (runtime errors) on your Web pages by now. If you're running your programs under IIS on your local machine (localhost), you can view detailed information about the error, including a stack trace. On the other hand, if you run programs on a shared server, such as the one used in college computer labs, error information is not as complete. In this section, we will show how to control the level of detail.

    The **Custom Errors** setting determines the way in which error messages are displayed on Web pages. Three possible settings exist, and are documented in the **Custom Error Messages** section of an application's Web.config file:

◆ On: Always display custom (friendly) error messages.

◆ Off: Always display detailed error information.

◆ RemoteOnly: Remote users see custom (friendly) error messages. Meanwhile, users on the local machine see detailed error information.

Following are the default settings in Web.config:

```
<configuration>
    <system.web>
        <customErrors mode="RemoteOnly" />
    </system.web>
</configuration>
```

(Additional entries in the system.web group are not shown here.)

Example: Unhandled Exception

Suppose a program attempts to convert the contents of a text box to an integer and fails. Figure 8-1 shows the type of detailed information a programmer needs to see. It includes line numbers and a stack trace. Understandably, this is not the type of information that should be seen by end users. It might reveal sensitive information such as the program's source code and database name.

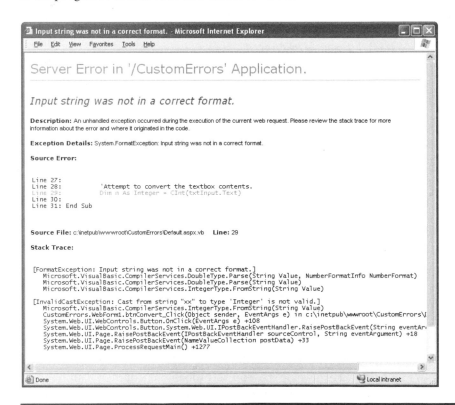

Figure 8-1   Unhandled Exception, viewed by local user.

Figure 8-2 shows what happens when a remote user connects to the example program and generates the same error. The resulting message does a good job of hiding secret information, but it tells the user nothing about what went wrong. If you ever hope to correct the problem, you will need users to supply useful feedback.

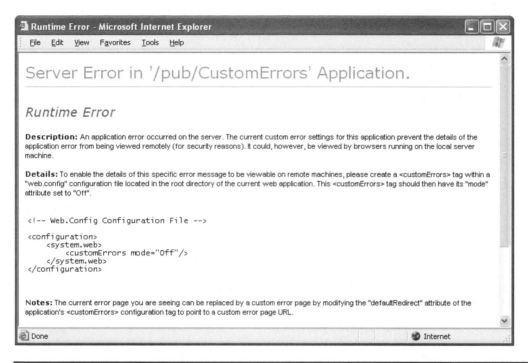

Figure 8-2   Unhandled exception, viewed by remote user.

A good approach to error handling is to create a custom error page similar to the one in Figure 8-3. The URL that loads this page includes a request parameter named **aspxerrorpath**, which is the path of the Web page that was executing when the error occurred. The example custom error page displays aspxerrorpath and has an email link so the user can notify the support department about the error (Figure 8-4).

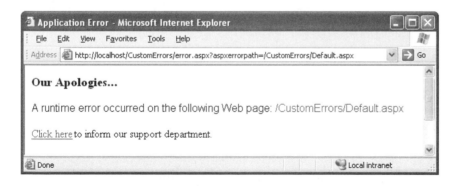

Figure 8-3   CustomErrors program.

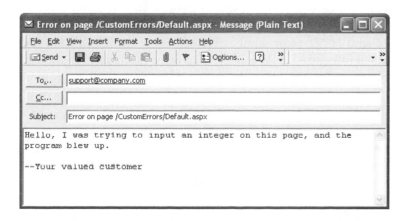

Figure 8-4   Sending an email report.

All that is required to redirect the user to a custom error page (here named error.aspx) is the following line in the Web.config file:

```
<customErrors mode="RemoteOnly" defaultRedirect="error.aspx" />
```

You can test a redirected error handler on your local machine without having to copy your program to a public Web server. Just temporarily change the mode to **On**:

```
<customErrors mode="On" defaultRedirect="error.aspx" />
```

Handling HTTP Errors

Most Web sites have custom error pages that handle HTTP errors generated by a Web server. For example, error 404 is generated by a server when a requested Web page is not found. Rather than displaying a generic error page (seen earlier in Figure 8-3), you can designate a specific page for error 404 in the Web.config file. In the following example, the **notFound.aspx** file displays whenever error 404 occurs:

```
<customErrors mode="On" defaultRedirect="error.aspx">
  <error statusCode="404" redirect="notFound.aspx" />
</customErrors>
```

The error page used in the CustomErrors program appears in Figure 8-5.

Figure 8-5 Custom error page for 404 Not Found.

Configuring Error Messages in IIS

You can create a set of custom HTTP error pages for all applications running on your Web site. Rather than adding individual entries to each program's Web.config file, use Internet Information Services (IIS) to map HTTP error codes to Web pages. To run the IIS adminstrator program, select **Start | Control Panel | Adminstrative Tools | Internet Information Services**. Right-click on **Default Web Site** and select **Properties**. Click on the **Custom Errors** tab.

A separate HTML file is bound to each HTTP error number. We will use error 404 (file not found) as an example. The default error page is shown in Figure 8-6. If you select an error (such as 404) and click on Edit Properties (Figure 8-7), you can link the error number to either a file or a virtual Web path on the same machine as the server (Figure 8-8).

Figure 8-6 Default error page for HTTP error 404.

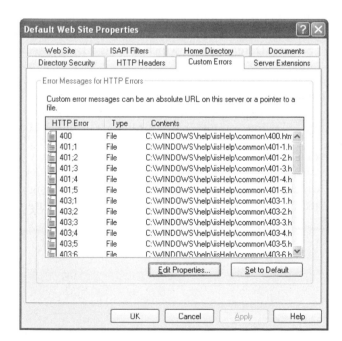

Figure 8-7 IIS error messages.

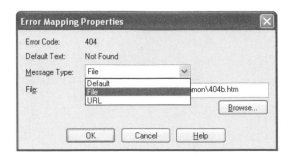

Figure 8-8   Error mapping properties for HTTP error 404.

▶8.2 Calendar Control

The Calendar control is one of the most convenient and powerful Web Forms controls. The user can scroll forward and backward through monthly displays and select individual dates and sets of dates. When the user selects a date, a program can query a Calendar control's **SelectedDate** property, which returns a Date object. The following gets the date from a Calendar named calTours:

```
Dim dt As Date = calTours.SelectedDate
```

SelectedDate can be set programmatically, as in the following example that sets calTours to July 2, 2004:

```
calTours.SelectedDate = New Date(2004,7,2)
```

The control has a **SelectedDates** collection, which can hold multiple Date objects. You can assign values to this collection, causing the dates to appear selected in the control. For example, the following statements add date selections to the calTours Calendar control:

```
With calTours.SelectedDates
    .Add(New Date(2004, 5, 1))
    .Add(New Date(2004, 5, 4))
    .Add(New Date(2004, 5, 6))
    .Add(New Date(2004, 5, 8))
    .Add(New Date(2004, 6, 12))
End With
```

All but one of the dates is in the month of May, shown in Figure 8-9. The final date selection appears when the user scrolls the calendar forward to the month of June (Figure 8-10). If the user returns to May, the selections we saw in Figure 8-9 are automatically restored.

Figure 8-9   Displaying multiple selected dates.

Figure 8-10   Showing the date selected in June.

Useful Tips

You can use the Calendar control as a display-only device by setting its **SelectionMode** property to **None** (the default is **Day**). Users will not be able to select any dates, but they will able to scroll forward and backward through the months. If you want to prevent the user from scrolling to the previous and next months, set the **ShowTitle** property to False. The **VisibleDate** property can be used to control which month is displayed when the Web form is loaded. By default, VisibleDate is set to the current date.

Kayak Tour Scheduler Example

KayakTourScheduler

The **Kayak Tour Scheduler** program lets the management of a kayak store schedule upcoming kayak tours. The user selects a date from a calendar control and inputs the name of a kayak tour (Figure 8-11). When the Add button is clicked, the tour name and date are added to the list box. Although we will not do it now, it would be easy to store the list in a database. Table 8-1 lists the controls used in the program along with their relevant property values.

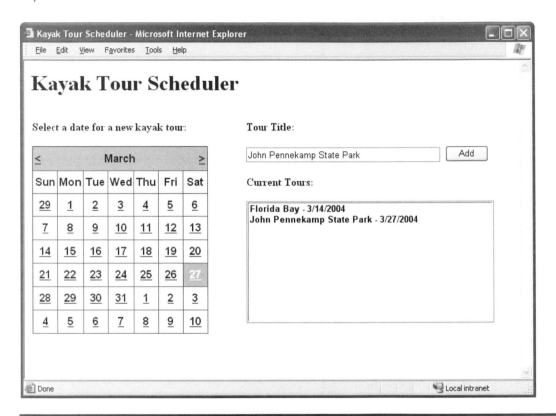

Figure 8-11   Kayak Tour Scheduler program.

Table 8-1

Controls used in the Kayak Tour Scheduler

Control Type	Control Name	Properties
Web Form	(document)	Title: Kayak Tour Scheduler
Calendar	calTours	BorderStyle: Inset
		BorderColor: Blue
		Font.Name: Arial
		Font.Bold: True
		TitleFormat: Month
TextBox	txtTitle	
Button	btnAdd	Text: Add
ListBox	lstTours	Font.Name: Arial
		Font.Bold: True
Label	lblMessage	ForeColor: Red

Implementation

In the event handler for the Add button, if the tour name is blank or no date has been selected for the tour, a message indicates the error and the procedure exits:

```
If Trim(txtTitle.Text).Length = 0 Or calTours.SelectedDates.Count = 0 Then
    lblMessage.Text = "Please select a date and enter a title for the tour"
    Exit Sub
End If
```

If a date and tour name have been selected, the program adds an entry to the list box containing the name of the tour and the tour date:

```
lstTours.Items.Add(txtTitle.Text & " - " & calTours.SelectedDate())
```

Program Listing

A complete listing of the Kayak Tour Scheduler appears below:

```
Public Class KayakTour
    Inherits System.Web.UI.Page
```

```
+ Web Form Designer generated code
```

```
    Private Sub btnAdd_Click(ByVal sender As System.Object, _
     ByVal e As System.EventArgs) Handles btnAdd.Click

        'Skip if either no title was entered or no date was selected.
        If Trim(txtTitle.Text).Length = 0 _
           Or calTours.SelectedDates.Count = 0 Then
           lblMessage.Text = "Please select a date and enter a " _
            & "title for the tour"
           Exit Sub
        End If

        lstTours.Items.Add(txtTitle.Text & " - " & calTours.SelectedDate())
    End Sub
End Class
```

Checkpoint

8.5 Which Calendar control property returns a single date selected by the user?

8.6 What is the best way to select multiple dates in a Calendar control, using program code?

8.7 How can you make the Calendar display date selections without allowing the user to make any changes?

8.8 How would you make the Calendar control display the month of April?

▶ 8.3 Data Binding with Arrays

The ListControl class defines the properties, methods, and events that apply to the ListBox, DropDownList, CheckBoxList, and RadioButtonList classes. You cannot create a ListControl object because it is an abstract class. Since the ListBox, DropDownList, CheckBoxList, and RadioButtonList classes all extend ListControl, they inherit the same properties, methods, and events. In particular, there are a number of common properties listed in Table 8-2.

Table 8-2

ListControl properties.

Property	Description
AutoPostBack	Determines whether a postback will occur when the user selects an item.
DataMember	The specific table in the DataSource that will be bound to the control.
DataSource	The data source that fills the controls Items collection.
DataTextField	The field within the DataSource that provides the visible list of items.
DataTextFormatString	The format string applied to the displayed items.
DataValueField	The field in the data source that provides the value of each list item.
Items	The collection of items in the list control (read-only).
SelectedIndex	The lowest index of the selected items in the list.
SelectedItem	The selected item with the lowest index in the list control (read-only).

All ListControl objects can be bound to arrays, ArrayLists, and datasets at runtime. In fact, any object type that supports what is called the *IEnumerable interface* can be bound. In this chapter, we will show how to bind to arrays and ArrayLists, and Chapter 9 will show how to bind to datasets. Web forms controls only support one-way binding. Data can be transferred from a data source to a control, but modified data in the control are not copied back to the data source.

The following example creates a String array named Members and binds it to a DropDownList:

```
1: Dim Members() As String = {"Adams, Ben", "Baker, Shauna", _
2:    "Chong, Harry", "Davis, Angie", "Firenzie, Georgio"}
3: ddlMembers.DataSource = Members
4: ddlMembers.DataBind()
```

On Line 3, the array name is assigned to a dropdown list's **DataSource** property. On Line 4, the DataBind method is called on the dropdown list.

The Items array of any list-type control contains ListItem objects, each of which has Text and Value properties. When you bind an array to the control, each item's Text and Value properties are assigned the same array element value. In our ddlMembers example, both the Text and Value properties of the first ListItem equal "Adams, Ben".

Example Program: Computer Club Tasks

ComputerClubTasks

Let's look at a short program (**ComputerClubTasks**) that permits the user to assign tasks to individual computer club members. First, the user selects from a dropdown list containing names of club members (Figure 8-12). Then a task is selected from another dropdown list. When the Assign button is clicked, the assigned task is inserted into the Value property of the selected member (a ListItem object) and the task appears in a label. From that point on, whenever the same member name is selected again, their assigned task appears in the label.

Figure 8-12 Assigning computer club tasks.

Implementation

Code Listing 8-1 displays the complete source code of the Computer Club Tasks program. The ddlMembers DropDownList control is bound to the Members array. The ddlTasks DropDownList is bound to the Tasks array. The Page_Load event handler sets up the data binding:

```
If Not IsPostBack Then
   Dim Members() As String = {"Adams, Ben", "Baker, Shauna", _
     "Chong, Harry", "Davis, Angie", "Firenzie, Georgio"}
   Dim Tasks() As String = {"President", "Vice-President", _
     "Treasurer", "Secretary", "Membership Director"}
   ddlMembers.DataSource = Members
   ddlMembers.DataBind()
   ddlTasks.DataSource = Tasks
   ddlTasks.DataBind()
End If
```

The **If Not IsPostBack** statement assures that the initialization code will execute only once—when the page is first loaded.

When the user clicks the Assign button, the task name is assigned to the Value property of the currently selected member, and is displayed in a Label:

```
ddlMembers.SelectedItem().Value = ddlTasks.SelectedItem.Text
lblTask.Text = ddlTasks.SelectedItem.Text
```

When the user selects a name from the ddlMembers dropdown list, the program uses the SelectedIndexChanged event handler to display the item's SelectedValue:

```
Dim val As String = ddlMembers.SelectedValue
If val = ddlMembers.SelectedItem.Text Then
   lblTask.Text = ""
Else
   lblTask.Text = val
End If
```

When the ddlMembers list was initialized, SelectedValue and SelectedItem for each item were automatically assigned the same value. But when the user selects a member name, we only want to display SelectedValue value if an actual task (such as President) has been inserted in the list item.

Because the SelectedIndexChanged event handler needs to execute every time the user selects a member name, the AutoPostBack property of ddlMembers was set to True.

Code Listing 8-1 (Computer Club Tasks)

```
Public Class ComputerClub
    Inherits System.Web.UI.Page

+ Web Form Designer generated code

    Private Sub Page_Load(ByVal sender As System.Object, _
     ByVal e As System.EventArgs) Handles MyBase.Load

        If Not IsPostBack Then
            Dim Members() As String = {"Adams, Ben", "Baker, Shauna", _
             "Chong, Harry", "Davis, Angie", "Firenzie, Georgio"}
            ddlMembers.DataSource = Members
            ddlMembers.DataBind()

            Dim Tasks() As String = {"President", "Vice-President", _
             "Treasurer", "Secretary", "Membership Director"}
            ddlTasks.DataSource = Tasks
            ddlTasks.DataBind()
        End If
    End Sub

    Private Sub btnAssign_Click(ByVal sender As System.Object, _
     ByVal e As System.EventArgs) Handles btnAssign.Click

        ddlMembers.SelectedItem().Value = ddlTasks.SelectedItem.Text
        lblTask.Text = ddlTasks.SelectedItem.Text
    End Sub

    Private Sub ddlMembers_SelectedIndexChanged(ByVal sender As _
     System.Object, ByVal e As System.EventArgs) _
     Handles ddlMembers.SelectedIndexChanged

        Dim val As String = ddlMembers.SelectedValue
        If val = ddlMembers.SelectedItem.Text Then
            lblTask.Text = ""
        Else
            lblTask.Text = val
        End If
    End Sub
End Class
```

Binding to a Class Type

You can further explore ListControl binding by creating a class that describes each item to be inserted. For example, we can define a Person class (Code Listing 8-2) having two properties, Name and Email. The class needs a parameterized constructor and two property procedures.

Code Listing 8-2 (Person class)

```
Public Class Person
   Private _name As String
   Private _email As String

   Public Sub New(ByVal name As String, ByVal email As String)
     _name = name
     _email = email
   End Sub

   Public Property Name() As String
      Get
         Return _name
      End Get
      Set(ByVal Value As String)
        _name = Value
      End Set
   End Property

   Public Property Email() As String
      Get
         Return _email
      End Get
      Set(ByVal Value As String)
        _email = Value
      End Set
   End Property
End Class
```

Then we can design a form with a CheckBoxList control, an OK button, and a label to display the email addresses of all selected members (Figure 8-13).

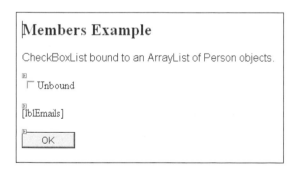

Figure 8-13   Bound CheckBoxList, design mode.

Code to perform the data binding is placed in the Page_Load event handler. First, an ArrayList is filled with Person objects:

```
If Not IsPostBack Then
   Dim members As ArrayList = New ArrayList
   With members
      .Add(New Person("Chong, Gary", "gchong@fiu.edu"))
      .Add(New Person("Fujikawa, Hiroko", "hfujikawafiu.edu"))
      .Add(New Person("Gonzalez, Luis", "lgonz001@fiu.edu"))
      .Add(New Person("Habib, Majaraf", "mhabib002@fiu.edu"))
      .Add(New Person("Jones, Sam", "sjones@fiu.edu"))
   End With
```

We assign the ArrayList to the DataSource property, and assign the two Person property names (Name, Email) to the DataTextField and DataValueField properties:

```
With chkMembers
    .DataSource = members
    .DataTextField = "Name"
    .DataValueField = "Email"
    .DataBind()
End With
End If
```

Visual Basic uses the strings "Name" and "Email" to look up the corresponding property values in the Person object as the CheckBoxList is being filled. Figure 8-14 shows the program running, after the user has selected several members and clicked on OK.

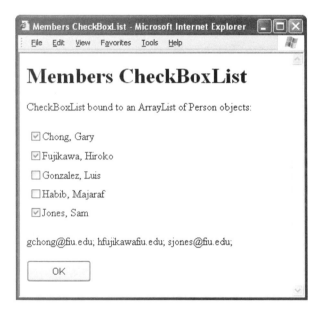

Figure 8-14 Data-bound CheckBoxList.

The OK button handler uses a loop to iterate through the chkMembers.Items collection; for each selected item, we use the Value property to obtain the person's email address and append it to a string. The complete source code in the Members CheckBoxList form appears in Code Listing 8-3

Code Listing 8-3 (Members CheckBoxList)

```
Public Class Members
    Inherits System.Web.UI.Page

+ Web Form Designer generated code

    Private Sub Page_Load(ByVal sender As System.Object, _
    ByVal e As System.EventArgs) Handles MyBase.Load

        If Not IsPostBack Then
            Dim members As ArrayList = New ArrayList
            With members
                .Add(New Person("Chong, Gary", "gchong@fiu.edu"))
                .Add(New Person("Fujikawa, Hiroko", "hfujikawafiu.edu"))
                .Add(New Person("Gonzalez, Luis", "lgonz001@fiu.edu"))
                .Add(New Person("Habib, Majaraf", "mhabib002@fiu.edu"))
                .Add(New Person("Jones, Sam", "sjones@fiu.edu"))
```

```
        End With

        With chkMembers
            .DataSource = members
            .DataTextField = "Name"
            .DataValueField = "Email"
            .DataBind()
        End With
    End If
End Sub

Private Sub btnOk_Click(ByVal sender As System.Object, _
  ByVal e As System.EventArgs) Handles btnOk.Click

    lblSelected.Text = ""
    Dim item As ListItem
    For Each item In chkMembers.Items
        If item.Selected Then
            lblSelected.Text &= item.Value & "; "
        End If
    Next
End Sub
End Class
```

Checkpoint

8.9 Name two types of non-database objects that can be bound to a DropDownList control.

8.10 How would the behavior of the Computer Club Tasks program be different if the AutoPostBack property of ddlMembers were equal to False?

8.11 If a RadioButtonList control is bound to an array of String and the contents of the control are modified, will the array of String be modified as well?

▶8.4 Uploading Files

Allowing users of Web applications to upload files to a Web site opens up many possibilities: Users can send email with attachments; users can upload pictures to an online photo album; students can upload assignments; and groups collaborating on projects can share documents. The HTMLInputFile control lets users upload any type of file, but you have the option of restricting the permitted file types and maximum sizes. Because it is an HTML control, it generates no events and does not support ViewState.

An important requirement for using this control is to change the default encoding format used by the enclosing form to **multipart/form-data**. To do this, display the form in design mode and click on the HTML tab. Here's an example of an acceptable form tag:

```
<form id="Form1" method="post" encType="multipart/form-data" runat="server">
```

The HTMLInputFile control does not appear in the Visual Studio .NET toolbox, so you must declare it directly in your form's HTML. If we named the control **btnSelectFile**, the declaration would be as follows:

```
<input id="btnSelectFile" type="file" runat="server">
```

HTMLInputFile Properties

Table 8-3 lists HTMLInputFile control properties. The Accept property contains a list of acceptable file types (called MIME) that are universally understood by Web and email software. If you leave it blank, any type of file can be uploaded. Table 8-4 lists a number of common MIME types. The HTMLInputFile control has no methods or events.

Table 8-3

HTMLInputFile properties.

Property	Description
Accept	A list of the MIME file types that can be uploaded, separated by commas.
MaxLength	Sets the maximum length of the filename and path.
PostedFile	An HttpPostedFile object that contains information about the file being uploaded.
Size	Width of the text box containing the filename.

Table 8-4

Common MIME types.

MIME	Type Description
image/gif	GIF image file
image/pjpeg	JPEG image file
image/*	any type of image file
text/plain	plain text file
application/octet-stream	Java source code file
application/java	Java .class file
text/html	HTML file
application/x-zip-compressed	ZIP (compressed) file
application/msword	Microsoft Word document
application/pdf	Adobe Acrobat™ file

PostedFile Property

The PostedFile property, a HttpPostedFile object, represents the uploaded file. Following are the class properties:

Property	Description
ContentLength	The length of the uploaded file, in bytes.
ContentType	Identifies the MIME content type of the uploaded file.
FileName	Uploaded file's complete file path on the client computer.
InputStream	Returns a stream containing the raw contents of the uploaded file.

The FileName property may produce a blank value when running under Web browsers other than Internet Explorer. HttpPostedFile has a **SaveAs** method, which receives a full path that determines the location of the saved file on the server. Here's an example that calls SaveAs:

```
btnSelectFile.PostedFile.SaveAs( "c:\temp\picture.gif" )
```

In other words, the name of the file on the client's computer and the name of the saved file do not have to match.

If you want to use the client's filename directly, you have to write a little bit of code to extract just the filename from the control's PostedFile.FileName property. The following function extracts just the filename from a full file path. If the path is empty or it contains no backslash (\), the function returns an empty string:

```
Private Function JustFileName(ByVal fullPath As String) As String
    Dim pos As Integer = fullPath.LastIndexOf("\")
    If pos < 1 Then Return ""
    Return fullPath.Substring(pos + 1, (fullPath.Length() - pos) - 1)
End Function
```

The following example calls JustFileName and uses the return value to save the file on the server:

```
With btnSelectFile.PostedFile
    .SaveAs( "c:\temp\" & JustFileName( .FileName ))
End With
```

Figure 8-15 shows a demo program that uploads a file. The HTMLInputFile control appears as a text box and button, side by side. When the user clicks the Browse button, their Web browser displays a file chooser window, letting them locate a file. The complete file path appears in the text box. When the user clicks on **Upload Now**, the file is transferred to the server computer.

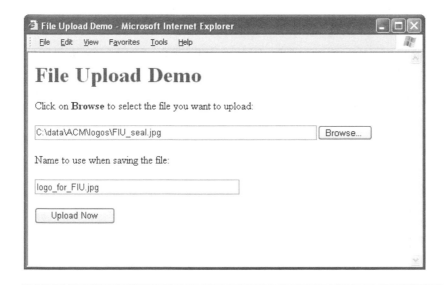

Figure 8-15 File Upload program, just before uploading.

Once the file has been uploaded, the program displays information about the file (Figure 8-16). The filename has disappeared from the HTMLInputFile control because the **Upload Now** button caused a postback and the HTMLInputFile control did not preserve its contents. A possible advantage to this behavior is that if the user accidentally clicks twice in a row, the file will not upload a second time.

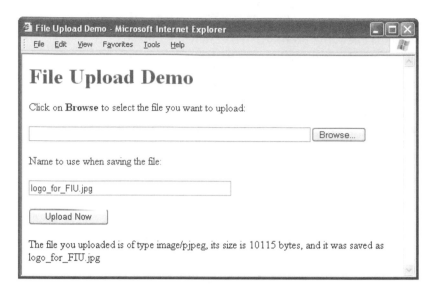

Figure 8-16 File Upload program, after uploading the file.

Implementation

The HTMLInputFile control is described in the form's HTML as:

```
<input id="btnSelectFile" style="WIDTH: 504px; HEIGHT: 22px" type="file"
size="64" runat="server">
```

The encoding method in the form tag is specified thus:

```
encType="multipart/form-data"
```

Following is the source code:

```
Const UPLOAD_PATH As String = "c:\temp\"

Private Sub btnUpload_Click(ByVal sender As System.Object, _
  ByVal e As System.EventArgs) Handles btnUpload.Click

    With btnSelectFile.PostedFile
        .SaveAs(UPLOAD_PATH & txtFileName.Text)
        lblInfo.Text = "The file you uploaded is of type " & .ContentType _
          & ", its size is " & .ContentLength & " bytes, and it was " _
          & "saved as " & txtFileName.Text
    End With
End Sub
```

The complete source code of the File Upload demo program appears in Code Listing 8-4.

Code Listing 8-4 (File Upload Demo)

```
Public Class WebForm1
    Inherits System.Web.UI.Page
```

```
+ Web Form Designer generated code
```

```
    Const UPLOAD_PATH As String = "c:\temp\"
```

```
'Implementation Notes:
'HTML form tag must include the following:
'    <form EncType="multipart/form-data"

'The HTMLInputFile control must be declared as follows:
'<input id="(name)" type="file" runat="server">

'The HTMLInputFile control has no ViewState capability, so
'you must save its runtime properties yourself.

'justFileName:
'Extracts just the filename from a full file path. If the path is
'empty or if no "\" was found, the function returns an empty string.

Private Function justFileName(ByVal fullPath As String) As String
    Dim pos As Integer = fullPath.LastIndexOf("\")
    If pos < 1 Then Return ""
    Return fullPath.Substring(pos + 1, (fullPath.Length() - pos) - 1)
End Function

Private Sub btnUpload_Click(ByVal sender As System.Object, _
 ByVal e As System.EventArgs) Handles btnUpload.Click

    'Optional: save using the same filename
    'With btnSelectFile.PostedFile
    '.SaveAs(UPLOAD_PATH & justFileName(.FileName))
    'End With

    With btnSelectFile.PostedFile
        .SaveAs(UPLOAD_PATH & txtFileName.Text)
        lblInfo.Text = "The file you uploaded is of type " & .ContentType _
        & ", its size is " & .ContentLength & " bytes, and it was " _
        & "saved as " & txtFileName.Text
    End With
End Sub
End Class
```

Checkpoint

8.12 Which control makes it possible for users to upload files to a server from their browser?

8.13 What type of form encoding format is required when uploading files to a Web form?

8.14 Why is the HttpPostedFile class important in a program that lets users upload files?

▶8.5 Sending Mail

One of the most useful tasks an ASP.NET application can perform is to send email. For example, it might send a confirmation notice when customers order an item, or when members join a club. It could use email to send time-sensitive information to users. Or, if a runtime error occurs, a program could send an email notification to the program vendor. SMTP (*Simple Mail Transfer Protocol*) contains a standard set of commands all computer systems use for sending email. Programs such as Microsoft Outlook use SMTP when sending mail messages via your Internet service provider. You can locate your current SMTP server name by looking in Outlook's Tools | Accounts directory. Look for the "outgoing mail server" entry. All the mail classes we are about to demonstrate require that you import the System.Web.Mail namespace.

SmtpMail Class

The simplest way to send an email message is to use the SmtpMail class. Before sending a message, you must set the SmtpServer property to the name of the mail server used by your system:

```
SmtpMail.SmtpServer = "mail.myprovider.net"
```

The SmtpMail.Send method has the following parameters:

```
Send( sender As String, recipient As String,
    subject As String, message As String)
```

Many mail servers require the From and To fields to contain valid email addresses. Following is an example of calling Send:

```
SmtpMail.Send( me@myCollege.edu, you@somewhere.com, _
    "this is my subject", "this is my message")
```

The Send method does not do much else, so if you need additional email features, you must create a MailMessage object and pass it to the Send method:

```
SmtpMail.Send( new MailMessage( . . . ) )
```

MailMessage Class

The MailMessage class has a rich set of properties that lets you configure messages and include attachments. Some of the more useful properties are shown in Table 8-5. The Bcc field is convenient when sending a message to multiple persons, because each recipient cannot see the addresses of the other recipients. When a field contains a list of email addresses, they must be separated by semicolons.

Table 8-5

MailMessage class properties.

Property	Description
Attachments	Collection of MailAttachment objects that represent file attachments.
Bcc	Blind carbon copy recipient list. Email addresses. Recipients cannot see this field.
Body	Body of the message
BodyFormat	MailFormat enumeration value. Choices are Text and Html.
Cc	Carbon copy recipient list. Recipients can see this field.
From	The sender's email address.
Headers	Collection of headers used by the message.
Priority	MailPriority enumeration. Choices are High, Normal, and Low.
Subject	Message subject.
To	List of recipients.

Email Encoding

SMTP only works with 7-bit ASCII data. This presents a problem when sending files containing 8-bit bytes, such as binary files, or files that are not plain text. Non-ASCII files must be transformed (encoded) into a text-like representation before being sent. When an email message is received, its attachments must be decoded. Two popular encoding methods are supported by .NET: Base64 and UUEncode. Most email programs can decode files created using both types of encoding methods.

Sending Attachments

To send one or more attachments with a mail message, construct a MailAttachment object for each and add it to the MailMessage.Attachments collection. The MailAttachment class has two properties: **Encoding** and **Filename**. The Encoding property identifies the type of encoding used for the file. The two possible values are listed in the Mail.MailEncoding enumeration: Base64 and UUEncode. The Filename property must contain the complete path of the file you want to send.

There are two ways to construct a MailAttachment object. The first takes just a filename, and the second requires both a filename and encoding method:

```
new MailAttachment( filename As String )
new MailAttachment( filename As String, method As Mail.MailEncoding )
```

The UUEncode encoding method is the default if you pass only a filename. The following code demonstrates the basic steps required to create and send a message with a single attachment:

```
Dim objMail As New MailMessage
With objMail
    .From = "kip@fiu.edu"
    .To = "editor@scottjones.com"
    .Subject = "Chapter 8"
    .Body = "I have attached the finished version of Chapter 8."
    .Attachments.Add(New MailAttachment("d:\vb_book\ch08.doc"))
End With
SmtpMail.SmtpServer = "mail.myIsp.net"
SmtpMail.Send(objMail)
```

Messages Containing HTML Tags

You can embed HTML tags in a message body as long as you set the MailMessage.BodyFormat property to HTML. When the form is posted back, however, the HttpRequest class rejects HTML tags as being potentially harmful. Figure 8-17 shows the runtime error that results from inserting the <b> tag in the message body.

Figure 8-17   RequestValidation error message.

As the instructions in the error message explain, you can bypass this error by including the following assignment in the form's Page directive. To get there, click on the HTML tab in the Designer window.

```
validateRequest="false"
```

MailDemo Program

Figure 8-18 shows an ASP.NET program that sends mail to recipients using the MailMessage class. The program lets you send messages in either text or HTML format, depending on your choice in the dropdown list. If you select HTML, you can embed tags such as <b> or <h1> in your message. The Attachment field in this example is for demonstration purposes only. In a real program, the user would probably not know the exact path of a file on the server's system. We might prefer to let the user upload a file to the server and send the file as an attachment.

 Note:

Important! *Before running this sample program, you must customize the SERVERNAME setting in the program source code, to make it match the mail server name on your system.*

The lblMessage control at the bottom of the form indicates the success or failure to send the mail message. If errors occur because of invalid email addresses in the From or To fields, one message is seen frequently: **Error: Could not access 'CDO.Message' object.** If the attachment file path is incorrect, the following message is displayed: **Error: invalid mail attachment.**

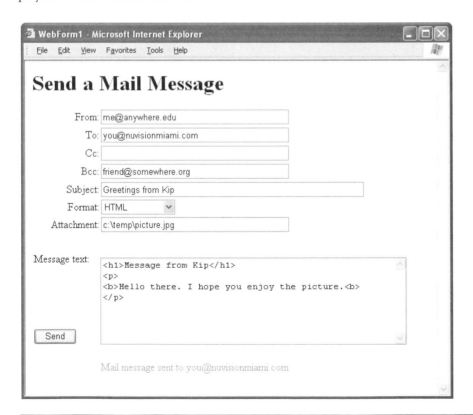

Figure 8-18 Sending a mail message.

Table 8-6 lists the controls used in the program. We must not forget to set validateRequest="false" in the Page directive of the form.

Table 8-6

Controls used in the MailDemo program.

Control Type	Name	Properties
TextBox	txtFrom	
TextBox	txtTo	
TextBox	txtCc	
TextBox	txtBcc	
TextBox	txtSubject	
TextBox	txtBody	TextMode: MultiLine
TextBox	txtAttach	
DropDownList	ddlFormat	Items: Text, HTML
Button	btnSend	Text: Send
Label	lblMessage	ForeColor: Red

Implementation

The SMTP server name must be customized on the following line to match your system:

```
Const SERVERNAME As String = "mail.MYISP.net"
```

The setFormat method receives a MailMessage object and sets its BodyFormat property according to the format selected by the user from the dropdown list:

```
Private Sub setFormat(ByVal objMail As MailMessage)
   Select Case ddlFormat.SelectedValue
      Case "HTML"
         objMail.BodyFormat = MailFormat.Html
      Case "Text"
         objMail.BodyFormat = MailFormat.Text
   End Select
End Sub
```

The Click event handler creates a MailMessage object from the contents of input controls, sets the server name, and sends the mail:

```
Private Sub btnSend_Click(ByVal sender As System.Object, _
 ByVal e As System.EventArgs) Handles btnSend.Click

   Try
      Dim objMail As New MailMessage
      setFormat(objMail)
      With objMail
         .From = txtFrom.Text
         .To = txtTo.Text
         .Cc = txtCc.Text
         .Bcc = txtBcc.Text
         .Subject = txtSubject.Text
         .Body = txtBody.Text
         If Trim(txtAttach.Text).Length > 0 Then
            .Attachments.Add(New MailAttachment(txtAttach.Text))
         End If
      End With
```

```
        SmtpMail.SmtpServer = SERVERNAME
        SmtpMail.Send(objMail)
        lblMessage.Text = "Mail message sent to " & txtTo.Text
    Catch ex As Exception
        lblMessage.Text = "Error: " & ex.Message
    End Try
End Sub
```

The call to the Trim method removes any leading or trailing spaces from the text box before checking its length. The Try-End Try statement handles exceptions caused by invalid email addresses, nonexisting attachment files, and an invalid SMTP server name. A complete listing of the MailDemo code appears in Code Listing 8-5.

Code Listing 8-5 (Mail Demo)

```
Imports System.Web.Mail

Public Class MailDemo
    Inherits System.Web.UI.Page

+ Web Form Designer generated code

    'Change the following server name to your server:
    Const SERVERNAME As String = "mail.MYISP.net"

    Private Sub setFormat(ByVal objMail As MailMessage)
        Select Case ddlFormat.SelectedValue
            Case "HTML"
                objMail.BodyFormat = MailFormat.Html
            Case "Text"
                objMail.BodyFormat = MailFormat.Text
        End Select
    End Sub

    Private Sub btnSend_Click(ByVal sender As System.Object, _
        ByVal e As System.EventArgs) Handles btnSend.Click
        Try
            Dim objMail As New MailMessage
            setFormat(objMail)
            With objMail
                .From = txtFrom.Text
                .To = txtTo.Text
                .Cc = txtCc.Text
                .Bcc = txtBcc.Text
                .Subject = txtSubject.Text
                .Body = txtBody.Text
                If Trim(txtAttach.Text).Length > 0 Then
                    .Attachments.Add(New MailAttachment(txtAttach.Text))
                End If
            End With

            SmtpMail.SmtpServer = SERVERNAME
            SmtpMail.Send(objMail)
            lblMessage.Text = "Mail message sent to " & txtTo.Text
        Catch ex As Exception
            lblMessage.Text = "Error: " & ex.Message
        End Try
    End Sub
End Class
```

▶8.6 Data Validation Controls

Validating user input is a time-consuming activity. The programmers we've met agree that a large portion of their code deals with data validation. A number of typical errors are encountered when a user has entered data into an input field:

◆ The field is empty.

◆ The value entered into a field is not in a reasonable range. An employee might have entered a salary value that is less than zero, for example.

◆ The field's value does not correlate with the contents of another field in a logical manner. A student, for example, might have entered a graduation date earlier than their initial enrollment date.

◆ The user's input does not match a standard expected format. For example, a user might have entered a date that does not match the way dates are expressed in their geographical locale.

In addition to these common errors, programs often perform more complex error checking. A user's input might violate a set of constraints expressed as logical rules. For example, tax calculation programs have a number of rules that govern whether or not exceptions for dependents can be claimed. Microsoft created several useful data validation controls for ASP.NET:

◆ RequiredFieldValidator

◆ RangeValidator

◆ CompareValidator

◆ RegularExpressionValidator

◆ CustomValidator

◆ ValidationSummary

The nice thing about using these controls is that validation can occur as the user is moving between input fields, providing a Windows desktop-like experience. When these controls detect that an error has been corrected, they hide the related error message. The validator controls are located in the Web Forms section of the Visual Studio .NET toolbox. Use the validator controls by associating one or more of them with input fields on a Web form.

RequiredFieldValidator

The RequiredFieldValidator control alerts the user when an input field cannot be left empty. For example, we can require the user's input into a text box by placing a RequiredFieldValidator control on the form next to the text box. In Figure 8-19, an error message is displayed when the user clicks on the OK button without having entered a value. The properties of the RequiredFieldValidator in this example are assigned as follows:

Property Name	Value
ControlToValidate	txtRentalRate
Text	*
ErrorMessage	Rental rate is required

Figure 8-19 RequiredFieldValidator example.

The Text property holds a string that displays at the location of the RequiredFieldValidator when the target control fails its validation check. The ErrorMessage property determines the string to display in the ValidationSummary control located just above the OK button. If we had other validation controls on the form, their error messages would display in the same ValidationSummary control. If you leave the Text property blank, the contents of the ErrorMessage property display in the same page position as the validator control. When the user corrects the error and clicks on the OK button, the * marker and error message disappear automatically. We can see this in Figure 8-20. The button has moved up to fill the position of the validation summary, since this form was designed in FlowLayout mode.

Figure 8-20 After the user corrects the error.

CausesValidation Property

Sometimes, the user does not want to enter any data and just wants to move to another Web page. In the Daily Rental Rate example we've been looking at, users can click on the LinkButton control entitled **Skip this page**, taking them to the page shown in Figure 8-21. By default, any button that navigates to a new page triggers validation events on the current page. If we set the button's **CausesValidationProperty** to False, however, validation events are suspended and the program is able to move to the new Web page.

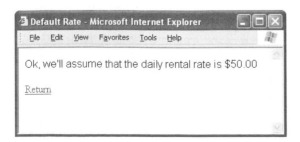

Figure 8-21 Skipping user input.

Multiple Validators

An input field can have multiple validation controls checking its contents. For our daily rental rate example, we might like to include a RangeValidator control. If an input field's contents are blank, only the RequiredFieldValidator is activated. Once the user enters data into the field, other types of validators become active.

Common Properties

A number of properties are common to all validator controls (Table 8-7).

Table 8-7

Common validator control properties.

Property Name	Description
ControlToValidate	Control whose contents are to be validated (called the *target control*).
Display	Determines how the message contained in the Text property is displayed. Choices are Static, Dynamic, and None.
EnableClientScript	Enable or disable client-side validation.
Enabled	Enable or disable validation of the target control.
ErrorMessage	The message displayed by the ValidationSummary control when an error is detected.
IsValid	Equals True when the control's contents are valid (runtime property).
Text	Text displayed on the form at the location of the validator control when the validation check fails.

Client vs Server

All of the Web server validation controls have a property named **EnableClientScript** which you can use to either enable or disable client-side validation. The property is True by default. Assuming this property to be True, validation can only be performed on the client when an *uplevel* Web browser (Internet Explorer version 5.5 or later) is used. The user is able to see error messages when tabbing between fields, even before the page is posted back to the server. On the other hand, if EnableClientScript is False or the client is using a *downlevel* browser, the current page must be posted back to the server before validation can be performed. Recall that clicking on a button is one way for a postback to occur.

 Note:
   Client-side validation for the validation controls is performed by predefined JavaScript functions, located in the file WebUIValidation.js, found in the aspnet_client subdirectory of your default Web server directory (usually c:\inetpub\ wwwroot).

RangeValidator

The RangeValidator control lets you specify minimum and maximum values for the user's input to a control. It becomes active after the user has entered some data into the input field. Using our previous validator example as a reference point, suppose we want to be sure that the user enters a daily rental rate between 1 and 100. Figure 8-22 shows what happens when the user enters an out-of-range value and clicks on OK. If the user corrects the error and clicks on OK, the error message disappears. The property settings of the RangeValidator are listed in Table 8-8. Ranges do not have to be numeric. For example, you can set MinimumValue to "s" and MaximumValue to "x" if you want to require input strings to fall between these two letters of the alphabet.

Table 8-8

RangeValidator settings

Property Name	Value
ControlToValidate	txtRentalRate
Text	*
ErrorMessage	Rental rate must be between 1 and 100
MaximumValue	100
MinimumValue	1

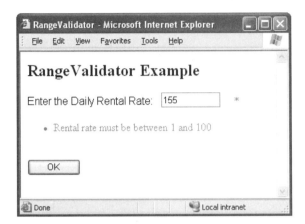

Figure 8-22 Using the RangeValidator control.

CompareValidator

The CompareValidator control compares a control's contents to the contents of another control. Properties not found in the other validator controls are listed in Table 8-9.

Table 8-9

CompareValidator properties

Property Name	Description
ValueToCompare	Constant value compared to the control's contents.
Operator	Used when comparing control contents to a constant value. Select from a list of predefined operator identifiers: equal, greater than, less than, etc.
Type	Type of data used in the control being validated. Select from String, Integer, Double, Date, or Currency.
ControlToCompare	Control whose contents will be compared to the control being validated.

Let's use the CompareValidator to check the values of starting and ending rental reservation dates. Naturally, the return date must be greater than or equal to the rental date. In Figure 8-23, the user has entered an invalid date range. Table 8-10 lists the assigned CompareValidator properties. As in previous validator examples, we have included a ValidationSummary control on the form to display error messages generated by the CompareValidator.

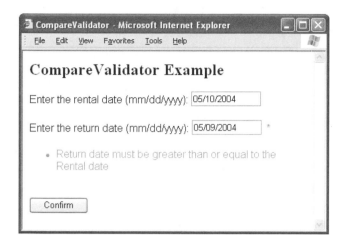

Figure 8-23 CompareValidator Example.

Table 8-10

CompareValidator assigned properties

Property Name	Property Value
ControlToValidate	txtReturnDate
ControlToCompare	txtRentalDate
ErrorMessage	Return date must be greater than or equal to the Rental date
Font	Arial
Operator	GreaterThanEqual
Text	*
Type	Date

Comparing to Today's Date

There may be times when you want to compare a date input by the user to today's date. Although the standard **Today** property returns today's date, you cannot assign it to the ValueToCompare property in design mode. On the other hand, you can assign the property at runtime:

```
cmpDate.ValueToCompare = CStr(Today)
```

RegularExpressionValidator

The RegularExpressionValidator control performs string pattern matching against the contents of another control. Regular expression syntax is somewhat complex, but you can select from a dropdown list of predefined expressions when setting the ValidationExpression property. Here are some of the predefined regular expressions you can choose:

- ◆ Internet URL
- ◆ Email address
- ◆ U.S. Phone number
- ◆ U.S. Social Security Number
- ◆ U.S. Zip code

In Figure 8-24, a regular expression is used to validate an email address entered by the user. Table 8-11 lists the RegularExpressionValidator's property values used in this example.

Figure 8-24   Validating an email address.

Table 8-11

RegularExpressionValidator property values

Property Name	Property Value
ControlToValidate	txtEmail
ErrorMessage	Invalid email format
Font	Arial
Text	*
ValidationExpression	\w+([-+.]\w+)*@\w+([-.]\w+)*\.\w+([-.]\w+)*

Regular expressions

Regular expressions are specification strings that conform to *regular expression syntax*. They are a powerful tool for pattern matching. You can match an expression against various input strings and accept or reject each string based on how it matches the expression. For example, a regular expression that specifies a 4-digit Personal Identification Number (PIN) would be encoded as "\d{4}". If this value were assigned to the ValidationExpression property, the control would accept or reject input strings:

```
1234     accept
2222     accept
333      reject
9999     accept
11111    reject
```

Numerous symbols are used by regular expressions to validate strings. We do not have the space to explain them all, but a few common ones are listed in Table 8-12

Table 8-12

Common regular expression symbols.

Symbol	Description
\w	Matches digits 0 through 9, underscore, and any other characters classified as alphanumeric in the Unicode character properties database.
\d	Matches digits 0 through 9 only.
+	Matches any number of occurrences of the preceding character.
\	Escape. Matches the next character following the backslash.
{*n*}	Specify the number of occurences *n* of the previous character.
( )*	Repeat the sequence inside the parentheses any number of times.
[*aaa*]	The set of characters specified inside the brackets.
[^*aaa*]	Matches all characters except the ones specified inside the brackets.

Table 8-13 lists a number of regular expression examples you can modify and use in your own programs. If you are interested in learning more, look up "Regular Expressions" in the *Visual Studio .NET Environment* section of the MSDN help.

Table 8-13

Regular expression examples.

Expression	Matches Strings Containing...	Sample Matching Strings
\d+ \d* (\d)*	any number of digits.	234249749875764392 1
\d{5}	exactly five digits.	98346 11111 00002
X(\d)*Y	strings beginning with X, ending with Y, containing any number of digits in between.	X2Y XY X23423424234Y
\w*	any number of alphanumeric characters, including the underscore.	sdjd6883sdfh_234AB
AB+	character A followed by any number of letter B's.	AB ABBBBBBB
[123]{5}	any digit from the set {1,2,3}, repeated five times.	11111 11222 13221 33333
000\d{3}	three zeros followed by any three digits.	000123 000444 000219
[A-Za-z]+	any number of capital or lowercase letters in the range A to Z.	aBytXnp B
[a-z]:\\[a-z]+	lowercase letter, colon, backslash, followed by any number of lowercase letters.	c:\xyz b:\z
[^aeiou]	any character not in the set of vowels.	X Z M

Validating an Email Address

The ValidationExpression used in our earlier example to validate an email address was \w+([-+.]\w+)*@\w+([-.]\w+)*\.\w+([-.]\w+)*. Table 8-14 breaks it into segments to make it more understandable. Examples of strings that match the first subexpression are show here:

```
ben123
any_one
fred.jones
dan+miller
comp-sci
microsoft.com
```

Tale 8-14

Email expression example

Subexpression	Description
\w+([-+.]\w+)*	Any number of alphanumeric characters can begin an email address (\w+) followed by a single occurrence of either minus, plus, or dot. This is followed by any number of alphanumeric characters.
@	The @ symbol.
\w+([-+.]\w+)*	Same as the first subexpression.
\.	A period (.)
\w+([-+.]\w+)*	Same as the first subexpression.

CustomValidator

The CustomValidator control can be used when you want to perform some type of validation not already covered by existing validator controls. Validation can be performed on either the server or the client. For the latter option, you must set the ClientValidationFunction property to the name of a JavaScript or VBScript function that will perform the validation.

In Figure 8-25, the user selects the academic status of a student who plans to register for classes and inputs the number of requested credits. When the Verify button is clicked, the program evaluates the request according to the following criteria:

- ◆ If the Advisor override box is checked, the student can register.
- ◆ Otherwise,...
  - ▶ If status = Satisfactory, the student may take no more than 18 credits.
  - ▶ If status = Warning, the student may take no more than 12 credits.
  - ▶ If status = Probation, the student may take no more than 8 credits.
  - ▶ IF status = Not eligible, the student may not take any credits.

Suppose a Satisfactory student tries to register for 19 credits. The result is shown in Figure 8-26.

Figure 8-25   CustomValidator example.

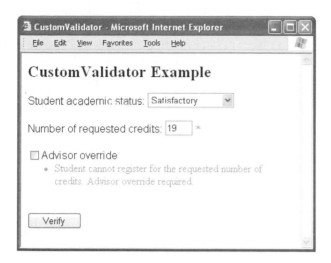

Figure 8- 26   Example error message.

ServerValidate Event Handler

In order to enable a CustomValidator control, you must create a handler procedure for the ServerValidate event:

```
Sub vldCredits_ServerValidate(ByVal source As Object, _
  ByVal args As ServerValidateEventArgs)...
```

The second parameter (*args*), has a property named **IsValid**. If your validation logic determines the user's input to be valid, set args.IsValid to True; otherwise, set it to False. Here is our implementation of the ServerValidate handler for the current course credits example:

```
Private Sub vldCredits_ServerValidate(ByVal source As Object, _
  ByVal args As ServerValidateEventArgs) Handles vldCredits.ServerValidate

    args.IsValid = True
    'If the advisor override box is checked, everything's OK.
    If chkAdvisorOverride.Checked Then Exit Sub

    'Determine the maximum number of credits the student can take.
    Dim maxCredits As Integer = 0
    Select Case ddlStatus.SelectedValue
       Case "S"
          maxCredits = 18
       Case "W"
          maxCredits = 12
       Case "P"
          maxCredits = 8
       Case "N"
          maxCredits = 0
    End Select

    If CInt(txtCredits.Text) > maxCredits Then args.IsValid = False
End Sub
```

The CustomValidator control offers unlimited possibilities for validation. You can, for example, combine it with a database table to look up information to use in the validation process.

►8.7 State Management

Web servers, as we have mentioned before, do not keep a link to a particular page active once the page has been sent to the client's browser. This presents a challenge when you have class-level variables in your Web forms that contain important data. Similarly, when users move from one Web page to another, it is often necessary to transmit data from the first page to the second. The following tools are used to manage state:

◆   ViewState: Holds runtime contents of controls when a page is posted back.

◆   Application State: Holds data that can be shared by all active sessions (users).

◆   Session State: Holds data belonging to a single session that can be accessed from any Web form.

◆   Cookies: Persistent strings stored in the user's computer.

Page-Level State (*ViewState*)

ViewState

The contents of many Web server controls are automatically saved when their enclosing page is posted back to the server. Web pages have a collection property named **ViewState** that holds the data in the server controls. You can use the ViewState collection to store and retrieve the values of variables that have been declared at the class level. Suppose a program lets the user input names, and it needs to keep track of how many names have been entered (Figure 8-27).

Figure 8-27   Counting names input by the user.

In a typical WinForms application, the counter variable would be declared at the class level so it could keep its value across multiple calls to btnOk_Click. We will try that in the current ASP.NET program:

```
Public Class NameList
    Inherits System.Web.UI.Page

    Dim nameCount As Integer

    Private Sub btnOk_Click(ByVal sender As System.Object, _
     ByVal e As System.EventArgs) Handles btnOk.Click

        nameCount += 1
        lblCount.Text = CStr(nameCount) & " names have been entered"
    End Sub
End Class
```

Unfortunately, every time the page posts back to the server, nameCount is reset to zero. When nameCount is incremented, the displayed value is always equal to 1. We can fix this problem by storing nameCount in the ViewState collection. In the btnOk_Click procedure, the following line retrieves the current value of nameCount:

```
nameCount = ViewState("count")
```

The following line saves the current value of nameCount in ViewState:

```
ViewState("count") = nameCount
```

Incorporating both techniques into our program solves the stated problem:

```
Public Class NameList
    Inherits System.Web.UI.Page

    Dim nameCount As Integer

    Private Sub btnOk_Click(ByVal sender As System.Object, _
     ByVal e As System.EventArgs) Handles btnOk.Click

        nameCount = ViewState("count")
        nameCount += 1
        ViewState("count") = nameCount
        lblCount.Text = CStr(nameCount) & " names have been entered"
    End Sub
End Class
```

We might just as easily have retrieved the value of nameCount inside the Page_Load event handler. Then it would be available to all class methods:

```
Private Sub Page_Load(ByVal sender As Object, _
 ByVal e As System.EventArgs) Handles MyBase.Load

    nameCount = ViewState("count")
End Sub
```

ViewState's Limitations

ViewState's most important limitation is that you cannot use it to hold objects unless those objects are serializable. Though we will not explain how to serialize objects (a specialized topic), we will demonstrate a more practical way to save object data. ViewState has another limitation: it does not save information when the user moves between Web pages.

Application State

Application state is an HttpApplicationState object that stores data which can be shared by all connected sessions. Every program has an **Application** property that can be accessed by code inside the Global.asax file or within Web forms. To create or modify a state variable, use its identifier as a key:

```
Application("userCount") = 1
```

To retrieve the value of a state variable, use a statement such as the following:

```
lblNumUsers.Text = Application("userCount")
```

To delete a state variable, call the Remove method:

```
Application.Remove("userCount")
```

To remove all state variables, call RemoveAll:

```
Application.RemoveAll( )
```

If you modify the Global.asax file while a program is running, application state is cleared.

Application-Level Events

Two important events are associated with ASP.NET applications:

- ◆ **Application_Start** fires when an application begins to execute.
- ◆ **Application_End** fires when the application stops executing.

You can start an application by connecting to its startup page with a browser. If you close the browser, the application will continue to run. If you modify and recompile the program, the application will end. (It will also end if you shut down the Web server.)

Examples

Suppose we want to create an application state variable that counts the number of connected users. We could set the variable to 0 when the application loads:

```
Sub Application_Start(ByVal sender As Object, ByVal e As EventArgs)
    Application("userCount") = 0
End Sub
```

Then when a new session begins (a user connects), we could increment the count:

```
Sub Session_Start(ByVal sender As Object, ByVal e As EventArgs)
    Application("userCount") += 1
End Sub
```

When the current session ends, we could decrement the count:

```
Sub Session_End(ByVal sender As Object, ByVal e As EventArgs)
    Application("userCount") -= 1
End Sub
```

Locking for Safety

If your application is run by simultaneous multiple users, there is a chance that two sessions might start at the same time and corrupt shared application variables. To prevent this from happening, you can use the Lock and Unlock statements to guarantee that only a single user's session can update an application variable. Here are safer versions of Session_Start and Session_End:

```
Sub Session_Start(ByVal sender As Object, ByVal e As EventArgs)
    Application.Lock()
    Application("sessionCount") += 1
    Application.UnLock()
End Sub
```

Once the current session calls Lock, no other sessions may modify sessionCount until the current session calls Unlock. When the current session ends, we can decrement the count:

```
Sub Session_End(ByVal sender As Object, ByVal e As EventArgs)
    Application.Lock()
    Application("sessionCount") -= 1
    Application.UnLock()
End Sub
```

As a general rule, do not insert much code between calls to Lock and Unlock. Doing so can slow down an application when there are lots of users.

Checkpoint

8.23 When a page is posted back to the server, how do TextBox controls avoid losing their contents?

8.24 (yes/no) If two users are running the same ASP.NET application, can one user access the session state of the other user?

8.25 Show an example of storing the contents of an Integer variable named **users** in an Application variable.

8.26 Write a statement that removes the **users** Application variable.

8.27 Why would you call the Application.Lock method when modifying an Application variable?

▶8.8 Session State and Browser Cookies

Session state is the name given for the mechanism that ASP.NET uses to associate information with a particular user. Session state is a great tool for passing object information when users navigate between the application's Web pages.

When a user connects to an application, a unique session ID is created and saved as a temporary cookie by the user's browser. The session ID is used when saving and retrieving session state information while the user's session is active. If the browser does not accept cookies, session state can only be saved if the *cookieless session* option is specified in the application's Web.config file. A session remains active as long as the user's browser is running. If the user leaves the browser window open with no postbacks, the session times out after a set time period. The default is twenty minutes.

Session state is stored on the Web server, which means that a significant amount of server time might be spent transfering data to users if large objects are stored in session state.

Session state items are stored in name-value pairs. The following example stores the value **A1234** in a session variable named **customerId**:

```
Session.Item("customerId") = "A1234"
```

The current value of customerId can be retrieved by the following statement:

```
Dim customerId As String = Session.Item("customerId")
```

Because Item is the default Session property, we can simplify references to customerId:

```
Session("customerId") = "A1234"
Dim customerId As String = Session("customerId")
```

Saving and Restoring Objects

Any object can be saved in session state. For example, we can create a Student object and save it in a session state variable named currStudent:

```
Dim S As Student = New Student(12345,"Smith")
Session("currStudent") = S
```

When retrieving the value of currStudent, the Session.Item property returns a generic Object. The following statement generates an error when Option Explicit is turned on:

```
S = Session.Item("currStudent")
```

Instead, we must cast the Session variable into its appropriate type (Student):

```
S = CType(Session.Item("currStudent"), Student)
```

Leaving out the implicit Item property name, the equivalent statement would be:

```
S = CType(Session("currStudent"), Student)
```

You may find it helpful at times to try to load a specific Session variable, and upon discovering that it doesn't exist, create the object:

```
If Session("currStudent") Is Nothing Then
   Session("currStudent") = New Student
End If
```

Similarly, you can use exception handling to prevent the runtime error that results from trying to cast a null value into an object:

```
Dim S As Student
Try
   S = CType(Session("currStudent"), Student)
Catch
   'S is null, but that's ok
End Try
```

HttpSessionState Properties and Methods

The HttpSessionState class lets you manipulate session state values, as well as the Session object itself. The properties are listed in Table 8-15, and the methods are listed in Table 8-16.

Table 8-15

HttpSessionState properties

Property	Description
Count	Returns the number of items in the session state collection.
IsCookieless	If True, the session ID is embedded in the URL; otherwise, the session ID is stored in a cookie.
IsNewSession	If True, the current session was created with the current request.
Item	Gets or sets individual session state values (default property).
Keys	Returns a collection of all keys stored in the session.
SessionID	Returns the ID number of the current session.
Timeout	Gets or sets the timeout period (in minutes) between requests before the current session is terminated.

Table 8-16

HttpSessionState methods

Method	Description
Abandon( )	Logs the user out of the current session.
Add(name As String, value As Object)	Adds a new item to the session state.
Clear( )	Clears all values from session state.
Remove(name As String)	Removes a named item from the session state.
RemoveAll( )	Removes all session state values.
RemoveAt(index As Integer)	Removes the item at position *index.*

SessionState Demo Program

Sessiondemo

The SessionState Demo program displays session state properties and uses Application state to save information about user connections. Figure 8-28 shows the program's output when the first user has connected. The session ID has been generated automatically, and we can see the date and time when the session began. In Figure 8-29 a second user has connected. Note how the session count has changed and the ID of the new session displays.

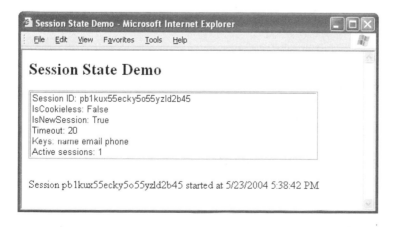

Figure 8-28   Session state demo program.

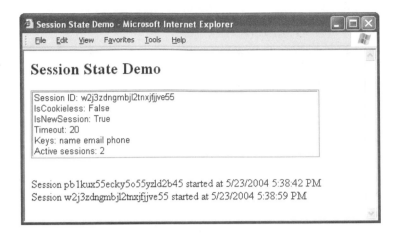

Figure 8-29 Connection by a second user.

The **Session_Start** event handler in the Global.asax file uses an Application state variable to log the session ID , time, and date. It also adds to the sessionCount state variable:

```
Sub Session_Start(ByVal sender As Object, ByVal e As EventArgs)

   Dim appLog As String = Application("appLog")
   appLog += " Session " & Session.SessionID & _
      " started at " & Now
   Application("appLog") = appLog
   Application("sessionCount") += 1
End Sub
```

In the startup form's **Page_Load** handler, we assign the appLog variable to a label on the form and save a few session state values:

```
Private Sub Page_Load(ByVal sender As System.Object, _
 ByVal e As System.EventArgs) Handles MyBase.Load

   lblAppLog.Text = Application("appLog")

   'Create some session state values
   Session.Add("name", "Joe Smith")
   Session.Add("email", "joe@anywhere.com")
   Session.Add("phone", "303-222-3333")
```

In the list box, we display several Session properties and call getKeys to convert the list of session keys to a string:

```
   lstbox.Items.Clear()
   With lstbox.Items
      .Add("Session ID: " & Session.SessionID)
      .Add("IsCookieless: " & Session.IsCookieless)
      .Add("IsNewSession: " & Session.IsNewSession)
      .Add("Timeout: " & Session.Timeout)
      lstbox.Items.Add("Keys: " & getKeys())
      .Add("Active sessions: " & Application("sessionCount"))
   End With
End Sub
```

The getKeys function iterates over the Session.Keys collection and builds a string:

```
Private Function getKeys() As String
   Dim temp As String, key As String
   For Each key In Session.Keys
      temp &= key + " "
   Next
   Return temp
End Function
```

Cookieless Session

Some browsers do not accept cookies, which presents a problem if a program needs to save session state information when moving between pages. Without a cookie, the user would appear to start a new session every time a new page was loaded. Fortunately, you can permit cookieless sessions in the Web.config file using the following code:

```
<sessionState
  cookieless="true"
/>
```

When the user first connects to the application, the server automatically modifies the application's base URL to include the user's session ID. From that point on, the session ID appears in the browser's address bar when the user navigates to other pages using relative links. (A relative link stores only the path from the current page to some other page.) Figure 8-30 shows a browser running the SessionDemo program using a cookieless session. The Session ID appears in the page's URL. A complete listing of the Session State Demo program appears in Code Listing 8-6.

Figure 8-30 Session ID added to URL.

Code Listing 8-6 (Session State Demo)

```
Public Class SessionStateDemo
   Inherits System.Web.UI.Page

+ Web Form Designer generated code

   Private Sub Page_Load(ByVal sender As System.Object, _
      ByVal e As System.EventArgs) Handles MyBase.Load

      lblAppLog.Text = Application("appLog")

      'Create some Session state values
      Session.Add("name", "Joe Smith")
      Session.Add("email", "joe@anywhere.com")
```

```
        Session.Add("phone", "303-222-3333")

        lstbox.Items.Clear()
        With lstbox.Items
            .Add("Session ID: " & Session.SessionID)
            .Add("IsCookieless: " & Session.IsCookieless)
            .Add("IsNewSession: " & Session.IsNewSession)
            .Add("Timeout: " & Session.Timeout)
            lstbox.Items.Add("Keys: " & getKeys())
            .Add("Active sessions: " & Application("sessionCount"))
        End With
    End Sub

    Private Function getKeys() As String
        Dim temp As String, key As String
        For Each key In Session.Keys
            temp &= key + " "
        Next
        Return temp
    End Function
End Class
```

Pizzicato Music Store Example

The Pizzicato Music Store program demonstrates the saving and retrieving of session state information. It begins with a form that lets the user accumulate an order (Figure 8-31). When the user clicks on **Confirm your order**, a confirmation page lists the items, prices, and total order amount (Figure 8-32).

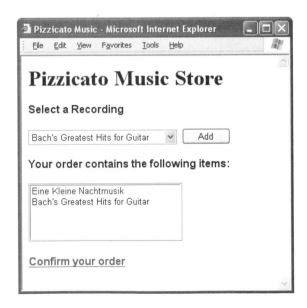

Figure 8-31   Placing an order at the Pizzicato Music Store.

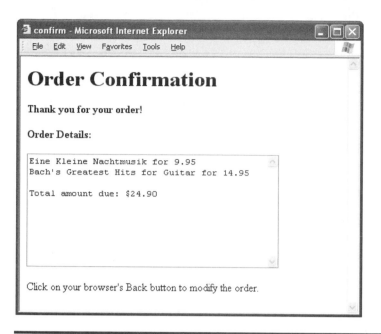

Figure 8-32 Confirming the order.

When the user clicks on the browser's back button, the list box on the startup page still shows the same selections. We have cleverly avoided the real problem: If the user clicked on a hyperlink to move from the confirmation page to the startup page, we would lose all selection information. With a minor amount of work, however, session state can be used to save the information. We will leave that problem as an exercise.

Designing the Startup Form

The startup form contains a dropdown list named ddlItems, a list box named lstOrder, a button named btnAdd, and a HyperLink control (to transfer to the confirmation page). Figure 8-33 lists the items added to the ddlItems.Items collection, although the titles and prices are not important.

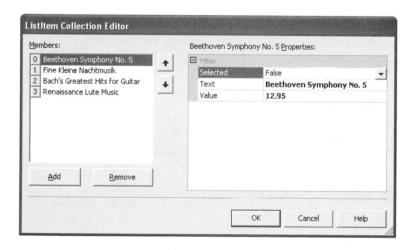

Figure 8-33 Items in the ddlItems dropdown list.

OrderItem and Order Classes

The OrderItem class holds the name and price of a single item that has been ordered (Code Listing 8-7).

Code Listing 8-7 (OrderItem class)

```
Public Class OrderItem
    Private _itemName As String
```

```
      Private _price As Decimal

      Public Sub New(ByVal nameVal As String, ByVal priceVal As Decimal)
         _itemName = nameVal
         _price = priceVal
      End Sub

      Public Property ItemName() As String
         Get
             Return _itemName
         End Get
         Set(ByVal Value As String)
              _itemName = Value
         End Set
      End Property

      Public Property Price() As Decimal
         Get
             Return _price
         End Get
         Set(ByVal Value As Decimal)
            _price = Value
         End Set
      End Property
   End Class
```

The Order class (Code Listing 8-8) is a container that holds any number of OrderItem objects. It contains an ArrayList (an expandable array) named _items, and it has a Total property that returns the total amount due for all items.

Code Listing 8-8 (Order class)

```
Public Class Order
   Private _items As ArrayList = New ArrayList

   Public Sub Add(ByVal itemName As String, ByVal price As Decimal)
      _items.Add(New OrderItem(itemName, price))
   End Sub

   Public ReadOnly Property Items() As ArrayList
      Get
          Return _items
      End Get
   End Property

   Public ReadOnly Property Total() As Decimal
      Get
          Dim sum As Decimal = 0
          Dim item As OrderItem
          For Each item In _items
             sum += item.Price
          Next
          Return sum
      End Get
   End Property
End Class
```

An ArrayList behaves more or less like a collection. It has an Add method that takes an Object, and you can iterate over its members. For example, the ArrayList named **_items** contains OrderItem objects, and this is how we declare the item variable:

```
Dim item As OrderItem
For Each item In _items
   '...
Next
```

Order Form

The program's startup form (shown earlier in Figure 8-31) doesn't have much to do. The Page_Load handler creates an Order object and saves it in a Session variable:

```
If Not IsPostBack Then
   Session("order") = New Order
End If
```

The Click handler for the Add button builds a ListItem from the name of the recording in the dropdown list, coupled with the item's value (the item price). This item is added to the list box:

```
lstOrder.Items.Add(New ListItem(ddlItems.SelectedItem.Text, _
   ddlItems.SelectedValue))
```

The session state named **order** is retrieved and cast into an Order object. The recording name and price are added to the order, and the Order object is stored back into the session state for safekeeping:

```
Dim currOrder As Order = CType(Session("order"), Order)
currOrder.Add(ddlItems.SelectedItem.Text, CDec(ddlItems.SelectedValue))
Session("order") = currOrder
```

Program Listing

The complete source code of the Pizzicato Music Store startup form appears in Code Listing 8-9. The comfirmation form appears in Code Listing 8-10.

Code Listing 8-9 (Pizzicato Music – Default.aspx)

```
Public Class PizzicatoMusic
    Inherits System.Web.UI.Page

+ Web Form Designer generated code

    Private Sub Page_Load(ByVal sender As System.Object, _
    ByVal e As System.EventArgs) Handles MyBase.Load

       If Not IsPostBack Then
          Session("order") = New Order
       End If
    End Sub

    Private Sub btnAdd_Click(ByVal sender As System.Object, _
    ByVal e As System.EventArgs) Handles btnAdd.Click

       lstOrder.Items.Add(New ListItem(ddlItems.SelectedItem.Text, _
       ddlItems.SelectedValue))
```

```
      Dim currOrder As Order = CType(Session("order"), Order)
      currOrder.Add(ddlItems.SelectedItem.Text, CDec(ddlItems.SelectedValue))
      Session("order") = currOrder
   End Sub
End Class
```

Code Listing 8-10 (Pizzicato Music — Confirm.aspx)

```
Public Class confirm
    Inherits System.Web.UI.Page

+ Web Form Designer generated code

   Private Sub Page_Load(ByVal sender As System.Object, _
   ByVal e As System.EventArgs) Handles MyBase.Load

      Dim myOrder As Order = CType(Session("order"), Order)
      Dim item As OrderItem
      For Each item In myOrder.Items
         txtResult.Text &= item.ItemName & " for " _
           & item.Price & vbCrLf
      Next

      txtResult.Text &= (vbCrLf & "Total amount due: " _
        & FormatCurrency(myOrder.Total))
   End Sub
End Class
```

Browser Cookies

Browser cookies are name-value pairs stored on a user's computer by their Web browser. Such cookies are only appropriate for small amounts of data that can be expressed as strings. You cannot store a Student object, for example, in a cookie. Browsers have the option to disable cookies, so your programs should be careful about assuming you can use cookies. Cookies are not encrypted, so you should never store passwords, credit card numbers, or other sensitive information in a cookie. Cookies can be stored temporarily or for days, months, years at a time. Each cookie has an **Expires** property (set to a date) that controls its lifetime. If you leave the property blank, the cookie is deleted when the user session ends. Programs create and assign cookies using the Response.Cookies property. The Request.Cookies property, on the other hand, is used to retrieve cookie values.

You can see a list of cookies currently on your computer by looking in the directory named *<drive>*:\Documents and Settings*<user>*\Cookies, where *<drive>* is your system drive letter, and *<user>* is your username. Each cookie is stored as a text file. For example, the following shows a cookie named **Name**, which is stored in a file named kip@localhost[1].txt:

```
Name
Kip Irvine
localhost/
1024
3984441856
29633514
3275258352
29633313
*
```

A *session cookie* is a cookie that expires as soon as the user closes the browser. A *persistent cookie* is stored in a file on the user's computer. To make a persistent cookie, you must set its expiration date to some time in the future.

Examples

The following declares an HttpCookie variable:

```
Dim aCookie As HttpCookie
```

The following creates a cookie named **FirstName** and assigns it a value of "Bill":

```
aCookie = new HttpCookie("FirstName", "Bill")
```

The following retrieves a cookie named **FirstName** from the Request object:

```
aCookie = Request.Cookies("FirstName")
```

The following assigns a cookie's value to a text box:

```
txtName.Text = aCookie.Value
```

The following adds a cookie to the Response object's Cookies collection:

```
Response.Cookies.Add(aCookie)
```

If you retrieve and modify a cookie, you must call the Set method if you want the change to be permanent. The following replaces a cookie:

```
Response.Cookies.Set(aCookie)
```

The following assigns an expiration date of three days in the future:

```
aCookie.Expires = Now.AddDays(3)
```

The following pair of statements delete a cookie:

```
aCookie.Expires = Now
Response.Cookies.Set(aCookie)
```

Cookie Example Program

The Cookie Example program uses a persistent cookie to remember the name of the person who last logged in from the same user account on a particular computer. Figure 8-34 shows the program after the user has entered their name and checked the "Remember me the next time I visit" option. Clicking on OK saves this information, hides the panel containing all the controls, and displays a closing message (Figure 8-35).

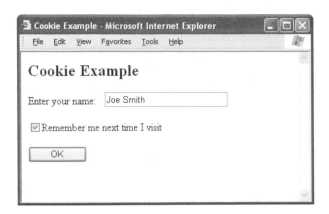

Figure 8-34   Cookie Example program..

Figure 8-35   After the user has clicked on OK.

The user should close the browser, start a new browser, and run the example again. The program will look for the cookie, and if found, copy the person's name from the cookie to the text box. The program uses a Panel control to hold all text and controls, making it easy to hide all of those elements with a single statement that sets the Panel's Visible property to False.

Implementation

First, the program's startup form declares a class-level variable named **nameCookie**:

```
Private nameCookie As HttpCookie
```

When the page is loaded for the first time, the Page_Load event handler attempts to retrieve the cookie named **Name**. If the cookie is found, we assign its value to the text box (txtName):

```
Private Sub Page_Load(ByVal sender As System.Object, _
   ByVal e As System.EventArgs) Handles MyBase.Load

   If Not IsPostBack Then
      nameCookie = Request.Cookies("Name")
      If Not nameCookie Is Nothing Then
         txtName.Text = nameCookie.Value
      End If
   End If
End Sub
```

When the user clicks the OK button, the program must first determine whether the **Name** cookie exists. If not, a new cookie is created and added to the Cookies collection:

```
1:   Private Sub btnOK_Click(ByVal sender As System.Object, _
2:      ByVal e As System.EventArgs) Handles btnOk.Click
3:
4:       nameCookie = Request.Cookies("Name")
5:      If nameCookie Is Nothing Then
6:          'Create and Add a new cookie
7:          nameCookie = New HttpCookie("Name", txtName.Text)
8:          nameCookie.Expires = Now.AddDays(1)
9:          Response.Cookies.Add(nameCookie)
10:     Else
11:         'Modify existing cookie
12:         If chkRemember.Checked = False Then    'don't remember user
13:            nameCookie.Expires = Now            'delete the cookie
14:         Else
15:            nameCookie.Value = txtName.Text      'put user name in cookie
16:            nameCookie.Expires = Now.AddDays(31) 'store it for 31 days
17:         End If
18:         Response.Cookies.Set(nameCookie)        'put back in collection
19:     End If
20:     mainPanel.Visible = False
21:     Response.Write("Thanks. Now close the browser window")
22:   End Sub
```

If the **Name** cookie exists, line 12 uses the check box value to decide whether or not to save the person's name in a cookie. Setting the Expires property to Now on line 13 automatically marks the cookie for deletion. If the user name is to be saved, lines 15 and 16 assign the user's name from the text box and set the cookie's Expires property to 31 days in the future. Line 18 replaces the existing cookie with the modified one. Line 20 hides the panel that holds all the form controls, and line 21 writes a message to the browser window. A complete listing of the Cookie Example program appears in Code Listing 8-11.

Code Listing 8-11 (Cookie Example)

```
Public Class CookieExample
    Inherits System.Web.UI.Page

+ Web Form Designer generated code

    Private nameCookie As HttpCookie

    Private Sub Page_Load(ByVal sender As System.Object, _
     ByVal e As System.EventArgs) Handles MyBase.Load

       If Not IsPostBack Then
       nameCookie = Request.Cookies("Name")
       If Not nameCookie Is Nothing Then
          txtName.Text = nameCookie.Value
       End If
    End If
End Sub
```

```
Private Sub btnOK_Click(ByVal sender As System.Object, _
  ByVal e As System.EventArgs) Handles btnOk.Click

    nameCookie = Request.Cookies("Name")
    If nameCookie Is Nothing Then
       'Create and Add a new cookie
       nameCookie = New HttpCookie("Name", txtName.Text)
       nameCookie.Expires = Now.AddDays(1)
       Response.Cookies.Add(nameCookie)
    Else
       'Modify existing cookie
       If chkRemember.Checked = False Then
        nameCookie.Expires = Now                 'delete the existing cookie
       Else
          nameCookie.Value = txtName.Text      'put user name in cookie
          nameCookie.Expires = Now.AddDays(31)'store it for 31 days
       End If
       Response.Cookies.Set(nameCookie)          'put back in collection
    End If
    mainPanel.Visible = False
    Response.Write("Thanks. Now close the browser window")
  End Sub
End Class
```

Checkpoint

8.28 How is session state different from application state?

8.29 Write a statement that creates an Employee object and stores it in a session variable named **employee**. Assume that the Employee constructor has no parameters.

8.30 Write a statement that retrieves an Employee object from a session variable named employee. Assume that Option Strict is On.

8.31 What type of information can be stored in a browser cookie?

▶ 8.9 Deploying a Web Application

Deploying a Web application can be simple when you deploy on the same machine used to develop the program. Select **Copy Project** from the Project menu. When the dialog shown in Figure 8-36 appears, select the path you want to use for the Destination project folder. Select the File share option, and the File share path. Select the option that copies only files needed to run this application, and click on OK.

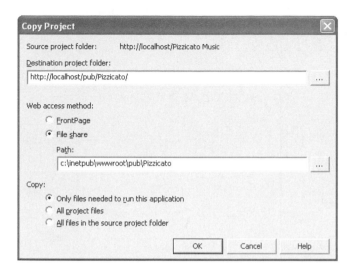

Figure 8-36   Deploying the Pizzicato Music application.

Deploying on a Network

If you want to deploy your program on a different computer from the development machine, the procedure is a little more complicated. On the target computer, use Windows Explorer to create a folder below the \Inetpub\wwwroot folder, or below an existing Web site folder. Next, you will use Internet Information Services (IIS) to designate the target folder as a Web application folder. Here are the steps:

1. From the Start menu on the target computer, select Control Panel, select Administrative Tools, and select Internet Information Services.

2. Expand the Web Sites entry.

3. Expand the Default Web Site entry.

4. Right-click on the folder you created (call it **MyWeb**) and select Properties.

5. Select the Directory tab and click on Create (Figure 8-37).

6. Click OK to save your changes.

Now you can copy the project files from the source computer to the target computer's folder, or you can use the Copy Project command from the Project menu.

Figure 8-37 Creating a Web application.

Once you have deployed your application, users anywhere on the Web can access your application if they know your computer's IP address. Suppose your IP address was **123.43.56.78**, your application was named **MyWeb**, and its startup page was **Default.aspx**. Your Web application could be reached by the following URL:

```
http://123.43.56.78/MyWeb/Default.aspx
```

There are companies on the Web that offer free domain-name forwarding services in which your computer's current IP address is kept in a database and associated with a domain name. For example, suppose your domain was called mydomain.com. Users could type the following:

```
http://mydomain.com/MyWeb/Default.aspx
```

If your Internet service provider does not provide a static IP address, domain forwarding services can install a program on your machine that sends them your current IP address. One such company we've used can be found at www.no-ip.com.

▶8.10 Chapter Summary

- ◆ *Custom error handling* refers to the ability ASP.NET programs have to configure the display of runtime error messages for both end users and program developers.
- ◆ The Custom Errors setting governs the way in which error messages are displayed on Web pages.
- ◆ Programs often create custom error pages to handle common HTML errors. The custom page references can be located in the Web.config file, or they can be set up using the Internet Information Services Administrator program.
- ◆ The Calendar control lets the user scroll forward and backward through monthly date displays and select individual dates.
- ◆ The Kayak Tour Scheduler program schedules tours for a hypothetical kayak store. The user selects tours from a dropdown list and selects dates from a Calendar control.
- ◆ Web forms controls such as DropDownList, ListBox, RadioButtonList, and CheckBoxList can be bound to array and ArrayList variables at runtime.

◆ Web forms controls only support one-way binding; that is, data are transferred automatically from a data source to a control.

◆ The Computer Club Tasks program binds array variables to DropDownList controls, permitting the user to assign tasks to individual members.

◆ The HTMLInputFile control lets users upload files to a Web site. Any type of file can be transferred, but there is an option to restrict file types and maximum sizes.

◆ Simple Mail Transfer Protocol (SMTP) is a service that responds to a standard set of commands for sending email.

◆ The simplest way to send an email message is to use the SmtpMail class. The Send method sends a message with few options.

◆ The MailMessage class has a rich set of properties that let you configure messages and include attachments.

◆ The MailDemo program sends mail to recipients using the MailMessage class. The program lets you send messages in text or HTML format and it sends file attachments.

◆ The RequiredFieldValidator control alerts the user when an input field cannot be left empty.

◆ The RangeValidator control checks minimum and maximum values against user input.

◆ The CompareValidator control compares one control's contents to that of another.

◆ The RegularExpressionValidator control performs string pattern matching against the contents of another control. *Regular expressions* are specification strings that conform to *regular expression syntax*. They are a powerful tool for pattern matching.

◆ The CustomValidator control performs advanced types of validation not available with existing validator controls.

◆ The ValidationSummary control displays error messages generated by other validation controls on the same Web form.

◆ Web servers do not keep a link to a particular page active once the page has been sent to the client's browser. At the same time, programs often must preserve data when moving between pages.

◆ Web pages have a ViewState property that holds the contents of input controls when forms are posted back to the server.

◆ An ASP.NET program can store common application-wide information in the application state collection.

◆ Each user has a distinct collection named *session state* that can be used to store objects and other data.

◆ The SessionState Demo program displays session state properties, and uses application state to save information about user connections.

◆ The Pizzicato Music Store program demonstrates the use of session state to save objects. The program lets users place orders for music recordings. An order summary is displayed on a separate Web page.

◆ *Cookies* are name-value pairs stored on a user's computer by their Web browser. Such cookies are appropriate for small amounts of data, which can be expressed as strings.

◆ Cookies can be stored temporarily or for days, months, years at a time. Each cookie has an **Expires** property (set to a date) that controls its lifetime.

◆ A *session cookie* is one that expires as soon as the user closes the browser. A *persistent cookie* is stored in a file on the user's computer.

◆ The Cookie Example program uses a persistent cookie to remember the name of the person who last logged in from the same user account on a particular computer.

▶8.11 Key Terms

Application State

Base64

Browser Cookie

Calendar control

CheckBoxList

CompareValidator

Cookieless session

CustomValidator

DropDownList

HTMLInputFile

HTTP errors

Internet Information Services (IIS)

ListBox

ListControl

MailMessage class

MIME types

persistent cookie

RadioButtonList

RangeValidator

regular expressions

RegularExpressionValidator

relative link

RequiredFieldValidator

Session cookie

Session ID

Session State

Simple Mail Transfer Protocol (SMTP)

SMTPMail class

UUEncode

ValidationSummary

ViewState

▶8.12 Review Questions

Fill-in-the-Blank

1. The _____ Errors setting in the Web.config file lets you determine the way in which error messages are displayed on Web pages.

2. The _____ property of a Calendar control returns the date selected by the user.

3. The Kayak Tour Builder program features the _____ control.

4. The _____ property of a DropDownList control can be used to bind the control to an array.

5. In an HTMLInputFile control, the _____ property provides information about the uploaded file.

Multiple Choice

1. The best way to let end users of your site see a friendly error message and simultaneously allow you to see detailed error information is to set the Custom Errors mode to which of the following?
   a. On
   b. Off
   c. RemoteOnly
   d. LocalOnly
   e. none of the above

2. Which of the following statements selects a specific date in the Calendar control named **cal**?
   a. cal.SelectedDates.Add("02/20/2004")
   b. cal.SelectedDate.Add("02/20/2004")
   c. cal.SelectedDates.Add(new Date("02/20/2004"))

d. cal.SelectedDates.Add(new Date(2, 20, 2004))

e. cal.SelectedDate = new Date(2004, 2, 20)

3. Which property in the HttpPostedFile class holds the file size?

a. ContentSize

b. FileSize

c. FileLength

d. ContentLength

e. none of the above

4. Which of the following is the class that lets you send email with attachments?

a. MailMessage

b. SmtpMail

c. SmtpMessage

d. MailServer

e. SmtpServer

5. Which of the following properties is **not** common to all types of validator controls?

a. ControlToValidate

b. Display

c. ErrorMessage

d. IsValid

e. ControlToCompare

True or False

1. Browser cookies can hold strings of limited length, but not complex objects.

2. When the user clicks on the browser's Back button to return to a page containing listbox selections, the selections remain visible.

3. Browser cookies automatically remain on the client's computer for 24 hours.

4. The sessionState setting in the Web.config file permits cookieless sessions.

5. The Obtain and Release statements are used to lock Application variables when there is a chance that two sessions might simultaneously modify the same data.

Short Answer

1. When you use IIS to modify the properties of a Web site, how do you designate specific Web pages to handle HTTP errors such as 404 (file not found)?

2. How can you prevent users from scrolling a Calendar control forward and backward through different months?

3. After setting the DataSource property of a DropDownList to the name of an array, what additional step must be taken before the items will appear in the list?

4. Which HTMLInputFile property lets you specify the types of files that users will be permitted to upload?

5. What property in the MailMessage class must be set before sending an HTML message?

What do You Think?

1. Why do you think sending an HTML message triggers a Request Validation error?

2. What advantages might there be to using the IIS administrator program to link custom Web pages to specific HTTP error numbers?

3. If you were to redesign the Calendar control, what changes or improvements would you make?

4. Do you think the HTMLFileInput control reveals too much information about the client's computer setup?

Algorithm Workbench

1. Write a statement in Web.config that routes all HTTP error 403 instances to a Web page named error403.htm.

2. Write a statement that adds February 10, 2005 to the collection of selected dates in a Calendar control named myCal.

3. Write a statement that makes February 10, 2005 visible in the Calendar control named myCal.

4. Write a statement that saves an uploaded file as "c:\temp\x.doc", for the HTMLInputFile control named uplFile.

5. Write a single statement that sends an email message from me@fiu.edu to you@fiu.edu with the subject "Grades" and the body "Your grades are ready for viewing".

6. Given a MailMessage object named myMsg, add a file attachment named "c:\classes\grades.htm".

▶8.13 Programming Challenges

1. **Computer Club Meeting**

   Write a program for a computer club that lets the user schedule a meeting date by selecting from a Calendar control, entering the meeting title as the message subject, and list of email addresses for the message recipients. (Multiple email addresses must be separated by semicolons.)

2. **Kayak Tour Scheduler**

   Using the Kayak Tour Scheduler program from Section 8.2 as a starting point, do the following:

   ◆ Do not permit two tours to be scheduled on the same date.

   ◆ Add a second Web page that displays all the tour dates as selections in a Calendar control.

3. **MailDemo with File Attachment**

   Improve the MailDemo program from Section 8.5 to allow the user to upload the file attachment from their own computer.

4. **MailDemo with Validation**

   Improve the MailDemo program from Section 8.5 by adding validation controls. Specifically, make sure that the From, To, and Subject fields are not blank. Also, verify that all email fields are correctly formatted.

5. **Pizzicato Music Store**

   Improve the Pizzicato Music Store presented in 8.8 by doing the following: Place a hyperlink on the Confirmation form that returns to the startup form. When the startup form reappears, it must display the user's existing order selections. In other words, use Session state variables to restore the list box items.

   Hints: You can save the Items collection of the list box in a Session variable, and then retrieve the variable when the startup form is loaded. You might want to use an exception handler to prevent a runtime error caused by a nonexistent session variable.

6. **Best Brew Coffee Shop**

   Start with your solution program for **Best Brew Coffee Shop Version 3** from Chapter 7. Make the following improvements:

   ◆ Fill the list box of drink types from a data-bound array. Use another array to hold the prices of the corresponding drinks (Figure 8-38).

   ◆ Use Session state variables to hold all information passed to the Receipt Web page (Figure 8-39). In other words, do not pass request parameters in the URL.

Figure 8-38   Best Brew Coffee Shop.

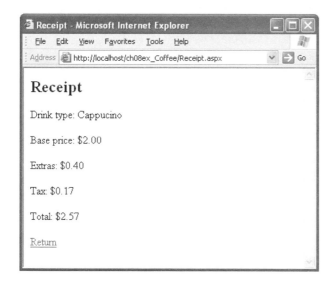

Figure 8-39   Displaying the receipt.

ASP.NET Databases

▶9.1 Using a DataReader

Reading Rows from a Table

ADO.NET permits databases to be accessed in *connected* mode, in which rows are read directly from a database. To do that, you must use a DataReader, an object that efficently reads data only in a forward direction. DataReaders are lightweight in that they do not keep a dataset in memory. For that reason, they are ideal when filling list-type controls on Web pages. By list-type controls, we can include the ListBox, DropDownList, CheckBoxList, RadioButtonList, Repeater, DataList, and DataGrid controls.

Datasets, nearly always used in desktop applications, consume valuable memory resources. Web pages automatically store datasets in ViewState, but doing so can greatly increase the time it takes to reload a Web page. DataReaders have three limitations:

1. No other processing can be done with the same Connection object until the DataReader is closed.

2. The rows can only be read in a forward direction, which causes the DataReader to be nicknamed a *firehose cursor*.

3. The rows are read-only, so you cannot modify the data.

Using a DataReader entails a few simple steps:

1. Open a Connection object.

2. Create a Command object, passing it a query string (or the name of a stored procedure) and a reference to the Connection.

3. Call the ExecuteReader method on the Command object. The return value is a DataReader object.

We are using generic names for Connection, Command, and DataReader. The actual class names depend on the type of connection:

Connection	Command	DataReader	Imports
SqlConnection	SqlCommand	SqlDataReader	System.Data.SqlClient
OleDbConnection	OleDbCommand	OleDbDataReader	System.Data.OleDb

The SqlDataReader and OleDbDataReader classes both implement the IDataReader and IDataRecord interfaces. SqlDataReader and OleDbDataReader share all the properties and methods defined in these two interfaces. Here are the essential ones:

♦ The **FieldCount** property returns the number of fields in the current row.

♦ The **Item** property returns a single column from the result set, identified by index position or column name.

♦ The **Close** method closes the DataReader, releasing the resources it was using.

♦ The **Read** method reads the next row in the query's result set. It returns True when a row is found and returns False when it reaches the end of the data.

Examples

Assuming we have have a connection to the pubs database named **conPubs**, the following lines open the connection and create a Command that gets two columns from the jobs table:

```
conPubs.Open()
Dim sql As String = "SELECT job_id, job_desc FROM jobs"
Dim cmd As New SqlCommand(sql, conPubs)
```

ExecuteReader executes the query and returns a DataReader:

```
Dim drJobs As SqlDataReader = cmd.ExecuteReader()
```

The Read method reads a single row from the database and returns a boolean value indicating whether or not more rows can be read:

```
drJobs.Read()
```

The following expression returns the number of fields (columns) in the current row:

```
drJobs.FieldCount
```

The following expression retrieves the job_id column from the current row:

```
drJobs.Item("job_id")
```

Item is the IDataReader's default property, so the following two expressions are equivalent:

```
drJobs.Item("job_id")
drJobs("job_id")
```

The following loop adds each job description from the jobs table to a list box:

```
Do While drJobs.Read()
    lstJobs.Items.Add(drJobs("job_desc"))
Loop
```

A loop is not required when filling a list box or any other list-type control. You can use data binding. Assign the DataReader to the control's DataSource property, and assign the column name to DataTextField:

```
With lstjobs
    .DataSource = drJobs
    .DataTextField = "job_desc"
    .DataBind()
End With
```

Keep a DataReader open only long enough to read the result set. The following statement closes the DataReader:

```
drJobs.Close()
```

When a DataReader is closed, its resources are released and the connection becomes available for other purposes. If you need to keep all rows in memory, one option is to copy them into a collection. Another option would be to use a dataset rather than a DataReader.

 If you pass a nonexistent column name to a DataReader's Item method, it throws an IndexOutOfRangeException.

DataReader Example

 DataReader

We will look at a short program that uses a DataReader to read the names of publishers from the pubs table. Names are displayed in a ListBox control (Figure 9-1). The following code is used in the Page_Load event handler:

```
Private Sub Page_Load(ByVal sender As System.Object, _
 ByVal e As System.EventArgs) Handles MyBase.Load

    If Not IsPostBack Then
       conPubs.Open()
       Dim sql As String = "SELECT pub_name FROM publishers "
       Dim cmd As New SqlCommand(sql, conPubs)
       Dim drPublishers As SqlDataReader = cmd.ExecuteReader()
       With lstPublishers
          .DataSource = drPublishers
          .DataTextField = "pub_name"
          .DataBind()
       End With
       drPublishers.Close()
       conPubs.Close()
    End If
End Sub
```

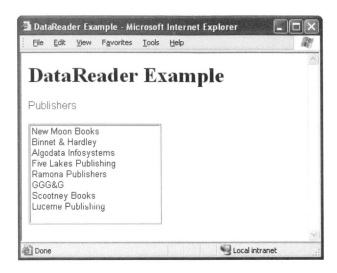

Figure 9-1 DataReaderTest output.

►9.2 CheckBoxList and RadioButtonList Controls

In Chapter 8, you learned how use the ListBox, DropDownList, CheckBoxList, and RadioButtonList controls. In addition, they can be data-bound to arrays, collections, and ArrayLists. We can expand their use by binding to datasets. A copy of the dataset is held in the form's ViewState property, which can cause efficiency concerns if the dataset is large. The RadioButtonList, CheckBoxList, ListBox, and DropDownList controls are all bound to dataset tables in the same manner, using the properties listed in Table 9-1.

Table 9-1

Properties used by List-Type controls for data binding.

Property	Description
DataSource	The DataSet or DataReader supplying the data.
DataMember	A DataTable object that exists within the DataSource.
DataTextField	Identifies the table column that will display in the Text properties of the buttons.
DataValueField	Column used to identify which row of the table the user selected.

Calling DataBind

If you modify a control's data binding properties, be sure to call its DataBind method. Following is an example that fills the lstPublishers ListBox from the the publishers table:

```
With lstPublishers
    .DataSource = DsPublishers1
    .DataMember = "publishers"
    .DataTextField = "pub_name"
    .DataValueField = "pub_id"
    .DataBind()
End With
```

Authors Example

Authors

Suppose we want to fill a DropDownList control with the first and last names of authors, sorted by last name. We can create a Command object, call its ExecuteReader method, and bind the reader to the DropDownList. When the user selects an author, we display the author's ID number. Sample program output is shown in Figure 9-2. The following SQL query retrieves the ID, first name, and last name of each author:

```
Dim cmd As SqlCommand = New SqlCommand( _
    "SELECT au_id, au_fname + ' ' + au_lname AS fullName " _
    & "FROM authors ORDER BY au_lname ", conPubs)
```

The following statements bind the ddlAuthors DropDownList to the DataReader:

```
conPubs.Open()
Dim reader As SqlDataReader = cmd.ExecuteReader()
With ddlAuthors
    .DataSource = reader
    .DataMember = "authors"
    .DataTextField = "fullName"
    .DataBind()
End With
reader.Close()
conPubs.Close()
```

When the user selects an author from the list, the following statement displays the author's ID number:

```
lblId.Text = ddlAuthors.SelectedValue
```

The program's complete source code appears in Code Listing 9-1.

Figure 9-2 Selecting authors.

Code Listing 9-1 (Authors Example)

```
Public Class Authors
    Inherits System.Web.UI.Page

+ Web Form Designer Generated Code

    Private Sub Page_Load(ByVal sender As System.Object, _
      ByVal e As System.EventArgs) Handles MyBase.Load

      If Not IsPostBack Then
          Dim cmd As SqlCommand = New SqlCommand( _
            "SELECT au_id, au_fname + ' ' + au_lname AS fullName " _
            & "FROM authors ORDER BY au_lname ", conPubs)

          conPubs.Open()
          Dim reader As SqlDataReader = cmd.ExecuteReader()
          With ddlAuthors
              .DataSource = reader
              .DataMember = "authors"
              .DataTextField = "fullName"
              .DataValueField = "au_id"
              .DataBind()
          End With
          reader.Close()
        conPubs.Close()
      End If

    End Sub

    Private Sub ddlAuthors_SelectedIndexChanged(ByVal sender As Object, _
      ByVal e As System.EventArgs) Handles ddlAuthors.SelectedIndexChanged

        lblId.Text = ddlAuthors.SelectedValue
    End Sub
End Class
```

Hands-On Tutorial: Kayak Types

 RadioButtonKayakTypes

We will create a short program that displays a list of kayak types (Figure 9-3). The user has selected one of the kayaks, and the label on the right side displays the kayak category ID. The radio button list is bound to a database table. A new database will be introduced, named KayakStore. Before starting this tutorial, take a few minutes to review the structure of this database. It is attached to your SQL Server instance, and is available as an MS-Access file in the c:\vbdata directory.

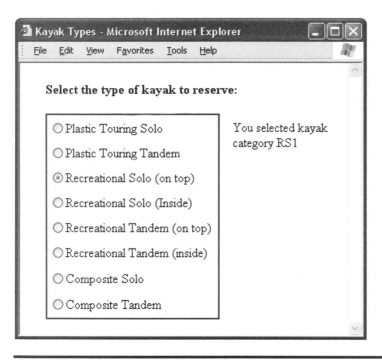

Figure 9-3 RadioButtonList showing kayak types.

Step 1. Create a new ASP.NET project named **RadioButtonKayakTypes**.

Step 2. Add a connection to the KayakStore database.

Step 3. Create a data adapter for the categories table named **daCategories** and use it to generate a dataset named **dsCategories**. The dataset variable will be named **DsCategories1**.

Step 4. Insert text on the Web form equal to "Select the type of kayak to reserve:". Use a bold font.

Step 5. Place a RadioButtonList control to the Web form and set the following property values:

Property	Value
ID	radKayakTypes
AutoPostBack	True
BorderStyle	Solid
BorderWidth	2px
BorderColor	Blue
DataSource	DsCategories1
DataMember	Categories
DataTextField	cat_name
DataValueField	cat_id

RadioButtonList controls do not automatically post back to the server when a selection is made. By setting the AutoPostBack property to true, we can change the default behavior.

Step 6. Insert the following code in the Page_Load event handler:

```
If Not IsPostBack Then
    daCategories.Fill(DsCategories1)
    radKayakTypes.DataBind()
End If
```

Step 7. Save and run the program. The radiobutton list should display the kayak types, and you can click each radio button to select a kayak type.

Next, you will display the category ID for the type of kayak selected by the user. A few modifications are required:

Step 8. Add a label named **lblCategory** to the right side of the radio button list.

Step 9. Add the following code to the SelectedIndexChanged event of radKayakTypes:

```
lblCategory.Text = "You selected kayak category " _
    & radKayakTypes.SelectedValue
```

Step 10. Run the program and select various kayak types from the list. As each is selected, you should see the selected kayak's cat_id value (such as PTS or RS1).

Notes on the RadioButton KayakTypes Example

You may be wondering why we had to check the value of IsPostBack in the Page_Load event handler. As an experiment, comment out the following If and EndIf statements and run the program again:

```
If Not IsPostBack Then                      'disabled
    daCategories.Fill(DsCategories1)
    radKayakTypes.DataBind()
'End If                                      'disabled
```

Now when you select a kayak type, the selection immediately disappears and the kayak's cat_id is blank. What happened? Clicking on the RadioButtonList posted the page to the server, and the Page_Load procedure executed. The dataset was filled again, and the existing radio button selection was cleared.

Not Posting Back

If your Web form consists of multiple lists and controls, you might not want to post the page back to the server every time the user selects a radio button. An alternative design to the program we just finished would be to set the RadioButtonList's AutoPostBack property to False. You could use a button on the form to post the page back when the user had finished making all selections.

▶9.3 Repeater Control

 Repeater

The Repeater control displays a list of data-bound items, with the option of adding formatting to each item. As we learned in the previous chapter, controls such as RadioButtonList and ListBox can be bound to arrays. The same is true of the Repeater control. What distinguishes the Repeater from many other controls is its ability to hold complex formatting expressions in containers called *templates*.

Example: Repeater Listing Kayak Types

Suppose we want to display a list of kayak types, taken from the categories table of the KayakStore database. The table contains two columns: **cat_id** (category ID), and **cat_name** (description of the kayak type). Figure 9-4 displays the cat_name column in a Repeater control. The data source can be a dataset or a DataReader. Each row displayed by the Repeater is called an *ItemTemplate*. Following is the item template for the current example, expressed in HTML:

```
<ItemTemplate>
   <li>
      <%# Container.DataItem("cat_name") %>
   </li>
</ItemTemplate>
```

The notation <li> is the HTML tag for a list item. The <%# tag begins a data-binding expression, and %> is the ending tag. The data-binding expression used in this example retrieves the cat_name column from the control's data source.

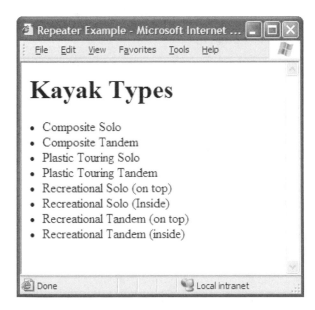

Figure 9-4 Repeater control listing types of kayaks.

When you insert a Repeater control on a form, it displays a message that directs you to the form's HTML view:

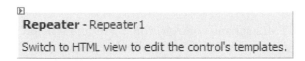

Editing HTML directly may be an unfamiliar skill for you, but if you're careful about punctuation, you should have no problem. In the long run, any competent ASP.NET programmer must be fluent in HTML. The following statement defines a Repeater control:

```
<asp:Repeater id="Repeater1" runat="server"></asp:Repeater>
```

Break the beginning and ending tags into separate lines so you can more easily insert other HTML statements:

```
<asp:Repeater id="Repeater1" runat="server">

</asp:Repeater>
```

Template definitions are inserted as shown here for an ItemTemplate:

```
<asp:Repeater id="Repeater1" runat="server">
   <ItemTemplate>
      <li>
       <%# Container.DataItem("cat_name") %>
      </li>
   </ItemTemplate>
</asp:Repeater>
```

You may want to use indentation to make the HTML easier to read. Code Listing 9-2 contains the complete source code for this program.

Code Listing 9-2 (Repeater – RadioButtons class)

```
Public Class RadioButtons
    Inherits System.Web.UI.Page

 +  Web Form Designer generated code

    Private Sub Page_Load(ByVal sender As System.Object, _
    ByVal e As System.EventArgs) Handles MyBase.Load

       Dim cmd As SqlCommand = New SqlCommand( _
           "SELECT * FROM categories", conKayakStore)
       conKayakStore.Open()
       Dim reader As SqlDataReader = cmd.ExecuteReader()
       rptCategories.DataSource = reader
       rptCategories.DataBind()
       reader.Close()
       conKayakStore.Close()
    End Sub
End Class
```

Using Multiple Controls

The ItemTemplate can contain any combination of HTML tags and controls. You might find it helpful to create the HTML tags and controls somewhere else on your form using the Visual Studio designer, and copy and paste the resulting HTML tag inside the repeater. In Figure 9-5, each template contains two text boxes and a check box. The template is defined here:

```
<ItemTemplate>
   <asp:TextBox id="txtId" runat="server"
    Text='<%# Container.DataItem("cat_id") %>' Width="34px"
    Font-Names="Arial" ForeColor="White" BackColor="Blue">
   </asp:TextBox> 
   <asp:TextBox id="txtName" runat="server"
      Text='<%# Container.DataItem("cat_name") %>' Width="200px"
      Font-Names="Arial" ForeColor="White" BackColor="Blue">
```

```
        </asp:TextBox> 
        <asp:CheckBox id="chkSelect" runat="server"></asp:CheckBox><br>
    </ItemTemplate>
```

In any event, the Repeater control gives you an excellent chance to develop your HTML skills.

Figure 9-5 Repeater template with TextBoxes and Checkbox.

Header and Footer Templates

The **HeaderTemplate** definition for a Repeater lets you define HTML tags that appear before the repeated items. The **FooterTemplate** defines tags that occur after the last repeated item. Combining these provides an excellent way to format Repeater items as an HTML table. For example, Figure 9-6 displays the list of kayak types in a table, using a blue background for the header row.

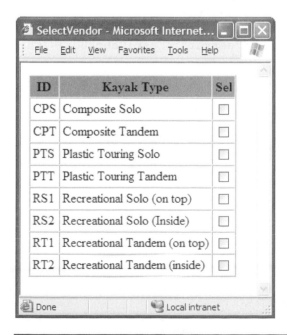

Figure 9-6 Repeater, using table form.

The <table> tag should appear in the HeaderTemplate, along with the table header. Here is the definition used in our example:

```
<HeaderTemplate>
   <table border="1" cellpadding="3" cellspacing="0">
    <tr bgcolor="#00A0FF">
     <th>ID</th>
     <th>Kayak Type</th>
     <th>Sel</th>
    </tr>
</HeaderTemplate>
```

The ItemTemplate definition should include the <tr> (table row) and <td> (table column) tags. Here is the one we used:

```
<ItemTemplate>
   <tr>
      <td><%# Container.DataItem("cat_id") %></td>
      <td><%# Container.DataItem("cat_name") %></td>
      <td><asp:CheckBox id="chkSel" runat="server"></asp:CheckBox></td>
   </tr>
</ItemTemplate>
```

The FooterTemplate definition closes the <table> tag begun inside the header template:

```
<FooterTemplate>
      </table>
</FooterTemplate>
```

The Repeater control's **AlternatingItemTemplate** can be used to change the formatting of alternating list items. Typically, the item's background color is changed to enhance the overall appearance. Following is an example that sets the background color of our sample program's alternating items to light blue:

```
<AlternatingItemTemplate>
   <tr bgcolor=#99ffff>
      <td><%# Container.DataItem("cat_id") %></td>
      <td><%# Container.DataItem("cat_name") %></td>
      <td><asp:CheckBox id="chkSel" runat="server"></asp:CheckBox></td>
   </tr>
</AlternatingItemTemplate>
```

You can find the examples in this section demonstrated in the program named **Repeater**.

▶9.4 DataList Control

The DataList control provides a flexible way to combine multiple controls into a data-bound sequence that repeats for each row of a dataset. It has a lot in common with the Repeater control, with one important difference: the DataList control generates events.

Templates

As we saw during the discussion of the Repeater control, templates provide an effective way to insert controls and formatting into each repeated row. They can be used to format headers and footers. Templates can be used in more ways, depending on the type of control. Table 9-2 shows how various template types are supported by the Repeater (RP), DataGrid (DG), and DataList (DL) controls.

Table 9-2

DataList template types.

Template Type	Description	RP	DG	DL
ItemTemplate	Formats the display of each row item.	X	X	X
AlternatingItemTemplate	Formats the display of alternating row items.	X		X
SeparatorTemplate	Formats the separators between items.	X		X
HeaderTemplate	Formats the heading row.	X	X	X
FooterTemplate	Formats the footer row.	X	X	X
SelectedItemTemplate	Formats items that have been selected.			X
EditItemTemplate	Formats items that are being edited.		X	X

If possible, set a DataList's EnableViewState property to False to allow the Web form to load more quickly. You will most likely have to refresh the dataset every time the form posts back.

The DataList control has a **SelectedIndex** property that sets or returns the index of the currently selected row. If you assign a value, the row becomes selected. In a DataList named dlAuthors, for example, the following statement selects row 2:

```
dlAuthors.SelectedIndex = 2
```

When a list row is selected, the DataList's SelectedItemTemplate is displayed. Any formatting or controls in the template becomes visible.

Handling Events

The **ItemCommand** event handler executes when the user clicks on a button embedded within a DataList template. The handler has a parameter named **e** containing important information about the selected item:

```
Private Sub dlAuthors_ItemCommand(ByVal source As Object, _
    ByVal e As System.Web.UI.WebControls.DataListCommandEventArgs) _
    Handles dlStores.ItemCommand
```

The **Item.ItemIndex** property, for example, returns the current row index of the selected item. If we assign the index value to the SelectedIndex property, the DataList's SelectedItemTemplate will become visible:

```
dlAuthors.SelectedIndex = e.Item.ItemIndex
```

DataKeys

The DataList control has a **DataKeyField** property that identifies a column in the data source as a unique identifier for each row. For example, we would probably select the **au_id** field from the authors table:

```
dlAuthors.DataKeyField = "au_id"
```

The DataList control contains an array of these key values named **DataKeys**. The following expression returns the au_id value from row 3:

```
dlAuthors.DataKeys(3)
```

Example: Stores and Book Titles

DataList

We will create a program that displays a list of bookstore names in a DataList control. We will create a data-bound ItemTemplate for each bookstore's name and address. A SelectedItemTemplate will display a DropDownList of books sold by the store. The program uses data from the stores, sales, and titles tables in the pubs database. The table relationships are shown in Figure 9-7. Figure 9-8 shows the program at startup. Each entry contains the store name, store address, and a Select button (LinkButton control).

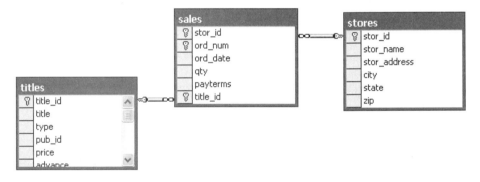

Figure 9-7 Stores, sales, and titles table relationships.

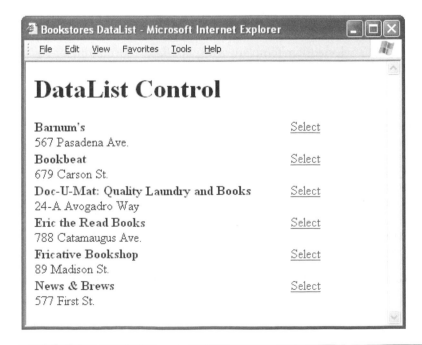

Figure 9-8 Displaying bookstores in a DataList.

When the user selects an item (Figure 9-9), the SelectedItemTemplate activates, showing two horizontal rules (lines), the store name, and a ComboBox containing all books from the **sales** table sold by the selected bookstore. If the user selects a different bookstore, the DataList displays a combo box for the new bookstore (Figure 9-10).

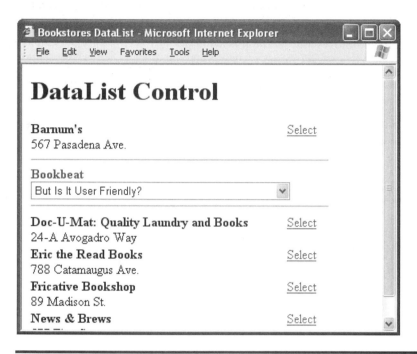

Figure 9-9 Selected item contains list of book titles.

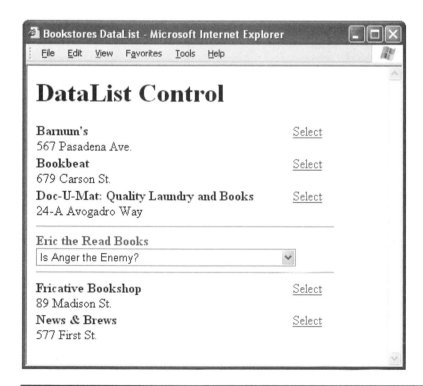

Figure 9-10 Selecting a different bookstore.

Implementation

Step 1. Create ASP.NET Web application named **DataList**.

Step 2. On the startup form, create a data adapter named **daStores** and a dataset named **dsStores** (DsStores1) for the stores table in the pubs database. Sort on the **stor_name** column. Include the **stor_id** column in the SQL query.

Step 3. Add a DataList control named **dlStores** and set the following properties: EnableViewState = False; DataSource = DsStores1; DataMember = stores; DataKeyField = stor_id.

Step 4. Insert a Label control named **lblMessage** on the form just below the DataList. Set its foreground color to red.

Step 5. Right-click on dlStores and select **Edit Template**, then select **Item Templates**. In the ItemTemplate area, insert a Label named lblStoreName, a Label named lblAddress, and a LinkButton control named lnkSelect. For the latter, set Text = Select.

Step 6. Select the DataBindings property of **lblStoreName** by selecting **stor_name** from the DataItem category under the Container category (Figure 9-11).

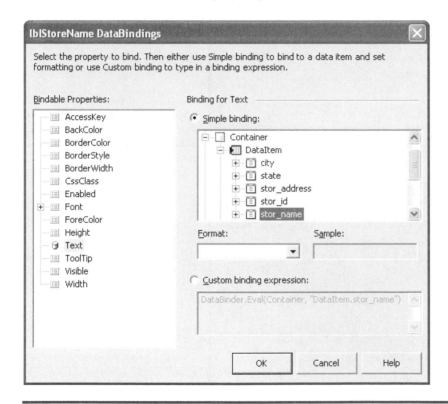

Figure 9-11 DataBindings property of lblStoreName.

Step 7. Using the DataBindings property of **lblAddress**, bind it to **stor_address**. Right-click on the DataList and select **End Template Editing**.

Step 8. Add the following lines to the Page_Load event handler:

```
daStores.Fill(DsStores1)
dlStores.DataBind()
```

We did not include the `If Not IsPostBack` statement because this code should execute each time the form is posted back. The datalist will need to be refreshed when the user clicks on any of the Select buttons.

Step 9. Run and test the program. You should see the list of store names in the DataList control. Clicking on the Select link doesn't do anything yet.

In the next part of this tutorial, you will create a data adapter that joins the sales and titles tables from the pubs database. You will create a template in the DataList for selected items, and bind the template to a dataset.

Step 10. Create a data adapter named **daSales** that joins the sales and titles tables. It should have a single query parameter named **@stor_id**:

```
SELECT titles.title
FROM sales INNER JOIN
     titles ON sales.title_id = titles.title_id
WHERE (sales.stor_id = @stor_id)
ORDER BY titles.title
```

Step 11. Create a dataset from daSales named **dsSales** (variable name: DsSales1).

Step 12. Create a template for selected items by right-clicking on the DataList control and selecting **Item Templates**. In the SelectedItemTemplate area, insert a Label control and bind it to the **stor_name** field. Insert a DropDownList control and set the following properties: DataSource = DsSales1; DataMember = sales; DataTextField = title.

Step 13. Locate the **Horizontal Rule** control from the HTML section of the ToolBox. Insert one rule before the Label control and insert the other rule after the DropDownList. Right-click on the DataList and select **End Template Editing**.

Step 14. In the form's code window, create the following **ItemCommand** event handler for the DataList:

```
1:    Private Sub dlStores_ItemCommand(ByVal source As Object, _
2:      ByVal e As System.Web.UI.WebControls.DataListCommandEventArgs) _
3:      Handles dlStores.ItemCommand
4:
5:      Try
6:         'Cause the SelectedItemTemplate to display
7:         dlStores.SelectedIndex = e.Item.ItemIndex
8:         'Use the store ID to fill a dropdown list with book titles.
9:         Dim storeId As Integer = CInt(dlStores.DataKeys(e.Item.ItemIndex))
10:         daSales.SelectCommand.Parameters("@stor_id").Value = storeId
11:         daSales.Fill(DsSales1)
12:         dlStores.DataBind()
13:      Catch ex As Exception
14:         lblMessage.Text = ex.Message
15:      End Try
16:    End Sub
```

Line 9 gets the store's ID number from the DataKeys collection, using the selected item's row number (stored in e.Item.ItemIndex). Line 10 assigns the store ID to the query parameter for the daSales data adapter's SelectCommand. Line 11 fills the dataset, and Line 12 binds the dataset to the DataList control. At runtime, the dropdown list in the SelectedItemTemplate should contain a list of book titles matching the selected Store ID number (books sold by the store).

Step 15. Run and test the program. Select different stores, and notice that the dropdown list of book titles is different for each store. If you want to test the program's error-handling, modify the name of the @stor_id parameter inside the ItemCommand event handler and run the program again.

(End of tutorial. The complete source code is shown in Code Listing 9-3.)

Code Listing 9-3 (DataList program)

```
Public Class WebForm1
    Inherits System.Web.UI.Page

    + Web Form Designer generated code

    Private Sub Page_Load(ByVal sender As System.Object, _
       ByVal e As System.EventArgs) Handles MyBase.Load

       'This code must also execute during postbacks:
       daStores.Fill(DsStores1)
       dlStores.DataBind()
    End Sub

    Private Sub dlStores_ItemCommand(ByVal source As Object, _
     ByVal e As System.Web.UI.WebControls.DataListCommandEventArgs) _
      Handles dlStores.ItemCommand

      Try
          'Cause the SelectedItemTemplate to display
          dlStores.SelectedIndex = e.Item.ItemIndex
          'Use the store ID to fill a dropdown list with book titles.
          Dim storeId As Integer = CInt(dlStores.DataKeys(e.Item.ItemIndex))
          daSales.SelectCommand.Parameters("@stor_id").Value = storeId
          daSales.Fill(DsSales1)
          dlStores.DataBind()
      Catch ex As Exception
          lblMessage.Text = ex.Message
      End Try
    End Sub
End Class
```

Checkpoint

9.1 Name at least one template type supported by the DataList control, but not supported by the Repeater control.

9.2 Which DataList property, when set, causes the SelectedItemTemplate to appear?

9.3 Which DataList property identifies a column in the data source as a unique identifier for each row?

9.4 In the DataList program that displays store names, if you set the DataList's EnableViewState property to True and changed the code in Page_Load to the following,

```
If Not IsPostBack Then
  daStores.Fill(DsStores1)
  dlStores.DataBind()
End If
```

What effect would these changes have on the program's behavior?

▶9.5 DataGrid Control

The Web Forms DataGrid control is a counterpart to the WinForms DataGrid. Though the two controls look similar, they vary considerably in their details. Table 9-3 lists properties common to the two controls. Table 9-4, on the other hand, lists Web DataGrid properties which have no counterpart in the WinForms DataGrid.

Table 9-3

DataGrid properties common to Web and Win forms.

Property	Description
AllowSorting	If True, permits the user to sort on any column.
DataSource	Object containing a list of values used to populate the control.
DataMember	A specific member of a multimember data source that will be bound to the grid.
BorderStyle	Style of border displayed around the control.
Enabled	Determines whether the user can interact with the control.
Visible	Determines whether the control shows on the form.

Table 9-4

Unique Web DataGrid properties.

Property	Description
AllowPaging	If True, allows the user to view individual pages of data rather than the entire rowset.
Columns	Collection of objects representing the displayed columns.
CurrentPageIndex	Index of the currently displayed page.
DataKeyField	The key field in the dataset specified by the DataSource property.
DataKeys	A collection of key values of each record (displayed as a row) in the control.
FooterStyle, HeaderStyle	Styles associated with grid footer and header.
Items	Collection of DataGridItem objects representing the individual items in the DataGrid control.
SelectedIndex	Index of the currently selected Item.
SelectedItem	A DataGridItem object representing the selected item.
ShowFoooter, ShowHeader	Indicates whether the footer and header will be displayed.

Use the DataKeyField property to identify the record key of the table loaded into the grid. If the user selects a row from the grid by clicking on a Delete, Edit, or Select button, the index of the selected row can be used to retrieve the record key value of the row. Suppose the grid **dgrCourses** displays the **courses** table, for which the record key is named **courseid**. We would set DataKeyField in this way:

```
dgrCourses.DataKeyField = "courseid"
```

The following expression would return the course ID stored in row 3 of the grid:

```
dgrCourses.DataKeys(3)
```

Filling a DataGrid

The DataSource property typically holds DataTable, DataView, and DataSet objects. Any object type that implements either the IListSource or IList interface can be assigned to DataSource. For example, a DataGrid named dgrAuthors is bound to a dataset named DsAuthors1 using the following statement:

```
dgrAuthors.DataSource = DsAuthors1
```

The following binds a DataView control named dvAuthors to the same grid:

```
dgrAuthors.DataSource = dvAuthors
```

If the dataset contains more than one table, assign a table name to the grid's DataMember property:

```
dgrAuthors.DataMember = "authors"
```

To fill a DataGrid, you must also fill the bound dataset and call the DataBind method on the grid:

```
daEmployee.Fill(DsAuthors1)
dgrAuthors.DataBind()
```

If you have several controls to bind on the same form, you can write a single call to the form's DataBind method:

```
Me.DataBind()
```

Column Formatting

A DataGrid can be automatically formatted to the default column order in the dataset (Figure 9-12). The result is a little rough, so you may prefer to create a custom format. You can specify the set of columns and their order, using the Property Builder tool. To launch Property Builder, right-click on the grid, select **Property Builder** and select the **Columns** page by clicking in the list on the left side of the dialog. Figure 9-13 shows sample column definitions for the employee table.

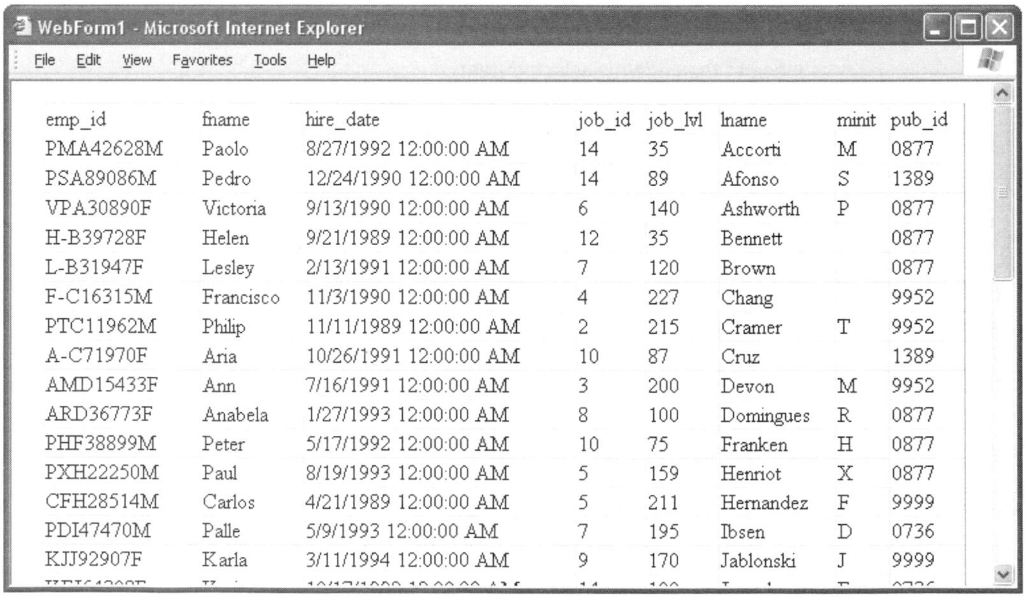

Figure 9-12 Employee table DataGrid (default columns).

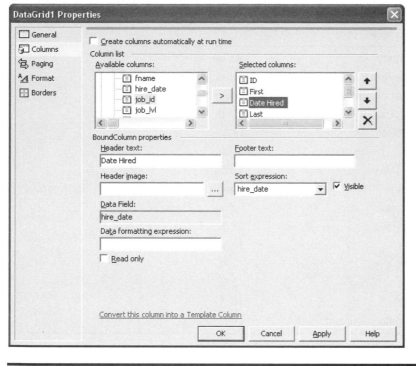

Figure 9-13 Setting DataGrid column properties.

Employee DataGrid Example

DataGridExample

We will show a program that fills a grid from the employee table in the pubs database. We will format the columns, sort the grid on any column, and divide the grid items into pages. Figure 9-14 shows a preliminary version of the program, with formatted columns. Table 9-5 lists the column properties used.

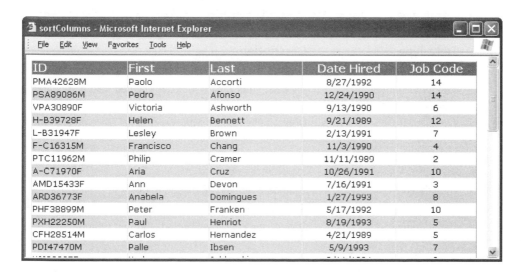

ID	First	Last	Date Hired	Job Code
PMA42628M	Paolo	Accorti	8/27/1992	14
PSA89086M	Pedro	Afonso	12/24/1990	14
VPA30890F	Victoria	Ashworth	9/13/1990	6
H-B39728F	Helen	Bennett	9/21/1989	12
L-B31947F	Lesley	Brown	2/13/1991	7
F-C16315M	Francisco	Chang	11/3/1990	4
PTC11962M	Philip	Cramer	11/11/1989	2
A-C71970F	Aria	Cruz	10/26/1991	10
AMD15433F	Ann	Devon	7/16/1991	3
ARD36773F	Anabela	Domingues	1/27/1993	8
PHF38899M	Peter	Franken	5/17/1992	10
PXH22250M	Paul	Henriot	8/19/1993	5
CFH28514M	Carlos	Hernandez	4/21/1989	5
PDI47470M	Palle	Ibsen	5/9/1993	7

Figure 9-14 Employee DataGrid with custom formatting.

Table 9-5

Column properties in the DataGridExample program.

Column	Property	Value
(all)	HeaderText	(shown in Figure)
DateHired	Data formatting expression	{0:d}
Header	ForeColor	White
Header	BackColor	Gray
Header	Font	Bold
Normal items	Font name	Verdana
Normal items	Font size	Smaller
Alternating items	BackColor	Aqua
ID column	Width	12 %
First column	Width	10 %
Last column	Width	12 %
Date Hired column	Width	12 %
Job Code column	Width	10 %
Date Hired, Job Code	Horizontal alignment	Center

Formatting Expressions in DataGrid Columns

The DateHired column in Table 9-5 contains the formatting expression {0:d}, which produces a short date format in the form mm/dd/yy. A rich set of formatting expressions may be used in DataGrid columns. To specify a formatting expression for any column in a data grid, select the **Columns** sheet in the grid's Property Builder window. The formatting expression must be appropriate for the type of column data. Table 9-6 contains a number of sample formatting expressions. Note that {0} is the digit zero and not the letter O. To read about format expressions in more detail, look for "Formatting types" in the .NET Framework documentation.

Table 9-6

Sample formatting expressions.

Format Expression	Data Type	Description
Price: {0:C}	numeric/decimal	Displays the literal "Price:" followed by numbers in currency format.
{0:D4}	integer (cannot be used with decimal numbers.)	Integers are displayed in a zero-padded field four characters wide.
{0:N2}%	numeric	Displays the number with two-decimal place precision followed by the literal "%".
{0:000.0}	numeric/decimal	Numbers rounded to one decimal place. Numbers less than three digits are zero padded.
{0:D}	date/datetime	Long date format ("Thursday, August 06, 1996").
{0:d}	date/datetime	Short date format ("12/31/99").
{0:yy-MM-dd}	date/datetime	Date in numeric year-month-day format (96-08-06).

Manipulating Columns

The DataGrid class makes it easy to manipulate the appearance of DataGrid columns at runtime. You might, for example, want to hide certain DataGrid columns from users who should not view sensitive information. The following statement changes the caption of column 0 in the dgrEmployee grid. The change does not show until a postback occurs:

```
dgrEmployee.Columns(0).HeaderText = "Employee ID"
```

The following example hides column 2 in the dgrEmployee grid if the person's user (security) level is less than 3:

```
If userLevel < 3 Then
    dgrEmployee.Columns(2).Visible = False
EndIf
```

Sorting a DataGrid

To sort a grid, bind it to a DataView control and set the latter's Sort property in design mode or at runtime. Set the DataView's **Table** property to the name of the dataset table (in our case, *employee*). If you want to allow users to sort on any column by clicking on its heading, set the data grid's **AllowSorting** property to True. Create a **SortCommand** event handler to modify the DataView's Sort property. For example, suppose a grid named **dgrEmployee** is attached to a DataView named **dvEmployee.** The following implementation of the SortCommand handler assigns the SortExpression property of the parameter **e** to the DataView's Sort property:

```
Private Sub dgrEmployee_SortCommand(ByVal source As Object, _
    ByVal e As System.Web.UI.WebControls.DataGridSortCommandEventArgs) _
    Handles dgrEmployee.SortCommand

    dvEmployee.Sort = e.SortExpression
    Me.DataBind()
End Sub
```

You must call DataBind, which posts the page back to the server and refreshes the grid. In Figure 9-15, the user has clicked on the ID column header.

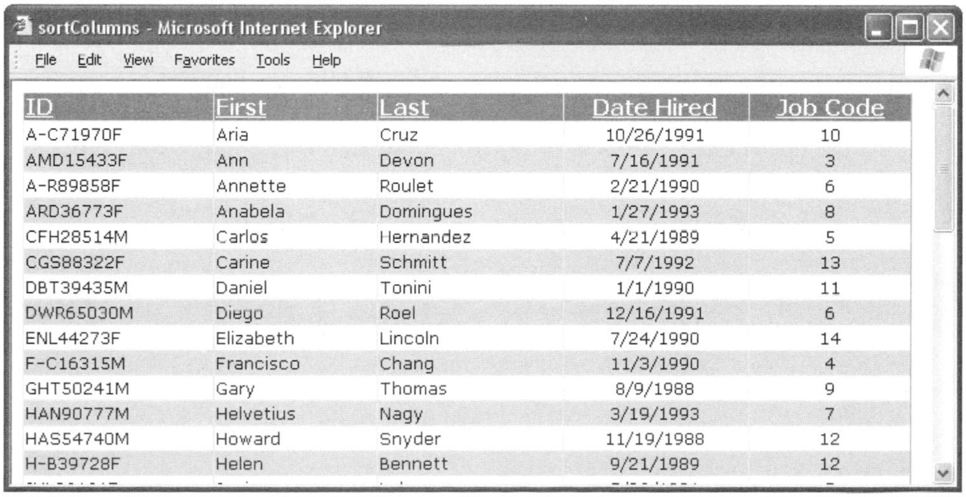

Figure 9-15 Sorting on the ID column.

Paging a DataGrid

When a grid is filled from a dataset, the grid contents are encoded into a hidden field in the HTML sent to the client's browser. Here is an example:

```
<input type="hidden" name="__VIEWSTATE" value=
"dDwtMTI1NDM3ODk4Njt0PDtsPGk8MT47PjtsPHQ8O2w8aTwxPjs+O2w8dDxAMDxwPHA8bDxQYWdlIQ
291bnQ7XyFJdGVtQ291bnQ7XyFEYXRhU291cmNlSXRlbUNvdW50O0RhdGFLZXlzOz47bDxpPDE+O2k
8NDM+O2k8NDM+O2w8Pjs+Pjs+Ozs7Ozs7Ozs7Oz47bDxpPDA+Oz47bDx0PDtsPGk8MT47aTwyPjtpPP
DM+O2k8ND47aTw1PjtpPDY+O2k8Nz47aTw4PjtpPDk+O2k8MTA+O2k8MTE+O2k8MTI+O2k8MTM+O2k
8MTQ+O2k8MTU+O2k8MTY+O2k8MTc+O2k8MTg+O2k8MTk+O2k8MjA+O2k8MjE+O2k8MjI+O2k8MjM+O
2k8MjQ+O2k8MjU+O2k8MjY+O2k8Mjc+O2k8Mjg+O2k8Mjk+O2...etc.
```

If the dataset filling a grid is large, it may take some time to send back an HTML page with all of the data. The user would be forced to scroll the window to see the data. If you prefer not to display too much data at once, you can enable grid paging. In Figure 9-16, only ten rows display at a time, and page numbers are displayed at the bottom. The hidden HTML field only contains the rows shown on the current page. Users can see that the dataset contains about fifty rows, and they can jump to any selected page.

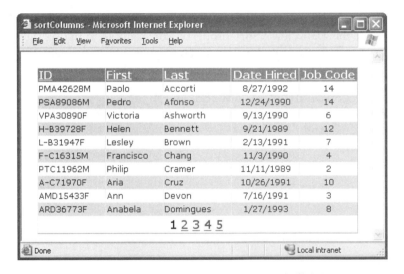

Figure 9-16 DataGrid with paging enabled

To enable paging in a DataGrid, open the Property Builder window for the grid and select **Paging** (Figure 9-17). Check the **Allow Paging** option, which sets the grid's AllowPaging property to True. Optionally, you can set **Mode**, which lets you choose either page numbers or next/previous buttons. The Position property has three options: top, bottom, and top & bottom. You can set the Page size to the number of rows you want to display (the default is 10).

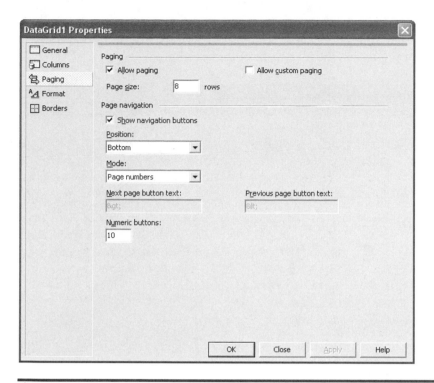

Figure 9-17 Setting the paging properties.

Event Handler

To enable paging, you must create a **PageIndexChanged** event handler for the grid. The argument named **e** has a property named **NewPageIndex** you can use to modify the grid's page index:

```
Private Sub dgrEmployee_PageIndexChanged(ByVal source As System.Object, _
    ByVal e As System.Web.UI.WebControls.DataGridPageChangedEventArgs)

    dgrEmployee.CurrentPageIndex = e.NewPageIndex
    Me.DataBind()
End Sub
```

This code shows that runtime code can modify the grid's CurrentPageIndex at any time. You can format the hyperlinks placed on the form when paging is enabled. Figure 9-18 shows the Property Builder's **Format** page, which lets you set the colors, font properties, and alignment of the hyperlinks.

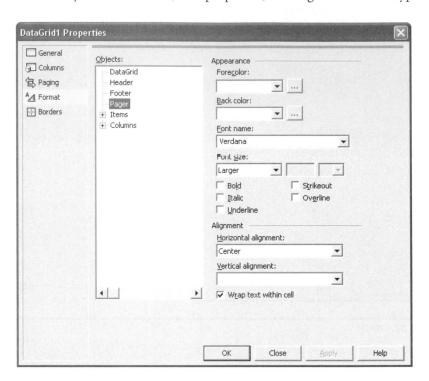

Figure 9-18 Formatting the paging hyperlinks.

Changing Paging Options at Run Time

All paging options are visible in the grid's property window under the **PagerStyle** property. You may at times want to set the PagerStyle property options at run time. For example, the following changes the PagerStyle.Mode from numeric page numbers to next/previous symbols (< and >):

```
dgrEmployee.PagerStyle.Mode = PagerMode.NextPrev
Me.DataBind( )
```

The complete source code for the Employee DataGrid Example program appears in Code Listing 9-4.

Code Listing 9-4 (Employee DataGrid Example)

```
Public Class EmployeeDataGrid
    Inherits System.Web.UI.Page

+ Web Form Designer generated code

    Private Sub Page_Load(ByVal sender As System.Object, _
     ByVal e As System.EventArgs) Handles MyBase.Load

        daEmployee.Fill(DsEmployee1)
        dgrEmployee.DataBind()
    End Sub

    Private Sub btnMode_Click(ByVal sender As System.Object, _
     ByVal e As System.EventArgs)

        dgrEmployee.PagerStyle.Mode = PagerMode.NextPrev
```

```
        dgrEmployee.DataBind()
    End Sub

    Private Sub dgrEmployee_SortCommand(ByVal source As System.Object, _
      ByVal e As System.Web.UI.WebControls.DataGridSortCommandEventArgs) _
        Handles dgrEmployee.SortCommand

        dvEmployee.Sort = e.SortExpression
        dgrEmployee.DataBind()
    End Sub

    Private Sub dgrEmployee_PageIndexChanged(ByVal source As System.Object, _
      ByVal e As System.Web.UI.WebControls.DataGridPageChangedEventArgs) _
        Handles dgrEmployee.PageIndexChanged

        dgrEmployee.CurrentPageIndex = e.NewPageIndex
        dgrEmployee.DataBind()
    End Sub
End Class
```

Checkpoint

9.5 Which DataGrid property specifies the key field in the dataset specified by the grid's DataSource property?

9.6 Which DataGrid property returns an object that represents the currently selected row?

9.7 If a dataset connected to a DataGrid contains more than one table, which property identifies the correct table?

9.8 In addition to calling the data adapter's Fill method, which other method must be called in order to fill a DataGrid?

▶9.6 Adding Buttons to DataGrids

One of the most useful features of the DataGrid control is its ability to display one or more buttons in each row. The standard button types are Cancel, Delete, Select, Edit, and Update. When the user clicks on a button embedded in a grid row, one of several events are fired (Table 9-7).

Table 9-7

DataGrid button event types

Event	Description
CancelCommand	Occurs when the Cancel button is clicked for a DataGrid item.
DeleteCommand	Occurs when the Delete button is clicked for a DataGrid item.
EditCommand	Occurs when the Edit button is clicked for a DataGrid item.
ItemCommand	Occurs when any custom command button is clicked for a DataGrid item. Fired, for example, when the user clicks on the Select button.
UpdateCommand	Occurs when the Update button is clicked for a DataGrid item.

Delete Button

Buttons are inserted into a grid from its Property Builder window, in the Columns pane. In Figure 9-19, we have selected **Delete** under the **Button Column** heading in the **Available columns** list. When the arrow pointing right is clicked, the button is copied into the **Selected columns** list. We can then customize the button's appearance by altering the ButtonColumn properties.

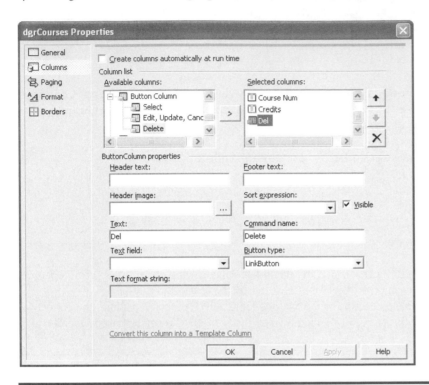

Figure 9-19 Creating the Delete button column.

You can create an ItemCommand event handler to respond to button clicks in the grid rows:

```
Private Sub dgrCourses_ItemCommand(ByVal source As Object, _
  ByVal e As System.Web.UI.WebControls.DataGridCommandEventArgs) _
    Handles dgrCourses.ItemCommand
```

The parameter named **e** holds important information about the grid row containing the clicked button. Here are its properties:

Property	Description
CommandArgument	Gets the argument for the command.
CommandName	Gets the name of the command.
CommandSource	Gets the source of the command.
Item	Gets the DataGridItem containing the clicked button.

CommandName identifies the command string associated with the clicked button. If each grid row contains multiple buttons, the event handler uses a Select Case statement to identify the current Command name. In the following example, the ItemCommand handler for the dgrCourses grid uses e.CommandName to determine which button was clicked:

```
Private Sub dgrCourses_ItemCommand(ByVal source As Object, _
  ByVal e As System.Web.UI.WebControls.DataGridCommandEventArgs) _
    Handles dgrCourses.ItemCommand

    Select Case e.CommandName
        Case "Delete"
            'delete the current row
        Case "Select"
            'select the current row
        Case "Edit"
            'edit the current row
    End Select
```

Selecting Grid Items (Select Button)

A DataGrid column can contain Select buttons, represented as hyperlinks or button controls. If you add a Select button to each row of a DataGrid, use the ItemCommand event handler to carry out actions related to selecting grid rows. The e.Item property holds the currently selected grid row (a DataGridItem). The e.Item.ItemIndex property returns the index of the selected grid row:

```
Dim item As DataGridItem = e.Item
Dim index As Integer = e.Item.ItemIndex
```

If you need to get the contents of one of the columns within a grid row, use the Cells property, which returns a TableCell object. The following expression returns the contents of column 0 as a String:

```
e.Item.Cells(0).Text
```

The Items property of a DataGrid contains all of the rows. The following, for example, returns the contents of the first grid row:

```
Dim item As DataGridItem = dgrCourses.Items(0)
```

If a dataset is attached to the grid, you can use the ItemIndex to obtain the matching dataset row (a DataRow object):

```
Dim row As DataRow
row = DsCourses1.courses.Rows(e.Item.ItemIndex)
```

Using the DataRow object, you can iterate over the column values, stored in the ItemArray array:

```
Dim column As Object
For Each column In row.ItemArray
    '...
Next
```

You can highlight the selected row by changing its background color and font style. Using the row's Controls collection, you can hide individual columns:

```
With e.item
   .BackColor = System.Drawing.Color.Cyan
   .Font.Bold = True
   'Hide the first column.
   .Controls(0).Visible = False
End With
```

Hands-On Tutorial: Deleting College Courses

GridButtons

The campus database introduced in Chapter 6 contains a table named **courses**. Each row contains information about a college course, including its ID number, year, semester, course number, and number of credits. We will create a program containing a DataGrid that displays the course table, and add a column containing Delete buttons (Figure 9-20). When the user clicks on a button, the course is removed from the table (Figure 9-21).

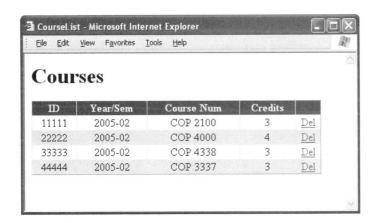

Figure 9-20 Displaying the course list.

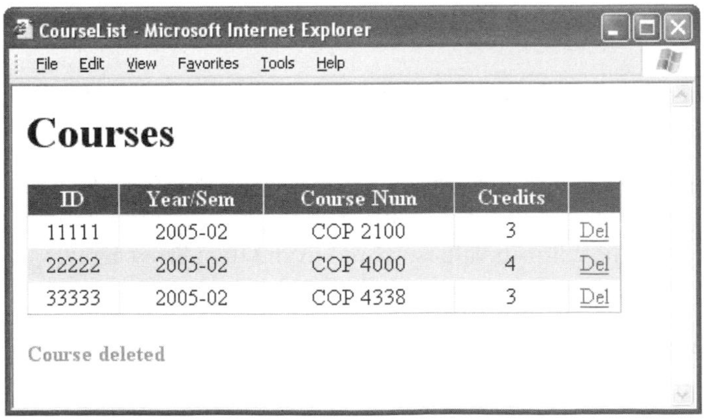

Figure 9-21 After deleting a course.

Before You Begin

You may have deleted the courses table when running the College_Courses application in Chapter 6. If so, run the program again and create the courses table in the campus database. Using Enterprise Manager (or Server Explorer), add a few extra rows to the table.

Begin the Tutorial

Step 1. Create a Web Forms application named **GridButtons**.

Step 2. Create a connection named **conCampus** and a data adapter named **daCourses**. Generate a dataset class named **dsCourses**. Name the dataset object **DsCourses1**.

Step 3. In FlowLayout mode, add the title "Courses" to the form, using style Heading 1.

Step 4. Add a DataGrid control to the form and name it **dgrCourses**.

Step 5. Add a label control to the form and name it **lblMessage**. Set the ForeColor property to Red, and set Font.Bold to True.

Step 6. Right-click on the DataGrid and select **Property Builder**. In the **General** pane, assign the following properties:

Property	Value
DataSource	DsCourses1
DataMember	courses
DataKeyField	courseid

Step 7. In the Columns view of the Property Builder, uncheck the *Create columns automatically at run time* option and add the columns manually. Use Figure 9-20 (shown earlier) as a guide.

Step 8. Select the Columns pane. Select **Delete** under the *Button Column* heading in the *Available columns* list. Transfer the column to the *Selected columns* list.

Step 9. Select the Format pane and configure the headings, columns, and detail lines so they resemble Figure 9-20.

Code Window

Step 10. Insert the following lines in the Page_Load handler:

```
daCourses.Fill(DsCourses1)
dgrCourses.DataBind()
```

Step 11. Create a **DeleteCommand** event handler for dgrCourses. DeleteCommand is not the default event, so select dgrCourses from the ClassName list, and select DeleteCommand from the Method Name list.

Step 12. Add the following code to the DeleteCommand event handler:

```
Try
    conCampus.Open()
    Dim cmd As SqlCommand = New SqlCommand("DELETE FROM courses " _
        & "WHERE courseid = @courseid", conCampus)
    With cmd
        .Parameters.Add("@courseid", _
            dgrCourses.DataKeys(e.Item.ItemIndex))
        .ExecuteNonQuery()
    End With
    lblMessage.Text = "Course deleted"
    'Refresh the grid.
    DsCourses1.Clear()
    daCourses.Fill(DsCourses1)
    dgrCourses.DataBind()
Catch ex As Exception
    lblMessage.Text = ex.Message
Finally
    If conCampus.State = ConnectionState.Open Then conCampus.Close()
End Try
```

Step 13. Save and run the program. Test the program by deleting one or two courses.

(End of tutorial. The complete program source code appears in Code Listing 9-5.)

Code Listing 9-5 (CourseList form, GridButtons example)

```
Public Class CourseList
    Inherits System.Web.UI.Page

    + Web Form Designer generated code

    Private Sub Page_Load(ByVal sender As System.Object, _
        ByVal e As System.EventArgs) Handles MyBase.Load

        daCourses.Fill(DsCourses1)
        dgrCourses.DataBind()
    End Sub

    Private Sub dgrCourses_DeleteCommand(ByVal source As Object, _
        ByVal e As System.Web.UI.WebControls.DataGridCommandEventArgs) _
        Handles dgrCourses.DeleteCommand

        Try
            conCampus.Open()
            Dim cmd As SqlCommand = New SqlCommand("DELETE FROM courses " _
                & "WHERE courseid = @courseid", conCampus)
            With cmd
                .Parameters.Add("@courseid", _
                    dgrCourses.DataKeys(e.Item.ItemIndex))
                .ExecuteNonQuery()
            End With
```

```
        lblMessage.Text = "Course deleted"
        'Refresh the grid.
        DsCourses1.Clear()
        daCourses.Fill(DsCourses1)
        dgrCourses.DataBind()
    Catch ex As Exception
        lblMessage.Text = ex.Message
    Finally
        If conCampus.State = ConnectionState.Open Then conCampus.Close()
    End Try
    End Sub
End Class
```

Jobs/Employee DataGrid Example

JobsEmployeeGrid

The Jobs/Employee DataGrid program demonstrates a simple way to display related tables in separate DataGrid controls. The program begins by displaying a list of job descriptions in a DataGrid along with Select buttons (Figure 9-22). When the user clicks on the Select button next to a job description, all employees who have a matching Job ID are displayed in a second grid (Figure 9-23). The relevant job category conveniently displays above the list of employees.

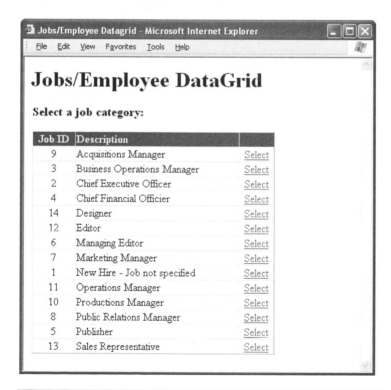

Figure 9-22   Listing the job categories.

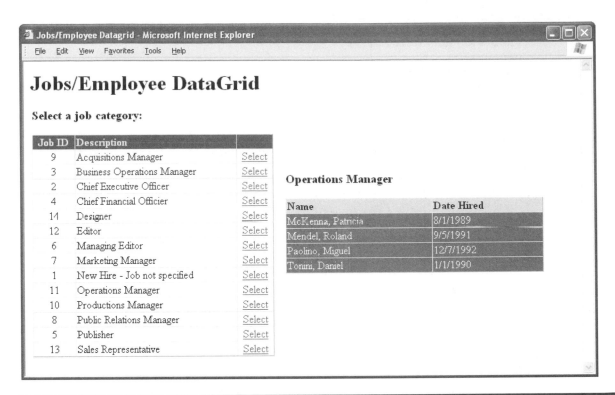

Figure 9-23 Selecting the Operations Manager category.

Implementation

The program's form is designed in flow layout mode (Figure 9-24), using a table that holds two Panel controls. The Panel control for the employees grid can be hidden or displayed, depending on whether any matching employees are found.

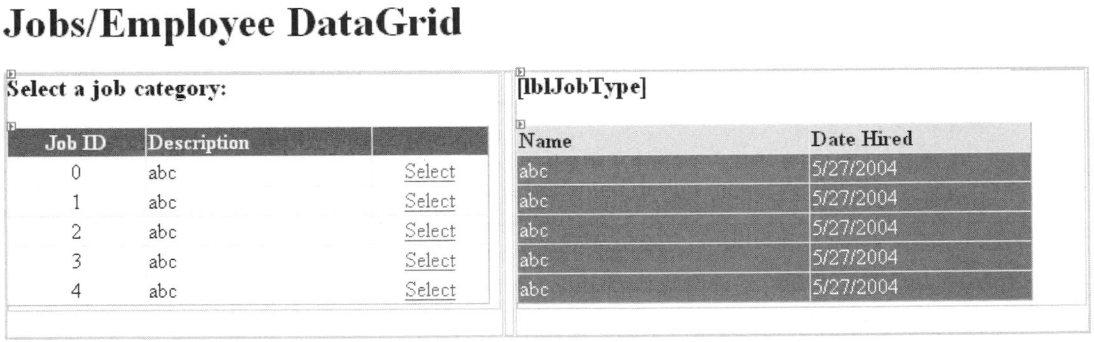

Jobs/Employee DataGrid

Figure 9-24 Design mode.

The program uses the following data components:

Component	Description
conPubs	Connection to the pubs database.
daJobs	Data adapter for the jobs table.
DsJobs1	DataSet object that holds the jobs table.
daEmployee	Data adapter for the employee table.
DsEmployee1	DataSet object that holds the employees table
dvEmployee	DataView linked to the DsEmployee1.employee table.

The DataSource of the dgrJobs DataGrid is DsJobs1. The DataSource of the dgrEmployee DataGrid is dvEmployee. The Page_Load event handler fills the dgrJobs grid on the left-hand side of the form:

```
If Not IsPostBack Then
   daJobs.Fill(DsJobs1)
   dgrJobs.DataBind()
End If
```

The ItemCommand handler for dgrJobs activates when the user clicks on a Select button:

```
1:      Private Sub dgrJobs_ItemCommand(ByVal source As System.Object, _
2:       ByVal e As System.Web.UI.WebControls.DataGridCommandEventArgs) _
3:       Handles dgrJobs.ItemCommand
4:
5:         Dim jobId As Integer = CInt(dgrJobs.DataKeys(e.Item.ItemIndex))
6:         dvEmployee.RowFilter = "job_id = " & jobId
7:         daEmployee.Fill(DsEmployee1)
8:         dgrEmployee.DataBind()
9:
10:        lblJobType.Text = e.Item.Cells(1).Text
11:        employeePanel.Visible = dgrEmployee.Items.Count > 0
12:     End Sub
```

Line 5 gets the key value of the currently selected row, which is the job ID. Line 6 uses the job ID to set the RowFilter property of the DataView control named dvEmployee. Line 7 fills the DsEmployee dataset, and Line 8 binds the dgrEmployee grid to the DataView control. Line 10 gets the job description from the Cells collection of the selected grid item and copies it to the label appearing just above the employee grid. Line 11 makes the panel containing the employee grid visible if the grid contains items. The complete program source code appears in Code Listing 9-6.

Code Listing 9-6 (Jobs/Employee DataGrid)

```
Public Class JobsEmployee
   Inherits System.Web.UI.Page

┌─────────────────────────────────────┐
│ + Web Form Designer generated code  │
└─────────────────────────────────────┘

   Private Sub Page_Load(ByVal sender As System.Object, _
    ByVal e As System.EventArgs) Handles MyBase.Load

      If Not IsPostBack Then
         daJobs.Fill(DsJobs1)
         dgrJobs.DataBind()
      End If
   End Sub

   Private Sub dgrJobs_ItemCommand(ByVal source As System.Object, _
    ByVal e As System.Web.UI.WebControls.DataGridCommandEventArgs) _
    Handles dgrJobs.ItemCommand

      'Assume that e.CommandName = "Select"
      Dim jobId As Integer = CInt(dgrJobs.DataKeys(e.Item.ItemIndex))
      dvEmployee.RowFilter = "job_id = " & jobId
```

```
            daEmployee.Fill(DsEmployee1)
            dgrEmployee.DataBind()
            lblJobType.Text = e.Item.Cells(1).Text
            employeePanel.Visible = dgrEmployee.Items.Count > 0
        End Sub
End Class
```

Hands-On Tutorial: Kayak Selection Program

KayakGrid

Chapter 4 showed how to display related tables using the Windows DataGrid control. We can perform a similar operation using the DataGrid server control, using slightly different techniques.

The DataGrid server control cannot use a DataRelation object to navigate between tables, so we must do more coding. Our approach will be to fill a DropDownList with a list of kayak types from a kayak rental store. When the user selects a kayak type, we will display a grid containing all kayaks from the store's inventory that match the desired kayak type. The user can click on a *Select* button in the grid and accumulate a list of selected kayaks. This program uses the KayakStore database, which contains the following tables:

◆ **inventory**: Keeps track of all kayaks currently on hand. Primary key is inven_id. Foreign keys are model_id, vendor_id, cat_id, and color_id.

◆ **models**: Lists the various types (models) of kayaks. Primary key is model_id.

◆ **vendors**: Lists the companies that supply kayaks to the store. Primary key is vendor_id.

◆ **colors**: Lists the various kayak colors. Primary key is color_id.

Figure 9-25 shows the relationships between the tables, along with the column selections you will be using in this program.

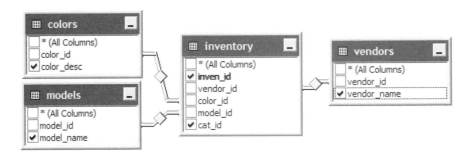

Figure 9-25 Relationships between tables.

User Interface

The startup form (Figure 9-26) contains a list of kayak types in a dropdown list. When the user selects a kayak type, a DataGrid control displays kayaks from the store's inventory that match the given type (Figure 9-27). Each kayak in the grid has a *Select* button that could be used to reserve it for an upcoming rental.

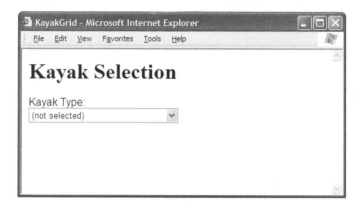

Figure 9-26   Kayak Selection startup form.

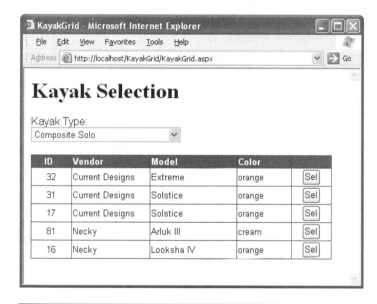

Figure 9-27   Showing selected kayaks.

When the user clicks on *Select* next to a kayak (Figure 9-28), the grid row is highlighted in a contrasting color. As each kayak is selected, its Select button is removed. As the user views different kayak types and selects individual items, the program has to remember all previous selections. If the user returns to a kayak type which had previously contained selected items, those items must still appear selected.

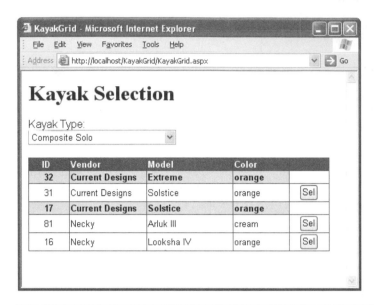

Figure 9-28 Selecting kayaks.

Implementation

A parameterized query will fill the DataGrid. We will create a session state variable named **kayaks** to hold an ArrayList of selected kayak ID numbers. This list must be retrieved when the user selects a different type of kayak. When the user selects a kayak, the kayak ID must be appended to the list of selected kayaks.

Step 1. Create a Web project named **KayakGrid.**

Step 2. Rename the startup form to KayakGrid.aspx and add Web controls, using Figure 9-27 as a guide along with the properties listed in Table 9-8.

Table 9-8

Control properties, KayakTypes form.

Control Type	Name	Properties
Web Form	KayakGrid	
DropDownList	ddlCategories	AutoPostBack: True
DataGrid	dgrInventory	AutoGenerateColumns: False
		DataSource: DsInventory1
		DataKey: inven_id
		Font: Arial
		(custom columns: ID, vendor, model, color)
		Select button in each row

Step 3. Create a data adapter named **daInventory** that joins the inventory, models, vendors, and colors tables. Select the following columns: inventory.inven_id, inventory.cat_id, models.model_name, vendors.vendor_name, and colors.color_desc. Add a WHERE clause to the CommandText containing the query parameter @cat_id, along with an ORDER_BY clause:

```
WHERE cat_id = @cat_id
ORDER BY vendor_name, model_name
```

Step 4. Generate the **dsInventory dataset** from the daInventory data adapter. The database connection should be named **conKayakStore**.

Step 5. Open the form's code window and add the FillCategoriesList procedure, which uses a DataReader to fill the dropdown list with kayak categories and ID numbers:

```
Private Sub FillCategoriesList()
   conKayakStore.Open()
   Dim sql As String = "SELECT * FROM Categories"
   Dim cmd As New SqlCommand(sql, conKayakStore)
   Dim drCategories As SqlDataReader = cmd.ExecuteReader()
   With ddlCategories
      .DataSource = drCategories
      .DataTextField = "cat_name"
      .DataValueField = "cat_id"
      .DataBind()
   End With
   conKayakStore.Close()
   'Add a dummy entry to the beginning of the list.
   ddlCategories.Items.Insert(0, "(not selected)")
End Sub
```

Step 6. Add the following code to the **Page_Load** event handler. If the "kayaks" session variable is not found, an ArrayList is created and stored in the variable. Then the dropdown list of kayak categories is filled:

```
If Not IsPostBack Then
   If Session("kayaks") Is Nothing Then
      Session("kayaks") = New ArrayList
   End If
   FillCategoriesList()
End If
```

Step 7. Add a **SelectedIndexChanged** handler for the dropdown list. The first step is to assign the SelectedValue of the dropdown list to the @cat_id query parameter.

```
Private Sub ddlCategories_SelectedIndexChanged(ByVal sender As _
   System.Object, ByVal e As System.EventArgs) _
   Handles ddlCategories.SelectedIndexChanged

   daInventory.SelecCommand.Parameters("@cat_id").Value = _
      ddlCategories.SelectedValue
   daInventory.Fill(DsInventory1)
   dgrInventory.DataBind()
   'Refresh highlighting of any existing selected items.
   RefreshGridSelections()
End Sub
```

Step 8. Create the **RefreshGridSelections** method. Its job is to iterate through the current contents of the grid and match up the ID numbers of selected kayaks. The selected IDs are in the ArrayList named selectedKayaks, which must be retrieved from Session state:

```
Private Sub RefreshGridSelections()
    Dim selectedKayaks As ArrayList = CType(Session("kayaks"), _
        ArrayList)
    Dim item As DataGridItem
    For Each item In dgrInventory.Items
        Dim id As Integer = CInt(dgrInventory.DataKeys _
            (item.ItemIndex))
        If selectedKayaks.Contains(id) Then MarkItem(item)
    Next item
End Sub
```

Let us briefly review the meaning of the expression **dgrInventory.DataKeys(item.ItemIndex)**. The DataKeys collection contains all the matching key values for the grid items. The grid's DataKeyField property, set in design mode, determines which field from the attached dataset will be stored in DataKeys. DataKeyField was set to **inven_id**, so our DataKeys collection contains inven_id values.

The loop in RefreshGridSelections gets each kayak's ID number. If the ID is found in the selectedKayaks array, the grid item is highlighted by calling the **MarkItem** method.

Step 9. Create the **MarkItem** method, which changes a grid item's background color to Cyan, sets the font to bold, and removes the Select button:

```
Private Sub MarkItem(ByVal item As DataGridItem)
    With item
        .BackColor = System.Drawing.Color.Cyan
        .Font.Bold = True
        'Remove the button so it cannot be selected twice.
        .Controls(4).Visible = False
    End With
End Sub
```

Step 10. Create the ItemCommand event handler for the grid. First, it calls MarkItem to show the current item as selected. Next, the selectedKayaks array is retrieved from Session state, and the new kayak's ID number is added to the list:

```
Private Sub dgrInventory_ItemCommand(ByVal source As Object, _
    ByVal e As System.Web.UI.WebControls.DataGridCommandEventArgs) _
    Handles dgrInventory.ItemCommand

    If e.CommandName = "Select" Then
        MarkItem(e.Item)
        'Add the kayak's ID to the list of selected kayaks.
        Dim selectedKayaks As ArrayList = CType(Session("kayaks"), _
            ArrayList)
        selectedKayaks.Add(CInt(dgrInventory.DataKeys( _
            e.Item.ItemIndex)))
        Session("kayaks") = selectedKayaks
    End If
```

Step 11. Save, run, and test the program. Select individual kayaks from different categories. Return to categories you've already selected, and verify that your earlier kayak selections reappear.

(End of tutorial. The complete program source code appears in Code Listing 9-7.)

Code Listing 9-7 (Kayak Selection)

```
Public Class WebForm1
    Inherits System.Web.UI.Page

+ Web Form Designer generated code

    Private Sub Page_Load(ByVal sender As System.Object, _
     ByVal e As System.EventArgs) Handles MyBase.Load

        If Not IsPostBack Then
            If Session("kayaks") Is Nothing Then
                Session("kayaks") = New ArrayList
            End If
            FillCategoriesList()
        End If
    End Sub


    'Refresh highlighting of selected grid items.
    Private Sub RefreshGridSelections()
        Dim selectedKayaks As ArrayList = CType(Session("kayaks"), _
            ArrayList)
        Dim item As DataGridItem
        For Each item In dgrInventory.Items
            Dim id As Integer = CInt(dgrInventory.DataKeys( _
                item.ItemIndex))
            If selectedKayaks.Contains(id) Then MarkItem(item)
        Next item
    End Sub


    'Highlight a grid item so the user knows it's been selected.
    Private Sub MarkItem(ByVal item As DataGridItem)
        With item
            .BackColor = System.Drawing.Color.Cyan
            .Font.Bold = True
            'Remove the button so it cannot be selected twice.
            .Controls(4).Visible = False
        End With
    End Sub

    Private Sub dgrInventory_ItemCommand(ByVal source As System.Object, _
     ByVal e As System.Web.UI.WebControls.DataGridCommandEventArgs) _
     Handles dgrInventory.ItemCommand

        If e.CommandName = "Select" Then
            MarkItem(e.Item)
            'Add the kayak's ID to the list of selected kayaks.
            Dim selectedKayaks As ArrayList = CType(Session("kayaks"), _
                ArrayList)
```

```
                selectedKayaks.Add(CInt(dgrInventory.DataKeys( _
                    e.Item.ItemIndex)))
                Session("kayaks") = selectedKayaks
            End If
        End Sub


        'Fill the dropdown list with a list of kayak types from
        'the categories table.
        Private Sub FillCategoriesList()
            conKayakStore.Open()
            Dim sql As String = "SELECT * FROM Categories"
            Dim cmd As New SqlCommand(sql, conKayakStore)
            Dim drCategories As SqlDataReader = cmd.ExecuteReader()
            With ddlCategories
                .DataSource = drCategories
                .DataTextField = "cat_name"
                .DataValueField = "cat_id"
                .DataBind()
            End With
            conKayakStore.Close()
            'Add a dummy entry to the beginning of the list.
            ddlCategories.Items.Insert(0, "(not selected)")
        End Sub

        Private Sub ddlCategories_SelectedIndexChanged( _
            ByVal sender As System.Object, _
            ByVal e As System.EventArgs) Handles _
            ddlCategories.SelectedIndexChanged

            SqlSelectCommand1.Parameters("@cat_id").Value = _
                ddlCategories.SelectedValue
            daInventory.Fill(DsInventory1)
            dgrInventory.DataBind()
            'Refresh highlighting of any existing selected items.
            RefreshGridSelections()
        End Sub
    End Class
```

Stored Procedure Option

If you would like to use a stored procedure in this program, here's the one we used:

```
CREATE PROCEDURE spSelectInventory
@cat_id varchar(3)
AS
SELECT inventory.inven_id, inventory.cat_id, models.model_name,
    vendors.vendor_name, colors.color_desc
FROM inventory INNER JOIN
    models ON inventory.model_id = models.model_id INNER JOIN
    vendors ON inventory.vendor_id = vendors.vendor_id INNER JOIN
    colors ON inventory.color_id = colors.color_id
WHERE cat_id = @cat_id
ORDER BY vendor_name, model_name
```

The DataAdapter Wizard in Visual Studio can generate stored procedures for you. This feature is particularly helpful when a query contains multiple tables. When you reach the **Choose a Query Type** step, select **Create New Stored Procedures**. If you select the Advanced Options button, you can choose to generate only a SELECT statement.

▶9.7 Adding Rental Reservations

 RentalReserve

A random survey of Web applications would probably indicate the two most common database actions performed are to (1) retrieve and display information from a database, and (2) to collect user input and save in a database. We have explored ways to perform the first action, using the Repeater, DataList, and DataGrid controls. Let us now turn to the second basic type of action, the one you are likely to use many times in the future.

If you were to insert a row into a dataset, the dataset would have to be retained in Session state until the data adapter's Update method was called. Instead, Web applications usually save database rows using Command objects containing INSERT queries. This direct update approach, introduced in Chapter 4, is simple and efficient. Update queries can be made even more efficient by compiling them into stored procedures.

In this section, we present a program that lets customers of a sports rental store reserve items they plan to pick up later. Once each reservation is confirmed, the customer can show up at the store on the stated date and rent the item. This is the runtime scenario:

1. The user enters the date, customer's first and last name, phone, email address, and the rental duration (Figure 9-29). They also select a rental item.

2. The Web form checks for any missing fields or fields containing out-of-range values. If any are discovered, error messages notify the user.

3. When all input fields are correctly entered, the program writes a new row to the Reservations table (Table 9-9) of the SportsRental database. If the database update is successful, an appropriate message is displayed. If an error occurs while saving the reservation, the user is shown an error message. The user can correct values in the input fields and try to save the reservation.

Figure 9-29 Filling in the Reservation form.

Table 9-9

Reservations table design

Field Name	Type	Description
rental_id	Autonumber	Integer; Record key
item_id	Long integer	Identifies the item to be reserved
cust_name	varchar (50)	Customer's first and last name
cust_phone	varchar (20)	Customer's phone number
cust_email	varchar (30)	Customer's email address
res_date	smalldatetime	Date and time when reservation was made
start_date	smalldatetime	Date when reservation starts
duration	Integer	Duration of rental, in hours

Validation

RequiredFieldValidator controls are used for the Date, First name, Last name, Phone, Email, and Rental duration fields. The Email field is also validated using a RegularExpressionValidator control. A RangeValidator is used for the Rental duration field. Figure 9-30 shows what happens when the user tries to save a reservation containing missing fields.

Figure 9-30 Showing field validation.

Selecting the Date

When the user clicks on the Select link next to the date field, a separate form displays a calendar control (Figure 9-31). The user selects a date and clicks on Return. When the Reservation form appears again, the selected date appears in the text box. The Enabled property of the text box is False, so the user cannot enter a date without using the Calendar control.

Figure 9-31 Selecting a Rental Date.

Data Components

The Connection object is named conSports. There are two data adapters: **daItems** (based on the Items table) and **daReservations** (based on the Reservations table). The dsItems dataset is bound to the ddlItems DropDownList control.

Globally Defined String

This program creates a session state variable named **startDate** and references it several times. Because the name of a session variable is so easily misspelled, we have declared its name as a constant in the Global.asax.vb file:

```
Public Const SESSION_STARTDATE As String = "startDate"
```

Statements accessing the variable use the constant name. The compiler can easily detect a misspelling before a hard-to-find bug enters the program:

```
If Not Session(Global.SESSION_STARTDATE) Is Nothing Then ...
```

Reservation Form

In the startup form (Reservation.aspx), the Page_Load event handler looks for a Session variable containing the rental date. If one is found, the date is copied into the txtDate text box. The ddlItems dropdown list is filled with descriptions of rental items:

```
If Not IsPostBack Then
    If Not Session(Global.SESSION_STARTDATE) Is Nothing Then
        txtStartDate.Text = CStr(Session Global.SESSION_STARTDATE))
    End If
    daItems.Fill(DsItems1)
    ddlItems.DataBind()
    'Initialize the CompareValidator control with today's date.
    'It will be compared to the rental date.
    cmpDate.ValueToCompare = CStr(Today)
End If
```

btnSave_Click Event Handler

The Click event handler for btnSave is a bit more complicated. First, it converts the rental duration from days to hours, if the user has input the length of rental in days:

```
Dim duration As Integer, reservId As Integer
Try
    'If the user has specified the rental duration in days,
    'convert the value to hours.
    duration = CInt(txtDuration.Text)
    If ddlHoursDays.SelectedValue = "Days" Then duration *= 24
Catch ex As Exception
    lblStatusLine.Text = "Error: " & ex.Message
    Exit Sub
End Try
```

Next, it opens the connection and passes parameters to the daReservations data adapter's InsertCommand object. It executes the command, which inserts the new table row:

```
Try
    Dim rightNow As DateTime = Now()
    conSports.Open()
    With daReservations.InsertCommand
```

```
.Parameters("@item_id").Value = CInt(ddlItems.SelectedValue)
.Parameters("@cust_name").Value = txtLast.Text _
   & ", " & txtFirst.Text
.Parameters("@cust_phone").Value = txtPhone.Text
.Parameters("@cust_email").Value = txtEmail.Text
.Parameters("@res_date").Value = rightNow
.Parameters("@start_date").Value = Session( _
   Global.SESSION_STARTDATE)
.Parameters("@duration").Value = duration
.ExecuteNonQuery()
```

No value is assigned to the rental_id column because it is auto-generated. We want to get the rental_id and display it for the user, so we retrieve the row just added to the table. The CommandText property is assigned a SELECT statement:

```
'Retrieve the auto-generated rental_id.
.CommandText = "SELECT rental_id, cust_email FROM Reservations " _
   & "WHERE res_date = '" & rightNow & "' AND cust_email = '" _
   & txtEmail.Text & "'"
reservId = CInt(.ExecuteScalar())
End With
lblStatusLine.Text = "Your reservation has been saved. Your " _
   & "reservation ID is " & CStr(reservId)
Catch ex As Exception
lblStatusLine.Text = "Error: " & ex.Message
Finally
If conSports.State = ConnectionState.Open Then conSports.Close()
End Try
```

The SELECT statement finds the row having the same time/date value, along with the customer's email address. The ExecuteScalar method returns the first column of the row returned by a query. The complete listing of the Reservation form appears in Code Listing 9-8.

Code Listing 9-8 (Reservation class)

```
Public Class Reservation
   Inherits System.Web.UI.Page
```

```
+ Web Form Designer generated code
```

```
   Private Sub Page_Load(ByVal sender As System.Object, _
     ByVal e As System.EventArgs) Handles MyBase.Load

      If Not IsPostBack Then
         If Not Session(Global.SESSION_STARTDATE) Is Nothing Then
            txtStartDate.Text = CStr(Session( _
            Global.SESSION_STARTDATE))
         End If
         daItems.Fill(DsItems1)
         ddlItems.DataBind()
         'Initialize the CompareValidator control with today's date.
         'It will be compared to the rental date.
         cmpDate.ValueToCompare = CStr(Today)
      End If
   End Sub
```

```
    Private Sub btnSave_Click(ByVal sender As System.Object, _
     ByVal e As System.EventArgs) Handles btnSave.Click

       Dim duration As Integer, reservId As Integer
       Try
           'If the user has specified the rental duration in days,
           'convert the value to hours.
           duration = CInt(txtDuration.Text)
           If ddlHoursDays.SelectedValue = "Days" Then duration *= 24
       Catch ex As Exception
           lblStatusLine.Text = "Error: " & ex.Message
           Exit Sub
       End Try

       Try
           Dim rightNow As DateTime = Now()
           conSports.Open()
           Dim cmd As SqlCommand = SqlInsertCommand2
           With cmd
               .Parameters("@item_id").Value = CInt(ddlItems.SelectedValue)
               .Parameters("@cust_name").Value = txtLast.Text _
                  & ", " & txtFirst.Text
               .Parameters("@cust_phone").Value = txtPhone.Text
               .Parameters("@cust_email").Value = txtEmail.Text
               .Parameters("@res_date").Value = rightNow
               .Parameters("@start_date").Value = Session(Global.SESSION_STARTDATE)
               .Parameters("@duration").Value = duration
               .ExecuteNonQuery()

               'Retrieve the auto-generated rental_id.
               .CommandText = "SELECT rental_id, cust_email FROM Reservations " _
                  & "WHERE res_date = '" & rightNow & "' AND cust_email = '" _
                  & txtEmail.Text & "'"
               reservId = CInt(.ExecuteScalar())
           End With
           lblStatusLine.Text = "Your reservation has been saved. Your " _
              & "reservation ID is " & CStr(reservId)
       Catch ex As Exception
           lblStatusLine.Text = "Error: " & ex.Message
       Finally
           If conSports.State = ConnectionState.Open Then conSports.Close()
       End Try
    End Sub
End Class
```

Date Selection Form

The Date Selection form (Code Listing 9-9) looks for an existing date in Session state, and if it finds one, selects the date in the Calendar control. This feature is important if the user selects a date, returns to the reservation form, and opens the date selection form again. Their previously selected date is highlighted in the Calendar control:

```
If Not IsPostBack Then
   If Not Session(Global.SESSION_STARTDATE) Is Nothing Then
      calDate.SelectedDate = CDate(Session(Global.SESSION_STARTDATE))
   End If
End If
```

The Date Selection form has a Click event handler that saves the selected date from the Calendar control into Session state and returns to the Reservation form:

```
Session(Global.SESSION_STARTDATE) = calDate.SelectedDate
Server.Transfer("Reservation.aspx")
```

Code Listing 9-9 (selectDate.aspx)

```
Public Class selectDate
   Inherits System.Web.UI.Page

+ Web Form Designer Generated Code

   Private Sub Page_Load(ByVal sender As Object, _
      ByVal e As System.EventArgs) Handles MyBase.Load

      If Not IsPostBack Then
         If Not Session(Global.SESSION_STARTDATE) Is Nothing Then
            calDate.SelectedDate = CDate(Session(Global.SESSION_STARTDATE))
         End If
      End If
   End Sub

   Private Sub lnkReturn_Click(ByVal sender As System.Object, _
    ByVal e As System.EventArgs) Handles lnkReturn.Click

      Session(Global.SESSION_STARTDATE) = calDate.SelectedDate
      Server.Transfer("Reservation.aspx")
   End Sub
End Class
```

Checkpoint

9.12 Why do Web applications usually avoid using datasets for inserting and updating rows in databases?

9.13 How does the Rental Reservation program validate the user's email address?

9.14 How does the Rental Reservation program display currently selected dates in the Calendar control?

9.15 In the button click event handler, why is a SELECT command executed immediately after the INSERT command?

▶9.8 Chapter Summary

◆ A DataReader reads rows directly from a database, in forward direction only. The rows are read-only. DataReaders are ideal for filling list-type controls on Web pages.

◆ An SqlCommand object's ExecuteReader method returns a SqlDataReader object.

◆ DataReaders can be bound to the DataSource property of a list-type control.

◆ CheckBoxList and RadioButtonList controls can be bound to datasets.

◆ DataBinding on Web pages is in one direction only, which is from the data source to the control.

◆ Setting AutoPostBack in list-type controls slows down the program's response time because the Web page must be posted back to the server each time a list item is selected.

◆ The Repeater control displays a list of data-bound items, with the option of adding formatting to each item. Each row displayed by a Repeater is formatted using an ItemTemplate.

◆ Data binding expressions can be coded directly in HTML.

◆ The HeaderTemplate definition for a Repeater lets you define HTML tags that appear before the repeated items. The FooterTemplate defines tags that occur after the last repeated item.

◆ The DataList control provides a flexible way to combine multiple controls into a data-bound sequence that repeats for each row of a dataset. Visual Studio .NET provides a designer for DataList templates.

◆ The Web Forms DataGrid control is the ASP.NET counterpart to the WinForms DataGrid. Though the two controls look similar, they have different sets of property names. The Web Forms version has many advanced capabilities, including sorting and paging.

◆ One of the most useful features of the DataGrid control is its ability to include special button columns. The available button types are Select, Edit, Update, Cancel, and Delete.

◆ The Jobs/Employee DataGrid program demonstrates a simple way to display related tables in separate DataGrid controls.

◆ The Kayak Selection program lets the user select a kayak type, and displays a data grid containing a list of matching kayaks. The user can select multiple kayaks, highlighted in the data grid.

◆ The Rental Reservations example program lets customers of a sports rental store reserve items they would like to rent in the future.

▶9.9 Key Terms

AllowPaging	firehose cursor
AlternatingItemTemplate	FooterTemplate
connected mode	HeaderTemplate
DataKeyField	ItemCommand
DataKeys	ItemTemplate
DataList	PageIndexChanged
DataReader	PagerStyle
ExecuteReader	Repeater
FieldCount	SelectedItemTemplate

▶9.10 Review Questions

Fill-in-the-Blank

1. A _____ reads rows directly from a database, in forward direction only.

2. Each row displayed by a Repeater control is formatted using an _____.

3. The _____ definition for a Repeater control lets you define HTML tags that appear before the repeated items.

4. The available button types in a DataGrid control are Select, Delete, and _____.

5. The DataGrid control uses the _____ property to hold a collection of key values.

Multiple Choice

1. Which of the following controls support the SelectedItemTemplate?

    a. Repeater
    b. DataGrid
    c. DataList
    d. Repeater and DataGrid
    e. DataList and DataGrid

2. Which of the following controls support the SeparatorTemplate?

    a. Repeater
    b. DataGrid
    c. DataList
    d. Repeater and DataList
    e. DataList and DataGrid

3. Which of the following identifies a collection of key values in a DataGrid associated with grid items?

    a. DataKeys
    b. KeyValues
    c. Items
    d. ItemKeys
    e. SelectedItems

4. Which DataGrid event is fired when the user clicks on a Select button?

    a. SelectedIndexChanged
    b. SelectCommand
    c. ItemCommand
    d. EditCommand
    e. none of the above

5. Which of the following controls does not have a DataSource property?

    a. RadioButtonList
    b. Repeater
    c. DataList
    d. CheckBoxList
    e. none of the above

Short Answer

1. What is a common nickname given to DataReaders?
2. (y/n) Can a DataReader be used to insert rows in a table?
3. Which DataReader property returns the number of fields in the current row?
4. Which DataList template formats the display of selected items?
5. Which DataGrid property identifies the table column that will be used to fill the DataKeys collection?

What Do You Think?

1. Of the Repeater, DataList, or DataGrid, which requires the most knowledge of HTML when working in Visual Studio .NET?
2. Regarding the DataGrid control, how are the functions of the DataValueField and DataKeyField properties different?
3. Compare the features of the Windows Forms DataGrid control to those of the Web Forms DataGrid.
4. How does the Paging feature of a DataGrid affect an application's runtime speed?

Algorithm Workbench

1. Write a statement that uses a Command object named **myCmd** to create and return a DataReader.
2. Write a statement that hides column 0 of a DataGrid named **dgrAuthors**.
3. Write an HTML tag for a data-bound column named **firstName** that will be placed inside the ItemTemplate of a Repeater control.
4. Write an expression that returns the key value of the currently selected item in a DataList control named **dlAuthors**.
5. Assume you are writing code for the following event handler in a DataList control. Write a statement that causes the SelectedItemTemplate to display:

```
Private Sub dlStores_ItemCommand(ByVal source As Object, _
  ByVal e As System.Web.UI.WebControls.DataListCommandEventArgs) _
    Handles dlStores.ItemCommand
```

▶9.11 Programming Challenges

1. Rental Reservations History

Using the Rental Reservations program from Section 9.7, add the following improvement: Create a form that lists all reservations made by the customer. We will assume each customer has a unique email address. *Optional:* Create a stored procedure to handle the row selection.

2. Rental Reservations, Item Details

Using the Rental Reservations program from Section 9.7, add the following improvements:

◆ Add an Item Details form (Figure 9-32) containing a DataGrid that displays details about the rental items. Link to the Item Details form from the Reservation page.

◆ Suppose a user has begun to fill out the reservation and then switches to the Item Details form. When they return to the reservation form, all inputs and selections should remain as before.

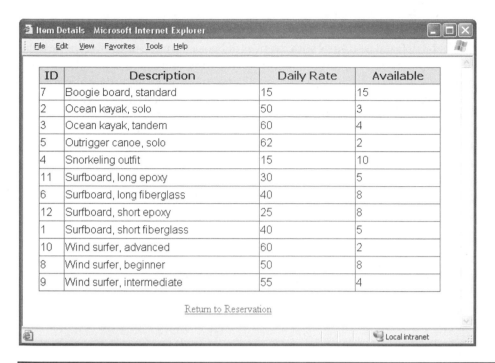

Figure 9-32 Item Details form.

3. Rental Reservations, Removing Reservations

Modify the Rental Reservations program from Section 9.7 as follows: Display a DataGrid containing all reservations, with a Delete button at the end of each row. Let the user remove individual reservations by clicking on the button. *Optional:* Create a stored procedure to handle the deletions.

4. Jobs and Employees

Modify the Jobs/Employee DataGrid program as follows: Use DataReaders to populate the grids, rather than data adapters and datasets. *Note: a DataReader can be assigned to the DataSource property of a DataGrid control.*

5. Unselecting Kayaks

Modify the **Selecting Kayaks** program in Section 9.6 as follows: When a kayak is selected, change its button caption to "UnSel". When the button is clicked a second time, return the selected row to its default color and font, and remove the kayak's ID number from the ArrayList of selected kayaks.

6. Showing Selected Kayaks in a Grid

Modify the **Selecting Kayaks** program in Section 9.6 as follows: Add a button that displays a new form containing the category, vendor name, model name, and color of each selected kayak. Consult with your professor about which of the following approaches should be used:

Approach #1: Use an SQL stored procedure to add a temporary table to the database and fill it with the selected ID numbers. Create a data adapter that joins your table with the other tables containing related information (color, model, vendor, and category). Use the data adapter to fill the grid. Remove the temporary table using another stored procedure.

Approach #2: Create a class that represents each DataGrid row (id, vendor, model, and color). Fill an ArrayList with objects representing the selected kayaks. Bind the ArrayList to the DataGrid.

7. **Book Titles DataList**

Create a program that fills a DataList control with the titles of books from the titles table in the pubs database. Each title should be displayed in a LinkButton control. When the user clicks on a title, details about the book must be displayed to the right of the DataList (Figure 9-33). Do not display any null field values. *Hint:* Strongly typed DataRow objects have built-in properties that make it easy to check for null field values. Suppose a dataset named dsTitles contains rows from the titles table. Then the specific DataRow type is dsTitles.titlesRow:

```
Dim myRow As dsTitles.titlesRow
```

You can reference predefined Boolean property values in the DataRow class. For example, the following checks the pub_name field for a null value:

```
If Not myRow.Ispub_nameNull
```

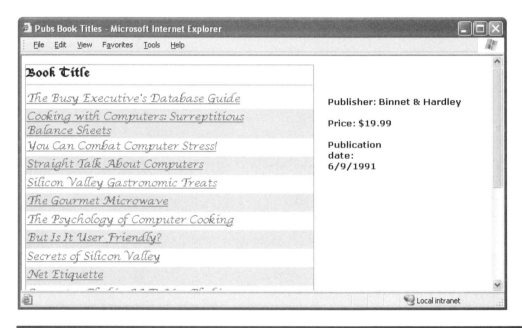

Figure 9-33 Book Titles DataList.

Web Services

▶10.1 Introducing XML Web Services

XML Web Services is a new technology introduced with the .NET Framework. A *Web service* is a component class that is compiled and stored on a Web site. It has no visual interface, but it exposes methods and properties that may be accessed by other programs on a network. Web services are usually consumed by Windows desktop applications or ASP.NET applications. Web services make it convenient for programs to acquire and distribute data across the Internet.

Web browsers provide a human-readable visual interface to Web sites. Many applications, however, require information to be directly transferred between programs. Imagine a Web application that lets users compare prices of consumer items sold by different online stores. The following events might take place:

1. The user enters an item name or description in a text box.

2. The program accesses multiple remote shopping sites and requests the price and related information for the requested item at each site.

3. Each remote site responds with the item's price and related information.

3. The application displays the company name, price, and related information for each shopping site. If users click on a store link, they are taken directly to a dialog that handles the purchase.

Initially, background communication on the Web was accomplished by custom-designed programs using proprietary methods of communication. They often sent text streams through network sockets. But Web services have made it possible for Web sites to standardize the interactions between programs on the Web. The following are just a few of the ways Web services can be useful:

◆ Credit card companies can provide Web services for card authorizations and transactions.

◆ Manufacturers and distributors can provide prices and inventory availablity on demand.

509

◆ Government agencies can provide weather and satellite information.

◆ Real-time stock market data can be sent to subscribers.

◆ Sports events results can be obtained on demand.

◆ Companies can embed statements in their software that order products from other companies over the Web.

Web services are another step in an evolutionary series that began with Microsoft Distributed Component Object Model (DCOM), Common Object Broker Resource Architecture (CORBA), and Remote Method Invocation (RMI). Web services take advantage of several enabling technologies and specifications:

◆ **eXtensible Markup Language (XML):** A text markup language for the exchange of structured documents and data across the Web. Designers can create their own XML tags to indicate specific types of information. Network firewalls are often configured to prevent binary data from passing through because they may contain malicious programs. XML data, because they are in text format, can pass through firewalls more easily.

◆ **Simple Object Access Protocol (SOAP):** An industry-standard protocol for handling requests and responses. It includes class names, method names, and parameters. SOAP, like XML, is represented as plain text and can pass through firewalls.

◆ **Web Services Description Language (WSDL):** Specifies the formatting of calls to Web services methods. A WSDL file is created in the Web References folder of a consumer program. For each method exposed by the Web service, the WSDL file contains information about the method name, parameter list, and return type.

◆ **Universal Description, Discovery, and Integration (UDDI):** A directory service that makes information about Web services publicly available. You can use it to search for available Web services. Look for the XML Web Services tab on the Visual Studio .NET Start Page (Figure 10-1).

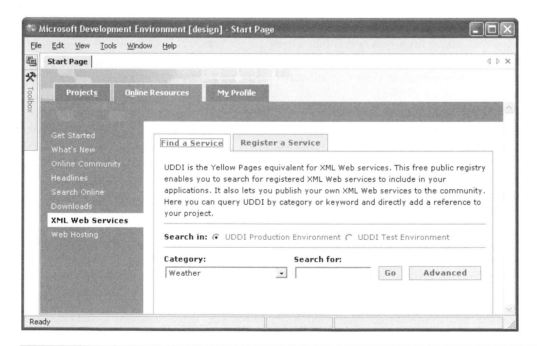

Figure 10-1 Finding Web services (Visual Studio .NET Start page)

▶ 10.2 Example: BookInfo Web Service

The titles table from the Pubs database contains information about book titles. The titleId column is the primary key, the title column contains the book title, and the price column contains the book's price. Following are sample rows:

titleId	title	price
BU1032	The Busy Executive's Database Guide	19.99
BU1111	Cooking with Computers: Surreptitious Balance Sheets	11.95
BU2075	You Can Combat Computer Stress!	2.99
BU7832	Straight Talk About Computers	19.99
MC2222	Silicon Valley Gastronomic Treats	19.99

Suppose we create a Web service named **BookInfo** that exposes two methods named getTitle and getPrice:

```
'Returns the title of a book identified by titleId.
Function getTitle( ByVal titleId As String ) As String

'Returns the price of a book identified by titleId.
Function getPrice( ByVal titleId As String) As Decimal
```

A Web consumer application could use these methods in various ways. For example, it could prompt the user for a titleId of a book, and call getTitle and getPrice to get information about the book. Also, it could iterate through a collection of titleId values and produce a listing of the titles and prices of all the books.

Creating the Web Service

BookInfo

We can create a Web Service project in Visual Studio .NET (Figure 10-2). As in Web Forms applications, the Web service is most easily created as a subdirectory of localhost. The physical location of localhost will usually be the Inetpub\wwwroot directory. The startup form has no visual interface (Figure 10-3), but it holds components. Web service forms always have an .asmx filename extension.

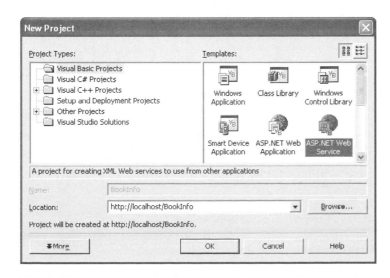

Figure 10-2 Creating a Web Service project

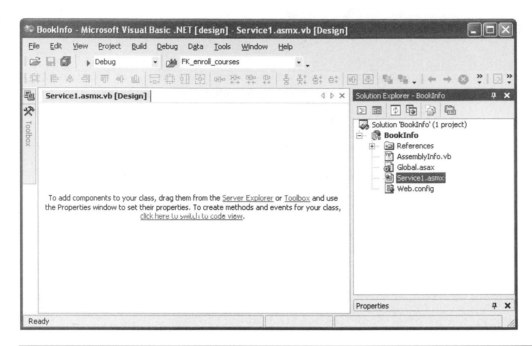

Figure 10-3 Startup form (design mode)

The default filename for the startup form in a new project is **Service1.asmx**. We will rename our startup form to **Default.asmx**, and in the code window (Code Listing 10-1), rename the class to **BookInfo**.

Code Listing 10-1 (BookInfo class, starting version)

```
Imports System.Web.Services

<WebService(Namespace:="http://tempuri.org/BookInfo")> _
Public Class BookInfo
    Inherits System.Web.Services.WebService

+ Web Services Designer Generated Code

' WEB SERVICE EXAMPLE
' The HelloWorld() example service returns the string Hello World.
' To build, uncomment the following lines then save and build the project.
' To test this web service, ensure that the .asmx file is the start page
' and press F5.
'
'<WebMethod()> _
'Public Function HelloWorld() As String
'    Return "Hello World"
'End Function
End Class
```

All Web service programs must import the System.Web.Services namespace. The Web service's class name is prefaced by the **WebService** attribute tag, which assigns a value to the **Namespace** property. The value is a fully qualified class that will be exposed by our Web service:

```
<WebService(Namespace:="http://tempuri.org/BookInfo")> _
Public Class BookInfo
    Inherits System.Web.Services.WebService
```

Attribute tags generate information exported to the services that register and identify Web services. The tags enable other programs to access both the Web service class and its methods. The domain name http://tempuri.org is a default, but you should change it to a name that helps differentiate you or your company from other Web service providers. The name used in the Namespace property does not have to be a real domain name. The WebService attribute has a **Description** property, to which you can assign a string describing the Web service:

```
Description:="Returns book information from the pubs database"
```

WebMethod Attribute

The **WebMethod** attribute begins the declaration of a method exposed to consumer programs. Here is an example of a Web method named HelloWorld:

```
<WebMethod()> Public Function HelloWorld() As String
```

There is an optional property named **Description** you may find useful. The information placed there appears on the public documentation page for the method. The property value is inserted between parentheses, and the := operator denotes assignment:

```
<WebMethod(Description:="This method says Hello")> _
```

Adding Web Service Methods

Our next action is to define two Web service methods. The **getTitle** method receives a book's identification number (named titleId) and returns the book title. We have included a short description in the WebMethod attribute:

```
<WebMethod(Description:="Returns a book title")> _
Public Function getTitle(ByVal titleId As String) As String
    Dim title As String = "Advanced Visual Basic .NET"
    Return title
End Function
```

The **getPrice** method receives a book's identification number and returns its price:

```
<WebMethod(Description:="Returns a book price")> _
Public Function getPrice(ByVal titleId As String) As Decimal
    Dim price As Decimal = 65D
    Return price
End Function
```

The complete program appears in Code Listing 10-2.

Code Listing 10-2 (Revised BookInfo)

```
Imports System.Web.Services

<WebService(Namespace:="http://scottjonespub.com/BookInfo")> _
Public Class BookInfo
    Inherits System.Web.Services.WebService

+ Web Services Designer Generated Code

    'Version 1: return default values

    'Given the titleId of a book, return its title.
    <WebMethod(Description:="Returns a book title")> _
    Public Function getTitle(ByVal titleId As String) As String
        Dim title As String = "Advanced Visual Basic .NET"
```

10

```
      Return title
   End Function

   'Given the titleId of a book, return its price.
   <WebMethod(Description:="Returns a book price")> _
   Public Function getPrice(ByVal titleId As String) As Decimal
      Dim price As Decimal = 65D
      Return price
   End Function
End Class
```

Testing the Web Service

A Web service can be tested from Visual Studio .NET by running it from the IDE or by typing its URL in the browser's address bar. The browser displays a test page containing the names of the methods supported by the Web service, along with a service description (Figure 10-4). The Service Description link displays a description of the Web service methods using WSDL (Figure 10-5).

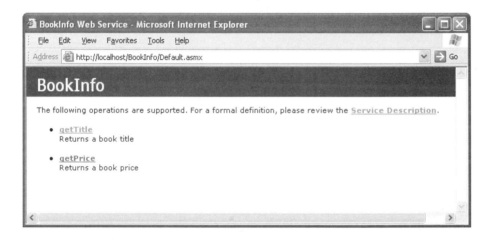

Figure 10-4 Test the Web service in a browser

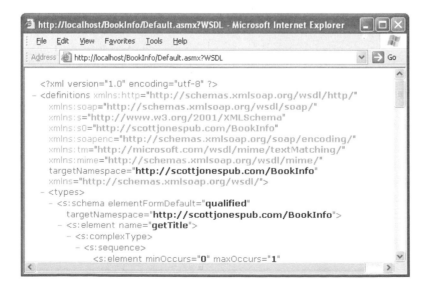

Figure 10-5 Web Service Description Language (WSDL)

When we click on the **getTitle** method name, a new Web page displays, containing a box in which we can pass a parameter value and invoke the method (Figure 10-6). When the **Invoke** button is clicked, the method executes and the return value (a book title) is displayed in XML notation (Figure 10-7).

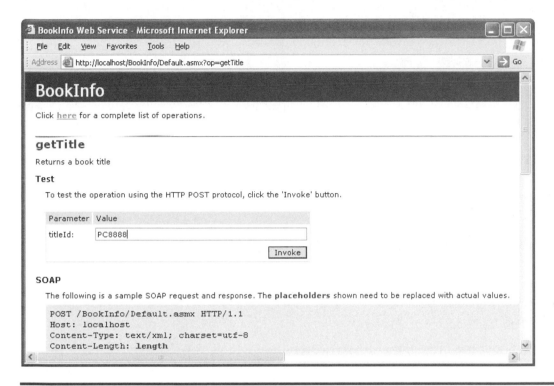

Figure 10-6 Ready to invoke the getTitle method

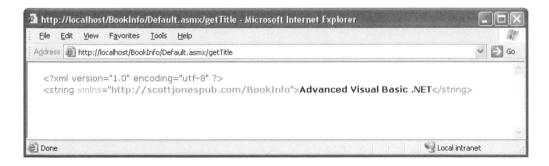

Figure 10-7 Return value from the getTitle method

Consuming the Web Service

ConsumeBookInfo

We will create an ASP.NET project named **ConsumeBookInfo** that consumes the BookInfo Web service. After renaming the startup form to Consume.aspx, we insert a title, a TextBox named txtTitleId, two buttons named btnGetTitle and btnGetPrice to invoke the Web methods, and a Label control named lblResult that displays the return values (Figure 10-8).

 When creating Web services and consumer programs to test them, you may find it useful to add both projects to the same solution. Then you can edit both programs without having to close one solution and open another.

Consume the BookInfo Web Service

Title ID

Get Title   Get Price

[lblResult]

Figure 10-8   Consume.aspx form design

Adding a Web Reference (localhost)

The most important step in creating a Web service consumer is to add a **Web Reference**. The Web Reference can be a URL on the local machine, or it can be a URL on a remote computer. If we right-click on the project name in the Solution Explorer window and select **Add Web Reference**, the page in Figure 10-9 appears.

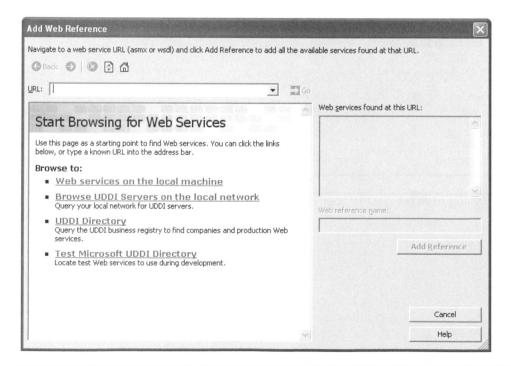

Figure 10-9   Add Web reference

When we select the link entitled **Web services on the local machine** and select the BookInfo.Default.asmx file, the list of methods exposed by the BookInfo service appears (Figure 10-10). To save the reference and close the window, click on the **Add Reference** button. The name localhost appears in the Web References folder (Figure 10-11).

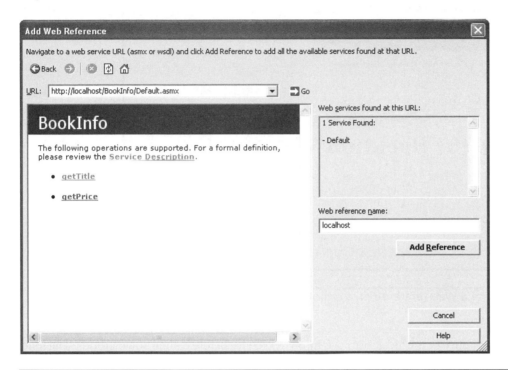

Figure 10-10   Locating the BookInfo Web service

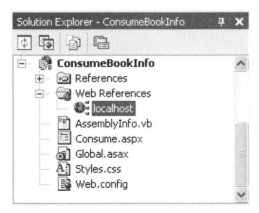

Figure 10-11   localhost added to Web References folder

Adding a Reference to a Remote Service

You can use the **Add Web Reference** window to locate Web services on remote computers. In Figure 10-12, the Web service is typed into the URL window and we click on the **Go** button just to the right of the URL. Once the BookInfo service displays, we click on the **Add Reference** button. Similarly, if the Web service is located on a local network, you can use a machine name in place of a domain name. Suppose the machine was named GOOFY and the Web service was located in its \Inetpub\wwwroot\BookInfo directory. The following URL would find the Web service:

```
http://GOOFY/BookInfo/Default.asmx
```

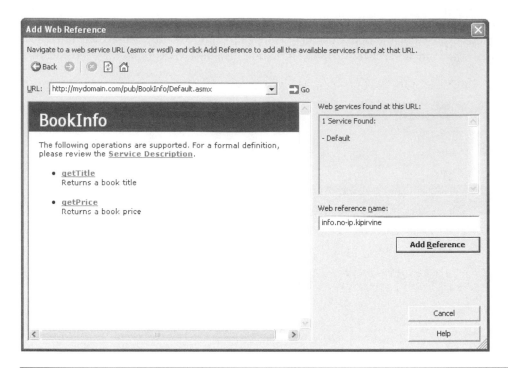

Figure 10-12 Finding a Web reference on a remote site

Calling the Methods

We must create an instance of the localhost.BookInfo Web service before calling any methods. The following line is added to the Click handler for the Get Title button (btnGetTitle):

```
Dim service As New localhost.BookInfo
```

The BookInfo class referenced by the consumer program is called a *proxy class* because it is a look-alike copy of the BookInfo Web service class. The proxy class has the same methods and properties as the server's BookInfo class, but its internal code differs. Its job is to receive function calls from the Web service consumer, convert the function calls to a SOAP-compatible format, and forward them to the Web service program. Using the BookInfo object, we invoke the **getTitle** method and assign its return value to a Label on the form:

```
lblResult.Text = service.getTitle(txtTitleId.Text)
```

The method argument is the value typed by the user into the txtTitleId TextBox. We must add similar code to the Click handler for the Get Price button (btnGetPrice), which displays the return value in Currency format:

```
Dim service As New localhost.BookInfo
Dim price As Decimal = service.getPrice(txtTitleId.Text)
lblResult.Text = FormatCurrency(price)
```

If we run the program, we can enter any book ID number, and click on Get Title (Figure 10-13). Then we click on Get Price (Figure 10-14). The current version always displays the same book title and price. We will modify the Web service so it searches for books in the titles table of the pubs database.

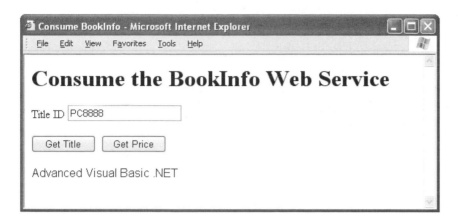

Figure 10-13 Calling getTitle

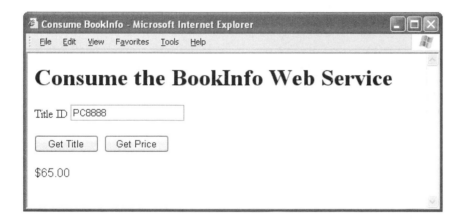

Figure 10-14 Calling getPrice

T
I
P If you modify the public interface of a Web service, be sure to update its Web reference in your consumer program. To do that, right-click on the Web reference in the Solution Explorer window and select **Update Web Reference**.

Connecting to a Database

 BookInfoDb

Let's create a new version of the BookInfo Web service that connects to the pubs database and looks up information in the titles table. It will expose the same two Web methods named getTitle and getPrice. First, we create a new Web service project named **BookInfoDb**, and set the class name in Default.asmx to **BookInfo**. We run the Data Adapter Wizard to create a parameterized query that locates any book in the titles table of the pubs database. Here is the query:

```
SELECT  title_id, title, pub_id, price, ytd_sales, pubdate
FROM    titles
WHERE   (title_id = @title_id)
```

If the data adapter is named **daTitles**, we can generate a dataset class named **dsTitles** and a corresponding dataset variable named **DsTitles1**.

Adding a WebService Description

The WebService attribute will include a Description property:

```
<System.Web.Services.WebService( _
Description:="Returns book information from the pubs database", _
Namespace:="http://scottjonespub.com/BookInfoDb")> _
```

New Web Methods

With the database connection added to the Web service, we can rewrite the getTitle and getPrice methods. All we have to do is assign a value to the query parameter and call the Fill method (which executes the query). Here is the code for getTitle:

```
<WebMethod(Description:="Returns a book title")> _
Public Function getTitle(ByVal titleId As String) As String

    daTitles.SelectCommand.Parameters("@title_id").Value _
       = titleId
    daTitles.Fill(DsTitles1)
    If DsTitles1.titles.Count > 0 Then
       Return CStr(DsTitles1.titles(0).Item("title"))
    Else
       Return ""
    End If
End Function
```

If the titleId value is not found, getTitle returns an empty string. The coding of the getPrice method is similar. Complete source code for the BookInfoDb Web service appears in Code Listing 10-3.

Code Listing 10-3 (BookInfoDb Web service)

```
Imports System.Web.Services

<System.Web.Services.WebService( _
   Description:="Returns book information from the pubs database", _
   Namespace:="http://scottjonespub.com/BookInfoDb")> _
Public Class BookInfo
    Inherits System.Web.Services.WebService

┌─────────────────────────────────────────┐
│ + Web Services Designer Generated Code   │
└─────────────────────────────────────────┘

    'Given the titleId of a book, return its title.
    'If the book is not found, return an empty string.
    <WebMethod(Description:="Returns a book title")> _
    Public Function getTitle(ByVal titleId As String) As String

        daTitles.SelectCommand.Parameters("@title_id").Value _
           = titleId
        daTitles.Fill(DsTitles1)
        If DsTitles1.titles.Count > 0 Then
           Return CStr(DsTitles1.titles(0).Item("title"))
        Else
           Return ""
        End If
    End Function

    'Given the titleId of a book, return its price.
    'If the book is not found, return zero.
```

```
    <WebMethod(Description:="Returns a book price")> _
    Public Function getPrice(ByVal titleId As String) As Decimal

        daTitles.SelectCommand.Parameters("@title_id").Value = titleId
        daTitles.Fill(DsTitles1)
        If DsTitles1.titles.Count > 0 Then
            Return CDec(DsTitles1.titles(0).Item("price"))
        Else
            Return 0
        End If
    End Function
End Class
```

Revised ConsumeBookInfo Program

ConsumeBookInfoDb

The ConsumeBookInfo program we created earlier needs a minor change before it can work with the BookInfoDb Web service. We right-click on **localhost** in the Web References folder of the Solution Explorer window, select **Properties**, and change the Web reference URL to the following:

http://localhost/BookInfoDb/Default.asmx

As an optional modification, we can check the return value from getTitle, and if it is blank, display an appropriate message:

```
    Private Sub btnGetTitle_Click(ByVal sender As System.Object, _
        ByVal e As System.EventArgs) Handles btnGetTitle.Click

        Dim service As New localhost.BookInfo
        Dim title As String = service.getTitle(txtTitleId.Text)
        If title = "" Then
            lblResult.Text = "(book not found)"
        Else
            lblResult.Text = title
        End If
    End Sub
```

The revised ConsumeBookInfo program is ready to run. When we enter a Title ID that exists in the database, the matching book title appears (Figure 10-15). In Figure 10-16, the program displays the book's price.

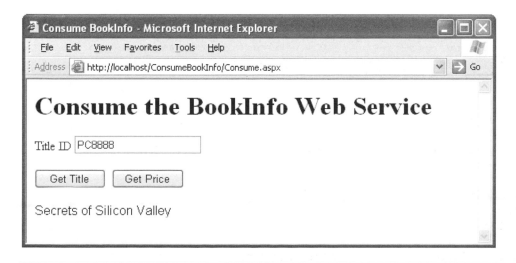

Figure 10-15 Consuming the BookInfoDb Web service

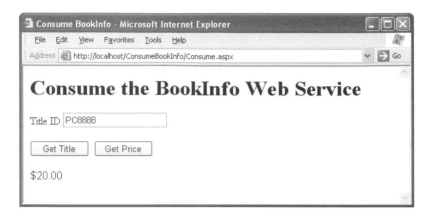

Figure 10-16 Obtaining the book price

Returning a Dataset

The BookInfoDb Web service from the previous section returned information for a single book. A more useful Web service would return an entire dataset containing rows from the titles table that match an SQL query. SOAP permits object types to be passed to Web service methods and to be returned from the methods. This is a powerful capability, given that complex objects must be converted to a text stream before being transported across the Web and through firewalls.

Hands-on Tutorial: Finding Book Titles

BookInfoDb2

We will take you through a hands-on tutorial to build a Web service that searches for book titles in the pubs database using partial string matching. A consumer of the service will pass part of a book title, and the service will return a dataset containing matching books. You will create a Web consumer application that displays the dataset in a DataGrid. In Figure 10-17, the grid contains a list of books containing the word "computer" somewhere in their titles.

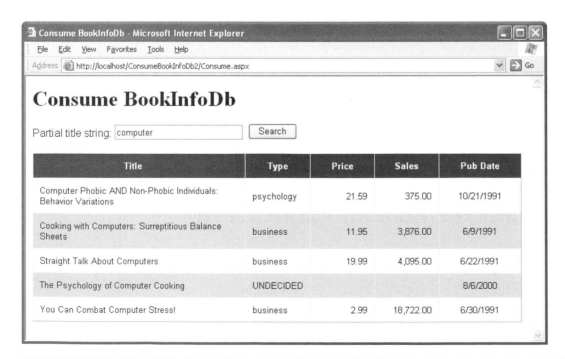

Figure 10-17 Searching for books

A conditional expression in SQL can combine the % character with the LIKE operator to match string patterns. The % is usually placed on both sides of a specific string to indicate that any characters can precede the string and any characters can follow the string. The following expression, for example, matches all titles containing "computer" anywhere within the title:

```
WHERE title LIKE '%computer%'
```

Your program will use a query parameter named @title to make the SELECT statement more flexible:

```
SELECT tile_id, title,...
FROM titles
WHERE (title LIKE '%' + @title + '%')
```

The **BookInfoDb** Web service will expose a method named **getTitleRows** that receives a string parameter named **matchStr** and returns a dataset containing rows generated by the SQL query:

```
Public Function getTitleRows(ByVal matchStr As String) As DataSet
    daTitles.SelectCommand.Parameters("@title").Value = matchStr
    daTitles.Fill(DsTitles1)
    Return DsTitles1
End Function
```

Create the Web Service

Step 1. Create a Web service project named **BookInfoDb2**. *The names of the Web service class and its enclosing project can be different.*

Step 2. Rename the startup form to **Default.asmx** and rename the Web service class to **BookInfoDb**.

Step 3. Using the Data Adapter Wizard from the Visual Studio ToolBox, create a data adapter named **daTitles** using the following query:

```
SELECT title_id, title, type, pub_id, price, advance, royalty,
    ytd_sales, notes, pubdate
FROM titles
WHERE (title LIKE '%' + @title + '%')
```

Step 4. Generate a dataset class named **dsTitles** and a corresponding object named **DsTitles1**.

Step 5. Modify the code inside Default.asmx so that it matches Code Listing 10-4.

Step 6. Run the Web service, input the string "computer" (Figure 10-18), and click on **Invoke**. Scroll through the XML produced by the Web service (Figure 10-19), and verify that it contains matching rows from the titles table.

Next, we turn our attention to the Web consumer program.

Code Listing 10-4 (BookInfoDb2 code)

```
Imports System.Web.Services

<System.Web.Services.WebService( _
    Namespace:="http://scottjonespub.com/BookInfoDb2")> _
    Public Class BookInfoDb
        Inherits System.Web.Services.WebService
```

```
+ Web Services Designer Generated Code

   <WebMethod(Description:="Returns a DataSet containing rows from the " _
      & " titles table (pubs database) in which the book titles match " _
      & " the wildcard query passed in this method's input parameter." _
   )> _
   Public Function getTitleRows(ByVal matchStr As String) As DataSet
      daTitles.SelectCommand.Parameters("@title").Value = matchStr
      daTitles.Fill(DsTitles1)
      Return DsTitles1
   End Function
End Class
```

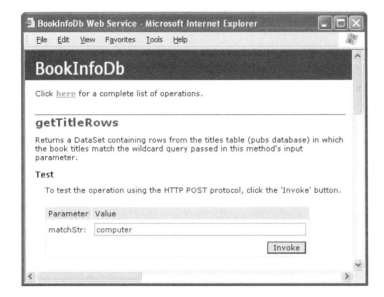

Figure 10-18 Testing the Web service

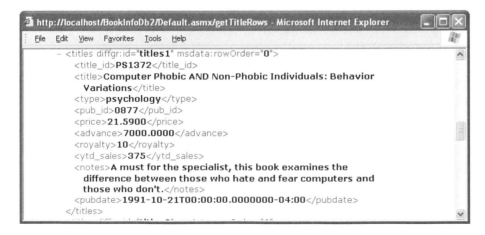

Figure 10-19 XML produced by Web service

Create the Web Consumer

ConsumeBookInfoDb2

Step 1. Create an ASP.NET application named **ConsumeBookInfoDb2**.

Step 2. Rename the startup form to **Consume.aspx**. Rename the form's class to **ConsumeBookInfoDb2**.

Step 3. Right-click on References and add a Web Reference to the following:
http://localhost/BookInfoDb2/Default.asmx

Step 4. Add controls to the form (Figure 10-20), including a title (Heading 1 style), a text box named **txtTitle**, a button named **btnSearch**, and a DataGrid named **dgrTitles**. Set the DataGrid's DataMember property to **titles**, and format the headings as shown in the figure. Use the following formatting expression for the price and ytd_sales columns: {0:N2}. Use the following formatting expression for the pubdate column: {0:d}.

Consume BookInfoDb

Partial title string: [_____] [Search]

Title	Type	Price	Sales	Pub Date
Databound	Databound	Databound	Databound	Databound
Databound	Databound	Databound	Databound	Databound
Databound	Databound	Databound	Databound	Databound
Databound	Databound	Databound	Databound	Databound
Databound	Databound	Databound	Databound	Databound

Figure 10-20 Consume.aspx form design

When you design columns for the DataGrid control, here's a trick to make the database fields available: Create a data adapter and dataset for the titles table in the pubs database. Open the DataGrid Properties window and add the appropriate columns to the grid. Then delete the data adapter and datset components.

Step 5. Edit the form's source code so it is the same as Code Listing 10-5.

Step 6. Save and run the program. Enter various words into the text box and observe the resulting lists of books.

(End of tutorial)

Code Listing 10-5 (ConsumeBookInfoDb2)

```
Public Class ConsumeBookInfoDb2
    Inherits System.Web.UI.Page
```

```
+ Web Form Designer Generated Code
```

```
    Private Sub btnSearch_Click(ByVal sender As Object, _
        ByVal e As System.EventArgs) Handles btnSearch.Click

        Dim service As New localhost.BookInfoDb
        dgrTitles.DataSource = service.getTitleRows(txtTitle.Text)
        dgrTitles.DataBind()
    End Sub
End Class
```

▶10.3 Application State

Web services can take advantage of Application state to save information while the service is active. A service, once started, will remain active until the computer is restarted or the Web service is recompiled. As in ordinary ASP.NET applications, Application state variables are most easily created in the Application_Start event handler in the file named Global.asax. The variable is created by assigning a key value that uniquely identifies it. The following example creates a variable named userCount:

```
Application("userCount") = 0
```

A Web service consumer can call a Web method that returns the value of an Application state variable. In that way, a consumer program can participate in the sharing of information with other consumers using the same Web service.

The UserList Web Service

 UserList

Web services frequently have some form of authentication, to control who consumes their methods and data. They might also charge a fee for using the service. In our next example, the **UserList** Web service maintains a list of users who have accessed the service since it was last started.

In the consumer program (a Windows desktop application), the user enters a username and password, which are passed to a Web method named **AddUser**. If the user is approved, the Web service adds the username to an ArrayList and returns a Boolean result of True. Another Web method named **GetUserList** returns an array holding the names of all users. The Web service uses Application state to save the ArrayList between method calls. The following code in the Global.asax file creates the Application state variable when the Web service is launched:

```
Sub Application_Start(ByVal sender As Object, ByVal e As EventArgs)
    Application("userList") = New ArrayList
End Sub
```

Code Listing 10-6 contains the UserList Web service source code. The current version of AddUser automatically approves all users. An improved version would look up the usernames and passwords in a database.

Code Listing 10-6 (UserList Web service)

```vbnet
Imports System.Web.Services

<System.Web.Services.WebService(_
    Namespace:="http://scottjonespub.com/UserList")> _
Public Class UserList
    Inherits System.Web.Services.WebService
```

```
+ Web Services Designer Generated Code
```

```vbnet
    'Add name parameter to the ArrayList definied in Application
    'state. Return True, indicating the user was authenticated.
    <WebMethod()> _
    Public Function AddUser(ByVal name As String, _
       ByVal passwd As String) As Boolean

       'Authenticate the user...
       'Get the list of current users.
       Dim userList As ArrayList = CType(Application("userList"), _
          ArrayList)
       'Add the new user and save the list.
       userList.Add(name)
       Application("userList") = userList
       Return True
    End Function

    'Return the ArrayList as an array of Object.
    <WebMethod()> _
    Public Function GetUserList() As Object()
       Return CType(Application("userList"), ArrayList).ToArray()
    End Function
End Class
```

10

Web Service Consumer (User Login)

UserListConsume

The Web service consumer program in our example, **User Login**, is a Windows Desktop application that lets the user input a name and password. The values are passed to the **AddUser** Web method. The program uses a Timer control to refresh the display of current users by calling the GetUserList Web method once per second. Figure 10-21 shows two consumer programs simultaneously using the Web service. Each displays a list of current users. When additional users log in, each program connected to the service is notified. Table 10-1 details the controls used on the program. Complete source code for the program appears in Code Listing 10-7.

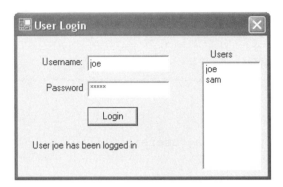 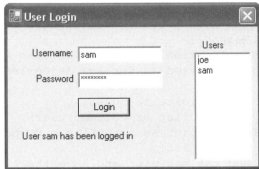

Figure 10-21   Consuming the UserList Web service

Table 10-1

Controls in the User Login program.

Control Type	Name	Property Values
TextBox	txtName	
TextBox	txtPass	PasswordChar: *
Button	btnAdd	Text: Login
ListBox	lstUsers	
Timer	Timer1	Enabled: True
		Interval: 1000
Label	lblStatus	
Label	(default)	Text: Username
Label	(default)	Text: Password

Code Listing 10-7 (Login form: Consumes UserList)

```
Public Class Login
    Inherits System.Windows.Forms.Form

+ Windows Form Designer generated code

    Private service As New localhost.UserList

    Private Sub btnAdd_Click(ByVal sender As System.Object, _
        ByVal e As System.EventArgs) Handles btnAdd.Click

        If service.AddUser(txtName.Text, txtPass.Text) Then
            lblStatus.Text = "User " & txtName.Text & _
            " has been logged in"
        Else
            lblStatus.Text = "User " & txtName.Text & _
```

```
            " not recognized"
        End If
    End Sub

    Private Sub Timer1_Tick(ByVal sender As System.Object, _
        ByVal e As System.EventArgs) Handles Timer1.Tick

        Dim users As Object() = service.GetUserList()
        lstUsers.Items.Clear()
        Dim name As String
        For Each name In users
            lstUsers.Items.Add(name) 'add to ListBox
        Next
    End Sub
End Class
```

▶ 10.4 Chapter Summary

◆ A Web service is a component class compiled and stored on a Web site. It has no visual interface, but it exposes methods and properties accessed by other programs across a network.

◆ Programs that use Web services are called consumers.

◆ eXtensible Markup Language (XML) is the standard protocol used to represent data on the Web.

◆ Simple Object Access Protocol (SOAP) is an industry-standard protocol for handling requests and responses. It includes class names, method names, and parameters.

◆ Web Services Description Language (WSDL) specifies the formatting of calls to Web methods.

◆ Universal Description, Discovery, and Integration (UDDI) is a directory service that makes information about Web services publicly available.

◆ The BookInfo Web service example obtains the title and price of a book, which is identified by a unique ID number. The BookInfoDb service uses a database to retrieve the information.

◆ The most important step in creating a Web service consumer is to add a Web Reference. The Web Reference can be a URL on the local machine, or it can be a URL on a remote computer.

◆ A Web service consumer program must create an instance of a Web service before calling any of its methods.

◆ SOAP permits object types to be passed to Web methods and returned by Web methods.

◆ The UserList Web service example shows how to use Application state and share the contents of a state variable with Web service consumers.

10

▶ 10.5 Key Terms

eXtensible Markup Language (XML)

proxy class

Simple Object Access Protocol (SOAP)

Universal Description, Discovery, and
    Integration (UDDI)

WebMethod attribute

Web Reference

Web Service consumer

Web Service

WebService attribute

Web Services Description Language (WSDL)

XML Web Services

▶10.6 Review Questions

Fill in the Blank

1. A Web service exposes properties and —————.
2. SOAP stands for Simple Object ————— Protocol.
3. WSDL stands for Web Services ————— Language.

Multiple Choice

1. Which of the following is a protocol for handling requests and responses, and which includes class names, method names, and parameters?
   a. XML
   b. SOAP
   c. WSDL
   d. UDDI
2. Which of the following is helpful when you want to locate available Web services?
   a. XML
   b. SOAP
   c. WSDL
   d. UDDI

True or False

1. A Web service consumer must be an ASP.NET application.
2. A Web service must have file extension **asmx**.
3. The WebMethod attribute is required for Web service functions.
4. The Namespace property for all Web services should be tempuri.org.

Short Answer

1. What is the attribute tag used just prior to the class name in a Web service?
2. If you are writing a program to consume a Web service, how do you let the program find the Web service's methods and properties?
3. What type of object can be returned by a Web service when it has completed a SELECT query?

What do You Think?

1. In the UserList Web service, consumers call a method named GetUserList. What efficiency issues do you think are raised by this method?
2. Suppose a Web site produces a continuous stream of stock market data. Do you think it would work well as a Web service?
3. Once a Web service has identified a valid connection by a consumer program (as in the User Login example), how might the Web service identify the same consumer when it calls other methods from the service?

Algorithm Workbench

1. Write a statement declaring a Web service class named WeatherService. Set the Namespace to mydomain.com/WeatherService.
2. Write a Web method declaration for a function named GetTemperature that returns a value of type Single.
3. In a program that consumes WeatherService methods, write code that creates an instance of the Web service and calls its GetTemperature method.

▶10.7 Programming Challenges

1. Currency Conversion Web Service

Create a Web service that converts currency values between U.S. Dollars and several other world currencies. Consumers can pass each currency code as a two-character or three-character string. One method, named **GetDollarValue**, returns the amount in US dollars corresponding to the **amount** parameter:

```
Public Function GetDollarValue( ByVal Country As String, _
    ByVal amount As Decimal ) As Decimal
```

The other method, named **GetCurrencyValue**, returns the value in a foreign currency that corresponds to the dollars parameter:

```
Public Function GetCurrencyValue( ByVal Country As String, _
    ByVal dollars As Decimal ) As Decimal
```

Assign values to the Description properties of both the WebService attribute and the WebMethod attributes.

Consumer Program

Create a Windows Desktop consumer program that lets the user select a currency type from a ComboBox, and input a U.S. dollar amount or a foreign currency amount. In Figure 10-22, the user can click on the button with the arrow pointing right to convert $55 US into the equivalent amount in Euro-dollars. If the user enters the foreign currency amount in the right-hand text box (Figure 10-23) and clicks on the arrow pointing left, the equivalent amount in Dollars should appear.

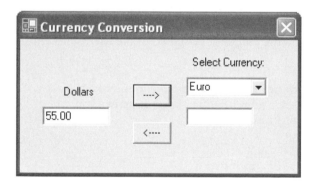

Figure 10-22 Converting Dollars to Euros

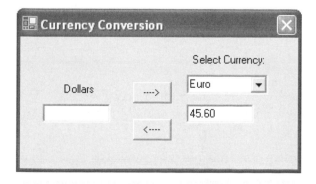

Figure 10-23 Converting Euros to Dollars

2. UserList Web Service – Removing Users

Improve the UserList Web Service program by adding a method named RemoveUser that removes a user from the ArrayList. Modify the UserList Consumer program so it calls RemoveUser.

3. UserList Web Service with Database

Convert the UserList Web service to a database component. Create a database table named Users and use the table to authenticate calls to the AddUser Web method. Return True if the username and password match; otherwise return False. Here is a sample table:

username	password
joe	abc123
sam	xyz876
ann	&#2yte
maria	@@34ab2

4. Asynchronous Message Web Service

Create a Web service that permits users to send short text messages to other users and receive messages from other users. The Web service is termed *asynchronous* because messages are not received as soon as they are sent; users decide when they want to receive messages.

When a user logs in with a name and password, the Web service authenticates them by searching a database table. If the user is accepted, a unique Id number is created and sent to the user. The Web service uses this ID number to identify the user in all subsequent calls to Web methods.

A user sends a message by calling a Web method and passing a user ID, the name of the recipient, and the message text. A user receives his/her messages by passing a user ID to a Web method that returns an array of message strings. When the user logs out, the unique ID assigned to the user is discarded. Here are the suggested method declarations:

```
'Log into the the message service with a username and password.
'Returns a unique integer to be used in subsequent transmissions.
Public Function Login(ByVal user As String, _
    ByVal passwd As String) As Integer


'Send a message to a specific user. Parameters:
'userId: unique identifier returned by Login method.
'recipient: username of the receiver of the message
'msg: the text of the message
'Returns True if the userId is recognized.
Public Function Send(ByVal userId As Integer, _
    ByVal recipient As String, _
    ByVal msg As String) As Boolean


'Get all messsages addressed to the current user.
'If the userId is recognized, an Array of String containing
'the messages is returned; otherwise, the array is empty.
Public Function GetMessages(ByVal userId As Integer) As String()


'Log out of the mail service. Discards the the unique userId.
Public Sub Logout(ByVal userId As Integer)
```

Advanced Classes

☞ *Note:*

The Windows Console applications in this chapter call the System.Console.WriteLine method. When writing your own programs, add the System.Console namespace to the Common Properties | Imports area of the Project Properties dialog.

▶11.1 Value Types

As we mentioned in Chapter 1, Visual Basic .NET has two basic types: value types and reference types. Value types include all the numeric types such as Integer and Decimal, as well as Boolean. Four features distinguish value types from reference types:

◆ The assignment operator copies their contents.

◆ They can be compared using relational operators (<, >, =, etc.).

◆ They can be created without using the New operator.

◆ Programs execute more quickly when manipulating value types because no extra time is required to look up an address before accessing data.

You can define your own value types in two ways. The first is to define an Enum, and the second is to define a Structure.

Enums

 Object.Enums

The Enum class is the base class for enumerated types containing a limited set of integral values. Enum inherits from the System.ValueType class, which in turn inherits from System.Object. Your own Enum types implicitly inherit from System.Enum. Enum types define the set of values an Enum instance can hold. For example, the SqlConnection.State property is an Enum with the following set of possible values, defined in the ConnectionState type: Broken, Closed, Connecting, Executing, Fetching, and Open. When you press the dot after an Enum variable, Visual Studio's *intellisense* makes the list of choices pop up. The following Enum type named **AccountType** differentiates between various types of accounts:

```
Enum AccountType
    Checking = 100
    Savings = 101
    Trading = 102
    Annunity = 103
End Enum
```

You don't have to assign specific values to the Enum members. If omitted, the integer values of AccountType would default to 0, 1, 2, and 3. When we declare an AccountType variable, only values from the prescribed list can be assigned to it:

```
Dim acct As AccountType
acct = AccountType.Checking
acct = AccountType.Trading
```

The following statement is illegal though it appears to match one of the constants associated with the Enum type:

```
acct = 101
```

The Enum.GetName method returns a string containing an Enum variable's value. Pass it the enumerated type and the variable name:

```
Public Shared Function GetName( _
    ByVal enumType As Type, _
    ByVal value As Object _
) As String
```

The following code displays "AccountType.Checking". The Type object returned by calling Object.GetType is passed to the GetName method:

```
Dim acct As AccountType
acct = AccountType.Checking
WriteLine(AccountType.GetName(acct.GetType, acct))
```

Structures

Objects.PointDemo

Structures are the other value type you can create in Visual Basic. A structure can contain all the same elements as classes, such as constructors, methods, properties, and fields. Unlike classes, structures use value semantics:

◆ You can declare a structure variable without using New.

◆ When you pass a structure ByVal to a method, the method cannot change the structure's state.

◆ When you call the Equals method, the structures are compared using their contents (their state).

Let's demonstrate all three of these features. First, we declare a **Point** structure with fields X and Y, and a constructor:

```
Structure Point
    Public X As Integer
    Public Y As Integer

    Public Sub New(ByVal xx As Integer, ByVal yy As Integer)
        X = xx
        Y = yy
    End Sub
End Structure
```

The program shown in Code Listing 11-1 creates two points p1 and p2, both having the same X and Y field values. The call to Equals returns True, showing that p1 and p2 are being compared according to their contents (what we call *value semantics*). When p1 is passed to the Show method, the latter modifies field **X** of the **pt** parameter. When Show is called a second time, the output shows p1 has not changed.

Code Listing 11-1 (Using the Point Structure)

```
Sub Show(ByVal pt As Point)
    WriteLine(pt.X & ", " & pt.Y)
    pt.X = 0
End Sub

Public Sub Start()
    Dim p1 As Point
    p1.X = 10
    p1.Y = 20
    Dim p2 As New Point(10, 20)
    WriteLine("p1.Equals(p2): " & p1.Equals(p2))
    Show(p1)         'displays: 10, 20
    Show(p1)         'displays: 10, 20
End Sub
```

Public Fields

Whereas we almost never would create Public instance fields in a class, the practice is far less dangerous in structures. In particular, if the instance fields are value types, the only reason for using property procedures might be to include error checking before assigning values to the fields.

Checkpoint

11.1 *(true/false)* When using the assignment operator (=) with value types, the contents of one variable are copied into another variable.

11.2 *(true/false)* Enum types can represent floating-point numbers.

11.3 *(true/false)* A structure variable can be created without using the New operator.

11.4 *(true/false)* Structures are reference types.

▶11.2 Objects and Reflection

Introducing Reflection

 Objects.Reflection

Reflection is the technique of finding out information about objects at runtime. Given any arbitrary object, you can find out its type. If its type is a class, you can uncover an extensive amount of information about its class members. Reflection is called an *enabling technology* because it makes possible many advanced features in .NET such as serialization and Web services.

Runtime Type Identification

The TypeOf—Is expression verifies the runtime type of an expression. The first operand must be a reference type, and the second operand must be a type name. The expression returns a Boolean value:

```
TypeOf ("abc") Is String              'True
```

Assuming the Account class had been defined, the following expression would also return True:

```
Dim myAcct As New Account
Dim result As Boolean = TypeOf (myAcct) Is Account
```

TypeOf returns True when comparing a derived object to a base class name. Suppose we have a dataset variable named DsAuthors1. Because all datasets inherit from the DataSet class, the following expression returns True:

```
TypeOf( DsAuthors1 ) Is DataSet       'True
```

The Type Class

Visual Basic .NET has a class named **Type** that represents type declarations of classes, interfaces, arrays, value types, and enumerations. It becomes useful on those occasions when you need to know the type of an object. The Object class has a method named **GetType** that returns a **Type** object. For example, using the same Account class shown earlier, T contains the type Account:

```
Dim myAcct As New Account
Dim T As System.Type
T = myAcct.GetType()
```

You can obtain a string containing the fully qualified class name by calling either FullName or ToString on the Type object:

```
WriteLine(T.FullName())         'Objects.Account
WriteLine(T.ToString())         'Objects.Account
```

System.Object Class

 Objects.Comparing

The System.Object class is called the *ultimate superclass* (base class) of all classes in the .NET Framework. Any class you create is implicitly derived from System.Object, and it inherits Object's public members. From this point on, we will shorten its name to the Object class.

Comparing Value Types

Value types such as Integer, Double, and Decimal can be compared using operators such as =, <, and >. Strings are the only reference types that can be compared using these operators. Other reference types, known as *objects*, must be compared by calling methods. The following statements define two integers, assign one integer to the other, and compare them. The = operator and the Equals method (a shared method in the Object class) return True:

```
Dim x As Integer = 5
Dim y As Integer = x
WriteLine((x = y) & ", " & Equals(x, y))          'True, True
```

Strings behave like value types. The following comparisons both return True:

```
Dim s1 As String = "aaa"
Dim s2 As String = s1
WriteLine((s1 = s2) & ", " & Equals(s1, s2))      'True,True
```

Comparing Reference Types

Reference types cannot be compared using relational operators such as <, >, and =. They can be compared by calling the Equals method, but it does not compare their states. Instead, it compares their object references. The term for this type of comparison is *reference equality*. Two object references are equal if and only if they refer to the same object. To illustrate, suppose we define an Account class in which every instance has the same ID value:

```
Class Account
    Private ID As Integer = 5
End Class
```

If we declare two instances of Account, a1 and a2 are reference types:

```
Dim a1 As New Account
Dim a2 As New Account
```

The following call to Equals returns False because a1 and a2 do not refer to the same object instance:

```
WriteLine(Equals(a1, a2))              'False
```

Chapter 1 pointed out you can use the assignment operator (=) to copy an object reference into another reference variable. In the next example, after assigning a2 to a3, the Equals method returns True because the two variables refer to the same object instance:

```
Dim a3 As Account = a2
WriteLine(Equals(a2, a3))              'True
```

11

Object.Equals Method

Two versions of the Equals method exist in the Object class. The one we just demonstrated was the shared method. The Object class also contains an Equals instance method:

```
Overloads Overridable Public Function Equals(Object) As Boolean
```

 Review:

A shared method can be called using the class name as a qualifier. An instance method requires an object instance to qualify the method call. Here are two examples:

```
Dim x As New Bird
Bird.Fly( 50 )              'shared
x.Fly( 50 )                'instance
```

Because all reference types are derived from Object, they can invoke the Equals method. For example, Accounts can be compared:

```
Dim a1 As New Account
Dim a2 As New Account
a1.Equals( a2 )                    'False
```

The semantics (meaning) of the Equals instance method is the same as the shared Equals method. It is possible, however, to override the Equals method in your own classes and change its behavior. We will show how to do it when we talk about inheritance.

Object.ReferenceEquals Shared Method

The Object class contains a shared method named **ReferenceEquals**, which behaves like Equals:

```
Overloads Public Shared Function ReferenceEquals(Object, Object) As Boolean
```

Following is an example:

```
Dim a1 As New Account
Dim a2 As New Account
WriteLine(ReferenceEquals(a1, a2))                'False
```

Overriding a shared method is imposssible, so the meaning of ReferenceEquals will not change when comparing any types of objects.

ToString

The ToString method, defined in the Object class, returns a string representation of an object:

```
Public Overrides Function ToString() As String
```

The Object class implementation displays the fully qualified name of the object type, which includes its namespace path and class name. Here are examples:

```
System.Object
System.IO.Data.DataSet
```

User-created classes usually override the ToString method to provide a more useful string representation. Suppose the Account class had two instance fields named AccountId and Balance. Th following ToString method would be useful:

```
Public Overrides Function ToString() As String
   Return "AccountId = " & AccountId & ", Balance = " _
      & FormatCurrency(Balance)
End Function
```

This is a sample of what the output might look like:

```
AccountId = 1001, Balance = $50.25
```

Overriding the Equals Method

Objects.Accounts

We have said the Object class implementation of the Equals method returns True only if the two object instances are the same. You can change its behavior to *value equality* in your own classes by overriding the method so it compares the state of the objects. For example, if we consider two Account objects to be equal when they have the same unique account number, we can create the following implementation of Equals:

```
1:    Public Overrides Overloads _
2:    Function Equals(ByVal obj As Object) As Boolean
3:
4:        If obj Is Nothing Then Return False
5:        If Not obj.GetType Is Me.GetType Then Return False
6:        Return AccountId = CType(obj, Account).AccountId
7:    End Function
```

Line 4 compares the **obj** parameter to null (Nothing), in case a client program compares an Account to an uninitialized variable. Line 5 prevents an Account object from being compared to some other object type; if we neglected to check for this possibility, the call to CType in Line 6 would throw an InvalidCastException. Line 6 compares the Account ID numbers.

 Note:

The Overloads keyword must be included when overriding Equals because the Equals instance method overloads the shared Equals method in the Object class. We could omit the Overrides keyword, but the method definition would be misleading.

Code Listing 11-2 shows an Account class with ToString and Equals methods. In the following test code, accounts are equal only if they have the same AccountId value:

```
Dim a1 As New Account(1001, 50.25D)
Dim a2 As New Account(1001, 400D)
Dim a3 As New Account(2002, 50.25D)
WriteLine(a1.Equals(a2))              'True
WriteLine(a1.Equals(a3))              'False
```

When we discuss interfaces later in this chapter, we will demonstrate other ways to compare objects.

Code Listing 11-2 (Account class with Equals and ToString)

```
Class Account
   Private AccountId As Integer
   Private Balance As Double

   Sub New(ByVal id As Integer, ByVal bal As Decimal)
      AccountId = id
      Balance = bal
   End Sub

   Overrides Function ToString() As String
      Return "AccountId = " & AccountId & ", Balance = " _
      & FormatCurrency(Balance)
   End Function

   Public Overrides Overloads _
   Function Equals(ByVal obj As Object) As Boolean

      If obj Is Nothing Then Return False
      If Not obj.GetType Is Me.GetType Then Return False
      Return AccountId = CType(obj, Account).AccountId
   End Function
End Class
```

Checkpoint

11.5 What does reflection tell you about an object?

11.6 *(true/false)* TypeOf returns True when comparing the class of an object to one of its base classes.

11.7 The Object.Equals method uses reference equality when comparing objects.

11.8 What is displayed by the Object.ToString method?

▶11.3 Interfaces

Visual Basic .NET, along with other languages, supports a feature named *interfaces*. An interface specifies a set of methods, properties, types, and events that must be supported by classes implementing the interface.

Defining an Interface

An interface is defined much in the same way as a class, except it uses the Interface keyword:

```
Interface identifier
   property-definition
   method-definition
   event-definition
   type-definition
End Interface
```

Interfaces can contain properties, methods, events, and type definitions. Method and property definitions appear as prototypes, each consisting of a return type, name, and parameter list. All members are implicitly public, so you cannot use a Public or Private modifier. You are permitted to use Overloads and Default.

For example, payroll software for an organization might declare an interface named **IPayable**, which contains properties and methods relating to paying individuals:

```
Interface IPayable
    Function CalculateTax() As Decimal
    ReadOnly Property NetPay() As Decimal
End Interface
```

CalculateTax returns the amount of withholding tax for the current pay period. NetPay returns the person's bi-weekly pay after subtracting taxes.

Interface names in the .NET Framework always begin with the letter I, helping to distinguish them from class names. You may want to adopt the same practice.

Implementing an Interface

 Interfaces.IPayableExample

A class implementing an interface must signal its intent by using the **Implements** keyword. For example, here is how the Employee class would implement IPayable:

```
Class Employee
    Implements IPayable
```

A class may implement multiple interfaces:

```
Class Employee
    Implements IPayable, IComparable
```

The IPayable interface can be implemented by classes representing people who can be paid. For example, the Employee class (Code Listing 11-3) implements the NetPay property by subtracting the tax amount from the bi-weekly salary. Though it's not required, the implemented methods and properties should be declared Public as a reminder that all interface members are public.

The following code creates an Employee, calculates the taxes and net pay, and displays the results:

```
Dim emp As New Employee("Jones, Dan", 35000D)
WriteLine(emp.ToString() & _
    ", Tax=" & FormatCurrency(emp.CalculateTax()) & _
    ", Net Pay=" & FormatCurrency(emp.NetPay))
```

Here is the output produced by the example:

```
Jones, Dan    $35,000.00, Tax=$134.62, Net Pay=$1,211.54
```

Renaming Methods and Properties

Visual Basic allows you to rename a method or property when implementing an interface, as long as the Implements clause has the same name as the interface. Here, for example, we rename CalculateTax to **CalcFederalTax**:

```
Public Function CalcFederalTax() As Decimal _
   Implements IPayable.CalculateTax

   Return mSalary * (TAX_RATE / 26D)
End Function
```

We recommend against renaming when implementing an interface because it can easily confuse others reading your source code.

Code Listing 11-3 (Employee Class Implements IPayable)

```
Class Employee
   Implements IPayable

   Sub New(ByVal name As String, ByVal salary As Decimal)
      mName = name
      mSalary = salary
   End Sub

   Public ReadOnly Property NetPay() As Decimal _
      Implements IPayable.NetPay
      Get
         Return (mSalary / 26D) - CalculateTax()
      End Get
   End Property

   Public Function CalculateTax() As Decimal _
    Implements IPayable.CalculateTax
      Return mSalary * (TAX_RATE / 26D)
   End Function

   Public Overrides Function ToString() As String
      Return mName & vbTab & FormatCurrency(mSalary)
   End Function

   Const TAX_RATE As Decimal = 0.1D
   Private mName As String
   Private mSalary As Decimal
End Class
```

 When you type "Implements IPayable" and press Enter in Visual Studio .NET, the editor automatically creates empty versions of CalculateTax and NetPay. In other words, all properties and methods declared in the interface are created within your class.

Interface Parameter Type

When an Interface type is used as parameter type, any instance of a class that implements the interface can be passed as an argument. Suppose we declare a method having a IPayable parameter type:

```
Sub ProcessPayroll(ByVal P As IPayable)
    WriteLine("Tax     = " & FormatCurrency(P.CalculateTax()))
    WriteLine("Net Pay = " & FormatCurrency(P.NetPay))
End Sub
```

We can pass an Employee object because it implements IPayable:

```
Dim emp As New Employee("Jones, Dan", 35000D)
ProcessPayroll(emp)
```

The output appears as follows:

```
Tax     = $134.62
Net Pay = $1,211.54
```

Consultant Class Implements IPayable

We can imagine other classes implementing the IPayable interface. Consultants, for example, are often paid by the hour. During a two-week payroll period, we can keep track of the hours they have worked. The Consultant class (Code Listing 11-4) implements the CalculateTax and NetPay interface members in a manner appropriate to hourly consultants. The following statements create a Consultant object and pass it to the ProcessPayroll method:

```
Dim cons As New Consultant("Ramirez, Manuel", 55D, 125D)
WriteLine(cons.ToString())
ProcessPayroll(cons)
```

This is the resulting output:

```
Ramirez, Manuel Hourly rate=$125.00, Hours=55
Tax     = $687.50
Net Pay = $6,187.50
```

Code Listing 11-4 (Consultant Class)

```
Class Consultant
    Implements IPayable

    Sub New(ByVal name As String, ByVal hours As Single, _
        ByVal hourlyRate As Decimal)
        mName = name
        mHours = hours
        mHourlyRate = hourlyRate
    End Sub
```

11

```
Public Function CalculateTax() As Decimal _
    Implements IPayable.CalculateTax
    Return CDec(mHourlyRate * mHours) * TAX_RATE
End Function

Public ReadOnly Property NetPay() As Decimal _
    Implements IPayable.NetPay
    Get
        Return CDec(mHourlyRate * mHours) - CalculateTax()
    End Get
End Property

Public Overrides Function ToString() As String
    Return mName & vbTab & _
        "Hourly rate=" & FormatCurrency(mHourlyRate) _
        & ", Hours=" & mHours
End Function

Private mName As String
Private mHours As Single
Private mHourlyRate As Single
Const TAX_RATE As Decimal = 0.1D
End Class
```

IComparable Interface

Suppose we wanted to be able to compare Employee objects, possibly with the idea of inserting them into a collection and sorting the data. Employee would have to implement the **IComparable** interface. IComparable contains only one method, **CompareTo**:

```
Interface IComparable
    Function CompareTo(ByVal obj As Object) As Integer
End Interface
```

The SortedArray class in the .NET Framework automatically keeps elements in sorted order. When an element is inserted, SortedArray automatically calls CompareTo. If your class defines the object type to be used as a key, you must implement IComparable. Similarly, if you plan to create an array of objects and call the Sort method in the Array class, you must implement IComparable. The general behavior of CompareTo when comparing objects A and B is the following:

◆ A.CompareTo(null) returns a positive integer.

◆ A System.ArgumentException is thrown if A and B are different types.

◆ If A is less than B, A.CompareTo(B) returns a negative integer.

◆ If A is equal to B, A.CompareTo(B) returns zero.

◆ If A is greater than B, A.CompareTo(B) returns a positive integer.

Employee Class Example

Interfaces.EmployeeCompare

We can implement CompareTo in the Employee class by subtracting the salary of another Employee from the current Employee:

```
Public Function CompareTo(ByVal obj As Object) As Integer _
   Implements IComparable.CompareTo

   Dim emp2 As Employee = CType(obj, Employee)
   Return CInt(mSalary - emp2.mSalary)
End Function
```

Subtracting the salaries produces the following results: Given two employees e1 and e2, the following are true regarding the return value of e1.CompareTo(e2):

◆ Negative if e1's salary is less than e2's salary

◆ Positive if e1's salary is greater than e2's salary

◆ Zero if the salaries are the same

One might ask why we cannot make the parameter an Employee rather than an Object, as in the following:

```
Public Function CompareTo(ByVal emp2 As Employee) As Integer _
   Implements IComparable.CompareTo
   ...
```

This code would not compile because CompareTo must have the same parameter types as the method declaration in IComparable.

Improved CompareTo

A correct implementation of CompareTo requires two more statements. The first statement returns a positive value if an Employee is compared to null (Nothing). The second throws an ArgumentException if the parameter's type is different from Employee:

```
If obj Is Nothing Then Return 1
If Not Me.GetType() Is obj.GetType() Then Throw New ArgumentException
```

A simplified version of the Employee class implementing IComparable appears in Code Listing 11-5.

Code Listing 11-5 (Employee class with IComparable)

```
Class Employee
   Implements IComparable

   Sub New(ByVal name As String, ByVal salary As Decimal)
      mName = name
      mSalary = salary
   End Sub

   Public Function CompareTo(ByVal obj As Object) As Integer _
      Implements IComparable.CompareTo
```

11

```
        If obj Is Nothing Then Return 1
        If Not Me.GetType() Is obj.GetType() Then _
           Throw New ArgumentException

        Dim emp2 As Employee = CType(obj, Employee)
        Return CInt(mSalary - emp2.mSalary)
    End Function

    Public Property Salary() As Decimal
        Get
            Return mSalary
        End Get
        Set(ByVal Value As Decimal)
            mSalary = Value
        End Set
    End Property

    Public Overrides Function ToString() As String
        Return mName & vbTab & FormatCurrency(mSalary)
    End Function

    Private mName As String
    Private mSalary As Decimal
End Class
```

Comparing Employees by Name

 Interfaces.CompareNames

Suppose we wanted to compare Employees by their names rather than salaries. We cannot subtract one person's name from another, as was done with the salaries. Fortunately, the String class implements IComparable, so it has a CompareTo method that performs a case-sensitive string comparison. Our new version of Employee.CompareTo compares the values of the **mName** fields. Only one line of code is different from the version that compared salaries:

```
    Public Function CompareTo(ByVal obj As Object) As Integer _
      Implements IComparable.CompareTo

       If obj Is Nothing Then Return 1
       If Not Me.GetType() Is obj.GetType() Then _
        Throw New ArgumentException

       Dim emp2 As Employee = CType(obj, Employee)
       Return mName.CompareTo(emp2.mName)          '* changed *
    End Function
```

Sorting an Array of Employee

The following statements create an array of Employee objects and call the **Sort** method from the System.Array class. Sort is a shared method that takes an array as its parameter:

```
    Dim staff(3) As Employee
    staff(0) = New Employee("Jones, Dan", 65000D)
    staff(1) = New Employee("Ramirez, Julio", 45000D)
    staff(2) = New Employee("Bond, Barry", 55000D)
    staff(3) = New Employee("Chong, Gary", 75000D)
    System.Array.Sort(staff)
```

We will use a For-Each loop to display the array:

```
Dim person As Employee
For Each person In staff
   WriteLine(person)
Next
```

The output generated by this code shows the array sorted by employee name:

```
Bond, Barry     $55,000.00
Chong, Gary     $75,000.00
Jones, Dan      $65,000.00
Ramirez, Julio  $45,000.00
```

A perceptive reader might ask how the array of Employees could be sorted in descending order. For that matter, how might the same program sort an array of Employees several different ways, given that CompareTo has only a single implementation. To answer these questions, we need to introduce the IComparer interface.

IComparer Interface

The **IComparer** interface declares a single method named **Compare**. It compares two objects and returns an integer in the same manner as IComparable.CompareTo:

```
Interface IComparer
   Function Compare(ByVal x As Object, ByVal y As Object) As Integer
End Interface
```

Unlike CompareTo, the Compare method is not declared in the class it compares. It is declared in its own class, one that implements the IComparer interface. A general template for the class shows you can choose arbitrary names for the class and the method:

```
Class className
   Implements IComparer

   Public Function methodName(ByVal A As Object, _
      ByVal B As Object) As Integer _
      Implements IComparer.Compare

   End Function
End Class
```

When an IComparer object is created using the New operator, we call it a *comparator*. The following code passes an array of Point objects and a comparator to the Array.Sort method:

```
Array.Sort( pArray, new ComparisonClass )
```

11

Windmill Example

Interfaces.Comparators

The way you implement a comparator determines how it will be used. For example, Code Listing 11-6 declares a structure named **Windmill** and a comparator named **RpmComparator**. The comparator returns a positive number if x.rpm is greater than y.rpm; it returns zero if the rpms are equal, and it returns a negative number if x.rpm is less than y.rpm. The following statements create an array of Windmills and sort them in ascending order by rpm:

```
Dim wind(10) As Windmill
'...assign Rpm values to the array members...
Array.Sort(wind, New RpmComparator)
```

Code Listing 11-6 (Windmill and RpmComparator)

```
Structure Windmill
    Public rpm As Integer
End Structure

Class RpmComparator
    Implements IComparer

    Public Function Compare(ByVal x As Object, ByVal y As Object) _
        As Integer Implements IComparer.Compare

        Return CType(x, Windmill).rpm - CType(y, Windmill).rpm
    End Function
End Class
```

Employee Example

Interfaces.Comparators

The primary advantage to using comparators lies in their ability to sort a collection multiple ways without having to rely solely on CompareTo. If, for example, Employee.CompareTo currently orders Employees by name in ascending order, we can create comparators to sort in other ways. Code Listing 11-7 contains comparators that sort Employees by salary in ascending order and descending order, respectively. If you look closely, you can identify the difference between the two implementations. The following output is from a program that sorts and displays the same Employee array four different ways:

```
Ascending Name:
Bond, Barry      $55,000.00
Chong, Gary      $75,000.00
Jones, Dan       $65,000.00
Ramirez, Julio   $45,000.00
Descending Name:
Ramirez, Julio   $45,000.00
Jones, Dan       $65,000.00
Chong, Gary      $75,000.00
Bond, Barry      $55,000.00
```

```
Ascending Salary:
Ramirez, Julio  $45,000.00
Bond, Barry     $55,000.00
Jones, Dan      $65,000.00
Chong, Gary     $75,000.00
Descending Salary:
Chong, Gary     $75,000.00
Jones, Dan      $65,000.00
Bond, Barry     $55,000.00
Ramirez, Julio  $45,000.00
```

Code Listing 11-7 (SortBySalaryAsc and SortBySalaryDesc)

```
Class SortBySalaryAsc
   Implements IComparer

   Public Function Compare(ByVal emp1 As Object, _
      ByVal emp2 As Object) As Integer _
      Implements IComparer.Compare

      Dim e1 As Employee = CType(emp1, Employee)
      Dim e2 As Employee = CType(emp2, Employee)
      Return CInt(e1.Salary) - CInt(e2.Salary)
   End Function
End Class

Class SortBySalaryDesc
   Implements IComparer

   Public Function Compare(ByVal emp1 As Object, _
      ByVal emp2 As Object) As Integer _
      Implements IComparer.Compare

      Dim e1 As Employee = CType(emp1, Employee)
      Dim e2 As Employee = CType(emp2, Employee)
      Return CInt(e2.Salary) - CInt(e1.Salary)
   End Function
End Class
```

Checkpoint

11.9 *(true/false)* An interface definition can include type definitions.

11.10 *(true/false)* Interfaces are not permitted to have method implementations.

11.11 *(true/false)* A method implementation must have the same name as the interface method it implements.

11.12 *(true/false)* The IComparable interface includes the Equals and CompareTo methods.

11

▶ 11.4 Inheritance

Inheritance in object-oriented programming means the ability of classes to specialize the properties, methods, and events in other classes. The **Inherits** clause in Visual Basic identifies an inheritance relationship between the class being defined and another class called the *base class*.

```
Class derivedClass
    Inherits baseClass
```

The base class must be within the current namespace, or within a namespace imported by the program, or it must be a fully qualified class name such as com.scottjones.Payable. Throughout this book, we have made references to base classes that establish behaviors and attributes of more specialized classes. The class behind a Windows Form, for example is derived from the Form class in the System.Windows.Forms namespace:

```
Public Class frmMain
    Inherits System.Windows.Forms.Form
```

In the simplest terms, this declaration means frmMain contains all of the methods, properties, and events in the Form class and all of its base classes. In fact, there is a long inheritance chain leading up to the Form class:

```
System.Object
    System.MarshalByRefObject
        System.ComponentModel.Component
            System.Windows.Forms.Control
                System.Windows.Forms.ScrollableControl
                    System.Windows.Forms.ContainerControl
                        System.Windows.Forms.Form
```

Among the various Form properties (Table 11-1), many are inherited from one of the base classes. Some, like AcceptButton, have been declared for the first time in the Form class.

Table 11-1

Partial list of Form properties (from MSDN help)

Property	Description
AcceptButton	Gets or sets the button on the form that is clicked when the user presses the ENTER key.
AccessibilityObject *(inherited from Control)*	Gets the AccessibleObject assigned to the control.
AccessibleDefaultActionDescription *(inherited from Control)*	Gets or sets the default action description of the control for use by accessibility client applications.
AccessibleDescription *(inherited from Control)*	Gets or sets the description of the control used by accessibility client applications.
AccessibleName *(inherited from Control)*	Gets or sets the name of the control used by accessibility client applications.
AccessibleRole *(inherited from Control)*	Gets or sets the accessible role of the control.
ActiveControl *(inherited from ContainerControl)*	Gets or sets the active control on the container control.

Inheriting common members from base classes helps to reduce the amount of duplicate code in an object-oriented program or code library. Inheritance improves consistency of member names and common operations throughout a class hierarchy. For example, the Object class defines the ToString method. Because all classes implicitly inherit from Object, you can call ToString on any object. Similarly, the Component class has a Container property. An instance of any class derived from Component will have a Container property. Such uniformity of naming and function is a great help to programmers when dealing with a large object library.

Other Terms

In discussions with other programmers, you may hear conflicting use of terms relating to object-oriented programming. The following table compares terms used in Visual Basic with those used by Java programmers:

Visual Basic, C#, and C++	Java
base class	superclass
derived class	subclass
inherits from	extends

Programmers who use multiple languages often switch back and forth between naming systems without realizing it.

Access Modifiers

Before starting to create derived classes, let's review the various member access modifiers. Table 11-2 lists all access modifiers from most permissive (Public) to least permissive (Private). If no access modifier is used, the default is Public. If a field is declared using Dim, it is automatically Private:

```
Class Demo
    Dim mCount As Integer           'Private
    Property Count As Integer...    'Public
    Sub foo()...                    'Public
    Class Inner                     'Public
        ...
    End Class
End Class
```

Table 11-2

Access modifiers

Modifier	Description
Public *(default)*	No restrictions on access to the member.
Protected Friend	Union of Protected and Friend access.
Friend	Accessible only within the same program as the declared member.
Protected	Accessible within the declaring class and classes that inherit from the current class.
Private	Accessible only within the declaring class.

Creating a Derived Class

A class that inherits from a base class is called a *derived class*. It must include the **Inherits** keyword in the class definition. The following indicates the SalariedEmployee class is derived from the Employee class:

```
Class SalariedEmployee
    Inherits Employee
```

All classes implicitly inherit from the Object class, so it requires no declaration. A class can only inherit from one other class. Some programming languages such as C++ permit multiple inheritance, but Visual Basic .NET achieves a similar result using interfaces.

Access to Base Class Members

 Inheritance.Heroes_0

Derived classes can reference base class members declared Public, Protected, or Friend. They cannot reference members declared Private. Suppose the Person class contains the following members with various access specifiers:

```
Class Person
    Public Sub Display()
        WriteLine("Person: " & mName)
    End Sub

    Friend Property Name() As String
        Get
            Return mName
        End Get
        Set(ByVal Value As String)
            mName = Value
        End Set
    End Property

    Protected ID As Integer
    Private mName As String
End Class
```

If the Hero class inherits from Person, the following code shows which Person members can be accessed:

```
Class Hero
    Inherits Person

    Sub TestAccess()
        Display()                   'ok: Public
        Name = "Sam Jones"          'ok: Friend
        ID = 12345                  'ok: Protected
        mName = "Joe Smith"         'error: Private
    End Sub
End Class
```

The derived class may optionally use the **MyBase** identifier to show when a member belongs to the base class:

```
MyBase.Display()
MyBase.Name = "Sam Jones"
```

Heroes and Villains

Inheritance.Heroes_1

Suppose we were to create a set of classes representing characters in a computerized role-playing game. We could look for characteristics identifying the following types of characters: Hero, Villain, and Wizard. We will call this the **Heroes** application, with outlines of classes shown in Code Listing 11-8. (To keep the classes brief, we have used public fields. In a real program, we would create public properties and make the fields private.)

A UML diagram of the class relationships (Figure 11-1) uses arrows pointing from derived classes toward Person, the common base class. Although Object is the implicit base class of Person, it is not shown in object-oriented design diagrams.

Code Listing 11-8 (Person, Hero, Villain, Wizard)

```
Class Person

    Public Name As String
End Class

Class Hero
    Inherits Person

    Public Ability As String
End Class

Class Villain
    Inherits Person

    Public BadDeeds As ArrayList()
End Class

Class Wizard
    Inherits Person

    Enum MagicSpecialty
        casts_spells
        casts_out_spirits
        vanishes
        speaks_in_tongues
        wisdom
    End Enum

    Public Specialty As MagicSpecialty
End Class
```

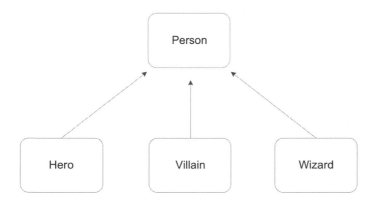

Figure 11-1 Hero class hierarchy

Hero, Villain, and Wizard objects implicitly contain the Name field declared in Person, as well as fields declared in their own classes. Figure 11-2 shows the overlapping of data in each of these objects. The following code is from a test program that illustrates the additive nature of inheritance. A Hero has a name and ability:

```
Dim H As New Hero
H.Name = "Superman"
H.Ability = "Invincible"
```

A Villain has a name, along with a list of bad deeds:

```
Dim V As New Villain
V.Name = "Evil Witch"
V.BadDeeds.Add("Casts spells")
V.BadDeeds.Add("Turns princes into frogs")
```

A Wizard has a name and a specialty:

```
Dim W As New Wizard
W.Name = "Merlin"
W.Specialty = Wizard.MagicSpecialty.wisdom
```

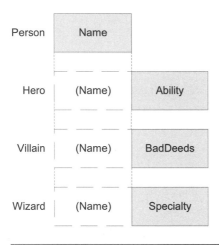

Figure 11-2 Overlapping members in Hero classes

Inheritance with Constructors

Inheritance.Heroes_2

When a derived object is constructed, its base class constructors execute before the object's own constructor executes. This an important concept because the object's constructor might make references to fields declared in its superclasses. We have to know the superclass fields have been properly initialized. When a Hero is constructed, the compiler automatically calls the default constructor for Person. Here is an example:

```
Class Person
   Sub New()
      WriteLine("Person.New executing...")
   End Sub
End Class

Class Hero
   Inherits Person
   Sub New()
```

```
        WriteLine("Hero.New executing...")
      End Sub
    End Class
```

If we construct a Hero object, the program's output displays the constructor calls:

```
Person.New executing...
Hero.New executing...
```

If Person has a parameterized constructor, however, the first statement inside Hero's constructor must call Person's constructor. In the following example, the **MyBase.New** statement passes the **name** parameter to Person.New:

```
Class Person
   Sub New(ByVal name As String)
      mName = name
   End Sub
   Private mName As String
End Class

Class Hero
   Inherits Person

   Sub New(ByVal name As String, ByVal ability As String)
      MyBase.New(name)
      mAbility = ability
   End Sub
   Private mAbility As String
End Class
```

Inherited Properties and Methods

Inheritance.Heroes_3

In the same way fields are inherited, properties and methods are also inherited by derived classes. In Code Listing 11-9, we have added a Display method and Name property to the Person class. We have added an Ability property to the Hero class. The following statements show a Hero can access any member of the Person class:

```
Dim H As New Hero("Batman", "Agility")
H.Display()
WriteLine(H.Name & ": " & H.Ability)
```

But a Person cannot access the Ability property declared in the Hero class:

```
Dim P As New Person("Joe")
P.Display()                          'ok
WriteLine(P.Ability)                 'error
```

Code Listing 11-9 (Person and Hero)

```
Class Person
   Sub New(ByVal name As String)
     mName = name
   End Sub

   Sub Display()
     WriteLine("Person: " & mName)
   End Sub

   Property Name() As String
     Get
         Return mName
     End Get
     Set(ByVal Value As String)
        mName = Value
     End Set
   End Property

   Private mName As String
End Class

Class Hero
   Inherits Person

   Sub New(ByVal name As String, ByVal ability As String)
     MyBase.New(name)
     mAbility = ability
   End Sub

   Property Ability() As String
     Get
         Return mAbility
     End Get
     Set(ByVal Value As String)
        mAbility = Value
     End Set
   End Property

   Private mAbility As String
End Class
```

Assigning Object References

Object references can always be assigned upward in the inheritance hierarchy from a derived type to a base type. This is termed an *upward cast*:

```
Dim P As Person
Dim H As New Hero("Aquaman", "Swims")
P = H
```

The compiler will not let you directly assign a base type to a derived type:

```
Dim P As New Person("Joe")
Dim H As Hero
H = P                         'error
```

If such an assignment were permitted, one might be tempted to reference a member of Hero using an object that was, after all, just a Person. It is possible to satisfy the compiler using a *downward cast*, accomplished by calling CType:

```
Dim P As New Person("Joe")
Dim Z As Hero = CType(P, Hero)
```

The Common Language Runtime throws an exception when it discovers P holds a reference to a Person, not a Hero.

Downward casts are legitimate and useful in certain situations when you know a variable of a base type holds a reference to a derived type. The following example uses a valid cast:

```
Dim P As Person = New Hero("Aquaman", "Swims")
  .
  .
WriteLine(CType(P, Hero).Ability)      'ok
```

To be on the safe side, we recommend you surround downward casts with a Try-Catch block.

Overriding and Overloading

Inheritance.Overriding

The terms overriding and overloading can easily be confused with each other:

- To *override* a method is to replace a base class method with a derived class method having the same signature. Properties can also be overridden.

- To *overload* a method is to create a new method having the same name as an existing method in the same class or a base class. The new method must have a different signature.

Table 11-3 lists the modifiers that relate to overriding methods and properties. A method or property must be declared Overridable before it can be overriden in a derived class. A method or property that overrides another method must use the Overrides qualifier.

Table 11-3

Modifiers related to method overriding

Modifier	Description
Overridable	Property or method **can** be overridden in a class derived from the current class.
Overrides	Overrides an existing property or method in a base class.
NotOverridable	Property or method **cannot** be overridden (default)
MustOverride	Property or method **must** be overridden in a class derived from the current class. (Only a prototype is used in the declaration.)

11

Code Listing 11-10 shows two classes named Base and Derived. The Derived.foo method overrides Base.foo. Suppose the following two statements are executed:

```
Dim obj As New Derived
obj.foo()
```

The output is **foo in Derived Class**, because the compiler knew obj's type and generated a call to Derived.foo(). Perhaps we can fool the compiler by declaring obj as type Base and assign a Derived object to the variable:

```
Dim obj As Base
obj = New Derived
obj.foo()
```

Again, the output is **foo in Derived Class**. Although the compiler regarded obj as a Base object, the .NET Common Language Runtime identified the object's type and generated a call to Derived.foo(). The term for this technique is called *late binding*, when the address of a method is not bound to a variable calling the method until the program is executing.

Code Listing 11-10 (Overriding the foo Method)

```
Class Base

    Overridable Sub foo()
        Console.WriteLine("foo in Base Class")
    End Sub
End Class

Class Derived
    Inherits Base

    Overrides Sub foo()
        WriteLine("foo in Derived Class")
    End Sub
End Class
```

Changing Access Levels

A member declared Private in a base class cannot be overridden, because derived classes have no access to private base class members:

```
Class Base
    Private Overridable Sub foo()          'error
```

You can use Overridable with Friend, Protected, or Public:

```
Class Base
    Protected Overridable Sub foo()        'ok
```

You cannot change the access level of a method when overriding a member. The following use of Overrides is an error:

```
Class Base
    Overridable Sub foo()

Class Derived
    Private Overrides Sub foo()            'error
```

Method Overloading by a Derived Class

Inheritance.Overloading

A derived class can overload methods located in any of its base classes. In Code Listing 11-11, the **foo** method in the **Derived** class has a different signature from the foo method in the **Base** class. The Overloads qualifier is required as it would be if both methods were in the same class. Suppose we executed the following statements:

```
Dim obj As New Derived
obj.foo()
obj.foo("abc")
```

The output would be the following:

```
foo in Base Class
foo in Derived Class
```

The difference between the method signatures is enough for the program to distinguish between the two versions of foo.

Code Listing 11-11 (Overloading in a Derived Class)

```
Class Base

    Sub foo()
        Console.WriteLine("foo in Base Class")
    End Sub
End Class

Class Derived
    Inherits Base

    Overloads Sub foo(ByVal str As String)
        WriteLine("foo in Derived Class")
    End Sub
End Class
```

Abstract Classes and Methods

Inheritance.Abstract

A class declared with the **MustInherit** keyword is known as an *abstract class*. You cannot create an instance of an abstract class, but it's a great place to put fields, properties, and methods common to all of its derived classes. A method declared **MustOverride** is an *abstract method*. It contains a method prototype with no implementation. It must be overridden and implemented in a derived class before instances of the derived class can be created.

In Code Listing 11-12, the **Base** class is declared **MustInherit**, making it an abstract class. It contains a **MustOverride** method named **foo**. If we want to create an instance of **Derived**, the class must override the foo method. We can execute the following statements to test the methods:

```
Dim obj As New Derived
obj.foo()
```

If we removed foo from the Derived class, a compiler error would say that Derived must be declared MustInherit or it must override the foo method.

11

Code Listing 11-12 (Abstract class)

```
MustInherit Class Base

    MustOverride Sub foo()
End Class

Class Derived
    Inherits Base

    Overrides Sub foo()
        WriteLine("foo in Derived Class")
    End Sub
End Class
```

Employee Classes Example

 Inheritance.AbstractEmployee

The Employee class in Code Listing 11-13 is an abstract class (a MustInherit class) that implements the IComparable interface. Combining inheritance with interfaces is commonly done because it combines a rich set of attributes and behaviors. The GrossPay property is declared MustOverride because Employee does not contain enough information to calculate a person's pay. NetPay and CalculateTax, on the other hand, are implemented in Employee because the calculations will probably work for all types of employees. NetPay and CalculateTax are declared Overridable in case future derived classes need to calculate the net pay and taxes differently. The ToString method is not declared Overridable because it inherits this attribute from the Object class:

```
Public Overrides Function ToString() As String
    Return mName
End Function
```

CompareTo relaxes the type checking rules by allowing obj to be any type of Employee. The **TypeOf** operator returns True if **obj** is derived from Employee:

```
If Not TypeOf (obj) Is Employee Then _
    Throw New ArgumentException
```

Code Listing 11-13 (Abstract Employee class)

```
MustInherit Class Employee
    Implements IComparable

    Sub New(ByVal empId As Integer, ByVal name As String)
        mEmpId = empId
        mName = name
    End Sub

    MustOverride ReadOnly Property GrossPay() As Decimal

    Overridable Function CalculateTax() As Decimal
        Return GrossPay * TAX_RATE
    End Function

    Overridable ReadOnly Property NetPay() As Decimal
        Get
            Return GrossPay - CalculateTax()
        End Get
```

```
        End Property

        ReadOnly Property EmpId() As Integer
            Get
                Return mEmpId
            End Get
        End Property

        Property Name() As String
            Get
                Return mName
            End Get
            Set(ByVal Value As String)
                mName = Value
            End Set
        End Property

        Public Overloads _
        Function CompareTo(ByVal obj As Object) As Integer _
            Implements IComparable.Compareto

            If obj Is Nothing Then Return 1
            If Not TypeOf (obj) Is Employee Then _
                Throw New ArgumentException
            Return mName.CompareTo(CType(obj, Employee).mName)
        End Function

        Public Overrides Overloads _
        Function Equals(ByVal obj As Object) As Boolean

            If obj Is Nothing Then Return False
            If Not obj.GetType Is Me.GetType Then Return False
            Return mEmpId.Equals(CType(obj, Employee).mEmpId)
        End Function

        Public Overrides Function GetHashCode() As Integer
            Return mEmpId.GetHashCode()
        End Function

        Public Overrides Function ToString() As String
            Return mEmpId & ": " & mName
        End Function

        Private Const TAX_RATE As Decimal = 0.1D
        Private mEmpId As Integer
        Private mName As String
    End Class
```

SalariedEmployee and HourlyEmployee Classes

The SalariedEmployee and HourlyEmployee classes are shown in Code Listing 11-14. Each must override the GrossPay method and calculate the employee's pay in a manner appropriate to the class. A SalariedEmployee receives 1/26 of their annual salary every two weeks, and an hourly employee receives hours worked multiplied by the hourly pay rate.

Code Listing 11-14 (SalariedEmployee and HourlyEmployee)

```
Class SalariedEmployee
    Inherits Employee

    Sub New(ByVal empId As Integer, ByVal name As String, _
        ByVal salary As Decimal)
        MyBase.New(empId, name)
        mSalary = salary
    End Sub

    Overrides ReadOnly Property GrossPay() As Decimal
        Get
            Return (mSalary / 26D)
        End Get
    End Property

    Overrides Function ToString() As String
        Return MyBase.ToString() & "  " & FormatCurrency(mSalary)
    End Function

    Private mSalary As Decimal
End Class

Class HourlyEmployee
    Inherits Employee

    Sub New(ByVal empId As Integer, ByVal name As String, _
        ByVal hours As Decimal, ByVal payRate As Decimal)

        MyBase.New(empId, name)
        mHours = hours
        mPayRate = payRate
    End Sub

    Overrides ReadOnly Property GrossPay() As Decimal
        Get
            Return mHours * mPayRate
        End Get
    End Property

    Public ReadOnly Property PayRate() As Decimal
        Get
            Return mPayRate
        End Get
    End Property

    Overrides Function ToString() As String
        Return MyBase.ToString() & "  Hrs/Rate = " & mHours & "/" & mPayRate
    End Function

    Private mHours As Decimal
    Private mPayRate As Decimal
End Class
```

Derived class constructors should always call their base class constructors. The SalariedEmployee constructor demonstrates the way to do it by calling MyBase.New:

```
Sub New(ByVal empId As Integer, ByVal name As String, _
 ByVal salary As Decimal)
    MyBase.New(empId, name)
    mSalary = salary
End Sub
```

Similarly, SalariedEmployee's ToString method calls the same method in its base class:

```
Overrides Function ToString() As String
    Return MyBase.ToString() & "   " & FormatCurrency(mSalary)
End Function
```

Testing the Classes

The following code creates two employees and invokes the payroll calculations on each:

```
Dim S As Employee, H As Employee
S = New SalariedEmployee(1001, "Johnson, Cal", 57000)
H = New HourlyEmployee(2002, "Ramirez, Ben", 85, 35.5D)

WriteLine(S.ToString() & ": " & _
    FormatCurrency(S.GrossPay) & " - " & _
    FormatCurrency(S.CalculateTax) & " = " & _
    FormatCurrency(S.NetPay))

WriteLine(H.ToString() & ": " & _
    FormatCurrency(H.GrossPay) & " - " & _
    FormatCurrency(H.CalculateTax) & " = " & _
    FormatCurrency(H.NetPay))
```

Here is the output produced by our code:

```
1001: Johnson, Cal  $57,000.00: $2,192.31 - $219.23 = $1,973.08
2002: Ramirez, Ben  Hrs/Rate = 85/35.5: $3,017.50 - $301.75 = $2,715.75
```

Polymorphism

Inheritance.Polymorphism

Webster's dictionary defines *polymorphic* as "having, occurring, or assuming various forms, characters, or styles." Object-oriented design commonly defines polymorphism as a base type's ability to reference various derived types. If we declare a variable of type Employee and assign it a derived type, we're using polymorphism:

```
Dim emp As Employee
emp = New SalariedEmployee(1001, "Johnson, Cal", 57000)
```

At a later point in the program's execution, we might decide to assign an HourlyEmployee to the same variable:

```
emp = New HourlyEmployee(2002, "Ramirez, Ben", 85, 35.5D)
```

This assignment is permitted because it gives programs the flexibility to create arrays and collections of various employee types. Programs can use generic methods to handle objects of many different types.

Using the recent example containing Employee, SalariedEmployee, and HourlyEmployee classes, we can create a method that calculates and displays the pay and taxes for all types of employees:

```
Sub DoCalculations(ByVal emp As Employee)
    WriteLine(emp.ToString() & ": " & _
        FormatCurrency(emp.GrossPay) & " - " & _
        FormatCurrency(emp.CalculateTax) & " = " & _
        FormatCurrency(emp.NetPay))
End Sub
```

The parameter is type Employee, but we can pass any derived type as a parameter. If, in the future, new types of employees are added to the inheritance hierarchy, they can be passed to the DoCalculations method. Having a method that works for all types of employees greatly reduces the amount of duplicate code in programs. We can add new types of employees to our system without having to revise and rewrite existing methods that handle employees.

An important issue in regard to methods like DoCalculations can be raised. Assuming the parameter is type Employee, why doesn't the DoCalculations method call the GrossPay property procedure located in the Employee class? One reason is GrossPay is only prototyped in the Employee class. Another is that Visual Basic is able to wait until runtime to decide whether to call SalariedEmployee.GrossPay or HourlyEmployee.GrossPay. Suppose we call DoCalculations with the following code:

```
Dim emp As Employee
emp = New SalariedEmployee(1001, "Johnson, Cal", 57000)
DoCalculations(emp)
```

During the program's execution, the Common Language Runtime looks up emp's type, and upon discovering it is a SalariedEmployee, calls the GrossPay property procedure in the SalariedEmployee class.

Polymorphism seems a little like magic, yet its usage has become commonplace in programming languages such as Java, C#, C++, and Visual Basic .NET.

Checkpoint

11.13 *(true/false)* A class may inherit from more than one base class.

11.14 *(true/false)* Protected members of a base class can be referenced by methods in its derived class.

11.15 *(true/false)* Base class constructors execute before derived class constructors.

11.16 *(true/false)* Casting an object from a base class type to a derived type is called *upward casting*.

▶11.5 Collections

Nearly every modern industrial-strength programming language has an extensive library of classes called *collections*. Instances of these classes hold sets and ordered lists of objects. The class names vary, yet the principles behind their design and use are the same. The .NET Framework collection classes are as good as you will find in any programming language.

Relational databases such as SQL Server and MS-Access do a good job of storing data in related tables, but they are nowhere near as adept as collections at storing hierarchical data. For example, suppose you had a list of customers (Figure 11-3). Attached to each of those customers was an array of lists, each containing orders placed by the customer during a particular month. Within a single month's list, a list of orders existed for each date. Each order had a list of items. Each item contained an item number, quantity, and price. You would hard-pressed to code such information in database tables without losing the conceptual structure of the data. Collection objects, on the other hand, can hold other collection objects, which can hold other collections, etc. You can go as deep as you want and efficiently access data as long as it will fit in memory.

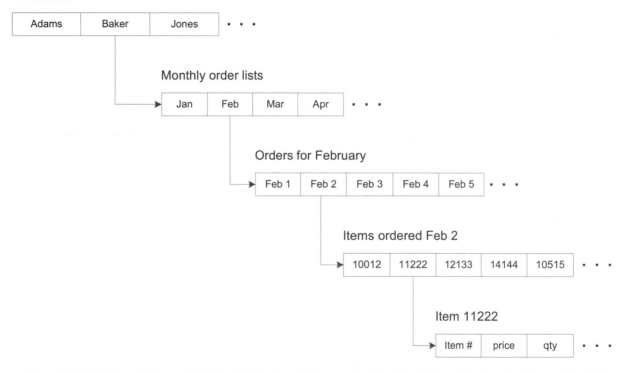

Figure 11-3 Hierarchical order item structure

The System.Collections namespace in the .NET Framework contains a number of useful classes, summarized in Table 11-4. We will only discuss the Hashtable and SortedList classes in this chapter, but you can check our book's Web site for examples that use the other collections.

Table 11-4

Classes in the System.Collections namespace

Class Name	Description
ArrayList	An array-type collection that expands as needed. Permits sequential and random access to elements.
BitArray	A collection of boolean values; permits both sequential and random access to elements.
CollectionBase	Abstract class, from which you can use inheritance to create a strongly typed collection; minimal set of methods, but you can enhance the class capabilities.
DictionaryBase	Abstract class, from which you can create your own class that maps keys to values. Known as a *dictionary* or *map*.
Hashtable	Dictionary-type collection containing keys mapped to values; automatically sorted by the keys, optimized for rapid lookup.
Queue	Specialized type of sequential list that uses the first-in, first-out (FIFO) principle for adding and removing items.
SortedList	A collection of key-value pairs sorted by the keys and accessible by key or by index; cross between a HashTable and an Array.
Stack	Specialized type of sequential list that uses the last-in, first-out (LIFO) principle for adding and removing items.

Hashtable

A Hashtable is a dictionary-type collection that stores keys and their associated values. A *dictionary* lets you look up information on any type of object, called a *key*. Hashtables are optimized for quick storage and retrieval, and the keys must be unique. Inserting a duplicate key throws an ArgumentException. The Hashtable class implements the **IDictionary** and **ICollection** interfaces, which determine the set of properties and methods it must contain. The IDictionary interface is shown in Table 11-5.

Table 11-5

The IDictionary interface

Properties	Description
IsFixedSize	Returns a Boolean value indicating whether the IDictionary has a fixed size.
IsReadOnly	Returns a Boolean value indicating whether the IDictionary is read-only.
Item	Gets or sets the element matching a specified key.
Keys	Returns an ICollection of keys.
Values	Returns an ICollection of values.
Methods	
Add	Adds an element containing a key and value to the dictionary.
Clear	Removes all elements.
Contains	Returns a Boolean value indicating whether an element with the specified key exists.
GetEnumerator	Returns an enumerator that can be used to iterate over the dictionary.
Remove	Removes the element with the specified key from the dictionary.

The ICollection interface has a single property named **Count** that returns the number of items in a collection. It has a method named **CopyTo** that copies the collection elements into an Array object. Therefore, Count and CopyTo are implemented in Hashtable. Each entry in a Hashtable (or any IDictionary) is a **DictionaryEntry** object, which has two properties named **Key** and **Value**. Both are type Object.

Batting Averages Example

 Collections.HashTableEx

Suppose we wanted to keep track of the batting averages of a group of baseball players. Our keys could be the players' names, and the value associated with each key would be the person's batting average. The Hashtable's Add method inserts each key-value pair:

```
Dim averages As New Hashtable
With averages
    .Add("Joe", 230.2)
    .Add("Dan", 330.2)
    .Add("Ann", 210)
    .Add("Bob", 430.2)
    .Add("Sam", 160.6)
    .Add("Jim", 200.7)
End With
```

If Hashtable keys are strings, they are compared in case-sensitive mode. Therefore, a key of "ann" is distinct from "Ann".

Looking Up Values

The **Item** property can be used to get the value associated with a key. For example, looking up a person's batting average is accomplished using the key as an index into the Items collection. The return value is an Object:

```
Dim obj As Object = averages.Item("Dan")
```

Because Item is the default property, the statement can be abbreviated:

```
Dim obj As Object = averages("Dan")
```

We might cast the value into a String or numeric type:

```
WriteLine("Dan's average is " & CSng(obj))
```

The **Contains** method returns True if the key passed to it is found in the Hashtable:

```
If averages.Contains("Bob") Then...
```

The **ContainsKey** method also returns True if a key is found in the Hashtable:

```
If averages.ContainsKey("Bob") Then...
```

Another method, **ContainsValue**, returns True if it finds a matching element in the Values collection. This method does not work when the keys are floating-point numbers because such numbers do not have an exact storage representation. If your keys are objects that implement the Equals method, ContainsValue will work.

Hashtable keys are stored using a hashing function that calculates an index position in memory according to a sophisticated integer calculation. The purpose of a hash function is to identify a unique location for each key. When a program retrieves the value associated with the key, the same hash function calculates the value's location. In fact, sometimes two keys can produce the same hash code, causing a collision which is dealt with internally by the Hashtable class designer.

11

Display the Keys Collection

You can display the keys in a Hashtable using a For-Each loop. The ordering of the keys cannot be predicted, because their memory locations are determined by the hashing function:

```
Dim name As String
For Each name In averages.Keys
   WriteLine(name)
Next
```

Here, for example is the output from the display loop in our example program. The order is not alphabetical, and it does not match the order in which keys were inserted:

```
Ann
Jim
Dan
Joe
Sam
Bob
```

Display the Values Collection

A For-Each loop can be used to iterate over the Values collection in a Hashtable. The following displays all batting averages:

```
Dim score As Single
For Each score In averages.Values
   WriteLine(score)
Next
```

Display the Entries

You can use a For-Each loop to iterate over all the **DictionaryEntry** objects in the collection. The Key and Value properties are Objects, so you must cast them into appropriate types:

```
Dim entry As DictionaryEntry
For Each entry In averages
   WriteLine(CStr(entry.Key) & "-->" & CSng(entry.Value))
Next
```

Produces the following output:

```
Ann-->210
Jim-->200.7
Dan-->330.2
Joe-->230.2
Sam-->160.6
Bob-->430.2
```

Replacing Values

The Item property of a Hashtable replaces the value associated with a key. Each of the following statements replaces Dan's batting average:

```
averages.Item("Dan") = 275
averages("Dan") = 275
```

Untyped Elements

Hashtables have a feature that can be thought of as either good or bad, depending on its use. A Hashtable can contain any types of objects. For example, we might accidentally reverse the parameters when adding a member to the averages Hashtable:

```
averages.Add(250, "Buz")
```

Our error would not show up until we tried to iterate over the values, which we thought were all numbers:

```
Dim score As Single
For Each score In averages.Values        'throws InvalidCastException
    WriteLine(score)
Next
```

We would also not find Buz's score:

```
Dim score as Single = averages("Buz")        'not found
```

If we were careful to insert objects related to each other by inheritance or implementation (interfaces), we could take advantage of polymorphism when performing operations on Hashtable elements. A popular design approach is to create a strongly typed collection class that inherits from DictionaryBase. Then one can specify the types of objects permitted in the Hashtable.

SortedList

 Collections.SortedListEx

The SortedList collection class implements the IDictionary interface, so you can look up values associated with keys. Most notably, it maintains the keys in sorted order. The keys must be unique, or a System.ArgumentException is thrown. Each entry in SortedList is a DictionaryEntry object.

For our example program, we will insert Employee objects into a SortedList. The Employee class (Code Listing 11-15) is kept as simple as possible. Code Listing 11-16 adds some Employee objects to a SortedList named **list**.

Code Listing 11-15 (Employee for SortedList)

```
Class Employee
   Sub New(ByVal empId As Integer, Optional ByVal name As String = "")
      mEmpId = empId
      mName = name
   End Sub

   Public Overrides Overloads _
   Function Equals(ByVal obj As Object) As Boolean
      If obj Is Nothing Then Return False
      If Not obj.GetType Is Me.GetType Then Return False
      Return mEmpId = CType(obj, Employee).mEmpId
   End Function

   Overrides Function ToString() As String
      Return mEmpId & ": " & mName
   End Function
```

```
    ReadOnly Property EmpId() As Integer
       Get
           Return mEmpId
       End Get
    End Property

    ReadOnly Property Name() As String
       Get
           Return mName
       End Get
    End Property

    Private mEmpId As Integer
    Private mName As String
End Class
```

Code Listing 11-16 (Adding Entries to SortedList)

```
Dim list As New SortedList
Dim emp As Employee
emp = New Employee(1001, "Jones, Dan")
list.Add(emp.EmpId, emp)
emp = New Employee(3001, "Baker, Sam")
list.Add(emp.EmpId, emp)
emp = New Employee(2001, "Gonzalez, Julio")
list.Add(emp.EmpId, emp)
emp = New Employee(1501, "Chong, Gary")
list.Add(emp.EmpId, emp)
```

Display the Entries

The following loop displays all entries:

```
    Dim entry As DictionaryEntry
    For Each entry In list
       WriteLine(CInt(entry.Key) & "-->" & entry.Value.ToString())
    Next
```

The following statement gets the value associated with key 1001:

```
    WriteLine("Found key 1001: " & list(1001).ToString())
```

The **ContainsValue** method searches for a matching object in the Values collection and returns True if one is found. We construct an Employee from an ID number before searching:

```
    emp = New Employee(1501)
    WriteLine("Contains Chong: " & list.ContainsValue(emp))
```

ContainsValue automatically calls Employee.Equals during the search. Our Employee class overrides Equals, so Employees are compared by their ID numbers. If we did not override Equals, the default Equals method in the Object class would compare the objects by their instances.

Inserting, removing, and finding entries in a SortedList are much slower than the same opertions on a Hashtable. If you have a large number of keys that do not have to be sorted, use a Hashtable rather than a SortedList.

Checkpoint

11.17 *(true/false)* Collection classes are adept at expressing hierarchical data relationships.

11.18 *(true/false)* You cannot create an instance of CollectionBase.

11.19 *(true/false)* The Hashtable class requires you to calculate the hash code of a key before inserting an entry in the table.

11.20 *(true/false)* Hashtable keys are always kept in strict sequential order.

▶11.6 Visual Inheritance

Windows Forms and Web Forms are declared as classes in .NET. Controls are declared as class members, and Form classes inherit from existing classes in the .NET Framework. The powerful concept implicit in this design is that you can use *visual inheritance* to create new forms that build on other forms.

You can create a base Form class containing visual and functional elements common to other forms in your program. If you import a base Form class into other programs, their forms can inherit the same appearance and functionality. Suppose a company logo was on such a form; every program would display the same logo. Should the company later change its logo, the change would be made only in the base Form class. All programs inheriting from this form would be updated as soon as they were recompiled.

Web pages at educational and corporate sites usually have a standard look and feel, with logos, borders, banners, and hyperlinks. All such information can be defined in a base Web forms class and inherited by the other Web forms.

Hands-On Tutorial

BaseForm and Login Classes

 VisualInherit

In this hands-on tutorial, you will create a Form class that acts as a base class for other forms. You will then create two derived Form classes with different sets of controls.

Step 1. Create a new Windows application named **VisualInherit**.

Step 2. Delete the startup form and create a new form named **BaseForm**.

Step 3. Remove the Minimize and Maximize buttons, and set the form's Text property to **Base Form**.

11

Step 4. Add a Label control along the bottom of the form and set its Text property to **Copyright Scott-Jones Publishing, 2004.** Center the text. A sample of the form is shown in Figure 11-4.

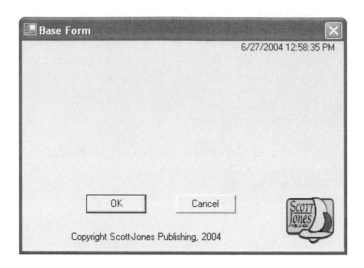

Figure 11-4 Base Form, run mode

Step 5. Add a PictureBox control to the form in the lower right corner. Set the SizeMode property to **StretchImage.** Set the Image property by navigating to the **SJlogo.gif** file in the Chapter 11 examples directory.

Step 6. Add a Label control to the upper-right corner and name it **lblDateTime**.

Step 7. Add a Timer control to the form and set its Enabled property to **True** and its Interval property to **1000**. The timer will update the date and time display on the form.

Step 8. Add two buttons to the form, named **btnOk** and **btnCancel**. Set their Text properties to **OK** and **Cancel**.

Step 9. Double-click on the Timer control and insert the following line of code in its Click event handler:

```
lblDateTime.Text = CStr(Now)
```

Step 10. Double-click on the Cancel button and insert the following code in its Click event handler:

```
Me.Close()
```

Step 11. Run the program and verify that it looks like the output in Figure 11-3. The time display should update once per second. When you click on the Cancel button, the form should close.

Creating a Derived Form

Now you will begin the most interesting part of the program design, which is to create a new form derived from the BaseForm class. It is a simple login form, into which the user can enter a username and password.

Step 1. Right-click on the project name in the Solution Explorer window, select **Add**, and select **Add Inherited Form**. Name the form **LoginForm**. After the Inheritance Picker dialog appears (Figure 11-5), select the base class from which your form will inherit. Select **BaseForm** and click on OK.

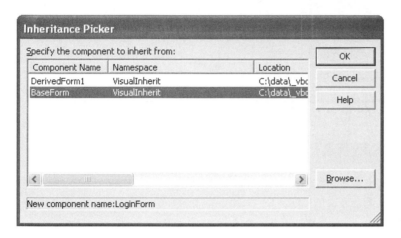

Figure 11-5 Inheritance Picker dialog

Step 2. Notice the form looks almost like BaseForm, except for the small blue and gray icons at the corner of each control (Figure 11-6) showing it is inherited.

Step 3. Set the form's Text property to **Login Form**. Add the following controls to the form, using Figure 11-7 as a guide:

Control Type	Name	Properties
Label	(default)	Text: Username
Label	(default)	Text: Password
TextBox	txtUserName	
TextBox	txtPassword	

11

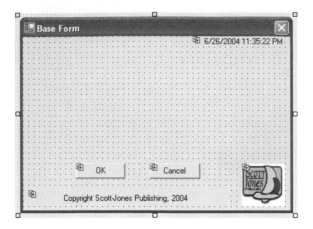

Figure 11-6 Starting to design the Login form

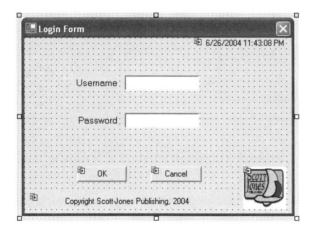

Figure 11-7 Login form, finished design

Step 4. Right-click the project properties and set the Login form as the startup form.

Step 5. Double-click on the OK button and insert the following statement in its Click event handler:

```
MessageBox.Show("Thank you for logging in.", "Login Form")
```

Step 6. Save and run the program. You should be able to enter a username and password, and click on OK or Cancel.

 If you make any changes to a base form class, save and rebuild the project before making any changes to derived form classes.

Controlling Scope of Controls

The default access for controls on a base form is Friend, which permits any method in the current project to reference the control. It is better to use **Protected** access, which can be set using a control's **Modifiers** property. If a control has Protected access, you can modify its properties while designing the derived form. You can reference the control in your derived form's code.

If you set a control's Modifiers property to **Private**, the control cannot be moved or modified when designing a derived form. Now we continue the **VisualInherit** program:

Step 1. In the BaseForm designer, set the Modified property of the PictureBox control to Private. Do the same for the label control at the bottom of the form.

Step 2. Set the Modified properties of the two buttons to Protected.

Step 3. Save and rebuild the project.

Step 4. Open the Login form in the designer, and attempt to move the Picture box or modify any of its properties. It should not be possible to do so.

Step 5. Move the two Button controls and experiment with changing their properties. You should be able to do so.

Step 6. Save the program.

Event Handling in Derived Forms

If a control defined in a base class has no handler, you can create an event handler in its derived class. If the base class contains a handler, you have to use special coding to process the event handling.

A derived form can define event handlers that work in tandem with event handlers already written for base class controls. The BaseForm class in the VisualInherit program has an event handler for the Cancel button that closes the form. Suppose, when creating the Login form, we would like to create a Click handler for the same button. Logically, we should override the event handler in the base class, but event handlers are not declared Overridable. Instead, we will use the approach suggested in Francisco Balena's book[1].

Step 7. Insert a call to OnCancelClick in the Cancel button's Click event handler in the BaseForm class:

```
Private Sub btnCancel_Click(ByVal sender As System.Object, _
 ByVal e As System.EventArgs) Handles btnCancel.Click
   OnCancelClick()
End Sub
```

Step 8. Add a Protected Overridable method to the BaseForm class named OnCancelClick:

```
Protected Overridable Sub OnCancelClick()
   Me.Close()
End Sub
```

Step 9. In the Login form class, Override the OnCancelClick method, and insert code that performs actions prior to calling the BaseForm.OnCancelClick method:

```
Protected Overrides Sub OnCancelClick()
   Dim result As Integer
   result = MessageBox.Show("Are you sure you want to cancel?", _
    "Cancel", MessageBoxButtons.YesNo, MessageBoxIcon.Question)

   If result = DialogResult.Yes Then
     MyBase.OnCancelClick()
   End If
End Sub
```

---

[1] *Programming Microsoft Visual Basic .NET*. Microsoft Press, 2002.

11

Step 10. A clever mechanism is working here (Figure 11-8). When the user clicks on the Cancel button, the object receiving the Click event is a Login object. Because Login has no event handler for the Cancel button, the BaseForm.btnCancel_Click handler executes. The handler calls OnCancelClick, which is overridded in the Login class. Control transfers to Login.OnCancelClick, which makes a call to BaseForm.OnCancelClick, which closes the form.

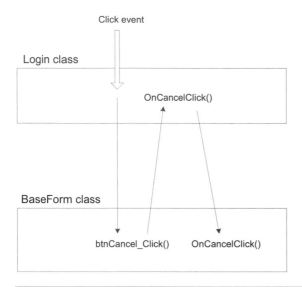

Figure 11-8   Handling a click event

You can find many uses for visual inheritance, by enhancing the behaviors of individual controls or by building forms with common properties. You might explore this technique with Web forms, and create a common Web form inherited by all other Web forms in the same application.

Checkpoint

11.21 *(true/false)* Controls placed on a base form appear on all of its inherited forms.

11.22 *(true/false)* A control declared Private in a base form class can be moved and modified when viewed in a derived form's designer window.

11.23 *(true/false)* If a base class control has no event handler, you can define a handler in a derived class.

►11.7 Advanced Topic: Delegates

Delegates

A *delegate* is a method type declaration that permits methods to be called using their addresses. This powerful technique is used extensively by .NET, particularly when handling runtime events such as Button_Click or Text_Changed. A delegate must be declared outside of all classes, so it usually appears at the beginning of a code module. The **Delegate** keyword appears before Sub or Function.

Example

The following **Sub_NoParms** delegate defines a method type with no parameters:

```
Delegate Sub Sub_NoParms()
```

The Delegate statement does not define a method—instead, it defines a method *type*. To say it another way, the Delegte statement defines a class of methods containing a specific argument list. It cannot be called directly. Suppose a method named **Hello** exists that matches the signature of Sub_NoParms:

```
Sub Hello()
    System.Console.WriteLine("Hello there")
End Sub
```

The following statements declare a variable of type Sub_NoParms and assign it the address of Hello:

```
Dim deleg As Sub_NoParms
deleg = AddressOf Hello
```

The following **Invoke** statement calls the Hello method, using the address stored in **deleg**:

```
deleg.Invoke()
```

If you can call a method by name, it's always best to do so. But when the name of the method to be called is not known at compile time, a delegate can offer more flexibility. We can assign the addresses of different methods to the same variable, using information acquired at runtime. The .NET runtime, for example, uses delegates to store addresses of event handlers. When events are generated for a particular control, the appropriate handler methods are called using delegates.

The next example will show how a method can act as an intermediary between a calling program and the method it calls.

Indirectly Calling a Method

Indirectly calling a method means calling the method using its address. A method address can be stored in a variable or passed as a parameter between other methods. Let's define a method type with a single String parameter and two methods having the same parameter lists:

```
Delegate Sub Sub_OneString(ByVal parm As String)

Sub ShowColor(ByVal color As String)
    System.Console.WriteLine("Color: " & color)
End Sub

Sub ShowFruit(ByVal fruit As String)
    System.Console.WriteLine("Fruit: " & fruit)
End Sub
```

Next, we create a method named **Call_a_proc** that receives two parameters, the address of a method and a String. This is an intermediary method that uses **Invoke** to execute the method whose address was received, passing it the String parameter:

```
Sub Call_a_proc(ByVal deleg As Sub_OneString, ByVal parm As String)
    deleg.Invoke(parm)
End Sub
```

We set the program in motion by calling Call_a_proc twice, passing different information each time:

```
Call_a_proc(AddressOf ShowColor, "Green")
Call_a_proc(AddressOf ShowFruit, "Orange")
```

When the program runs, the output is as follows:

```
Color: Green
Fruit: Orange
```

Function Methods

You can declare delegates for function methods. Each delegate defines a method type having a different signature. You can define any number of delegate types within the same module or class. The delegates are strongly typed, preventing you from assigning the address of a method with the wrong signature to a delegate variable. The following code does not compile because the Hello method has no parameters and Sub_OneString requires a single String parameter:

```
Dim deleg As Sub_OneString
deleg = AddressOf Hello            'error: wrong signature
```

For this reason, delegates are often called *type-safe function pointers* because the compiler performs type checking on values assigned to a delegate variable.

►11.8 Chapter Summary

- Value types include all the numeric types such as Integer and Decimal, as well as Boolean. Reference types include Strings and objects.

- The Enum class is the base class for enumerated types. An Enum type can contain a limited set of integral values.

- A structure can contain all the same elements as classes, such as constructors, methods, properties, and fields. Unlike classes, structures use value semantics.

- Reflection is the technique finding out information about objects at runtime.

- An program statement using **TypeOf--Is** can verify the runtime type of an expression.

- The Type class represents type declarations of class types, interface types, array types, value types, and enumeration types.

- The System.Object class is the ultimate superclass, or base class, of all classes in the .NET Framework.

- Reference types cannot be compared using relational operators such as <, >, and =. They can be compared by calling the Equals method, but it does not compare the states of two objects. Instead, it compares their object references.

- An interface specifies behaviors for classes that implement the interface. Interfaces can contain properties, methods, events, and type definitions.

- The IComparable interface contains only the CompareTo method, which compares two objects and returns an integer.

- The IComparer interface declares a single method named Compare that compares two Objects and returns an integer. When an IComparer object is created using the New operator, we call it a comparator.

- Inheritance in object-oriented programming means the ability of classes to specialize the properties, methods, and events of base classes.

- Inheriting common members from base classes helps to reduce the amount of duplicate code in an object-oriented program or code library. Inheritance improves consistency of member names and common operations throughout a class hierarchy.

- When a derived object is constructed, its superclass constructors must execute before the object's own constructor executes.

- To override a member is to replace a base class member with a derived class member having the same name and signature.

- To overload a method is to create a new method having the same name as an existing method in the same class or a base class, but with a different signature.

- A class declared MustInherit is an abstract class. You cannot create an instance of an abstract class.

- A method declared MustOverride is an abstract method. It has a declaration and no implementation.

- Polymorphism permits a base type to reference objects of various types derived from the base.

- Nearly every modern industrial-strength programming language has an extensive library of collection classes. Instances of these classes hold sets and ordered lists of objects.

- A Hashtable is a dictionary-type collection that stores keys and their associated values.

- The SortedList class implements the IDictionary interface, which lets you look up values associated with keys. Most notably, it maintains the keys in sorted order.

- You can use visual inheritance to create customized forms that build on other forms.

▶11.9 Key Terms

abstract class

abstract method

base class

collection

comparator

dictionary

derived class

downward cast

enabling technology

Enum

Hashtable

IComparable

IComparer

IDictionary

interface

overload

override

polymorphism

reference type

Reflection

runtime type identification

SortedList

Structure

TypeOf

value equality

value type

visual inheritance

▶11.10 Review Questions

Fill in the Blank

1. Value type variables can be created and assigned a value without using the —————— operator.

2. A —————— is like a class, except it creates value types.

3. The —————— method in the Type class returns an object's type.

4. The CompareTo method is part of the —————— interface.

5. A comparator is a class that implements the —————— interface.

Multiple Choice

1. Which of the following modifers prevents a base class method from being overriden?
   a. CannotOverride
   b. NotOverridable
   c. (no modifier)
   d. two of the above are correct

2. Which of the following is **not** a rule regarding overloading methods?
   a. Signature of overloaded method must be different.
   b. The method name cannot be a member of a base class
   c. Access type (public, private, protected, friend) must be the same as overloaded method.
   d. Overloads keyword must be used.

3. Which of the following collection classes is best suited to the first-in-first-out principle?

    a. Queue

    b. Stack

    c. SortedList

    d. Hashtable

4. Which of the following is **not** an IDictionary property?

    a. Item

    b. Keys

    c. Values

    d. Count

Short Answer

1. Which Hashtable method returns True when the table contains an element with a specified key?

2. Which method should be overridden in a class to check for equality using the states of objects?

3. How can an Array of Employee objects be sorted on various fields, such as name and salary?

4. Which keyword in a derived class definition identifies the base class?

5. Which class executes insert operations more quickly—Hashtable or SortedList?

Algorithm Workbench

1. Define the **Colors** Enum, with members red, yellow, and blue. Write a statement that declares an Enum variable and assigns it one of the colors.

2. Write a statement that displays the type of an object referenced by obj.

3. Write a expression that returns True if variables A and B refer to the same object instance.

4. If the Student class implements IComparable, show how to declare Student.CompareTo.

5. Write a statement that adds a Student object to a Hashtable named students. The entry should contain the student's ID property, and a Student object as the value.

6. Write a statement that sorts an Array of Student objects named students using a comparator named CompareNames.

7. Write a statement that declares a public method named Print having no parameters that must be overriden in a derived class.

8. Declare an abstract class named StudentBase.

9. Write statements that create a SortedList named courses. Each entry contains a course ID (String) and a course title. Insert three entries. Write a loop that displays the keys.

10. Write a loop that iterates over the entries in a SortedList named myList and displays both the keys and values. The keys are integers and the values are strings.

11

▶11.11 Programming Challenges

1. **Sorting Accounts**

   Write a Windows Desktop program that creates an array of five employees and displays the sorted array in a ListBox. Use the Employee class from Code Listing 11-5. Modify the implementation of CompareTo so it can sort an array of employees in descending order by salary.

2. **Bobsled Race Results**

   Create a class named BobsledRace that holds results from a single run in a Bobsled race. The results are the following: dateAndTime (DateTime), teamName (String), and totalTime (Single). Create a parameterized constructor, a ToString method, and other property methods as needed.

   Create and fill an array with five BobsledRace objects. Create comparators (IComparer interface) that permit you to sort the array in ascending order by dateAndTime, teamName, and totalTime. Write testing code that displays the array after sorting it each of the three ways.

3. **SalesEmployee Class**

   Use the Employee class from Code Listing 11-13 to inherit a SalesEmployee class. The class will have fields named basePay, salesQuota, salesAmount, and comissionRate. The person's gross pay is calculated this way:

   basePay + ((salesAmount − salesQuota) * commissionRate)

   If salesAmount is less than salesQuota, however, the gross pay equals the basePay value. Create several instances of SalesEmployee and demonstrate the use of all properties and methods. For each person, display their name, gross pay, tax, and net pay.

4. **Accounts SortedList**

   Write a Windows Application program that lets users interact with a list of Account objects. Create a SortedList of Account objects. Use the Account class defined in Code Listing 11-2, and add any properties or methods you deem necessary. When the user inputs the Account ID and balance, use the information to create an Account object and insert it in the SortedList.

   Let the user search for accounts by ID number. When an account is found, display it on the form. Let the user delete an account. Let the user view a list of all accounts by displaying the account ID and balance of each account.

5. **Authors Hashtable**

   Read the authors table from the pubs database into a Hashtable. Define a class named **Author** that holds the au_id, au_lname, au_fname, and city columns from the authors table. As you read the database, save each row in an Author object and insert the object into the Hashtable. When the user enters an author ID, display the complete Author object from the HashTable.

Crystal Reports

▶12.1 Introduction

Crystal Reports is an easy-to-use, yet powerful report design tool that retrieves and displays data from databases, recordsets, and other data sources. Crystal Reports has sophisticated formatting capabilities, its own formula editor, advanced formatting capabilities, and the ability to sort, group, and select records. It can generate running group totals as well as final totals. The output can be displayed by both Windows Desktop and Web Forms applications. Crystal Reports.NET is fully integrated into the .NET Framework, so it takes advantage of .NET's object-oriented features.

You can use Crystal Reports to generate a variety of report and chart types. For examples, look in the Crystal Reports\Samples subdirectory of your Visual Studio .NET installation. The sample reports use a MS-Access database named **Xtreme Mountain Bike Company** (xtreme.mdb).

When you add a Crystal Report to your program, the report is defined as a class, with properties, methods, and embedded source code. Reports can be accessed from program code as programmable objects. Reports are displayed on forms using a custom control named **CrystalReportsControl**, in both the Windows Forms and Web Forms sections of the Visual Studio .NET Toolbox.

Creating a Report

To create a Crystal Report, select **Add New Item** from the Project menu, then select **Crystal Report** (Figure 12-1). You must select a name for the report file (extension .rpt). The first time you create a report, you may see a Registration Wizard window (Figure 12-2). You can defer registration until later, or fill out the registration information. The Crystal Report Gallery window (Figure 12-3) offers three choices:

◆ Create a new report using Report Expert, which guides you through the required steps in creating a report. Figure 12-3 lists several types of reports.

◆ Create a blank report. Using this option gives you great flexibility, but you must set all report columns, totals, and other features manually.

◆ Create a new report by making a copy of an existing report and modifying the copy.

A Crystal Report is defined by its own class. You can see the source code file associated with a report in your project by selecting the *Show All Files* button in Solution Explorer.

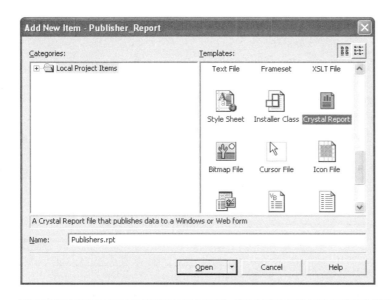

Figure 12-1 Add a Crystal Report to the project.

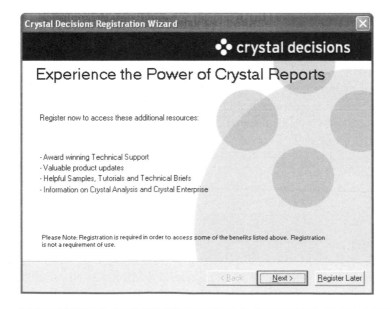

Figure 12-2 Registration Wizard.

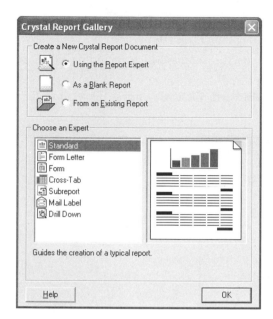

Figure 12-3 Crystal Report Gallery.

►12.2 Report Expert

In almost all cases, you will use Report Expert to design and modify reports. It takes you through a series of steps, identified by tabs at the top of the window (Table 12-1). Not all steps are used in every report.

Table 12-1

Steps in Report Expert, identified by tabs.

Step	Purpose
Data	Select a data source (database, recordset), a data provider (such as SQL Server or Jet SQL), and dataset tables.
Links	Create/edit links between two or more related tables.
Fields	Select individual fields from report tables.
Group	Select one or more field groupings, generate group headings and footings.
Total	Identify fields that generate final group and final totals.
Top N	Sort report rows based on selected group totals.
Drill	Select which group fields will be displayed when the report starts, versus fields that appear only after the user double-clicks the mouse. Possible only when one or more groups have been selected.
Chart	Add various types of bar, line, pie, and area charts to a report, and customize the chart attributes.
Select	Select table rows using criteria, similar to the SQL WHERE clause.
Style	Select from a variety of report styles and specify a report title.

Report Data Sources

When you create a report, you are permitted to choose from several types of data sources (Figure 12-4):

- ◆ **Project Data:** Your report can retrieve data from ADO.NET datasets inside your application.
- ◆ **OLE DB (ADO):** The OLE DB provider is the most up-to-date and generalized way to retrieve database data in ADO.NET. For example, you can access SQL Server, Oracle, and MS-Access databases, as well as Excel spreadsheet data.

◆ **ODBC (RDO):** If you cannot find an OLE DB provider for a particular type of data source, chances are an ODBC driver exists. ODBC uses an older technology than OLE DB.

◆ **Database Files:** Your report can import data from specific database files, including MS-Access, Excel, Text, and XML files.

◆ **More Data Sources:** You can generate a report from XML files, MS-Access, Excel, and Crystal Field Definition files.

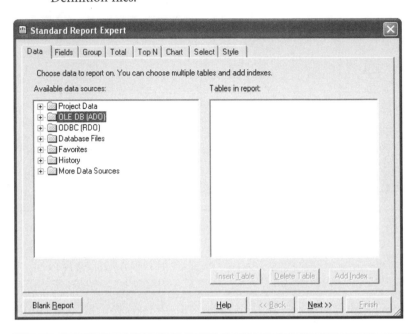

Figure 12-4 Select the data source type.

We will show examples in this chapter that generate reports from ADO.NET datasets, SQL Server, and MS-Access databases. Data sources can include multiple database tables. Crystal Reports can automatically join related tables using primary and foreign keys.

Data Providers

Once you have selected a data source (such as OLE DB), you must also select a data provider. In Figure 12-5, for example, the Microsoft OLE DB Provider for SQL Server has been selected.

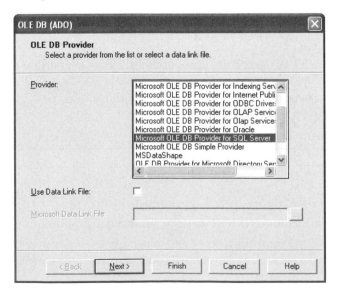

Figure 12-5 Select OLE DB Provider for SQL Server.

Connection Settings

After you select a data provider, you are prompted for connection information. For example, if you were connecting to the MS-Access database named karate used in Chapter 3, the entries would be the following:

Database name: **C:\vbdata\karate.mdb**

Database type: **Access**

User ID: **Admin**

If you were connecting to SQL Server using SQL Server 2000 on a home computer, the entries would be the following:

Server: **(local)**

User ID: **sa**

Password: **(blank)**

If you were connecting to the NetSDK server (MSDE), the entries would be the following:

Server: **(local)\NetSDK**

Integrated Security: (*checked*)

Selecting Tables

Once a data connection has been established, Report Expert displays one or more databases belonging to the connection. You can then expand a database's entry in the data sources panel (Figure 12-6), select a table name, and click on the **Insert Table** button to transfer the table name to the **Tables in report** panel.

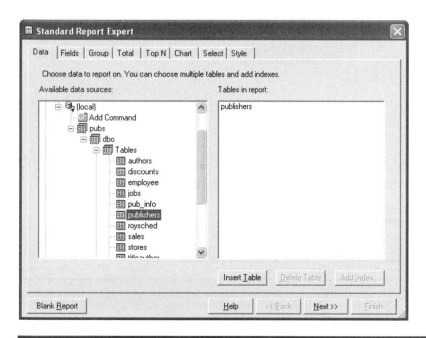

Figure 12-6 Selecting the publishers table.

If you select multiple tables as in Figure 12-7, Report Expert adds a new tab named **Links**. It lets you view and modify the way tables have been joined on common key fields (Figure 12-8). In our example, the au_id field is common to the authors and titleauthor tables. The title_id field is common to the titleauthor and titles tables.

12

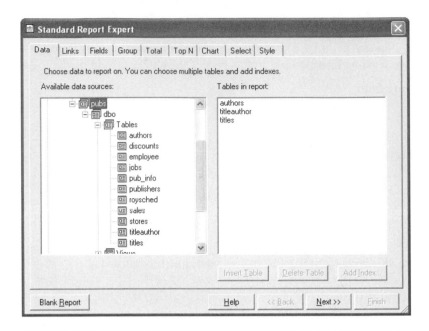

Figure 12-7 Selecting multiple tables.

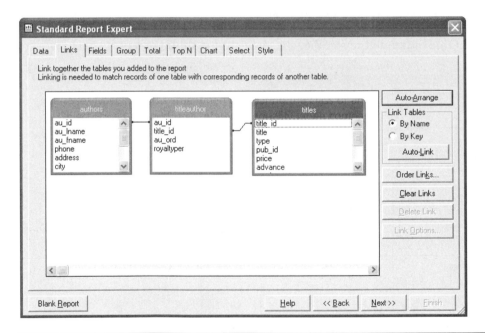

Figure 12-8 Reviewing the links between tables.

Selecting Fields

The **Fields** tab lets you select fields (columns) from all tables belonging to the report. In Figure 12-9 we have selected fields that produce lists of books written by authors. At the time you are selecting fields, you can click on the Formula button to create additional report fields based on formulas.

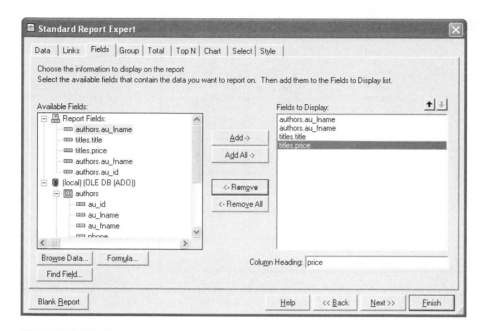

Figure 12-9 Selecting fields from multiple tables.

Formula Editor

The Formula Editor is activated in one of two ways:

◆ By clicking the **Formula** button in the Fields tab of Report Expert

◆ By right-clicking on **Formula Fields** in the Field Explorer window (Figure 12-10).

Formulas are created interactively by selecting report fields from one list, functions from another, and operators from a third list (Figure 12-11). There are two choices for the syntax option: Crystal Syntax and Visual Basic Syntax. The formula shown in the figure concatenates the last name, a comma, a space, and the first name into a single field named **fullName**:

```
Formula = {authors.au_lname} & ", " & {authors.au_fname}
```

Field names are surrounded by curly braces, but the Visual Basic syntax should be familiar. When referring to formula fields in reports, their names begin with the @ sign.

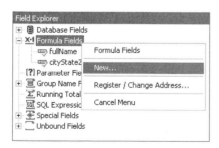

Figure 12-10 Field Explorer.

12

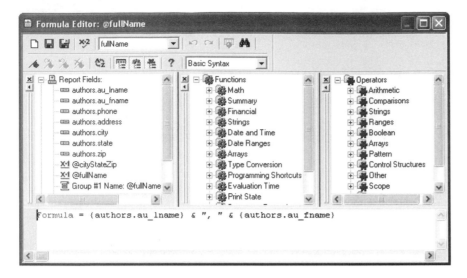

Figure 12-11 Formula Editor window.

Selecting Groups

The **Group** tab lets you optionally group report rows according to one or more fields (Figure 12-12). Suppose you want to see a list of books written by each author. Then you can group them by author's last names and author's first names. When the report is executed (Figure 12-13), a + sign appears next to each grouped item in the Group Tree (left panel). The user can click on a + to view the contents of its group.

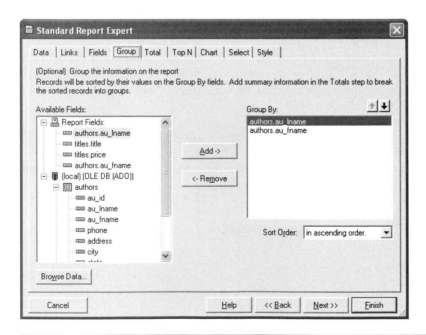

Figure 12-12 Grouping report rows by last name and first name.

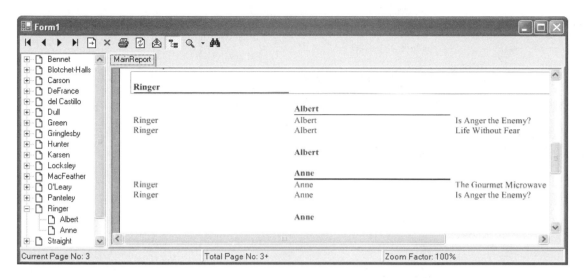

Figure 12-13 Showing groups at runtime.

Adding Totals

When report groups are created, Report Expert automatically generates subtotals on all numeric columns. You can alter the defaults by clicking on the **Total** tab (Figure 12-14), add and remove fields, and change the **Summary Type** selection. A checkbox near the bottom of the panel determines whether grand totals will appear at the end of the report.

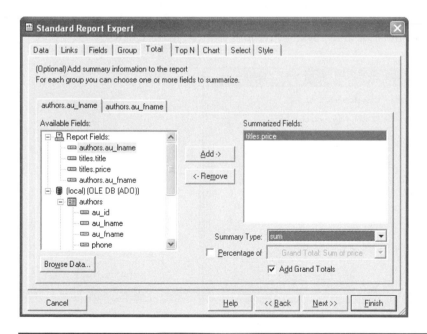

Figure 12-14 The default report total, summing the price column.

Selecting TopN Rows

The **Top N** tab lets you sort report groups based on one of the subtotals. In Figure 12-15, the five authors having the highest total book prices will be printed, followed by a single group containing all other authors. Top N can only be used if you have selected one or more report groups.

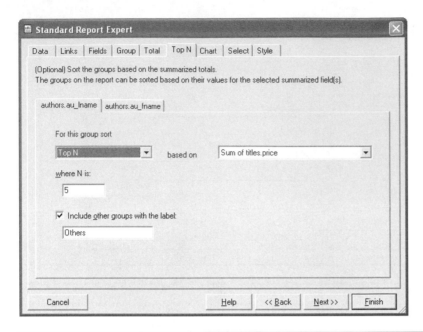

Figure 12-15 Using the Top N tab to sort by the sum of book prices.

Drill Down

The **Drill** tab lets you hide and display detailed sections. It appears in Report Expert when you have selected one or more report groups. In Figure 12-16, we have chosen to display the first and last names of authors, but not their book details. Figure 12-17 shows part of a report based on the selected drill-down options. To see the details for Albert Ringer, the user must double-click the author's name (Figure 12-18).

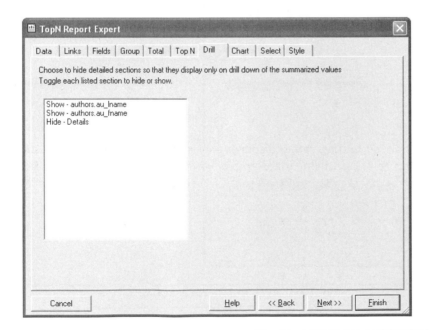

Figure 12-16 Selecting the Drill option.

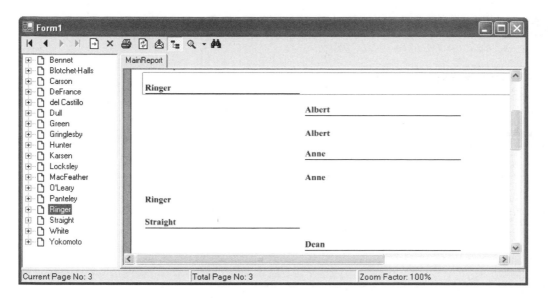

Figure 12-17 Displaying fields before drill-down.

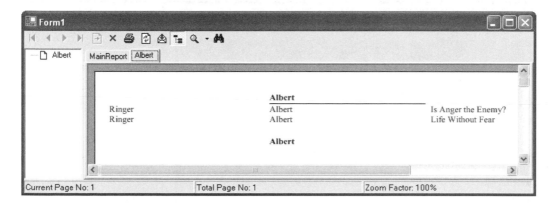

Figure 12-18 Drilling down into details.

Selecting Rows

The **Select** tab activates row selection, permitting you to display a subset of all rows from the data source. You can enter selection criteria interactively. We might, for example, want to create a report with no groups, but sorted by last name and first name. We can select only rows having a book price greater than $14.99 (Figure 12-19). Figure 12-20 shows the resulting report.

12

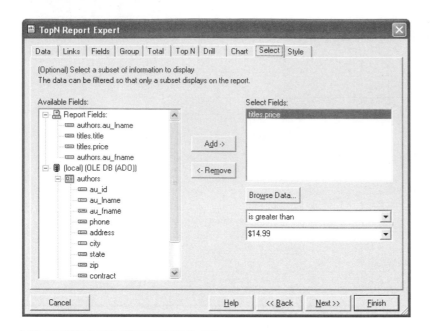

Figure 12-19 Selecting rows by price.

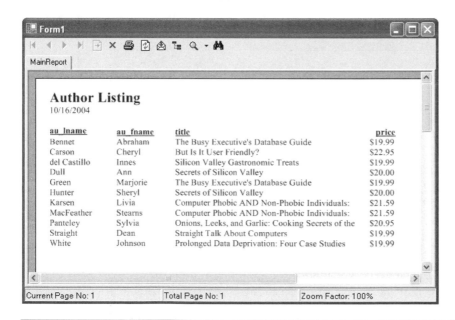

Figure 12-20 Report with rows selected by book price.

Report Style

The **Style** tab of Report Expert lets you select from a set of predefined report templates (Figure 12-21). The report shown in Figure 12-20 was based on Standard style. The same report data using Table style appears in Figure 12-22. When you change a report's style, the change cannot be automatically undone. You must modify the style a second time, setting it back to your original preference.

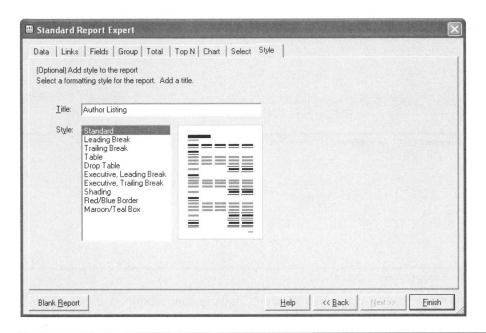

Figure 12-21 Adding a title, selecting Standard report style.

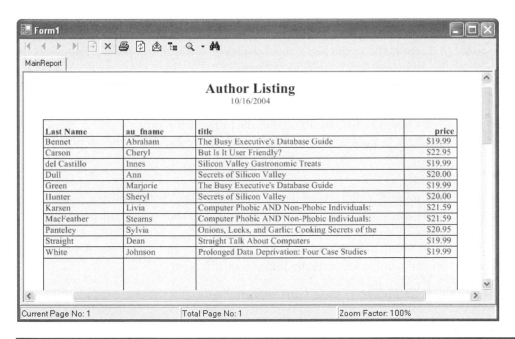

Figure 12-22 Author Listing report, using the Table style.

Running a Report

Windows Desktop Programs

To run a Crystal Report from a Windows Desktop application, place a **CrystalReportViewer** control on your program's form (Figure 12-23). You can find the control at the end of the Windows Forms section of the Visual Studio .NET ToolBox. You may want to set the control's Dock property to **Fill** (middle selection button in Figure 12-24) so it fills the entire enclosing form. Or, if you want part of the form to be exposed, position the control on the form and select the control's Anchor property.

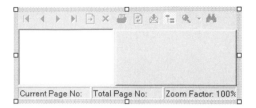

Figure 12-23 The CrystalReportsViewer control.

Figure 12-24 Setting the Dock property to Fill.

A report can be run in one of two ways from a Windows Desktop application:

◆ Create an instance of the report class and assign it to the ReportSource property of the CrystalReportViewer control. The following code runs a report named **Publishers**, using a control named **crvPublishers**:

```
crvPublishers.ReportSource = New Publishers
```

◆ Assign the name of a report file to the ReportSource property. Assuming the file *Publishers.rpt* is in the project directory, the following statement runs the report:

```
crvPubs.ReportSource = "..\Publishers.rpt"
```

Visual Basic .NET projects run from the EXE file located in the project's bin directory. The "..\" at the beginning of the filename tells MS-Windows to back up one directory level before looking for the report file.

Web Applications

Web applications run Crystal Reports using a Web server version of the CrystalReportsViewer control. All you have to do is drag the control onto a Web form and add a statement to the Page_Load event handler assigning a report instance to the control's ReportSource property.

Assuming a report named **Publishers** belongs to the current project and the CrystalReportsViewer control is named **crvPublishers**, the following code correctly initializes the report:

```
crvPublishers.ReportSource = New Publishers
```

If a report is not included in the current Web project, you must specify its absolute file path:

```
crvPublishers.ReportSource = "c:\vbdata\Crystal\Publishers.rpt"
```

When running a report from a Web form, a navigation bar is automatically placed on the client's Web page (Figure 12-25). The user can search for text and zoom in and out.

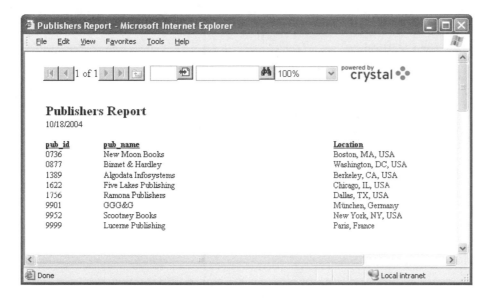

Figure 12-25 Running a report from a Web form.

Hands-On Tutorial: Publisher Report

Publisher Report

In this hands-on tutorial, you will create a report from the **publishers** table in the **pubs** database. You will use Report Expert to select the data source, data table, and report type.

Step 1. Create a new Windows Application project named **Publisher_Report**.

Step 2. Select **Add New Item** from the Project menu, then select **Crystal Report**. Name the file **Publishers.rpt** and click on **Open** to create the report.

Step 3. When the Crystal Report Gallery window appears and the **Report Expert** option is selected, click on **OK**.

Step 4. With the **Data** tab selected, double-click on **OLE DB (ADO)**.

Step 5. Select **Microsoft OLE DB Provider for SQL Server** and click on **Next**.

Step 6. Enter the connection settings you typically use for the **pubs** database and click on **Finish** to return to Report Expert.

Step 7. In Report Expert, expand the pubs database entry in the available data sources pane, and select the **publishers** table. Click on **Insert Table** to copy publishers to the pane on the right side of the window. Click on **Next**.

Step 8. Next, you will select fields to display on the report (Figure 12-26). Click on the **Add All** button, which copies all field names from the publishers table to the field list on the right side. (Optionally, you can assign a custom column heading to each field.)

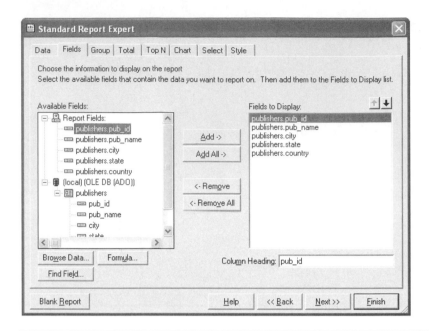

Figure 12-26 Selecting fields to display.

Step 9. Click on the **Style** tab and enter **Publishers Report** as the report title. We will leave the report style set to Standard. Click on the **Finish** button to create the report. (We are skipping some report options that will be discussed later in this chapter.)

Step 10. The Report Designer window should appear, in which you can make various formatting changes to the report. Select the **PrintDate** field in the header area, and expand its size about ¼ inch to the right. Save your report.

Step 11. Next, you will add a control to the program's startup form to display the Publishers report. Switch to the program's startup form, expand its size to approximately two-thirds the screen size, and place a **CrystalReportViewer** control on the form. Set its Dock property to **Fill**. Name the control **crvPublishers**.

Step 12. Set the control's **DisplayGroupTree** property to False. (The *GroupTree* is a separate panel used when grouping report items.)

Step 13. Double-click crvPublishers and insert the following statement in its **Load** event handler:

```
crvPublishers.ReportSource = New Publishers
```

Step 14. Save and run the project. The report should look like Figure 12-27, except with a different date.

At this point, you would normally spend some time adjusting finer elements of the report's appearance. There's no need to make changes now.

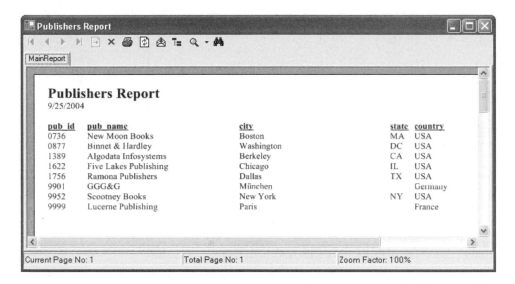

Figure 12-27 Run the program and view the report.

Adding a Formula Field to the Publishers Report

Next, you will add a formula to the Publishers report that concatenates the City, State, and Country fields.

Step 15. Display the Publishers report in the Report Designer window.

Step 16. In the Field Explorer window, right-click on **Formula Fields** and select **New**.

Step 17. When prompted, name the formula **cityStateCountry**.

Step 18. In the Formula Editor, select **Basic Syntax** from the dropdown list in the upper right corner.

Step 19. Type **Formula** = into the editing area.

Step 20. Under Report Fields, double-click on **Publishers.city**.

Step 21. Add the following string to the formula: **& "," &**.

Step 22. Double-click on the **Publishers.state** field.

Step 23. Continue editing the formula until it looks like the following:

```
Formula = {publishers.city} & ", " & {publishers.state}
    & ", " & {publishers.country}
```

(The formula wraps around on the printed page, but not in the Formula Editor window.)

Step 24. Save the formula and close the Formula Editor.

Step 25. Run Report Expert, click on the **Fields** tab, and replace the city, state, and country fields with the **@cityStateCountry** formula field. Change the column heading to **Location**.

Step 26. Click on Finish. Save the report and run the program. The displayed report should appear as in Figure 12-28.

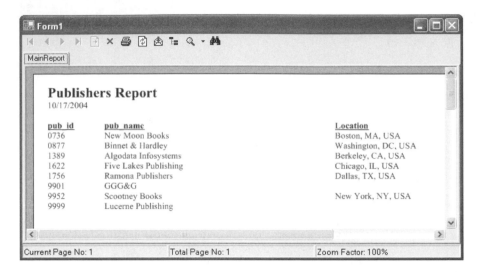

Figure 12-28 Publishers report, using a formula field.

Do you notice something wrong with the output? The locations of two publishers are blank. If you refer to Figure 12-27, notice that the same two publishers did not have a value in their state field because they were from outside the United States. When a Crystal Reports formula encounters a null field, processing of the formula is aborted. Fortunately, there is a function named **IsNull** that returns true when a database field is null. We will use it to check the value of publishers.state, and build a location string appropriately.

Step 27. Edit the **@cityStateCountry** formula in the Formula Editor. Change the formula to the following:

```
If IsNull({publishers.state}) Then
    Formula = {publishers.city} & ", " & {publishers.country}
Else
    Formula = {publishers.city} & ", " & {publishers.state} _
        & ", " & {publishers.country}
End If
```

Step 28. Save the formula, close the Editor, and run the program again. The output should appear as in Figure 12-29.

A complete coverage of Crystal Reports formulas is beyond the scope of this chapter. You can, however, download the documentation for the Crystal Reports Visual Studio .NET SDK from the Crystal Decisions Web site.

(End of Tutorial)

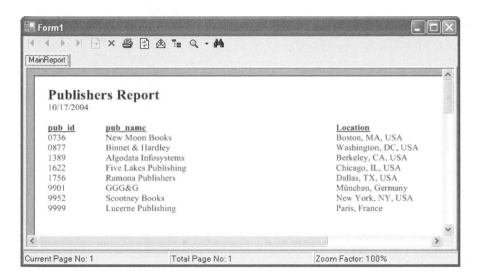

Figure 12-29 Publishers report, using the revised formula field.

Displaying a Report on a Separate Form

Sometimes, you will find it useful to offer the user a list of report names. When one is selected, your program can display the report in a separate window. The best way to do this is to create an instance of the report form, set the control's ReportSource property, and call the form's ShowDialog method.

Hands-On Tutorial: Modifying the Publishers Report Program

Publisher_Separate

In this tutorial, you will make a copy of the Publishers_Report program. You will add a menu to the startup form, and display the Publishers report in a separate form.

Step 1. Make a copy of the Publisher_Report project directory and rename it to **Publisher_Separate**. Open the new program. O*ptionally, you can rename the project and solution in the Solution Explorer window*.

Step 2. Add a new form to the project named **frmReport**. Move the crvPublishers control from the startup form to frmReport. To do this, select the control, select Edit | Cut from the menu; open frmReport, and select Edit | Paste from the menu to paste the control into frmReport.

Step 3. Add a MainMenu control to the startup form, and insert the following menu selections:

Menu Selection	Name
File	Exit	mnuFileExit
Report	Publisher Report	mnuReportPublisher

Step 4. Insert a line of code that closes the form in the mnuFileExit_Click handler.

Step 5. Delete the crvPublishers_Load event handler.

Step 6. Insert the following lines of code in the mnuReportPublisher handler:

```
Dim frm As New frmReport
frm.crvPubs.ReportSource = New Publishers
frm.ShowDialog()
```

Step 7. Save and run the program. Use the menu on the startup form to display the Publishers report.

(End of Tutorial)

▶12.3 Report Designer

Modifying an Existing Report

Crystal Report Designer is seamlessly integrated into the Visual Studio .NET environment. Two toolbars, Crystal Reports Insert, and Crystal Reports Main, are added to the toolbar area by default. You can turn them on or off from the View | Toolbars menu. Use the Field Explorer window (Figure 12-30) to add fields to a report. You can add database fields, formula fields, parameter fields, group name fields, running total fields, SQL expression fields, special fields, and unbound fields.

Figure 12-30 Field Explorer.

Report Expert

You may be lucky enough to make just the right choices when using Report Expert, and not have to change your mind later. But more likely, you will want to modify some report settings after the fact. To do this, right-click in the Report Designer window (outside of detail and grouping sections), select **Report**, then select **Report Expert** (Figure 12-31). When you are warned that Report Expert will replace your existing report definition, click on **Yes** to continue.

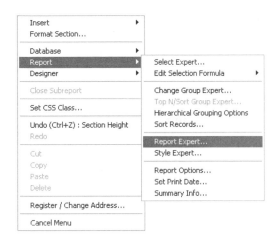

Figure 12-31 Starting Report Expert.

Report Expert displays your existing report settings, lets you modify the settings, and saves your changes. You do not have to work sequentially through the tabs—you can select tabs in a more or less random order. There's one important point to consider—manual changes you have made using Report Designer may be overwritten when you run Report Expert.

Report Sections

Reports can contain the following sections:

- ◆ **Report Header:** Displayed once at the top of the first page of the report.
- ◆ **Page Header:** Displayed at the top of each page. May include the page number, column headings, date, and other information.
- ◆ **Group Header:** Displayed at the beginning of each group. Usually displays the group name.
- ◆ **Details:** Displayed once for each row in the data source.
- ◆ **Group Footer:** Displayed at the end of each group. Usually displays counts, totals, and averages for the group.
- ◆ **Page Footer:** Displayed at the bottom of each page.
- ◆ **Report Footer:** Displayed once at the end of the report. Usually displays totals, averages, counts, and so on, relating to the entire report.

Reports can have multiple grouping levels, which result in a separate Group Header and Group Footer for each group. Figure 12-32 shows the Publishers report created in our first hands-on tutorial, which contains a Report Header, Page Header, Details, Report Footer, and Page Footer. The shading on the Report Header and Report Footer indicate they are suppressed (not displayed). You can hide any report section by right-clicking on its identifier bar and selecting **Hide** or **Suppress**. The Hide option permits the user to drill down into a group at runtime, whereas the Suppress option does not permit drill-down.

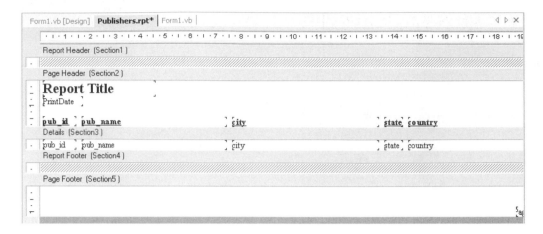

Figure 12-32 Report designer (Publishers).

Formatting Report Fields

Formatting Items

To modify the format of a report item, right-click on the item and select **Format**. The Format Editor window (Figure 12-33) has five tabs: Common, Border, Font, Paragraph, and Hyperlink. Suppose we want to change the font of the report title. We open the Format Editor, select the Font tab, and enter choices (Figure 12-34).

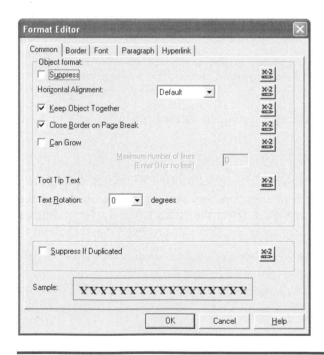

Figure 12-33 Format Editor window.

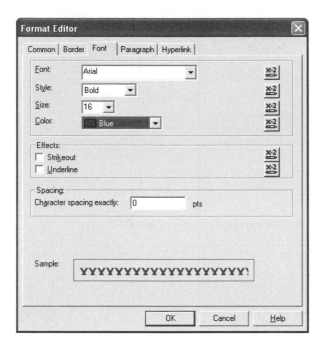

Figure 12-34 Changing fonts.

Modifying Text Objects

To modify a text object such as a heading or label, right-click on the object, select **Edit Text Object**, and place the cursor inside the object's text area. When you finish editing, click the mouse outside the field.

Formatting Multiple Items

To format multiple report items, hold down the Ctrl key and select the items with the mouse. Right-click on any member of the group and select **Format Multiple Objects** from the popup menu. Your will enter your selections in the **Format Editor** window.

Changing Field Selections and Headings

After running Report Expert, you may change your mind about the placement of columns, heading values, or other report details. Report Expert lets you change field selections and heading names. To change the heading of the pub_id report field, for example, rerun Report Expert, select the **Fields** tab, and select publishers.pub_id in the Report Fields box (Figure 12-35). Change the Column Heading value to **Pub ID** and click on **Finish**.

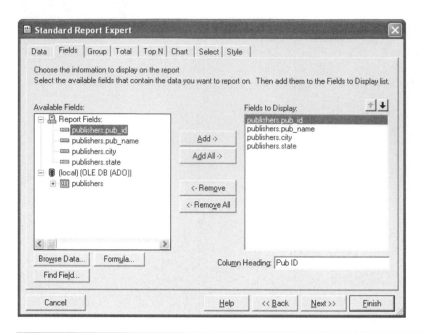

Figure 12-35 Modifying the pub_id report field.

Selecting Records

Using the **Select** tab in Report Expert, you can insert criteria that select which rows display in the report. A simple relational expression is created interactively by selecting from a list of predefined operators. Suppose you want to limit the rows displayed by the Publishers report to cities with names less than the letter N. You can run Report Expert, click on the Select tab, and enter the values shown in Figure 12-36. Similarly, you can select only records in which the country contains **USA** (Figure 12-37). It is not necessary to surround string and date values with quotation marks. In this respect, Crystal Reports syntax differs from that of SQL queries.

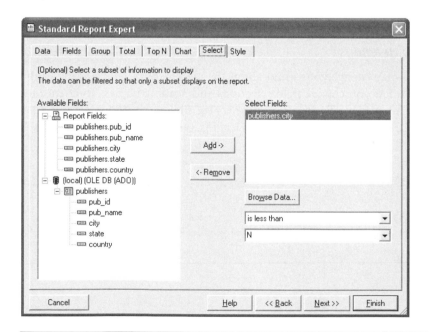

Figure 12-36 Selecting publisher.city < N.

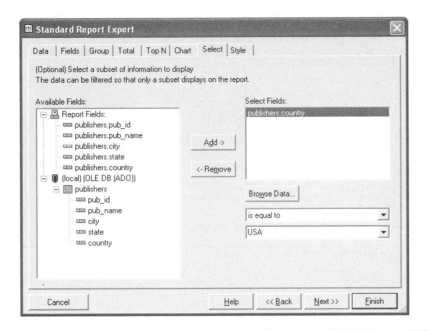

Figure 12-37 Selecting publishers.country = USA.

Sorting Reports

A report can be sorted on one or more columns by selecting **Sort Records** from the **Report** popup menu (Figure 12-38).

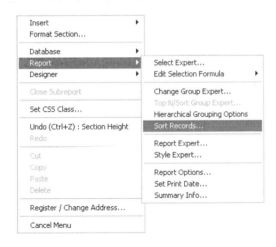

Figure 12-38 Sort Records popup menu.

The **Record Sort Order** window lets you select each sort field, starting with the top-level sort. In Figure 12-39, we have selected an ascending sort on the publishers.city column.

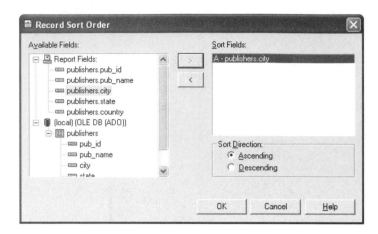

Figure 12-39 Sorting the Publishers report by city.

Using Report Groups

Grouping Report Rows

If you group the rows of a report on one of the table columns, group header and group footer sections are automatically added to the report. Each grouped column contains its own header and footer sections. To specify a group, run Report Expert, click on the **Group** tab, select a report field, and add it to the **Group By** box. You can choose the sort order at the same time.

Suppose you use Report Expert to group publishers by City (Figure 12-40). Group Footer #1 and Group Footer #2 appear in the report designer. When the report executes, group headings print automatically (Figure 12-41). *(Earlier releases of Crystal Reports .NET did not generate group headings unless you added a group summary.)*

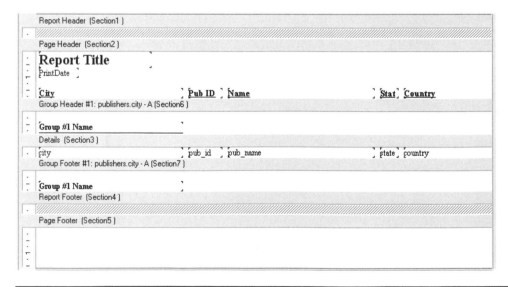

Figure 12-40 Grouping publishers by city.

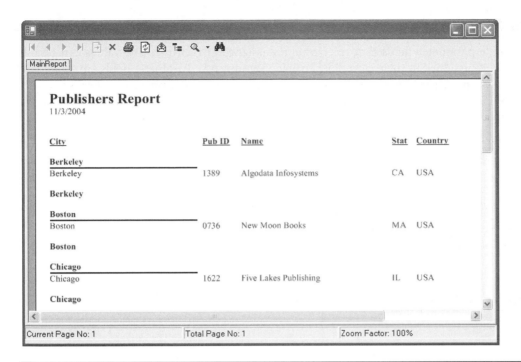

Figure 12-41 Sorted and grouped by city.

To add a total or count to a section group, run Report Expert, select the **Total** tab, select the summarized field (such as City), and select the Summary Type (such as count). Figure 12-42 shows the Publishers report grouped and summarized by City.

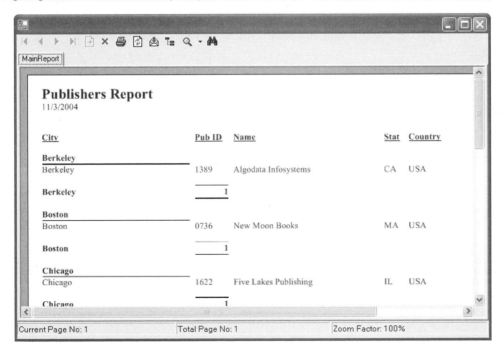

Figure 12-42 Counting the members in each group.

Generating Final Totals

In order to generate a grand total for any field (column) using Report Expert, you must first create a group on the field and then select a final total. Once the report has been created, you can hide the group header and group footer sections, leaving only the grand total in the report footer area.

12

Parameter Fields

Reports can include parameter fields that receive values assigned at runtime. The values can be interactively entered by the user or assigned to the report object using program code. Parameter fields are created in the **Field Explorer** window of the Report Designer. To create one, right-click on **Parameters** and select **New**. When the Create Parameter Field window displays (Figure 12-43), you can select a parameter name, text to be used when prompting the user, and the parameter's type.

Figure 12-43 Creating a parameter field.

Suppose we have created a parameter field named **GeneratedBy**. We can add it to the Authors report by dragging the parameter name from the Field Explorer window to the Page Header area. At runtime, the user is automatically prompted for the parameter value (Figure 12-44) before the report displays. Figure 12-45 shows an Author Listing report with the user's name (Joe Smith) displayed in the page header.

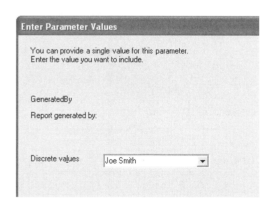

Figure 12-44 Entering the GeneratedBy parameter at runtime.

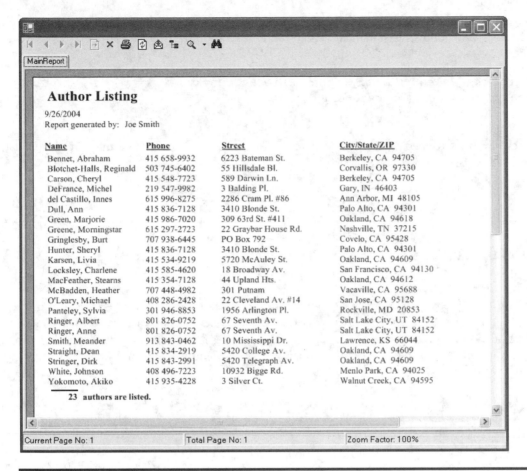

Figure 12-45 Displaying the finished report.

Assigning Parameter Fields in Code

You can assign parameter fields in program code by calling the report object's **SetParameterValue** method. In the following example, we set the GeneratedBy parameter to "Joe Smith" before assigning the report source:

```
Dim auth As New Authors
auth.SetParameterValue("GeneratedBy", "Joe Smith")
crvPubs.ReportSource = auth
```

As a result, the report executes without prompting the user for the parameter value.

Connecting a Report to a Dataset

You can connect a Crystal Report to a dataset within your application. This powerful idea makes it possible to use your own queries to join tables, select rows, and sort, before the data is passed to the Crystal Reports Viewer. All you have to do is call the report's **SetDataSource** method, passing it the name of a dataset. Suppose our program has a data adapter named **daCustomer** and a dataset named **DsCustomer1**. First, we fill the dataset:

```
daCustomer.Fill( DsCustomer1 )
```

12

Suppose the report we want to display is named **SalesByCountry** and the Crystal Reports Viewer control is named crvXtreme. The following statements create an instance of the report and call the SetDataSource method:

```
Dim report As SalesByCountry = New SalesByCountry
report.SetDataSource(DsCustomer1)
crvXtreme.ReportSource = report
```

Aside from these few lines, connecting a Crystal Report to a dataset is the same as connecting directly to a database.

▶ 12.4 Xtreme Bike Sales Example

Hands-On Tutorial

Xtreme_sales

In this hands-on example, you will create a report from the Xtreme Mountain Bike database in the Crystal Reports Samples directory. The report will list yearly mountain bike sales by various companies in Southeast Asia (Figure 12-46). Rows will be grouped by country, and total sales for each country will appear in group footers. Country names will be sorted in ascending order, and within country, customer names will be sorted in ascending order.

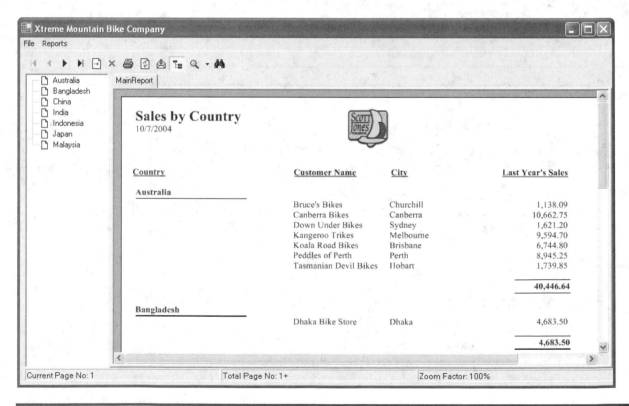

Figure 12-46 Xtreme Mountain Bike sales, Southeast Asia.

Step 1. Create a new Windows Desktop project named **Xtreme_sales**.

Step 2. Change the Text property of the startup form to **Xtreme Mountain Bike Company**.

Step 3. Add a database connection to Server Explorer: find the MS-Access database named **xtreme.mdb**, located in the **Crystal Reports\Samples\Database** directory in the folder where Visual Studio .NET was installed.

Step 4. Drag the Customer table from the xtreme database onto the form. Rename the connection to **conXtreme**, rename the data adapter to **daCustomer**.

Step 5. Edit the SelectCommand.CommandText property of daCustomers, and select only the following fields from the Customers table: Customer ID, Country, Last Year's Sales, Customer Name, and City.

Step 6. Generate a dataset class named **dsCustomer**. The dataset object name will be named **DsCustomer1**.

Step 7. Add a MainMenu control, and insert a File | Exit menu entry named **mnuFileExit**. Insert a Reports | Regional Sales menu entry named **mnuRegionalSales**.

Step 8. Add a CrystalReportsViewer control to the form and name it **crvXtreme**.

Step 9. Open the code window and insert the following line in the Form_Load event handler:

```
daCustomer.Fill(DsCustomer1)
```

Step 10. Insert the following statement in the mnuFileExit handler:

```
Me.Close()
```

Step 11. Insert the following statements in the mnuRegionalSales_Click handler:

```
Dim report As SalesByCountry = New SalesByCountry
report.SetDataSource(DsCustomer1)
crvXtreme.ReportSource = report
crvXtreme.ReportSource = New SalesByCountry
```

Create the SalesByCountry Report

Now you will create a report that displays customer sales in the SouthEast region of the world, grouping the records by country.

Step 1. Create a new Crystal Report named **SalesByCountry**. Select the Standard Report Expert.

Step 2. In Report Expert under the **Data** tab, expand the **Project Data** entry (Figure 12-47) until you see the Customer table. Select **Customer** and click on **Insert Table** to make it part of the report.

12

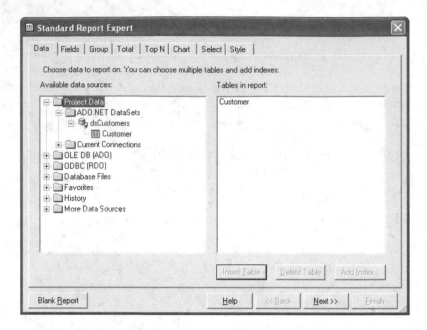

Figure 12-47 Selecting project data.

Step 3. Click on the **Fields** tab. Add the Country, Customer Name, City, and Last Year's Sales fields to the *Fields to Display* box.

Step 4. Click on the **Group** tab and select **Customer.Country** as the Group By field.

Step 5. Under the **Total** tab, select the **Customer.Last Year's Sales** field for the total. Leave the check box selected for Add Grand Totals.

Step 6. Under the **Select** tab, choose **Customer.Country** (Figure 12-48), select **is one of** from the dropdown list, and input three country names: Australia, Bangladesh, and China.

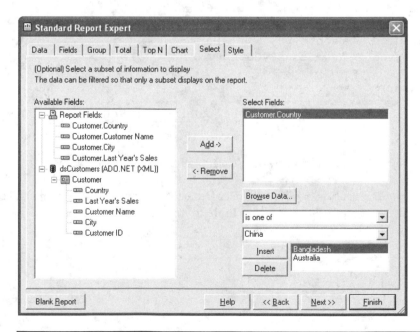

Figure 12-48 Select records.

Step 7. Under the **Style** tab, enter **Sales by Country** as the report title, and select the Standard report style.

Step 8. Save and run the project. Select **SE Regional Sales** from the Reports menu. The displayed report is somewhat rough-looking, with headings for the Last Year's Sales column truncated.

Editing the Report in the Report Designer

Now you will use Report Designer to refine the report's appearance.

Step 1. Decrease the space between columns. You can reduce the size of columns by resizing the box surrounding the heading and detail fields. You can move columns by selecting their header and detail fields, and dragging them with the mouse.

Step 2. Widen the **Print Date** field.

Step 3. Delete the **Country** field from the Details section. Because Country appears in the group heading, there is no reason to repeat it on every detail line.

Step 4. Remove the **Group #1 Name** field from the Group #1 Footer section.

Step 5. Remove the **Grand Total** field name from the Grand Total sections.

Step 6. Expand the Page Header area vertically and add a Picture field to the center. Use the sjlogo.bmp file supplied in the \Examples\Crystal directory of your book's CDROM, or supply another logo of your own choosing. Right-click in the Page Header area and select Insert | Picture from the menu.

Step 7. Run the program again and view the report (Figure 12-49).

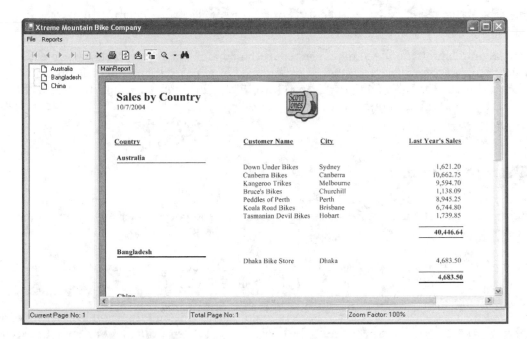

Figure 12-49 Revised report.

Modify the Record Selection Formula

When you entered the three country names under the Select tab of Report Expert, a selection formula was created automatically. In the next several steps, you will edit the formula and add more country names. You will also sort within each country on the customer name.

Step 1. Right-click on the report (in design mode) and select Report | Edit Selection Formula... | Records. The Record Selection Formula Editor window (Figure 12-50) appears.

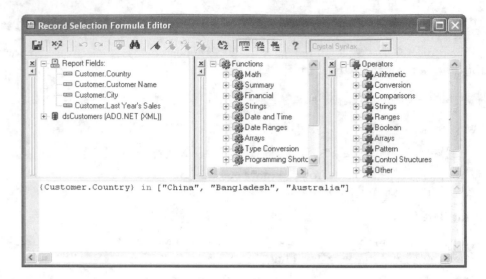

Figure 12-50 Edit the record selection formula.

Step 2. The formula in this window shows country names surrounded by quotes, separated by commas. Add each of the following country names, surrounded by double quotes, separated by commas, to the formula: **India, Indonesia, Japan, and Malaysia**. (There are other countries from the same region in the database, but we will leave them out to save time.) When you are finished, click on the Save and Close icon (first button on the toolbar).

Step 3. Right-click on the report and select Report | Sort Records. Select **Customer.Customer Name** and add it to the list of sort fields.

Step 4. Save and run the project one last time. The report should look like Figure 12-46, shown earlier. As you click on each country name in the left pane, a red box appears around the matching country heading in the report. This rapid search capability is useful for multi-page reports because the page containing the matching country displays automatically.

(End of Tutorial)

Adding Charts to Reports

When you use Report Expert to create a chart, you have the option to include a chart. Even if you decide to omit the chart, you can add a chart later. Charts are usually placed in the Report Header or Report Footer section. There are many chart types to choose from (Figure 12-51), including Bar, 3-D Bar, Pie, Line, Area, Doughnut, and so on.

After selecting a chart type, select the **Data** tab to specify the chart location and data ranges to be used when generating the chart. In Figure 12-52 for example, the chart will be displayed once at the beginning of a report. It will group the sum of last year's sales for each country.

The **Text** tab of the Chart Expert (Figure 12-53) lets you modify the default titles and labels. If you want to change a title, remove its check mark in the Auto-Text column, and enter a title of your own. In the sample figure, the chart title has been modified.

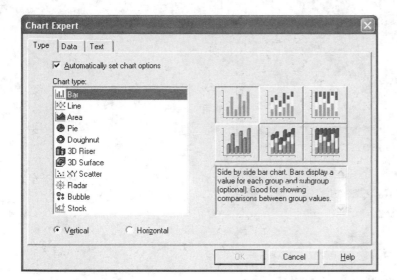

Figure 12-51 Chart Expert window.

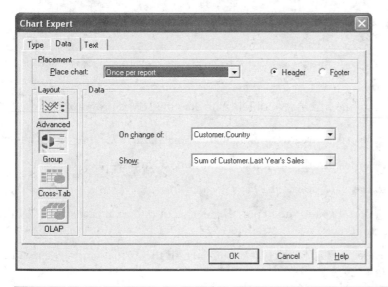

Figure 12-52 Chart data panel.

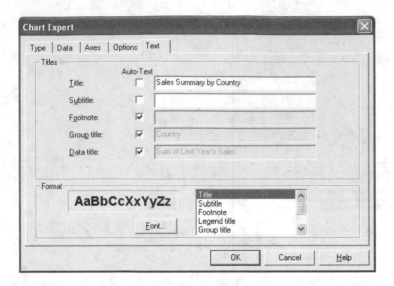

Figure 12-53 Modifying the chart titles.

Adding a Bar Chart to Xtreme Bike Sales

Hands-On Tutorial

Xtreme_sales_chart

In this tutorial, we will add a bar chart to the Xtreme Mountain Bike Regional Sales program.

Step 1. Copy the project in the **Xtreme_sales** directory to a new directory named **Xtreme_sales_chart**.

Step 2. Open the new project and rename both the project and solution to Xtreme_sales_chart.

Step 3. Move the Scott-Jones icon to the right side of the Page Header area.

Step 4. Open the **SalesByCountry** report. Expand the Report Header section to a vertical size of 3.5 inches (a ruler displays along the left margin).

Step 5. Right-click in the Report Header area and select **Insert | Chart**. In the dialog window, select a horizontal, 3-D bar chart (Figure 12-54).

Step 6. Click on OK to close the Chart Expert. Save and run the program. Your report and chart should look like the one in Figure 12-55, except your bars will be in color rather than the grayscale on our printed page.

Step 7. Next, you will change the chart to a pie chart. Right-click in the Report Header area, and select the **Pie** type (two-dimensional). Save and run the program again. Your output should appear similar to Figure 12-56.

You may want to experiment with various chart formatting options. To edit the chart, right-click on it and select **Chart Expert**. Select the **Text** tab to change the chart title, group title (Y axis), or data title (X axis). There are many formatting options you can modify.

(End of Tutorial)

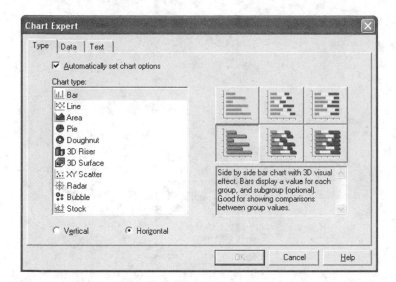

Figure 12-54 Selecting horizontal bar chart.

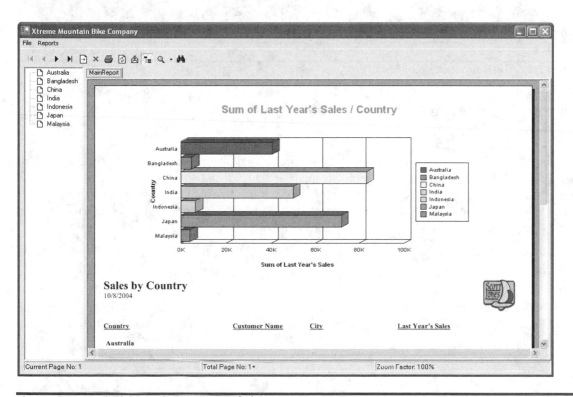

Figure 12-55 Displaying the report and chart.

12

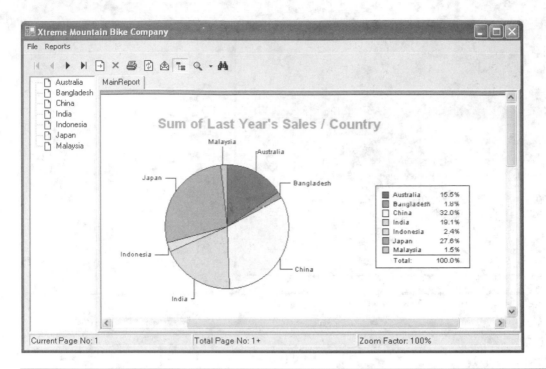

Figure 12-56 Sales summary pie chart.

Creating Reports from Joined Tables

Xtreme_Sales_Joined

There are two ways to create a Crystal Report from multiple database tables. You can create an SQL join query, as we did beginning in Chapter 5, or you can join the tables using the expert supplied by Crystal Reports. Suppose we want to create a Drill-Down report showing orders by customers. After selecting the Customer and Orders tables using the Drill Down Report Expert, the **Links** tab shows the tables connected by Customer ID (Figure 12-57). We can then select the following report fields:

```
Customer.Customer Name
Orders.PO#
Orders.Order Date
Orders.Order Amount
```

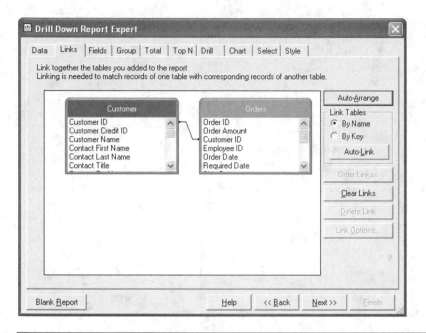

Figure 12-57 Linking the Customer and Orders tables.

Let's group the report by Customer Name, and create a total on the Order Amount field. To limit the number of records, we can use the **Top N** option to display individual customers having the ten highest values in the sum of Orders.Order Amount (Figure 12-58). The **Drill** option (Figure 12-59) lets us hide the detail rows and show the group headers containing customer names.

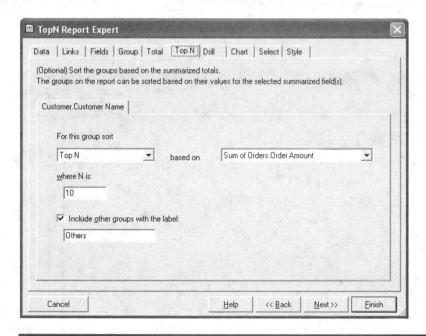

Figure 12-58 Selecting the top ten customers.

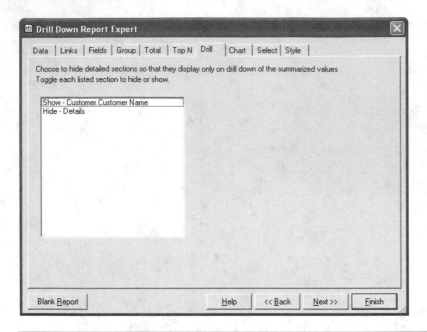

Figure 12-59 Selecting the Drill option to hide order details.

When we attach the report to a CrystalReportViewer control and run the report (Figure 12-60), customer names appear in the Group Tree panel and customer order summaries appear in the MainReport pane. For example, the total order amount for **The Great Bike Shop** is $76,266.44. The group headings (PO#, Order Date, Order Amount) indicate hidden detailed information. When the user double-clicks on a customer name in the report, a new Tab is created and a report showing individual orders by the selected customer is displayed on a separate sheet (Figure 12-61). The user can switch between reports by clicking on the named tabs above the reports.

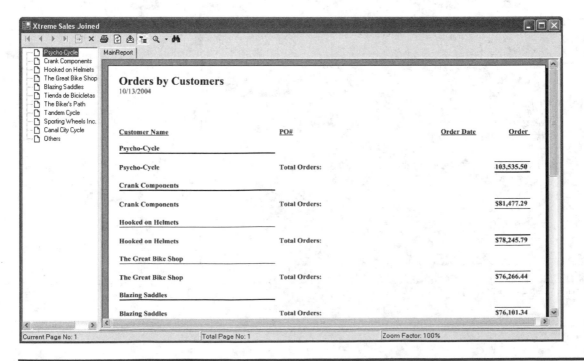

Figure 12-60 Customer Orders report.

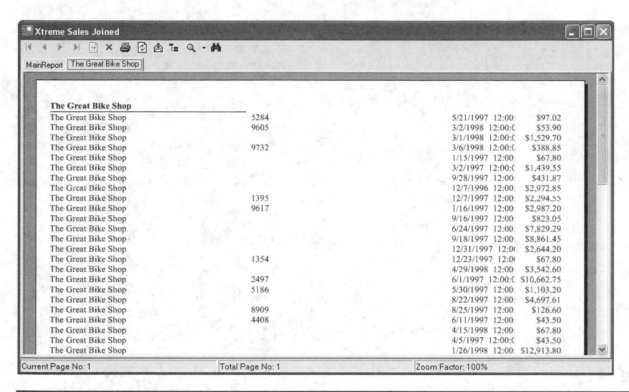

Figure 12-61 Drilling down into a single customer's details.

Refining the Report Format

The report created by Report Expert can use some refinement. Some columns must be narrowed, others widened, and the Order Date needs to be formatted. Here are some suggested changes:

◆ Widen the Print Date field.

◆ Remove the Group Name field from the Group Footer section.

◆ Reduce the width of the Customer Name and PO# columns.

◆ Right-click on the Order Date field, select Format, and select the mm/dd/yyyy format (listed as 03/03/1999).

◆ Widen the Order Amount column.

◆ Move the PO#, Order Date, and Order Amount column headings from the Page Header section to the Group Header section.

The finished report appears in Figure 12-62 and Figure 12-63.

12

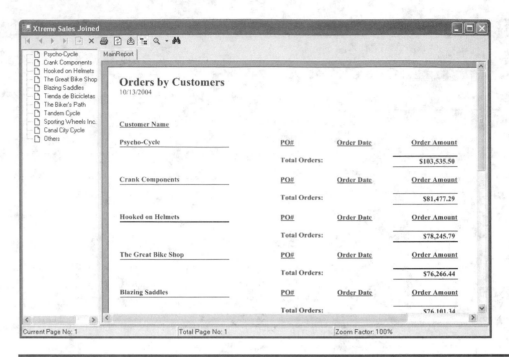

Figure 12-62 Revised Customer Orders report.

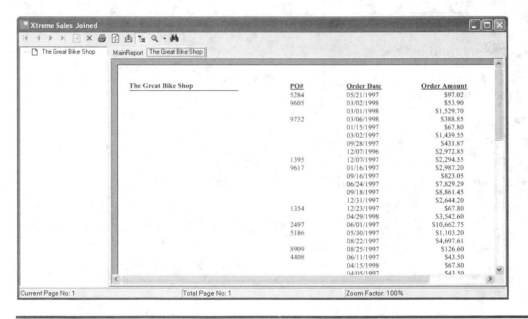

Figure 12-63 Customer Order details.

▶12.5 Chapter Summary

◆ Crystal Reports is an easy-to-use, yet powerful report design tool that retrieves and displays data from databases, recordsets, and other data sources.

◆ Crystal Reports has sophisticated formatting capabilities, its own formula editor, advanced formatting capabilities, and the ability to sort, group, and select records.

- When you add a Crystal Report to your program, the report is defined as a class, with properties, methods, and embedded source code.

- Reports are displayed on forms using a custom control named **CrystalReportsControl**, available for both Windows Forms and Web Forms.

- Report Expert is the primary tool for designing and modifying reports.

- You can use the interactive Formula Editor to create formula fields for reports.

- A report can be run from an application by assigning a report instance to the ReportSource property of the CrystalReportsViewer control. Alternatively, you can assign the report's file path to the ReportSource property.

- Reports can be selected on one form and displayed on a different form. This approach makes it possible for the user to select different forms to view at runtime.

- If you group the rows of a report on one of the table columns, group header and group footer sections are automatically added to the report.

- Reports can include *parameter fields* that receive values assigned at runtime. The values can be interactively entered by the user or assigned to the report object using program code.

- You can connect a Crystal Report to a dataset within your application. You can write database queries that join tables, select rows, and sort, before the data is passed to the Crystal Reports Viewer.

- When you use Report Expert to create a chart, there is an option to include a chart. Even if you decide to omit the chart, you can add a chart later.

- There are two ways to create a Crystal Report from multiple database tables: You can create an SQL join query, or you can join the tables using Report Expert.

▶12.6　Review Questions

Fill in the Blank

1. The _____ control is required when displaying a Crystal Report from a Visual Basic .NET application.

2. The _____ tab in Report Expert is used when showing table relationships.

3. The _____ tab in Report Expert is used when grouping and sorting records.

4. The _____ tab in Report Expert is used when deciding which group fields and detail fields display when a report is displayed.

5. The _____ tab in Report Expert is used when limiting the output to report rows satisfying some criteria.

Multiple Choice

1. Which of the following is not a data source type in Crystal Reports?
   a. OLA (BDO)
   b. ODBC (RDO)
   c. Database files
   d. Project data (datasets)
   e. Two of the above are correct

12

2. Which of the following identifies the tab in Project Expert that sorts report rows based on selected group totals?
   a. Select
   b. Top N
   c. Drill
   d. Sort
   e. Two of the above are correct

3. Which of the following sections in Report Expert lets you create a Formula field?
   a. Total
   b. Group
   c. Fields
   d. Data
   e. Two of the above are correct

4. Which of the following cannot be assigned to the ReportSource property of a CrystalReportsViewer control?
   a. The report filename
   b. An instance of the report object
   c. None of the above
   d. The report's URL
   e. Two of the above are correct

True or False

1. The Group Tree panel on a Crystal Report lets the user drill down into the detail records belonging to a group.

2. Formula fields must be created using Crystal Syntax.

3. To check for a null database field value in a formula, check the field's DbNull.Value property.

4. To hide a report section in Crystal Reports Designer, right-click on its identifier bar and select either **Hide** or **Suppress**.

5. When a report is grouped on a certain field, you cannot select the **Top N** option for the same field.

Short Answer

1. Which window in the Report Designer is used when creating parameter fields?

2. Which sections of a report typically contain charts?

3. What is the easiest way to make a CrystalReportsViewer control fill an entire form?

4. Which report group displays only once at the end of a report?

5. How do you modify the contents of a text object in a report?

What Do You Think?

1. Suppose a report drawn from thousands of database records filters out all but a few of those records. Will the report display more quickly if the record filtering is accomplished using a stored procedure as opposed to using a selection formula in the report itself?

2. When you edit a report in Report Designer and subsequently revise the report using Report Expert, which of the original modifications are lost? *(You may have to experiment before answering this question.)*

3. What aspects of Crystal Syntax do you prefer over Basic Syntax when creating formula fields?

4. What characteristic must your report have in order for the Group Tree panel entries to have + (plus) signs next to each entry?

5. How would rate the ease of use of the record selection formula editor in Report Expert?

Algorithm Workbench

1. Create a formula field named @joined using Basic Syntax that joins together fields X, Y, and Z, with hyphen (-) characters between the fields.

2. Write statements that assign a dataset named DsEmployees to a CrystalReportsViewer control named crvEmployees. Assume the report is named Employees.rpt.

▶12.7 Reporting Challenges

The following reports can be built and tested in a Windows Desktop or Web Forms application.

1. Xtreme Sales – Select a Country

Using the Xtreme_Sales program example as a starting point, add a **country** parameter to the SQL query in the data adapter. Fill a combo box with all possible country names and let the user select the country to be used when generating the report.

2. Titles by Authors

Using Figure 12-13 as a reference, create a report that lists all books written by each author in the authors table of the pubs database. Instead of showing the author's first and last names in separate columns, create a single column containing the last and first name together, in the following format: **Last, First**.

3. Jobs and Employees

Create a report that groups employees by job description. Use the jobs and employees tables from the pubs database. Display the job description, employee name (concatenate the first and last names), and hire date.

4. Karate Payments

Create a report that lists the amount and date of each payment made by members of the karate school. Use the Members and Payments tables of the Karate database, and make it a drill-down report.

5. Karate Payments – Single Member

Create a report that lists the amount and date of each payment made by single member of a karate school. Let the user select the member name from a combo box or dropdown list, and display a report for only that member. Use the Members and Payments tables of the Karate database.

12

Answers to Review Questions

(Corrections to this Appendix will be posted at: http://kipirvine.com/vbnet/corrections.htm)

▶Chapter 1

Checkpoint Questions

1. Definition of a type, with attributes and behaviors

2. Dynamic heap

3. No variables must reference the object.

4. Garbage collector

5. When the program runs low on memory, depending on how the garbage collector works.

6. To design classes in such as way that the resulting objects will effectively cooperate and communicate

7. yes

8. Portion of the class that is hidden from client programs. Members are private.

9. The Form class receives messages based on user actions, and delivers information to the user.

10. Syntax:

    ```
    Public Class classname
       member-declarations
    End Class
    ```

11. Console application writes to an output text stream and reads from an input text stream. No graphics are used.

12. (code example)

    ```
    Class clsEmployee
       Private mDepartmentID As String
    End Class
    ```

13. (code example)

    ```
    Public Function GetGradeAverage() As Single
       If mCreditsEarned <> 0 Then
          Return mTotalGradePoints / mCreditsEarned
       End If
    End Function
    ```

14. To avoid direct references by client programs that could cause unintended side effects and break the encapsulation of the class.

15. (code example)

```
Property Years() As Integer
   Get
       return mYears
   End Get
   Set(ByVal Value As Integer)
      mYears = Value
   End Set
End Property
```

16. (code example)

```
Property Years() As String
   Get
       return mDepartmentID
   End Get
   Set(ByVal Value As String)
      mDepartmentID = Value
   End Set
End Property
```

17. Because it is calculated from private fields.

18. (code example)

```
Public Property Name() As String
   Get
       Return mName
   End Get
   Set(ByVal Value As String)
      If Value <> "" Then
          mName = Value
      End If
   End Set
End Property
```

19. No

20. (code example)

```
Sub New(ByVal id As String, ByVal balance As Decimal)
   mID = id
   mBalance = balance
End Sub
```

21. (code example)

```
Private Sub New()
   '...
End Sub
```

22. (code example)

```
Sub New(Optional ByVal id As String)
   mID = id
End Sub
```

23. The Account class. Business Tier methods are: Deposit, Update, and Withdraw.

24. The BankTeller program has a combined Business/Data tier, containing the Account class. The Data tier methods are Open and ReadFromFile.

25. The WithDraw method returns False and no money is withdrawn.

26. The Leave event handler calls the IsNumeric method. If the value is not a number, the Leave handler displays a message and resets the focus to the same control.

27. The Leave event

28. An Automobile object contains an Engine object.

29. If classes are like components with standard interfaces, they can be "plugged into" each other. Visual Basic .NET controls are good examples.

30. (Diagram: Box containing Department class, with black diamond at the base of a line that connects to another box containing the Employee class).

31. clsPersonalInfo, clsProject, and clsSalaryItem

Review Questions

Fill-in-the-Blank

1. Business rules

2. classes (objects)

3. Modeling

4. containing, or aggregation

5. Garbage Collector

Multiple Choice

1. B

2. A

3. B

4. C

5. D

True or False

1. False

2. True

3. False

4. False

5. False – an instance of Employee would be required

Short Answer

1. runtime stack

2. Visual Interface tier

3. As methods

4. The business tier would contain rules for tasks such as the following: (1) determine how long members can rent movies. (2) what to do when a membership has expired. (3) what to do when a rental is overdue.

5. Business tier

6. The Account.Update method.

7. The Account.Deposit method

8. StreamReader object

9. A shared variable can be referenced using the class name, rather than an instance of the class. All class instances share the same variable.

10.　(code example)

```
Class Window
   Private Shared mColor As Integer

   Public Shared Property Color As Integer
      Sub Get
         return mColor
      End Get
      Sub Set(ByVal Value As Integer)
         mColor = Value
      End Set
   End Property
End Class
```

Algorithm Workbench

1.　(UML diagram for a class named Employee that has two attributes named ID and Salary.)

2.　Create a String property named LastName that provides access to a private class variable named mLastName.

```
Property LastName As String
   Sub Get
      return mLastName
   End Get
   Sub Set(ByVal Value As String)
      mLastName = Value
   End Set
End Property
```

3.　Write a simple code example that demonstrates passing an object variable by reference. Show how the object variable can be reassigned to a new object.

```
Sub ChangeIt(ByRef obj As Object)
   obj = New Object
End Sub
Sub test
   Dim X As New Object
   ChangeIt( X )
   'X now references a different object
End Sub
```

4.　(code example)

```
Sub New(Optional ByVal str As Integer, Optional ByVal intell As Integer)
   Strength = str
   Intelligence = intell
End Sub
```

5.　(code example)

```
Class Course
   Private courseId As String
   Private courseName As String
End Class

'Student contains an array of Course objects
Class Student

   Private courses As Course()
End Class
```

▶ Chapter 2

Checkpoint

1. Menu-driven interface with context-sensitive help
2. Use case scenarios (use cases)
3. Steps:
    1. Program displays an input form with two date fields
    2. User enters a beginning date and an ending date
    3. Program searches for all nonreturned items that fall within the two dates.
    4. Program displays the list of items.
4. Use a menu.
5. Use a Panel with Tabs that expose individual boxes when the user clicks on a tab.
6. user input errors
7. Validation using rules that reflect company policy. The rules might involve cross-checking user inputs against a database.
8. The user can remember why they entered the value.
9. CausesValidation property
10. Displays visual cues. Makes it easy to prevent validation when the user wants to close the form.
11. ImageList property
12. ImageIndex property
13. No
14. Yes
15. Select the Buttons property.
16. View.Details, View.LargeIcon, View.List, and View.SmallIcon.
17. AllowColumnReorder
18. SubItems property
19. ItemCheck event
20. (code example)

    ```
    lvwEmployees.Items.Remove(empItem)
    ```
21. Unhandled exception
22. No, it unwinds the execution stack, following the sequence of method calls that led to the exception being thrown.
23. No, the variable is optional.
24. Yes

Review Questions

Fill-in-the-Blank

1. user interface
2. use-case
3. Office
4. CausesValidation
5. ListItem

Multiple Choice

1. C
2. E
3. E
4. D
5. A
6. D

True or False

1. True
2. False
3. False
4. True
5. False
6. True
7. False
8. True
9. True
10. False
11. True
12. False
13. True
14. True
15. False

Short Answer

1. Pre-set sequence of actions, limited choices, little reliance on user knowledge.
2. The user may want to enter the data in nonsequential order.
3. SetError
4. Buttons
5. AllowColumnReorder
6. ItemCheck
7. ExpandAll method
8. unhandled (uncaught) exception
9. ApplicationException
10. FormatException
11. StackTrace

Algorithm Workbench

1. Use-Case scenario for "Display the complete store inventory":

   a. User logs into the system.

   b. User inputs the display complete inventory command.

   c. Store inventory displays on screen.

   d. User logs out of the system.

2. Sprinkler system wizard:

   a. What is the current date and time?

   b. How often do you want the system to come on?

   c. what time of day should it come on?

   d. how long should the sprinkler stay on?

3. (code example)

```
If Not(txtZIP.Text.Length = 5 And _
    IsNumeric(txtZIP.Text)) Then e.Cancel = True
```

4. (code example)

```
If txtName.Text.IndexOf(" ") = -1 Then
    errProvider.SetError(CType(sender, Control), _
        "The name must be two words")
End If
```

5. (code example)

```
lvwCustomer.Columns.Add("Address", CInt(.Width * 0.2), _
    HorizontalAlignment.Left)
```

6. (code example)

```
Dim item As ListViewItem
item = New ListViewItem("Surfboards Hawaii")
item.SubItems.Add("100 North King Street")
```

7. (code example)

```
Dim aNode As TreeNode
With tvwSurfspots
    aNode = .Nodes.Add("Hawaii")
    aNode.Nodes.Add("Maui")
    aNode.Nodes.Add("Oahu")
End With
```

8. (code example)

```
Dim aNode As TreeNode
With tvwSurfspots
    aNode = .Nodes.Add("Hawaii")
    aNode.Nodes.Add("Maui")
    aNode = aNode.Nodes.Add("Oahu")
    aNode.Nodes.Add("Velzyland")
    aNode.Nodes.Add("Pupukea")
End With
```

►Chapter 3

Checkpoint

1. Loose connection, disconnected datasets.
2. ADO.NET can create XML files and send across the Web.
3. tables
4. Open connection, read table (data adapter), fill dataset
5. Field
6. permits controls to display the contents of the current dataset row
7. CurrencyManager
8. SelectCommand.CommandText
9. drag a table from the ServerExplorer onto a form
10. Look for an XSD file having the same root name in the Solution Explorer window.
11. Position
12. Create empty row, fill in fields, add row to table.
13. call CancelEdit
14. call RemoveAt from the CurrencyManager
15. Update
16. SELECT
17. SELECT (field-list) FROM Employees WHERE Years > 9.
18. Fill
19. double-click on XSD file; add new line to table definition containing E; add field name, field type, and set the Expression property.
20. SelectedIndexChanged

Review Questions

Fill-in-the-Blank

1. loosely
2. Extensible
3. adapter
4. relation
5. dataset
6. Rows
7. Position
8. CommandText

Multiple Choice

1. C
2. D
3. E
4. C
5. D
6. C

True or False

1. False
2. False
3. True
4. True
5. True
6. False
7. False

Short Answer

1. OleDbConnection
2. BindingContext
3. Select the data adapter's Generate dataset command.
4. ConstraintException
5. RemoveAt
6. Query Builder

Algorithm Workbench

1. daEmployees.Fill(DsEmployees1)
2. currManager = Me.BindingContext(DsEmployees1, "Employees")
3. SELECT DeptID, ManagerName FROM Departments
4. myCurr.Position = myCurr.Count - 1
5. Dim myRow As System.Data.DataRow = DsEmployees1.Employees.NewRow
6. myCurr.RemoveAt(0)
7. SELECT DeptID, Salary FROM Departments WHERE Salary <= 50000
8. daEmployees.SelectCommand.Parameters("Salary").Value = 30000

►Chapter 4

Checkpoint

1. yes
2. Type on the bottom line and fill in the field values
3. Enabled
4. CurrentCell

5. CurrentCellChanged

6. dvMembers.Sort="LastName"

7. By setting its Table property to the dataset and datatable.

8. dvEmployees.Sort="Salary DESC"

9. dvEmployees(5).Item("LastName")

10. The DataView has both Sort and RowFilter properties.

11. Presentation, Business, Data

12. Data

13. no

14. yes

15. SportsRental=Data; Items=Business; frmRentalIncome=Presentation

16. The program displays a dialog window containing a list of employee names.

17. The program displays the current customer information.

18. The program calculates the suggested prepayment amount.

19. Employee table

20. To identify the toolbar buttons by index position.

21. When the user closed the frmCustomer window by clicking the OK button.

22. select, insert, update, and delete

23. SqlCommand, OleDbCommand

24. INSERT INTO

25. Parameters collection

Review Questions

True or False

1. True

2. False

Short Answer

1. DataGrid

2. ListView

3. RowFilter

4. ReadOnly

►Chapter 5

Checkpoint

1. Its value is unique.

2. (1) single table would be too detailed or have too many columns; (2) supplementary text or graphics might be too large; (3) security restrictions on certain columns

3. Create an intermediate table

4. Stores and titles

5. Requires every value in the primary key column(s) to be unique.

6. One-to-one

7. Many-to-many

8. Look for the linking column between the tables, and note which table contains duplicate values in the column data.

9. pub_id

10. job_id

11. SelectedValue property (assigned to the DataView's RowFilter)

12. employee table

13. The name of the relation created in the Edit Relation window (XSD schema definition window)

14. parent

15. In the Schema view of the XML Designer.

16. A DataRelation object

17. sales table

18. SELECT employee.lname, jobs.job_desc FROM employee INNER JOIN jobs on employee.job_id = jobs.job_id

Review Questions

Fill-in-the-blank

1. tables

2. one-to-one

3. foreign

4. titles

5. INNER JOIN

6. primary key

7. Navigate

Multiple Choice

1. C

2. C

3. B

4. D

True or False

1. True

2. False

3. True

4. False

5. True

6. False

Short Answer

1. pub_info

2. foreign key constraint (or referential integrity constraint)

3. cascading update

4. TableStyles

5. GridColumnStyles

6. GetParentRow

Algorithm Workbench

1. SELECT sales.title_id, stores.stor_name FROM (sales INNER JOIN stores ON sales.stor_id = stores.stor_id)

2. dvEmployee.RowFilter = "job_id = " & cboJobs.SelectedValue

3. dvSales.RowFilter = "stor_id = " & cboStores.SelectedValue

4. employeeRows = drJobs.GetChildRows("relJobsEmployee")

5. SELECT jobs.job_desc, employee.lname, employee.hire_date FROM (jobs INNER JOIN employee ON jobs.job_id = employee.job_id)

▶Chapter 6

Checkpoint

1. ANSI SQL

2. Jet SQL

3. Data Manipulation Language (DML)

4. String

5. tinyint

6. They permit fast searching for column values

7. Select two of the followoing: (1) To restrict certain users from accessing columns containing senstive information. (2) To join together existing tables or views. (3) To rename table columns, making them more user-friendly. (4) To filter table rows.

8. A key made up of more than one table column.

9. Windows NT integrated security.

10. Insert the names into the Alias column of the grid pane.

11. To create table relationships.

12. CREATE TABLE

13. address varchar(50)

14. none

15. ALTER TABLE employees ADD serviceYears int

16. UPDATE employees SET bonus = 0

17. UPDATE employees SET salary = salary * 1.10

18. UPDATE employees SET bonus = 1000 WHERE hireDate < '01/01/1998'

19. DELETE from payroll WHERE hours < 40

20. SQL query string

21. CommandType and Connection

22. In the Finally block of a Try-End Try statement.

23. NETSDK uses integrated security and includes NETSDK in the data source parameter. SQL Server has a user id parameter and the data source is "(local")".

24. They are compiled and they use the Tabular Data Stream protocol.

25. Insist on the use of stored procedures, and require approval before the procedures can be used in production.

26. Between the /* and */ symbols.

27. no

28. SqlCommand cmd = new SqlCommand(spMyproc, myConn)

29. CommandType.StoredProcedure

30. Create table, delete table, add rows, remove rows, and update rows.

31. cmdParameters.Add("@age", SqlDbType.Int)

32. SqlException

Review Questions

Fill-in-the-blank

1. ANSI

2. action

3. Definition

4. primary

5. INSERT INTO

Multiple Choice

1. C

2. B

3. C

4. B

5. A

True or False

1. True

2. False

3. True

4. False

5. True

6. False

7. False

8. False

9. True

10. True

11. True

12. False

13. True

14. True
15. False
16. False
17. False
18. True

Short Answer

1. (LOCAL)
2. Diagrams
3. integrated security
4. DROP temp
5. DELETE FROM temp

Algorithm Workbench

1. (code example)

```
INSERT INTO target SELECT * from source
```

2. (code example)

```
CREATE TABLE employee
   (id int PRIMARY KEY,
   name varchar(30) NOT NULL,
   salary real NOT NULL)
```

3. (code example)

```
ALTER TABLE employee
   ADD hireDate datetime
```

4. (code example)

```
ALTER TABLE employee
   ALTER COLUMN salary decimal
```

5. (code example)

```
INSERT INTO employee
   VALUES( 1001, "Bill Jones", 35000, '10/01/2004')
```

6. (code example)

```
DELETE FROM employee
   WHERE hireDate < '1/1/1995'
```

7. (code example)

```
ALTER TABLE employee
   DROP COLUMN salary
```

►Chapter 7

Checkpoint

1. Scripting languages do not provide compile-time type checking.
2. Interactive program that communicates with web browsers over a network.

3. When you use a Web browser such as Internet Explorer to access a Web site, your browser is the client, and the Web site is the server.

4. When the contents of a web page are sent to the Web server, and the server resends the page to the user's browser.

5. It provides development tools, code libraries, and visual controls for Web programming.

6. Web form, containing text, images, HTML controls, and Web forms controls.

7. Page displayed by an uplevel browser can perform error checking before the page is posted back to the server.

8. Select two from the following: Language, AutoEventWireup, Codebehind.

9. System.Web.UI.Page

10. Contains event handlers for the Web forms controls, as well as other class methods.

11. Because the Web server generates generic HTML.

12. Hidden field that stores runtime property values within the pages HTML.

13. HttpApplication

14. Which two classes make it possible to read, write, add, and remove HTTP cookies? HttpCookie and HttpCookieCollection

15. HttpResponse

16. HttpSessionState

17. System.Web.Mail

18. Causes page to be immediately posted back when the user makes a list selection.

19. Page_Load

20. LinkButton generates a click event, whereas HyperLink does not.

21. Assign the same GroupName property value to each button.

22. CheckChanged

23. Items (collection), Text property

24. Use a For-Each loop to examine the Selected property of each check box.

25. DropDownList

26. Set the DataSource property to the array name.

27. TabIndex

28. pageLayout

29. HTML Table control

30. Create a table outlining the rows first. Then insert a new table in each row, breaking it into internal rows and columns.

31. DropDownList, ListBox, CheckBoxList, and RadioButtonList.

Review Questions

Multiple Choice

1. C
2. C
3. A
4. B
5. D
6. C
7. A

Fill-in-the-blank

1. Web server
2. HTML
3. postback
4. platform
5. Web forms controls
6. Web.config

True or False

1. False
2. True
3. True
4. False
5. True
6. False
7. True
8. True
9. False
10. False
11. True
12. True

Short Answer

1. From the menu, select Tools > Options > Projects and Solutions > Visual Studio projects location.
2. Server.Transfer
3. reboot the computer
4. LinkButton
5. HttpRequest
6. ImageButton
7. CheckChanged
8. RepeatDirection
9. SelectionMode
10. Page_Load (before SelectedIndexChanged)
11. Panel
12. zero

Algorithm Workbench

1. (code example)

```
'(insert in the Page_Load method)
If Not IsPostBack Then
    Dim depts As String() = {"Art", "Chemistry", "Music", "Physics"}
    lstDepts.DataSource = depts
    lstDepts.DataBind()
End If
```

2. (code example)

```
lstDepts.Items.Add(txtDepartment.Text)
lstDepts.SelectedIndex = lstDepts.Items.Count - 1
```

3. (code example)

```
Response.Redirect("Page2.aspx?dept=" & lstDepts.SelectedValue)
```

4. (code example)

```
Dim dept As String = Request.Params("dept")
Response.Write("Department = " & dept)
```

5. (code example)

```
Dim strList As String
Dim item As ListItem
For Each item In chkDepts.Items
   If item.Selected Then
      strList &= item.Text & " "
   End If
Next
```

6. (code example)

```
Dim strList As String
Dim item As ListItem
For Each item In chkDepts.Items
   If item.Selected Then
      strList &= item.Value & " "
   End If
Next
```

►Chapter 8

Checkpoint

1. Off
2. <customErrors mode="RemoteOnly">
3. error 404 (file not found)
4. Internet Information Services Administrator
5. SelectedDate
6. Call the SelectedDates.Add method.
7. Set the SelectionMode property to None.
8. Set the VisibleDate property to any date in April.
9. Array and ArrayList
10. The selected person's assigned task would display only when the Assign button was clicked.
11. No, because data binding only works in one direction.
12. HTMLInputFile control
13. multipart/form-data
14. The PostedFile property of HTMLInputFile is a HttpPostedFile object.
15. SMTP
16.

    ```
    SmtpMail.Send( me@myCollege.edu, you@somewhere.com, _
    "this is my subject", "this is my message")
    ```
17. MailMessage class
18. Base64 and UUEncode.
19. RequiredFieldValidator

20. ControlToValidate, MaximumValue, MinimumValue
21. CompareValidator
22. RegularExpressionValidator
23. Saved in ViewState property
24. no
25. Application("users") = users
26. Application.Remove("users")
27. Because two sessions might try to access the variable at the same time
28. Session state preserves information for a single user; application state preserves the same information for all active users.
29. Session("employee") = new Employee()
30. Dim emp As Employee = CType(Session("employee"), Employee)
31. small amounts of data that can be expressed as strings.

Review Questions

Fill-in-the-blank

1. Custom
2. SelectedDate
3. Calendar
4. DataSource
5. PostedFile

Multiple Choice

1. C
2. E
3. D
4. A
5. E

True or False

1. True
2. True
3. False
4. True
5. False

Short Answer

1. Click on the Custom Errors tab, select an error number, select Edit Properties, then change either the File or URL setting.
2. Set ShowTitle to False.
3. call the DataBind method
4. Accept property
5. BodyFormat

Algorithm Workbench

1. <error statusCode="403" redirect="error403.htm" />

2. myCal.SelectedDates.Add(new Date(2005, 2, 10))

3. myCal.VisibleDate = new Date(2005, 2, 10)

4. uplFile.PostedFile.SaveAs("c:\temp\x.doc")

5. SmtpMail.Send("me@fiu.edu", "you@fiu.edu", "Grades", "Your grades are ready for viewing")

6. myMsg.Attachments.Add(New MailAttachment("c:\classes\grades.htm"))

▶Chapter 9

Checkpoint

1. Choose one: SelectedItemTemplate, EditItemTemplate

2. SelectedIndex

3. DataKeyField

4. The list of stores would disappear after clicking on a Select button.

5. DataKeyField

6. SelectedItem

7. DataMember

8. DataBind

9. DeleteCommand

10. ComandArgument, CommandName, CommandSource, Item.

11. The DsEmployee1 dataset would be empty when the user selected a job category. No employees would display.

12. Extra memory required to keep dataset in session state

13. RegularExpressionValidator control

14. Retrieves current date from Session state and assigns it to the Calendar control's SelectedDate property.

15. To get the auto-generated reservation ID number.

Review Questions

Fill-in-the-Blank

1. DataReader

2. ItemTemplate

3. HeaderTemplate

4. Edit

5. DataKeys

Multiple Choice

1. C

2. D

3. A

4. C

5. E

Short Answer

1. firehose cursor
2. no
3. FieldCount
4. SelectedItemTemplate
5. DataKeyField

Algorithm Workbench

1. reader = myCmd.ExecuteReader()
2. dgrAuthors.Columns(0).Visible = False
3. <%# Container.DataItem("firstName") %>
4. dlAuthors.DataKeys(dlAuthors.SelectedIndex)
5. dlStores.SelectedIndex = e.Item.ItemIndex

▶Chapter 10

(There are no Checkpoint questions for Chapter 10.)

Review Questions

Fill in the Blank

1. methods
2. Access
3. Description

Multiple Choice

1. B
2. D

True or False

1. False
2. True
3. True
4. False

Short Answer

1. WebService
2. Right-click on Web References in the Solution Explorer and select Add Web Reference.
3. DataSet

Algorithm Workbench

1. (code example)

```
<WebService(Namespace:="http://mydomain.com/WeatherService")> _
Public Class WeatherService
Inherits System.Web.Services.WebService
```

2. (code example)

```
<WebMethod> Public Function GetTemperature() As Single
```

3. (code example)

```
Dim temp As Single
Dim service As New localhost.WeatherService
temp = service.GetTemperature()
```

►Chapter 11

Checkpoint

1. True
2. False
3. True
4. False
5. Its class, and the list of class members.
6. True
7. True
8. fully qualified class name
9. True
10. True
11. False
12. False
13. False
14. True
15. True
16. False
17. True
18. True
19. False
20. False
21. True
22. False
23. True

Review Questions

Fill in the Blank

1. New
2. Structure
3. GetType
4. IComparable
5. IComparer

Multiple Choice

1. D
2. B
3. B
4. D

Short Answer

1. Contains
2. Equals
3. Create a comparator for each type of sort, and pass it to the Array.Sort method.
4. Inherits
5. Hashtable

Algorithm Workbench

1. (code example)

```
Enum Colors
    Red
    Green
    Blue
End Enum
Dim X As Color = Colors.Red
```

2. (code example)

```
WriteLine(obj.GetType().ToString())
```

3. (code example)

```
A.InstanceEquals(B), or Object.Equals(A, B)
```

4. (code example)

```
Public Overrides Function CompareTo(ByVal obj _
    As Student) As Boolean _
    Implements IComparable.CompareTo
```

5. (code example)

```
Student S
students.Add(S.ID, S)
```

6. (code example)

```
Array.Sort(students, New CompareNames)
```

7. (code example)

```
Public MustOverride Sub Print()
```

8. (code example)

```
MustInherit Class StudentBase
```

9. (code example)

```
Dim courses As New SortedList
courses.Add("COP 1110", "Intro to Programming")
courses.Add("BUS 2210", "Management Principles")
courses.Add("ART 1000", "Art Appreciation")
Dim courseId As String
For Each courseId In courses.Keys
    WriteLine(courseId)
Next
```

10. (code example)

```
Dim entry As DictionaryEntry
For Each entry In myList
    WriteLine(CInt(entry.Key) & "-->" & entry.Value)
Next
```

►CHAPTER 12

(There are no Checkpoint questions for Chapter 12.)

Review Questions

Fill in the Blank

1. CrystalReportsViewer
2. Links
3. Group
4. Drill
5. Select

Multiple Choice

1. A
2. B.
3. C.
4. D.

True or False

1. T
2. F
3. F
4. T
5. F

Short Answer

1. Field Explorer
2. Report Header and Report Footer
3. Set the Dock property to **Fill**
4. Report Footer
5. Right-click on the object and select **Edit Text Object**

Algorithm Workbench

1. Formula = {X} + "-" + {Y} + "-" + Z
2. (code example)

```
Dim report As Employees = new Employees
report.SetDataSource(DsEmployees1)
crvEmployees.ReportSource = report
```

Index